Praise for Nancy Caro Hollander's *Up*

"While reading *Uproo* 5/14 become a giant among a handful of psychoanalytic investigators who have taken psychoanalysis beyond the couch and utilized it in the examination of social, political, historical, and economic conditions. An esteemed authority on the psychology of the era of state terror in Latin America between the 1960s and 1990s, she contributes to our understanding of Latin American psychoanalysts' moving, soul-searching response to it. In this book, her psychoanalytic insights also illuminate topics ranging from terror and torture to "American Exceptionalism," globalization to political leaders' personalities, and new economic/military alliances to despair as well as hope about humankind's future. This is one of the most significant books of our time, and it should be read not only by persons who are interested in expanding the influence of psychoanalysis beyond its clinical application, but by everyone who wishes to be more than a passive bystander to the dangerous world we live in."

Vamik D. Volkan, M.D.
President, American College of Psychoanalysts

"This subtle and penetrating inquiry weaves together the hideous record of state terror in the Americas and the terrible human cost of economic fundamentalism, and explores how social–psychological theory and direct engagement can ameliorate the traumas left in their wake and help overcome the institutional framework of repression and domination that bars the way to personal and social liberation."

Noam Chomsky, Ph.D.
Author, *What We Say Goes: Conversations on U.S. Power in a Changing World* (2007) and *Essential Chomsky* (2009)

"Nancy Hollander's book makes its welcome appearance just as Argentina has moved toward a much-needed social reparation by reopening the legal cases against the perpetrators of the Dirty War, who four decades ago disappeared, tortured, and assassinated tens of thousands of Argentine citizens. Intimately familiar with the history of dictatorship in the Southern Cone, Hollander alerts us to the dangerous road traveled by the United States since 9/11. Books like Hollander's, which represent a socially engaged psychoanalysis, take their place alongside the courageous work of human rights activists that have made social justice possible. *Uprooted Minds* is a must-read for all who are concerned about the future of humanity."

Julia Braun, Argentine Psychoanalyst
Winner of the IPA's Hayman Prize for published work pertaining to traumatizes in children and adults, and mother of a disappeared son

"In the tradition begun by Freud when he turned his psychoanalytic gaze toward the deeply conflicted human condition in *Civilization and Its Discontents*, Nancy Caro Hollander critically explores the discontents of *our* culture. She has produced a book that inserts itself in the crossroads between the individual and the social, the personal and the political, between neoliberalism and the progressive movements that challenge it, between democracy and authoritarianism, and between the September 11s of the two Americas. With an artist's sensibility and a depth that only personal experience can engender, she examines the impact of traumatic events that deeply affect people's subjectivity and social experience. *Uprooted Minds* is a testimonial text that is not dispassionate and 'objective,' but, on the contrary, a revelation of life lived, suffered, felt, and thought about: history incarnate. Hollander's style is rigorous, transparent, solidly researched, and colloquial, and with *Uprooted Minds* she delivers a social analysis that only a psychoanalyst could write."

Juan Carlos Volnovich, Argentine Psychoanalyst
Psychological Consultant to the Grandmothers of the Plaza del Mayo
and Honoree Professor, University of the Mothers of Plaza del Mayo

"Drawing on personal experience and conversations with psychoanalysts who lived through and witnessed torture and murder in Argentina, Chile, and Uruguay over the last four decades, Nancy Hollander has written a book that will be an eye-opener and a consciousness-raiser for many of us about U.S.-sponsored oppression. For U.S. psychoanalysts in particular, there is much to be learned from the experience of Latin American analysts' struggles to relieve individual suffering in the context of state-sponsored terror, while deploying psychoanalytic understanding in the service of creating a more humane society. Bringing lessons learned from this Latin American experience to an analysis of the social trauma represented by 9/11 and the consequent erosion of political and social democracy in this country, Hollander shows how a social psychoanalysis has emerged here as well. She has given an essential guide to those of us in North America who, using a socially situated psychoanalysis, want to help the individuals we work with in the context of post–9/11 political crises and to make a reparative contribution to the world we live in."

Neil Altman, Ph.D.
Author, *The Analyst in the Inner City*, Second Edition (2009)

"*Uprooted Minds* inherits and develops psychoanalytical social psychology through a brilliant analysis of the historical roots of disturbances in the social matrices of several contemporary societies. Hollander weaves interviews with eminent analysts and social activists with her own personal recollections to create a book unlike any other I have ever read. Informative, challenging, disturbing, passionate, and good-humored, I think it will inspire a new generation of psychoanalytical investigations of social dreaming."

Christopher Bollas, Ph.D.

"Nancy Hollander has once again ventured into domains few psychoanalysts have dared to explore. As in her previous highly acclaimed *Love in a Time of Hate: Liberation Psychology in Latin America*, she brilliantly exposes the intersection of psychology and politics. This time she examines the post–9/11 impact on political culture, covering a wide range of topics, from Argentina's economic debacle to today's challenges in America's democracy. *Uprooted Minds* accomplishes the almost impossible task of establishing a long-overdue dialogue between social sciences and psychoanalysis. Hollander, an historian and psychoanalyst, has delivered an original work that illuminates readers from the South and the North. Her work empowers psychoanalysts, mental health practitioners, and social scientists to build bridges between practice and political activism."

Isaac Tylim, Ph.D.
Secretary, International Psychoanalytic Association,
Committee on the United Nations

"*Uprooted Minds* is an important and riveting critique of our times. At present, globalization is linking us in violence as well as environmental and economic collapse. Integrating history, politics, memoirs, and psychoanalysis, this book is an incisive study of this disintegration. Hollander illuminates our despair, but she also exhorts us toward hope, courage, and resistance. This is a passionate, humane, and scholarly work."

Sue Grand, Ph.D.
Author, *The Hero in the Mirror: From Fear to Fortitude* (2009)

Uprooted Minds

RELATIONAL PERSPECTIVES BOOK SERIES

LEWIS ARON & ADRIENNE HARRIS
Series Editors

The Relational Perspectives Book Series (RPBS) publishes books that grow out of or contribute to the relational tradition in contemporary psychoanalysis. The term "relational psychoanalysis" was first used by Greenberg and Mitchell (1983) to bridge the traditions of interpersonal relations, as developed within interpersonal psychoanalysis and object relations, as developed within contemporary British theory. But, under the seminal work of the late Stephen Mitchell, the term "relational psychoanalysis" grew and began to accrue to itself many other influences and developments. Various tributaries—interpersonal psychoanalysis, object relations theory, self psychology, empirical infancy research, and elements of contemporary Freudian and Kleinian thought—flow into this tradition, which understands relational configurations between self and others, both real and fantasied, as the primary subject of psychoanalytic investigation.

We refer to the relational tradition, rather than to a relational school, to highlight that we are identifying a trend, a tendency within contemporary psychoanalysis, not a more formally organized or coherent school or system of beliefs. Our use of the term 'relational' signifies a dimension of theory and practice that has become salient across the wide spectrum of contemporary psychoanalysis. Now under the editorial supervision of Lewis Aron and Adrienne Harris, the Relational Perspectives Book Series originated in 1990 under the editorial eye of the late Stephen A. Mitchell. Mitchell was the most prolific and influential of the originators of the relational tradition. He was committed to dialogue among psychoanalysts and he abhorred the authoritarianism that dictated adherence to a rigid set of beliefs or technical restrictions. He championed open discussion, comparative and integrative approaches, and he promoted new voices across the generations.

Included in the Relational Perspectives Book Series are authors and works that come from within the relational tradition, extend and develop the tradition, as well as works that critique relational approaches or compare and contrast it with alternative points of view. The series includes our most distinguished senior psychoanalysts along with younger contributors who bring fresh vision.

RELATIONAL PERSPECTIVES BOOK SERIES
LEWIS ARON & ADRIENNE HARRIS
Series Editors

Vol. 47
Uprooted Minds:
Surviving the Politics of Terror in the
Americas
Nancy Caro Hollander

Vol. 46
A Disturbance in the Field:
Essays in Transference-
Countertransference Engagement
Steven H. Cooper

Vol. 45
First Do No Harm:
The Paradoxical Encounters of
Psychoanalysis, Warmaking, and
Resistance
Adrienne Harris & Steven Botticelli (eds.)

Vol. 44
Good Enough Endings:
Breaks, Interruptions, and Terminations
from Contemporary Relational
Perspectives
Jill Salberg (ed.)

Vol. 43
Invasive Objects: Minds Under Siege
Paul Williams

Vol. 42
Sabert Basescu:
Selected Papers on Human Nature and
Psychoanalysis
George Goldstein & Helen Golden (eds.)

Vol. 41
The Hero in the Mirror:
From Fear to Fortitude
Sue Grand

Vol. 40
The Analyst in the Inner City, Second
Edition:
Race, Class, and Culture Through a
Psychoanalytic Lens
Neil Altman

Vol. 39
Dare to be Human:
A Contemporary Psychoanalytic Journey
Michael Shoshani Rosenbaum

Vol. 38
Repair of the Soul:
Metaphors of Transformation in Jewish
Mysticism and Psychoanalysis
Karen E. Starr

Vol. 37
Adolescent Identities:
A Collection of Readings
Deborah Browning (ed.)

Vol. 36
Bodies in Treatment:
The Unspoken Dimension
Frances Sommer Anderson (ed.)

Vol. 35
Comparative-Integrative Psychoanalysis:
A Relational Perspective for the
Discipline's Second Century
Brent Willock

Vol. 34
Relational Psychoanalysis, Vol. III:
New Voices
Melanie Suchet, Adrienne Harris, & Lewis
Aron (eds.)

Vol. 33
Creating Bodies:
Eating Disorders as Self-Destructive
Survival
Katie Gentile

Vol. 32
Getting From Here to There:
Analytic Love, Analytic Process
Sheldon Bach

Vol. 31
Unconscious Fantasies and the Relational
World
Danielle Knafo & Kenneth Feiner

Vol. 30
The Healer's Bent:
Solitude and Dialogue in the Clinical
Encounter
James T. McLaughlin

Vol. 29
Child Therapy in the Great Outdoors:
A Relational View
Sebastiano Santostefano

Vol. 28
Relational Psychoanalysis, Vol. II:
Innovation and Expansion
Lewis Aron & Adrienne Harris (eds.)

Vol. 27
The Designed Self:
Psychoanalysis and Contemporary
Identities
Carlo Strenger

Vol. 26
Impossible Training:
A Relational View of Psychoanalytic
Education
Emanuel Berman

Vol. 25
Gender as Soft Assembly
Adrienne Harris

RELATIONAL PERSPECTIVES BOOK SERIES
LEWIS ARON & ADRIENNE HARRIS
Series Editors

Vol. 24
Minding Spirituality
Randall Lehman Sorenson

Vol. 23
September 11: Trauma and Human Bonds
Susan W. Coates, Jane L. Rosenthal, &
Daniel S. Schechter (eds.)

Vol. 22
Sexuality, Intimacy, Power
Muriel Dimen

Vol. 21
Looking for Ground:
Countertransference and the Problem of
Value in Psychoanalysis
Peter G. M. Carnochan

Vol. 20
Relationality:
From Attachment to Intersubjectivity
Stephen A. Mitchell

Vol. 19
Who is the Dreamer, Who Dreams the
Dream?
A Study of Psychic Presences
James S. Grotstein

Vol. 18
Objects of Hope:
Exploring Possibility and Limit in
Psychoanalysis
Steven H. Cooper

Vol. 17
The Reproduction of Evil:
A Clinical and Cultural Perspective
Sue Grand

Vol. 16
Psychoanalytic Participation:
Action, Interaction, and Integration
Kenneth A. Frank

Vol. 15
The Collapse of the Self and Its Therapeutic
Restoration
Rochelle G. K. Kainer

Vol. 14
Relational Psychoanalysis:
The Emergence of a Tradition
Stephen A. Mitchell & Lewis Aron (eds.)

Vol. 13
Seduction, Surrender, and Transformation:
Emotional Engagement in the Analytic
Process
Karen Maroda

Vol. 12
Relational Perspectives on the Body
Lewis Aron & Frances Sommer Anderson
(eds.)

Vol. 11
Building Bridges:
Negotiation of Paradox in Psychoanalysis
Stuart A. Pizer

Vol. 10
Fairbairn, Then and Now
Neil J. Skolnick and David E. Scharff (eds.)

Vol. 9
Influence and Autonomy in Psychoanalysis
Stephen A. Mitchell

Vol. 8
Unformulated Experience:
From Dissociation to Imagination in
Psychoanalysis
Donnel B. Stern

Vol. 7
Soul on the Couch:
Spirituality, Religion, and Morality in
Contemporary Psychoanalysis
Charles Spezzano & Gerald J. Gargiulo
(eds.)

Vol. 6
The Therapist as a Person:
Life Crises, Life Choices, Life Experiences,
and Their Effects on Treatment
Barbara Gerson (ed.)

Vol. 5
Holding and Psychoanalysis:
A Relational Perspective
Joyce A. Slochower

Vol. 4
A Meeting of Minds:
Mutuality in Psychoanalysis
Lewis Aron

Vol. 3
The Analyst in the Inner City:
Race, Class, and Culture through a
Psychoanalytic Lens
Neil Altman

Vol. 2
Affect in Psychoanalysis:
A Clinical Synthesis
Charles Spezzano

Vol. 1
Conversing With Uncertainty:
Practicing Psychotherapy in a Hospital
Setting
Rita Wiley McCleary

Uprooted Minds

Surviving the Politics of Terror in the Americas

psychoanalysis • history • memoir

Nancy Caro Hollander

Routledge
Taylor & Francis Group
New York   London

Routledge   Routledge
Taylor & Francis Group   Taylor & Francis Group
270 Madison Avenue   27 Church Road
New York, NY 10016   Hove, East Sussex BN3 2FA

© 2010 by Taylor and Francis Group, LLC
Routledge is an imprint of Taylor & Francis Group, an Informa business

Printed in the United States of America on acid-free paper
10 9 8 7 6 5 4 3 2 1

International Standard Book Number: 978-0-88163-490-7 (Hardback) 978-0-88163-491-4 (Paperback)

Library of Congress Cataloging-in-Publication Data

Hollander, Nancy Caro, 1939-
    Uprooted minds : surviving the politics of terror in the Americas / Nancy Caro Hollander.
        p. cm. -- (The relational perspectives book series ; v. 47)
    Includes bibliographical references and index.
    ISBN 978-0-88163-490-7 (hbk.) -- ISBN 978-0-88163-491-4 (pbk.) -- ISBN 978-0-203-88823-0 (e-book)
    1. State-sponsored terrorism--Psychological aspects--America. 2. Terrorism--Psychological aspects--America. 3. Psychic trauma- America. 4. Crises--Psychological aspects--America. 5. Social justice--Psychological aspects--America. 6. Psychoanalysts--Political activity--America. I. Title.

HV6433.A45H65 2010
303.6'25097--dc22   2009053228

Visit the Taylor & Francis Web site at
http://www.taylorandfrancis.com

and the Routledge Web site at
http://www.routledgementalhealth.com

For Rafa, his generation, and a world rooted in reparative justice.

Contents

Acknowledgments   xv
Introduction   xvii

1 Scared stiff: Social trauma and the post–9/11
  political culture   1

2 Political culture and psychoanalysis in the Southern Cone:
  Coming attractions of the Dirty Wars   33

3 A psychoanalysis for tumultuous times: The psyche and
  social revolution   61

4 The psychosocial dynamics of state terror   91

5 The culture of fear and social trauma   121

6 Exile: Paradoxes of loss and creativity   157

7 Neoliberal democracy in Latin America: Impunity and
  economic meltdown   191

8 U.S. neoliberal / neoconservative democracy:
  Psychoanalysis without the couch   225

9 Impunity and resistance: Saving democracy in the heart of
  empire   265

10 The future's uprooted minds   301

   References   347
   Index   367

Acknowledgments

My profound gratitude goes to Mimi Langer, who will always be *presente*, and to my other Latin American psychoanalytic *compañeros* with whom I have shared and learned so much about the political psyche. I am, as well, grateful to and for Hedda Bolgar, whose insight and commitment to the importance of psychoanalytic perspectives on the social world and enduringly gracious energy have been inspirational. I am enormously appreciative of the network of progressive psychoanalytic friends and colleagues in the United States, especially members of Section 9 of the Division of Psychoanalysis (39) of the American Psychological Association and the members of the Los Angeles–based Uprooted Mind Committee, whose commitments to "psychoanalysis beyond the couch" in its various forms have been so important to me and to the writing of this book. A special note of acknowledgment to Blase and Theresa Bonpane of the Office of the Americas, with whom I have had a home for activism since the early 1980s, on behalf of the Global Justice Movement's principle that "another world is possible." As well, I wish to recognize the significant work of my fellow members of Psychologists for Social Responsibility (http://psysr.org/), psychologists and other advocates for social change who apply psychological knowledge and expertise to promote peace, social justice, human rights, and sustainability.

I am eternally appreciative to Stephen Portuges for our loving partnership, our mutual commitment to the development of a social psychoanalysis, and our active participation in struggles for redistributive justice. For Susan Gutwill, I am deeply grateful, as always, for her steadfast intellectual and emotional sisterhood, which is always sustaining and has been so helpful during the writing of this book. And for my many friends and colleagues, especially Lynne Layton, Stephanie Solomon, Nina Thomas, Maureen Katz, and Andrew Samuels, I want to express my heartfelt thanks for many years of important discussions that helped to hone my own perspectives on the convergences of psychic and social reality.

Finally, I want to offer my warm thanks to Lew Aron, who believed in this project from the beginning and was unflaggingly supportive during its execution, and to the editorial staff at Routledge, including Kristopher Spring, Linda Leggio, and Eleanor Reading, who were most helpful every step of the way.

Introduction

There is no hope if you don't recognize the real.

— Chris Hedges (2009a)

And although forgetfulness, which destroys all, has killed my old dreams
I keep concealed a humble hope that is my heart's whole fortune.

— Argentine Tango

This is a book about paradoxes: how to courageously face the terrors of
our era and to live with optimism and hope. It is a social psychoanalytic
exploration of the tension between, on the one hand, our identifications
with hegemonic values and social institutions, and on the other, our ability
to develop a critical consciousness about the political and economic forces
that are destabilizing our lives. In this troublesome era, the feminist assertion that "the personal is political" is incontrovertibly lived on a daily basis.
By weaving together psychology, history, and memoir, this book's narrative
strives to illustrate how it is equally true that "the political is personal."

Many of the familiar markers of predictability and continuity in our
lives seem to have been uprooted. In our post–9/11 environment we have
been subject to the traumas of international terrorism, authoritarian governance, war, and economic meltdown. Our customary sense of relative
security and stability associated with the privilege of living in the heart of
the U.S. empire has been profoundly shaken. As we are forced to negotiate
increasing anxieties about dramatic changes in our society, we live in an
environment saturated with information about droughts, floods, pandemic
viruses, crime, terrorism, hunger, and indebtedness; the loss of health care,
jobs, retirement plans, and a sense of safety. Moreover, our daily personal
struggles with work, family, friends, and community are punctuated by
inescapable moments of awareness of the threat of global warming, terrorism, and nuclear proliferation. We experience what sociologist Zygmunt
Bauman calls "liquid fears" in our increasingly unsafe globalized world.

This book endeavors to make sense of the historical forces that have brought us to this critical juncture. It does so by analyzing the role played by the neoliberal economic paradigm and conservative political agenda that emerged in the United States and Latin America over the past three decades with devastating consequences for the majority of the hemisphere's citizens. My historical account is informed by a psychoanalytic elaboration of how the sociosymbolic order is an important constituent of the psyche and how subjectivity is formed in light of hegemonic ideology. I have woven into the theoretical material and historical narrative testimonies of U.S. and Latin American psychoanalysts who share their experiences and observations about living under authoritarian political conditions. I show how these progressive psychoanalysts engage in social activism on behalf of human rights and redistributive justice they believe to be the fundamental social matrix for collective psychological health. By illuminating themes related to the mutual effects of social power and ideology, large group dynamics and unconscious fantasies, affects and defenses, I hope to encourage reflections about our experience as social/psychological subjects.

The complex psychological and social sequelae of living in our post–9/11 culture of fear imposed by the neoconservative agenda has yet to be fully appreciated, as does the significance of the economic catastrophe that now haunts most citizens' lives. Vexing questions remain as to the fundamental nature of the crisis of democracy in this country and its relationship to the neoliberal political/economic model that predated the Bush administration and threatens to sustain itself under the stewardship of Barack Obama and the Democratic Party. We do not yet know if the new administration represents enough of a fundamental departure from the policies of the past to effectively address the systemic sources of the growing social and psychological dislocation haunting this country. Our post–9/11 environment continues to be a traumatogenic one in which individual and group physical safety, social security, and symbolic capacities are being assaulted.

An interdisciplinary psychoanalysis can illuminate what it means when a person's experience is traumatic and rendered unnamable and unspeakable. It can appreciate how the profound human need to attach to others extends to the larger society, which when it does not function to provide a holding environment leaves individuals and groups vulnerable to uncontainable anxieties that in turn affect the social world. Thus, from my perspective, taking account of the past and assessing the current direction of this country involve thinking about how psychology and politics intersect, how intrapsychic and intersubjective dynamics converge with economic, ideological, and political forces to reinforce or alter an inequitable social order. Because I was trained first as a Latin American historian and then as a psychoanalyst, I have learned to think about the intersection of psychic and social reality in the context of extreme political crisis. My analysis of the nature and impact of our post–9/11 authoritarian political culture and the challenges that we face in this country today have been informed by my experience during the last four decades of researching and writing about the more tumultuous conditions of dictatorship and revolution in Latin America.

In 1997, I published *Love in a Time of Hate: Liberation Psychology in Latin America*, in which I analyzed a number of themes related to state terror and social trauma. In part, the book was the product of my efforts to work through my own traumatic encounter with Latin American authoritarianism. I had lived in Argentina for some years prior to the Dirty War. During the transition to the 1976 military coup, the environment was already inundated with repressive state policies marked by right-wing death squads' disappearance and murder of many Argentine citizens, including some of my close friends and colleagues. These losses only multiplied following the military seizure of state power. Thus the book was written from the perspective of both participant and witness/observer. I explored the subjective meanings of the politically repressive conditions provoked by the military dictatorships in Argentina, Chile, and Uruguay that endured from the 1970s through the 1980s. Although my research included interviews with individuals from many sectors of society who lived through the agonizing experience of state terror, I chose to elaborate the systemic roots of these authoritarian regimes and the psychology of perpetrators, bystanders, victims, and political activists through the real-life experiences of 10 Argentine, Uruguayan, and Chilean psychoanalysts. Their desire to forge an integration of their progressive political concerns with their commitments to their psychoanalytic profession make them spokespersons for colleagues throughout the world who stand apart from a mainstream psychoanalysis that has all too often chosen to remain isolated from pressing social issues. A central figure in this drama is Austrian-born Argentine psychoanalyst Marie Langer, whose history prior to her immigration to Latin America in the late 1930s included training at Freud's Vienna Psychoanalytic Institute and participation as a physician in an International Medical Brigade in the Spanish Civil War. Langer was one of the six founders in 1942 of the Argentine Psychoanalytic Association and by the 1960s had become a prominent figure in the political struggles that linked mental health issues with the need for progressive social change.

Langer and the nine other protagonists in *Love in a Time of Hate* lived through their countries' politically repressive conditions and found ways to engage in struggles for democracy and human rights, either from within their countries or as political refugees, often at great personal risk to themselves and their families. Their psychoanalytic and radical political perspectives shed light on the subjective meanings of collective social action. When I met her in 1983, Marie Langer was living in exile in Mexico City and cochairing a group of psychoanalysts who were helping the Sandinista Revolution construct Nicaragua's first national free and psychoanalytically oriented mental health care system. She and other psychoanalysts also provided psychotherapy to survivors of torture and refugees from many Latin American military dictatorships. My own research with individuals who had survived horrendous abuses by the state and my experience with these psychoanalysts highlighted irrefutable convergences between psychic and social reality and demonstrated the importance of understanding the psychology of violent group conflict and the social trauma it engenders. Moreover, my collaboration with these Latin American psychoanalysts in the context of the more extreme social situation of their countries has informed my understanding of the authoritarian trends that have characterized the post–9/11 U.S. political culture designed by the neoconservatives, as well as the subjective meanings of the emergence of a progressive movement that has challenged their hegemony. The activism of my psychoanalytic colleagues in the Global South on behalf of social justice and economic equity has been an inspiration to my own participation during the past eight years with other psychoanalysts in this country engaged in projects whose principles reflect a socially responsible psychoanalysis.

In the past decade, a number of psychoanalysts in the United States have found their own journeys toward a psychoanalysis beyond the couch. *Uprooted Minds* tells this story through the myriad projects that have been developed in response to the neoliberal economic model and social strategy that has had deleterious psychological effects for millions of people. Progressive psychoanalysts in the United States have also been engaged in struggles to defend democracy from its assault by the neoconservative policies of the past eight years. This aspect of the history is framed by the testimony of Hedda Bolgar, a European-born, Los Angeles–based psychoanalyst whose personal history and commitment to a social psychoanalysis is similar to that of our Latin American protagonists. Bolgar, who recently celebrated her 100th birthday, shares her psychoanalytic understanding of the psychological significance of the multiple social and political challenges facing us in this country. As young girls, Langer and Bolgar attended the same private girls' school in Red Vienna, where their feminist and radical social consciousness took root. With the rise of the Nazis, both were forced to flee Europe, Langer to Argentina and Bolgar to the United States. We learn through these pages how each, Langer in the Global South and Bolgar in the heart of the U.S. empire, developed her own version of a socially committed psychoanalysis.

As we will see, the human suffering that was produced by Latin America's military regimes has for years been represented by the signifier "September 11"—the day in 1973 of the infamous coup in Chile—which has stood for the military-imposed twin oppressions of political authoritarianism and neoliberal free-market economic fundamentalism. The constitutionally elected governments that succeeded state terror in Latin America from the 1980s on proved to be thoroughly corrupt: They became more

benign administrators of a culture of impunity that sustained the unregulated free-market economic model and protected the former perpetrators
of state terror from prosecution for their crimes against humanity. Latin
Americans lived through several decades of these cultures of impunity until
the inherent contradictions became so intense that they produced radical
mass movements that demanded change. In the past decade, throughout
the region, grassroots activism has brought to power progressive regimes
that are challenging the hegemony of the U.S. and national elites, known as
the Washington Consensus, in favor of radical reforms of the institutional
sources of the region's condemnation of the majority of people to lives of
poverty and powerlessness.

I believe that Latin America's last half-century's experience of state terror and its aftermath foreshadowed similar trends, although not so extreme
and in a more condensed period of time, that developed in this country during our post–9/11 political culture and economic priorities. The relationship between Latin American and U.S. experiences with authoritarianism
is captured in the signifier of the date by which both are known. While
Latin America's September 11 has functioned as an icon signifying U.S.-
supported-and-financed state terror throughout the hemisphere, our 9/11
was interpreted by the U.S. state as a symbol of our unprovoked victimization, and it was manipulated opportunistically by the neoconservative
movement for a domestic and foreign policy agenda that predated it. In this
country, the state launched an authoritarian assault on democratic process,
constitutional guarantees, checks and balances of the three branches of
government, and citizens' civil liberties. Domestic laws were undermined
in the construction of a surveillance society. After 9/11 our government's
aggressive foreign policy of preemptive invasion was predicated on an
unwillingness to acknowledge the long history of U.S. interventionism in
the Global South as one cause of anti-American animosity. This failure
produced a politics in which the "Axis of Evil" became a repository for
the state's denied and projected aggression that could then be attacked and
destroyed through war and occupation in the name of keeping us safe.
Under cover of 9/11, the neoconservatives also developed a corrupt form
of crony capitalism through a bloated military budget and a deregulated
financial structure, which has thrown this country into an unprecedented
economic catastrophe that mirrors the Latin American economic debacle at
the turn of the millennium. Such a profound crisis has added many voices
to the radical critique of this authoritarian era of U.S. history. Typical of
a rising chorus denouncing the nature of U.S. politics during the Bush
administration is international human rights lawyer Scott Horton, who
has recently claimed that "We may not have realized it at the time, but in
the period from late 2001 to January 19, 2009, this country was a dictatorship" (Stockwell, 2009).[1]

Uprooted Minds is a book about psychoanalysis and the politics of terror in the Americas. In my elaboration of the themes indicated above, I am always mindful of the complex interplay of psychological dynamics and social forces. The book begins in this country, and in chapter 1 I elaborate a social psychoanalytic conceptualization of how the psyche is inserted in the larger social order and how intrapsychic and intersubjective dynamics affect the social world. This perspective serves as the context for my analysis of how the convergence of ideology and psychological defenses framed the U.S. response to the shared traumatic significance of 9/11. The chapter then traces the psycho-political factors responsible for the drift toward authoritarianism and the evolution of a bystander population in the early years of the Bush administration.

In chapters 2 through 7, I retell the stories of our Latin American psychoanalytic colleagues as they traversed the terrible experience of state terror and engaged in movements that challenged the corrupt democratic regimes that replaced military dictatorships. We learn about how they managed the demands of progressive political activism with their professional lives and how their psychoanalytic theoretical perspectives shed light on the subjective experience of living with the destructiveness of oppressive political and economic structures. I examine the Argentine economic meltdown in December 2001 brought on by the neoliberal free-market paradigm and describe the radicalized grassroots citizens' responses, which included the collaboration of many psychoanalysts. The chapters' additional themes, including the losses and challenges of migration experienced by political and economic refugees and the relationship between social activism and mental health, shed light on some of the most important contemporary issues facing people throughout the world.

These chapters provide a referent that serves to illuminate the nature of our own recent history with political authoritarianism and economic catastrophe in the heart of the U.S. empire. In chapter 8 we turn our attention back to this country in order to further understand the psychosocial dynamics of our post–9/11 political culture. An elaboration of the historical roots of this culture's high value on individualism serves as a context for my analysis of neoliberalism as an economic policy and social theory that came to be internalized as an aspect of normative subjectivity. I then elucidate the convergences between the neoliberal paradigm and the neoconservative agenda that have compromised this country's democracy and economic stability. We see how psychoanalysts in this country have responded to social trauma by becoming engaged in projects that integrate their psychoanalytic expertise with their commitment to activism on behalf of social justice.

In chapter 9, I interpret the growing concerns in civil society about the rightward drift of the Bush administration and explore the psychological and social significance of the oppositional movement that emerged to successfully challenge the neoconservative agenda and to mobilize support for

the election of Barack Obama. We also revisit our Latin American protagonists, who share their perspectives on the significance of post–9/11 political
and economic crises in the United States and their impact on their own progressive struggles to challenge the hegemony of the Washington Consensus.
In chapter 10, I assess the implications of the election of Barack Obama
and show how psychoanalysis can shed light on the dynamic relationship
between leaders and the groups they represent. I also explore the potential
for altering the institutional and ideological sources of the U.S. and global
economic meltdown in 2008. In this context, a series of discourses are
delineated that I argue contribute to a psychoanalytic conceptualization of
the relationship between psychic and social reality.

In a related vein, I elaborate a social psychoanalysis that takes seriously
the clinical as well as the theoretical significance of how psychic life bears
the mark of the social order. I argue for the importance within the clinical
experience of including rather than marginalizing the anxieties and fears
stimulated by political realities, which inevitably manifest themselves in
the transference/countertransference dynamic and relationship. Finally, I
examine the important role that psychoanalysts can play in engaging in
struggles for social justice and democracy upon which the very practice of
our profession depends.

ENDNOTES

1. Scott Horton is a New York attorney, specialist in human rights law, and
   contributor to *Harper's Magazine*.

Chapter 1

Scared stiff

Social trauma and the post–9/11 political culture

May you live in interesting times.

—Chinese proverb

Vengeance is a lazy form of grief.

—Silvia Broome
The Interpreter (Pollack, 2005)

"I left Vienna on March 15, 1938, the very day Hitler himself entered the city as part of the official Anschluss. I remember that it was a beautiful, sunny, cool day, and a spontaneous popular celebration of the Führer's arrival had erupted. The streets were packed with wildly cheering crowds waving Nazi flags. I knew I would be arrested and wouldn't survive because I had published many anti-Nazi articles in magazines that had circulated in Paris and Amsterdam. Besides, because of what I had learned growing up in my highly politicized family and from my training at the University of Vienna, I was really clear about the horrors that lay in store for everyone under Nazi rule." So begins Hedda Bolgar's response to my question about how her experiences as a young woman living in Europe as it succumbed to fascism have influenced her reactions to the increasing threats to our democracy by the Bush administration's "war on terror."

It is a sunny day in July 2006, and Hedda, now 97 years old, is a psychoanalyst and social activist who still has a full-time practice. She is a training and supervising analyst at the Los Angeles Institute and Society for Psychoanalytic Studies, which she cofounded in the 1980s. Hedda's comfortably elegant Brentwood home serves as a hospitable hub for many of the institute's functions, and she hosts a salon on the first Wednesday of the month for colleagues to discuss a variety of topics ranging from clinical and theoretical psychoanalytic issues to the psychological implication of social problems. She and I are sitting in her earth-toned, informal living room, walls covered with original paintings and framed posters, many of which are visual representations of Hedda's commitment to the significant political struggles of the last half century. Her gracious charm is reflected in the sumptuous gardens that surround the entranceway and the enticing fruits and pastries spread before us to energize our discussion. She periodically utters playful side comments to her beloved cats as they wander in and out, lazily curious about what their doting owner is up to now. In this same room, along with eight other psychoanalytic colleagues, Hedda and I have met on a monthly basis over the past three years, organizing a series of conferences for mental health professionals and the community at large that feature psychoanalytic perspectives on the crucial social issues of our times. On this day, as I listen to Hedda recount the details of her life, I am reminded once again about her finely tuned memory, which is the envy of her "younger" colleagues in our 50s and 60s. Each of us has had the experience during one meeting or another of struggling to remember a specific name or date and invariably turning to Hedda, who always amazes us with her reliable instant recall of all kinds of details. We are accustomed to chuckling every once in a while when, as we settle into our evening's agenda and heave exhausted sighs after attending to patients all day, Hedda's alert attentiveness is blunted as she mentions that she is a bit tired, having had a full schedule of patients on the heels of a rigorous, weekend, out-of-town conference. When we demand to know what accounts for her boundless energy at the age of 97, her answer is always the same: "Diet," she responds. "I've been a vegetarian for 85 years." And then she adds with a twinkle in her eye but quite seriously, "Oh, yes, and being engaged in the world, always fighting for the truth."

Now the two of us are involved in the specific project of this book. Like my Latin American psychoanalytic colleagues whose personal testimonies illuminate my analysis of their countries' traumatogenic political and economic crises, Hedda has agreed to share aspects of her history and self-reflections that help to contextualize my interpretation of the subjective experience of the drift toward authoritarianism and economic catastrophe in the United States since 9/11. Her lifelong social concerns mirror the commitments of much of the political activism that has emerged among psychoanalysts in the post–9/11 environment. I am intrigued by Hedda's narrative in that much of it parallels Marie Langer's experience of growing up in the cultural ferment of the interwar years in Europe. Both were forced to flee their homeland and, as immigrants in new countries, to integrate their progressive political views with their psychoanalytic theory and practice—Marie Langer in the context of the turbulent conditions of third-world Latin America, and Hedda in the less extreme circumstances of the U.S. superpower.

"I had been studying for my Ph.D. at the University of Vienna," Hedda continues, now focusing on what life had been like before the Nazis extended their power into Austria. "I majored in psychology, and although the department was not psychoanalytic, nor were we involved in Freud's free clinics,[1] some faculty had connections to Freud's Institute. It was the 1930s, during the time that Vienna was exploding with all kinds of wonderful social and cultural programs supported by the progressive Social Democratic municipal government, including much of the mental health enterprise, some of it related to the work at the university's psychology department. Many of the faculty were Marxists, members of the Socialist Party and the youth movement, and they were very much committed to social issues. The work was very intense. We studied child development, the importance of the mother–child relationship, and even the social effects of unemployment on communities. The orientation was one of understanding the individual in the context of family and community, and this reinforced in me a sensitivity to the internal and external—or the psychic and social— continuum in human experience. The department also had connections to American universities, and because I was interested in clinical training, which was not offered there, colleagues suggested I apply for a postdoctoral fellowship at the University of Chicago. My successful application turned out to be a life saver, because I was accepted just as Social Democracy was being vanquished by the Austro-fascist movement that later merged with the even more repressive Nazi Party. Many of the psychology faculty were arrested in the process."

I ask Hedda what it was like living in the transition to fascism. "During the time the political situation worsened," she says, "I noticed that as a manic defense people often joked about the really terrible events occurring all around us. We lived in an increasingly schizophrenic Vienna, with rising unemployment, poverty, and even homelessness for the first time. People were really suffering, but the opera and symphony and galleries were still operating, as was some semblance of informative news reportage for the middle and upper-middle classes. The privileged could often easily deny the frightening signs of terrible social dislocation and the looming political threat. For me, it was the writing on the wall, and I knew we had to leave. My fiancé, Herbert Bekker, was resistant to leaving. Like many others I argued with, he thought that since he was not publicly political, he would encounter little trouble with the Nazis and would therefore have plenty of time to take care of his family before departing. So he would emigrate later, and I would have to flee alone. I packed a small suitcase and set out to negotiate the labyrinthine Nazi-dominated border crossings and train routes that would take me to the coast of France, where I would set sail for New York."

As Hedda describes in a matter-of-fact manner the often terrifying details of her flight, the images in my mind are like a cinematic thriller. I interrupt her to ask how she was able to tolerate what I imagine must have been intense anxiety given the personally threatening situations she frequently found herself in during her journey. How had she not been unbearably frightened? "No, I wasn't scared," she responds. "I wasn't supposed to be scared of anything. I was raised not to be frightened." She recalls how as a child just after World War I, her Marxist parents had been deeply involved in the short-lived leftist revolution that had brought socialism to Hungary for some brief months. "That was a very exciting period for me, even when as a nine-year-old my first real party was cancelled because my parents had to make the revolution. When I told my father that he had ruined my party, he said to me with a straight face, 'I'm so sorry; I wish you'd have told me, and we would have postponed the revolution!' But even with that major upset, I also remember it being glorious. My parents weren't scared; they were remaking the world, and their attitude was, 'If there's a problem, you solve it; a need, you meet it.'" But there were also the more difficult aspects of experience during these tumultuous times, and Hedda's early life was characterized by overstimulation, loss, and even depression. She has described the multiple losses she suffered brought on by war, her parents' divorce, her frequent family moves from one country to another, and the loss of her first nanny. Although the political and social environment was exciting, Hedda (2001) has written that "…life during those years now feels like a manic defense against the chronic mourning everybody in the family was constantly feeling…today I know that what I knew not consciously then was that very little was experienced deeply" (p. 41).

I wonder aloud if the combination of political consciousness and manic defense learned early in life permitted her to endure with such equanimity the frightening conditions under which she fled fascist Austria. "Yes," Hedda says, pondering the question. "The fear was probably there, but the terror and helplessness were really repressed. That was certainly the case for me as a child when the reactionary forces overturned the brief Hungarian socialist government and enacted a brutal backlash. Years later, when I flaunted my own safety to do some of the things I needed to do as I fled the Nazis, I didn't permit myself to feel the fear either. On my way to France from Austria, for example, I took some risks going to Switzerland and Czechoslovakia and back into Germany to collect some of my father's important papers and money from bank accounts that I knew would be needed later. In several potentially compromising situations when I was confronted by Nazi authorities, I remembered the lessons my father taught me about the importance of assuming a cool, disdainful demeanor with those in power, and I managed to save myself. On the other hand, I had a choice: I could have joined the resistance and stayed, but it never occurred to me. I don't know why. I did not feel guilty about leaving because I had the conviction that after I left, I would be able to help more people than if I had stayed. It was true as it turned out, because I was able to bring a lot of people out and save their lives."

This discussion stimulates associations for both of us to our present political environment in the United States and the omnipresent sense of threat that pervades the culture. We share the conviction that the Bush administration is eroding democracy by compromising civil liberties and the right to dissent, all the while legitimizing practices, such as torture and extraordinary renditions, that violate international and national law. His preemptive war policy depends on a military budget that is compromising our welfare at home and making the United States a rogue state internationally. We are worried about how the neoconservative discourse continues to dominate the media, disenfranchising critical voices as antipatriotic threats to national security. Hedda says she is reminded of the question that plagued so many in Europe as the Nazis eviscerated democracy from one country to another: When do you pack your bags and flee? It brings back painful memories for me, as well, memories of Latin American friends and colleagues who were forced to decide when the pivotal moment had arrived to make the life-altering decision to save themselves and their families by fleeing their countries' state terrorist regimes. We ruefully agree that perhaps the scariest thing for us at this historical moment is that, in spite of so many citizens' fantasies of moving to another country, in this globalized world, there is actually no place to escape to.

"After the attacks on the World Trade Center and the Pentagon," Hedda is saying, "it was the first time in my life that I really allowed myself to be afraid. I've lived through all kinds of situations that were dangerous, and I always felt I had to—and could—do something. But after 9/11, I was suddenly scared to death. I couldn't understand why, because Ground Zero was more than 3,000 miles away, and there was no real indication that something similar was about to happen here in Los Angeles. But I had the grim feeling, which I couldn't put into words, that this was the beginning of something really bad. I just felt that Bush was going to use this tragedy in a very destructive way. It was nothing I could really consciously explain; it was just a general political mistrust. I was more afraid of the reaction to the terrorists than of the terrorists themselves, and that's where I still am. What kind of a question is, 'Why do they hate us?' We know that for years the aim of this country's foreign policy has been to control others' resources and governments. And there is this split: The United States keeps doing what it's been doing, and meanwhile we are caught up in this horrible trauma of 9/11 that is indelibly impressed on our psyches: the people who were in the towers burning to death, the dreadful images of those who leapt to their death, those who disappeared in the ashes that covered the city... and then the wonderful first responders. There is this constant battle: on the one hand, this terrible thing that has happened; and on the other, the retaliatory revenge strategy that was developed almost immediately, which I could not bear. I remembered how the Social Democrats caved in to the fascists in Vienna. Now I have this intense sense of complete helplessness in the face of something similar occurring among our elected representatives, Democrats and Republicans alike, in this government. We have to scramble even to get reliable information, and there is the feeling that we have lost whatever real democracy there was in the United States. Right after 9/11 I had the sensation that with the right wing in the White House, we were going to lose all the gains, like Social Security and other benefits of progressive state policies, that still existed. I had no idea then how bad it would actually get."

These thoughts spark recollections of our work together that began in 2003, two years after the terrorist attacks. In response to 9/11 and Hedda's urgent concerns about the problematic political realities she thought many citizens in this country were denying, including her psychoanalytic colleagues, she proposed organizing a conference on the reciprocal impact of psychic and social reality. She wanted to demonstrate that psychoanalysts have something to contribute to our understanding of how psychological experience is affected by and affects an increasingly dangerous world. When Hedda invited me to be a member of the committee that would organize the conference,[2] I was delighted because it represented in Los Angeles a bridge to the work I had been doing with my psychoanalytic social activist colleagues in Latin America. All the committee members wished to do something practical that would provide people with the opportunity to use their minds to think about the growing dangers of our new political reality that were emanating as much from domestic as they were from foreign influences. We wanted the conference to focus on how current social realities affect our individual psyches and how our psychic realities impact on and reorganize the larger social world. An additional goal was to help psychoanalysts and other mental health professionals think about external reality and social events as sources of their patients' and their own profound anxieties rather than interpret them as if they were only symbolic of unconscious anxieties provoked by unresolved childhood conflict and trauma. After one year of intense planning, the three-day conference, "The Uprooted Mind: Psychoanalytic Perspectives on Living in an Unsafe World," took place the last weekend of October 2004, on the eve of the highly contested 2004 national election. Keynote speakers included Robert Jay Lifton, who analyzed the U.S. experience of unprecedented vulnerability and its compensatory bellicose reaction to 9/11 as delineated in his book *Superpower Syndrome: America's apocalyptic confrontation with the world* (Lifton 2003); Maureen Katz, who explored the multiple and paradoxical psychological meanings to U.S. citizens of the spectacle of Abu Ghraib (see Katz, 2006); Andrew Samuels, who conveyed aspects of his pioneering ideas about political subjectivity detailed in his *Politics on the Couch* (2007); and myself, with a presentation elaborating on my work on trauma, ideology, and psychic defenses, originally developed in the context of state terror in Latin America and now conceptualized in terms of the traumatogenic political culture of post–9/11 United States (see Hollander, 2006; Hollander & Gutwill, 2006).

I was in part concerned with the difficulty citizens in this country were having in recognizing the crisis of our democracy and the tendency to disavow reality because of the long-held ideological assumption that although authoritarian rule can occur anywhere else in the world, "it can't happen here." This attitude was an eerie reminder of what my friend and colleague Uruguayan psychoanalyst Marcelo Viñar had once poignantly told me about how it felt to be living in his country in 1971 during the several years before its century-long democratic rule was forcibly ended by a military coup. With painful irony, Marcelo had commented:

> The process of political change and the capacity to subjectively absorb and understand this change operate at distinctly different rates...It's as if I continued to believe in democracy when I was living in a country that was already totalitarian. I believe that it is characteristic of the period of transition between democracy and dictatorship that people function by denying reality.

I proposed that Marcelo's observation of the tendency to deny a threatening reality could serve as a warning to us in this country as we, too, succumb to the wish to disavow the signs of our own transition toward an unprecedented centralization of political power and disenfranchisement of citizens. "The uprooted mind" was the metaphor for the painful and even traumatic impact of living in the post–9/11 environment permeated with dangers that were intensifying at a pace that felt overwhelming. The psychic residue of these social terrors, I argued, was apparent in our consultation rooms as patients experienced how the political is personal, the other side of the coin of the revolutionary idea proclaimed by feminists of the 1960s that "the personal is political."

Since the "Uprooted Mind" conference, I have continued to extend my work on trauma, ideology, and psychic defenses as a construct to explain the subjective meanings of the political and economic crises that have become more profound and complex since 9/11. Like Hedda, I have been arguing that if we ever had any doubts, under the extreme social conditions in which we now live, it is no longer possible to speak of psychic and social reality as if they were two exclusively separate registers. Indeed, from my perspective, subjectivity is fashioned out of the intimate interplay between the imaginary dimensions of the unconscious, which is characterized by representations, drives, defenses, and affects, and a relational matrix that reaches out beyond the family to include the sociosymbolic order, composed of asymmetrical relations of power and force.

THE SOCIAL MATRIX OF PSYCHIC EXPERIENCE

Psychoanalysts have been dealing for years from different theoretical perspectives with the concept of psychic reality and what role social reality plays in unconscious life. In the early 1990s, the International Psychoanalytic Association held its biannual congress in San Francisco, the theme of which was psychic reality. The invited presenters concurred that Freud's concept of psychic reality, together with the theory of infantile sexuality, the unconscious, repetition, and transference, constituted the foundations of psychoanalysis. There was agreement that external reality had to be taken into account in any conceptualization of psychic reality, but external reality for most of the presenters meant essentially the intersubjective encounter between the analyst's and the patient's unconscious minds. For some, the mechanism of projective identification was the essential link between the subject and the external world. But others, most notably a group of Argentine psychoanalysts, argued that the components of the unconscious are not only fantasy and object relations but internalized attributes of the sociocultural environment as well. They emphasized the importance of accounting for how the subject is constituted within specific historical moments and cultures and is likely to bear the signs of intergenerational transmissions of socially constructed trauma (Etchegoyen, 1996).

This view seems to me to take into account the insertion of the individual in the social order out of which the complex interplay between unconscious dynamics and social forces render human experience inevitably destabilizing. It is situated within an important trend stemming from Freud himself. Freud's revolutionary discovery was the decentered subject: Enlightenment man, rational, in charge of nature and the social order, was displaced by the psychoanalytic self, dominated by unconscious forces whose presence he did not control, like that of a foreign body—an internalized trace of parental others—that could never be completely assimilated. The disconcerting implications of this notion were softened by Freud's belief that psychoanalytic therapy could help human beings reassume some degree of reason over disorderly passions through making the unconscious conscious. As Stephen Frosh (1987) points out, this tradition within psychoanalysis promised mastery and a fantasy of completeness and integrated selfhood, for analysts and patients alike. However, perhaps in response to the relativism, narcissism, and nihilism associated with postmodern culture and global capitalism, many psychoanalytic theorists have returned to an interest in the social and psychological meanings of the Freudian decentered subject. Considerations of how social reality forms part of the psyche lead toward a focus on how the Other (from parent to the larger social order) governs our existence to impose an essential alienness or alterity of human subjectivity. My own understanding is that external reality is, indeed, a foundational aspect of the constitution of the self.

Most psychoanalytic research demonstrates that the social matrix either facilitates or impedes psychic development and integration. Libidinal and aggressive impulses are fated to be constructively or destructively expressed, depending on the existence and nature of container/contained relationships, not only in the intimacy of the family but in the culture at large. How can psychoanalysis help us understand the nature of human destructiveness, which is a major theme of this book? Two trends generally characterize psychoanalytic thinking, the first that sides with Freud's conviction of an innate destructive drive or instinct that is inevitably mobilized against the self or outward against others; and the second that conceptualizes aggression as a response to deprivations and frustrations in the environment, impingements that originate in the catastrophes of childhood trauma and are reproduced throughout the life span. My view as it is elaborated in my analysis of the violence of terror in the Americas parallels Stephen Mitchell's perspective in which aggression, like sexuality, does not represent a "a push from within," but a response to others, biologically mediated and prewired, within a relational context (Mitchell, 1998, p. 25). Hegemonic institutions and ideologies either exacerbate primitive anxieties and their manifestation in envy, greed, and hate or promote the capacities that form the basis of reparative guilt and love, concern, and responsibility for others (see Rustin, 1991; Peltz, 2005). Psychoanalytic theories have also elaborated how interpersonal experience is realized through the medium and psychological use of social symbols. D. W. Winnicott, for example, thought of symbolization as a constructive, expansive, intrapsychic capacity as well as a relational process in which one uses a transitional me/not me space to negotiate a balance between acceptance of authentic internal wishes and needs and responsiveness to external reality's expectations and demands. When the transitional space fails, it exacerbates what Melanie Klein called paranoid/schizoid states of mind, characterized by primitive defenses such as splitting, projection, idealization, and projective identification that protect the subject from being overwhelmed by annihilation anxiety stimulated by external as well as internal forces.[3] But Winnicott, Klein, and other object relations theorists did not take into account how external reality contains the hegemonic cultural symbols of the social order's asymmetrical forces of privilege and power, which are internalized to form an alienating aspect of identity. Several psychoanalytic traditions elaborate the relationship between the psyche and the larger social order, one represented by the group theorists associated with the work of S. H. Foulkes and Wilford Bion and the other by Jacques Lacan and Jean LaPlanche. Both approaches are useful in our analysis of the individual and group response in this country to 9/11.

Psychoanalysts in the group psychotherapy tradition account for a socially constructed subjectivity through the concept of the social unconscious, by which they mean the coconstructed and shared unconscious of members of particular social systems such as community, society, nation, or culture. The social unconscious includes shared anxieties, fantasies, defenses, myths, and memories, and its building blocks are made of chosen traumas and chosen glories (Weinberg, 2007). For some theorists in this tradition, the social unconscious represents the installation of social *power relations* within the core of psychic structure and functions as a bridge between the individual and the group that shapes drives, affects, and defenses. The *I* of the individual is constructed inevitably out of the preexisting *we*, which in turn exists in relation to a designated *not we*, always characterized by power hierarchies. Thus the psychology of individuals is constituted within the vicissitudes of the power-relational field they inhabit to shape how they feel about themselves and behave toward others (Dalal, 2001). In the British psychosocial studies tradition that examines subjectivity through a psychoanalytically informed lens, Wendy Hollway defines the concept *psycho-social* in this way:

> We are *psycho*-social because we are products of a unique life history of anxiety- and desire-provoking life events and the manner in which they have been transformed in internal reality. We are psycho-*social* because such defensive activities affect and are affected by material conditions and discourses (systems of meaning which pre-exist any given individual), because unconscious defenses are intersubjective processes...and because of the real events in the external, social world which are discursively, desirously and defensively appropriated. (Hook, 2008, p. 351)

In the language of Lacan and LaPlanche, the intersubjective unconscious is constituted by an alterity created by the "the Other," by which they mean that the subject is created by the intersubjective relationships that contextualize it, predate it, and extend beyond it. To put this in developmental terms, the infant is born without a sense of stable bodily or psychic integrity. The emergence of the self develops over time in the relationship with the primary adult(s), whose conscious and unconscious identity, saturated with constituents of the social order, is internalized by the infant as an aspect of its own psychic structure. At the same time, the child is shaped by larger external forces (unconscious expectations of others, language, patriarchy, and so on), and this otherness is also internalized to become part of the self. In this way, the individual's original state of diffuseness or decenteredness is partially transcended through the encounter with a consolingly coherent image of him- or herself mediated through the dominant ideological discourse that assigns a place in the social order based on attributes associated with class, race, and gender. But while the specific place of each subject in what Lacan calls the *symbolic order* renders an apparent integrative identity, it enforces a recognition of difference and prohibitions, both of which unavoidably entail loss and rupture. Lacan's perspective emphasizes the inevitability of divisions within the self and among subjects even as desire for unification persists (Elliot, 1939; see also Soler, 2006).

LaPlanche has stressed that the alien within the subject begins with mother and the enigmatic message the infant receives based on mother's unconscious conflicted sexuality and aggression. The child translates what it can into representations or fantasies, leaving the remainder that cannot be interpreted to become the foundation of the unconscious. LaPlanche's view that the child actively negotiates the parental enigmatic signifier through fantasy and unconscious defenses can be extended to show that these processes enjoy a recapitulation across the life span as the subject struggles with the enigmatic messages of authority figures in the social order that, even while they often refuse to yield coherent and consistent meanings, are compellingly seductive (Caruth, 2001; LaPlanche, 1999).

While the Symbolic Order, to use Lacan's term, provides the decentered subject with an apparently coherent identity and thus the possibility of covering over internal discontinuities, it simultaneously functions to sustain the repressive and constraining asymmetrical relations of authority and power. Many theorists have studied how the ruling classes of any given society are able to exercise their control through the dominant ideology, or system of ideas, which functions to justify their power and is internalized by the subjugated classes who come to identify with a world view that is not in their objective interests. This contradictory condition by which the oppressed identify with the dominant ideology has been referred to as *false consciousness* by many radical theorists (McCarney, 2003; see also Eagleton, 1994). However, political philosopher Antonio Gramsci (1971) argued that the ruling classes govern by securing consent from those they subjugate, not only in the realm of shared ideas but through a complex habitual social practice lived out through the unconscious and inarticulate dimensions of social experience. Gramsci postulated that the dominant social symbols of the culture—the whole range of values, attitudes, beliefs, cultural norms, legal precepts, and so on that infuse civil society—are transmitted through the vast range of institutions, including the family, religious groups, the legal apparatus, civic organizations, the media, and so forth, all of which generate a belief in a particular system. Together they constitute what Gramsci called hegemony, which is so powerful because it is experienced as the common sense of an entire social order. Hegemony lends a secure and enduring quality to power not achievable through the use of coercive institutions such as the military and the police, thus giving it a kind of psychological validity. Hegemony is not static; it has to be renewed, recreated, and defended. Multiple creeds, doctrines, and modes of perception may jostle for authority; but despite their differences, together they generate and reinforce citizens' belief in the existing system. By way of illustration, neoconservative and liberal perspectives represent different ideological trends, but they share unquestioned hegemonic assumptions about U.S. superpower strivings and the sacrosanct principles of individualism and private property (Boggs, 1984).

Elaborating upon Gramsci, French Lacanian Marxist Louis Althusser analyzed what he called *state ideological apparatuses*—social institutions that in his words interpellate or "hail" us to our place in the social order so that we unconsciously assume our position within it in a way that maintains the hidden relations of power. Althusser (1984) explored in more detail the important unconscious function of the dominant ideology. From his Lacanian perspective, the subject engages in an imaginary search for unity and coherence to escape the fractured and decentered nature of human experience. The individual locates him- or herself through ideology, which is a thought–practice—in other words, both an unquestioned set of ideas and engrained customs located in concrete behaviors of everyday life. Since hegemonic values are taken as natural, our conscious awareness about them is preempted and we are habituated to them. In Lacanian philosopher Slavoj Zizek's words, "They do not know it, but they are doing it" (Myers, 2003, p. 63). Sociologist Zygmunt Bauman stresses this invisible quality and shared experience of existing power relations: "Power," he argues,

> is not an object stocked in governmental safes that can be acquired by revolutionaries storming and occupying the Winter Palace; it cannot be "taken over" by assaulting and removing its present holders "on high." It is present in every tissue and cell of society—and it is also constantly reproduced and replenished by daily routine conduct. (Haugaard, 2008, p. 112)

This discussion raises the important question of how we can account for the capacity of citizens to disengage from hegemony to develop a critical ideological position about their lived experience that counters the "official story" of those who rule. We will explore how this capacity has been exercised in the context of political struggles against authoritarian government in Latin America and in this country. But first I want to show how the social psychoanalytic orientation I have presented helps us understand the consensual support that the Bush administration secured for its domestic and foreign policies in the early years following 9/11. How, in other words, did the specificities of U.S. history and culture—what Gramsci calls hegemony and what I will refer to as hegemonic ideology—affect the U.S. experience and response to the traumatic trigger of the terrorist attacks on the World Trade Center and the Pentagon?

We might say that in the wake of the terrorist attacks on 9/11, ideology came to our rescue. Bush's aggressive policies were justified by a discourse that split the world into a struggle between U.S. democracy and totalitarian fundamentalism. Most citizens could uncritically identify with the ideological assumptions underlying Bush's crusade. That is, citizens were unconsciously identified with the hegemonic ideological justifications of the

policies instituted by the powerful who rule this nation. Ideology rationalized a government strategy aimed at ensuring U.S. hegemony, all the while
it functioned to cover over the psychological experience of individual and
group decentering, vulnerability, and discontinuity provoked by 9/11. An
aggressive foreign policy justified as self-defense protected us against the
narcissistic injury of impotence and helplessness triggered by the terrorist attacks, and in so doing, ideology worked. Indeed, military expansionism as a response to the terrorist attacks was experienced by many people
as a familiar solution to feelings of insecurity and impotence on the one
hand and rage and aggression on the other. These conditions created a
sociosymbolic order characterized by what Thomas Ogden calls the pathology of the potential space. There was little negotiation between self and
Other; the symbol and the symbolized were collapsed. For example, in the
initial stages of the U.S. occupation of Iraq, ideological depictions of us/
America as all good and they/Iraq as all bad inhibited our capacity to see
the world in the more complex terms that would encompass the idea that
we as well as they are good *and* bad. It was assumed that if the Iraqis hated
Saddam's dictatorship, then they would want a U.S. military occupation,
a perspective still maintained in this country despite much evidence to the
contrary. The ideology of the "war on terror" required psychological-split-
ting mechanisms that inhibited citizens' abilities to tolerate the ambiguity
and ambivalence characteristics of reality, resulting in the paradox that if
we are all good, then we are endlessly threatened by the all bad Other, who
will attack us and thus whom we are inevitably driven to keep attacking in
"self-defense."

We all recall the initial mandate from the government: We were urged to
resume life as usual and to go shopping to support the American economy.
As citizens we were encouraged to buy things, thereby associating feeling
good and safe through consumption and the private relationship with commodities, rather than through engagement with others in communities of
shared critical thinking and informed civic participation. Surely no other
message could have captured the essence of the ideological underpinnings of
an individualistic consumer society. Because so many of us were frightened,
the lure of acting as if life could, indeed, go on as usual was compelling.
While we were shopping, our emboldened leaders promised to take care of
us, literally *with a vengeance.* But denial of danger was perforated with the
terrors of the immediate post–9/11 environment. Those who were closest
to Ground Zero, whose lives were directly affected, were most apt to suffer
deleterious effects to their core self, and capacities for agency, continuity,
cohesiveness, and affect were often compromised by dissociative defenses.[4]
The rest of the country's citizens were subjected to an ongoing onslaught of
the terrifying scenes of the planes flying into the Twin Towers that repeatedly intruded into our lives via all the mass media. People spoke of little
else, and many obsessively worried, both alone and with one another, as

they navigated an environment saturated with warnings of potential future suicide bombings and biochemical, nuclear, or anthrax attacks. Feelings of helplessness were exacerbated in the immediate aftermath by disclosures that the government was unprepared to protect us and an economic dislocation that threatened people's jobs, investments, and savings. America was scared stiff, and patriotism, in the form of a law that bore its name—the Patriot Act—was the prescription offered by the Bush administration and Congress to keep us safe.

Robert Jay Lifton (2003) speaks of this dilemma in contemporary America in a slightly different way when he analyzes the pathology of the "superpower syndrome," which he believes contains a basic contradiction stemming from the need to eliminate the experience of vulnerability. This need puts the superpower on what Lifton describes as a psychological treadmill. He writes, "The idea of vulnerability is intolerable, the fact of it irrefutable. One solution is to maintain an illusion of invulnerability. But the superpower then runs the danger of taking increasingly draconian actions to sustain that illusion. For to do otherwise would be to surrender the cherished status of superpower" (p. 129). Lifton's view suggests a pathological transitional space in which primitive defenses prop up a leadership unable to tolerate the narcissistic blow to their omnipotent control over material and symbolic supplies of every kind throughout the world. These defenses impede those in power from being able to move beyond their grandiosity to learn from experience; for example, that people inevitably resist foreign occupations and can now do so with weapons of mass destruction; that political and economic policies focused on control over the world's natural resources are based on short-sighted greed and unconscious denial of the immanent disappearance of oil and natural gas and the urgency with which we need to invest in research and development of alternative sustainable energy supplies; that the proliferation of nuclear weapons has a chance of being contained only if the world's superpower ceases to threaten other countries and models the way to contain proliferation through a dismantling of its arsenal. For those in this country who do not exercise power, the sense of vulnerability produces a frightened, angry, and aggressive population that seeks relief through various defenses, including an identification with "the agressor" leader(ship).

In Lacanian terms, the overwhelming nature of events such as 9/11 punctures through the socially constructed world's capacity to protect us from terror, leaving us in states of defenselessness as we encounter the Real, that which we cannot ever quite get hold of or register symbolically, that which stays beyond the mind's grasp and cannot be communicated between us. Its ominous and mystifying grip is manifested in the human capacity for destructiveness and violence. In *Welcome to the Desert of the Real* (Zizek, 2002), Zizek writes of the significance of the attack on the World Trade Center, "...on account of its traumatic/excessive character, we are unable to integrate it into (what we experience as) our reality, and are therefore compelled to experience it as a nightmarish apparition...the Real itself, in order to be sustained, has to be perceived as a nightmarish unreal spectre" (p. 19). Thus, for a time, consensual support of arbitrary government policies was secured because under dangerous social conditions that break through the barrier of threats that can be tolerated, the arousal of fear and insecurity adversely affects peoples' capacity for critical thought, thereby diminishing what Peter Fonagy (2002) calls mentalization and promoting the reliance on an ideologized mode of thinking. The mobilization of omnipotent defenses against feelings of vulnerability is typical of traumatized states, and in the wake of 9/11, this defensive posture characterized not only individual citizens but the large group response of a superpower nation. The government's bellicose policies in reaction to an unprecedented vulnerability reflected the need to reaffirm the hegemonic position of the United States in the world, all the while fulfilling citizens' fantasies of being rescued by a strong leader who would enact wishes for revenge.

An important component of the traumatic significance of 9/11 was our experience of ourselves as targets of an arbitrary and unfathomably aggressive act. Why did we become the innocent victims of such a monstrous assault? As an ostensibly puzzled President Bush put it, "But why do they hate us? We are so good." This stance represents what Christopher Bollas (1992) posits as "violent or radical innocence," a psychic defense by which the denial of one's own aggression is projected onto the other, who is then experienced as the source of one's innocent victimhood. This defense simplifies consciousness and inhibits the capacity for symbolization, promoting paranoid schizoid splitting and projective mechanisms that characterized the states of mind of both leaders and citizens in this country. Shortly after 9/11, Hedda had an experience that illustrates this phenomenon. She called together a group of her colleagues to discuss their responses to the attacks on the Twin Towers and the Pentagon. "Of course, early on, the question of 'why do they hate us' came up," she told me, with more than a little irritation, "and I thought, okay, I know a little about this, so I tried to explain something about this country's role in the world. I got resistance to this line of thinking, so I tried suggesting that we think together about how people are looking to Bush as a father figure who in fantasy we need to rely on to keep us safe. But that kind of minimal psychoanalytic thinking was not what they were interested in. They wanted to talk about revenge, how we could get even with the terrorists. They were afraid it might happen again, and no one but me was afraid of what *we* might do, what Bush might carry out in a kind of self-righteous vindication that would wind up being even more destructive. I felt isolated in my concerns, which were much more about our government than about the terrorists."

As Hedda feared, this theme of violent innocence was manifested in the Bush administration's adoption of an attitude of righteous entitlement to aggressive retaliatory tactics that risked an ever-expanding war whose product would be the manufacture of thousands of new terrorists who also experience violent innocence in their conviction that the United States is a mortal enemy they must destroy. The recourse to violent innocence as a strategy to deal with the destabilizing effects of the terrorist attacks was framed by aspects of hegemonic ideology that have informed this country's relationship to the rest of the world for centuries. Most U.S. citizens understand foreign policy through the government's ideological lens as it is monotonously transmitted and reiterated through the corporate-owned media and the host of other institutions through which circulate, as Gramsci showed, hegemonic notions and practices that are felt to be the shared common sense of the social order. Citizens were thus receptive to their government's self-representation of violent innocence based on the denial of U.S. expansionist policies that long predated 9/11. While we were in fact victims of hateful violence, the immediate conclusion of our innocent victimization and the assumption that the terrorists were motivated by envy—of our goodness, our freedoms, our material achievements—inhibited citizens' capacity to think about how U.S. policies in the Middle East and Asia may have been an important source of terrorist hatred, about which we might be able to do something constructive. In this regard, a poster carried by participants in antiwar marches ironically asked a significant question regarding a motive for the invasion of Iraq. It read: "How did *our* oil get under *their* sand?!" The grandiosity in the attitude satirized in the poster has a long tradition in this country's estimation of its superior institutions and values that are the foundation of U.S. foreign policy. Many citizens endorsed, however unknowingly, the ideological assumptions underlying the war on terror and its aggressive foreign and domestic policies. They identified with and thus gave consensual support to hegemonic depictions of this country's invasion and occupation of Iraq as a force for democracy, liberty, and justice. War was the culturally acceptable response to the terrorist attacks because the government could rely on a historical reservoir of racism and neocolonial sentiments that has driven U.S. foreign policy for centuries.

Indeed, from the early history of the American colonies through the era of nation building, the social imaginary has been infused with themes related to American Exceptionalism, the notion that from its inceptions, the many immigrant peoples who compose this country's population share a common bond based on self-evident truths that include freedom, inalienable natural and human rights, democracy, the rule of law, civil liberties, fair play, civic virtue, private property, and constitutional government. The idealized version of American Exceptionalism is that the people of the United States have been on a slow but continuous journey toward a destiny to perfect governance and to implement the hopes and ideas of its founding fathers. American Exceptionalism is related to Manifest Destiny, the historical belief that this country was ordained and destined by the God of Christianity to extend its civilization across the North American continent and beyond. The theme of American Exceptionalism, that is, the virtue of the American people and their institutions, was articulated by 19th and 20th century exponents of Manifest Destiny, who argued on behalf of the God-given mission of the United States to redeem and remake the rest of the world (Fresonke, 2003; see also Black, 1988). Manifest Destiny has rationalized the ethnic cleansing of Native Americans, the enslavement of Africans, the theft of one-third of Mexico and its citizens, the abusive exclusionary laws and customs aimed at immigrant workers, and the exploitation of labor and resources throughout the Global South. It is especially when the subjugated resist being dominated that U.S. superiority and entitlement are expressed through coercive violence to assure the maintenance of U.S. hegemony throughout the world. This tradition was reaffirmed in the mid-1990s, when a group of neoconservatives, many of whom later became major figures in the Bush administration, formed the Project for a New American Century. The PNAC was conceived as a post–Cold War strategy designed to maintain this nation's role as the world's only superpower in the 21st century by imposing a *Pax Americana* through force of arms. Control over the earth's strategic energy resources was essential to PNAC's vision, and long before 9/11, the invasion of Iraq was thought to be a necessary step toward achieving this objective (PNAC, 2007). Appropriation of Iraqi oil would be central to an agenda to increase defense spending, assume control over an essential commodity sought after by competing economies, including Europe and China; serve as a warning to other Middle East governments of U.S. power; and award government contracts through noncompetitive bidding to corporations close to and partially owned by PNAC members, such as Halliburton, Bechtel, and Blackwater (Gutwill, 2009).

The expansionist PNAC agenda was actualized by the Bush administration's "war on terror" and constructed around rhetorically simplistic equations that were reproduced endlessly by the corporate media, by that time so concentrated that only six corporate monoliths owned all but 10% of the country's newspapers, magazines, TV and radio stations, books, records, movies, videos, wire services, and photo agencies (Media Reform Information Center, 2004). Media discourse conflated a complex reality by first morphing Osama bin Laden into Saddam Hussein, who then was identified with 9/11, then with terrorism, then with Hitler, then with Iraq, and then with the Iraqis. The belligerent actions of government were inverted through language distortion, encouraging citizens to identify with familiar hegemonic signifiers of American democracy: "seeking peace" was the symbolic language used for waging war. Bombing civilians was referred to as "liberating" them. "Collateral damage" and "soft targets" were reported, rather than the number of mothers, fathers, and children being killed and maimed by U.S. bombs. "Unpatriotic" was a code used to justify the government's attack on anyone with a dissenting view from official policy. "Freedom is on the march" was a euphemism for the unilateral preemptive invasion and occupation of other countries.

The administration's simplistic discourse, which bifurcated the world into good and bad—civilization versus barbarism, the Christian world versus Islam, democracy versus an "axis of evil"—enabled citizens to identify with an all-powerful goodness, while all that was bad was projected onto a demonized other. This powerful emotional response exacerbated the difficulty of tolerating ambiguity and complexity typical of what Melanie Klein (1935, 1937) called the depressive position, characterized by the capacity to tolerate acknowledging one's own aggressive impulses, feeling guilt, and making reparation. As Hanna Segal has argued, groups tend to be narcissistic, self-idealizing, and paranoid in relation to other groups and to shield themselves from knowledge about the reality of their own aggression, which of necessity is projected into an enemy—real or imagined—so that it can be demeaned, held in contempt, and then attacked. Under the traumatogenic conditions provoked by the terrorist attacks and then by the aggressive U.S. response, the capacity for empathy for the suffering of others collapsed. Psychologist Sam Keen (1986) describes what happens to people who are vulnerable to unconscious splitting:

> Start with an empty canvas…Dip into the unconscious well of your own disowned darkness with a wide brush and stain the strangers with the sinister hue of the shadow. Trace onto the face of the enemy the greed, hatred, carelessness you dare not claim as your own. Erase all hints of the myriad loves, hopes, fears that play through the kaleidoscope of every finite heart…when your icon of the enemy is complete you will be able to kill without guilt, slaughter without shame. (p. 9)

As psychic defenses and ideology converged, shock and awe attacked U.S. citizens' minds as well as their purported enemy.

The defensive significance of the ideological response to 9/11 has to do with another theme related to the threat of species annihilation that people have lived with since the United States dropped atomic bombs on Hiroshima and Nagasaki. In this regard, Hedda once told me about an experience she had when she was deeply committed to the antinuclear movement to which she gave as much time, energy, and money as she could. She found that the psychoanalytic community was loath to take up social issues and struggles, even this overridingly important one. "I gave a paper at a psychoanalytic meeting about the threat of nuclear arsenals and proliferation," she recalled, "and before I spoke, a very prominent analyst confided that at the time of Hiroshima he had been on his way to Tokyo, and that if it hadn't been for the bomb, he and his fellow soldiers would surely have been killed. At least, that's what they were told. Therefore, he proclaimed, he found it hard to feel too worried and critical about the bomb. So I talked to him about denial. Following the presentation of my paper he wrote me a note to tell me that after listening to me, he could recognize in himself what I meant and that it was very hard to persist with his denial. That was a minor victory! But it wasn't often repeated." This defensive denial has worked even more effectively and therefore dangerously among the decision makers who manufacture and trade in nuclear arms. Hannah Segal (2002) argues that the leaders of the United States, as well as other countries with nuclear capabilities, have disavowed their own aggressive motivations as they developed weapons of mass destruction. For well over half a century, the military-industrial-congressional complex has produced an increasingly dangerous world, as U.S. arms manufacturers have engaged in annual sales of armaments and components of weapons of mass destruction to countries all over the world, including the Middle East and Asia. Geopolitical interests and access to strategic resources, such as oil and natural gas, have guaranteed U.S. governmental support of arms sales to nations and groups who have used them against one another and sometimes against the United States itself. Furthermore, over time, the complex process involving research, allocation of government contracts, and production and sales of armaments of all kinds has facilitated a fragmentation of responsibility and accountability, which has made it easy for those involved to hide from themselves the dangerous implications of their decisions and actions. Their denial has resulted in the gross absence of government involvement in constructing reasonable programs aimed at emergency preparedness that could protect—minimally at least—the civilian population in this country from anyone who might use a weapon of mass destruction against us. Denial has taken the form of "it won't happen" or "it won't be that bad." *New York Times* investigative journalists examined the reasons why the U.S. government has not done more over the past several decades to protect civilians in this country from the dangers of a chemical, biological, or nuclear attack. They quoted one officer in the U.S. military, who told them why the military had no real plans to defend this country against a germ threat: "There's an in-box, an out-box, and a too-hard-to-do box...We saw it as a threat, but we didn't want to deal with it, to put together a war plan. It was too difficult" (Miller, Engelberg, & Broad, 2002, p. 91). In this regard, 9/11 permitted the projection of responsibility for the menace to humanity posed by the arms race onto the immediate threat by terrorists who might very well have managed to buy or steal the components of germ warfare or radiation bombs from sources financed or supplied by the United States itself. This country has reconstructed itself from being a major player in the proliferation of weapons of mass destruction to that of a victim, whose current military escalation is defined exclusively as justifiable self-defense.

In the policies they developed following 9/11, our political leaders assumed a posture of self-vindication divorced from the reality of the history of U.S. imperial reach and their own declared designs to guarantee its superpower position in the world. Denial among the decision makers came in the form of projecting responsibility and guilt for their aggressive policies, insisting, for example, that their preemptive invasion of a sovereign country was the result of wrongs inflicted *on* them, not *by* them. In their arrogance they denied the reality of their motives and actions, had little respect for truth, and thus avoided any experience of shame. Most citizens were vulnerable to the ideological representations that mystified government policies, which converged with the need to maintain a sense of sanity and safety, often through disavowal. So, for example, some of us knew—and then "forgot"—that our ports, public buildings, nuclear power plants, waste sites, weaponry storage centers, and chemical and biological research facilities were not safe because of lack of oversight and protective strategies. We knew—and then "forgot"—that the budgets necessary for such protection were not supported by the government even as it warned of imminent terrorist attacks. Instead, we were told that our leaders would protect us through making war on other countries and expanding exponentially the definition of a terrorist to include anyone who opposes the policies of this country. And while U.S. citizens were still reeling from the devastation of 9/11, the government implemented a broad range of political and economic policies that expanded the influence of the executive branch at the expense of our constitutional system of checks and balances and developed an economic and military policy that favored the interests of a narrow sector of the population over those of the majority.

These developments were facilitated by the convergence of ideology and psychological defenses, demonstrating Zizek's notion of hegemony, that "they do not know it, but they are doing it." Thus were stifled critical reflection, restraint, and dialogue in the early years of the U.S. response to 9/11. A more long-range, thoughtful response might have included, in addition to pursuing and containing terrorist networks, an internationally collaborative constructive policy along the lines of the Marshall Plan, which underwrote European reconstruction after World War II, that could have helped to alter the social conditions that stimulate resentment, hatred, and impotence, all-too-fertile ground for terrorist movements. Such a shift in orientation would mean that we had discovered a national capacity to understand our history and to learn from experience. Indeed, it would take into account a reality-based, complex appreciation of this dangerous world and the United States's contribution to it, and thus represent the political equivalent of moving from the paranoid-schizoid to the depressive position, from primitive splitting and projection to integrative and reparative capacities.

But there is yet another factor that enabled the administration to implement its domestic and foreign policies with so little opposition for a time. I believe that in a paradoxical way, in addition to its traumatic significance, the crisis of 9/11 also represented a shared group opportunity. An aggressive foreign policy permitted Americans to experience a temporary, albeit illusory, reparation of the internally generated cumulative traumatic stressors due to the deep divisions in this country that predated 9/11. In this sense, the terrorist attacks symbolically constituted a defensive relief of persecutory anxiety experienced by citizens who had been living in a culture undergoing a deterioration from within. This phenomenon is related to Robert J. Lifton's concept of death anxiety. From early on in life, argues Lifton, we struggle for vitality and ultimately for symbolic immortality. Early experiences with separation, loss, and fears of disintegration represent death equivalents. In this sense they are precursors of imagery, symbolization, and meaning connected to "a life-death model or paradigm" (Caruth, 1995, p. 130). Lifton's concept of psychic numbing refers to the inability to work through trauma and deal with it symbolically. If the traumatized individual cannot reconstitute her former self as she metabolizes the traumatogenic experience, there is a perverse quest for meaning that includes the exploitation of other people psychologically. As Lifton puts it, in response to traumatic situations that are not integrated, "we reassert our own vitality and symbolic immortality by denying [others] their right to live and by identifying them with the death taint, by designating them as victims" (Caruth, 1995, p. 139). In other words, destructiveness entails the projection of death anxiety onto others, who become its container. Lifton adds that human beings cannot kill large numbers of people except by claiming a virtuous motive, "so that killing on a large scale is always an attempt at affirming the life power of one's own group" (Caruth, 1995, p. 140).

I employ Lifton's notion of death anxiety to suggest that 9/11 symbolically constituted a diminishing of persecutory anxiety that stemmed from living in a society that during prior decades had been imploding, the symptoms of which included the erosion of family and community, the corruption of government in league with the powerful, the abandonment of working people by profit-driven corporations going international, urban plight, a violence-addicted media (Hollander & Gutwill, 2002), a spiritually bereft culture held prisoner to the almighty consumer ethic, racial discrimination, misogyny, gay bashing, growing numbers of families joining the homeless, and environmental devastation. From my perspective, 9/11 permitted a respite among citizens from a general sense of internal decay by stimulating a renewed vitality via a reconfiguration of political and psychological forces: Profound tensions within this country yielded to a wave of nationalism in which a united people—*Americans* all—stood as one against external aggression. The generosity, solidarity, and self-sacrifice expressed by Americans toward one another immediately following 9/11 and the sacrifice of young Americans in Iraq during subsequent years served to reaffirm our sense of ourselves as capable of achieving the "positive" depressive position sentiments of love, empathy, and self-sacrifice for the group. Fractured social relations were promised symbolic repair. The threat to our integrity as a nation could be displaced from the web of complex internal forces difficult to understand and change onto a simple and identifiable enemy from outside of us that could be used as a blank screen for our collective projections. This country's response to 9/11 in part demonstrates how persecutory anxiety is more easily dealt with in individuals and in groups when it appears to be provoked from the outside rather than from internal sources.

My view is that our sense of American Exceptionalism, in this case, our exemption from living with economic deprivations and political polarizations that characterize life for *other* people in *other* countries, was already under attack several decades before 9/11. As I see it, many sectors of U.S. society were living in conditions of ongoing and repetitive stressors that constituted the social equivalent of strain or cumulative trauma (Khan, 1963). This was a time when the problems suffered beyond our borders became ours as well: In the early 1990s, in the aftermath of the fall of the Soviet Union, the United States announced a New World Order and a deregulated free-market version of corporate capitalism that would become a global system overseen by the only superpower in a newly unipolar world. Usually referred to as "globalization," for many social theorists it is the context for our increasingly dangerous world: Patterns of international investment and trade have concentrated wealth in fewer and fewer hands and have impoverished more and more people around the world. It is a system that uproots peoples' minds by diminishing their access to jobs, land, education, health care, resources, security, and predictability—the material foundation of psychological cohesion and stability.[5] As Brazilian President Lula put it, the biggest weapon of mass destruction in the world is hunger.[6] Although Lula was referring to the desperate condition of the poor throughout the world—the neocolonial peoples whom Franz Fanon called "the wretched of the earth"—many citizens in the United States have not been immune from the impact of corporate globalization.

By the early 21st century, citizens in the United States still benefited, as we had historically, from living in the richest county in the world—a country that represents 4.5 percent of the world's population but consumes 25 percent of the world's resources, including its energy. Although our general standard of living outdistanced every other country, in the past several decades class inequities dramatically increased. Disturbing patterns in the distribution of wealth not seen since the days immediately prior to the Great Depression had emerged by 2000: The top 1 percent of the population held almost 40 percent of the wealth in the United States. Downward trends in employment, wages, job security, and benefits for working people and increased bankruptcies for small businesses accompanied the shift from a manufacturing economy to a services-based economy, characterized by low wages and nonunionized jobs. As New Deal and Great Society social programs unraveled, along with the percentage of the work force organized into unions, a shift in poverty from female-headed households to two-parent families emerged. In the wealthiest country in the world, one in five children was living in poverty. And the income gap based on race continued: The median family income for whites had come to be 11 times that of Latino families and 14 times that of Black families (Economic Policy Institute, 2003). These patterns, although experienced by many working people and minority groups, were not understood by citizens as a manifestation of foundational problems characteristic of the neoliberal free-market system and war economy. Moreover, a mass-mediated culture promulgated ubiquitous narratives and images of violence that mirrored and stimulated cycles of violence in homes, at the workplace, in schools, and on the streets (Hollander & Gutwill, 2006). As cultural critic Mark Dery suggests, in *The Pyrotechnic Insanitarium* (1999), the mass media landscape was collapsing the sublime and annunciating the obscene, the horrific, and the hilarious, in which "thermonuclear weapons systems and soft drink commercials coexist in an overlit realm ruled by advertising and pseudoevents, science and pornography" (p. 36). Mark Selzer describes the pathological public sphere as "shock and trauma; states of injury and victim status; the wound, the disease, the virus, and epidemics of violence; disaster, accident, catastrophe, and mass death; the abnormal normality of paranoia and psychosis; the pornography of mass-mediated desires and other forms of addiction and artificial life" (Dery, 1999, p. 36). The real and virtual environment of violence from the 1990s on has expanded the customary legitimate parameters for the aggressive expression of frustration and anxiety.

The deindustrialization of America had serious political and ideological consequences as well. The geographical area known as the rust belt—the South and the prairie and mountain states—was most deeply affected, precisely where the neoconservative movement took root.[7] The neoconservatives won the hearts and minds of the underemployed, those without jobs, those who had lost their family farms, and still others whose small businesses had gone bankrupt. These people were vulnerable to the organizing efforts from the 1980s on by a right-wing movement whose neoconservative ideology replaced class as a category of social experience and political struggle with the "culture wars": support for prayer in the schools, and publicly funded religious social services, chauvinistic patriotism, and opposition to reproductive and gay rights. Religious fundamentalism was the glue that held the neoconservative movement together. The Republican Party, historically the political representation of the wealthy, was refashioned ideologically into the standard-bearer of the oppressed. Class rage was displaced from the bosses and an exploitative economic system onto the liberal establishment, geographically identified with the coastal states and politically with the Democratic Party and moderate Republicans. Liberalism and its affinity for secularism, acceptance of ethnic diversity, and support for female, gay, and workers' rights became the symbol for the persecution of traditional, God-fearing Americans. These citizens shielded themselves from the social, economic, and cultural shifts in this country by joining the battle for a return to the reliable, clear, and firm boundaries of the traditional family, control over women's reproductive rights, and religious fundamentalism (Frank, 2004; Bageant, 2007).

Thus ideology and manic defenses joined to ward off the vulnerability produced by complex social forces. This conservative populist movement was mobilized in part during the 2000 electoral campaign by the Republicans' ideological manipulation of Clinton's sexual dalliances as proof positive of liberalism's violation of family values and Christian morality to become a pillar of support that brought George W. Bush and his neoconservative coalition into the White House. During the first Bush administration, the conservative movement, including fundamentalist Christian religious organizations and right-wing media broadcasters and Internet bloggers, successfully mobilized support for neoconservative domestic and foreign policies.

For a time, the government's ideological use of 9/11 managed to succeed in suppressing critical voices, which were equated with anti-Americanism and antipatriotism in a time of national peril. This campaign was so effective that by the second Bush administration, the neoconservatives monopolized the political agenda, and it seemed as if no viable oppositional movement would arise to challenge its legitimacy.

This, then, was the social matrix of psychic experience that characterized the initial years of our post–9/11 era. As has occurred elsewhere under similar political conditions, the institutional and ideological hegemony of a powerful political group allied with core economic interests produced for a time a bystander population, by which I mean people who were either identified uncritically with the dominant ideology or became frightened, disinterested, cynical, or alienated by authoritarian control over the political process and discourse. Psychologist Ervin Staub (1989) has pointed out that bystander populations inadvertently, through low-level acceptance or active complicity, play a supportive role in their government's perpetration of all kinds of immoral and illegal policies in their name, and in so doing, inhibit the healthy functioning of democracy.

SOCIAL TRAUMA AND THE PROBLEM OF THE BYSTANDER

One of the signs of the assault on the healthy functioning of our democracy has been the shocking evidence of the U.S. practice of torture of detainees from Iraq to Afghanistan to Guantanamo Bay. How do citizens deal psychologically with the knowledge that they live in a country whose democracy violates international human rights conventions in its treatment of prisoners and detainees? What is the impact of living in a society whose president has assumed executive privilege to declare any individual, including American citizens, to be an enemy combatant and thus suffer an indeterminate imprisonment without charges or access to due process? Just as in Argentina during the Dirty War, citizens in this country are obliged to psychologically manage the generalized threat when the law becomes an arbitrary tool, and no one can be certain if and when any specific individual might become a target of the random implementation of authoritarian power.

It is June 10, 2006, and these issues emerge as Hedda and I talk together during the lunch break at a one-day conference in the series that the Uprooted Mind Committee has organized over the several years since our initial three-day conference in October 2004. Today's event is called "Psychoanalytic Ethics in a Time of War," and our speaker is Nina Thomas, a New York–based psychologist/psychoanalyst who has specialized in trauma related to war, ethnic conflict, and state-sponsored repression.[8] In her morning presentation, "Our Times Are Not Times for Silence," Nina described the struggles that a group of psychoanalysts within the American Psychological Association have been engaged in to oppose the participation of psychologists in interrogations of enemy combatants, prisoners, and detainees.[9] Hedda and I are sharing our impressions of the audience's responses to Nina's analysis of the conflicting reports of the use of torture by U.S. forces against the country's declared enemies and the controversies surrounding the participation of psychologists in the teaching, training, and supervising of "enhanced interrogations methods" carried out by the U.S. military and Central Intelligence Agency (CIA). We note the contradiction inherent in the fact that many of the audience members, most of whom are educated, middle-class professionals, acknowledged feeling shocked as they learned about the practices of their profession and their government, even while news reports related to Abu Ghraib, Guantanamo Bay, and CIA extraordinary renditions have already filtered through the information barriers to create contentious debate in many corners of U.S. society. It seems to us to be a good example of how individuals employ disavowal in the face of a disconcerting, decentering, or dangerous reality, which they can be aware of at one moment, only to "forget" about the next, with the result that it has no coherent psychic significance. This, Hedda and I agree, is a frequently encountered defense that in the context of the larger social world contributes to citizens' becoming bystanders to their government's problematic actions.

Hedda is telling me that she is profoundly bothered by how so many people in this country appear to be disinterested in the multiple dangers facing us, not the least of which are the policies of the Bush administration that represent more danger, violence, and death in the world. "I think about the difference between the repressive period of the 1950s and what's happening now. During the McCarthy period, I wasn't nearly as worried as I am now. Maybe it was because I was busy building a career and working on my marriage, but it seemed less dangerous then. Although it was scary, I always thought the constitutional structures of this country would be able to sustain themselves in the face of that right-wing campaign, that the American people would go to the edge, then find their minds, retreat, and opt to salvage their democracy. I think that happened with McCarthy and even finally in response to the Vietnam War. I don't see that now, and even though the polls show that 60 percent of the people are opposed to Bush's policies, I'm convinced that he will take care of that through his discourse around terrorism—the "war on terror," the terrorists, the "axis of evil." Ironically, in response to Bush's foreign policy, there is increasing hatred against the United States, so it's also likely there will be a retaliatory attack here. But I'm still more worried about the evidence of state terror in this country through all the attempts of the government to take away civil liberties, the abuse by the media, the fact that the president can do whatever he wants. We don't know how many phones are tapped, how many personal records are being investigated, how many people are in jail, or what's happening to them when they're there. No Geneva Conventions apply here now. And what's really disturbing is that with all of Bush's rhetoric about homeland security, his administration's done nothing to protect our nuclear reactors or ports. In the meantime, this abuse of power is very dangerous. It's the lying to people, the distortion of facts, the inane discourse coming out of the White House that imperils us."

I agree that the social environment we live in is indeed riddled with these frightening paradoxes, and I ask Hedda what her psychoanalytic perspective is regarding the difficulty people have in understanding how their anxieties, apprehensions, and depressive states may have something to do with the larger social world beyond their personal relationships and work situations. "It's too overwhelming," she muses, "...and defenses set in. Denial is the first defense, and then a kind of isolation from political concerns takes place. There's a good deal of repression, and then there is the helplessness: 'I can't do anything about this overwhelming mess.' And when you feel helpless, anyone who makes you feel that way becomes an object of hate and rage. Hate is an unpleasant feeling—it's potentially dangerous because the people you hate can retaliate. And then there's the complication for people who suffer superego conflicts, people whose ethics don't permit them to act on rage; these people want to deny any relatedness to the grave political situation because the hatred they feel makes them feel helpless. The opposite happens for some of those who go to fight in Iraq because they want to act and help. Volunteering can help them feel there is something they can do. They feel they've made a choice without realizing that an external force is responsible for imposing it on them."

Hedda is describing some aspects of the dynamic that produces bystander populations, which, as I indicated earlier, Ervin Staub argues inadvertently support their government's perpetration of immoral and illegal policies in their name. Denial operates on many levels, both conscious and unconscious, and can be manifested in a lack of emotional responsiveness, a cognitive process that blocks factual information, an inability to assume a moral position of responsibility, and an incapacity to take action in light of knowledge. As Hedda indicates, we often try to protect ourselves from the annihilation anxiety stimulated by our threatening social reality by creating an illusion of safety. Denial helps to ward off feelings of intolerable vulnerability as we retreat into the narrow dimensions of personal concerns we want to believe are disconnected from social issues. There are additional psychological recourses we have at our disposal. We can assume an absolutist state of mind whose paranoid-schizoid defenses transform fear into hatred, which is typical of anti-immigrant vigilante organizations and fundamentalist religious movements. We can identify with aggressive political leaders and policies whose ideological discourse involves splitting—us versus them—that permits the projection of badness onto an enemy whose destruction is then experienced as a form of manic invulnerability. We also disavow the ubiquitous dangers we face, letting ourselves know about them at one moment and turning away from knowing the next in an effort to reestablish something akin to what D. W. Winnicott called a sense of going-on-being. Disavowal thus reinstates a temporary (and illusory) sense of psychic equilibrium. Many of us simply lose ourselves in the manic retreat offered by postmodern consumer culture or willfully refuse to read the papers and watch the news so as to push away the dread produced by our threatening social world.

In addition to the need to protect ourselves from anxieties produced by a dangerous external world, an attitude of disinterest can be a defensive maneuver to avoid potential internally generated conflict: If we actually let ourselves know about what is real, in this case what lies behind the official story of an authoritarian regime, we run the risk of having to act and thereby threaten our sense of personal safety. To put it psychoanalytically, we face the peril of an intrapsychic dilemma: the price we pay if we do not satisfy superego or ego-ideal mandates for internal moral consistency between our convictions and our willingness to behave in concert with them. The bystander position thus not only protects us from the experience of external threats but from the internal danger of self-indictment. However, this safety is secured at the risk of perpetuating the conditions that provoke the need for the employment of the defenses of the bystander in the first place, thus maintaining us in a repetitive need to adapt to hegemonic structures and discourses that oppress us. All of these defenses employed in the bystander position are deeply permeated by the internalization of hegemonic ideology, which is defended because it is experienced as a core part of identity.

But we also have the capacity to assess the nature of the threats in the social world and to actively engage in myriad ways to reform the very conditions we find unacceptable. In so doing, we can make possible a sense of personal agency and connection to community that helps to contain fear, anxiety, and dread. The disengagement from hegemony represents new possibilities that are liberating but also experienced as potentially threatening: When one's belief in and attachment to political authorities and hegemonic ideology is undermined, a potential psychological as well as political destabilization is often experienced. Just as in the therapeutic experience, in the political domain, disengaging from attachments to bad objects, individuating from destructive relationships, and acknowledging painful realities can lead to feelings of despair and dread. The capacity to mourn one's losses, face uncertainty, and tolerate vulnerability can enable individuals to make new attachments that help them move from feelings of impotence toward a new sense of engagement and thus hopefulness.

How can we explain this capability of people to disengage from hegemony? In the Freudian account of the subject, our earliest experiences are rooted in dependence on parental authority, a dependence out of which the formation of the superego constitutes such a powerful identification with authority because it is saturated with the vicissitudes of sexuality and aggression. We can deduce that this conflictual relationship provides the foundation for a subjectivity that is constituted through identification with as well as resistance toward authority. This ambivalence is so deep-seated that it is destined to be repeated throughout life, not only within the family but in one's relationship to the larger social group. Resistance to authority may be understood from a Kleinian perspective as the depressive position capacity that permits the subject to tolerate the uncertainty and complexity of psychic and external reality; to rely less on splitting, projection, and omnipotent control over others; to take responsibility and feel guilt for one's own aggressive impulses; and to make creative reparation. This victory of love over hate can be realized through engagement in political movements that stress libidinal connections in the struggles for social structures of equity and justice. Gramsci emphasized that the consciousness of subordinated social groups is fissured and uneven, in part drawn from the "official story" of the ruling ideology, and in part from their own experience of social reality. The inchoate, ambiguous aspects of experience can at moments be raised to the status of a coherent critique and alternative world view that coalesce in oppositional movements. A Lacanian point of view suggests that hegemonic practices can never provide the suture that completely covers over or permanently repairs the original gap or wound that forms the basis of the subject's alienation. As Zizek declares with respect to the interpellation performed by hegemonic ideological apparatuses, "for psychoanalysis, the subject emerges when and in so far as interpellation...fails. Not only does the subject never fully recognize itself in the interpellative call: Its resistance to the symbolic identity provided by interpellation *is* the subject" (p. 121). For Zizek, our salvation lies in recognizing the importance of and engaging in the act that goes beyond the horizons of what appears to be possible and redefines the very contours of what is possible (Butler, Laclau, & Zizek, 2000).

Even before the United States attacked Iraq, the first signs of resistance to authority occurred in the historically unprecedented internationally coordinated antiwar demonstrations on March 20, 2003, in which millions of people all over the world and within the heart of the empire opposed a U.S. invasion of that sovereign country. Since then, initially on the margins in a variety of progressive organizations, and then in the political center of U.S. society, a vast and multifaceted oppositional movement grew to salvage our democracy and to fight for social justice. A transitional space emerged for citizens to think about alternatives and to question the neoconservatives' agenda, a process that in the 2008 presidential election won a victory for progressive Democrat Barack Obama.

But we are getting ahead of ourselves. It is time first to turn to the part of our story that has to do with the Latin American experience, which touches on another aspect of the problem of the bystander. Most U.S. citizens, if they think about U.S.–Latin American relations at all, have been uncritically identified with the tenets of Manifest Destiny and the assumption that U.S. policy toward Latin America represents a force for democracy, liberty, and modernization in a backward region of the world lucky to receive the beneficent interest of their wealthy neighbor to the north. Most people in this country have known little about their government's long-term strategy to ensure U.S. hegemony in the region, which has included for well over a century political and military interference in the internal affairs of Latin American countries. U.S. citizens have had little real notion of how, in their name, their government's policies pursue the interests of U.S. and Latin American political and economic elites to the detriment of the well-being and human rights of the majority of Latin American middle- and working-class families. Too few of us have been aware of our government's ideological and material support for authoritarian regimes and repression of progressive movements and governments committed to social and economic reform. U.S. citizens have stood by, immobilized ideologically, as their government supplies weaponry and counterinsurgency training, including torture, to Latin American governments intent on preserving the neoliberal economic model whose devastating effects on working people have now directly affected us in the very heart of the empire.

During the era of state terror in Latin America from the 1960s through the 1990s, the U.S. National Security Doctrine functioned as the ideological frame for this country's geopolitical interests that supported military dictatorships from Guatemala to Argentina. As Alfred McCoy (2006) has shown in his study of the CIA's role in the dissemination of torture throughout the Americas, "...U.S. training programs provided sophisticated techniques, up-to-date equipment, and moral legitimacy for the practice [of torture], producing a clear correspondence between U.S. Cold War policy and the extreme state violence of the authoritarian age in Latin America" (p. 11).[10] It is to this authoritarian era and its legacy in the cultures of impunity in Argentina, Chile, and Uruguay that we now turn our attention. Our Latin American psychoanalytic colleagues' experiences and their perspectives on living with terror and resisting it will help to illuminate the book's final chapters when we return to an analysis of our own recent history of terror and the ongoing struggles against it.

ENDNOTES

1. Freud was the inspiration for the development of free and low-fee psychoanalytic treatment for working-class families in Berlin and Vienna. For a description of this socially responsible psychoanalytic project, see chapter 8.
2. This was the first time that all psychoanalytic institutes in Los Angeles cosponsored an event and the first time in the city's history that psychoanalysts had organized a conference focused on thinking psychoanalytically about multiple threats in the social environment. The original committee was composed of two representatives from each of the seven psychoanalytic institutes and groups in Los Angeles. In addition to the principal speakers and the breakout sessions, the final day of the conference featured presentations on resilience and community activism by psychoanalysts engaged in specific projects in the Los Angeles area. Following the initial three-day conference, its success motivated some of the committee members—including Hedda Bolgar, Joy Schary, Carol Mayhew, Bonnie Engdahl, Barry Miller, Samoan Barish, and myself—to remain together for several additional years, during which we have organized a series of one-day conferences on specific topics that are described in chapter 7.
3. For a more detailed analysis, see Hollander and Gutwill (2006).
4. For an in-depth and integrative analysis of adult onset trauma and dissociative mechanisms, see Boulanger (2007).
5. See Hardt and Negri (2001), Roy (2001), Petras and Veltmeyer (2001), and Chomsky (2003).
6. Statement by Brazil's President Luiz Inácio Lula da Silva on the occasion of the meeting between France's President Jacques Chirac, Chile's President Ricardo Lagos, and United Nations' Secretary-General Kofi Annan, Geneva, January 30, 2004.

7. For detailed accounts of this history and contemporary manifestations, see Frank (2004) and Sperling (2004).

8. Nina Thomas is a psychologist/psychoanalyst who has worked extensively in the area of trauma attendant to war, ethnic conflict, and state-sponsored repression. Among her activities, she volunteers with Doctors of the World conducting psychological evaluations of asylum seekers. See Thomas (2004, 2006).

9. This story of how Section 9 of the American Psychological Association's Division of Psychoanalysis, Psychoanalysis for Social Responsibility, led the struggle within the organization against the participation of psychologists in interrogations of detainees held by the state, is recounted in detail in chapter 8.

10. For U.S. involvement in repression in Latin America, see also Harbury (2005) and Perkins (2005, 2007)

Chapter 2

Political culture and psychoanalysis in the Southern Cone ˎ
Coming attractions of the Dirty Wars

> Historical memory...has to do with recovering not only the sense of one's own identity and the pride of belonging to a people but also a reliance on a tradition and a culture, and above all, with rescuing those aspects of identity which served yesterday, and will serve today, for liberation.
>
> — Ignacio Martín-Baró (1994)

I first became enamored with Argentina when I was living there in the late 1960s and 1970s as a UCLA Latin American History graduate student on a Fulbright dissertation fellowship. As an undergraduate at the University of Madrid, I had studied the political economy of underdevelopment and the human suffering that is its consequence. But my formative childhood experiences had early on established a baseline of identification with the psychology of marginalized peoples and the dynamic relationship between the oppressor and the oppressed, which would ultimately inform my academic and psychoanalytic work. I grew up in an apolitical family, and when I was seven, we moved from San Francisco to a small town in the San Joaquin Valley midway between the Bay Area and Los Angeles. We were among the five Jewish families out of 12,000 inhabitants and almost as many Catholic, Protestant, and Evangelical churches. I knew that we were "different," and I also knew that different was not good, but rather a source of mystifying shame and fear that if my identity was discovered, I would be rejected by my peers. When I was 12, we moved to Los Angeles, and being Jewish was suddenly transformed into something positive—membership in the mainstream culture, which, because of the prominence of Jews in the city's professions and entertainment industry, was associated with material wealth and social status. My extended family and my new friends' families fit into this culture, but for multiple reasons, I felt alienated from it. My first positive group identification came in my late adolescence when I met a network of Jewish artists and poets involved with the Los Angeles progressive underground avant-garde culture critical of the 1950s' politics of conformity.

My subsequent activism at the university during the 1960s in the anti-war, civil rights, and women's movements reinforced my identification with those who had been excluded from opportunity and power in a culture divided by class, race, and gender privilege. My identification with "the other" developed theoretical and political depth. My training as a Latin American historian gave me the scholarship and real-life experiences in Latin America to understand and identify with how Latin Americans have been depicted in this country not as subjects but as an other—people whose histories and destinies were interpreted in light of U.S. cultural values and geopolitical priorities.

By the time I began to live in Buenos Aires in late 1968, Argentina was in turmoil, and I soon became immersed in its turbulent political atmosphere. These were heady times: The country, with a history of intermittent military rule, was yet again under the sway of the generals. But this was a time during which progressive peoples' movements, from grassroots union dissidents to liberation theology activists, were becoming increasingly audacious in their challenges to authority. I lived in Buenos Aires for several years, followed by three more years divided between Buenos Aires and Los Angeles. My ongoing research provided me with material for presentations at academic conferences about the growing economic crises and political polarization throughout Latin America. As we shall soon learn, by 1975, Argentina was in a transition period of increasing political repression that would culminate in the draconian military coup the following year. In this transition period, I returned to live in Los Angeles, where I became professor of Latin American history and gender studies at California State University. In the years during the military dictatorship, I maintained contact with a network of Argentines, many of whom were in exile, and I continued to speak and write about the structures and ideology of military rule in Latin America and their deleterious effects on the peoples of the region.

Meanwhile, shortly following the military coup in Chile on September 11, 1973, I joined a group of filmmakers and Latin American specialists to form a production team we called Lucha Films, which would make feature documentaries about Latin America for a North American audience. We organized ourselves on the model of the New Latin American Cinema movement, which emerged in the cultural ferment from the late 1960s to produce feature films for Latin American audiences that explored the historical forces responsible for poverty, class antagonisms, and political repression. We finished one film, *Communiqué from Argentina*, just after the military coup on March 24, 1976, and although it was banned in Argentina, it won awards at several international film festivals. Our most thrilling experience in distributing the film took place in Mexico City in 1978, when it was screened at the Argentine Cultural Center, where several thousand Argentines living in exile responded in enthusiastic endorsement of the film's analysis and message. They laughed and sang and cried during many of the film's scenes, and we were deeply moved to see that we had captured these Argentines' history—and their pride at having built an effective mass movement for change, which had been overshadowed by the painful losses produced by the reign of terror the military dictatorship was imposing on their country.

A few years after that emotional evening, an Argentine sociologist colleague living in Mexico City who had been present at the screening asked me if I knew an Argentine psychoanalyst named Marie Langer, because, he said, we shared so many political and feminist perspectives. Intrigued and somewhat perplexed, I confessed that I did not even know her by name. Within a short period of time, I received a copy of a book in the mail, with a note from my colleague saying that he believed it would be especially significant for me. Indeed, the book would change my life in ways I could not anticipate, in part by introducing me to a socially engaged psychoanalysis.

That was how I first met Marie Langer: through the pages of *Memoria, Historia y Diálogo Psicoanalítico*, an autobiographical narrative based on several lengthy interviews with her, published in Mexico in 1981. I was transfixed by the woman who emerged from its pages. Langer's life encompassed some of the pivotal historical developments of the 20th century. A prominent Latin American psychoanalyst, her professional practice was informed by her feminism and political radicalism. As I read her book, the contours of Langer's extraordinary life became apparent. An Austrian Jew born in 1910, she grew up in the exciting, politicized culture of Vienna, which was governed by an elected Marxist party, the Social Democrats. After graduating from medical school in the mid-1930s, she attended Freud's Psychoanalytic Institute until her antifascist convictions prompted her to join an International Medical Brigade bound for the Spanish Civil War. After the fall of the Spanish Republic, Langer emigrated to Buenos Aires, where in 1942 she was one of the six founders of the prestigious Argentine Psychoanalytic Association.

During the next several decades, Langer worked tirelessly to develop psychoanalysis in Latin America, and from the late 1960s on, when Argentina was ruled by a series of military governments, she became a prominent figure in the human rights movement among mental health professionals in the Southern Cone. She called for a psychoanalysis whose theory of psychic malaise would embrace a Marxist conceptualization of class society in order to shed light on the inevitable psychological suffering that was the product of a social order composed of inherently exploitative relations. Several years before the military coup, because of her outspoken denunciation of the human rights violations of Argentina's repressive government, the infamous right-wing death squad, the Argentine Anticommunist Alliance (Triple A), included her name on its death list. Thus in 1974 Langer was forced into exile for the second time in her life, and she joined the Argentine exile community in Mexico City. She resumed a private practice, taught and supervised at the National Autonomous University of Mexico, and actively participated in the human rights movement among refugees from the Southern Cone living in exile in Mexico. She provided psychological treatment in the refugee communities to survivors from military-run Argentina, Chile, Uruguay, and Central America.

Even before I finished her book, I knew I wanted to write Langer's biography. I sent her an introductory letter, and when I called her to discuss my proposal for a biographical project, in response to my respectfully formal *"Buenos días, Doctora Langer...,"* she quickly interrupted me, and in a friendly Viennese-accented Spanish said, "Nancy, how nice to receive your letter. But, my dear, don't you remember? I met you at the screening of your film in the Argentine Center in Mexico City several years ago. Ah...," she continued, "but how could you recall everyone who spoke with you that night? What an exciting evening that was, no? How your film captured so much of the history we lived through. Well, how nice to hear from you, my dear, and what is this about writing my biography?"

I was completely disarmed and quickly realized that I was already considered a friend and colleague. In fact, the *doctora* was quite willing to entertain my proposal. As we chatted about it, she exuberantly told me that shortly after her book was published, she became the co-coordinator of the Internationalist Team of Mental Health Workers, Mexico-Nicaragua, whose purpose was to help the Sandinistas develop Nicaragua's first national system of mental health care. The 12 members of the team—psychoanalysts, psychiatrists, and psychologists from Argentina, Chile, and Mexico—were all residing in Mexico City. "Imagine," she said excitedly, "the first country undergoing radical social transformation that has enlisted a psychoanalytically informed model of mental health to help create its health care system. It's the first time in history, so you can see I'm very passionate about this. Suddenly this unhappy exile has turned into a victorious adventure for me!"

In more ways than I could have imagined, Marie Langer would profoundly enrich my life. My relationship with her was an important factor in my deciding to pursue psychoanalytic training in Los Angeles shortly after we began working together. After our initial contact, I was a frequent visitor of Mexico City, where I observed her professional work and human rights activism. I taped 60 hours of interviews with her and many more with family members and colleagues. Her home was in the old colonial section of Mexico City, nestled behind massive walls that shut out the hustle and pollution of the city's noisy, congested streets. We would sit in front of the enormous window in the living room looking out onto the verdant gardens, and she would curl up in the same corner of the couch and smile. "Okay, *compañera*, where do we begin today?" Her physical presence belied her 70-odd years. She was slim and tan, with a shock of white hair and startling blue eyes that alternated between penetrating directness and sidelong coquettish glances. Often dressed in jeans and a Latin American peasant shirt, she gesticulated dramatically as she spoke and puffed on her omnipresent cigarette. Her discourse was punctuated by frequent coughing, and I would gently chide her for smoking excessively. In one of our first discussions about radical politics and psychology, she told me, "Listen, I'll tell you what Marxism and psychoanalysis have in common: If you've once understood the concept of surplus value [the part of the value produced by the worker's labor that is not paid for by the capitalist but expropriated in the form of profit] and thus the exploitation of one class by another, you can never forget it. In the same way, if you've understood the concept of the unconscious, even if only through the analysis of a dream or a Freudian slip, you can't forget that either. Marx and Freud, each in his own way, delved below the mere appearance of things, and in so doing exposed the latent reality that directs our lives."

Over several years, I came to know the exile community of mental health professionals from Argentina, Chile, and Uruguay. Whenever I could, I participated in the weekly meetings of the Internationalist Team that took place every Monday night in Marie's home for the purposes of organizing the overall strategy of the work in Nicaragua. The members of the team traveled to Nicaragua in twos and threes on a rotational basis for 10 days out of each month, and the work had to be coordinated so as to provide continuity to their training efforts in hospitals, clinics, and universities. I realized how profoundly Marie affected those around her, how her charismatic strength and charm, which I had first gleaned from reading her book, drew people to her like a magnet.

The most fascinating part of this research experience was my trip to Nicaragua with Marie and her colleague Ignacio Maldonado. There I was able to participate directly in the creative work of the Internationalist Team and to witness the response she sparked in the appreciative physicians, teachers, social workers, and psychologists she taught and supervised. During this trip I adopted the habit of calling her "Mimi," a nickname she claimed she did not relish but which most everyone who knew and loved her affectionately called her. Following this trip, Mimi and I returned to our respective activism in the solidarity movements with the peoples of Central America, she in Mexico City and I in Los Angeles. As I worked on my book, the horrifying news arrived that Mimi was suffering from inoperable cancer. I visited her twice more in Mexico during the next year, after which she returned to Argentina, her adopted homeland, once again under democratic rule. There she spent the last months of her life. We spoke frequently by telephone, conversations in which she oscillated between lucid observations about the social issues that had brought a sense of meaning and dignity to her life and saddened admissions of her deteriorating emotional and physical strength. I felt I could hear her very life slipping away through the tenuous transcontinental connection. Her death, which came in December 1987 at the age of 77, was a profound blow to all of us who had known her well and whose personal, professional, and political lives had been deeply affected by her. Public commemorations were held in Buenos Aires, Managua, and Mexico City, where the mass media covered the events, as they too paid homage to one of Latin America's most important psychoanalysts and spokespersons for justice and human rights.

It took time to move through the grief that the loss of Mimi signified. And then I began to travel to Buenos Aires to interview her two sons and their families as well as colleagues with whom she had worked during her four decades in Argentina. As I spent more time in Latin America, my relationships with other politically progressive Argentine psychoanalysts and with their counterparts in Uruguay and Chile strengthened and deepened. All of them had known Mimi, and most felt their lives to have been deeply affected by her. Moreover, as I developed closer ties with those who had remained in Argentina during military rule, I was able to explore in depth their personal experiences and ideas about the psychological effects of living in state terror. My involvement with the Grandmothers of the Plaza de Mayo and the mental health professionals who aided them in their struggles to locate their disappeared children and grandchildren deepened my understanding of the relationship between political activism and mental health. Meanwhile, partially motivated by these relationships and my understanding of the importance of grappling with the psychological as well as the political aspects of subjectivity, I continued my own formal training in psychoanalysis in Los Angeles.

Over time, in Argentina, Chile, and Uruguay, I established close bonds with individuals who represent three generations of psychoanalysts and psychoanalytically oriented psychologists who are dedicated to the integration of radical social theory and psychoanalytic scholarship in order to analyze the different axes of crisis in their societies. Their professional practice in different ways and in a variety of settings is devoted to helping people develop a critical consciousness not only about their unconscious minds but also about the social forces that contribute to their psychological pain. In the politically polarized societies of Latin America, engagement rather than neutrality defines their lives and work. These stories are infused with fear, victory, loss, bereavement, joy, achievement, and survival. They represent many of the collective experiences of the citizens of Argentina, Chile, and Uruguay, whose lives were profoundly disrupted by the violence of state terror.

HISTORY AND MEMORY

What is the historical context that explains the emergence of state terror in Latin America? Ironically, like other areas on the periphery of the world capitalist economy, from the beginning of its "discovery" by Europe, Latin America has been cursed by its extraordinary wealth. One power-ful nation after another from the center has exploited its prolific natural and human resources for its own ends. For centuries the "open veins" of the continent have spilled forth their gold, silver, wheat, bananas, sugar, coffee, cotton, copper, rubber, hides, and petroleum to enrich and develop other continents in what Eduardo Galeano (1973) calls "five hundred years of pillage."[1] During the colonial period, mercantilists Spain and Portugal imposed their monopolistic policies on their colonies, and following inde-pendence in the early 19th century, new foreign powers exerted their neo-colonial influences. By the early 20th century, the United States became the dominant foreign political and economic force in the hemisphere. Liberal economic theory underwrote free trade policies that privileged landholding elites and foreign merchants and industrialists. The contemporary struggles within Latin America against neoliberalism are but the latest manifesta-tion of almost two centuries of political struggles during which nationalist movements have stressed the importance of using the state to promote pro-tectionist policies under which national capital could facilitate economic development.[2] Such aspirations have repeatedly collided with U.S. policy and this country's presumed right to expand its interests southward with little opposition from nationalist ideas and movements. From the 19th cen-tury on, the ideology of Manifest Destiny asserted that Providence had given the United States the mission of spreading its superior institutions and values to other (inferior) peoples for their own good, thereby redeeming the world in its own image.[3] This country's hegemonic ideology has justified its interventions in domestic Latin American affairs as a strategy for spreading its democratic institutions and values of free enterprise, effectively denying its own self-serving economic, geopolitical, and military objectives in the region. Latin American governments have often come to power because of support from U.S. dollars, arms, or military forces, irrespective of their citizens' preferences. Popularly supported nationalistic governments have just as frequently fallen as a result of the material and ideological interven-tion of the United States and its alliance with the dominant ruling classes against middle- and working-class demands for reform. For millions of people, "Yankee go home" has been a battle cry protesting what from their perspective has been the heavy-handed manipulation of Latin American political life in order to assure a privileged position for U.S. corporate interests.[4]

Most of the Latin American protagonists of this book grew up in the tumultuous post–World War II period, influenced by nationalist cultural movements and learning about politics in the context of the growing ten-sions between the United States and their countries. As the United States indulged in repeated interventions in the internal affairs of its southern neighbors, our protagonists joined a host of Latin American critics who became ever more radical in their denunciation of the United States as an imperialist power.[5] Their claims seemed to be confirmed in 1954, when the U.S. State Department and the Central Intelligence Agency (CIA) organized a military coup to oust the democratically elected reformist government of Guatemala after it nationalized unused United Fruit holdings as part of its land reform program.[6] Denunciations became even louder in 1961, when the United States trained and armed Cuban mercenaries for the Bay of Pigs invasion of Cuba to overturn the revolutionary government that two years earlier had successfully overthrown the U.S.-backed military dictatorship of Fulgencio Batista.[7] The Cuban Revolution was depicted in the United States as the extension of the Soviet Union's determination to erode free enterprise and democracy in that country. But to millions of Latin Americans, it signified a social transformation that sought to end the U.S.-supported economic inequities and human rights violations of military rule and to redistribute wealth and opportunity for the Cuban people. Fidel Castro and Ernesto "Che" Guevara embodied resistance to U.S. expansionism and the exercise of the principle of national self-determination.

Throughout the 1960s, U.S.-sponsored political and military programs suppressed local demands for reform. Both the State Department and advocates from the private sector argued that when U.S. corporations earned high profits from their investments and trade, Latin Americans also benefited and that U.S. and Latin American interests were in harmony, not contradiction. In fact, they believed that Latin American development required the continual flow southward of U.S. capital, technology, and the cultural values associated with the Protestant work ethic.[8] Moreover, they contended that capitalism and democracy were inextricably linked and that any other economic system would inevitably lead to undemocratic government. They ignored the fact that authoritarian government in Latin America was often the result of intensified class struggle in which the elites used political repression to enforce oppressive structures within Latin American dependent capitalism.

Progressive Latin Americans have critiqued existing institutions and hegemonic ideology in favor of restructuring class, ethnic, and gender relations toward alternative social formations based on equity and justice. From the late 19th century on, the left has been an important sector within the labor movement throughout the region and has been a significant player in electoral politics as well. It has exercised a predominant role in the rise of welfare states in various countries, which, while inefficient and unable to spark development due to a number of international and national factors, have saved significant sectors of the population from uncontrolled exploitation and exclusion. Through their ongoing struggles against authoritarian governments, many sectors of the left have also put their weight behind the democratic process. In recent years, where constitutional governments have replaced dictatorships, they have done so in part because of the pressure from the left. Grassroots struggles in rural and urban areas alike have often been organized to elect left candidates because of the belief that they will improve living and working conditions for the majority.[9] But the United States used Cold War rhetoric to label as a "communist threat" any reformist or nationalist party or movement that sought to control Latin American resources for Latin Americans, so that by the late 1960s, many Latin Americans would come to believe that working within the system for change was doomed to failure and that only revolution would enable their countries to achieve independence and development.

Argentina, Uruguay, and Chile all manifested the general social, economic, and political patterns described above. In spite of their different political histories, by the late 1960s, each country was imprisoned in the contradictions attendant on an export-oriented economy dominated by foreign capital and vulnerable to the oscillations of the international market. Each country experienced an economic crisis that provoked significant sectors of the middle and working classes to demand redistributive policies from governments unwilling or unable to respond. And in each country it appeared that social revolution would succeed in challenging the existing order.[10] This profound social polarization ultimately led to military coups in all three countries—June 1973 in Uruguay, September 1973 in Chile, and March 1976 in Argentina. The era of state terror was marked by authoritarian dictatorships with similar ideologies and strategies, whose assault against the civilian population was unprecedented in the Southern Cone.[11] Although our story emerges from this broad tapestry, it also contains the specific textures of the unique traditions of each of these nations. Three of our psychoanalytic protagonists and their personal, professional, and political experiences reveal their shared experience growing up in the Global South as well as their ties to the specific history of their countries.

It is the autumn of 1996, and I am interviewing them as part of my research on the convergence of psychology and politics in the context of Latin American state terror and the struggles against it.

URUGUAY AND THE ASSAULT ON WELFARE STATE POLITICS

Marcelo Viñar is a big bear of a man, with a deep, gravelly voice and twinkling eyes. He has a magnetic and robust appeal; when serious, he speaks slowly and reflectively, making his way carefully through his words. Although there is sometimes a vague sadness about him, he often chuckles as he speaks ironically about life, politics, and the human condition.

Marcelo and his Chilean wife and colleague, Maren Ulriksen de Viñar, have been talking into my tape recorder for seven hours straight in their Montevideo home. They have responded candidly to my difficult questions about their lives first under military rule and then in exile. Our only interruptions have been Maren's periodic searches for their articles and books on trauma and survival and Marcelo's preparations of a typical *asado gaucho*, an elaborate grill of the delicious beef grown on the pampas. We need to take a break, and while Maren grabs a quick nap, Marcelo and I walk through their genteel, middle-class neighborhood to see Montevideo's newest shopping mall.

The mall, he tells me, has been fashioned out of a prison, where the Uruguayan military dictatorship had tortured its political opponents. For years, the victims' screams had pierced the silence of the late-night hours, reminding neighbors of the price of speaking out. Today, the turrets and cells of the prison have been integrated into the fanciful architecture of the mall's boutiques and shops, whose bright lights and lively music beckon the public to a fantasyland of consumerism. "You must see it with your own eyes," Marcelo insists and then muses, "I can't tell which is worse, the before or after of this terrible place."

I am struck speechless by the sight of the people from all social classes who are crowding through the prison/mall archway, hurrying to spend their hard-earned money. It is a visual symbol of forgetting and remembering all at once. The huge complex is reminiscent of LaPlanche's notion of the enigmatic signifier, for it is the symbolic representation of a mystifying source of hegemonic power in two forms: It is both an enduring monument to its past function—the annihilation of citizens' human rights—and a declaration of the triumph of an economic system that manipulates desire and need by seducing governments and individuals alike into debt and dependency. As we wander around the mall trying to figure out how the fashionable architect decided which parts of the prison to leave intact, I wonder whether this hybrid structure is meant as a warning: Submit to the system, or the mall will easily be reconverted into a prison.

As we turn to walk back toward Marcelo's house, the sudden sound of music from a loudspeaker coming closer and closer interrupts our somber thoughts. We turn to see a pickup truck drive slowly by. It is covered with progressive political slogans for an upcoming election and loaded with young people yelling political greetings, waving, and throwing leaflets to the people on the sidewalks. Marcelo's face slowly lights up. Proudly gesturing with his chin at these activists, he smiles, "You see, it is the next generation coming back to life." Marcelo is optimistic that these resilient youths will overcome the legacy of silence from the years of military rule and bring this pastoral country back toward its traditional embrace of political pluralism. Our day of discussions has revealed his pride in his country's generally pacifist and conciliatory history and his acute awareness of its profound influence on his own psychological and political formation.

Marcelo's grandparents emigrated from Russia and Romania in the early 20th century, arriving first in Argentina as part of the plan to establish rural Jewish colonies, but ultimately settling in Uruguay in the small provincial town of Paisandú. As Marcelo is quick to point out, "It's true that I am the grandson of the famous *gauchos judíos* [Jewish cowboys], but my family soon came to this country and became part of the European immigrant communities that would have a great impact on Uruguayan culture and society." Indeed, by the early 20th century, an enlightened middle class emerged from among the European immigrants and brought advanced legislation to the country's citizens that guaranteed workers the right to unionize, a minimum wage, an eight-hour day, pensions, accident insurance, and paid holidays. In the 1930s, the government endorsed an industrialization plan and subsequently invested in cultural activities and scientific endeavors, including, as Marcelo points out, psychiatry and child psychiatry, which received significant support in the early 1950s. Even the Uruguayan Psychoanalytic Association, which was established in 1955, received subsidies from the government for many of its activities.[12]

But in the late 1950s, a severe economic crisis provoked by declining prices for its agricultural exports deeply affected the living standards of the middle and working classes, resulting in the emigration of nearly 20 percent of its economically active population. For increasing numbers of Uruguayans, including Marcelo, the revolution that had just taken place in Cuba seemed a beacon, shining its light in the direction of agrarian reform and nationalization of industry as strategies for treating the ailing political economy of their country. Tumultuous political debates about underdevelopment and social justice were the backdrop for Marcelo's education at the National University in Montevideo. "The university provided an environment that encouraged a social sensibility, a radical questioning of how to alter society so as to improve it. Politics was always for me associated with education, intellectual curiosity, and exploration. The university offered the opportunity to study to make oneself better, and the emphasis was on morality and ethics. I felt that it was necessary to understand the world in order to change it."

In 1965, Marcelo graduated from medical school and began to study psychoanalysis. In the same year he met and married Maren, a beautiful young Chilean who was a fifth-year student at the University of Chile Medical School. Maren fascinated Marcelo. She came from a very different background than he, the product of fourth-generation Danish immigrants on her father's side, and on her mother's, the Catholic oligarchy, whose origins could be traced to the 18th-century landowning aristocracy. Since childhood she had learned the value of fighting for humanitarian principles—ethics gleaned from her father's anti-Nazi activities in Santiago's German community and her family's involvement in the solidarity movement with the Spanish Republic. Maren had first learned about torture as a little girl when a young Spanish refugee staying with her family cried constantly for her brother, a political prisoner who had been brutally tortured by Francisco Franco's fascists. Maren's wish to study medicine seemed to her a logical outcome of growing up in a family that taught her about the many cultures within Chile and how professionally trained people could help to improve the conditions of the poor and contribute to struggles for social justice.

"I met Maren and began my psychoanalytic treatment in the same year," says Marcelo, "and I don't know which changed my life more profoundly." Typically, Maren's version is the "more romantic one," as she puts it, illustrated by the vivid details of their first encounter in 1959 at an international conference on medical psychology in Brazil. Together they were introduced to the Argentine founders of psychoanalysis, which was for both a thrilling experience. They were especially drawn to Marie Langer, says Maren, "who was a true teacher and whose thought opened up a whole new world for us to identify with. Mimi was so smart and sensitive, so easy to admire and to get close to. We named her the godmother of our relationship."

In the late 1960s, while Marcelo was still a candidate in training at the Uruguayan Psychoanalytic Association, Uruguay's economic crisis deepened, provoking thousands of strikes to which the government responded by instituting "emergency security measures" to censor the press, ban strikes, and repress leftists. Many people were accused of hiding "subversives" or supporting strike actions and were rounded up and thrown in jail. Under such conditions, the left attracted increasing numbers of intellectuals, students, white-collar professionals, service employees, and peasants and workers. Marcelo and Maren, both of whom were respected psychoanalysts by then, participated in the political mobilization. "This period was so exciting because it was a collective process," recalls Maren. "And Marcelo was an important part of it. As a professor in the medical school, for example, he led the shift in orientation of the entire approach to medical education. One fundamental thing they changed was to get the students out of a purely biological introduction into medicine to one that focused on the totality of the human system, including psychological and social factors as well as physiology. They linked students' training to outreach in the community in order to encourage a social consciousness about the various determinants of the health of individuals, families, and groups." Marcelo adds nostalgically, "It was a great period, when the Physicians' Union and the Central Confederation of Workers would meet together on campus to discuss the social priorities in education. There was such engagement and expectation of change."

The traditional left—activists in the unions and on the campuses—was composed of the Socialist and Communist Parties, legal parties that worked within the established political system. But by the mid-1960s, an armed urban guerrilla organization, called the National Liberation Movement (Tupamaros), was attracting mainly middle-class youths inspired by the

Cuban Revolution and the Christian radicalism of liberation theology. The Tupamaros raided business, government, and foreign embassy offices to capture documents that exposed widespread corruption. In true Robin Hood tradition, they kidnapped high officials for ransom and carried out bank robberies, using the money to distribute basic necessities to poor communities. Like their counterparts emerging throughout the continent, the Tupamaros had great popular appeal. But as the state came down full force against them, the guerrilla group's popularity waned because they were blamed for intensifying government repression. For several years the political confrontations grew, while the military stood in the wings, primed by their Brazilian counterparts who had engineered a repressive military coup in their country in 1964. In April 1972, the Congress voted for a "state of internal war," granting the military unlimited powers. Many people were arrested, usually accused of supporting or sympathizing with the Tupamaros. During this period, Marcelo was among the thousands taken away in the middle of the night and imprisoned, in his case for several months. Maren helped to organize an international campaign of support for him, which ultimately secured his release. The months in prison were a brutal personal experience that taught him much about the psychological effects of political repression.

By early 1973, the military declared the Tupamaros totally destroyed, but public protest continued, and military and police repression mounted. As the country moved inexorably toward a military coup, thousands of Uruguayans with means fled into exile. In June 1973, the military, counseled by their Brazilian counterparts, made their de facto rule official, dismissing the Congress, banning left organizations, closing the National University, and instituting press censorship. Thus was inaugurated a reign of terror that would strangle the tiny nation for the next decade through an all-out offensive to erase its tradition of liberal democracy. The Viñars would be among those forced into exile, where as part of the refugee community in Paris they would observe, treat, and write about the individual and social repercussions of state terror.

CHILE AND THE MILITARY DEMISE OF DEMOCRATIC SOCIALISM

Elizabeth Lira and I sit in her study, an improvised second floor of her modest home in a working-class section on the outskirts of Santiago, where she lives with her 25-year-old disabled son and 24-year-old daughter. The study is a treasure chest of books, journals, and unpublished papers, the likes of which would excite any historian. Because it is her life's passion to educate about state terror and to repair its profound injustices, Elizabeth eagerly pulls from this shelf and that file cabinet papers that shed light on the past several decades of turbulence in her country. Now she locates a volume of unpublished articles written in the mid-1970s by the participants of a clandestine conference on psychology and political repression, for which Marie Langer had written the introduction. Knowing of my special interest in Mimi, she hands me this prize, smiling at me as I gratefully take it.

An attractive woman who appears much younger than her 50 years, Elizabeth has donned an old, oversized heavy sweater to warm her short and compact body in the study's cold interior. When she responds to my questions about her life and work as a Chilean psychologist who has dedicated years to the fight against authoritarianism, her gentle manner and lilting voice carry a sense of urgency, and she speaks rapidly, as if there were no time to lose.

Elizabeth tells me that just several blocks away from her humble neighborhood is the community of La Victoria, one of the most militant neighborhoods in the outskirts of Santiago. Because of its combative history, La Victoria became a specific target of the military when it launched its bloody coup on September 11, 1973. The walls of the homes and small shops in La Victoria still bear the bullet holes that are visual reminders of the brutal repression of its inhabitants by soldiers and police. "We could hear and see the helicopters overhead and tanks forcing their way through the improvised barricades the neighbors had erected," Elizabeth tells me. "We knew what was in store for La Victoria's families, who refused to give up their elected socialist government without a fight."

Such visual signs of the military regime are ubiquitous, a subtle part of everyday life. Elizabeth shows me how her street dead-ends some 10 blocks away in a partially constructed towering edifice, whose open-air floors seem to ascend to the clouds. Planned as a hospital that would serve the local community, it is a monument to the sudden termination of the social programs of the Popular Unity (Unidad Popular, or UP) government, when following the coup the military junta withdrew the funds needed for its completion. This skeleton of a building is an eerie reminder of what the poor lost in the military's assault on Chilean democracy in 1973. When Elizabeth speaks of the days, weeks, and months following the bloody coup, she describes the sense of chaos, unpredictability, and terror into which she was plunged. A political activist left alone with two small children after her husband was forced into hiding, she struggled to maintain her equilibrium while she evaluated the media's distorted claims and interpreted the (often coded) information arriving from comrades in order to calculate how best to protect her family. For security reasons, contact with others had to be measured, and except for the infrequent visits from fellow activists from around the country passing through Santiago on their way into exile, she was all too often alone. Twenty-one years later, however, amid the frightening recollections, Elizabeth is able to relate with a wry humor the details of tragic–comic incidents that make us both laugh.

Elizabeth tells me that even the most seasoned Chilean progressive activists could not have imagined the extreme violence that would encompass their country once the military usurped power from their elected representatives. Alongside Uruguay, Chile had one of the strongest traditions of democratic rule in Latin America. Others would have bet their lives on the will of the people to fight in the streets to defend their democratic government. "Too many who wanted social change overestimated the level of commitment of the grass roots, the workers, and peasants, to stand firm in defense of the Popular Unity government when things began to get rough and it was clear that the right wing was organizing a coup. The left leadership didn't understand the impact of the brilliant ideological and economic war waged against the UP, which demoralized and devastated even its ardent supporters." For Elizabeth, who defines herself as politically cautious by nature, neither the coup nor the peoples' reluctance to challenge the soldiers was surprising.

Even though the popular classes in Chile have a long history of fighting for their rights, Elizabeth believes she has learned an important lesson from her years of work with peasant communities in the countryside. "I have always encountered class-conscious peasants, people who are willing to fight the large *hacendados* [landowners] for the land that was once theirs or to fight an unjust system for the right to education and decent wages. But we need to remember the power of the dominant class, especially the tenacious power of its ideology, which has been internalized by the very classes whose interests would be served by overturning the wealthy and their value system." She says that any strategy for change in Chile should be based on a dispassionate assessment of what is possible and that it is important to learn from history. Chile's history does, indeed, reveal both the militancy of the popular classes and the ability of the elite to maintain its hegemonic position in society.

Chile is a long and narrow land with the Pacific Ocean on its coastal western shores and its neighbor Argentina on its mountainous eastern border.[13] It has been a center of agriculture and mining, and even though its population is a mix of the indigenous peoples and European immigrants, most Chileans prefer to think of themselves as European in lineage and tradition. A highly urban society, Chile's wealth has come from the world demand first for its silver, then for its nitrates, and finally for its copper. The export-oriented ruling class fashioned an elite parliamentary democracy that in response to the emergence of a militant working class passed social welfare legislation as a preemptive strategy to head off more extensive organizing by independent radical unions. By 1920, class struggle in Chile had an anti-imperialist character given the fact that its most important economic sector, the copper industry, was controlled by three companies, two of which were owned by Anaconda and the third by Kennecott, both U.S. corporations. In the period following World War II, Elizabeth grew up in the midst of full-scale social conflict, with violent strikes waged throughout the country. Economic conditions deteriorated during the 1950s, and the high cost of basic necessities, including utilities and transportation, stimulated popular protest. Elizabeth's middle-class family struggled to sustain a decent standard of living. She recalls that her household was rather typical of Chilean homes in that politics were hotly debated and "everyone— including my 10 siblings and I—had a strong opinion, whether or not we knew what was really going on!" Following her high school graduation in 1960, Elizabeth entered the Catholic University in Santiago to study psychology, a major she chose because of her interest in philosophy. Her social awakening, however, came as a result of her relationship with "a group of people unaffiliated with the university who were studying in Chile from all over Latin America and exploring the major issues facing our countries." In 1964, she participated with other university students in a summer project that took them to the countryside to work with poor peasant families. "I went to a small town in the Cordillera [the Andes mountain range to the east of Santiago] and there encountered a host of problems that affected the lives of the rural poor. There were many different illnesses, no main road, massive amounts of insects—things that really impressed us students from the city. It seemed to me the only way to resolve these dramatic problems was through a profound political change, altering things at the root. At this point I realized that the discipline of psychology was isolated from the social issues of the day, and I abandoned it in favor of the social sciences."

The issue of extreme poverty in the country, as well as Chile's dependence on copper, still owned by U.S. corporations, became important aspects of the heated 1964 presidential election. The victor was the Christian Democratic candidate, Eduardo Frei, whose presidential campaign was paid for principally by the CIA. Frei's lukewarm reformism grew unappealing in Chile's deteriorating economic conditions, and during the 1960s, more people identified with a radical left perspective. Elizabeth, by this time married and the mother of a small child, remembers this period as exciting, one in which people were interested in all kinds of political questions and involved in many different social projects. "Chile wasn't as polarized as it would later become. The cultural environment was open and included voices of the left in all domains. It was natural to go to a meeting at the university and hear the poet Pablo Neruda or the New Song composer Violeta Parra or listen to any number of leftist leaders. We would go to a demonstration to hear the famous poet Nicolás Guillén talk about the Cuban Revolution or to listen to an ex-political prisoner or a writer from Spain speak about Franco and the Spanish Civil War." In this increasingly politicized environment, despite frantic U.S. covert interventions in the 1970 electoral process, the people of Chile voted for Salvador Allende, the candidate of the Communist and Socialist coalition called Popular Unity, as their new president.

Throughout the world, social theorists and political activists interested in strategies for social change looked to Chile to see whether it was possible to use the ballot box to vote in socialism. That is, could a radical transformation of the inequities of unregulated capitalism be altered peacefully rather than through revolution? Allende set about the difficult task of implementing substantive reforms, even though the judiciary and parliament were still controlled by representatives of the conservative elites. Although his initial strategy was to freeze prices and raise wages to produce a short-term redistribution of income, Allende soon began to carry out the economically nationalist policies promised in his electoral campaign. He extended the modest nationalization of copper firms begun under Frei to the entire copper industry, a move that was popular even among the opposition. But as Allende carried out more nationalizations—especially of U.S. firms—the U.S. government was quick to react, mounting an international "invisible blockade" against Chile. While preventing all loans and lines of credit from going to the country, the United States simultaneously increased aid to the Chilean armed forces. Meanwhile, pushed by militant workers and impatient peasants, Allende continued to extend the state's role in the economy, nationalizing more firms and initiating a land reform program. His government also supported the efforts of hundreds of thousands of people who took part in community-based construction, health care, educational, and cultural projects throughout the country.

This was a euphoric period for Chileans like Elizabeth, and she remembers that "it was like an enormous fiesta. We were so enthusiastic. It felt like we were creating something big, something important. Many people came from all over Latin America, and we were especially pleased that North Americans came to participate, to demonstrate solidarity. There was a cultural explosion, with films coming from all over the world, book exhibits from other countries, artisan fairs, cultural conferences, all free. The center of Santiago was filled with people from the popular classes. I'd never seen the city belong to its inhabitants like that. Of course, our excitement was matched by the terror growing among the wealthy, who had the sensation that the poor were invading their space and taking over."

Clearly this mobilization of the popular classes along with sympathetic students and cultural and professional sectors made the UP's redistributive policies even more frightening to the elite and its entrepreneurial middle-class allies, whose antipathy was reinforced by U.S. dollars and propaganda in a massive anti-UP campaign. Even though the ideological and strategic differences among the political parties of the UP coalition often compromised the effectiveness of their response to the intensification of a climate of crisis in the country, their popularity grew. When the midterm parliamentary and municipal elections indicated an increase of support for UP candidates rather than the usual decline in attractiveness of incumbent parties, the right-wing sectors of the military won the go-ahead to abandon the long-time respect for the democratic process in Chile in favor of a coup to oust the UP.

A strategy of economic destabilization was carried out during 1972 and 1973. The combination of a U.S.-backed international boycott of Chilean products and credit sources, a right-wing media campaign blaming increasing economic difficulties on the UP, and a series of CIA-backed-and-financed strikes by entrepreneurial sectors, including truckers and doctors, threatened total chaos. Elizabeth remembers how the open environment of increased liberties and economic opportunities shifted to one of grinding difficulty. "Basic necessities became more scarce, and every day people were forced to wait in long lines in the hopes of obtaining an ever-declining supply of foodstuffs, heating oil, diapers, and other essential goods," she recalls. "All the while storekeepers were hoarding supplies to sell to the rich on the black market." As the economic situation worsened, a right-wing propaganda war blamed the UP government and claimed the crisis would only extend under its rule, in this way successfully reducing the potential opposition to the military coup that would overthrow a democratically elected government.[14]

The stage was set, and on September 11, 1973, the military attacked the presidential palace, which resulted in the death of President Allende. A military junta declared itself the new government and began a draconian attack on the Chilean population. Civilian politicians, including ex-President Frei, supported the coup in the belief that the democratic tradition of Chile would prevail and that they would inherit the reins of government. But the military defied tradition by holding on to power for the next 18 years and by instituting a repressive culture of fear. The impact of state terror on the Chilean people would bring Elizabeth Lira back to psychology. Her participation in the human rights movement would prompt her to develop an understanding of social trauma and to explore ways to help the victims of political repression to deal with its psychological sequelae.

ARGENTINA AND THE FATAL PARADOX OF POPULISM

As always, Buenos Aires is teeming with life, its colorful streets jammed with people, kiosks, flower stands, automobiles, motorcycles, and buses in a kind of nonstop visual dance that never ceases to excite the senses. It is especially beautiful on this early fall day in 1996, for the trees that line the streets have not yet lost their leaves, and the sun crisply lights up the multicolored buildings. Like Rome and Paris, cosmopolitan Buenos Aires has a magical attraction and is a wondrous surprise spread out along the wide, silver-hued La Plata River, whose waters empty into the South Atlantic. I think about how thrilled I am to be back in this intense environment as I walk along the narrow sidewalk with Juan Carlos Volnovich. I struggle to keep up as his six-foot, two-inch frame moves ahead at a rapid clip. He is talking excitedly as he guides me to one of the neighborhood's hundreds of charming restaurants. As we are seated, I note the fresh, white tablecloth and wine glasses, which remind me that the noontime meal in this Latin American capital is always an elaborate and tasty ritual. With a tango hauntingly playing in the background, we continue our discussion about the conference Juan Carlos has helped to organize for the Grandmothers of the Plaza de Mayo, whose sessions we have been attending for three days and nights.

The conference has featured public presentations by legal and mental health professionals from Argentina, the United States, and Europe. Since the late 1970s these professionals have aided the Grandmothers in their efforts to locate their grandchildren who were disappeared by the military junta during their seven-year-long Dirty War, the name given to the military's illegal detentions, torture, and murder of tens of thousands of Argentine citizens, a terrorist strategy chosen to eliminate all actual and potential opposition to the established order. The conference participants include Argentine colleagues in both fields, as well as the general public. "This is so important," Juan Carlos tells me in his typically animated fashion. "The Grandmothers are among the few voices still urging us to deal with the legacy of the Dirty War. And look how many people are attending these sessions. The press coverage is fantastic, don't you think?" I am to present a paper in the afternoon's plenary session about the psychological impact of social violence in the United States. Having read it, Juan Carlos assures me that it will stimulate much concern among the participants, who need to think about the new manifestations of violence in Argentine society since the end of military rule. "We must understand the nature of this historical moment in order to intervene appropriately," he says. This is what is so engaging about Juan Carlos—his enthusiasm, his passion, his sense of being in the middle of significant events and of participating in movements that will make a difference in people's lives.

He is also very funny. As we recount an especially dramatic session of the previous afternoon, his ability to capture the humor and irony of an incident that was simultaneously disturbing has us both giggling irrepressibly. The session had been planned as an open dialogue with the audience to follow presentations by some of Buenos Aires's most prestigious psychoanalysts, who are also well known as outspoken human rights advocates. They had just finished brilliantly analyzing the psychosocial significance of various aspects of the Grandmothers' struggle. A young university student in the audience rose and addressed them, arguing that they did not understand the plight of her generation. "Look," she said, "you speak of 'the struggle.' But you have no idea what it is like for us. We grew up without heroes; we have no Che or Fidel; we've known only a society run by the military, and now its gruesome aftermath…a decadent society, with the torturers walking among us. We have no hope. Now there is just this New World Order, which isn't so new after all. It provides us with little more than the hope of surviving. There are fewer and fewer jobs, with less and less meaning. And yet there seems to be an endless supply of the latest consumer goods, which is all many people think about. What are the alternatives for those of us who know something is wrong? What do human rights mean in this so-called democratic society filled with corruption at every level?"

When the young woman finished, there was a dead silence. She had caught the usually articulate speakers off guard, and they were unable to muster a response. The session ended there, in the silence. Though Juan Carlos had felt a chill at this young woman's remarks, in retrospect he cannot help being amused at the discomfort of his colleagues. He knows that in his own generation's wish to find continuity with the meaning that past political struggles had given their lives, they often forget that the younger generation is bereft of their certainty about what to fight for and what to fight against.

But, then, nothing has ever been crystal clear in Argentine politics. And Juan Carlos is the first to acknowledge that his generation of political activists, including the mental health professionals among them, often had recourse to denial in order to endure the contradictions of their political culture and radical struggles. These contradictions are perhaps the legacy of a society whose self-image has been a conflicted one. Argentina is a little piece of Europe in the Global South, a sophisticated, first-world culture bound up with a neocolonial economy and revolutionary agenda. The roots of this conflict lie of course in the distant past.

From the beginning, Argentina's fate was locked to that of Europe.[15] Initially a backwater of the Spanish empire, Argentina, with its fertile pampas, did not become a major producer and exporter of cattle and agricultural products until the mid-19th century after independence, enriching its European-identified landowning class. British capital provided the infrastructure, and waves of immigrants from mainly Italy and Spain supplied the growing economy with professionals, artisans, and skilled workers. Many immigrants achieved middle-class status in one generation, enriching the language, culture, and politics of their new *patria* (homeland). Such was the case with the forebearers of Juan Carlos Volnovich, who, like most Argentine psychoanalysts and psychologists, traces his roots to an immigrant past. In the late 19th century, Juan Carlos's paternal grandparents, Romanian and Polish Jews, came to Buenos Aires, where his grandfather made a relatively good income as a tailor. Although neither grandparent ever learned to speak or write Spanish, clinging instead to their native Yiddish, their four sons achieved significant upward mobility in one generation. Two of them became doctors, and the other two were successful businessmen. The contributions of the burgeoning immigrant middle class were matched by their working-class counterparts, who also made their mark on Argentine culture that gave it a rich political texture. They built a militant trade union movement that from the 1870s on adapted European anarchist and socialist thought and strategies to their New World circumstances. Immigrant influence on political life was thoroughgoing, and by the 1920s, men of the middle and working classes won the vote and formed new political parties, including the moderate Radical Party and the Socialist and Communist parties.

During the 1930s, economic crisis provoked a military coup, and in response to the dramatic decline of imports and immigration due to the world Depression, the government was forced to support policies that fostered industrialization. The new factories surrounding Buenos Aires depended increasingly on workers from among the ethnically mixed population from the interior of the country, which became stigmatized as *cabecitas negras* (blackies or greasers) by the city's racist European-identified elites and middle class. In the early 1940s Colonel Juan Domingo Perón became the Secretary of Labor and Social Welfare, and he strengthened the unions, backed extensive labor legislation, and raised the dignity and improved the standard of living of the increasingly mixed-race working class. When he ran for president in 1946, Perón, an outspoken nationalist, was supported by a populist coalition of the new nationalist owners of industry and the working class. He handily won against his opposition, an alliance of forces ranging from the traditional landowning right wing and its U.S. supporters, which feared his economic nationalism, to the traditional Marxist left, which mistakenly saw him as an American variant of European fascism.[16]

From 1946 until 1955, Perón, with his charismatic wife, Evita, at his side, built a populist movement based on the principles of national sovereignty and social justice. His nationalization of U.S. and British investments in strategic sectors of the economy and his elaborate social welfare programs made him popular with industrialists and workers, but his anti-European nationalism, redistributive politics, and populist appeals to the poor and working population alienated not only the elite but a majority of the intellectuals because of their marked preference for European culture and values over the country's indigenous cultural roots. Class and ethnic tensions were made more acrimonious by Perón's use of strong-arm tactics where necessary to secure implementation of his policies.

Although Juan Carlos's family was not particularly political, he says of himself that his "childhood was marked by Peronism." Like all Jews in Argentina, young Juan Carlos was aware of the Holocaust. But, unlike most Jews in the country, he was infatuated with the Peróns. With a mischievous smile he remembers that when he started elementary school, he "fell in love with Evita," whose engaging photograph was in every classroom and whose book *The Reason for My Life* was required reading. "It was Perón's power as a leader and Evita's charismatic beauty, her lavish dresses, her impassioned speeches for the downtrodden, that awakened my fantasies as a boy. I guess now I would say that my Oedipus complex was lived out with Perón and Evita, but most especially with her!" Following Evita's premature death in 1952 at the age of 33, a series of economic crises destabilized the coalition supporting Perón. He was overthrown in a military coup that sent him into exile in Madrid, where he continued to influence the direction of Argentine political life for the next 18 years. Until 1972, inept civilian and repressive military regimes took turns attempting unsuccessively to guide Argentina's roller-coaster economy and to eliminate Peronism as a legitimate political force.

Juan Carlos entered medical school several years after the coup, at the precocious age of 16. Like many middle-class intellectuals, he partook of the boom in cultural life that followed Perón's ouster. Students, professionals, and intellectuals joined the film clubs, philosophical societies, and literary groups that multiplied during this period and flooded Buenos Aires with the latest in European art, literature, and cinema. Psychoanalysis was an important element in every aspect of cultural expression. Slowly, by the early 1960s, the first signs of new radical politics, influenced by the Cuban Revolution and liberation theology, began to make themselves felt among Argentines who were seeking a way of understanding their society, which seemed to be in endless turmoil politically and increasing difficulty economically.

In 1962, Juan Carlos met Silvia Werthein, a university student majoring in psychology. "She opened up a whole new world to me," he says, "and lifted me out of the narrow parameters of my medical studies and preoccupation with music and the arts. All at once, through Silvia, politics and psychology entered my life. The second time we saw each other, we fell in love, and we've been together ever since." Silvia introduced Juan Carlos to radical politics through her personal connection to the Cuban Revolution. In 1960, her physician brother, Leonardo, had written to his former medical school friend, Argentine Che Guevara, who invited him to come to Cuba to work as a physician in the rural zones where the Revolution was building clinics and hospitals for the peasantry and rural workers. Later, Leonardo became the director of epidemiology in the young Revolution's Ministry of Health. In 1960, Silvia had also gone to Cuba for some months to take part in the celebrated literacy campaign. "Cuba came to mean hope," Juan Carlos recalls. "When the Bay of Pigs failed, my previous cynicism about the impossibility of anything new happening in Latin America under the nose of the United States changed to one of optimism—maybe we can do something, I thought." So during the 1960s, Juan Carlos and Silvia felt a growing identification with revolutionary movements. "A Latin American revolution," he explains, "not a variant of the Soviet Union, but a revolution secured through an armed struggle that could put the 'salt of the earth' in power. We didn't join any of the leftist parties that were either reinvigorating themselves or sprouting up anew, like so many other young people we knew. Instead, we read Camus, Sartre, and de Beauvoir and applauded revolutionaries like Che Guevara in Bolivia and the priest Camilo Torres in Colombia." Meanwhile, through Silvia, Juan Carlos also came to know the world of psychoanalysis, which he would ultimately choose as his profession.

By the late 1960s, Argentina was drawn into a cauldron of intensifying contradictions. As U.S. multinational corporations fairly gobbled up the country's industrial and commercial sectors, nationalistic sentiment intensified, lending fuel to the fire of increasing class confrontation in response to declining wages, soaring prices, and rising unemployment. Middle-class aspirations were choked off by the combination of stagnation and hyperinflation, and many professionals, entrepreneurs, and intellectuals did an about-face with respect to Peronism. Juan Carlos and Silvia were among the middle class who came to believe that the Peronist movement was the vehicle through which much-needed radical social change would occur in Argentina. They found their niche within the movement being led by the new, combative, grassroots Peronist labor unions and revolutionary Peronist organizations, which had become radicalized over the years as their attempts to win economic and social reforms met with tenacious resistance from conservative politicians bent on preserving the status quo. The revolutionary-armed Peronist groups ultimately coalesced into one organization called the Montoneros, which drew popular support from militant workers and youth.

Even the ivory tower of psychoanalysis was penetrated by the effervescent social upheavals. By the late 1960s, Juan Carlos, now a candidate in training at the Argentine Psychoanalytic Association, was involved with other politically progressive analysts and candidates in attempting to link the psychoanalytic enterprise to the national agenda for radical change. Especially significant to him was his supervisor, Marie Langer, whose own radical politics he would come to know and admire and whose political path would often cross his own in subsequent years.

In 1972, in the first national elections since 1966, a Peronist coalition won, placing a progressive, mild-mannered doctor in the presidency and ushering in a short-lived period of free expression and political mobilization popularly referred to as "The Euphoria." Political prisoners were freed, mass demonstrations were organized to articulate support for a more open society and implementation of social reforms, and people from every social sector became engaged in working on community-improvement projects in the most economically and socially deprived neighborhoods. During this period, Juan Carlos participated with other politically progressive psychoanalysts and psychologists in a variety of community-based projects to bring psychoanalysis to the popular classes. He and his colleagues wrote articles and books analyzing the dynamics of authoritarian society and postulated ways of understanding the relationship between oppressive class relations and psychic pain.[17]

Some months after the election, Perón returned from exile with his wife, Isabel, and extraordinary elections took place shortly afterward. Perón and "Isabelita" were elected president and vice president, but, as the military had hoped, by this time old man Perón identified himself with the conservative factions of his movement, and he turned on the revolutionary forces whose efforts had brought him back to Argentina from his 18-year exile. When Perón died in 1974, his incompetent wife assumed the presidency, guiding the country into economic disaster, political corruption, and increasing repression of the Peronist and Marxist left by right-wing death squads, the most infamous of which was the Argentine Anticommunist Alliance (Triple A).

Life in Argentina became a nightmare for many citizens. Juan Carlos continued his political activism in legal community-based groups allied with the Montoneros, mainly providing desperately needed psychological interventions for the children of political activists. Like thousands of professionals, he and Silvia lived a double life, maintaining their private practices to support themselves, protecting their family as best they could, and continuing their work in a radical movement that was falling under the heavy weight of government-organized paramilitary repression. "It was terrifying," Juan Carlos remembers with a frown. "Our young son and daughter could never tell anyone where we lived. It was an environment that induced complete paranoia. We constantly thought about leaving Argentina but always concluded that we owed it to our country to stay."

Anyone associated with radical politics felt endangered by the increasingly open presence of right-wing death squads. Already during the prior year and a half there had been a steady emigration as people fled the growing violence. Marie Langer and other colleagues of Juan Carlos, whose names had appeared on the death list of the Triple A, had long ago been forced to leave the country. But the chaotic and frightening economic and political conditions were affecting more than political activists. Indeed, they were wearing down the entire society. Hyperinflation was making each family's struggle to obtain food and other basic necessities more and more unpredictable, while the incompetent and decadent rule of Isabel and her advisors was each day less defensible.

These uncertain conditions caused intolerable anxiety in the population at large, so that many, especially among the middle class, welcomed the inevitable military coup when it happened on March 24, 1976. Accustomed to the generals' occupation of the presidential palace, they told themselves they were once again simply trading democracy for longed-for law and order. They could not guess what lay in store for them: the Dirty War. Under the guise of eliminating the armed left opposition, which in reality had already been vanquished, the military carried out an unparalleled assault on civil society. Its aim was to eliminate all vestiges of progressive thought and organization, even if it meant the massacre of a good percentage of several generations of Argentine citizens.

Juan Carlos and Silvia remained in Argentina for nine months following the coup. With their political comrades dead, arrested, or in exile, they "felt like orphans." Although still reluctant to leave, a twist of fate propelled them from this nightmare, and in December 1976 they and their two children tearfully left their country. They would spend the years of the Dirty War in exile in Cuba, where Juan Carlos would have a unique opportunity to practice psychoanalysis and treat children from Argentina, Chile, and Uruguay whose parents had disappeared or been killed by these countries' terrorist states.

* * *

Marcelo and Maren Viñar, Elizabeth Lira, and Juan Carlos Volnovich all knew one another, as well as the other protagonists of our story whom we shall presently encounter, during the tumultuous period when they came of age professionally and politically. Their relationships deepened as they met over the subsequent years to work together or to share their observations of and experiences in the maelstrom of state terror and its aftermath. But first there is a bit more history to discover about the socially committed psychoanalysis that developed in the Southern Cone. What, indeed, was the nature of the movement within psychoanalysis that emerged in the explosive sixties to consider the radical parameters of a revolutionary enterprise of social and psychic emancipation? And why was it that on seizing power in March 1976, the Argentine military, like its counterparts in Uruguay and Chile, declared its Dirty War not only on its armed revolutionary enemy but on all manifestations of progressive thought? As the junta tightened its noose around every institution that threatened its authoritarian rule, a significant target was the mental health community. "Civilians are also warriors," the generals asserted, "ideas a different form of weapon" (Staub, 1989). In Buenos Aires the National University's Psychology Department was closed, entire staffs at community mental health clinics were summarily fired, and books by well-known psychological theorists were added to the public bonfires of banned reading materials. The junta marked psychoanalysts and psychologists as fair game in their onslaught against civil society, declaring that "Marx and Freud are the two main enemies of Western Christian Civilization."[18]

ENDNOTES

1. Galeano's book (1973) is a brilliant and passionate analysis of the continued existence of colonial patterns, especially the dominant role played by the
developed capitalist countries in the exploitation of Latin American natural
resources.
2. Many authors have written about the persistence of economic, social, and political colonial institutions in the independence period; see, for example, Burns
(1990) and Stein and Stein (1970). The 1969 Gillo Pontecorvo film *Burn* is a
powerful depiction of British imperialism in a fictional Caribbean island called
Quemada; Marlon Brando as the brilliant and opportunistic British agent gives
us a carefully constructed cinematic history lesson on the shift from colonial to
neocolonial patterns in Latin America.
3. See Chapter 1 for the historical and current context of the ideology of the
Manifest Destiny.
4. The U.S. interventionist policies of the 1980s stimulated much academic interest in the region's social and political conflicts, which resulted in the publication throughout the decade of many important studies. For an especially lively
depiction of U.S. intervention from the late 19th century on in Central America
and the Caribbean, see Black (1988), LaFeber (1983), and Chomsky (1985).
For a critical view of U.S. interventionism in Mexico and its impact on the
United States, see Zinn (1990).
5. Discussions within the State Department and the Commerce Department in
the postwar era revealed that U.S. policymakers and their colleagues in the
private sector understood all too clearly the nature of the threat to the United
States. While the U.S. government framed its policies to the public in terms
of Cold War rhetoric, insiders spoke to one another in exclusively economic
terms about the nationalist threat in Latin America to U.S. financial and investment expansionism in the region. Documents published by the Commerce
Department are especially revealing and are available in government publications archives in university libraries.
6. For background on the State Department–CIA organization of the 1954 coup
in Guatemala and the brutal military rule that flourished in subsequent decades,
see Immerman (1982) and Schlesinger and Kinzer (1983).
7. See, for example, Wyden (1980). For background on relations between the
United States and Cuba before and after the revolution, see Foner (1963),
Huberman and Sweezy (1961), and Halebsky and Kirk (1990, 1992).
8. Johnson (1958) is the classic academic source in English for this point of
view.
9. Castañeda (1994) offers an analysis of the central role that Marxism has
played philosophically and politically in Latin America since the 19th century,
a critical evaluation of the armed struggles in the 1960s and 1970s, and an
indictment of the current conditions that make Marxism still a viable theory
of Latin American economic underdevelopment and political turmoil. For an
approach that analyzes the conditions that sparked armed struggle as well as
an assessment of its various strategies and tactics, which the author argues are
still aspects of political struggles in today's Latin America, see Pereyra (1994).

For analyses of the contemporary strategies of progressive and left struggles in contemporary Latin America, see North American Congress on Latin America (1992a, 1995).

10. For an elaboration of dependency theory, see Cardoso and Faletto (1979), Frank (1974), and Collins (1986).

11. An analysis of authoritarian regimes in the Southern Cone as a response to popular demands may be found in O'Donnell (1973, 1978); see also Collier (1979) and O'Donnell, Schmitter, and Whitehead (1986).

12. Background on the history of Uruguay may be found in Weinstein (1988), Fitzgibbon (1954), and Kaufman (1979).

13. Background on Chile may be found in Roxborough (1977), Debray (1971), and Drake (1978).

14. For information on the Allende years and the U.S. role in the Chilean coup, see Johnson (1973); Gil, Lagos, and Landsberger (1979); Constable and Valenzuela (1991); and North American Congress on Latin America (1983, 1988).

15. For background on Argentina, see Corradi (1985), Hodges (1976), and Waisman (1988).

16. For the historical significance of Peronism, see Turner & Miguens (1983), Fraser and Navarro (1980), Page (1983), and Hollander (1974). The stage play *Evita*, whose brilliant music captures something of the angst and drama of this period in Argentine history, does so by depicting Argentine politics from a conservative, Eurocentric, and misogynist perspective.

17. This period is described by Hodges (1973, 1976).

18. For a brilliant and complex analysis of remarks like this and their ideological and unconscious symbolic meanings (from a Lacanian psychoanalytic perspective), see Graziano (1992).

Chapter 3

A psychoanalysis for tumultuous times

The psyche and social revolution

Behind what appears to us as reality, Freud and Marx both discovered the actual forces that govern us: Freud, the unconscious; and Marx, class struggle.

— Marie Langer (1971)

"It began early one morning in late December...it was 1974," Mimi Langer tells me. She is answering my question about why she left Argentina. We are sitting in her brightly colored living room in Mexico City for one of our many discussions about her life and work, and even though nine years have passed and her voice is calm, I notice how she lights a cigarette and looks away when she speaks. Her words evoke the scene. She had begun work as usual. Her consultation room in her expansive luxury apartment, situated in the heart of the prosperous Palermo neighborhood of Buenos Aires, felt cozy from the heat of the early sun's rays. But when her first patient arrived, his greeting pierced the tranquility. "Doctora," his voice was ominously hushed, "I've just discovered that your name is on the Triple A's death list." Somewhat disconcerted, she nonetheless told herself to remain calm, that perhaps his news was only an unfounded rumor. Similar communications from overwrought patients and colleagues throughout the day punctured Mimi's denial and compelled her to take these warnings seriously.

In a hastily arranged family meeting that evening, her daughter Veronica and two sons, Tomás and Martin, insisted that their 64-year-old mother leave the country. "But I was torn," she recalls. "On the one hand, I was truly terrified and wanted to run; and on the other, I felt guilty at the prospect of abandoning the other mental health professionals who were active in the movement with me. I knew many of them would also become targets of the paramilitary groups sanctioned by the government." In the end, Mimi acquiesced to her family's demands. She would go to Mexico, where her older daughter had recently relocated following her marriage to a Mexican writer. "Besides Ana and my professional connections in Mexico City," Mimi told herself, "I know lots of the political refugees in the exile community there."

Suitcases were packed hurriedly, and the details of Mimi's professional and personal life were left unattended in the last-minute rush to make the scheduled flight bound for Mexico City. She remembers that as the plane took off, "I stared out of the window and felt the sting of tears pushing through the numb feelings that had helped to move me like a sleepwalker through the past 24 hours." The lights of Buenos Aires sparkled as the plane ascended, and she eagerly searched the bright scene below to locate the familiar landmarks of the cosmopolitan city. As the proud South American center of European culture faded from view, Mimi abruptly sat back, feeling as if she were being plummeted into the black hole of an uncharted future. "I looked around at the other passengers, feeling bitter as I wondered how many of them, appearing composed just like me, were also being run out of their country. How many, just like me, were being forced at gunpoint to follow thousands of professionals and intellectuals before us who had spoken out against the repression? I was scared, and I wondered whether I would ever return. I remember thinking that this was the second time in my life that I was forced to abandon my home to become a political refugee. I also knew that it was the logical outcome of all that had come before."

"Tell me about it," I say. "Ah," she replies, her eyes lighting up. "That takes us back to Vienna, where it all started."

EUROPE: THE STRUGGLE AGAINST FASCISM

"I was born Marie Lisbeth Glas in 1910, the younger of two daughters in a wealthy and progressive Jewish family. What a time it was. I grew up nurtured by privilege, on the one hand, and on the other, by the exhilarating cultural environment of a city ruled by Europe's only mass-based Social Democratic Party...I remember as a little girl my father telling me about the Russian revolutionary women like Aleksandra Kollontai and Vera Figner. Their exciting lives and professional ambitions made a great impression on me. Later on I would learn about the feminist and socialist ideas that enabled them to go beyond the limiting parameters of respectable bourgeois women like my mother."

A Marxist critique of the exploitative nature of capitalist class relations inspired the politics of the labor movement and leftist parties, including the ruling Social Democrats, who instituted in Vienna progressive programs in education, housing, social security, and health. Mimi speaks enthusiastically about "the workers' universities, sports clubs, and summer camps—some of which I attended—that extended access to education and recreation beyond the privileged classes." The city's cultural renaissance brought provocative themes related to class struggle, sexuality, and the role of women to popular culture, the theater, and the arts. At her exclusive girls' school, the Schwarzwaldschule, Mimi was introduced to the work of the era's artists, writers, and social scientists, in which psychoanalysis and Marxism were employed to address the subjective and external inhibitors of human productivity and pleasure in contemporary society.

For them, Marx challenged the hegemonic bourgeois ideology of equal opportunity for all in capitalism by exposing its exploitative foundation in the capitalist expropriation of the surplus (unpaid) labor of the working class. And Sigmund Freud challenged Enlightenment beliefs in human rationality by uncovering the unconscious mind, whose powerfully irrational and impulse-ridden nature was harnessed to serve civilization at the heavy cost of individual freedom and contentment. In the 1920s, Wilhelm Reich, Otto Fenichel, Siegfried Bernfeld, and Edith Jacobson represented a generation of psychoanalysts whose psychological sensibilities were framed by their commitment to progressive political struggles for justice and equality.

The radical politics of the day embraced the new sexual mores, which challenged the deeply rooted Victorian legacy within Austrian culture. The feminist movement provided new role models for Mimi's generation, encouraging an open expression of sexuality and professional ambitions in women. Mimi describes her adolescence as "a time of excited experimentation with romantic involvements that distracted me from my academic demands. I was really curious about men and sex but resentful that I had to think about marrying 'well.' I remember envying poor women who weren't pressured by their families to fall in love with the 'right man.' I was quite relieved when my family lost their fortune in the Depression, making it impossible to provide me with a dowry. I felt liberated!" When, at the age of 19, Mimi decided to go to medical school, she received the enthusiastic support of her father, "for whom I was the son he never had," and reluctant agreement from her mother.

The subsequent direction in her life toward both political activism and psychoanalysis was determined by the rise of Austro-fascism in the early 1930s. During a research semester in Kiel, Germany, in 1932, Mimi experienced "the chilling effect of seeing a mass rally of the National Socialists [Nazis] and the mesmerizing impact of Hitler's speech on the demonstrators. When I returned to Austria, the Nazis began winning regional and municipal elections, and the Austro-fascists threatened the Social Democratic hold on Vienna. I decided to become active in the struggle against fascism. It seemed to me absurd for us to give up without a fight." A short time later, all political opposition—including the majority Social Democratic Party—was declared illegal by Austro-fascism, and Mimi became part of the clandestine movement with all its attendant dangers.

At the same time, and quite apart from her activism, Mimi pursued her studies, graduating from medical school in 1935. Her attempt to obtain training in psychiatry was circumvented when Jews were forbidden by the Austro-fascists to work in the public hospitals that had been part of the

Social Democratic–inspired socialized medical system. Mimi tells me that, ironically, "Austro-fascism was a decisive factor in my decision to be trained at Freud's institute." Following an interview with Anna Freud, she was accepted as a candidate for training in the Vienna Psychoanalytic Institute, where her formal education brought her into contact with luminaries of the psychoanalytic world, including her professor, Helene Deutsch, and her supervisor, Jeanne Lampl de Groot. "Once again, just as in high school, I wasn't a brilliant student—only this time for political reasons. My mind was elsewhere, on the political battles we were waging to hold on to civil rights in Austria. I led a double life, split between my psychoanalytic treatment and course work at the institute and my underground activism."

However, this activism had to be hidden from the psychoanalytic community. Fascism had succeeded in smothering the cross-fertilization between progressive politics psychoanalysis that had flourished under Social Democracy in Austria and that in Germany had been reflected in the innovative practice of Wilhelm Reich, who, for a brief time, integrated his psychoanalytic theory and clinical work with his political activism in the Communist Party. Now, in the deteriorating political situation, there was little time for theoretical discussion, especially in the midst of an intensifying mutual suspicion of psychoanalysis by political parties on the left and of leftist politics by psychoanalytic institutions. Under these conditions, "I felt increasingly self-indulgent and guilty about my psycho-analytic treatment and training. With worsening fascist repression and the imprisonment of growing numbers of my rank-and-file comrades, I began to feel that I was studying my umbilical cord while the world was blowing up around me."

The situation became more complicated when, alarmed by the Nazi per-secution in Germany of psychoanalysts who were viewed as representa-tives of a "subversive ideology," and by fascist repression in Austria, the Vienna Psychoanalytic Institute formally declared a position of neutrality with respect to politics. A regulation was passed that prohibited analysts and candidates from participating in clandestine organizations. Given the illegality of all opposition parties, this rule essentially forbade individuals related to the institute to participate in the antifascist struggle, in effect requiring that a choice be made between psychoanalysis and political activism. Either analysts had to end the treatment of politically involved patients, thereby ignoring medical ethics, or patients who were political activists had to agree not to speak about politics during their analytic ses-sions, countermanding the psychoanalytic rule of free association. "This development deeply affected my attitude toward the institute. I believed the administrators had withdrawn from the challenge facing all democratic sectors of Austrian society." It would, in fact, be a pivotal factor in Mimi's struggles later in life and on a faraway continent to bridge the gap between politics and psychoanalysis. But for now she believed psychoanalysts had acted naïvely or in bad faith, manifesting a severe form of "psychological denial," as if their refusal to respond to the persecution of Jewish analysts in Berlin and to the elimination of all civil rights in Austria could assure the survival of individual analysts or of their profession. "I was enraged, and I devalued psychoanalysis. And I knew that the revolution was more important." When the Spanish Civil War broke out in 1936, like thousands of political progressives, she was drawn to the Spanish Republic, whose progressive social experiment was being consumed in the flames of Franco's fascist onslaught.

Along with Max Langer, a surgeon and her future husband, Mimi joined an International Medical Brigade and spent months on the military front operating on the Spanish Republic's wounded and dying soldiers. Her first contact with Spanish political culture made her marvel at its passion, joy, and comradeship, but months later she felt ground down by the grim reality of war. Working first as Max's anesthesiologist, Mimi eventually performed surgical procedures as well. At the end of 1937, Max and Mimi were sent to Nice, France, to purchase equipment they would need to manufacture prosthetic devices. But before they could return, word arrived that the Republic was beyond saving. Thus the couple rejoined Mimi's parents, who had moved to the Sudetenland, Czechoslovakia, to be near her father's relocated business.

This final chapter of Mimi's life in Europe was filled with personal as well as political tragedy. After having suffered a series of miscarriages in Spain, she gave birth to a premature baby girl in Nice, who died after living only a few hours. "I entered into the deepest depression of my life." Shortly following her reunion with her family in what was now called Sudetenland, she realized she was once again pregnant. At the beginning of her second trimester, she began to hemorrhage, and as she was rushed by ambulance to a hospital located in the small town of Reichenberg, she suffered another miscarriage. "I'll never forget what it was like lying in the hospital bed at night, alone, my gown soaked with blood...Through the open window of my room I could hear the terrifying sounds of a passing Nazi demonstration and hundreds of voices yelling, 'Kill the Jews.'"

Mimi pauses for a moment, then collects herself. "You see," she resumes, "these devastating experiences were partly why I later became interested in psychosomatic disturbances in women's reproductive life. At the time I recognized that my miscarriages were a manifestation of a terrible conflict between my wish to have a baby and my fear of bringing a child into a world torn apart by violence and death. Later on, as a psychoanalyst, I would discover that they were symptoms, as well, of deeper conflicts about sexuality and motherhood typical of modern woman."

LATIN AMERICA: PSYCHOANALYSIS
IN THE NEW WORLD

In 1939, with the growing Nazi threat on the continent, Mimi and Max fled the escalating conflagration. "This opportunity brought me out of my depression. I viewed our departure as an adventure, a chance to start anew." They sailed for Uruguay, where together they endured several difficult and impoverished years. However, they found that in the New World, European immigrants with skill and fortitude could in fact begin again. During the three years in Uruguay, Mimi worked as a cook and a tutor in English and German, and she and Max had the first two of their five children. The couple maintained their political activism by joining the solidarity movement with the Spanish Republic.

Gradually Mimi wended her way back to psychoanalysis. "My reencounter occurred when a German immigrant from the solidarity movement asked me to give a lecture on Marx and Freud as a fund-raiser for the Spanish Republic. At that time I recalled much more of Marxism than of psychoanalytic theory, but I succeeded by focusing on how both of these great thinkers had discovered the latent meaning behind manifest reality." Shortly after, Mimi, Max, and their two children relocated to Buenos Aires, where Max's medical degree was eventually approved by the Argentine authorities and Mimi made her first explorations into the psychoanalytic community of that sophisticated city.

By 1942, when the Langers moved to Buenos Aires, psychoanalysis had already been influential for several decades among the city's medical profession and literati. In the twenties, the middle class in general, always avid consumers of the latest intellectual currents from Europe, had been reading the many journals and attending the numerous conferences that were dedicated to exploring a variety of themes in psychoanalysis. And, as in Europe, during the Depression, a significant number of Argentine professionals and academics politically opposed to their country's conservative government had explored the possible intersection between Marxism and psychoanalysis.

Once in Buenos Aires, Mimi dedicated herself to studying all of Freud's works, and this effort, in addition to her training at the Vienna Psychoanalytic Institute, gave her sufficient credentials in those early days to join a group about to launch a training center for psychoanalytic theory and clinical practice in Argentina. In 1942, she became the youngest and the only woman among the six official founders of the Argentine Psychoanalytic Association (APA). She was in formidable company, for her colleagues represented an impressive variety of interdisciplinary, scholarly, and progressive political interests in addition to their medical specializations. Several brought to the task of institution building the benefits of their own training in Europe with prominent individuals in the field and their friendships with outstanding figures in the arts, such as Salvador Dali and

Federico García Lorca. In Buenos Aires, the group attracted friends and colleagues whose fascination with psychoanalysis was connected to their ardent and multifaceted interests in philosophy, the arts, and democratic political struggles (see Hollander, 1990). The APA developed a full-fledged training program and was soon formally recognized by the International Psychoanalytical Association (IPA).

The founders of the APA represented a microcosm of Porteño society (the port city of Buenos Aires or one of its residents). They belonged to a generation formed by the dramatic economic and political upheavals of the period. Several, for example, came from families who had, like millions of others, responded to the Depression by migrating from the impoverished interior of the country to Buenos Aires, where they had achieved appreciable upward mobility. Several others, including Mimi, were recent refugees from Europe seeking a safe haven from a world that had come apart before their eyes. For them all, psychoanalysis became the central passion of their lives, something they fervently believed in as a vision of general human liberation as much as a treatment for individual suffering.

To Mimi in particular, psychoanalysis became "a new kind of militancy, one that replaced politics for several decades," during which time she committed her exceptional energies to the creation of the most vital and productive center of psychoanalytic thought and practice in Latin America. "I think my immersion in professional life and my isolation from left politics was partially a defense against my insecurity as an immigrant and my need to find a niche for myself and my family in a new society." It was, as well, a fearfulness about the unfamiliar political culture of Argentina, whose unpredictability provoked a fair amount of anxiety. The decision to keep a low political profile appeared especially advisable during the mid-1940s, when populist President Perón instituted a decade of nationalist antipathy toward British and U.S. economic influence and European cultural hegemony over Argentina. Although progressive in the context of Argentine history, Perón's politics threatened the traditions associated with the middle-class European and European-identified psychoanalytic community, as well as their counterparts in the arts and sciences.

However, in spite of the populist spirit of the Peronist government, during the 1940s and 1950s Buenos Aires proved a hospitable cultural environment for the growth of Latin America's most prestigious center of psychoanalytic training. Mimi and the other founding members immersed themselves in the task of constructing their institute, which soon won accolades from colleagues around the world for its contributions to the field. The founders of the APA made great efforts to disseminate psychoanalysis among not only the professional community but the lay public as well. Its journal *Revista de Psicoanálisis*, for example, was sold throughout Buenos Aires in the many bookstores that served an educated clientele interested in the social sciences and the arts.[1]

During this period, Mimi and other immigrant professionals felt it important not to call attention to their leftist leanings nor to be active in leftist politics. One had to keep a low profile so that the young psychoanalytic association would not be at risk. Even so, Mimi recalls that "in the APA we never prohibited political activism in an authoritarian way, as had been the case in Vienna, though there was an isolationist climate that discouraged it. Any progressive political activities I engaged in, for example, I did quite apart from my role as an analyst in the APA." The fact that the road to the left for politically progressive psychoanalysts had been closed by Stalinism also spurred the replacement of Mimi's political ideology with a psychoanalytic *Weltanschauung*. Communist psychiatrists in Argentina—as elsewhere throughout the world—were forced by the party to adopt behaviorism as their orientation and to reject psychoanalysis as idealist and a tool of a crumbling social order. "Thus at that time it seemed that my seniors in Vienna had been right: One had to choose between psychoanalysis and Marxism."

The extraordinary impact of psychoanalysis in Buenos Aires may be understood as a simple matter of supply and demand.[2] The culture and institutions of Buenos Aires consumed what the analysts had to give, and by the mid-1950s psychoanalysis enjoyed high visibility. The founding generation and their junior colleagues lectured at hospitals, where they instituted programs for primary prevention and taught courses at the medical school and the new Department of Psychology at the University of Buenos Aires. Among the most popular instructors was José Bleger, who in later years would become known in the APA as the "Red Rabbi" because he was the grandson of two rabbis and was himself a Marxist theoretician. Bleger's lectures attracted standing-room-only audiences that included university students as well as the public at large. Juan Carlos Volnovich remembers how he and Silvia would arrive at Bleger's lectures hours early just to get seats and enjoy the festive classroom scene. "When he began to speak, people were everywhere—in the aisles and passageways, sitting on the floor. He explained psychoanalysis in very accessible terms that drew adherents to the field." The presence of Bleger and other analysts from the APA at the university meant that the generation of students awakening to the era's new political activism were equally versed in radical political theory and in psychoanalysis.

Porteños became accustomed to seeing analysts' columns in newspapers, hearing them interviewed on the radio, and buying their publications in bookstores. Private practices burgeoned as the upper-middle and middle classes flocked to psychoanalysis, aware of its prestige in Europe and eager to emulate their counterparts in the metropolis. Being in analysis was an important symbol of upward mobility and status, often within easier financial reach than a new car or a condominium in an upscale neighborhood. And the intelligentsia sought answers on the analyst's couch to the larger existential questions of human angst and the meaning of life. In a fundamental way psychoanalysis was a good fit with prevailing themes in Argentine intellectual life, which, given the extraordinarily high percentage of immigrants and foreign-born in the population, revolved obsessively around the question of who and what Argentines were as a people and a nation. For all these reasons, by the mid-1950s, psychoanalysts were clearly among the Port City's most prestigious professionals. From the 1960s on, much of psychoanalysis even permeated popular culture to the extent that it is a generally accepted idea that in Buenos Aires, one is likely to encounter taxi drivers who, independent of their formal education, are quite comfortable holding forth on the oedipal complex as they traverse the chaotic traffic dedicated to disobeying as many traffic rules as possible.

Mimi's contributions to psychoanalysis were multifold. Her significant impact within the profession was due, in no small part, to her personal charisma as well as her brilliance as an analyst. A complex woman whose serious attitude toward work was complemented by her youthful good looks and charming Viennese-accented Spanish, Mimi attracted a loyal following that gave her voice considerable weight in the internal struggles within the APA. She lent her formidable organizational skills to APA's training program and its relations with other institutions and organizations. Her colleagues were sometimes resentful of her obvious popularity among the candidates, a sentiment that may have found expression when, in response to her "hard-line" critique of any analyst's abuse of transference,[3] they nicknamed her *la virgen María*. This appellation never failed to irritate her. "I resented it profoundly," she says indignantly. "I was especially proud of my liberated views about sexuality because of my own upbringing, and I certainly passed them onto my children." Perhaps this nickname reflected the resentment caused by Mimi's independence of spirit, for in controversial matters she tended to follow her own internal voice rather than succumb to pressures exerted by her colleagues. Such was the case regarding her interest in the application of psychoanalytic theory and clinical practice to group treatment. Although opposed by most of her colleagues, who believed psychoanalysis appropriate only for in-depth individual treatment, Mimi's work in group therapy encompassed techniques honed in England and based on Melanie Klein and Wilfred Bion's psychoanalytic studies of group behavior. "It extended my clinical skills and helped me develop a more social application of psychoanalysis beyond the limited parameters of the APA and the privileged social class it catered to."

Although Mimi wrote and lectured on many topics during this period, she was most interested in female psychosexual development and the unconscious conflict women experience in relation to their reproductive lives. "When I reread Freud in the early years in Buenos Aires, I was put off by his phallocentric views on women. It seemed to me he knew nothing of the female experience. I was asked to help translate into Spanish the work of Melanie Klein. I was very excited because I felt that Klein returned to women our femininity. Unlike Freud, who viewed the female as a castrated male and female unconscious conflict as a reflection of her envy of men, Klein showed how woman's unconscious conflict is partially rooted in her anxieties related to her reproductive capacities."

In the early years, Mimi was referred many female patients by the other founding members of the APA, among whom were women who suffered from infertility. Thus she had ample opportunity to test Klein's theories in her clinical practice. She was especially interested in what she viewed as an intensifying conflict among middle-class women between their professional aspirations and their maternal role. As a therapist, she observed their psychological responses to a sociological phenomenon that had occurred since the mid-1930s—namely, an industrial expansion that had resulted in widening work opportunities for women. By 1950, women constituted over a quarter of the country's wage earners and salaried employees. In Buenos Aires alone, almost half of the women between 18 and 29 worked outside the home. Working-class women increasingly found employment in factories and offices, although they were still also the domestic servants of middle-class women, who were rapidly entering the professional world.

Beginning in the 1930s, Argentine academic and popular cultural pundits had become preoccupied with what they claimed were the catastrophic effects of the entrance of women into the wage labor force, including a declining birth rate, a deterioration in the moral significance of the family, a rise in male unemployment due to "unfair" competition with cheap female labor, and a consequent decline in the dominant position of the father within the family (see Hollander, 2000a). This view of the threat to society caused by rising opportunities for women was countered in the 1940s and 1950s by Perón and his charismatic wife, Evita, who advocated women's rights, legalized women's suffrage, introduced protective legislation for working women, and encouraged women's political activism within the Peronist women's movement. Although Peronism appealed mainly to working-class women, its progressive politics widened the parameters for all women in the public sphere. These gains, on the one hand, irritated conservatives, who argued for the return of women to their traditional domestic roles, and, on the other, enraged leftists, whose own long history of struggles on behalf of women's rights was being co-opted by the Peróns, who had the political clout to institute massive reforms on behalf of gender equity. From Mimi's perspective, her middle-class female patients and their conflicts about motherhood and career represented an unconscious response to rising opportunities for women and to the growing contradictory attitudes and expectations regarding femininity and appropriate female roles in Argentine culture.

When Mimi became aware that a similar social phenomenon was occurring in the United States at the time, she was dismayed to learn that psychoanalysts responded in a generally conservative way to the changing role of women, offering prescriptive solutions that encouraged women to resolve their role conflicts by returning to the traditional sphere of maternal domesticity. Mimi's own reaction was to posit an alternative perspective based on her radical political and feminist intellectual formation. Contemporary female conflict about sexuality and motherhood, she believed, would best be resolved by institutional reforms and publicly supported social programs that embraced the expansion of the acceptable domains of female activity and facilitated their integration with women's maternal role.

In her clinical practice, Mimi focused on the psychosomatic disorders of female reproductive life. She wrote *Motherhood and Sexuality* (2000) as her contribution to the psychoanalytic literature about the vicissitudes of contemporary female experience. The book, first published in 1951, was an important departure from the conservative views articulated within psychoanalysis in the post–World War II era. She introduced her study with the argument that until the 20th century social restrictions had favored the development in women of their maternal functions while fostering repression of sexuality and creativity. As a result, women had frequently suffered symptoms of hysteria and other neurotic disorders. But, she argued, since the turn of the century, unprecedented sexual and social liberties and new economic and social imperatives had created conflicts within women regarding their maternal roles. Consequently, hysteria as the typical female disorder had been replaced by an increase in psychosomatic problems of infertility in women. Her book elaborated through psychoanalytic theory and clinical examples the unconscious conflicts women suffer at various stages in their reproductive lives.

Motherhood and Sexuality was sold in several editions throughout Latin America to lay as well as professional readers, giving Mimi an international reputation and substantial recognition within the IPA. Her prestige as an analyst soared, especially among Porteño middle-class women, resulting in a full patient schedule that brought many complaints from APA candidates, who were obliged to wait years before obtaining a training analysis, much less a weekly supervision session, with her.

Indeed, by the early 1960s, all the senior psychoanalysts were in great demand. The profession was attractive to an expanding number of candidates who had first been introduced to psychoanalytic theory as part of the cultural flowering that took place following the 1955 ouster of Perón. His exit closed a chapter on populist hostility to highbrow culture, and these young people seemed now to encounter psychoanalysis everywhere. As the sixties wore on and the political right gained ascendancy, psychoanalysis became an increasingly popular professional choice for many who would otherwise have chosen careers in the social sciences. After the military took power once again in 1966, social scientists were frequently targeted for persecution because of their progressive politics and community research. In contrast, because psychoanalysis retained its isolation from political and social questions, it became a haven for liberal and left professionals. For them, as for Marie Langer and her generation, psychoanalysis functioned as a substitute for a political ideology.[4]

The centrality of psychoanalysis in the intellectual and popular cultures of Buenos Aires and several other provincial cities of Argentina was not mirrored in Uruguay or Chile, where it followed two different courses. In Uruguay, the emergence of psychoanalysis as a profession in the mid-1950s was indebted to the help directly offered by the APA in Buenos Aires. The progressive nature of the Uruguayan state since the turn of the 20th century had resulted in an expansive social welfare program that subsidized cultural and scientific activities associated with the university and the private sector as well. By the early 1950s, the stimulating and pluralistic intellectual environment encouraged an interest in psychoanalysis among the country's physicians. Because there was no psychoanalytic institute in Montevideo, the first generation of physicians who sought training moved to Buenos Aires, where they were admitted to the APA. In order to respond to the growing demand in Uruguay for a formal training center, two British-trained APA analysts, Madelaine and Willy Baranger, moved to Montevideo in 1955 to help found the Uruguayan Psychoanalytic Association (APU). Marcelo Viñar remembers the Barangers as analysts of "very high quality and a seriousness that would leave its mark on the APU. Their tremendous capacity as clinicians and teachers helped to create an institute with profound integrity." Marcelo adds that "the tradition in my country of political pluralism, as well as the deep commitment among scientifically oriented professionals to social questions, also influenced the tenor of the APU." By 1965, when Marcelo, recently graduated from medical school, became a candidate in the APU, he was typical of his generation in his "wish to examine the correlation between psychological and social forces and to understand contemporary human problems as manifested in psychopathological symptoms of the disintegration of the family, abandoned children, and juvenile delinquency—in short, to seek the integration of psychoanalysis and a social project."

Thus, from its inception, psychoanalysis in Uruguay was considered to be more than a methodology for treating mental illness and was identified with social and cultural concerns. Classical psychiatry—which emphasized the physical or chemical treatment of mental and behavioral disorders rather than the psychoanalytic "talking cure"—battled the growing influence of psychoanalysis among mental health professionals in general. When psychology became a specialization at the university, psychoanalysis won hands down as the major influence in the young field. Perhaps this victory was due not only to the scientific differences between psychiatry and psychoanalysis but also to their tendency to be identified with disparate orientations to the world in general. Marcelo smilingly captures the difference in the kind of people attracted to the two orientations, commenting that a leader of the Physicians' Union once told him that "he did not know which was better, psychoanalysis or classical psychiatry, but he did know that during elections psychoanalysts voted for the progressive candidates and psychiatrists for the conservatives!"

In Chile, psychoanalysis made a somewhat later appearance than in Argentina and Uruguay, where scientific and cultural developments had been more directly affected by trends in Europe. Chile's location on the west coast meant that its major external influence had traditionally been the United States, where psychoanalysis did not occupy such a central position in cultural and academic life. Until the late 1960s, for example, Chilean psychology was dominated by classical psychiatry and behaviorism.

In the late 1950s, the Chilean Psychoanalytic Association (APC) was founded under the auspices of the chair of psychiatry of the University of Chile Medical School. The discipline developed under the tutelage of prominent analyst Ignacio Matte-Blanco and a small group of young psychoanalysts, including Otto Kernberg, who taught classes at the university. As Maren Viñar recalls, the curiosity of students was awakened by the provocative ideas of psychoanalysis. She was a medical student at the time, and she and a group of classmates would read Freud and spend hours at coffee houses "discussing the unconscious, holistic medicine, and the relationship between Marxism and psychoanalysis." For Maren, whose parents were political radicals and whose father had a copy of the first edition of Freud's *Civilization and Its Discontents*, these discussions were intriguing, not because, as she puts it, she understood anything of psychoanalysis. "Mainly I was reacting to the anonymity of the university hospital, where patients were treated like numbers...a deplorable situation that stimulated my interest in the social and psychological aspects of medicine." Although an autonomous psychoanalytic institute was founded in Santiago in the early 1960s, an exodus from Chile of the more intellectually vital individuals, including Matte-Blanco and Kernberg, for professional challenges elsewhere struck a blow to Chilean psychoanalysis from which it took many years to recover.

But Chileans interested in psychoanalysis had the opportunity to learn about it from other sources as well. Such was the case, for example, when in 1959 a group of students that included Maren attended an international meeting on medical psychology in Porto Alegre, Brazil. During the month-long conference the Chileans were exposed to analysts from all over Latin America. It was, however, only in the politically tumultuous late 1960s, before the election of the Popular Unity government, that Chilean psychology students began to read Wilhelm Reich and Herbert Marcuse and became aware of the radical currents within psychoanalysis these and other theorists represented. Some Chileans even left the country to study with Marcuse in California and, on their return, formed discussion groups among Chilean psychologists interested in the radical social philosophy underlying Marcuse's use of psychoanalytic theory.[5]

ARGENTINA: SOCIAL COMMITMENT
AND PSYCHOANALYSIS

Mimi says proudly that it was in Argentina that psychoanalysis offered a coherent analysis of the institutional fetters placed on psychological freedom by a repressive political order and that psychoanalysts actively challenged their profession to become part of the radical movement for social change. In Argentina the works of Marcuse, as well as those of Reich, Fenichel, and Erich Fromm—psychoanalysts with socialist convictions and social theorists with a psychoanalytic critique of bourgeois society—were read in the search for a new theory and praxis of liberation. Throughout the late 1960s and early 1970s, a new generation of psychoanalysts would design a politics of engagement, urging their profession to come down from its ivory tower to address the dramatic social crises facing the country.

The first battles took place within the APA as the younger candidates critiqued the institute's intellectual stagnation, which they attributed to the founders' theoretical rigidity and marked lack of interest in exploring new currents within psychoanalysis. They demanded a return to the broader social questions that had once preoccupied psychoanalysts interested in the relationship between individual and social repression. The candidates also protested the APA's hierarchical organization, which they argued enabled the founding members to maintain a tight-knit, elitist control over the administration and training programs and to prevent the participation of younger, nonvoting faculty and candidates.

Gradually, however, the struggles within the APA became more openly political as conditions in Argentina worsened following a military coup in 1966. Through the early 1970s, a series of military governments implemented politically repressive measures and economic policies that polarized Argentine society. The national parliament was shut down, choking off legitimate political representation of the country's citizens. One military regime after another instituted antiworker legislation with the intent of breaking the strong Peronist union movement that had been organized during the previous two decades. Rising unemployment and dramatic inflationary spirals cut deep into the standard of living of the working and middle classes. Social welfare legislation was rolled back, threatening access to medical care and retirement pensions for all working people. In addition, the military's antagonism to free expression brought censorship of the press and the arts, which alienated all sectors interested in the free flow of ideas and open cultural expression. This explosive situation erupted in the general strikes of 1969, in which major economic sectors of Buenos Aires and provincial cities were brought to a standstill. For the first time in the country's history, a general popular uprising was underway, involving industrial workers as well as middle-class professionals and students, and only the military's occupation of the cities in armored columns backed by air support suppressed the revolts (see Hodges, 1976; Corradi, 1985). Little did Argentines know at the time that these military governments were but a tepid version of what they would face following the military coup some years later that would launch the infamous Dirty War.

THE INSTITUTIONAL DEBATE

The psychoanalytic community was directly affected by these political confrontations throughout the country. Traditional struggles for influence within the APA based on contending factions of training analysts and their analysands or different orientations within the field gave way to a more clearly articulated political battle. "I felt so grateful," remembers Mimi, "that the younger candidates were unabashed about their leftist views. It gave me great encouragement to leave my political silence behind." Indeed, many of the younger candidates had been activist leaders at the university or were members of leftist political parties and movements, and together they denounced the APA's isolation from the crises facing Argentina. Mimi was one of the vocal senior analysts who joined the younger analysts and candidates in arguing that legitimate discourse within the APA should include the political questions facing the citizens of their country and that psychoanalysis must embrace a social perspective of psychic experience. The dissidents accused the APA of becoming a self-enclosed and self-congratulatory safe house for an elite professional sector bound to maintain its privilege and thus its alignment with the ruling class and the existing social order.

The conservative voices within the APA defended its insulation, arguing for the necessity of neutrality in the psychoanalytic enterprise. They claimed that value-free scientific inquiry and clinical treatment demanded that the patient know nothing about the analyst in order to facilitate the transference and fantasies revealing the nature and etiology of the patient's neurosis. A posture of neutrality on the part of the analyst was required. "We answered with the obvious," Mimi tells me. "We argued that analytic neutrality is an impossibility. Scientific inquiry is, after all, always designed in the context of the ideological frame of the investigator. Besides, everything about the analyst—our language, the location of our offices, our demeanor, how we dress, our fees—represents an identity based on class attitude and affiliation. So how could a completely neutral transference on the part of the patient ever really exist? We insisted that the psychoanalyst is no different from any other individual in society and that the APA's position on neutrality in the face of dramatic social, economic, and political injustices was an instance of identification with ideological hegemony as well as psychological denial."[6]

In the face of this open political confrontation, Mimi was ecstatic. For the first time since the painful days in the Vienna Psychoanalytic Institute, she was no longer bound to choose between psychoanalysis and politics. She became more outspoken, emboldened by the younger faculty and candidates, who had entered the APA with the view that psychoanalysis should not be a vehicle for adaptation to an oppressive society but rather an instrument for the development of a critical consciousness. Many of them came to psychoanalytic training with a background in social psychiatry and had received their training at the famous Lanus Hospital, a public institution located in the industrial belt of Buenos Aires that served a poor and working-class population. There they had developed a firsthand understanding of the grinding social and economic realities of working-class family life. Irrespective of their political orientation, they all became acutely conscious of the social components of individual physical and psychological illness.

Juan Carlos Volnovich was among those who gained precious medical and sociological training in Lanus Hospital, and in 1968, in the midst of the emerging struggles in the APA, he applied for psychoanalytic training. By this time he and Silvia, now married, had been to Cuba many times and were enthusiastically supportive of the goals of the revolution. "Sometimes," he says, "I don't understand the workings of the unconscious," referring to the irony of his interview with Marie Langer as a part of the application process. "She asked me whether I'd already had interviews with other training analysts, and I said, 'Yes, two.' And she replied, 'Pobrecito, how unpleasant to have to tell your life story so many times!' I felt, 'Thank goodness, she understands me,' and during that interview the only thing I talked about was Cuba! I don't know why. When I left I wanted to die. I didn't know Mimi was a leftist then, and I thought, 'You're nuts, how could you talk about Cuba to get into the APA?' I was convinced it was all over for me." Not only was Juan Carlos admitted to the APA, but, in retrospect, he credits that interview with his subsequent good luck in obtaining supervision with Mimi, who was so popular with the candidates that she had a seven-year waiting list!

Juan Carlos was the youngest candidate in the APA, and he finished his classes in a record three years amid growing tensions in the institute. He was still naïve about political theory, but he identified idealistically with the liberation movements throughout Latin America and was thus naturally drawn to the dissident movement within the APA. "There had been José Bleger at the Psychology Department, my experiences at Lanus Hospital, and my connection with Cuba through Silvia. I was 'condemned' to think on the left and in terms of radical change!" He became an ally of those within the APA who postulated that psychoanalytic theory must embrace a Marxist conceptualization of class society and hegemonic ideology in order to understand the external factors inhibiting the possibility of individual psychological change (see Bigliani, Bigliani, & Capdouze, 1971).

One of the articulate spokespersons of this position was Eduardo "Tato" Pavlovsky, an analysand of Mimi's who became one of the leaders of the dissidents in the APA. Tato was a third-generation Argentine of Russian and Italian background who had come to psychoanalytic training following his graduation from medical school in 1958. It had seemed the appropriate path to follow since he came from several generations of medical specialists. Besides, his own experience in psychoanalytic treatment as a lovesick adolescent had deeply impressed him, not only because of its salutary effects on his personal life but also because of the psychoanalytic conceptualization of human subjectivity. By the time Tato finished his training and became a faculty member of the APA in 1968, he had developed a unique specialty within the field. Early on he had discovered the value of psychodrama, a variant of play therapy, as a method of working with children. After studying with prominent specialists in psychodrama in the United States, he became a pioneer of the method in Argentina. "I consider myself a group therapist and a creator/coordinator of groups, rather than a psychoanalyst in the limited sense of the word," he says. This perspective continued to evolve as Tato found it increasingly difficult to identify with the APA, which he considered to be "a closed world, religious and theological."

In the volatile late 1960s, according to Tato, "the historical situation was impacting on our consciousness. I myself had come from rather reactionary parents who raised me in an oligarchic social and cultural environment. There was some tradition, however, of political engagement. My paternal grandfather had suffered persecution under the czar in Russia and had written books about the prerevolutionary climate, especially the phenomenon of nihilism. I always had the impression that there was a family secret because even though you couldn't find a more anticommunist or anti-Semitic family than mine, my grandfather kept a photograph of Lenin on his desk! My father was a middle-class, white-collar employee and an avid anti-Peronist. He was imprisoned for a short while in 1952, after which he went into exile in Montevideo and then Asunción, Paraguay. Even though I don't agree with his political ideas, I think I owe a debt to my father for his being a role model, someone willing to act in coherence with his ideals."

Tato's own politicization came slowly, at first through a romantic identification with the Cuban Revolution and then in response to the great social struggles taking place in Argentina. His search for personal meaning led him to become disillusioned with the typical life of a psychoanalyst, "which was reduced to the radius of a single social class. One could live quite well from analyzing only six patients who were wealthy businessmen. This produced in me a sense of unbearable emptiness." Tato's attraction to the theater led him to explore the postwar vanguard movement of Samuel Beckett and Eugène Ionesco and eventually to study with a group of leftist activists who produced an important and innovative theater movement in Buenos Aires. Tall, good-looking, and with a forceful personality, he was a powerful presence on stage. And even though he remained actively engaged in the dissident movement within the APA, he continued to be drawn toward cultural expression because "life in the theater put one much more in touch with the community and with the social context of individual human experience. It provided me with the opportunity to leave behind the bourgeois life style and consciousness in which psychoanalysis was steeped."

Tato's increasingly public persona offended many of the conservatives within the APA, who dismissed his involvement as self-indulgent acting out. "From my perspective, the theater helped me a lot with what amounted to an existential crisis. I knew that my profound discontent was healthy." He founded a group of physicians dedicated to studying alternative theater, which made a significant impact on Argentine cultural life. At the same time, he began to write plays whose themes brought him fame as a politically conscious and psychologically astute playwright. His *Señor Galindez*, an insightful exploration of the psychology of the torturer, first appeared in the early 1970s and became a classic for its intuitive depiction of the type of political repression that would beset Argentina in future years.[7] No wonder, then, that he became one of the principal organizers of the efforts within the APA to bring psychoanalysis and radical social theory together.

As tensions within the APA grew, the dissidents realized that similar developments were taking place in the psychoanalytic community in other countries. By 1968, the student and worker protests in many European countries and the antiwar movement in the United States prompted youthful candidates in a number of psychoanalytic associations to protest their institutes' isolation from the dramatic questions plaguing society the world over. At two congresses of the IPA, the first in July 1969 in Rome and the second in July 1971 in Vienna, concerned candidates and faculty from many countries held simultaneous counter-congresses to voice their social and political concerns. The Argentines played a pivotal role in these meetings, where the social relevance of psychoanalysis was examined in a host of different languages.

Mimi represented the dissident Argentine presence within the official congress of 1971 in Vienna, where the IPA was meeting for the first time since the Nazi repression of psychoanalysis and Freud's flight to England more than three decades earlier. In the luxurious Hofburg Imperial Castle and among some of the most prominent psychoanalysts in the world, Mimi presented a highly controversial paper entitled "Psychoanalysis and/ or Social Revolution," which was covered extensively by the international press. Mimi says that it was quite fitting that her paper would be presented in Vienna, where she had first been forced to choose between her professional and her political commitments. "It was precisely in Vienna that I would speak not only of psychoanalysis but of Marxism and revolution to boot!" Her paper traced the points of convergence between Marx and Freud, and she urged her illustrious colleagues to use their psychoanalytic knowledge to facilitate rather than to oppose the process of change. She admonished them not to follow in the footsteps of the analysts who had left Cuba following the revolution or those who were at that very moment departing from Chile on the heels of the election of Allende. "This time," she declared, "we will renounce neither Marx nor Freud" (Langer, 1971, p. 268).

And, as if to prove Mimi's point, participants in the counter-congress were establishing Platform, an international organization that would permit dissident analysts and candidates in their respective countries to articulate their critiques and develop alternatives to institutionalized psychoanalysis. The Argentines returned to Buenos Aires and under the leadership of two young analysts, Armando Bauleo and Hernán Kesselman, formed Plataforma, which became the organized challenge to the hierarchy of Argentine psychoanalysis. Only three months following the Vienna congress, in response to what the dissidents viewed as the APA's reactionary refusal to respond adequately to the growing political repression perpetrated by the military government, even when it directly affected members of the mental health community, they concluded that they had no choice but to leave. Another group, called Documento, which had been formed by those opposed to censorship within the APA, reluctantly joined Plataforma in severing its tie to the APA institute.

THE INSTITUTIONAL RUPTURE

Heated discussions and agonizing decisions preceded the rupture. For some, including Mimi, Tato, and Juan Carlos, it was clear that in order to develop an interdisciplinary and socially relevant psychoanalytic praxis, it was necessary to depart from the APA. For others, however, who agreed with the dissidents' critique, the only legitimate approach was to stay and fight from within the citadel for democratization. As the storm gathered, Mimi felt exhilarated at the chance to take a principled stand. "I was no longer encumbered by family responsibilities. Max had died in 1966, and my grown children were all politically active in their own right. I could now assume the consequences of a radical position. I felt that at last my life would represent coherence with my political convictions. And, best of all, I would now become an activist psychoanalyst and be able to bring my professional skills to the struggle against social and political oppression." All around Mimi, this passionate stance was being expressed. Not only psychoanalysts but musicians, writers, and filmmakers as well were abandoning their citadel—the U.S.- and European-dominated mass media—in the search for an authentically indigenous and critical expression of Latin American reality. Their militancy was captured by Argentine filmmakers Fernando Solanas and Octavio Getino, producers of the now classic revolutionary film *Hour of the Furnaces*, in their 1969 manifesto announcing the New Latin American Cinema Movement. "The camera is a gun," they wrote, "that shoots twenty-four frames a second." In a similar sense, Mimi believed that psychoanalysis was an explosive weapon in the ideological war against class, ethnic, and gender oppression.

From Tato's perspective, official psychoanalysis was suffocating the creativity and intellectual growth of its members. No longer able to bear the APA hierarchy, which he believed reflected the hierarchical relations of bourgeois society in general, he argued strongly for the rupture. "We did not want to be psychoanalytic practitioners in the narrow sense of the word, insulated and successfully sharing the elite lifestyle of our wealthy patients. Traditional psychoanalysis, which requires a patient to come four times a week and to use the couch is, after all, an economic as well as a scientific model. We were intellectuals, Latin American intellectuals, who wished to utilize our psychoanalytic expertise to understand more profoundly our Latin American reality and to develop new models befitting other social classes. As psychoanalytic intellectuals, our project in the grand scheme of things was to contribute to the popular will to change our society."

It all happened at once for Tato. "So much occurred in just one year: 1971. First, our 'Latin American Manifesto of Psychodrama' in an international congress in Amsterdam in August, where we denounced the North American use of encounter groups as a methodology of adaptation and argued for a group experience that could be an instrument to expose authoritarian structures, both in the mind and in society. Then came Plataforma and *Señor Galindez*." Tato's personal life reflected the tumultuous overturning of custom, as well; his first wife and he separated, and he moved into a commune with some ex-APA colleagues to explore "nontraditional forms of family life." At the moment of the rupture, according to Tato, "we did not have it all clearly thought out; we deeply needed to liberate ourselves, and we identified with the Latin American project of social justice and national liberation. We knew we had a psychological tool of colossal importance, but we had only sketchy ideas of how it could be brought together with a political analysis. Each of us would pursue this project in different ways afterward."

Juan Carlos experienced the rupture as a logical extension of his personal relations and his political sensibilities. By this time, he and Silvia had become politically active in the left-Peronist movement. "We lived a completely divided life. On the one hand, we were bourgeois analysts, and on the other, we were political activists, going poorly dressed to a working-class neighborhood to work in a local community center organized by the Montoneros." Juan Carlos wrote an article critiquing the APA criteria for mental health, which, as he summarized them, were "good work relations, good sexual relations, and good relations with friends." He added another criterion for mental health that he considered to be of fundamental importance: "a sensibility toward social injustice." This stand identified him with those who were deciding to leave the APA, and he was willing to risk his family's financial security in order to be politically consistent. As he humorously recalls, "During the night of the final discussion before the rupture, at one point an enthusiastic training analyst suddenly stopped the heated debate and exclaimed, 'Wait, do you realize what we're doing? You know what this means? It's like burning our Diners' Club card!'" In fact, leaving the APA had global consequences: It meant the rejection of membership in a small, elite, professional group that enjoyed financial success, social status, and the guarantee of a completely secure future. "We were willing to do it, to reach for a kind of continuity between our ideals and our practice. I remember that afterward, when a colleague said to several of us that he agreed with our ideas but believed we should stay and fight from within the institute, my friend replied, 'You know what? To be inside the APA is to be outside the country.'"

The split had a dramatic impact on the APA. To some it was a relief that the political activists had left. To others it represented a threat to the vitality of psychoanalysis. Still others were sorry to see some of the best minds in their profession leave the institute but believed in the importance of maintaining a separation between political conviction and professional life.[8] The rupture also had significant repercussions beyond the psychoanalytic community. Juan Carlos was in charge of Plataforma's public relations, and he was inundated with requests for interviews by the press. Newspaper and magazine articles described for the public at large the issues that had prompted the rupture within psychoanalysis, presenting the flurry of debates on the concept of neutrality, which, in the rapidly polarizing conditions of Argentina, was relevant to all citizens.

Plataforma was to last for little more than a year, during which, as Juan Carlos puts it, "we fought like crazy amongst ourselves over different theoretical positions. But we had the good sense to disband the organization before we reproduced the same errors for which we had criticized the APA." Plataforma dissolved, but it had provided the significant function, according to Tato, of creating "a new subjectivity, a new way of thinking, a new consciousness about the possibilities of a noninstitutional psychoanalysis, a socially committed psychoanalysis."

In this period of great intellectual productivity, social alternatives to both capitalism and Soviet Stalinism were explored. Mimi recounts how the analysts formed study groups to read Reich, Fromm, Louis Althusser, and other theorists whose ideas they could apply to the specific psychosocial situation of repression in Argentina. They elaborated critiques of the concept of neutrality. Some dissidents maintained that in co⌐ ⌐⌐⌐⌐ to the APA conservatives, who continued to delude themselves about the possibility of clinical and social neutrality, their consciousness of their nonneutrality made possible its elaboration, thus preventing its interference in their patients' treatment. Some argued that denial, not neutrality, motivated an analyst to interpret all aspects of a patient's concern about troublesome social conditions as evidence of childhood anxieties emerging in the transference relationship with the analyst. Others argued that only repression could account for a lack of affect on the part of either patient or analyst regarding the experience of living in the midst of military rule. These dissident analysts argued for the importance of being responsive to patients' fears and anxieties about the dramatic social crisis confronting Argentina.

Loss was a theme that permeated their discourse; both patient and analyst experienced losses in many domains as civil society was increasingly threatened by military and paramilitary forces whose repressive brutality indiscriminately targeted individuals engaged in legal public protest as well as members of clandestine organizations. In one case, a student was abducted by the army in the north of Argentina. When it was later discovered that he had died under torture, the provincial authorities attempted to investigate the case but were eventually dissuaded by death threats. Such incidents in the early 1970s were an omen of what was to come in the not too distant future.

Mimi edited and published two journal volumes called *Cuestionamos* (We Question, or Question Authority), in which the contributors analyzed different aspects of the relationship between psychoanalysis and social change.[9] Many themes were explored, including the nature of violence and aggression within repressive societies; the character of mourning in societies where imprisonment, torture, disappearances, and assassinations pervade citizens' daily experience; and the role of reparation in revolutionary struggles. Mimi's paper "Psychoanalysis and/or Social Revolution" appeared in the first volume, and in the second she contributed "Woman: Her Limitations and Potential," a synthesis of her views on the convergence of Marxist, psychoanalytic, and feminist theories in the interpretation of the specific nature of the oppression of women. She also coauthored an article in the same volume that critiqued the complicity of the Brazilian Psychoanalytic Society with the repressive military government that had ruled that country since 1964. She described how a candidate in the Rio Psychoanalytic Society worked with a team of army torturers, teaching them about the psychological responses to torture. "Evidently a training analyst does not know how to stop the psychoanalytic formation of a candidate who is a torturer without bringing inevitable reprisals on himself and the institute," she wrote. "In all its crudeness this situation captures the relationship between institutionalized Freudianism and the dominant system. Without a doubt, institutional survival can require a very heavy price."

PRAXIS: CLASS STRUGGLE AND PSYCHOANALYSIS

The split within psychoanalysis occurred as military rule produced an even larger mass movement of opposition to a system that clearly benefited the privileged few at the expense of everyone else. And reflecting the political theory popular throughout Latin America that arose in the ashes of failed reformist strategies to alter existing political and economic structures, many Argentine radicals argued that only an armed struggle would dislodge the ruling class from power. Guerrilla organizations, the two most important of which were the Marxist People's Revolutionary Army (ERP) and the left-Peronist Montoneros, named after the guerrilla fighters who fought the Spanish in the war for independence, carried out armed attacks against military targets and representatives of foreign capital. This violence was a response to unremitting economic exploitation and the systematic repression of progressive organizations and trade union movements by military and paramilitary forces. The Montoneros had a base within the radicalized Peronist working class, and their romantic appeal to the previously anti-Peronist middle class and students grew rapidly because they were believed to be the uniquely Argentine expression of a mass-based people's struggle against class exploitation and foreign domination by the United States. Many of the political psychoanalysts, like Juan Carlos, were sympathetic to the Montoneros and became activists in the legal political organizations allied with them.

Mimi and other dissident analysts had for several years been active in the politically progressive Argentine Psychiatric Federation (FAP), an organization that criticized the illegal actions of the military government, such as counterinsurgency policies that included the disappearance and murder of political militants and union activists. As members of FAP, they engaged in research and the development of programs that addressed serious social problems, such as alcoholism, among the popular classes. Now that they were no longer members of the medically controlled APA, they sought to democratize psychoanalytic training through the creation of the Organization of Mental Health Workers. For the first time, the traditional status and hierarchical divisions among mental health professionals with different specializations were eliminated, and everyone—irrespective of prior training—had access to psychoanalytic classes and supervision. This effort put the Argentine dissidents in the forefront of the demedicalization of psychoanalysis, which would later become an international trend. As Mimi puts it, "We believed that a common professional formation of all mental-health professionals would create a mutually shared sense of professional and political identity. This would increase our solidarity in union struggles and the organized opposition to the military government."

The Organization of Mental Health Workers created the Research and Training Centers (CDIs), the most important of which was in Buenos Aires. The CDI curriculum was divided into three areas of professional preparation: The first two areas elaborated psychoanalytic and radical social theory, and the third dealt with the relationship between these theories and clinical practice. Mimi recalls fundamental points of convergence between

Marx and Freud that were elaborated in the classes. "For example, we taught that both Marx and Freud agreed on the essential irrationality of the prevailing human condition and the idea that humanity is driven by forces it does not understand and therefore cannot control, in spite of its belief to the contrary. We stressed their agreement on the fundamental difference between appearance and reality, by which they meant that what we tell ourselves about what we do and why are the mere manifest surface below which operate forces we know nothing about. Marx argued that while the French Revolution proclaimed itself on the side of liberty, equality, and fraternity, in actuality, it represented a new historical era and mode of production—capitalism—that was built on compulsion, exploitation, and competition. Marx showed how the wage labor system, with its ideology of individual responsibility, hid [its] essentially exploitative nature...and hence the systemic sources of inequity in class relations. We linked Marx's idea that the ruling class could permit no challenge to its domination to Freud's notion of how the superego functions. Freud showed how the superego, which from our point of view is the repository of the hegemonic values and attitudes of any social era and its dominant class, relies on defenses such as denial, repression, and displacement to eliminate from the conscious mind thoughts and feelings that challenge its domination."

Mimi continues, "We also explored how in both Marx and Freud there is the theme of human alienation. Marx showed how in capitalism workers came to produce commodities in a complex process they don't understand or control. Thus they experience the products as having a life of their own and the organization of the process itself as being characterized by a kind of permanence. In the face of this illusion of permanence it is impossible for one to act as historical agent to change things. Freud dealt with this state of alienation and how it is reproduced through his concept of transference, by which he meant the way we all attribute to present figures in our lives the traits and qualities of significant figures from our early past. Freud showed how patients resist change and become ill because they do not remember their past. The repressed individual does not understand his or her history and is overwhelmed by it, and the neurotic symptom becomes a substitute for the past not remembered. For both Marx and Freud, the inability to comprehend the past condemns one to repeat it. Marx called for revolution, for him an act of revindication through which the oppressed would reappropriate power from the exploitative bourgeoisie and go on to develop a social order that would enable humanity to make its own history. Freud postulated a psychic revindication, a process based on the recovery of that which has been forced out of consciousness, through the psychoanalytic method of overcoming resistance to remembering and knowing. The resolution of the conflict between the rational ego and important components of unconscious life would permit a degree of unity between the different parts of the mind that have been divided against themselves."

Mimi points out that in Argentina the influence of Melanie Klein's thought informed psychoanalysts' particular reading of the Marx–Freud dialogue. "We didn't believe that all 'evil' resides only in external reality—that is to say, exclusively within the social and economic institutions of class society. We believed that hate, cruelty, envy, and destructiveness are as much a part of the human psyche as love and creativity. Klein showed us how the child's growing awareness that the parent it loves is the same person it also hates results in the capacity to feel guilt and the consequent urge to make amends for—to repair—the effects of one's destructive urges. We agreed with Klein that it is the recognition, rather than the disavowal, of the capacity for envy, greed, and destructiveness that produces the reparative impulse in human beings. So we—unlike Erich Fromm, for example—didn't subscribe to the thesis that all we had to do was change the oppressive structures of capitalism in order to create a sane and decent society. We were convinced that only when the conflict and ambivalence that characterize the psyche and all human relations are recognized and worked with, rather than denied, could people act out of concern for others and build a just social order."[10]

These theoretical postulates were a part of the core curriculum of the CDI classes. Under the clinical supervision of Mimi and her colleagues, students were also required to fulfill a minimal number of clinical hours by working in hospitals, community clinics, and unions. Although the CDI was a relatively short-lived experiment, Mimi believed it to have accomplished three important tasks before it became a victim of government repression. "It broke the stratification among mental health professionals and integrated them into one union; it demonstrated the possibility of acquiring psychoanalytic training outside the APA at a minimal cost; and it showed that psychoanalytic theory and technique could be used with all social classes in a variety of settings." Mimi's political activism in the CDIs and her role as president of the FAP put her in constant danger of being targeted by right-wing paramilitary groups. But she experienced a sense of elation and optimism rather than fear. "At last I could act in concert with my values and beliefs—with my ego ideal—and dedicate myself to the things that really mattered to me...[Now] I could utilize my training as a psychoanalyst in the service of the popular classes."

Many of the political analysts treated patients whose involvement in underground revolutionary activism they often knew nothing about for security reasons. Because he was a child analyst, Juan Carlos saw activists' children, who, in response to the growing tension all around them, were beginning to suffer nightmares, learning disabilities, insomnia, and psychosomatic illnesses. He and other analysts began to treat people in nontraditional ways, a strategy that would expand in future years when the repression deepened. He would meet a parent and child in a public plaza, for example, neither adult knowing the identity of the other. Sitting on a bench while the child played, the parent would communicate information about the child's difficulties to Juan Carlos while he observed the child's play. In subsequent meetings, arranged in parks and restaurants, he would bring his customary therapeutic materials, including clay, crayons, and toys, and hold informal sessions with the child. "What an ironic situation...for security reasons, neither of us learned each other's names, even though I knew very intimate details about their lives."

Tato chose another route toward political activism, which ultimately exposed him to the same risk of reprisal from a repressive state. He developed a high profile in the cultural world, where his fame was due to his prominence as a playwright and actor and his innovative contributions to psychoanalytic psychodrama. He remained in the public eye as well through the articles he published in the media critical of the authoritarian culture and politics of military-run Argentina.

Both Juan Carlos and Tato recall the excitement they shared about their activities during this period, which permitted them to feel, like Mimi, a euphoric "coherence with their ego ideal." In retrospect, though, both believe that they, like the rest of the left, could sustain their political involvement only by denying the risk their activism posed to their personal safety. "It was a kind of omnipotence; I was convinced that nothing could happen to me," recalls Juan Carlos. "My grandfather had written of survivors, and I saw myself in that tradition." Tato was in analysis with Mimi at the time, and when *Señor Galindez* appeared in the theaters, she told him, "Look, Tato, I don't know whether you're conscious of what you've written, but it seems to me they won't forgive you for it." It would take him years to realize that she was correct and that he had been in profound denial about the potential repercussions to his personal safety that would result from his outspoken political stance.

However, the political analysts would enjoy a brief respite before having to deal with such issues, a kind of calm before the storm. The military was on the defensive. Hundreds of thousands of activists were participating in antigovernment demonstrations, lending extensive support to strikes and factory occupations and volunteering their labor to improve housing, sanitation, and medical and legal services in the ubiquitous shantytowns where the injustices that resulted from the state's economic and social priorities were the most glaring. New struggles were being articulated as well: In 1972, a feminist movement emerged among middle- and working-class women. Small groups read and translated seminal works of U.S. and European feminist thinkers, started consciousness-raising to build solidarity among women, and took public positions critical of the repressive military government. One such organization was the Argentine Feminist Union, whose initials in Spanish—UFA—were the same as the expression commonly used by Argentines when they are exasperated; *ufa* means "enough" or "I've had it up to here."[11]

In fact, millions of Argentines were crying *ufa* to the military. As the signs of mass disaffection with the system became more clear, the military, the elite, and their international allies were prompted to recall Perón from his 18-year exile in Madrid in the belief that only he could forestall a revolution in their country. Perón's return was also desired by the left-Peronist mass movement, whose members were convinced that he would facilitate, rather than prevent, radical social transformation. For some months during 1973–1974, following the democratic elections that brought a Peronist-led coalition to power, the progressive forces within the movement dominated the presidency and the congress. This short period provided a political opening for mobilization among many different sectors. The left tendency within the Peronist movement, led by the Montoneros, opened up community centers, called *unidades basicas*, and led workers in the formation of new unions in radical opposition to the old labor bureaucracy. Women activists took part in these various activities, but a special organization for women, called the Agrupación Evita, was also created to deal with the special problems women faced. Influenced by the women's movements in other countries, activists produced a radical analysis of the exploitation of women's labor in the family and of the sexual objectification of women in the mass media. They also made demands for reproductive rights and for day-care centers and other institutions that would support women in the domestic and public spheres (see Hollander, 1974, 1977; Fraser & Navarro, 1980).

Within this heady political environment, the challenges were multifold for the political analysts. Mimi and her colleagues in FAP entered the most notorious maximum-security prison for political prisoners to investigate and denounce torture and to treat political prisoners who had been jailed during the long years of military rule. Members of FAP and the Organization of Mental Health Workers went to working-class neighborhoods and squatter settlements to volunteer their labor in public-health projects initiated by progressive and left political organizations. They threw themselves with buoyant spirits into radical union and movement activities, seeing themselves as socially conscious citizens who, trained as psychoanalysts, could help people free themselves of the psychological impediments to social engagement. Mimi coauthored (unpublished) articles, including "Psychoanalysis, Class Struggle, and Mental Health," analyzing this valuable experience. "In our therapeutic work, we remained faithful to our psychoanalytic technique of interpreting unconscious conflict. While we refrained from offering advice, suggestions, or didactic interventions, our interpretations of our working-class patients' discourse included a critical perspective of the class and gender determinants of their unconscious pain and rage."

Caught up in the fervor of the times, most of the political analysts, like militants in general, failed to comprehend the short-lived nature of this political opening. Indeed, it even seemed that their country was becoming a sanctuary for the refugees streaming into Argentina in desperate flight from the state terrorist regimes of Uruguay and Chile. They brought with them the horrendous reports of the unprecedented reprisals against anyone who had been identified with progressive politics in those two countries.

The situation in Argentina began to clarify by early 1974, when the continuing economic crises and intensifying class confrontations blew the inherently contradictory Peronist coalition apart. The right-wing and corrupt sectors within the movement captured the government apparatus and, in league with the elite and its military allies, began to repress the left Peronist and Marxist opposition. Unofficial death squads, often composed of junior army officers, and paramilitary right-wing gangs stepped up their operations, enjoying impunity in their violent assaults on the left. The Triple A and other death squads eliminated well-known revolutionaries and others regarded as sympathetic to them. These disappearances and murders were designed not only to kill off the left but to instill terror in the general populace. In anticipation of what would follow on the heels of the military coup in 1976, General Jorge Videla was already warning that "as many people will die in Argentina as is necessary to restore order" (Amnesty International, 1982).

The general's vision of order was translated into a daily atmosphere of ominous threat. Under such conditions, new priorities emerged for the political analysts. The demand grew among victims of political repression for psychotherapy with progressive analysts. People sought psychotherapy as a means of managing anxieties and fears that were more and more the product not only of individual and family histories but of current social reality. Increasingly, Mimi and her colleagues were called on by the leadership of the Peronist and Marxist left to help activists who had suffered the trauma of torture or to make an assessment about whether particular individuals with paranoid tendencies or other psychological disorders compromised their comrades' security.

Meanwhile, people were leaving the country, voluntarily seeking a haven from the political storm gathering momentum. Others, including psychoanalysts, left unwillingly in response to certain knowledge that they were no longer safe in Argentina. "When we'd receive a call from a friend who didn't want to talk on the phone but suggested meeting at a café," recalls Juan Carlos, "we knew it would be a goodbye encounter. It was a real blow when Mimi was targeted by the Triple A and left for Mexico. We began to feel abandoned, alone, isolated."

Feeling equally abandoned, alone, and isolated as her plane landed in Mexico, Mimi walked into the airport and a new chapter in her life. Once again a political refugee, she joined thousands of exiled Argentines who faced the challenge of reconstructing their lives far from their country, families, and the political struggle that had given them a sense of personal value and purpose. "It was a crucial turning point in my life, a forced separation from everything familiar, like stepping into an unknown abyss. I felt that I'd had a small taste of the joy of building something important together with thousands of other people who shared my values and principles. Now that was gone, and I had no idea what awaited me."

For our protagonists who remained in Argentina, an equally uncharted future lay in store. They would live through the transition to full-fledged military dictatorship with its unparalleled assault on democracy and human rights. Each would be faced with the excruciating decision of when to leave or how to survive the vicissitudes of the culture of fear that would be perpetrated by the terrorist state.

ENDNOTES

1. This and subsequent information about the formative years of psychoanalysis in Buenos Aires was gathered through interviews with first- and second-generation Argentine psychoanalysts, including, in addition to Marie Langer over a number of years, Arnaldo Rascovsky, Jorge Mom, and Mauricio Abadi in Buenos Aires during August 1990. See also Asociación Psicoanalítica Argentina (1982), Balán (1991), and Hollander (1990).
2. Author interview with the past president of the APA, Buenos Aires, August 1990.
3. *Transference* is a psychoanalytic term that refers to the patient's projection onto the analyst of thoughts and feelings associated with primary people in the formative period of the patient's life; *abuse of the transference* refers to an analyst's taking advantage of the patient's dependence, occasionally through an erotic flirtation or even seduction. Langer was consistently critical of any manifestation of such behavior on the part of any analyst. Several colleagues claimed, however, that her critique was somewhat hypocritical because her charismatic personality, intentional or not, wound up having the same impact on the candidates; because she was such a fascinating person, the candidates wished to become her analysands or supervisees. Her critics argued that this situation could be seen as a kind of indirect transference abuse.
4. Author interviews with Julia Braun and Argentine psychoanalyst Edmundo Zimmerman, Buenos Aires, August 1990.
5. Author interviews with Chilean psychologists María Isabel Castillo and Juana Kovalsky, Santiago, October 1995.
6. The dissident Argentines' criticism in the 1960s of the psychoanalyst as a neutral participant or a blank screen was one that would be treated at length and in a variety of ways in the psychoanalytic literature on countertransference that emerged during the next several decades in that country as well as in the United States and Europe; since the mid-1980s, the relational and intersubjective orientations within U.S. psychoanalysis have come to view the psychoanalytic process as a two-person enterprise in which the social world—culture—intervenes and is manifested. For the contemporary development of these ideas, see Mitchell (1993) and Altman (1995). Also see *Psychoanalytic Dialogues*, a journal that features conversations among psychoanalysts about contemporary trends in the field.

7. *Señor Galindez* has been performed in theaters in the United States, where it has been received with interest and where audiences have had the opportunity to discuss with Tato the provocative questions the play raises with respect to what makes a torturer.

8. Author interview with Antonio Barrutia, Buenos Aires, August 1990.

9. These two volumes, published by Gránica Editor (Buenos Aires) in 1971 and 1973, included contributions from many of the participants in the social movement within the profession; they raised significant issues regarding the relationship between psychoanalysis and ideology, politics, and violence.

10. For discussions on this perspective, see Langer (1989), Altman (1995), Alford (1989), Women's Therapy Centre Institute (1994), and Rustin (1991).

11. When I lived in Buenos Aires in the late 1960s and early 1970s, I participated in the emerging "second-wave" women's movement and, together with Gabriela Cristeller, founded the Unión Feminista Argentina (UFA), a center that offered women a lending library of feminist literature from around the world, lecture series about the history of women and the women's movements in other countries, and the opportunity to participate in consciousness-raising groups. Participants in UFA, as well as in a number of other feminist groups that grew up in that period, were middle-class and upper-middle-class professionals and students, individuals from the arts, and those with activist experience in progressive and left movements. The movement also attracted working-class women with long histories of union militantism.

Chapter 4

The psychosocial dynamics of state terror

First, we are going to kill all of the subversives, then their collaborators, then their sympathizers, then the indifferent, and finally the timid.

— General Iberico Manuel Saint-Jean
Governor of Buenos Aires Province (1977)
—Graziano (1992, p. 28)

What pardon, what "humanly possible justice" will bind with wire the windmills of our memory?

— Alicia Partnoy (2004)

Julia Braun smiles engagingly as she hands me a cup of espresso and invites me to partake of the delicious pastries before us. We are sitting in the charming, loft-like family room of her new, expansive penthouse, which towers high over the bustle of Buenos Aires. The apartment has a breathtaking, 180-degree view of the city, which in the northeasterly direction features the wide and serene La Plata River with the high-rises of Montevideo visible in the distance. The tranquility of the physical environment, with its casual blend of designer furniture, prized artwork, and rough-hewn paintings and statues created by Central American artisans, reflects the multiple facets of its owner's persona. Julia is 60, youthfully attractive and stylish, with a self-contained and gracious sociability. We have known each other for years, but this fall of 1998 is the first time that I am hearing the detailed chronology of her life. I am careful to take my cue from her, for we are speaking of difficult things. When she indicates her readiness to continue, I ask her to tell me what it was like to live in Argentina in the years leading up to the coup. "It was the most terrible time of my life," she begins haltingly, "except for later, with the disappearance of Gabriel..."

LIFE IN THE TRANSITION TO STATE TERROR

The metamorphosis of society toward military dictatorship, whether in countries accustomed to democratic institutions, such as Chile and Uruguay, or in ones familiar with the dynamics of military rule, like Argentina, is typically a period of confusion and disorientation. Only with hindsight can one say without a doubt that in such-and-such moment, the signs were incontrovertible. For a time, the contradictions in external reality, where the apparently reliable continuation of normal, everyday life is ominously punctuated by hints of profound disruption, dovetail with psychic defenses of denial and disavowal. In all three countries, the political analysts lived through agonizing uncertainty about the social drama unfolding before them, responding according to their psychological makeup. Julia believes her particular experience was affected by her lack of active political involvement and the fact that she had not analyzed or written about political repression before she experienced it herself.

When most of her friends in the Argentine Psychoanalytic Association (APA) left during the schism in 1971, Julia Braun remained in the institute along with others who agreed with the dissidents' critique but argued that it was better to stay and fight for reform from within. "Maybe I feared that I wouldn't be able to finish my training, or perhaps I wasn't brave enough. I don't know. And maybe I have tended to stand on the sidelines a bit. But I have always thought that one needs to have a posture of commitment toward society, toward politics, to contribute what one can. One should not pass through life leaving decisions to others."

Julia's sensibilities grew out of her awakening to politics as a young woman during the Perón era. A first-generation Argentine of Hungarian and Polish-Jewish parents, she grew up in a modest, middle-class neighborhood and attended public schools. Her politicization came in high school through her friendships with students who were interested in culture and politics, some of whom later attended medical school with her during the early 1950s. Julia was a delegate to the medical school's Student Center, a progressive organization whose anti-Peronist sentiments made it the object of government ire. When the center was declared illegal in October 1954, it went underground, and during a clandestine meeting at Julia's house, the police barged in and arrested everyone.

"I spent four and a half months in prison, but in comparison with the prisons later on, it was like being in a four-star hotel! There were 40 of us university women jailed, and although we were treated decently, the terrible part was that we had no right to a defense and no idea how long we'd be there." The students were finally released, although they never knew why. This episode occurred during the final days of the Perón government, with rumors abounding that the military was preparing for a coup. "I believe that this experience must have marked me in some way," Julia confides. "I think that in authoritarian governments the prison experience is a warning, a threat. It did not prevent me from being connected to politically active people or continuing to think politically, but in a sense it made me less willing to take bold risks."

In 1957, Julia married a fellow medical student and political comrade, Mariano Dunayevich, whose love she suspects was "imbued with a fair dose of idealization because he visited me in prison and must have viewed me as a kind of heroine." Julia was soon pregnant, and the couple, both struggling, young professionals, had their first son, Gabriel, in January 1958. Several years later, in the wake of an epidemic of unknown origins in the province of Buenos Aires, Mariano, a specialist in viruses, was offered a fellowship to study at the Communicable Disease Center at the University of California in Berkeley. When Julia obtained a residency in pediatrics at San Francisco Children's Hospital, they left for the United States, with their parents fairly bursting with pride, "as if we had each won a Nobel Peace Prize!"

They lived in San Francisco for two and a half years, which for Julia represented "from a psychoanalytic point of view, a moment of resignification in my life." During the sixties, the Argentine middle class and intelligentsia attached much significance to going abroad "to perfect oneself," so the experience perforce "had to be the best. We had to be enjoying it to the full. I had to love it, to learn a lot. Only years later could I understand the effort and the suffering it meant to be so far from home, to give birth to my second child, Bernardo, so far away from my family." Their return to Buenos Aires meant a new disruption and adjustment, which highlighted already-existing problems in Julia's relationship with her husband and her uncertainty about what she wanted to do with her life. Typical of her culture and class, she sought psychoanalysis to confront these troubling issues. At the same time, she began to work in the psychopathology department at the renowned Lanus Hospital, where she met many young doctors who were interested in psychoanalysis. Intrigued by her personal analytic experience and her work at the hospital, Julia decided to become an analyst. In 1967, she began her training at the APA.

Julia was a third-year candidate, just finishing her training analysis with one of the outspoken political analysts, when the rupture in the institute occurred. Most of her closest friends, as well as her analyst, left the APA. The only thing that tempered her bad feelings about staying was that José Bleger also remained, apparently unwilling to abandon the psychoanalytic home he had helped to create. "I allied myself with him, whom we all deeply admired, and felt in a minimal way justified."

Like so many other leftist intellectuals, Julia and Mariano lived through the turbulent early 1970s attracted to Peronism, voting for the progressive Peronists but not participating directly in the movement. Their radical sympathies were clear to their sons, the older of whom became active in his high school student federation, which was one of the student movements

influenced by the left Peronists. By 1974, however, the corrupt right-wing
Peronist government was targeting for repression the progressive sectors of
the movement. Julia became ever more nervous as she learned that Mimi
Langer and others were being chased from the country by the Triple A.
She remembers being anxiously preoccupied with her son's situation. Life
was dominated by family confrontations as Gabriel became increasingly
involved in political activism. "It was such a contradiction. Gabriel would
tell us that we were hypocrites, that he was only actualizing the political
principles he had learned from us. And he was right. Our position was difficult to defend. I respected his commitment to the values of justice and equality that we had always upheld. He argued that we couldn't teach him one
set of values and then ask him to be a traitor to his ideals and his comrades.
Like all the young people, he criticized us for our bourgeoisification."

Julia understood that an important aspect of the struggle with Gabriel
was characteristic adolescent rebelliousness toward parental authority with
its proclivity to criticize one's parents while simultaneously admiring and
identifying with them. "But the stakes were rising precipitously as the real
situation became more dangerous." Indeed, by the beginning of 1975, por-
tentous signs of disaster were multiplying. A deep deterioration in the economic situation produced spiraling inflation, speculation, hoarding, and
shortages in basic necessities. Industrial production dropped, unemployment increased, and sales of consumer goods shrank, resulting in demonstrations and strikes that by July culminated in a 48-hour general strike by
more than seven million workers throughout the country. In response, the
Congress passed legislation legitimizing repression of the opposition.

Progressive senators, artists, filmmakers, and journalists received telephone calls and letters ordering them to leave the country or face certain
assassination. Ads appeared in newspapers signed by the Triple A, giving
notice to selected individuals that they were on its death list. Lawyers were
warned on threat of death not to defend political prisoners; those who per-
sisted were killed, robbing the jailed of their legal defense. The press was
censored: Newspapers critical of the government were closed down, and
reporters who did not censor themselves were threatened, jailed, or murdered. Police cars appeared suddenly in different neighborhoods of Buenos
Aires, simultaneously cordoning off dozens of blocks in each area. Anyone
traveling by car, by bus, or on foot was stopped, searched, and forced to
provide identification. Police carried out house-to-house searches, demanding identification papers from inhabitants, who had to demonstrate their
right to be there. Telephones were tapped; mail was opened. Plainclothes
police frequented bars and restaurants, observing and listening. More bodies appeared in every city in Argentina, riddled with bullets, disfigured by
dynamite, burned beyond recognition. In Buenos Aires, a young political
activist—pregnant—was kidnapped from a family party and found shot
to death the next morning. Silvio Frondizi, the brother of the ex-president

and head of a Marxist party, was murdered in front of his family. A worker active in organizing a strike in his factory went missing and was later found murdered, his tortured body abandoned in an alley. A leftist Peronist deputy in the congress, Rodolfo Ortega Peña, was shot to death late one night. The executed bodies of three men and two women were found abandoned near a road outside Buenos Aires, each one bearing 140 bullets. Argentines were living in an environment that ominously presaged what was to come.

Perpetrated in the final months of Isabel Perón's reactionary government, the mounting repression represented the death rattle of populism. As with everyone they knew, Julia's and Mariano's anxieties intensified. Despite the undeniable danger, Gabriel was more and more politically involved every day, although in what his parents never knew for sure. "We did know, though, that at this point the movement had no chance of winning. Instead, they were heading for total destruction. We saw that the young activists were less and less protected by the leadership from the growing repression, and we were impotent to do anything."

They continued to try, convincing Gabriel and his *compañera* to participate in weekly family therapy sessions with a progressive and sympathetic psychoanalytic colleague. But the chasm between the desperately worried parents and their recalcitrant son remained. As more people began to disappear, Gabriel spoke little about his university-based activities, worried that he might compromise his parents. They sensed his fears, although he never articulated them. In the final days of 1975, when most Argentines assumed that a military coup was imminent, Julia and her husband made a last-ditch effort to protect their son. They suggested that the family leave the country for a time so he could gain some emotional distance to think about what he wanted to do. "We respect your ideals," they told him, "so if outside the immediacy of the situation you make a dispassionate assessment and decide that it is the best thing for you to come back, we will honor your wishes." Not surprisingly, Gabriel refused, perhaps sensing their unspoken agenda to try to stop him from returning to Argentina. On January 11, 1976, Gabriel turned 18, and his parents hosted a birthday celebration, a festive *asado* (Argentine barbecue) for all his friends at their weekend home in nearby Tigre. "It was the last party we ever had for him. I did not know then that it would be our farewell."

Julia lived through the transition to state terror as a politically conscious individual in anguish over the disastrous condition of her country but with an overriding maternal preoccupation about what might happen to her child. For others, like Juan Carlos Volnovich and Tato Pavlovsky, this period brought a daily paradoxical struggle to live their lives as normally as possible while simultaneously acting politically to help prevent the rapid drift toward a catastrophic resolution of the country's political tensions. Like the millions whose lives had been framed by activism, they vacillated between heart-rending dread and sublime denial as the noose tightened around them.

As with so many of his political *compañeros*, Juan Carlos's life became chaotic in the months leading up to the coup. For some time, he had been a psychoanalyst with much prestige in Porteño society, and his patients included foreign diplomats, prominent individuals in the arts, and members of the ruling elite families. The political activists he treated included the radical sons and daughters of the upper and middle classes as well as those from the most humble strata of Argentine society. As conditions in the country worsened, more patients sought therapy to help them face the unbearable anxieties of the intense political situation. Juan Carlos also continued to provide psychological interventions for Montonero activists. He witnessed the alarming effects of the state's repressive policies on the decision-making capacities of the Montonero leadership. Just as Julia had feared, the leaders began to demand compromising and perilous commitments from individual activists psychologically unprepared for the experience. As Argentina moved rapidly toward out-and-out fascism, Juan Carlos felt caught in a terrible conflict. Although he worried because of what he saw as the leaders' growing irresponsibility about exposing their young militants to predictable risks, he continued to collaborate because "we still believed we were going to make the revolution and because, especially given my psychoanalytic understanding of people, I accepted the fact that human beings are imperfect. I was not a romantic in that sense. Nothing is ideal, I thought; everything and everybody is characterized by contradictions. How could this not be true, I told myself, of the very revolutionaries with whom we were fighting for a better world. So I stayed."

Security became a primary issue, and everyone Juan Carlos knew moved constantly, sleeping in different locales every night. He, Silvia, and their two little children did the same, and they moved their offices frequently as well. In retrospect, Juan Carlos realizes that a combination of factors permitted him to bear the enormous tension during this period. One was his unconscious denial that the organized violence of the right-wing state had succeeded in derailing the progressive forces and that they were now in true disarray. "Once the repression reached a certain point, a cogent analysis of what was happening was impossible. At the time, I didn't realize that it was not feasible to analyze the situation, and I continued, like a technocrat, interpreting everything that happened and thinking I could understand it all. I continued to believe nothing could happen to me." However, in spite of their denial, he and Silvia also prepared for the worst, structuring a personal security system to protect their family. They never participated in the same political activities but took turns so as not to expose their children to the risk of losing both parents. And they had an escape strategy in place, with passports, visas, open plane tickets, and a plan elaborated for how on a second's notice they and their children could leave the country. But they stayed, keeping alive the hope that somehow the rapid drift toward disaster could be stopped.

Tato, too, refused to leave, although many of his psychoanalytic friends and colleagues in the theater were heading for exile. Even when a theater that featured *Señor Galindez* was bombed, Tato was resolute. "I think I unconsciously denied the danger because I could not bear giving up so many things—my country, my home, my work. I just told myself, they won't come for me." Meanwhile, he faced anguishing situations in his therapy groups, as individuals who had suffered imprisonment or torture sought psychological help. "Lots of people were dying, and it was impossible to be objective in this period. You couldn't speak only about the Oedipus complex now because we all shared the same fears. The issue of neutrality was dead along with the dying. I tried to be as neutral as possible in order to understand the nature of the more irrational conflicts that a patient might be suffering. But, given the conditions we were living through, sometimes the therapy provided the important function of helping patients with the difficult task of developing a language with which to articulate their experience of terror. In retrospect I realize that often the therapy group represented the only space in which people could put into words the fear, the panic. It was the only space where we could speak. It would be like that for years."

Uruguay's transition to state terror was much like Argentina's. By March 1972, when an ultra-rightist became the new Uruguayan president, the progressive democracy of the "Switzerland of South America" was being replaced by a military-dominated political system that successfully routed the Tupamaros and began the systematic elimination of the critical voices among organized labor and the middle class. Uruguay underwent a gradual militarization of daily life as soldiers carried out massive searches throughout neighborhoods in Montevideo and large-scale arrests in provincial Uruguayan cities. The media were utilized to sow fear among the population through daily radio and television broadcasts produced by the armed forces that reported on the "progress of the war." The "enemy" in the military's "war" turned out to include thousands of union activists, students, social workers, physicians, lawyers, journalists, and mental health professionals. The military saw them as constituting a vast network of subversion threatening the status quo.

Many of those targeted by the military, like Marcelo and Maren Viñar, had identified for years with progressive and leftist values and activities that had been a legitimate part of Uruguayan pluralistic political culture. Beginning in the tumultuous late 1960s, the Viñars participated in one of the first groups organized within the Uruguayan Psychoanalytic Association (APU) to study the intersection between the social and unconscious domains of human experience. The members of this group sought to break out of the fetters of mainstream psychoanalytic theory, which from their perspective had focused too exclusively on the intrapsychic world of the individual.

Maren recounts that "in that period it was clear that individual psychological experience was deeply influenced by the social world, and it forced us
to move beyond conceptualizing the internal world in a void." She stresses
how the themes of social violence and aggression prompted heated theoretical debates over issues about which analysts passionately disagreed—and
still do. "The new political violence that began with the death of students
and the repression of strikes forced many of us to see that the external
context of psychological life is not calm and stable, but on the contrary, its
dramatic unsettledness disturbs the internal world of the subject."

Maren and Marcelo point out that their involvement in the university,
the hospital, and working-class neighborhoods, where they treated families
struggling with deprivation and poverty, highlighted the social context of
their psychotherapeutic work. In 1970, during a congress in Caracas called
Social Reality and Psychoanalysis, the Uruguayan participants formed a
study group with Mimi Langer, José Bleger, and other Argentine analysts
to explore how psychoanalysis could contribute to an understanding of
the social crises in their countries. The group met every three months in
Montevideo or Buenos Aires to develop new paradigms for an analysis of
the role of the unconscious in group behavior. When their Argentine colleagues in Plataforma broke from the APA, Maren and Marcelo did not
feel compelled to leave the APU because it did not mirror the APA's hierarchical structures and closed ideological environment but in contrast, like
Uruguayan organizations in general, had tended toward a pluralistic open-
mindedness. So the Viñars remained in the APU but continued to work
with the dissident Argentines because they had parallel preoccupations.
In 1971 the Uruguayan group coauthored an article in *Cuestionamos I*,
asking whether therapeutic neutrality was possible within an increasingly
politically repressive society. They wrote about a specific situation in which
a patient of Maren's, a university student, had been shot by the military.
Should a psychoanalyst, they inquired, participate in the strike organized
to protest the murder? "We argued that in this situation no neutral position
was possible, that either position—to strike or not to strike—contained a
political posture in the face of deepening repression that affected patients
and analysts alike. Furthermore, as more of our patients began to be affected
by military and police actions, we postulated that when a patient or those
close to her are directly affected by political repression and she doesn't
speak about it, the analyst's refusal to raise the subject does not reflect
therapeutic neutrality but collusion with the patient's denial of reality."

But what Marcelo remembers most is his confusion during this period,
the difficulty of evaluating the meaning of events that were relentlessly altering reality as he had always known it. "There was the problem of timing,
if you will: how much time it took for an individual to be socialized in a
social democratic culture and then how much time it required to recognize
that it had changed into a terrorist and terrifying society. The process of

political change and the capacity to subjectively absorb and understand this change operate at distinctly different rates. I, for example, was very slow to realize the shift…it's as if I continued to believe in democracy when I was living in a country that was already totalitarian. I believe that it is characteristic of the period of transition between democracy and dictatorship that people function by denying reality. During those years we thought, 'I'm not a Tupamaro; I'm part of the democratic left. All I did was collect dues from three Communist Party members. But the party was legal, they won't put me in jail for that.' Or, 'Five years ago I signed a petition against the Vietnam War, but that wasn't against the law…the repression is against the Tupamaros, why would they come for me?' It's exactly as Freud describes, a splitting of the ego, in which one can believe two contradictory things at the same time but not be able to put them together to recognize the obvious truth. Thus two belief systems can coexist without entering into contradiction. This was how reality was characterized at the time. I couldn't believe that they would ever come after me to take me prisoner, and yet I did believe it."

Marcelo's state of disavowal had operated when, in 1971, he was approached by a colleague who requested advice about the medication and hospitalization of a Tupamaro militant who had suffered a psychotic break. Marcelo knew that the patient was a Tupamaro but told himself there was no problem because he was simply acting under the medical oath that obliged him to treat anyone needing medical intervention. A year later, he would be imprisoned for this professional decision, which was considered by the military a political rather than a medical act. His crime would come under the purview of "assistance to an association of delinquents." In this regard, Marcelo believes that "it wasn't until I was taken prisoner that my dissociation was challenged. In fact, I think I was helped tremendously by my first interrogations. It was only then that I began to understand that the mentality of my interrogators and my own were as different from one another as Martians and Earthlings. I am grateful to them, actually, because when the military came to get me a second time several years later, I was able to anticipate it and fled the country in time."

In Chile, the transition to state terror took a different course than in Argentina and Uruguay, but Elizabeth Lira's experience was similar to that of her *compañeros* in the other two countries. She lived through the destabilization of an already-existing leftist government and the creation of the conditions for its elimination. The Chilean military acted in league with President Nixon's 1970 mandate to the Central Intelligence Agency (CIA) to "utilize every appropriate resource" to get rid of Allende. By mid-1972, the international campaign of economic sabotage against Chile and the ongoing ideological attacks of the Chilean press blaming the Popular Unity (UP) for the ensuing economic difficulties created a state of continual crisis and foreboding.

"The country was in chaos, but it was clear that it was being orchestrated," remembers Elizabeth. At the height of the economic crisis, she had her second child, Cecelia. "Imagine, there were no diapers! There were terrible shortages of everything—bread, vegetables, cooking oil, meat. The right wing had control of the distribution networks and the wholesale suppliers, and the businessmen were hoarding products to sell on the black market at inflated prices. The people with money had no worry. The rest of us had to stand in long lines, sometimes for five or six hours a day beginning at 5 a.m. And, of course, it was the women who had to do it. Conflicts arose at home because there wasn't enough to eat." Increasingly, daily life became intolerable for millions of people who could not explain to themselves why they had to spend so many hours simply to obtain food. The UP ceased to represent an advantage or improvement in their lives. For many, their hope that the poor would one day run the country now seemed to have been a fantasy. The media kept up their threats, insisting that conditions would inevitably deteriorate if the UP continued in power. The media manipulated people's deepening anxiety about the uncertain future. The goal was to diminish popular support for Allende and to neutralize potential resistance to any illegal move to oust him from power.

Worst perhaps was the pervasive sense of confusion. Elizabeth says that "no one could imagine what was coming. I was frightened, though, because I had always felt that the Allende program was very idealistic, with the additional problem that the UP administrators had too little experience to implement the strategy of reforms in a way that could minimize the inevitable social conflict that comes with change." In the midst of the crisis, it was difficult to assess the balance of power. Many of Elizabeth's friends and comrades thought Chile was heading for civil war. Others viewed the huge demonstrations organized by the supporters of the UP as proof of the strength of progressive forces, which they believed could deter the right wing. Elizabeth thinks that the militant left misjudged the situation by overestimating the solidity of their support among the masses. "From my perspective they projected their own unshakable commitment to support Chilean democracy by any means necessary onto the hundreds of thousands who came to the spirited demonstrations they organized. They mistakenly assumed that the progressive forces would stand fast if the country moved into an armed confrontation. They were blinded to the difference for most people between taking part in a demonstration for a day and putting their lives on the line in the face of an increasingly violent enemy."

Elizabeth also believes that the decades-long leftist denunciation of U.S. imperialism had the paradoxical effect of diminishing the impact of the left's exposé of the United States as an active player in the unfolding drama in Chile. It sounded so fantastic: the U.S. State Department, the CIA, ITT Corporation, orchestrating from Washington a massive conspiracy with millions of dollars and hundreds of operatives to undermine their democratically elected government. "Fantastic, but true," she laments. "Many simply dismissed it as paranoid rhetoric, preferring to put blinders on so as not to heed the signs."[1]

During the three months leading up to the September 11 coup, conditions became increasingly catastrophic. Elizabeth's political organization met daily to evaluate the latest events, to calculate how best to support the government, and to figure out how to protect themselves. "But we were so naïve, we couldn't clearly identify what would happen. I remember meeting a friend one day, a sociologist, who advised me that we should learn from the experiences of comrades from other countries, the refugees among us from Brazil and Uruguay. 'If something happens,' he told me, 'we would have to burn our books, clean out our houses, disconnect from one another.' And I thought he was crazy. How in this country would I ever have to burn my books? Military dictatorship was something that characterized other countries, not Chile. This is a nation, I thought, where there is legality and where the armed forces are constitutionalists. We believed that. Allende believed it. We thought we were different."

As it turned out, in the Southern Cone there were no exceptions.

HEGEMONY AT WAR: THE IDEOLOGY OF STATE TERROR

The Lacanian concept of the discourse of the Other, which is internalized to become a constituent of unconscious life, is an important context for exploring the powerful significance of the ideology of state terror and its impact on citizens. The military juntas justified their repressive rule through an ideology that had been fine-tuned for three decades after World War II. Its origins can be found in the Doctrine of National Security designed in Washington at the outset of the Cold War. Its aim was to preserve the hegemonic role of the United States in the Western Hemisphere and to protect the capitalist order throughout the Americas from external and internal threat. By the late 1940s, a military division of labor between the United States and Latin American militaries had been elaborated: The United States would be responsible for the defense of the Western Hemisphere against outside aggression, and the Latin American armies would focus on the elimination of internal threats to stability of the existing socioeconomic order.[2]

The Doctrine of National Security was expanded during the Kennedy administration in the wake of the Cuban Revolution, and it provided the rationale in subsequent decades for the U.S. government's development of counterinsurgency programs in its struggle against genuine reformist governments as well as the spread of revolutionary movements in Latin America. Subversives were defined in broad terms to include anyone or any group whose aims were considered "inconvenient" to the existing system.

The United States organized centers where North American ideologues taught the principles of counterinsurgency to Latin American armed forces. Special advisers, instructors, and CIA operatives fanned out over the continent to disseminate the message and the know-how. Beginning in the 1960s, the Conferences of American Armies met to coordinate security operations among the various Latin American militaries. For most U.S. citizens, this country's involvement with torture is understood to have developed after our 9/11 as a defensive attempt to protect its interests from radical Islamist enemies. However, the truth is that the United States has practiced and taught torture beyond our borders for decades. The CIA coordinated with the Office of Public Safety (OPS) to recruit Latin American police forces for training at a clandestine center in Washington. Among the strategies for training Latin American police and military in the art of repression, CIA field offices in Panama and Buenos Aires responsible for psychological research were used to ship polygraph and electroshock machines in diplomatic pouches to public safety offices across the continent. From the Truman era through the Clinton presidency, thousands of Latin American military officers have attended special courses in the Doctrine of National Security and its tactics—including classes on the theory and practice of torture—at the School of the Americas, Fort Gulick in the Panama Canal Zone, and Fort Bragg in North Carolina.[3] Many of the officers who organized and implemented the coups in Argentina, Chile, and Uruguay had attended classes at these sites, where they developed collegial relationships and a mutual understanding of their historical task. They would cooperate when the time came to "go all the way" to implement the doctrine.

In the process, the liberals—the "soft-liners"—within the military would be forced to decide whether to acquiesce gracefully or get out (see Duhalde, 1983; Chavkin, 1989; and Fagen, 1992). The Uruguayan colonel appointed by the military to defend Marcelo after he was imprisoned was a case in point. Maren describes him as "avidly anti-Tupamaro." At first this officer scared her to death. She felt he was Marcelo's accuser rather than his defender. "But he was essentially a democratic man, and as the repression mounted, his personal ethic was deeply offended by the violation of human rights perpetrated by his military colleagues. After Marcelo was released, this colonel brought his daughters and wife for therapeutic consultations and also sent other associates for treatment. Shortly after, he took his family and left the country."

Ever since World War II, the United States has supplied heavy arms and lighter tactical weapons to Latin American militaries for counterinsurgency warfare against "internal enemies." As Defense Secretary Robert McNamara told Congress in 1963, "Our primary objective in Latin America is to aid, wherever necessary, the continual growth of the military and paramilitary forces, so that together with the police and other security forces, they may provide the necessary internal security" (Argentine

National Commission on the Disappeared, 1986, p. 444).[4] It was argued that World War III—the battle against communism—had many fronts and included political, ideological, and psychological warfare as well as military struggle. The U.S. military was so directly connected to the Latin American military apparatus that three years into the Argentine junta's Dirty War against its citizens, the United States organized a course in Buenos Aires that taught strategies in fighting subversion, which included classes in physical and psychological torture. It was attended by many members of the Latin American armed forces. And in the seventh year of military rule in Argentina, U.S. military personnel occupied offices in the army's head-quarters, with separate telephones in the Operations Section, Overseer of Operations and Central Division.[5]

During the period of state terror, the economic policies of Argentina, Chile, and Uruguay were based on the principles of neoliberalism, a conservative philosophy, so called because it accepts the free-trade tenets of 19th-century liberal economic theory advocated by the United States, Latin American business sectors, and international lending and trading institutions. The military governments, advised by the "Chicago boys," neoliberal economic technocrats associated with the University of Chicago monetarist Milton Friedman, dramatically reversed the previous trend toward state-sponsored industrialization and opened up their markets to foreign investors. The Chicago boys' blueprint for an unfettered marketplace called for the elimination of protective tariffs, minimum wage laws, social entitlements, and government safety and health regulations, and advocated government intervention in or destruction of unions. When corruption and unproductive speculative investments resulted in economic crises, the militaries exacerbated their countries' cycle of indebtedness by borrowing large sums from an enthusiastic International Monetary Fund and World Bank, where U.S. interests predominated. The close relationship between the Argentine junta and foreign capital was symbolized by Ford Motor Company, which in a full-page newspaper ad congratulated the military as "Argentines of good will" who were turning the country around. Ford pledged its participation "in the efforts to fulfill the nation's destiny," concluding with a self-congratulatory "Ford gives you more" (Fisher, 1989, p. 14). Indeed, Ford gave generously to the junta: its local subsidiary supplied government security forces with the unmarked Falcon automobiles that were used in the illegal abductions of Argentine citizens.

From Juan Carlos's perspective, "The historical function of the Southern Cone dictatorships was to eliminate those sectors of the population capable of mounting resistance to the uncontrolled, free-market economics sought by transnational corporations and international financial and trading institutions." He emphasizes that the revolutionary armed movement had already been destroyed in Argentina when the military took power, and thus the Dirty War it unleashed was equivalent to the use of the atomic bomb in Hiroshima. "It wasn't necessary to vanquish the Japanese, who had already admitted defeat, but rather to intimidate the Soviet Union: Look what we have and what we're willing to do. In the case of state terror in the Southern Cone, they utilized the strategy of counterinsurgency in a psychological war to attack all critical consciousness."

The mentality that engineered this ideological and military war against internal subversion was profoundly authoritarian. State terror was the product of a partnership in which U.S. political and military leaders shared a proclivity for authoritarianism with their Latin American counterparts. But because the violence occurred in Latin America, it could be depicted in the United States by government and media alike as the natural outcome of the inherently violent nature of the cultures to the south. The contributions of the U.S. government to the extreme political repression throughout the continent could be externalized onto other forces—immoral subversives, godless communists, bloodthirsty generals—and thus disavowed to its own citizens.

In addition to the Doctrine of National Security, each of the militaries in the Southern Cone brought to this partnership additional political and military theories garnered from their studies of 19th-century Prussian strategists and from their training with French veterans of the counterinsurgency wars fought in Algeria and Indochina.[6] These various orientations contributed to an authoritarian mindset among Latin American militaries, which was fully uninhibited and self-indulgent in its grandiosity. Military leaders and followers alike shared a psychology characterized by a set of paranoid/schizoid defenses: the splitting of the world into good and evil—Western civilization versus subversion; the projection of everything bad onto a hated object—the subversive—with the consequent need to control it for fear of being controlled by it; and an infantile sense of omnipotence that promotes attacks on free inquiry and political difference, with a corresponding incapacity for empathy. Like European fascism, the Latin American terrorist state was unable to abide political and philosophical pluralism. Repression of dissent was total. As the Argentine military succinctly put it, "Argentina has three main enemies: Karl Marx, because he tried to destroy the Christian concept of society; Sigmund Freud, because he tried to destroy the Christian concept of the family; and Albert Einstein, because he tried to destroy the Christian concept of time and space."[7]

With their strong sense of corporate identity, army officers saw themselves as members of an elite organization and were contemptuous of civilians and especially of politicians. Democracy was, from their perspective, an inappropriate medium for winning the war against "subversion." The militaries attacked all who might possibly be or become the enemy. The members of leftist organizations became demonized but were seen as the mere tip of the iceberg. According to the military, a vast subversive network of ideological conspirators had invaded every aspect of life, affecting the economy, the judicial and educational systems, the labor movement, and cultural expression. As Argentine President General Jorge Videla put it to the press in 1978, "A terrorist is not just someone with a gun or a bomb but also someone who spreads ideas that are contrary to Western civilization." Videla's military colleague in neighboring Chile, President Augusto Pinochet, agreed, reporting to journalists that minds armed with "envy, rancor and the irreconcilable struggle of classes" were more dangerous than guns (Fagen, 1992, p. 43).

The Argentine military elaborated a language that reflected the worldview of their colleagues in Chile and Uruguay as well. Their Dirty War was needed to cleanse Argentine society of the impurity of the subversives among the civilian population. Just as Hitler had seen the Jews as an "alien racial poison in our bodies" and Marxism as "eating deeply into the national body like a pestilence" (Binion, 1976, pp. 1, 24), the Argentine military described subversion as a disease infesting the nation, which in turn was viewed as a living organism. The Argentine military alluded to an "epidemic" similar to the plagues that had scourged the world in previous centuries (Immerman, 1982, p. 113). "The social body of the country is contaminated by a disease that corrodes its insides and forms antibodies," claimed Admiral Cesar A. Guzzetti, minister of foreign relations. "These antibodies must not be considered in the same way that one considers a germ. In proportion to the government's control and destruction of guerrilla warfare, the action of the antibodies is going to disappear." Guzzetti went on to justify military atrocities by arguing that right-wing terrorist acts were only "a natural reaction of a sick body" (Frontalini & Ciati, 1984, p. 21). An Uruguayan psychologist who was imprisoned for 13 months recalls that she and hundreds of other female prisoners were kept in military prisons because they were considered a "contagious infection" from which common criminals had to be protected.

In Argentina the military's repressive strategy was called the Process of National Reorganization, which offered a final solution to the problem of subversion. El Proceso, as it was known, identified for extermination not only the carriers of the germ—defined as social discontent—but those directly exposed to it as well. The military saw themselves as modern crusaders, convinced that theirs was a "just war" carried out in defense of the "natural order" designed by God. A popular handbook of military ethics encouraged the soldier to think of himself as a "perfect Crusading Knight for God and Fatherland," in which "the punishment of the guilty is not an evil but rather an act of goodness." Military discourse claimed that the authority for the Dirty War came from God and that it was "a sign of love and mercy in imitation of Christ...compelling [subversives] to goodness" (Graziano, 1992, p. 111).[8]

An important part of the ideological arsenal of state terror was its public discourse on gender, disseminated through the mass media by all three military dictatorships. In their crusade to uphold the customary class, race, and gender boundaries that privileged the male upper classes, they asserted a patriarchal solution to the subversion of the established social order. In all three countries of the Southern Cone, from the late 19th century on, middle- and working-class women had organized movements that over time had expanded female political, legal, and economic rights. But, like the Nazis before them, the military regimes reasserted an ideal feminine model of sublime domesticity and advocated traditional Christian and family values. Women were urged through ideological campaigns, sometimes buttressed by new laws, to withdraw from the public realm and return to the home. Femininity was defined as passivity, self-abnegation, and obedient adoration of men, traits viewed as the necessary compliment to male glory and heroic dominance.

But the paternalistic aspects of military gender ideology were contradicted by the harsh impact of state terror on women. For example, in spite of the domestic ideal of true womanhood and official discouragement of women's participation in the public sphere, in all three countries the economic disaster resulting from free-market policies pushed women out of the home in search of paid work to augment their husbands' declining wages or to earn a wage when their husbands fell victim to unemployment. Women workers were subjected to increased exploitation on the job and, as male abandonment of families grew in response to political and economic repression, increasing numbers of women found themselves heads of households, providing both financial and emotional resources to sustain themselves and their children. Moreover, the fundamentally misogynist attitudes of the military were expressed by officers and paramilitary forces, whose arbitrary arrests, rape, and torture of women fulfilled different functions: They were an official display of military domination over the civilian population, a self-indulgent ritual sport of off-duty officers, and a ritualized reenactment of power, which bonded the members of the military to one another. Female political activists, who represented the antithesis of bourgeois femininity, became a special target of the terrorist state. They embodied not only a revolutionary challenge to existing class relations but an assertion of self that challenged male hegemony in the psychological as well as the political domain. For this they paid dearly, and those who were among the disappeared became the victims in elaborate rituals of male domination exercised through psychological and physical torture. In addition, society in general suffered as the state's ideology and practice legitimized an intensification of the customary relationship between machismo and violence. Many men who found themselves the hapless victims of an authoritarian state, unable to express their rage directly at the military forces responsible, displaced their aggression onto women, who were safer and socially more acceptable objects of male violence.[9]

STRATEGIES OF STATE TERROR

State terror in Chile, Argentina, and Uruguay developed a strategy that made most of the population in each country victims of a doctrine of collective guilt.[10] The military governments engaged in a cleansing offensive against the enemies of Western Christian civilization, an important part of which was the construction of a public discourse aimed at paralyzing citizens with its contradictory and paradoxical content. The military's rhetoric turned the usual meanings of *order* and *violence* on their heads. Contrary to democracies, in which the function of government is ostensibly the creation and preservation of order through law and containment of violence, terrorist states created violence (while attributing it to political opponents) and disrupted law and order (while claiming to enforce it). Society was redefined as a war zone, and the military and paramilitary attack on civil society was reflected in the militarization of ideology, which imposed a sense of catastrophic danger and constant unpredictability. Fear was reinforced by the promulgation of laws whose goal was to sever social and public ties by prohibiting individuals from gathering in groups or organizations.

Psychic dysfunction was reinforced by the media, whose skewed information created a sense of ominous threat. Paradoxically, newspapers, radio, and television operated under strict censorship, obliged to follow a rule of silence. They simultaneously plied the public with overwhelming amounts of information about military arrests, detentions, and executions, all calculated to convey a terrifying and dangerous reality. As Chilean psychologists explain, the terrorist state appropriated language itself to mystify the perception of the past and the present. *Clean* and *dirty* were words repeatedly utilized by the media to create an unconscious identification with a range of governmental policies and attitudes: UP murals on city walls were whitewashed away—cleaned—along with the past; public employees were fired—cleaned out—and those who lost their jobs were political enemies—dirty—as were progressive politics, books, and foreigners in general, all designated as dirty enemy threats to the Chilean nation.

In Argentina, newspaper articles that began with accusatory headlines, such as "Parents: Do You Know Where Your Children Are?" described corpses of young people disfigured by bullets and torture found in city streets and along country roads. The papers identified them as hoodlums who had carried out illegal actions that forced confrontations with the police or military. The deceased were accused of being common criminals or subversives who had broken the laws of the nation and whose violent attacks on society had been legitimately responded to by the authorities. Responsibility for their deaths was displaced onto their parents, who were accused of inadequately supervising their children and failing to rear them with the appropriate respect for authority and private property.

Policies of disappearing, torturing, and murdering significant numbers of citizens were aimed at imposing a passive consensus within the population. Everyone knew about the "secret" concentration camps, woke to see or hear about the disfigured cadavers of torture victims rotting in the streets or floating in the rivers, knew someone whose relative or friend had disappeared. While the terrorist state spoke of the need to respect the family and social order, entire families were attacked, destroyed, and violated. Jacobo Timmerman (1982), the noted Argentine publisher abducted and tortured by the Argentine junta, wrote that "nothing can compare to those family groups who were tortured often together, sometimes separately but in view of one another. The entire affective world...collapses...Nothing is possible in such a universe, and that is precisely what the torturers know (p. 148)."

As each of the Southern Cone countries fell under military domination, political refugees fled from one nation to the other seeking asylum. But the military and security forces pursued them, driven by the U.S. Doctrine of National Security, which favored respect for ideological frontiers over national boundaries. Uruguayans were captured, tortured, and murdered by Uruguayan officers in Argentina, and Argentines fell victim to security forces from their own country operating in Uruguay. A Chilean hit squad even pursued Orlando Letelier, former foreign minister under Allende, to Washington, D.C., where they assassinated him and his U.S. assistant, Ronni Moffitt, with a car bomb in broad daylight.[11]

Political repression went hand in hand with a deteriorating economic situation for most sectors in all three countries. The terrorist state imposed economic policies that favored elite groups at the expense of the popular classes, whose traditional avenues for seeking economic redistribution had been smashed. The World Bank and the International Monetary Fund, along with U.S. neoliberal economic advisors, imposed harsh measures to attract foreign capital and international loans. A docile and inexpensive labor force was a prerequisite for multinational investment, and those who challenged such policies were abducted or jailed. Uruguayan journalist Eduardo Galeano's pithy remark captures his compatriots' plight: "In Uruguay, people were in prison so that prices could be free."[12]

Labor unions were closed down, taken over by the government, or declared to be illegal; and workers, employees, intellectuals, and professionals no longer had legitimate means of defending their class and sectoral interests. Rising unemployment rates, forced wage cuts, and an escalating cost of living all reflected the assault on the working and middle classes' quality of life. People's energies were drained in the frantic effort to survive. With freedom of speech and all forms of organized collective struggle prohibited, any kind of resistance or opposition brought life-threatening reprisals. In Argentina, the military found willing allies in the Church hierarchy, some of whom were present during torture sessions, and among factory owners and managers, some of whom, as at the Ford factory, permitted illegal detention centers to operate on the premises.

"This was the craziest time of our lives," says Juan Carlos. "Every minute Silvia and I would say, 'Let's go, let's go, let's go.' We fought incessantly. When I'd say, 'Yes, let's go,' Silvia would say no, and when I said no, she'd say yes. We'd talk constantly about it, but we were paralyzed. At one point I said, 'Basta, I'm going crazy; there's no good solution, either way it's a catastrophe, so let's stay and take our chances.' Silvia agreed and we settled in." Almost all their contacts had been caught. The president of the Psychological Association, of which Silvia was a member, had disappeared, and many of Carlos's colleagues in the FAP were also missing or detained. More people fled into exile, selling homes and other belongings for almost nothing in flea markets that were dubbed *férias americanas*. Juan Carlos bought a spectacular home and an office that was elegantly furnished with a balcony facing the neighborhood police station. He would water his plants and watch the military operatives come and go. He and Silvia had finally ended the torture of their indecision, and they told themselves that because they were cut off from everything political, they were safe. "We cleaned out our house of anything that could identify us with the left—books, posters, music. We focused on our patients and bought furniture, like good obsessives protecting ourselves from unwelcome thoughts and feelings. 'We were not doing anything wrong,' we told ourselves, and denied that we were at risk."

In December, nine months after the coup, Juan Carlos and Silvia received a phone call from Cuba, where Silvia's brother, Leonardo, had been working as an epidemiologist since the early sixties. Silvia's sister-in-law, Beatriz, announced that Leonardo had suffered a heart attack and was in serious condition, and she implored them to come to Cuba right away. Unable to speak clearly for fear the telephone was tapped, neither Silvia nor Juan Carlos could determine the real nature of the message and concluded it might be a warning in code. Finally Beatriz implored, "For once in your life, please, don't say anything more and take heed of what I'm telling you. Leave immediately and go to Lima, where everything will be arranged and waiting for you." Chilled by her words, they concluded that Silvia's family in Cuba had learned something about their circumstances in Argentina that they did not know. They suddenly were faced with an irrefutable fact: They would have to leave the country. And it would have to be fast.

It took them three days. Juan Carlos announced to his patients that he had to leave Argentina for political reasons, explaining that as a professor in the university medical school, he was among the psychoanalytic faculty who had been threatened by the new military dean's directive "to leave the country and go to live in Tel Aviv, Paris, or Moscow." In response, several of his patients, influential political conservatives, generously offered to use their contacts to escort him and his family safely out of Argentina. It turned out to be unnecessary. As he had always imagined, they would benefit from having lived in a state of constant alert, prepared to leave on a moment's notice. With all the necessary documents in order, their major decision was where to go and what to take. Although they both wanted to go to Cuba, Juan Carlos was apprehensive that he would not be able to work as an analyst in Cuba's behaviorist-oriented mental health care system. "I felt too old to retrain myself and deliberated over a tempting offer from the Piaget Center of Genetic Epistemology in Geneva to work for a year as a child analyst. It was a wrenching decision, but ultimately our affinity with Cuba won out."

They packed in a frenzy, their choices about what to take reflecting their manic response to the sudden reordering of their lives. Laughingly, Juan Carlos describes how they anguished over how many suitcases, the weight allowed by the airlines, which few precious things to carry away, perhaps forever. "We took some clothes, and I took the goose-down pillow I'd had since childhood, which had belonged to my mother and her mother before her in Europe. And Silvia, well, she fixated on a Swedish exercise machine she'd bought two days prior to our phone call from Cuba. It was a really complicated device that we'd thought would be the perfect accoutrement to round out our newly acquired bourgeois lifestyle. So that was what she chose to stuff into her suitcase. Its value was that she'd just bought it, and how could you leave behind a brand new thing like that? It weighed a ton, took up all the pounds the airlines allowed us to take on the plane! It was a testimony to our craziness. We'd never used it before nor did we after. But that's what we took into exile."

The next day when Juan Carlos, Silvia, and their two children went to the airport, many friends and family who had learned of their departure were there to see them off. "We went with the sensation that we would be gone for 40 years because that is what happened to the Spanish refugees when fascism overturned the Spanish Republic. We wept, all of us, and when the children and we boarded the plane, the four of us cried like babies all the way to Lima, Peru, our stopover to a new life." Several weeks later, when they landed in Cuba, they learned that Silvia's brother was in the hospital, recovering from a heart attack. The phone call had not been a code after all! No matter. They were safe. And the next eight years would prove to be the adventure of a lifetime.

Tato lasted in Buenos Aires several years into the Dirty War. "When the military finally came for me in March of 1978," he tells me, smiling, "believe it or not, my reaction was to feel outraged!" Tato had managed to survive emotionally by denying the danger and deluding himself with an omnipotent sense that he could stay, continue to speak out, and survive the wrath of the dictatorship. "More than denial," he says by way of self-criticism, "I employed an instrumental dissociation in order to go on. But my wife, Susana, was afraid, although she, too, escaped from her anxieties in her artistic activities." Tato felt that in staying he was sustaining a kind of political militancy by writing and producing plays whose themes would encourage people to think about the experience they were living through. "I told myself it would be all right, that I wasn't a guerrilla, only a playwright whose theater dealt with the human condition."

In 1977, his new play, *Telarañas* (Spiderwebs), opened, exploring for audiences the authoritarian characteristics in the patriarchal family system that made its members receptive to fascism. Immediately, Tato received a call from the authorities notifying him that he would have to close the production because, as they put it, he was an author without traditional Christian values. "To show you how much I denied my own vulnerability, I said to them in the most arrogant fashion, 'I can't do that. If you want the play shut down, you'll have to do it yourselves.'" Tato would pay a high price for this unfortunate miscalculation.

They came for him one day during a group psychotherapy session. His secretary interrupted the session to inform him that two men from the gas company were at the door downstairs. She signaled to him with a strange expression warning Tato that he was the object of a macabre reenactment of a scene in *Telarañas*, in which the paramilitary forces who come for the protagonists disguise themselves as *gassistas*. As he was telling his therapy group that he had to leave but that nothing would happen to them, he suddenly turned to see a hooded man standing behind him. Quickly, he leaped onto the balcony, where he caught a glimpse of two more hooded men in the kitchen below with two of his children.

"At that moment, panic overtook me. I did something truly mad. I leaped from the balcony to the house next door and went immediately to the police. I reported that two robbers—I couldn't say an armed group—had invaded my home. Then in the midst of it all, I did something really intelligent, something I think might very well have saved my life." While the police set off to investigate the robbery, the police chief sat across the desk from Tato, "viewing me with respect as an unfortunate doctor whose home was being vandalized rather than as a Marxist enemy who was being persecuted by a paramilitary operation." With his heart racing, Tato courteously requested the use of the telephone. He called his brother but pretended that the person on the other end was Raul Alfonsín, a prestigious figure internationally known at the time for his work in the human rights movement. "He was someone the police chief had to take seriously, given his high profile, and I said, 'Look, Raul, I'm here at the such-and-such police station with Police Chief Lopez,' and then I responded as if he were indicating that he was coming right over. I was convinced, though, that they were going to kill me on the spot."

When the police and the paramilitary group returned to the station together, a really mysterious thing happened. "They were trying to figure out what to do with me, when one officer approached me and asked, 'Tell me, are you Catholic or Jewish?' When I replied that I was Catholic, the officer said, 'Very good, Doctor. Look, you walk slowly until you get to the big avenue at the corner. Then get out of here.'" Tato started to walk, terrified, but when he got to the corner, he saw that his brother was waiting for him, having correctly interpreted the phone call. "Then the worst period of my life began. He told me that they'd destroyed my house and taken all my personal documents so that I wouldn't be able to leave the country. But, thank heaven, they did not harm my wife or children. I lived for weeks in Buenos Aires, moving from one friend's home to another, waiting until my departure could be arranged. My political *compañeros* demonstrated lots of solidarity, and they helped me get to Montevideo. Once there, in exile, I felt that there was a historical thread linking my grandfather, my father, and me, one that wove together our fate as émigrés. It gave me an eerie sense to be in the same bar in Montevideo on the Avenida 18 de Julio that my father had frequented when he was in exile 25 years earlier. It seemed that becoming a refugee was part of my destiny."

From Uruguay, Tato went to Madrid, where he would endure exile for the next three years. However, he was never able, in spite of personal growth and professional success, to transcend the sense that "my life had been shattered by the profound psychic disruption of exile."

FORCED DISAPPEARANCES AND TORTURE

Although Tato escaped from being abducted, thousands of citizens of Argentina, Chile, and Uruguay did not. Following the tradition of the infamous Nazi "night and fog" decrees, in which prisoners whose guilt could not be determined were transferred secretly in the darkness of night to undisclosed destinations, vanishing without a trace, the military governments ignored due process to simply abduct, torture, and murder citizens to whom they attributed the disturbing social, political, and economic crises of society. The disappeared—*desaparecidos*—became the metaphor for a dirty war. In Argentina, military discourse referred to "the incorporation of the enemy," and in line with the metaphor of disease and antibody, the enemy was in fact surrounded by the military, enclosed within it in the secret system of detention centers and concentration camps. The term used to refer to the strategy of disappearing people, *chupar*, means to suck, to absorb, to take in; *los chupados* were literally incorporated and taken in by the junta to be destroyed.

Why did the military choose this strategy? Why did they abduct individuals and families in often flagrant ways—openly witnessed by neighbors, coworkers, and bystanders—only to claim later that they knew nothing of the whereabouts of those they had kidnapped? The *desaparecidos* served many purposes, not the least of which was the military's imposition of the culture of fear. By disappearing people, the dictatorships could deny their crimes because there was no concrete evidence: no bodies, no arrests, no formal charges, no trials, and no imprisonments. And, even more to the point, the military needed the *desaparecidos* because as long as people continued to disappear, each dictatorship could argue that the nation was still under siege by subversives who continued to be caught. Indeed, the existence of an enemy was *the* raison d'être of repressive military rule. As scholar Frank Graziano has put it, "Were the Junta to neglect the constant invention of its Enemy, it too would soon be absent forever. The Hero thus found himself in the unhappy position of having a vital need for the very enemy he wishes to destroy" (Graziano, 1992, p. 133). The *desaparecidos* had an additional function: that of scapegoat. Military discourse depicted them as the embodiment of evil that had to be violently purged from the body politic, the community. Although they were members of the community, their persecution by the military was depicted as the purification of the community through the elimination of an evil rather than as violence directed against the entire community.

In Chile, although fewer people disappeared than in Argentina—approximately 1,000 in comparison with an estimated 30,000—the political and psychological functions were identical. The rumors of people vanishing made the security forces in Chile seem omnipresent and omnipotent. Elizabeth Lira indicates that "this policy of disappearing people evoked extreme states of anxiety in the community related to the sense that mysterious and uncontrollable forces were at work whose power everyone was impotent to contain." The individuals who disappeared left behind relatives—wives, children, husbands, mothers, fathers, grandparents—who were condemned to exhaust their energies in an endless search in the maze of federal, provincial, and municipal bureaucracies and police and military centers. Reminiscent of the universe in a Kafka novel, they were met with systematic denial of any knowledge of the whereabouts of their loved ones. Such fruitless endeavors often went on for years. The global effect of disappearing people was that it suggested "the inexplicable, the irrevocable, an absolute loss of knowledge" (Constable & Valenzuela, 1991, p. 94).

In Uruguay, with its tradition of the democratic rule of law, the terrorist state paid more attention to legal forms, even while it violated due process and norms of justice. The military established a classification system—called the A-B-C—to place each Uruguayan citizen into one of three categories, officially recorded in the central archives. "A" citizens were considered ideologically reliable, so they enjoyed employment rights with a modicum of civil freedoms; "B" citizens were politically suspect and thus did not qualify for government employment and were subject to continual harassment by the security forces; and "C" citizens were pariahs with no civil rights or rights of employment. Every citizen lived in constant terror of being reclassified into the "C" category.

Although Uruguayan state terrorists indulged in kidnapping people from their homes and in public settings, more often they relied on the imposition of lengthy prison terms to terrify not only the prisoners but the rest of society as well. In a country with only three million inhabitants, from the mid-1960s to the mid-1990s, 1 out of every 50 citizens was imprisoned and 1 out of 65 was tortured. Although far fewer individuals disappeared than in Argentina or Chile—an estimated 200—the large number of people who suffered lengthy imprisonment and unrelenting extreme mistreatment, including elaborate torture rituals, silenced dissent among all who feared the retribution of a brutal state.

Torture was, for the military in all three countries, more than a method of securing information by breaking individual prisoners. It was a political strategy, routinely practiced in a sophisticated and systematic way. It justified the military's war against the civilian population because it extracted confessions that "proved" the guilt of the *desaparecidos* and prisoners. Its object was not merely the body of the victim but the entire body politic. The overriding politics of torture was not to make a few individuals talk but to silence everyone.

The coerced confessions obtained through torture often had little to do with the actual identity or political experience of a prisoner. Individual victims were so totally destroyed through brutal physical and psychological torture that they confessed to anything demanded by their captors. In Uruguay, as in Argentina and Chile, many individuals who were arrested had been engaged in only peaceful and legal activities, so that torture drove them to admit to crimes they never would have imagined committing. The destruction of the true past and identity of prisoners reenacted thousands of times represented for the dictatorships the proof of their worldview and of the righteousness of their actions. As Graziano (1992) puts it, "Ceremonial acts of cruelty, particularly when performed by regimes lacking legitimacy, make clear how a body in the political sphere can be exploited for the generation of power as it can be in the work place for the generation of wealth" (p. 66).

The system of torture required a complex implementation, each point in the process demanding people with different kinds of psychological traits. For those who designed the system as a central pillar in the edifice of the National Security Doctrine, its key meaning lay in an authoritarian discourse that did not recognize the subjectivity of the victims. The extreme abuse was rationalized not as a wish to impose pain but as a necessary tool for securing the absolute subjugation of individuals perceived to threaten the institutions and ideology of the existing system. The second category of torturers were those who devised the torture strategies; they employed unconscious mechanisms of dissociation and denial in order to view their activity as if it were simply a particular form of work, no different from any other kind of employment. The third type of torturers, those who perpetrated the torture itself, experienced sadistic gratification from the attacks on the minds and bodies of their victims (see Abudara, 1986).

Each torture ritual was called by a specific euphemistic name. In Chile, the *picana*, an electrified prod used on sensitive body parts such as genitals and temples, was called "the grill"; repeated dunking in excrement, urine, or polluted water, "the submarine"; a waterless technique of strangulation or suffocation, "the dry submarine"; and prolonged suspension with the body twisted around a pole, "the parrot's perch." In Argentina, Timmerman's (1982) torturers referred to his sessions as "having a chat with Susan [the torture machine]" (p. 125). In all three countries the treatment was embellished in many ways: Victims were beaten with fists and rubber and metal weapons; enclosed in pens with vicious dogs that came close to dismembering them; tied into sacks with cats. Prisoners were burned with cigarettes on the breasts or with scalding water on the anus and genitals. They were submitted to repeated gang rapes and mock and real executions in front of other prisoners and relatives. Pregnant women were often tortured, resulting in miscarriage and even death. Innovations in torture techniques included a calculated manipulation of human needs and emotions, including sensory deprivation or overload interspersed with frightening sounds and images of the victim's loved ones being tortured or murdered. The injection of chemical substances induced a variety of agonizing physiological and psychological states.

In many cases torture rituals became the theater in which the instrumental torturers were able to enact their aberrant sexuality and transform it into political power, revealing an intimate link between violence and eroticism. Torturers engaged in autoerotic atrocities, alternating between assaulting and caressing their victims' bodies. The *picana* symbolized their eroticized violence and power. Just as weapons in every culture have symbolized masculinity, the *picana* crystallized the phallocentricity of the torture ritual. Its electrified onslaught was focused on the male and female genitalia, the breasts and nipples, the anus and the mouth. Central to a variety of torture rituals, the *picana* was forcibly intruded into every orifice, its impact made more effective by wetting the body to better conduct the electrical discharge. Some torture sessions were punctuated by jokes, laughter, music, and sadistic excitement. Masturbation often accompanied the brutal assaults on a victim's body. Through it all, the *picana* was omnipresent, a perverse representation of an autoerotic form of sadism perpetrated on the objectified body of the victim.

The system chose the instrumental torturers well. Individuals were screened according to criteria such as obedience, discipline, intelligence, and family or individual anticommunist background. The torturers were often of lower middle-class or working-class origin, lumpen in mentality; their lifelong powerlessness was suddenly transformed into the powerful ability to destroy life. Indeed, they were taught to see themselves as absolute rulers over their prisoners' lives, not subject to ordinary constraints. The psychological profile of the torturer revealed an identification with those in power, strong fears or anxieties, an inability to tolerate uncertainty, and a proclivity for fanaticism. The torturers' capacity to engage in the sadistic ritual of torture is made possible by the mechanism of projective identification, through which the perpetrator unconsciously evacuates the hateful and destructive aspects of himself into the victim, where they can then be destroyed through torture. The accompanying feelings of persecutory anxiety only further stimulate the torturer's sadism toward his victim (see Hollander, 1992; Godwin, 1993; Bendfeldt-Zachrisson, 1988).

Elizabeth believes that the training of torturers permits them to dissociate from their own emotions because a hierarchical structure takes moral and political responsibility for their brutality. However, she is convinced that each individual brings to the activity an unconscious motive—a personal passion and cruelty—that the system is able to mobilize. She gives the example of one torturer who was trained by the Chilean special security forces in torture methods and an ideology that depicted the UP and their goals as a cancer that had to be eliminated. "You know the worst thing of all?" he told her. "My father was a working-class leader, a communist... and he was an alcoholic who constantly abused me. He beat me a lot from the time I was a little kid." Elizabeth came to understand that this torturer had remained psychologically enmeshed in a complex relationship with his father, who had mistreated and devalued him. "In the position of the torturer, he fanatically abused men who had the same politics as his father. What's more, he wanted to understand where his victims got the internal resources to resist because it was a force he wanted to know how to vanquish."

Individuals underwent special indoctrination to become torturers. They were prepared psychologically for their work through basic training involving infantilization and psychological castration by superior officers whose aggression they predictably came to identify with. Their brutality was seasoned through courses on torture techniques in which they were required to torture one another (see Simpson & Bennett, 1985). As Marcelo indicates, "We have to study modern torture, which is not an act of barbarity. It is designed; it has a plan; it is not improvised. Torture is a system in the sense that there isn't a single torturer, but a group, a gang that enjoys a support system. It's as if they're intoxicated, getting drunk among friends. Group cruelty is cathartic in that it increases the sense of power of each participant."

The dehumanization of the potential victim was achieved through courses that stressed the necessity of the torture work for national security. In his study of German concentration camp guards, psychoanalyst Bruno Bettelheim pointed out the importance of the perpetrator's dehumanization of his victim. He recalled—from his own experience—how concentration-camp guards repeatedly said to their prisoners, "I'd shoot you with this gun but you're not worth the three pfennig of the bullet." The importance of this ritual lay not in its impact on the prisoners but in its affirmation for the guards of the worthlessness of their prisoners (Scarry, 1985). In Argentina potential torture victims were referred to as "delinquent subversives," the "enemy," "useful tools," "communist dupes." Such terminology, by facilitating an ideological and psychological splitting between the good object (the military) and the bad object (the prisoner), further diminished the torturers' respect for human life. The capacity for empathy and concern was stifled through the ongoing experience of torture and through the designation of the entire process in euphemistic terms. The torture chamber was often called the "intensive therapy room"; an individual to be killed had "gotten his ticket" or was a "transferee."

Once seasoned, torturers were allowed to perform unofficial or extracurricular tortures, which they devised to entertain themselves. In Argentina, low-ranking officers could indulge their perverse desires at any time with their helpless victims. Plunder, during or after an abduction, was also allowed. Not only people but their belongings were carried off as entire homes were ransacked and looted. In Argentina, the "spoils of war" often included babies, stolen and parceled out to childless couples among the military and their allies. This violation of family rights was justified by the messianic argument that the subversives' newborns would be brought up to respect the values of "Western and Christian civilization."

In 1973, Marie Langer had written in *Cuestionamos II* about the collaboration of a psychoanalyst with the Brazilian torturers. Such cooperation with state terror by health professionals, including physicians and psychiatrists, occurred in other countries as well. In Uruguay, for example, some health professionals were known to violate the human rights of prisoners in a variety of ways. They gave physical examinations and turned their medical records over to the military, who would then know how much they could torture without killing the victim; they wrote medical reports so as to hide the evidence of torture; they deliberately denied assistance to ill or injured torture victims; and they prescribed psychopharmaceutical medications to intensify the psychological and physical torture of prisoners. They participated in the "good torturer/bad torturer" syndrome, playing the part of the empathically concerned bystander who encouraged torture victims to tell all in order to save themselves from more suffering. This tactic had the effect of confusing the torture victim, who found it increasingly difficult to retain a coherent sense of what was happening and why, as well as to distinguish between good and bad, enemy and friend (Servicio Paz y Justicia, 1992).

Once the captors were finished with their prisoners, the prisoners were usually "transferred"—strangled, dynamited, or shot in executions that were frequently staged to appear as if a shootout had taken place between them and security forces. Many prisoners were injected with sedatives and dropped alive into the ocean from airplanes or helicopters. Less often, individuals were released from prisons or clandestine concentration camps after charges were determined to be unsubstantiated and then dropped. This part of the drama was important because the released torture victim, the *desaparecido* whose absence became real in his or her reappearance, was the link between the military and the public.

In Argentina, Julia's 18-year-old son, Gabriel, was one of the thousands of *desaparecidos* who vanished into thin air from the streets of Buenos Aires. On May 29, 1976, only two months after the generals had marched into the presidential palace to take control of the country, Julia was awakened by a telephone call in the middle of the night. "Julia," the wavering voice of an old friend punctured the silence, "I'm so sorry...Earlier this evening my daughter was walking with some friends downtown on Avenida Santa Fe when she saw the police grab Gabriel and haul him away." And, in a second, Julia's life turned upside down. Only then did she realize that all the horror she had been living with for so long had simply been a prelude to an unimaginable fear yet to come. As she sat there in the dark, paralyzed with dread, she could not guess that it would take eight long years to find out that her son had been tortured and murdered by the Argentine state.

ENDNOTES

1. See the report of the Senate Select Committee, headed by then-Senator Frank Church, that documented the U.S. conspiracy; the committee discovered, for example, that from 1969 to the day of the coup, the CIA generously gave financial support to anyone or any group that could be useful in bringing down the Allende government. As a former Chilean diplomat put it, "This meant that this CIA undertaking, first known as Track I and then as Track II, included everything...cloak-and-dagger operations, involving the murder of generals and civilians, the strangulation of [the] Chilean economy and subversion of its legally elected government" (Chavkin, 1982); see also Oppenheim (1973, 1993). For a history of the dictatorship that focuses on the personality, thought, and role of Augusto Pinochet, see Spooner (1994).
2. See Klare and Stein (1978) and Fleming (1961). Between 1950 and 1975, the following numbers of officers were trained in the United States or at U.S. bases in Panama: Argentina: 2,766 of a total 3,676 officer corps; Chile: 2,811 of a total 6,328 officer corps; and Uruguay: 1,120 of a total 2,537 officer corps (Wickham-Crowley, 1992, p. 79). For an analysis of the role of the United States in the creation of the ideology and strategy of state terror, see George (1991). Edward S. Herman and Gerry O'Sullivan, in their chapter, "'Terrorism' as Ideology and Cultural History," provide statistics that compare killings by state and nonstate terrorists in numbers and orders of magnitude and conclude that "the services of the terrorism industry have been very much needed in the West to cover over its own activities and crimes. During the past forty years

the Western states—including South Africa and Israel as well as the great pow-ers—have had to employ intimidation on a very large scale to maintain access, control, and privileged positions in the Third World, in the face of the national-ist and popular upheavals of the 'post-colonial' era. This has been a primary terrorism, in two senses: First, it has involved far more extensive killing and other forms of coercion than the 'terrorism' focused upon in the West... and second, it represents the efforts by the powerful to preserve undemocratic priv-ileges and structures from the threat of encroachment and control by popular organizations and mass movements" (pp. 40–43). See also chapters by Noam Chomsky, Richard Falk, and Michael McClintock, as well as The National Security Archive online for the files recently opened by the State Department on Argentina's Dirty War. The files include information related to the role of the U.S. government and private corporations operating in Argentina in sup-port of the military dictatorship.

3. See McCoy (2006), especially chapter 3, and Harbury (2005). As Argentine General Ramón J. Camps explained, "France and the United States were the great proponents of the antisubversive doctrine. They organized centers, par-ticularly in the United States, to teach the anti-subversive principles. They sent advisors, instructors. They sent out an extraordinary quantity of literature" (Argentine National Commission on the Disappeared, 1986, p. 442). In addi-tion, online reports are published by the School of the Americas Watch, an organization that exposes U.S. intervention in the Americas and is pressuring the Congress to close the infamous training center, School of the Americas (whose name was changed to Western Hemisphere Institute for Security Cooperation, but whose purpose of training Latin Americans in counterinsur-gency has continued).

4. My argument that the defense of neoliberalism was at the heart of state ter-ror in Latin America is borne out in the brilliant analysis of the relationship between authoritarianism and neoliberalism in an international context by Naomi Klein in *The Shock Doctrine: The Rise of Disaster Capitalism*, pub-lished in 2007 by Metropolitan Books to great acclaim throughout the world. Her study, a detailed exploration of Milton Friedman's free market economic theory and its forcible implementation at moments when populations are in a state of shock and upheaval, first accomplished by the Chicago Boys in Chile following the coup, confirms my argument that the goal of implementing and sustaining the unregulated free market economic system was the motive for political terror in Latin America.

5. *Nunca más* contains information about U.S. involvement in Argentina during the Dirty War.

6. See Hodges (1991), especially chapters 5 and 6.

7. Discussion of this and similar statements depicting the military's worldview can be found in Graziano (1992) and Hodges (1991).

8. For an elaborate discussion of this ideology, see Castillo (1979).

9. For a theoretical analysis of the relationship between gendered social arrange-ments in patriarchal capitalism and the impact on women of the terrorist state in Latin America, see Hollander (1996, 2010). For a detailed analysis and description of the various psychological and physical tortures applied to women, see Bunster (1993).

10. See Graziano (1992) and Hodges (1991); see also Brown (1985), Ferla (1985), Frontalini and Ciati (1984), Rouquié (1983), and Amnesty International (1984, especially pp. 143–180). For reports and analyses of the practice and psychological and physical impact of torture worldwide, see the quarterly publication of the Rehabilitation and Research Centre for Torture Victims, *Torture: Quarterly Journal on Rehabilitation of Torture Victims and Prevention of Torture*.
11. See the analysis of this military cooperation among Southern Cone countries in Argentine National Commission on the Disappeared (1986), pp. 254–272.
12. Radio interview with author, May 1988, Los Angeles.

Chapter 5

The culture of fear and social trauma

Visible colonialism is a process that openly mutilates you: it forbids you to speak, to act, to be. Invisible colonialism, in contrast, convinces you that enslavement is your destiny and impotence your nature. It convinces you that "you cannot speak, you cannot act, you cannot be."

— Eduardo Galeano (1992)

"We were afraid. I was afraid. Many times marching with the Mothers in the Plaza de Mayo, I'd feel terrified when they would take our photographs...and they would glower at us from behind their submachine guns. When I think about those years of terror, I remember that it was so hard to know at which moments people were specifically targeted and at which moments, not. There were times when you'd be convinced they had picked you out of the group, and others when you'd think no, not me. But you were never certain."

Psychologist Diana Kordon is recounting for me her participation in the famous Thursday afternoon marches of the Mothers of the Plaza de Mayo in Buenos Aires. The group, so-called because of their weekly demonstrations in the plaza that faces the Presidential Palace, carried posters with enlarged photographs of their disappeared children, demanding publicly that the military junta reveal their whereabouts. "You took them alive," was one of their slogans. "We want them back alive." Diana and her husband, Darío Lagos, along with Lucila Edelman, are members of the Team of Psychological Assistance to the Mothers of the Plaza de Mayo (Equipo de Asistencia Psicológica a las Madres de Plaza de Mayo)—known as the Equipo. We are sitting around a table in the Equipo's office in downtown Buenos Aires, where the three are explaining to me their emotional experiences and intellectual perceptions of the difficult years during the dictatorship. The sights and sounds of the office testify to the Equipo's continued activism during the 13 years since the return of constitutional rule in 1983. Its walls are plastered with posters announcing upcoming political and community events, and the hum of computers and fax machines can be heard from the adjoining rooms.

Diana is an attractive woman in her early 50s, her large, green eyes expressive as she explains the Equipo's perspective on the nature of trauma in conditions of state-inspired social violence. Lucila, also in her early 50s, emanates a calm self-assurance as she listens and interjects specific details that seem important to Diana's narrative. I am struck by their modest demeanor as they describe their astoundingly courageous activities in the human rights movement during the height of the junta's repressive rule. Darío, too, clarifies points as the discussion proceeds. In spite of his imposing physical presence and forceful demeanor, he demonstrates a marked respectfulness toward the two women, referring appreciatively to Diana as "my loving wife and a real *compañera* in the struggle."

They remind me about the conventional meaning of *trauma*, which generally refers to the disruption or breakdown of the psychic apparatus when it is affected by stimuli, external or internal, that are too powerful to be dealt with or assimilated in customary ways. The individual who has witnessed or been exposed to threatened or actual death or injury responds with a sense of terror, horror, humiliation, betrayal, or some combination of these states. An experience of helplessness results, ranging from complete apathy and withdrawal to an emotional storm often bordering on panic. "This description of trauma," Diana explains, "does not specifically capture the nature of group psychological reactions to violence produced by state terror." Lucila points out that many of the symptoms associated with posttraumatic stress disorder (PTSD) are noted in populations living under military dictatorships, such as psychic numbing or a lowered threshold for anxious arousal. "But," she clarifies, "we do not think the concept of PTSD is an adequate one to describe the psychological impact of state terror. It makes a psychiatric problem out of a social phenomenon." Diana adds that "we don't even speak of trauma because that is usually understood to mean an intrapsychic experience. We use the concept 'traumatic situation' in order to represent the social sources of the psychological suffering produced by state terror. And we do not speak of victims [*víctimas*] but of individuals and groups that are affected [*afectados*] by political repression."[1]

The Equipo echoes the perspective of other politically engaged analysts. For example, Elizabeth Lira argues that "PTSD does not capture the ongoing nature of state terror, because there is nothing 'post' about it. We could speak of a 'culture of trauma,' although I haven't because we need to appreciate that certain things will traumatize some individuals and not others, depending on their personal histories. But there is a traumatic impact on the society. I prefer to use 'the culture of fear' to emphasize that individual subjective experience is shared simultaneously by millions of people, with dramatic repercussions for social and political behavior." Julia Braun points out that although one can detect in the population at large or in individual patients a series of symptoms characteristic of PTSD, in state terror the syndrome is a "repetitive trauma," one trauma layered on another and then another. "The essence of social trauma," insists Julia, "is that it is not private but is a public and shared experience."[2]

THE PSYCHOLOGY OF SOCIAL TRAUMA

The military dictatorships in the Southern Cone created a traumatogenic environment that affected the psychic structures of the self and the systems of attachment and meaning that link the individual to the community. Although the outcome of any traumatic situation can affect the individual's ability to sustain attachments to others, in terrorist states, among the citizenry in general the attachment to community was eroded. In conditions of extreme political repression, the population was forced to work out a way of understanding the rules, the cues, what made a good citizen, and what made an enemy of the state. Citizens were compelled to feel that their homes, their jobs, their loved ones, their own lives were in jeopardy. Trust was difficult to sustain because contact with others could endanger. Citizens sought self-preservation in isolation, and their fearful hypervigilance resembled a kind of paranoid character disorder. Individual behavior in the terrorist state was characterized by silence, inexpressiveness, inhibition, and self-censorship, all of which resulted over time in depoliticization. In this situation, individuals became obedient and potentially punitive toward self and others.

In an endeavor to protect themselves, people engaged in active self-censorship as well, going beyond the limits imposed by official prescriptions and proscriptions. This personal vigilance led to the conscious creation of a false self, a partial and unrepresentative public portrayal of one's personality that was manufactured in order to survive the impingements of an environment that demanded extreme measures of adaptation. As a prominent Uruguayan sociologist writes, "Fear exterminated all social life in the public realm. Nobody spoke in the streets for fear of being heard. Nobody protested in the lines for fear of being reported to the police. One tried not to make new friends, for fear of being held responsible for their unknown pasts. One suspected immediately those who were more open or were less afraid, of being agents provocateurs of the intelligence service" (Weschler, 1990, p. 89).[3] The effects of this environment on children included an intensification of the fear of ghosts, states of confusion, fits of violence, all sorts of anxieties, learning disabilities, somatic disturbances, and accident-prone behavior (Kijak & Pelento, 1986).[4] Individuals who had participated in labor unions, peasant cooperatives, Christian base communities, women's groups, youth groups, or liberal and leftist political parties were forced to make an anguished choice. If they held firm to their political values and continued to commit themselves to struggle against the terrorist state, they lived with constant anticipatory anxiety about their own and their *compañeros'* and family's vulnerability. But activists' avoidance of anxiety necessitated the abandonment of the projects that had given their lives positive meaning, permitted them to practice their values, and contributed to their sense of community. This renunciation entailed significant guilt and the rejection of the person they once were, often experienced as the loss of personal identity. As Elizabeth Lira expresses it, "The loss is…of an idea of national identity centered around shared values and beliefs. The past seems lost within all the losses, symbolized by the dead, the disappeared, the tortured bodies, the broken hopes, the elimination of a future, the exiles, the disenchantment with politics. Each individual is conscious or unconscious of the losses and of the defenses that have been utilized to mourn less or to completely evade the necessary mourning."

In retrospect, Elizabeth Lira, Marie Langer, Juan Carlos Volnovich, and Maren Viñar all emphasize the unconscious defenses they employed as political activists to ward off anticipatory anxiety. They often refer to their recourse to denial and manic reactions, by which they mean inappropriately high spirits and hyperactivity that results in the conscious sense of accomplishment and omnipotent control over external circumstances; these feelings defend the self against the unconscious experience of loss and defeat. In a manic state, they were able to achieve a false sense of well-being, enabling them to deny both the unconscious fantasy and the external reality of terrifying danger that immobilizes.

Tato Pavlovsky, Marcelo Viñar, and the members of the Equipo stress especially their states of dissociation, an unconscious defense in which one group of mental processes is split off from the rest of a person's thinking or affect. This splitting permits the independent functioning of each group of discrete mental processes and thus prevents their customary integration from occurring. "I think," says Lucila, "that there's a good deal of reliance on the dissociative mechanisms under such circumstances. For example, we began to work in the office of the Mothers of the Plaza de Mayo during a time when people who met, even socially, in groups of more than five were automatically suspect in the eyes of the military government and subject to arrest or other kinds of intimidation. And this was very strange, something we noted often in the Equipo: We felt completely secure when we were inside the office of the Mothers and became anxious only when we had to leave. It was absurd," she laughs, "because in fact we were actually in more danger all gathered together in a well-known human rights center. But this dissociation permitted us to be there."

These defenses were utilized by a pacified population as well, not in the service of political activism but as coping strategies in the adaptation to authoritarian rule, which led them to become bystanders to their governments' terror. Elizabeth points to the psychological characteristics of citizens living in the Chilean militarized culture of fear. She asserts that "extreme vulnerability to arbitrary events beyond one's control produced a sense of personal weakness and a permanent state of alert, permitting no psycho-logical rest. In conditions that appeared to be life-threatening, people felt helpless and defenseless. Equally compromising was the distortion of reality purposefully created by the dictatorship through its control over informa-tion disseminated to the public." The media's focus on military operations, its downplaying of other news stories, and its manipulation of terrifying rumors, which frequently exaggerated the degree of repression, functioned to convince the population of their collective powerlessness. Rumors of ret-ribution against those who spoke out, while not necessarily experienced firsthand by many, exacerbated fantasies, which then functioned as inter-nalized self-repression. Citizens became guarded and self-protective, and because they did not venture out into the social world as much, they could not employ the important psychological process of reality testing to contain their fearful fantasies. "The boundaries between the real, the possible, and the imaginary were all erased," Elizabeth explains, "and reality thus became confused and threatening, no longer able to guide subjective perception. The state's domination was achieved as citizens engaged in self-regulatory processes that inhibited critical thinking and oppositional behavior."

Forced disappearances and torture were essential to the military's strategy of imposing on the entire population—not only those who actually disap-peared or were tortured—an acceptance of its absolute power. Many cultures have a centuries-old tradition of colorful, violent public sacrifice or spectacles of public punishment staged by those in power, who, by demanding the par-ticipation of the community as witness, impose on their citizens social involve-ment and responsibility.[5] But in Argentina, Chile, and Uruguay, torture was carried out secretly and clandestinely. Hidden from view and practiced on the *desaparecidos*, it nonetheless took hold of the public. As Graziano (1992) suc-cinctly describes it, "Instead of cheering or gasping or screaming beside the gallows, the public voice reached only a hushed whisper risked in the shad-ows, a mumble of rumors diffusing the spectacle by word of mouth through a population that was itself diffused, confused, frightened" (p. 73).

Torture created a multifaceted relationship between the military dicta-torships and their populations. The public became a participant–observer unable to do anything to stop it, as well as a potential (or actual) victim. The extreme anxiety resulting from this insoluble paradox often predis-posed people to undergo a regression in ego functioning that led to a passive reliance on a repressive leader(ship), viewed as omnipotent and omniscient. In this sense, the authoritarian state became a container for the profound anxieties that had been mobilized during its unpredictable transition to absolute power.[6] The military dictatorships succeeded in infantilizing citi-zens psychologically, prompting many of them to deliver themselves up to a superior agency that would decide everything for them.

Identification with the aggressor was an important defense against the fear and anxiety stimulated by the continuous flow of disappearances and rumors of torture. For the witness/victim citizens who survived in the violence of everyday life, identification, at both the unconscious and conscious levels, with an arbitrary state power enacting its wrath on the *desaparecidos* permitted them to symbolically choose victims outside themselves to sacrifice. People could tell themselves that the *desaparecidos* were persecuted legitimately, that they must indeed be guilty of some terrible crime deserving of the punishment they received. At base, the defensive identification with an aggressive power was wed to the already internalized identification with authority that had always been an aspect of hegemonic ideology. Violent impulses—which intensified and multiplied during state terror at every level—could be thus projected onto the socially created scapegoat, who would then be destroyed. In Chile, even though many people never witnessed the forced disappearances, they were nonetheless haunted by the stark images of people being hauled off, screaming and protesting to no avail. All were faced with the moral dilemma of whether to witness silently or denounce the abuses of state terror. As one Chilean put it, "I worry more about the fascist within than the fascist without...We became used to being in the cuckoo's nest, and we couldn't escape" (Constable & Valenzuela, 1991, p. 165).

The unconscious identification with officially sanctioned aggression was also revealed as the destructive behavior of the military and the torturers was gradually manifested within the general population as well. Among certain sectors military forms of thinking, feeling, and acting came to be accepted as normal modes of conduct. With social forms of response no longer available to permit the expression of aggression toward the real source of suffering and loss, aggressive attitudes and behavior were displaced onto less dangerous situations and onto safer objects in personal life. Explosive interactions increasingly characterized relations in work, family, and public encounters.

Many people simply refused to bear witness to the sinister events that unfolded before them. By disavowing reality, individuals shielded themselves from their consciences and the internal or external demand to defy the state's systematic violation of basic human rights. As parents, for example, altered their vocabulary and their vision of reality in response to their children's questions in order to protect them, they imposed denial, repression, and censorship within the family, which contributed to the creation of an apolitical and self-censoring generation. Thus, in the culture of fear, unconscious defenses converged with aspects of hegemonic ideology internalized as a core part of identity, which a terrorized people enacted in desperate self-defense. In grim paradoxical fashion, they became a bystander population that reinforced the power of the very social forces oppressing them.

What happened to people whose lives were directly affected by the state's repressive tactics of forced disappearances and torture? How did they cope with the catastrophic threat to their psychological equilibrium represented by such extreme situations?

FORCED DISAPPEARANCES AND SOCIAL TRAUMA

Psychological reactions of relatives and friends whose loved ones simply vanished without a trace were complicated by the anguishing and usually futile attempts to trace their whereabouts. The state consistently disavowed any policy of disappearing people, and thus petitioners seeking help at police stations and military headquarters encountered either denial of their predicament or the half-hearted pretense of an investigation that yielded nothing. Energies were absorbed in endless appeals and the pursuit of the smallest clues that might produce any evidence at all of missing loved ones.

This nightmare, which engulfed the psychic and physical energies of thousands of families of the *desaparecidos*, began for Julia Braun and her husband, Mariano, when they received the 3:00 A.M. telephone call that announced the disappearance of their son Gabriel. Stunned and then gradually overtaken by panic, Mariano pronounced, "It begins now, the cross we'll bear forever." He left immediately for the police station in their neighborhood, where the bureaucratic charade commenced. He was not permitted entrance, whereupon he rushed to another police station, only to be told by the officers who sent him home that there was no record of his son's having been picked up by the police. Desperate, he and Julia phoned several good friends, who the following day helped to secure a lawyer and develop a network of contacts who might be able to help. But it was all useless.

"In subsequent weeks and months, we lived in constant terror that they would come for us or our younger son, Bernardo. We slept in the homes of friends and stripped our house of everything we thought might be indicting. We destroyed half our personal library, hundreds of books—not our psychoanalytic literature, but our political books. It was horrible: We burned them, tore them up, threw them out, put them in bags, and hid them. We felt they were on our heels, about to invade our home. But they never came! Because they didn't descend on us to search our home, as in so many other cases, it was as if the earth had swallowed Gabriel up, as if they didn't even realize it was our son they had." This pattern of unpredictability was implemented by the terrorist state to foster confusion, doubt, panic. "There was no logic to depend on, no basis upon which to act. And it drove us crazy."

In the beginning, Julia denied what she might have guessed to be true. In spite of the fact that she knew of Gabriel's friends and *compañeros* who had also disappeared since the coup and had not been heard from since, she convinced herself that the police would soon release her son. Even when several months had passed, she still believed they would return him alive. She realized that her own prison experience several decades earlier had surely been different from Gabriel's under the current repressive conditions. But she could not let herself imagine that the military were torturing her son. "I knew he would be having a hard time, but I could envision nothing concrete, I think because I couldn't have stood it. I also couldn't conceive of the nature of the torture itself. I thought they hit people, put them in isolation. I couldn't imagine anything else."

Julia's life settled into a grim pattern of days divided between work and the search for Gabriel. For months, like other families whose relatives had disappeared, she and Mariano contacted lawyers and priests; wrote legal briefs and reports; visited barracks, jails, courts, the minister of the interior. "Daily life was divided between treating patients, searching for Gabriel, taking care of Bernardo, fear, denial, persecution, eating out, going to movies, hearing bombs exploding, celebrating a birthday, visiting friends, wondering when they would come for us, hearing about the dead, the tortured...all mixed up together." They did not leave Argentina. They could not. They had to keep searching.

In 1978, after two excruciating years had passed with no news of Gabriel, Julia listened to a speech by the president of the military junta and came to a painful conclusion. She interpreted his words to indicate that all the *desaparecidos* were dead. "Gabriel's fate was suddenly sealed in my mind: At that moment, I told myself that he was dead. Mariano was horrified and insisted that it was I who was killing Gabriel. I felt terrible. But I realized that something had changed inside me, that for me, the struggle to find Gabriel alive had ended. Yet I still had to do something."

Years later Julia would write about the psychological problems entailed in suffering the forced disappearance of a loved one. She would elaborate an analysis based on her own experience and those of the many people she observed and treated. She and other psychoanalysts would postulate that this mourning experience is characterized by unique difficulties. Those who suffer the disappearance of loved ones, they argue, can only partially work through the mourning process necessary for healthy mental functioning following traumatic loss. In contrast to the death of a relative or close friend, which usually stimulates community recognition of the significance of the deceased individual's life and death, when someone disappears as the result of governmental action, family and friends are left in a state of terrifying uncertainty, with no possibility of psychological closure (Pelento & Braun, 1985).

An important aspect of mourning is an acknowledgment of reality that ultimately entails a psychological separation from the individual who no longer exists. This mental process, which permits a gradual letting go of the deceased and the resumption of life in the present, is problematic and difficult to achieve when a family member has disappeared. There is no confirmation of his or her whereabouts or proof of death. The family is caught in a terrible contradiction: A husband, wife, parent, or child cannot mourn without risking intense guilt; for without proof of death, to go on with one's life is tantamount to a kind of murder of the disappeared loved one. However, to go on living and maintain the mental representation of the disappeared, to keep him or her alive, imposes a profound form of mental anguish. This terrible dilemma was one that Marie Langer noted among the refugee populations in Mexico from the Southern Cone and Central America. She called this unresolved mourning "frozen grief."

Not knowing about the actual fate of the disappeared person produces an intrapsychic elaboration that includes fantasies of the possible torments to the *desaparecido*'s mind and body, fantasies based on knowledge of the existence of secret concentration camps and other centers of torture. These fantasies cause acute anxiety and can result in the repression of fantasy life in general, which compromises mental functioning, especially in children. Life decisions are often frozen as the family waits for the return of the disappeared. The alternative reaction is the wish to free the victim from such suffering through the fantasy of his or her death, a wish that produces excruciating guilt feelings. In fact, the military dictatorship in Argentina demanded that the "missing" person be pronounced dead by the family itself in a variety of ways. For example, if the family needed to have access to money or property that was in the name of the disappeared person, they were forced to sign an official document declaring his or her death. For many Argentines caught in this dilemma, the psychological torture of a kind of arrested mourning often produced many apparently unrelated symptoms, such as psychosomatic illnesses, interpersonal conflicts, the inability to maintain healthy relationships, or a general alienation from one's immediate social group or society at large.

In Julia's case, at the moment she believed she had lost her son forever to the murderous forces of the state, she told herself that she had to act, had to do something. After Gabriel disappeared, she had returned to psycho-analytic treatment, this time with a sympathetic analyst whose nephew had also disappeared. "He was a kind person and a good analyst, and being in treatment helped me keep my sanity. But I knew that I needed something more, that I had to engage with others who were suffering the same trag-edy as I." For a time, Julia went to the Thursday afternoon marches of the Mothers of the Plaza de Mayo, and although she deeply admired their cour-age, her own fears at participating in this brazen challenge to the military government finally directed her to another kind of activism. "I am a psy-choanalyst," she thought, "and all of this has to do with human suffering and pain. I should use my skills to help."

Julia could see that her friend Graciela Fernández Meijide, whose son had also disappeared, was benefiting emotionally from her work with the Permanent Human Rights Assembly (Asamblea Permanente de Derechos Humanos). So when Graciela suggested that, for her own well-being, Julia become involved in a community health project organized by a colleague, Norberto Liwsky, she quickly agreed. Norberto was a pediatrician who was disappeared in 1975 and was brutally tortured.[7] After his release, he some-how found the psychological strength to return to his political activism. Now he was organizing medical services in a working-class community

church whose progressive priest had developed a network of professionals to respond to the legal, health, educational, and employment needs of
his poor parishioners. Julia immediately began to participate, and for the
next three years she worked with the church's population of working-class
Argentines and immigrant workers from Bolivia and Paraguay. She went
every Saturday for six hours and coordinated and supervised individual
therapy with children and group sessions with adults. "I felt utterly dismayed listening to these people's experiences, for if my story was terrible,
their stories were 50 times worse. Many of their *desaparecidos* had been
union activists, and not only had these women lost a son, a husband, an
uncle, or a brother, but they and their little ones had nothing to eat, nowhere
to live, nothing. Although it was difficult to sustain treatment in a formal
and continuous fashion, the powerful impact of these Saturday afternoons
at the Parochia lay in the fact that they provided the possibility of our being
together, to live some hours in a place of solidarity, where we could speak
about our traumas and listen to one another. Advice was given, help was
offered...some food...a little money. It was a shared space of suffering for
all of us who'd been affected by the dictatorship."

Although the project had been designed to bring professional aid to the
impoverished parishioners, Julia came to see it as a profound source of
mutual support. "It was a therapeutic community," she says, "that helped
to cure me." Thinking back on it, Julia believes that the experience was
healing for many reasons. This kind of activism permitted her to achieve
self-respect and a sense of integrity because it represented coherence with
her ego ideal. She could also give to these people something she herself
was desperately seeking and had not found before. Moreover, it was a significant source of continuity with her son because she was with people
who shared Gabriel's values and political commitments. "We experienced
a sense of gratification and mutual appreciation, they with me and I with
them. And it was, as well, a profound source of reparation. I could help
them with their losses in a way that I couldn't help the loved one whom I
myself had lost."

IMPRISONMENT, TORTURE, AND SOCIAL TRAUMA

Zizek writes that the Lacanian Real represents events or relationships characterized by their traumatic/excessive character, ones that we are unable to
integrate into what we live as our reality and are thus compelled to experience
as nightmarish specters. This notion of the Real captures the essence of life
in societies ruled by state terrorist regimes that disappear and torture their
own citizens. Most *desaparecidos* were subjected to violent torture rituals in
the prisons and concentration camps that spread like tentacles throughout
the Southern Cone. Designed to secure the complete submission of victim

(prisoner) and bystander (society) alike, torture was used as a weapon of power by states whose ability to ideologically control their populations had failed. Torture victims suffered thousands of deaths before their lives were completely obliterated. In Argentina, the omnipotence of the system was communicated through the torturers' arrogant and sadistic attitude and behavior toward their victims. As one of Timmerman's (1982) interrogators put it, "Only God gives and takes life...But God is busy elsewhere, and we're the ones who must undertake this task in Argentina" (p. 31).

Torture makes use of the body as a vehicle with which to secure psychic submission to the absolute power of the state. As Marcelo Viñar (1993) has understood it, in the terror of the torture experience and its aftermath, a moment exists when the suffering undergoes a shift from the subject's extraordinary physical anguish to the more desolate experience of complete and total psychological helplessness. He has written that along with

> the intensity of physical pain, including the sensory disorientation—the darkness, the hood covering one's head—and the rupture of all affective and loving ties with one's familiar and esteemed world comes the constant presence of a body in pain, agonizing, undone, completely at the mercy of the persecutor, who makes all other aspects of the world which are not central to the current experience disappear. We call this the moment of psychic demolition. (pp. 40–41)

This moment of demolition represents a traumatic threat to the victim's psychic structure. The imposition of a sense of total vulnerability entails multiple psychological repercussions. Because the victims have no possibility of defending themselves or others and are prohibited from expressing retaliatory aggression against their perpetrators, they often direct aggressive impulses inward. Self-blame and guilt are the result: Victims reproach themselves for having been caught, for failing to escape, for being weak and showing fear. Guilt is experienced when victims break down under torture or survive it when others do not. Political prisoners find ways to circumvent their isolation through the formation of deep attachments to those sharing their unfortunate fate.[8] As the renowned Uruguayan playwright Mauricio Rosencof recounts of his own prison experience, even in the most awful of Uruguay's prisons, La Libertad, he and other political prisoners sustained their courage and hope by using their knuckles to tap poetic messages of solidarity to one another on the prison's cement walls.[9]

However, the torture system is designed to sabotage this capacity for resistance. Often the inconsistent and unpredictable application of violence and the constant threat of imminent death successfully undermine the victim's clarity of thought and relations of solidarity with other prisoners in favor of relations of domination and submission. In the wake of several threats of death followed by sudden reprieves, in some cases prisoners succumb to the paradoxical state of viewing the perpetrator as their savior. The assault on the body transforms itself into the successful assassination of the victim's psychological autonomy. Similar to Nazi Germany, the Latin American terrorist state was often able to bring about the complete psychological regression of the victim so that a pathologically symbiotic relationship developed between the torturer and the tortured. Some torture victims came to feel they deserved their abuse. Their self-esteem demolished, they ceased to believe themselves worthy of decent relationships and turned to the torturer for salvation.[10]

The ability to maintain psychic integrity in the face of torture has become more difficult with the increasing sophistication of torture weapons, supplied by some of the technologically advanced nations. But the extent to which terror, humiliation, loss of dignity and physical anguish mark the victim depends on the structural characteristics of personality and the duration and intensity of the violence experienced. In this regard, Elizabeth Lira believes that in the victim's experience of helplessness the torture situation reproduces an already known but repressed universal infantile experience of helplessness and abandonment. Each individual's particular experiences in this state of early primitive helplessness affect and become enmeshed with the political and social experience as an adult under torture. This interaction of past and present partially determines the victim's reactions to the trauma.

Regardless of the psychic structure of individual torture victims, each suffers to some degree disturbing psychological sequelae. Symptoms are wide ranging in intensity and include sleep disorders, severe anxiety, psychosomatic illness, difficulty in thinking, loss of self-esteem, social withdrawal, decrease in productivity, abandonment of goals, and even premature death. In addition to the personal suffering these sequelae of torture represent, such reactions to trauma and even the specific symptoms associated with PTSD need here to be understood in light of the larger political goals of state-sponsored torture. Lira's point that "there is nothing 'post'" about this social trauma has to do with the legacy of state terror, which is that "the military dictatorships smashed important things not only in the torture victims but in the Chilean people in general. It destroyed the wish to construct a better future, the belief that it is possible, the conviction that people can do something worthwhile and make a difference. This is the context in which prisoners were tortured."

Marcelo knows about imprisonment, torture, and its aftermath, not only from treating survivors but also from his own experience when he was sequestered a year before the military coup. In June 1972, the government's declaration of the Law on State Security and Public Order gave the armed forces carte blanche to launch a witch hunt for any progressive individual who could be accused of being part of the legal solidarity movement connected to the Tupamaro guerrilla organization. They came for Marcelo two months later in the middle of a winter night. He and Maren were wrenched from a deep sleep by a group of armed men who had broken into their home. The terrified couple watched helplessly as the soldiers methodically ransacked their belongings, including their patients' files, searching for evidence. Of what? Neither Marcelo nor Maren knew. When they dragged Marcelo to the waiting van, they hauled off stacks of his clinical notebooks. Maren stared in shock as her husband disappeared. Later, when their six-year-old son, Daniel, realized what had happened, he whimpered, "Mama, do you think they're torturing Papa?" Maren asked what he thought torture was, and he replied, "Well, you get tied up and they hit you so much that you never, ever again can speak." As she recalls this reply, Maren chuckles bitterly, "It was like a summary of the goal of torture, to silence everyone. It was terrible. I told him that this was kind of what torture was like, but that we didn't know about Papa, that we hoped it wasn't happening to him."

For Marcelo, the entire experience of abduction and imprisonment was a prolonged torture. He insists on this interpretation. "Was I tortured? If you mean by that the infamous destructive attacks on the body, I have to say no. If I describe what my imprisonment was like, the answer would have to be yes—if a person is forced at gunpoint to go at 2:00 A.M. with 10 armed men, in the cold of winter, after they've gone through your whole house, turning it upside down, without respecting your personal life. They tell you they're taking you for a long time; they cover your eyes, handcuff you, tie your shoelaces together. They take you away; they don't tell you where. They don't tell you why. They isolate you and don't talk to you for a week. They make you do the *planton*, standing in one spot without knowing how long it's going to last. It goes on and on, interminably for five excruciating days. This for me is torture." He continues, "If I told you I was going to expose you to a very onerous experience for two months, you could accept it. But if I told you I was going to subject you to terrible things, who knows for how long, perhaps it will last forever, perhaps you'll die here, the situation of uncertainty and of the infinity of time, without limits, is very disorganizing mentally. The condition of sensory deprivation is itself a terrible torture. They deprive you of sight, of time and space referents, and they submit you to the unpredictable. For me this is torture."[11]

Marcelo describes how in such conditions one may even come to wish for punishment because at least it provides a concrete physical experience that punctuates the uncertainty. "As with head banging, the external pain helps to organize the disorganized internal world, but, in the case of torture, it's not self-inflicted." Echoing other prisoners, Marcelo emphasizes that torture is being deprived of knowing where one is, in such-and-such cell, in such-and-such prison, on such-and-such street. Although these facts may have no intrinsic meaning, they are profoundly important referents of one's location in the world. Knowing this, the torturers sadistically withhold such significant information from prisoners. "Often one of the only sources of orientation becomes the capacity to maintain control over one's sphincters. Enormous time is spent trying to control oneself to be able to pee or shit when they tell you you can and not to when they say no. Control over such functions can become everything, the central focus of orientation, the indicator of one's subjectivity. All the while, the effort reduces you to a completely infantile state."

As Marcelo indicates, torture is employed to impose on prisoners a "law of submission," every intimately small detail demonstrating to them their infantilized, dependent position. "One day I had the blindfold removed," he recalls, "with the instruction to look straight ahead at the wall. Here was my predicament: to obey and at least enjoy the relief of being able to see something, even if it was only a wall, or to resist and turn to see my persecutor. I obey because I am fearful of the punishment if I do not. I look straight ahead and time goes by, perhaps an hour. Suddenly I hear footsteps behind me, and before I realize it, I automatically turn to see who it is. They ferociously yank me away, punitively tie me up, and blindfold me again." Such apparently insignificant events function intentionally as psychological torture, ripping away from the prisoner any remnant of autonomy and dignity. "Who is going to risk dying because of not fulfilling one of these small details? And each time you obey, you acknowledge your impotence and their absolute power over you."

The torturers also deride prisoners about their isolation. "No one knows where you are," they taunt. "It doesn't matter what you do here or what we do to you, no one knows or cares. It's no use resisting. All your *compañeros* have talked. You've lost. You're lost. Everyone's given up on you. You're nothing because you've ceased to exist for others. You've been given up for dead."

How, Marcelo asks, and with what will the destroyed internal world of the torture victim be reconstituted? He asserts that two antagonistic realities fight for dominance in the victim's mind: the position identified with the torturer, who is incarnate in the present moment through his invasive control over life and death, and the other realities related to the past, now absent but promising coherence with the subject's identity prior to the torture, which he wishes to sustain but which is now gone, dead (Viñar & Viñar, 1993).

In Chile and Argentina, the majority of prisoners disappeared forever. In Uruguay, the disappeared were imprisoned, and relatives had to suffer sometimes for months before locating their loved ones. For Maren, suddenly Marcelo was gone, absent, disappeared, and she had no idea what was happening to him. "We didn't even know where he was. I couldn't deny reality to my son. There had been a media bombardment about the capture of Tupamaros, and about their grieving families, and everyone was talking about torture. So all the kids knew about it. Six months earlier, children had participated in the elections with their parents, going to festive Sunday picnics and then door to door campaigning for the progressive coalition, the Frente Amplio. Now it was all different. We couldn't get together, couldn't go out. There were roving police picking people up, surrounding entire city blocks, hunting people down. The kids knew they had to stop talking openly. They showed a great deal of solidarity with their parents, but at a great cost of self-control and anxiety." Maren's extensive experience as a child analyst had taught her about the pathogenic effects of parental lies to children. She had treated many a mother, after her husband with no history of illegal activity had been forced to go underground, who would tell her child that the father had gone away to work in the countryside or left town on a trip. "It is important, I think, to transmit reality to the child and to include her or him in the truth of what is happening. Children sense all of this anyway. Although it was difficult for the children to bear the truth, those who were lied to suffered in a worse way, their symptoms revealing that they understood much more than their parents told them. They often fell into depression, unable to symbolize what was happening or to elaborate it psychologically. If they are lied to, children are abandoned, alone without the truth."

As for Maren, the next two months were filled with nonstop action as she desperately fought to free her husband. "We didn't know where he was for two weeks. We were scared, and I just kept mobilized constantly, trying to do something, anything, everything I could. I was in constant motion, going to this military prison, that military headquarters, filling out papers, standing in lines, trying to leave packages of clothing. 'No, he's not on our list,' they'd say. 'We have no record of him,' I'd be told. 'But...but...they took him away,' I'd insist. There was a Kafka-like unyielding quality to the legal and penal bureaucracies. It was made even worse when we learned shortly after Marcelo's detention that several days earlier a colleague, a surgeon, had been taken away and that, like many others, he'd been tortured terribly with the *submarino* in the freezing cold."

Maren's torture was not knowing where Marcelo was or what they were doing to him. In a large meeting of the Uruguayan Medical Association, physicians' wives exchanged stories about how their husbands had been arrested and what they were suffering. "We mounted an international campaign of solidarity for Marcelo. From Buenos Aires, Marie Langer provided incredible help through the Argentine Psychiatric Federation (FAP), contacting people throughout the Americas and Europe. Within two weeks international support began to arrive from colleagues. Some members of the Uruguayan Psychoanalytic Association (APU) were scared and withdrew from us, but others showed generous and courageous support. They started a letter-writing campaign for Marcelo and even went to the parliament to demand information. Many never stopped coming to my house to see me and offer their help. In similar circumstances, other people had found themselves isolated, alone, abandoned by their intimidated friends. I was lucky."

Marcelo was in prison for two months—not so long, comparatively, but yet eternal, an endless two months of daily experiences that bore the contours of torture. It would require years for him to work through the psychological sequelae. Afterward, he would write about it as his contribution to the Latin American literature on political repression. Even at the moment of his imprisonment, he recognized that it represented a complete undoing of all his understanding and beliefs about the world, "a loss in the reliability of thought," as he puts it. "I felt like a fool, that I believed in things that no longer existed. I was perplexed, and, in the face of the torturers, I came to see that the diversity of human nature was greater than I, with all my university education and psychoanalytic training, could understand. I felt that the world was more complex and different than I'd imagined. This was a violent destruction of the reliability of thought and perception."

Marcelo describes his emotional reactions to the torturers, which others have documented as well. He felt a wish to enact a vengeful retribution, "an eye for an eye, a tooth for a tooth." The torturers wanted to liquidate him, and he wanted to do the same to them. Many prisoners tell of the wish to humiliate their torturers or of the fantasy of having the torturers in the same helpless position as they so that they might then demonstrate their superiority by renouncing the chance to torture them in kind. "My fantasy at times was to reverse the roles and for me to have total power over them. I would have them in the same helpless state, only to pardon them, so that their torture would be the realization of the differences between their humanity and mine."

Torture victims are sustained by another fantasy: the hope of leaving the prison or concentration camp and of reestablishing their former lives and social relations. But the fantasy and the reality are never the same. Marcelo's experience was similar to what is described by survivors of war and the Holocaust. "To be actually freed from prison," he says, "is not the same as the hopes one has kept alive during confinement. It is very difficult to transmit to others what has happened inside. People expect to encounter a hero or a traitor, but one isn't either of these. I don't deny that there are differences between the two, but I think reality is more complicated." The tendency to see torture victims in terms that bifurcate them into good and bad, Marcelo argues, is problematic. He believes there is a thin line between the hero and the traitor, the one who has withstood the torture and the one who has broken beneath the torturers' weapons. In either case, the torture victim is never the same afterward. "People expect you to be the same person who entered prison, and that, too, is never the case."

When Marcelo was released, people came to ask questions, to hear his story. He tried to describe the experience, thinking that it was necessary for political and humanitarian reasons. "My testimony was very radical in its description of the destruction of human beings inside prison. My friends listened, but I later learned that some said I was exaggerating. Several claimed I had been taken to a five-star hotel because I wasn't tortured as much as the average torture victim. Others didn't believe me, saying that I manifested a traumatic neurosis and didn't have the capacity to judge objectively what had happened. And I talked a lot, sometimes a little compulsively, like anyone who has seen hell of any kind. It was like a hemorrhage. I communicated things in an overwhelming way, I think, reproducing the details of my brutal experience. Now, with 20 years' hindsight, I can see that I said things the others didn't want to or couldn't hear. They wanted to know, but only what they thought they could bear. They emotionally spit back to me the things I told them that they couldn't take in."

This psychological collision was terrible for Marcelo, who says, "I felt my authority stripped from me, like something inside had been broken." Maren confirms its profound impact on the couple's relationship. "I wanted Marcelo to be whom he'd been before, but he had experienced two months that were like a hole in his life. He had no idea of what had happened outside during his imprisonment, as if history had abandoned him. A lot had gone on in the country during those two months—repression, people leaving, deaths, public demonstrations. I wanted to plug him into all that I had done in my life during his absence, the struggle, the battles, the mobilization of friends and colleagues. At the time, neither of us understood the disjuncture. I would get irritated at him because he seemed to have a fixed discourse, without variation. When people asked him whether he'd been tortured, he'd get mad. 'Having the *planton* is a torture,' he'd reply. It was as if he presented a story that hid the majority of things that had happened to him. 'Tell me about it,' I'd say. 'It's already passed,' he'd answer."

The impact on the family in general was dramatic. Years later, their son, Daniel, told his parents that he remembered his childhood as a happy one. It was filled with outings, camping trips, school, summer holidays, the house full of people—a life filled with vitality. "Then all of a sudden," he said, "it was broken."

Marcelo withdrew from much of his prodemocracy activism, although he was determined to stay in Uruguay. "I didn't leave at once because I believed there were values one had to defend. It seemed worthwhile to hang on to one's small place in the trenches." Although Maren lessened her activities, she would not stop completely. For three years, she treated many children whose parents had been imprisoned like Marcelo. She is convinced that her own experience helped her understand them. Indeed, it seemed to her that the families sought her out as a therapist because they trusted her and believed she could identify with them. For her part, she benefited from this work by having to assume a therapeutic distance in order to help her patients think about their painful emotional reactions, which in turn facilitated her capacity to bear her own. "It was therapeutic for me as well because it permitted me to leave my own trauma, my unthinkable situation, in order to think about theirs. It was a kind of reparation."

Marcelo also treated people who were in great need, militants who sought him out because they trusted him. "We were possessors of secrets," Marcelo comments ironically. "I knew many things. This is what scared me. But in Uruguay it wasn't that the military went after mental health professionals in particular. As people were imprisoned, the interrogators would ask them to name their doctor, their dentist, their therapist, their lawyer. When the same name came up again and again, it was assumed by the military that this particular professional was a movement sympathizer, and they'd go after him or her. Their technical name for this was 'the destruction of the sanitation apparatus of subversion.'" As in Argentina, the Uruguayan military believed that the intellectuals and their ideas were responsible for the radical challenge to the system they were defending.

Following the birth of their second son, Juan, in March 1975, Maren grew more frightened. The repression was intensifying and people all around them were being arrested and abducted. "But I felt I couldn't be a coward and flee," remembers Maren. "And one day in desperation I said to Marcelo, 'Well, lots of kids grow up without mothers.' He grabbed me and shook me, 'Are you crazy?' he demanded. 'Listen to what you just said. How could you say such a thing?' I was thinking to myself, 'Look at all the mothers in prison, their kids alone and abandoned. I can't leave because of the pain of leaving them.' I was in a kind of panic."

The feelings of vulnerability grew. No one could do anything without risk. They could not meet with anybody in the street, in the cafés, or at home. The only thing they now dared to do was collect funds for people who were leaving the country. By December 1975, Marcelo was convinced it was time to go, but still they stayed. They began to take security measures and slept in different locations. "One night in February, they came to get us. They occupied our house. Fortunately we weren't there, and we were alerted by friends though a preestablished code. We don't know why they came, but we imagined it was the result of someone naming one or both of us under torture. Daniel, who was only nine, was with relatives outside Montevideo. We had to leave the country without him. It was all so terrible; poor thing, he knew what had happened, and it was several days before he could join us. This experience really marked him."

When the Viñars were forced out of Uruguay, they fled to neighboring Argentina, only to realize immediately that a military coup was imminent. Then came the decision about where to go next. Several months earlier, Marcelo had been invited by psychoanalytic colleagues to Paris for a year's sabbatical. Although neither spoke French, their only alternative was Mexico, where they would at least be with Mimi Langer and other South American refugees. "But we wanted to convert exile into an intellectual and professional challenge, like a compensation for so much loss. So we didn't choose Mexico. We went to France."

In early March 1976, a mere two weeks before the Argentine armed forces marched into power, the Viñars sailed for Europe. As they stood on the ship's deck watching the American continent slowly recede into the horizon, Maren realized that Marcelo was suffering more than she. For her, this exile was a continuation of her history. She felt as if she were following in the footsteps of her father, whose life had been disrupted several times because of his political convictions. And she had already experienced the loss of her country when she had given up Chile to be with Marcelo. But for Marcelo this forced departure was complicated by a personal tragedy. "It's terrible," Maren thought, shivering in the wet ocean air. "It's different for him. Marcelo is leaving his dying father in Uruguay. And I have my little baby—the future—with me, in my arms, on this ship, now. With Marcelo and my two children here, it feels less daunting to face our unknown future on the other side of the Atlantic."

SOCIAL TRAUMA AND HUMAN DESTRUCTIVENESS

As my Latin American colleagues and I talk, we keep turning back to the relationship between social class and psychology. "When you speak of the culture of fear or social trauma or the people of a country affected by authoritarian repression," I would ask, "to whom are you referring? Does the class that objectively benefits from military dictatorship suffer the effects of social trauma? How do we explain the terrible, sadistic capacity of the torturer?"

Julia Braun responds to these questions by emphasizing that from her perspective "some people who approved the policies and ideology of state terror did not suffer. We may say that they could elude its implications. In fact," she tells me, "there are still individuals who actually say that the *desaparecidos* are on vacation in Europe! So when we speak of the 'culture of fear' or 'social trauma' or 'the Argentine people,' we are speaking of the majority who suffered, not the elite who were not harmed, who benefited from the stabilization of the traditional social order. But I also think it depends on the level of one's observation. It may be that if a wealthy person were on the analyst's couch, the analyst might detect the defenses that she or he had to mobilize in order to be shielded from feelings of empathy or guilt for the victims of the violence perpetrated in defense of his or her class interests."

Juan Carlos Volnovich holds the same view as Julia. "People who benefited from and agreed with the junta's project," he points out, "had to rely on the defenses of dissociation or denial in order to keep from recognizing the massive suffering imposed on the majority of people living in state terror." He believes that the need to organize one's mental life around these defenses has serious repercussions that impoverish the psyche. It is also Equipo member Diana Kordon's position that even the beneficiaries of the system were affected psychologically by the state's extreme violations of human rights. "To be a direct or indirect accomplice of massive assassination, of genocide, has to affect one's mental health in some way," she argues. "What we've seen in our experience is that even people who were directly involved in the repression have experienced sequelae, although few have sought psychological help. It is impossible that there is no impact. We know people who were torturers who have killed themselves and others who have reproduced very sadistic situations in their daily lives. For men—like the infamous Nazi doctors—who are capable of genocide all the while they are good family men, there is a primary schism involving profoundly dissociative processes. And those who were indirectly involved, if only by virtue of benefiting as a class, I think also manifested the impact in psychological terms. We could say that for them political repression is 'ego-syntonic,' by which we mean that such actions and ideas are compatible with the standards of the ego or the self. In this case, the aggression and dehumanizing ideology associated with state terror are acceptable to the social sectors whose interests are represented. But it impoverishes them as human beings because their focus on economic security and class domination leaves other attributes lacking. We especially note the restriction of the capacity for empathy and love."

Marie Langer believed that the cruelty manifest in state terror was the reflection in group behavior of the human capacity for cruelty and destructiveness. The perpetrators unconsciously disowned their own sadism, projecting it onto their victims and rationalizing it ideologically. But she also warned about the dangers inherent in psychologizing social phenomena. She maintained that "the problem of aggression expressed through class struggle is best thought about as a political question, not a psychological one." But she, too, strove to understand the psychological meanings of political life. She recalled Freud's view that during times of war the principles that guide superego functioning, including "thou shalt not kill," are countermanded by the legitimization of mass murder in the service of a higher cause. "People who torture are not just pathological but are responsible for their actions," Langer claimed. "The instrumental torturers are usually people from the marginal classes whose sadism—which we all have, isn't that true?—has been mobilized by class resentment. They are ordered to discharge—displace, we would technically call it—all their resentment for their powerlessness, which has been perpetrated by the system that marginalized them, onto the middle-class political activists and the class-conscious union militants. They operate on the basis of extreme dissociation reinforced by the prevailing anticommunist ideology."

Always in Langer's mind was the comparison between the Nazis and the Argentine torturers. From her point of view, the Germans were the more rational. They exploited the labor of the Jews in the camps, and those who could not work were put to death in the gas chambers. It was inhumane, to be sure, but they did not regularly torture inmates in the camps. The Argentines, she believed, acted more sadistically. "In Argentine state terror, people were tortured sometimes for years, and to what end? To diffuse terror in the population. The Argentine generals even killed people of their own class—families who were part of the opposition—including their own sons and daughters who had defected. The fathers, with their fear of losing everything to socialism, practiced filicide. I think the elites acted out of a kind of social guilt related to their historical role as the class whose privilege was based on the exploitation of the majority. They suffered persecutory fears of retribution by those they had brutally oppressed and went after them and their radical political allies with a vengeance."

Mimi pointed out that the elite and the generals congratulated themselves for the Dirty War and that their allies in other social classes justified the repression as a necessary tool for the cleansing of Argentine society. "But," she added, "we shouldn't forget the other responses. People also simply denied reality, which often permitted them, through identification with the repressors, to vicariously express their infantile sadism. And I know many people who, in order to remain in the country during the dictatorship or to return because they could not bear living in exile, had to disavow what they knew to be true."

Tato Pavlovsky agrees that Argentine society under state terror manifested a pattern similar to that of Nazi Germany or any nation ruled by dictatorship: Some of the population acquiesces to an authoritarian power. He cites Wilhelm Reich's classic study, *The Mass Psychology of Fascism*, to make the point that dictatorship does not exist without the complicity of the population. As he had elaborated in his play *Telarañas*, Tato argues that it is important to understand the subjective receptivity to fascism. From his perspective, the existence of an authoritarian consciousness among many sectors—including the middle and popular classes—stemming from bourgeois patriarchal society and its individualistic values predisposes people to identify with the forces of a repressive authority. "For example, when I returned from exile, I encountered my family, who had remained here during the military government. Nothing bad had ever happened to them. They had lived well, and they had no idea that there was even a problem with the dictatorship! There were so many people like my family, who had never lifted a finger, who had done nothing. On the other hand, I saw many people, including psychoanalysts, who were very traumatized, very affected, who had been courageous and valiant to stay here...people who were overjoyed to see me again, who wanted to struggle together, to do something meaningful. It was as if there were two countries."

Especially interesting to Tato is the discourse of those who benefited from state terror, "those who said, 'I didn't live badly during the dictatorship;

it went well for me economically. I had my little weekend country home. My children went to a good private school...there was order, there was no crime.'" This way of thinking, says Tato, is congruent with the bourgeois position in capitalist society, and it represents an ego-syntonic way of responding. "But such attitudes are shared by other social classes as well, who identify with the values of the dominant class. It's similar to what's been written about the Greek torturers. You couldn't find a more bloody dictatorship, but the torturers in Greece were more or less normal young men who were trained to have ideological convictions about their work." Tato thinks about Uruguayan writer Mauricio Rosencof's chilling description of his incarceration, in which he describes how a torturer could listen to a game of soccer on the radio with him and then subject him to the most unbelievably sadistic torture rituals. From Rosencof's perspective, the torturer did not suffer from any extreme pathology but had been ideologically trained to view him as an enemy of the Uruguayan nation. "I agree with Rosencof," says Tato, "and I think the torturer, in fact, doesn't have to be a sadist. That's what I tried to show in *Señor Galindez*, where I compared two torturers, both of whom were good examples of pathologically sadomasochistic personalities, with a third one, a nice young man who was in no way particularly aggressive but who had been deformed intellectually by his special forces training. To me, repression is a very complex phenomenon. Rosencof suggests that our biggest challenge is to understand what is in the heads of people for whom kidnapping, torture, beatings, the *picana* are syntonic with their affective and intellectual relationship to the world."[12]

Elizabeth Lira asserts that in the first years following the Chilean coup the global environment of fear affected everyone because there was a randomness to the violence as the military methodically imposed its complete and arbitrary power over the citizenry. Only later, when the repression was systematically aimed at political dissidents, was it clear that the military state protected some sectors and that these groups, although they might not necessarily like torture, found a way to rationalize it as a necessary evil to rid society of a "subversive cancer." Many who benefited from the coup could even claim that the danger had passed, in this way disavowing the continuing violent attacks on the sectors specifically targeted for repression. Elizabeth is reminded of the behavior of many Germans during the Nazi regime who denied that their government was carrying out genocidal policies against entire ethnic populations.

Elizabeth came to believe that there was nothing personal between the torturer and the tortured, only a symbolic relationship between the state and the "subversive." But she holds that the impersonal activity is fueled by what the torturers bring to the task in terms of their personal passions and cruelty. She, too, is reminded of the psychological studies of the Nazi doctors that postulate a phenomenon called *doubling*. An extreme form of dissociation, doubling refers to the existence of more than one ego, as if there are two subjects: one who is decent to people and a good family man, and the other who is perverse and capable of the most heinous crimes against humanity. "When I began to hear about the torture, from the perpetrators and from the victims, I felt I could hardly manage my reactions. I was filled with anxiety. I had terrible nightmares. But as I began to think about its meaning, what it entailed, how to denounce it, what we could do in the world so it would end, I could more easily listen to their stories."

PSYCHOANALYTIC PRACTICE
UNDER STATE TERROR

In all three countries, psychoanalytic treatment was affected by the advent of state terror. Marcelo explains that for the full exercise of psychoanalysis—"the talking cure"—which demands the articulation of fantasy life, a certain level of basic human rights in society is a necessary precondition. Free association, he stresses, is the fundamental rule of the psychoanalytic process, requiring that the patient attempt to relinquish conscious control over thoughts, wishes, and feelings so as to communicate to the analyst whatever comes to mind. The patient must often overcome conscious feelings of embarrassment, fear, shame, and guilt in the process. The analyst infers from the sequences, patterns, and content of the patient's associations the unconscious influences and conflicts underlying them. In the persecutory culture of fear, free association—and thus the practice of psychoanalysis—was seriously compromised because the distinction between psychic reality (fantasy) and external reality (state terror) collapsed. "In order for sadism, aggression, and so forth to be freely manifested in a patient's fantasy life, there has to be a guarantee that it's not happening in reality," says Marcelo.

In the culture of fear, not only was free association compromised, but patients also tended to increasingly repress thoughts and feelings that, if consciously acknowledged, might prove too dangerous. The conscious resistance to revealing information that might potentially be used to menace one's self and family, which characterized people's functioning in general, did not cease to operate at the analyst's door.

The work of the analyst was limited in other ways. As conditions deteriorated, the analytic function became more difficult to provide. When patients spoke of traumatic personal situations arising from the social conditions of state terror, analysts' ability to listen was compromised by associations to their own concerns, conflicts, and fears produced by the same conditions. Under such externally threatening conditions, working with the countertransference or intersubjective experience could threaten to overwhelm both patient and analyst rather than function as a source of learning and psychological growth. When Julia's son disappeared, for example, she attempted to separate her private life from her work as an analyst, to leave aside her terror, anxieties, and fears for Gabriel when she was with her patients. She strove to practice psychoanalysis as she had been taught. "Close the office door and try to understand my patients' terror related to the political repression as if my own terror were my private experience that should and could remain outside. I tried to arm myself psychologically in order to do the work and to keep everything the same—the schedule, the office, my own mental condition and physical appearance. I don't know how I did it or what I did! It was a terrible strain. I think I had to constantly disavow my fears that the police or military might interrupt a session to take either or both of us away. Several years later, my work with the church represented a tremendous emotional relief to me because I didn't have to hide behind the principle of psychoanalytic neutrality."

After his release from prison, Marcelo found it difficult to sustain the rule of neutrality and to keep his personal life from invading his patients' concerns. As the repression in Uruguay mounted, even though none of his patients left treatment with him for fear of being associated with an ex-prisoner, the possibility that he might still be "in the hornet's nest" was disturbing to both patient and analyst alike. "One of the reasons that I ultimately decided to leave the country was that I could not practice under those conditions. I realized I couldn't discriminate between what was happening to the patient and to me. Sometimes I reproached myself: If only I were stronger or better analyzed. At other times, I thought that the situation required a superhuman effort and that I was only human. For example, I was profoundly disturbed by the sounds in the environment: If a bus stopped, I got distracted wondering if it was just a city bus or something more sinister. One time during a session, two taxis stopped in front of my house, and I was convinced it was the armed forces coming to get me again. It turned out to be a priest who came to fetch me to treat a drunk who was threatening to harm himself with a knife."

Learning about aspects of a patient's life that might be of interest to the authorities put the analyst at risk of arrest, torture, and possible death. Some analysts did experience these forms of repression directly related to their work. In Argentina, on many occasions, analysts' offices were invaded during sessions, patients summarily arrested and carted off, sometimes never to be seen again.

But there were additional professional concerns: how to respect the injunction against imposing the analyst's perspective or point of view on the patient, as well as the mandate to focus on the patient's subjective reality rather than external events. Even the politically conscious analysts struggled to respect these aspects of prevailing psychoanalytic theory. It was often impossible. Marcelo recalls that he encouraged some of his activist patients whose lives were in danger to break off their analyses and flee the country. "In one case, a politically active friend of mine did not listen to his analyst's admonitions to leave the country immediately, and he paid dearly with seven years of prison and torture. Only years later, after studying psychoanalysis in France, did I finally understand that the world of unconscious fantasy is a mestizo—mixed breed—between the instincts and social reality and that the borders are much more porous than we used to think."

Juan Carlos also faced the conflict between professional responsibility to psychoanalytic technique and his ethical concerns about his patients. This problem emerged especially when he treated political activists who were in increasing danger as the repression in Argentina escalated. Concerned by what he viewed as a troublesome lack of attention to personal security on the part of the Montonero leadership toward their grassroots activists, he felt obliged to help his activist patients become conscious of the need to take precautionary measures to protect themselves from military persecution. "I realized my patients were in a state of denial about their extreme vulnerability. I'd intervene in ways that were not a direct expression of my opinion but rather my interpretation of the patients' unconscious concerns that emerged from their own discourse. Based on their associations, I could ask the important questions, which is, after all, the role of the analyst. 'Isn't it interesting that with what you're describing it never occurred to you that you might be in danger?' 'I wonder whether you're aware that when you talk about the revolutionary leadership, you're speaking as you do when you're describing your childhood and how you felt your mother didn't take care of you.'"

Yet another problem facing progressive analysts was the omnipresent threat that one of their patients might be an informant. Maren describes what happened to a psychotherapy group of adolescents when a participant's father was abducted. "Dealing with it was very difficult, and there was a great deal of censorship in the discussion. Free association wasn't possible because everyone knew that it took only one traitor within the group for a disaster to befall us all. The moral responsibility under such conditions was tremendous, and it was finally necessary to stop doing group therapy completely." On other occasions, patients become informants or collaborators. Maren relates one such incident about a high school boy who was taken prisoner and tortured. He became a hero, a symbol of resistance, and there were many demonstrations on his behalf. "When he was released, he sought therapy with me," recalls Maren. "But there was something about him that made me feel he was hiding, not telling the truth. I was frightened, and when he said he'd chosen me as a therapist because I was trusted by the left, I tried to minimize this connection in his mind. He didn't come back, and very soon after he was imprisoned again. Almost immediately he became a policeman and was often seen on the streets in our neighborhood, pointing out specific people to the military. When they later came for us, we hypothesized that it might have been he who denounced us."

In Chile, therapeutic issues confronting Elizabeth emerged within the context of her own journey back to psychology and the role of the therapist in the human rights movement. She recounts how during the several years following the coup, she was involved in solidarity work, helping people get out of jail, leave the country, or obtain economic help to feed their families. "It was really scary because you didn't know with whom you were working. Everything was anonymous for our own protection." She herself was always potentially in danger because of her history of militant activities with peasants, one of the sectors targeted for repression by the military. By 1976, she was once again drawn to psychology "because of my need to understand the subjective aspect of everything that had happened." A friend loaned her some books about Marxism and psychoanalysis, including one edited by Marie Langer that made a profound impression on her.[13] After that, she began to work in FASIC (the Catholic Foundation of Social Aid) in its psychiatric and medical section, where treatment was offered to former prisoners, families of the *desaparecidos*, and torture victims.[14] "That was when we began to write. In 1983, we put together two volumes of articles attempting to analyze what we observed, and Mimi wrote the introduction. We used pseudonyms for our safety and distributed copies of the volumes clandestinely within the country and internationally at congresses on human rights."

FASIC offered some degree of safety for Elizabeth and her colleagues who worked with torture victims. For several years, she and other mental health professionals listened to testimonies by hundreds of people who had been illegally imprisoned and tortured. It was an anguishing process. "It was so sad, men and women so young: 20-, 22-year-olds...so destroyed. I had a hard time psychologically containing both for them and for me something that was almost uncontainable. And we had no reliable therapeutic model to depend on to intervene clinically." The FASIC therapists began to tape their sessions, as well as testimonials of torture victims, so they could systematically study the psychic meaning of torture and its treatment. They read about the Nazi Holocaust and began an ongoing dialogue with therapists from other countries who practiced under similar conditions in order to elaborate a psychosocial analysis of state terror. "We noted similarities and differences between this experience and the Holocaust but felt lost because most of what was written dealt with the long-term effects on victims rather than with treatment interventions."

For Elizabeth and her colleagues, treatment issues were connected to the struggle to end the dictatorship. The testimonials were important for the victims because through them the reality of their experience could be validated by the therapists, who confirmed their sense of themselves and the world. Together they engaged in a political act by sending these testimonials to international human rights organizations and the United Nations to expose and denounce the dictatorship.

In 1988, in order to develop treatment interventions for victims of state terror and to research and publish analyses of the culture of fear and its sequelae, Elizabeth and her colleagues from FASIC formed ILAS (Latin American Institute of Mental Health and Human Rights). By this time, each had acquired psychoanalytic training. As Elizabeth says, "I came to realize that behaviorist treatment models were of no use in addressing the *afectados* of state terror and that only a psychoanalytic conceptualization of the psychic apparatus and psychoanalytic clinical techniques could make our therapeutic work effective. But I also became convinced that the patient's relationship with the analyst under these conditions needed to be thought of as more complex than simply a matter of transference. In fact, the patient–therapist relationship was often itself a transformative one, in which the patient learned to be able to depend on the analyst not only for psychological support but for practical help in resolving problems related to basic necessities like finding work, locating housing, and searching for the *desaparecidos*."

When working with victims of state terror, the notion of neutrality appeared totally irrelevant to Elizabeth. "We shared a political view with our patients, which helped us understand the depth and meaning of their trauma. We can't forget that in Chile we actually had won something in the election and presidency of Allende that then was brutally ripped away from us. That made the issue of loss different from [that in] the other countries in the Southern Cone. It was difficult for an analyst who didn't feel that the Allende government had constituted an extraordinary social project to comprehend how its loss could represent a profound catastrophe. Such sentiments in a torture victim would simply be devalued by a therapist who didn't understand this. The therapist who could identify with this experience—without necessarily telling the patient—could use it to work very productively. We have found the patients' knowledge that we are on their side to be fundamental to the working alliance. Without it, how could they speak, thinking that you might be on the side of the enemy? Because ILAS is publicly connected with the human rights movement and politically opposed to the dictatorship and state-organized violence, the patient who comes to us for help is never confused about our alliances. This shared context permits the patient to risk entering into the treatment and disclosing traumatic experiences related to torture and forced disappearances. In this sense, the therapeutic relationship is itself reparative."

THE EQUIPO AND THE MOTHERS OF THE PLAZA DE MAYO

"From the beginning, we were clearly identified with the Mothers' struggles to locate their disappeared children and grandchildren," Lucila says, "which is what made it possible for us to develop this unique therapeutic team effort on their behalf." Darío explains that their initial connection with the women who would later form the Mothers organization occurred shortly after the coup in March 1976, when Diana contacted some of them in the course of gathering names of *desaparecidos* for an Amnesty International delegation visiting Argentina. "It was in December," he recalls, "and after Diana and several colleagues delivered a list of names of university professors and students who had disappeared, they were followed and on the point of being detained. Luckily, the Amnesty delegates were alerted. Their immediate return to the scene prevented the arrest of Diana and the others because the military, already concerned about their international reputation as human rights abusers, feared a scandal."

During the next several years, Diana often encountered women as they anxiously traipsed from church to ministry to barracks seeking information about their disappeared children and grandchildren. Although Diana used a pseudonym in her human rights work, when some of the women learned that she was a psychologist, they asked her to meet with one of the mothers who was depressed. Diana began to meet her informally in relatively safe public places like churches and cafés. Soon there was a chain reaction because other mothers who heard about Diana's expertise created a permanent demand for her services. "Later," recalls Diana laughing, "when the Thursday afternoon marches in the Plaza de Mayo started, sometimes I'd be walking around in the march listening to a mother tell me about a disturbing dream and helping her understand its unconscious meanings!"

Out of this experience, Diana recognized the need to work with the Mothers as a mental health professional, not just a political activist. "That was the origin of the idea of forming a group, a team," says Lucila, "and Diana suggested the idea to Darío and me. Of course, we were very enthusiastic. We began immediately to deal with basic questions, such as what should be told to the children whose parent or parents had disappeared or how we should deal with the problems that emerged in the marital relationship of parents of a *desaparecido* or what could be done to help people tolerate the uncertainty and anguish of not knowing about the fate of their disappeared children and grandchildren. We quickly realized that these efforts would best be realized through the creation of small groups composed of the families themselves so they could participate in the elaboration of these issues."

The three organizers of the Equipo were not new to political activism, for each had been involved in the radical movement of mental health professionals that developed in the 1960s and 1970s in Buenos Aires. Their personal histories mirror the patterns of many psychoanalysts of their generation. Diana, whose grandparents had immigrated to Argentina from Russia and Romania, grew up in a politically progressive family who lived in a working-class neighborhood that had benefited greatly from the Peronist government's proworker policies. After graduating from high school, Diana entered the intensely politicized student environment of medical school, and she quickly came to identify with the left and Marxism. Then in the early 1970s, like many fellow medical students, she received an important professional and sociological education as a resident at Lanus Hospital. Lucila, too, is a second-generation Argentine whose grandparents arrived at the turn of the century from Russia, Romania, and Austria. Lucila's mother was one of Argentina's best-known leftist activists in the feminist movement from the 1920s on, and she had imparted her progressive values and principles to her daughter. "She left me an important legacy," Lucila notes, "for which I am grateful, although I must admit it has often been hard to be the daughter of the famous Fanny Edelman!" Darío is a fourth-generation Argentine of Spanish and Austrian heritage who also became politicized as a university student. During the early 1960s, medical school introduced him to professional training as well as progressive activism. His theoretical and clinical understanding of the relationship between social ills and individual sickness was honed in practice when he worked as a physician in a working-class community. Both his and Lucila's experiences as physicians among the poor stimulated their interest in psychology when they observed how frequently their patients' physical symptoms and requests for medical intervention seemed to be influenced by emotional difficulties and problematic social situations.

All three founding members of the Equipo developed a special interest in mental health. Their psychological training took place within the context of the great social turbulence in Argentina in the late 1960s. They were among the young generation of mental health professionals who were active in the Organization of Mental Health Workers, which was created by Marie Langer and other political analysts after their departure from the Argentine Psychoanalytic Association (APA). Diana remembers her work as a student on the committee to develop the Research and Training Center (CDI) curriculum. "It was fascinating to work with Mimi Langer in the CDIs, where we tried to develop a socially conscious psychoanalysis, one that would be responsive to the great social crises facing the country. We studied Freud, Klein, Laing, Lacan, Marx, and Althusser. It was incredibly exciting intellectually. And we were also developing activist projects, one of which was to put pressure on the state to implement programs of primary prevention. Hundreds of mental health professionals went into the communities, much like the social workers in the United States, to respond to the psychological and social needs of the poor."

Later, following the coup in 1976, when conditions became extremely repressive, the three focused on human rights work and treatment of victims of state terror, often at great risk to their own personal safety. Finally, in 1979, their efforts coalesced in the formation of the Equipo. They began to work in a formal manner with the Mothers of the Plaza de Mayo, providing them with psychological assistance in their struggles to confront the terrorist state.[15] The women who were engaged specifically in the search for their disappeared grandchildren had formed a separate organization, the Grandmothers—*Abuelas*—of the Plaza de Mayo.

Like their counterparts in other Latin American countries where Mothers organizations have fought for their disappeared children,[16] the women who became activists in the Mothers and Grandmothers of the Plaza de Mayo came from diverse backgrounds. Some had prior experience as political activists, while others were middle-class professionals and working-class women with no political experience. The majority were homemakers from all social sectors with no previous activity in the public realm. When they began to gather in the Plaza de Mayo in April 1977, the issue that united them was their commitment to their children and grandchildren and their unswerving refusal to passively accept their forced disappearance (and torture or murder) by a terrorist state. On behalf of their loved ones, with their own lives in constant danger, they tenaciously confronted the armed forces.

These women viewed their activism in very specific ways. They did not see themselves fighting in the tradition of the women's rights movements that had emerged at the turn of the century to demand social, economic, and legal equality with men, nor as part of the radical and socialist feminist movements that had made their appearance during the early 1970s. In fact, the Mothers repeatedly stated that they did not identify themselves as feminists but rather as a group of women whose activities were not politically motivated. Indeed, they purposefully designed their discourse to reflect their traditional domestic roles: Theirs was a struggle on behalf of motherhood and in defense of children. This self-presentation, symbolized by the white head scarves that became the motif of their struggle, coincided with the military's official rhetoric about Christian society and family values. Ironically, the military's adherence to the patriarchal ideal initially compromised their ability to respond to the Mothers with outright repression. Moreover, from the start, the armed forces' own prejudices against women led them to view the Mothers as an inept group of housewives, whom they disparagingly referred to as *las locas* (crazy women) of the Plaza de Mayo. The military's paternalistic underestimation of women prevented them from recognizing the Mothers as a potential threat to their authority, and this tactical error gave the women the time they needed to organize themselves. Even when the armed forces did attack the organization by kidnapping some of its members in late 1977, the Mothers' determination could not be broken. And although theirs was not a political struggle as they saw it, in the process of confronting the state, the Mothers educated themselves politically about the alliance of forces complicit with the military. They came to understand how the Catholic Church, the judiciary, and the capitalist elites cooperated with the crimes of the junta and then hid them from Argentine citizens.

The Mothers took up the search on behalf of their *desaparecidos* because, as they often publicly declared, their husbands were more vulnerable to the reprisals of the state. Their husbands, as well, had to maintain their jobs and thus could not risk being fired for missing work as a result of the labor-intensive search for their children and grandchildren. Many of the women speak warmly of their husbands' comradely support and willingness to take up the extra burden of housework so that their wives could go to the jails, police stations, hospitals, judges' chambers, and government bureaucracies to hunt for clues, to file papers, and to lodge formal denunciations. Diana explains that the women's activism created great solidarity among them, an important source of comfort in this grim activity that generally yielded nothing. "The solidarity often included their husbands, who did not participate themselves for a variety of reasons. Often the men stayed away because of the very real fear that they would be easier targets of the military and police than the women, but there was also the factor of psychological demoralization that many men felt in the face of their impotence to protect their children. And some mothers and grandmothers found it necessary to take to the streets and the plazas with little or no support from their husbands, who felt threatened by their wives' activist stance." For those women who were forced to deal with their husbands' passivity, fears, or even resentment of their own burgeoning assertiveness, conflicts in the marital relationship added additional stress to the politically provoked emotional burden of the loss of their children or grandchildren and their anxiety and fear for their own lives.[17]

However, membership in the Mothers organization has been extraordinarily positive for its participants. The Equipo members have written that the significance of this political activism must be understood within the context of the intended goal of state terror, which is the imposition of silence and total social isolation. Equipo members describe the pathological effects of complying with what they call "the silence rule," including extreme dissociative phenomena, the denial of reality, learning problems, and the impoverishment of fantasy life. The value of the Mothers, they argue, is their refusal to accept the terms of the terrorist state, their articulation of the existence of a responsible party that disappears their children, and their demand for an accounting from those responsible. Their slogans symbolize this posture: "They must appear alive"; "They took them away alive; we want them back alive"; "Punishment to culprits."

Although recognized as an important public stance, this political position of the Mothers brought debate within the organization and the Equipo. "We talked a lot about it," recalls Diana. "Many nonactivist therapists argued that families needed to mourn the loss of loved ones, to give up the *desaparecidos* as dead, in order to maintain their psychological connection with the real world. But we felt that for many people it was impossible to presume that their loved ones were dead, especially since we knew nothing about their fate. In that sense, we thought that what passed as 'neutral' psychological theory on mourning was an unconscious capitulation to the dominant discourse of state terror. This was a very complex question, and we supported the right of each family to go through their own subjective process about how to live with the situation of having had a child forcibly disappeared."

The Equipo has argued that, in their coming together to act, the Mothers give up the narcissistic dyad "I and my child" or "I and my grandchild" in their common concern for all the disappeared children and grandchildren. The Mothers do not seek revenge; their action is beyond the realm of retaliation. They demand the return of law and its ability to contain arbitrariness within the social order. They have occupied a geographical space—the Plaza de Mayo—where for centuries Argentines have assembled when fighting for their political rights. They have marched, their white kerchiefs indicating peace as well as the diaper—eternal symbol of mother–child unity—their large photographs of the disappeared a defiant message that their children are indeed *presente*.[18]

Diana and her colleagues postulate that the Mothers organization sheds light on the relationship between political resistance and mental health. They note that women such as these have been better able to work through the traumatic loss of their loved ones, in part because for them their activist group has become a new privileged relationship, and they have been able to give a new meaning to group links beyond the family. Many of them have emerged from the limited sphere of the home to assume new forms of active solidarity and to identify themselves as socially engaged human beings for the first time in their lives. "The struggle for peace and justice means another type of relationship with the [child]. The ego ideal system has been altered: To be a mother now means 'to fight for all our children' or 'to fight for life'" (Kordon & Edelman, 1986, p. 63).

The Equipo has noted that these activist women tend as a group to be better able to elaborate the trauma they suffered and to deal with the general impact of state terror than their husbands and those mothers who have not engaged in an organized confrontation with the political forces responsible for their traumatic loss.[19] As Diana points out, "Political activism does not necessarily eliminate the need for psychological attention. However, when we first began to work with the Mothers, we expected that, given their traumatic losses, they would all need psychotherapy. That was not the case. We discovered that, in and of itself, their involvement in the Mothers organization is potentially healing, precisely because the individual who has known traumatic loss is no longer cut off from the group. Her loss is no longer individualized, detached from its historical context, but is now part of the collective process that produced it and can now potentiate its reparation. The Mothers' transcendence of isolation and their commitment to act as historical agents are essential to the resolution of the pathological effects of social trauma."

Not only the Mothers about whom they write but Equipo members as well illustrate the positive use some individuals are able to make of social trauma. Their courage permitted them to preserve a sense of personal integrity and coherence with their ego ideals, which in turn empowered them. Hopefulness was nurtured as a result of their capacity to sustain a connection with others who shared their commitment to human rights. Marcelo and Maren Viñar have been especially interested in this human capacity for a creative response to traumatic situations. They have criticized the idea that the victims of the culture of fear are inevitably impaired, irrevocably changed for the worse, doomed to suffer lives deprived of creativity, productivity, and joy. The Viñars suggest that those who were the *afectados*, affected by the disappearances and torture in the Southern Cone, did not necessarily emerge "damaged" from the experience, as is implied by the diagnostic notion of "traumatic neurosis." Such a designation, they argue, may be more helpful to the therapist, whose work is framed by the comfort of a diagnosis, than to the victims, who can be hurt by the assumption that they have necessarily been psychically impoverished. The Viñars argue, "The person who has lost loved ones to the repressive state or has been tortured or forced into exile can emerge from such traumatic situations much worse off or much better off. The individual is altered, to be sure, but we ask the question: How? It may be that [one] matures as a human being. Extreme situations may deplete or enrich the subject, whose creative and symbolic capacities are either dramatically compromised or enhanced. Trauma is by its very nature something that resignifies one's life, not in the symptoms or the sequelae of the injury, but by the meaning one attributes to it through the psychic elaboration of the experience."

The Viñars' own responses to the traumatic events in their lives testify to this assertion. In addition to the social trauma they suffered within the citadel of state terror, they, like many other political analysts, were forced into exile. Far from home, they were obliged to deal with the additional trauma of making a new life for themselves, isolated from all the familiar cultural, historical, and familial indicators that are the profoundly important referents of one's location in the world. Like Juan Carlos Volnovich and Mimi Langer, they faced yet another challenge in the process of resignifying their lives. Through their capacity to embrace and transcend the potential pathological effects of this fundamental life disruption, a socially committed psychoanalysis would survive, not only in the courageous work continued by the analysts who stayed in Argentina, Chile, and Uruguay, but in the projects created amid the vicissitudes of exile.

ENDNOTES

1. Among mental health professionals in the United States who deal with the impact of ongoing trauma, such as child abuse and wife battering, there is a similar dialogue with respect to how to conceptualize the nature of trauma when it is imposed by external reality; see, for example, Herman (1992), Brown (1991), Lifton (1973), Davies and Frawley (1994), and Boulanger (2007).

2. Although she is stressing the ongoing nature of social trauma, Julia Braun would agree with the current literature on sexual abuse or wife battering, for example, which indicates the ongoing and repetitive nature of trauma within this private context.

3. See also Perelli (1992), Lira (1994), and Lira and Castillo (1991). For other sources on the dynamics of repression, see Sosnowski and Popkin (1993).

4. For additional sources on the impact on children of living in the culture of fear, see Suarez-Orozco (1987) and Movimiento Solidario de Salud Mental, Familiares de Detenidos y Desaparecidos por Razones Políticas (1987).

5. For an analysis of the psychopolitical functions of public forms of punishment, see Foucault (1979).

6. For a discussion of psychoanalytic thought regarding the notion of an environmental container (mother or social group or both) for intolerable and undigested or indigestible anxieties, see Winnicott (1965, 1971), Bion (1959b, 1967), and Ogden (1986).

7. The testimony about Norberto Liwsky's horrendous abduction and torture is published in *Nunca más*, pp. 20–26.

8. For discussions of this aspect of the experience of torture, see Bendfeldt-Zachrisson (1988) and Seminario Internacional (1987).

9. See Rosencof (1993a) for an evocative analysis of the experience of imprisonment, torture, and the capacity to maintain hope.

10. See Herman (1992), especially chapter 4, "Captivity," for a description of the similarities in the sadomasochistic relationships between the torturer and tortured and between the abuser and abused.

11. In *Fracturas de memoria*, Marcelo (Viñar & Viñar, 1993) describes in gruesome detail his torture in the chapter entitled "Un grito entre miles." It is interesting to note that in my interview with him, Marcelo did not describe the extent to which he had been tortured. For a profoundly moving exploration of the way that torture inflicts a sense of impotence and infantilization on prisoners through its attack on one's location in time and space and on one's control over basic biological functions, see Scarry (1985).

12. Simon Wiesenthal maintained that Adolf Eichmann, the bureaucrat in charge of deporting millions of Jews to death camps, was simply the logical product of a system that would have expected any order to be implemented in similar fashion—for example, "if he had been ordered to kill all men whose name began with P or B" (Askenasy, 1978, p. 28). Other studies of Nazi commanders of concentration camps reveal them to have been administrators interested in doing a good job who became desensitized to

the extreme human suffering they caused rather than perverse personalities deriving pleasure from their work; see, for example, Gilbert (1950) and Dicks (1972).

13. The books the friend loaned Elizabeth included *Cuestionamos I* and Gente, *Marxismo, psicoanálisis y sexpol* (1972); the Gente book was part of the publisher's Left Freudian Collection, a series edited by Marie Langer.

14. FASIC was a foundation within the Catholic Church involved in a variety of human rights activities during the dictatorship in Chile.

15. Their book (Kordon & Edelman, 1986) is an exploration of the particular type of research and political commitment that typified their work with the Mothers.

16. The following is a brief list of articles and books on the movements of mothers throughout the continent: Fisher (1989, 1993), Agosín and Galmozzi (2008), Golden (1991), Jelin (1990), Elshtain (1992), McLeod (1986), Thomson (1986), Manz (1982), and Menchú (1992). The first group in Latin America with the goal of locating disappeared family members emerged in Guatemala in 1967, following a wave of repression in that country a year earlier. A continent-wide movement was founded in 1980, the Latin American Federation of Associations of Relatives of the Detained–Disappeared. At its first congress, held in 1981 in Costa Rica, it was estimated that during the prior two decades more than 90,000 people had disappeared throughout the continent. The group meets annually so that member organizations can exchange information and strategies.

17. There seem to be gender differences in the psychological manner of responding to the impact of state terror; see Hollander (1996), Seminario Internacional (1987), and Golden (1991).

18. This term, which literally means "present," is used by Latin American progressives to indicate that a *compañero* or family member who has died in the struggle is still present in spirit and lives in the hearts and minds of the people who carry on the battle for justice and human rights.

19. In their interviews with me in 1994, the members of the Equipo and Julia Braun all referred to a recently finished epidemiological study they coauthored, in which they found that women who were activists in the Mothers organization during or after the military dictatorship had lower rates of serious illness and longer life expectancy than the population at large in their age cohort, including both men and women.

Chapter 6

Exile

Paradoxes of loss and creativity

> Exile, once it begins, never ends...ever. One experiences it as an internal migration that lasts forever.
>
> — Maren and Marcelo Viñar (2006)

It is a balmy summer morning in June 1984. Marie Langer, Ignacio "Nacho" Maldonado, and I are ordering espressos at the bar in Mexico City's international airport as we wait to board our plane for Managua, Nicaragua. Mimi has invited me to accompany her and Nacho, the two coordinators of the Internationalist Team of Mental Health Workers, Mexico–Nicaragua, as they return to the tiny Central American country whose revolution in 1979 has made it a target of President Reagan's new Cold War policies. For the past three years, the Internationalist Team has sent two or three of its members for 10 days of each month to teach, train, supervise, and offer direct services in the Sandinistas' new mental health system. This endeavor has brought new meaning to life in exile for Mimi and Nacho. We are excited to be going to Nicaragua, but a little anxious as well in anticipation of flying through nature's turbulent Central American winds and over the U.S.-sponsored civil war in El Salvador.

Soon, because it has become my custom to take advantage of free moments in Mimi's busy schedule to pursue our ongoing exploration of her life and work, and perhaps stimulated by the airport environment, I direct our attention to the theme of exile. Nacho, Mimi's close friend and a fellow veteran of the movement of political analysts in Argentina, has also lived in exile in Mexico City since 1974. A gentle and soft-spoken man in his 50s, Nacho contributes his own recollections as I pursue threads of previous conversations about Mimi's arrival in this country a decade earlier. I know that their perspectives can shed light on the experience of migration that has come to characterize the destinies of millions of people who are forced to leave their cultures of origin in the Global South for political reasons, or to search for economic opportunities in the developed world. Some of the subjective struggles and challenges of political exile are also shared by economic refugees, many of whom experience the problematic psychological sequelae of traumatic dislocation and uprooting.

"It's hard to describe," Mimi begins, her deep blue eyes becoming serious. "It's a daunting experience, arriving in a country and knowing from the moment you set foot on *tierra firme* that you are not here out of choice. Even more important, you have no idea how long your stay will be or whether you'll ever return home. You don't know what to feel, and in the beginning you oscillate from relief and excitement to fear and trepidation. At first you try to deny the gravity of the situation. Many of us plunged into a kind of defensive euphoria, playing at being tourists. 'Did you see how lovely Mexico City is?' 'Did you visit the pyramids—what beauty!' But our startled reactions to the sudden sound of an ambulance siren or the backfire of a car punctured the fiction that we were here on a planned vacation. We had come from a nightmare, and at night, when we slept, for months that nightmare persecuted us."

Nacho points out that after a while "the nightmare invaded our waking hours, and then we were even more psychologically disturbed." He and Mimi recall the impact of newspaper reports that detailed ongoing atrocities in Argentina. "There were the typical scenes," says Mimi. "An activist would comment anxiously to a *compañero*, 'Did you read that Heraldo went crazy under torture?' A distraught mother would tell a friend, 'You know the child my little girl plays with? Her mother just learned that they killed her husband.' And I'll never forget the evening when, during a meeting of a Freud study group, one of the female participants answered the phone, listened quietly to the voice on the other end, gasped, and began to scream, 'No, no...my god; they've killed my brother.'"

As exiles continued to learn about the horrors at home, the denial associated with the first phase of happy tourism shifted to a kind of depersonalization. Mimi recalls that "many friends and patients described 'out-of-body' experiences, observing themselves from outside as they went through the motions of daily life. And then there were the sudden attacks of self-reproach. One would walk the streets, thinking, 'What am I doing here? What is this city?' Or sit on the edge of the bed staring at the cheap ceramics purchased a day earlier with wild enthusiasm, thinking, 'But am I crazy? How did it occur to me to come here? I have to go back right away.' And then there were the slim hopes stimulated by rumors: 'Did you hear about the demonstration in Cordoba?' And 'What do you think? If the strike in Rosario continues a little more, will it be possible to return?'"

The worst was the guilt that everyone suffered, independent of their own histories, their political situations, or the circumstances of their leaving. It did not seem to matter whether they had left after being released from prison or had been deported by the government or had simply decided to flee. All the refugees suffered the pangs of guilt for having fled and survived when others could or would not. "The anguish of this 'survivor guilt' was bound up with our grief for the lost political project that was such a fundamental part of our lives," Nacho adds. "With its disappearance, we also lost our self-esteem. You could hear the self-recrimination in the frequently uttered remark, 'We are all deserters.'" Mimi nods in agreement. "I remember my worst moment in exile. It was the night I went to a solidarity meeting of the Chilean exiles to hear President Salvador Allende's sister, Laura, speak. She told about how she had been taken prisoner because she hadn't left Chile after the coup. She was from such a prominent family and so wasn't tortured, but one night they threw her, naked and blindfolded, on a pile of tortured bodies for the night. When she was released, she continued her activism in the opposition struggle. I went home that evening and collapsed on my bed in tears. I felt a terrible desperation because, unlike Laura, I had abandoned my commitments. I had not continued to struggle, and in Argentina people were suffering and dying."[1]

Mimi and Nacho are describing significant aspects of the psychological impact of exile.[2] The forcible uprooting of individuals and groups from their country of origin is experienced as a profound rupture that threatens the stable functioning of the psyche. Exile from everything familiar is a life crisis that stimulates emotional reactions comparable to the helplessness and futility felt by a baby or young child at the absence or loss of the parent, who is needed to help manage frustration, anxiety, loneliness, and fears of separation (see Bion, 1959b, 1962; Winnicott, 1975). Indeed, much like the defenseless child, refugees experience the loss of a containing environment when they are suddenly separated from their homeland, with its familiar and predictable language, cultural signifiers, and social relations. A state of psychic disorganization may result, especially if unresolved conflicts associated with earlier experiences of extreme vulnerability and loss are reawakened. Manic overcompensation in the form of an exaggerated enthusiasm about the new environment, such as Mimi describes, is frequently the first—and fragile—line of defense against a host of disturbing states of mind. Or the opposite may occur: The refugee cannot adapt to the new situation and rejects the culture, language, and people through an exaggerated devaluation and a nostalgic idealization of the country left behind. These reactions, while in some ways more extreme among political exiles, highlight the psychological experience that characterize the millions of people forced by deteriorated economic conditions of their home countries in the Global South to migrate to more developed countries in search of economic opportunities.

A variety of symptoms frequently appear among an exile population, including disorientation, confusion, acute self-doubt, nightmares, insomnia, the inability to focus, depression, anxieties, paranoia, and dissociation. Some individuals become accident-prone, as if reenacting the experience of being attacked by a harmful environment. Often psychological conflict is displaced onto the body, and psychosomatic problems emerge. Higher rates of fatal diseases, including cancer, are found among refugees in comparison with the general population. Somatic disturbances are frequently related to digestive symptoms, as if new foods—symbolic of the new experience in general—cannot be "digested" (Grinberg & Grinberg, 1984, p. 94). Marcelo Viñar recalls how, after living in Paris for a time, he received a letter from a friend whose philosophical advice hinged on eating as a metaphor for "taking in" the experience of exile. "I am happy to hear that you are in the process of putting down roots," the friend wrote. "One cannot continue to nibble a little at each thing, as if in passing through. It's necessary to sit down at the table and partake of what life offers us." His friend went on to advise Marcelo to embrace his current situation. "One must weave a kind of density and thickness around what is provisional in life," he counseled. "You and I have lived in a country that will never be the same. Something else will exist in the future. Other youth will make their history, others who will not be us. We must learn to live this grim existence that fate has dealt us. If not, when a new day dawns, we'll be asleep or daydreaming" (Viñar & Viñar, 1993, p. 87).

His friend wisely suggested that Marcelo recognize and accept the change in his life circumstances. He advised Marcelo to grieve the loss of his country and his own place in it, his own past identity, so as to get on with his life in the present. This mourning process is one of the central challenges facing the refugee, who must struggle to relinquish both the fantasy and the reality of what has been lost in order to make a psychological investment in the new situation and in new social relations.

Like any life crisis, exile is a transitional period in which deprivation and loss may chronically undermine mental health or else create the possibility for growth, depending on how the individual has negotiated early experiences of helplessness, separation, and loss. Some exiles find it difficult or impossible to overcome internal and external obstacles to adjustment and can experience an outbreak of latent pathologies, which often provoke serious psychological disturbances. Others are able to overcome the initial depressive and anxious responses that temporarily compromise the psychic structure to work through the mourning process related to lost loved ones and lost aspects of the self. Their resilience represents a positive use of the crisis of exile for the further development of creative and integrative capacities.

Such was the case with Marie Langer, Juan Carlos Volnovich, and Marcelo and Maren Viñar, all of whom were able to turn exile into an opportunity for growth and enrichment. As if sown by the wind, these activists landed in far-flung places whose distinct cultural and political circumstances presented new terrain on which to elaborate their various versions of a socially committed psychoanalysis.

MARIE LANGER AND MEXICO: 1974–1987

Almost from the start, Mimi was able to resolve the significant issue of economic survival in exile. "Mexico," as she puts it, "proved to be a hospitable
host." Well known among her Mexican colleagues, many of whom had been
trained years earlier by her in the Argentine Psychoanalytic Association
(APA), Mimi was welcomed by the academic and professional communities
alike. "Shortly after my arrival," she tells me, "I became a professor in clinical psychology in the postgraduate program at the National Autonomous
University of Mexico, where I supervised therapists who worked in institutions throughout the city offering low-fee or free treatment. It was very
gratifying, for, in a way, this supervision was a continuation of our work
in the public hospitals in Buenos Aires, where we brought quality mental
health treatment to the working class." Mimi also became an honorary
member of the Mexican Association of Group Psychotherapy and developed a private practice that included refugees from the Southern Cone
and Central America. This work with refugees taught her more about the
psychological responses to state terror and exile. "I had patients from the
sophisticated European cultural centers of Buenos Aires and Montevideo
and others from the indigenous highlands of Guatemala and El Salvador,
which gave me the chance to observe the role culture plays in shaping the
psychic responses to political repression."

   In spite of the relative ease of her professional adaptation, Mimi continued to experience the disconcerting anxieties and depressive affect typical of
other exiles whom she knew and even treated. At times she obsessed about
her departure from Argentina. Had she left too soon? Could she have withstood torture had she been abducted by the Triple A? Would she have been
killed had she stayed? It was hard to escape the doubts and the deep sadness
of feeling adrift, cut off from her friends and the movement in Argentina.
"I came to understand years later," she says, "that the exile community
was composed of two groups: first, those of us who had great difficulty
in adjusting to the loss of our political project. We became compulsively
involved in the work of denouncing the dictatorship. It wasn't only that
the right wing had won that was difficult for us but the fact of our defeat
that we found so hard to accept." The second group in exile did not remain
politically involved but instead assumed an extremely conservative lifestyle,
working hard, sending their children to the best private schools, and buying
homes and cars that demonstrated their material success. "They, too, found
it difficult to accept defeat at the hands of the military, but their reaction
was to reject their radical politics and return to the conservative ways of
their childhoods. We all need our self-esteem, and these people could feel
good about themselves through an adaptation to values acquired early on
in their conservative upbringing and internalized as superego morality and
expectations. For me, this was impossible. My self-esteem was related to

my ego ideal, which I felt I had betrayed by abandoning the struggle and my *compañeros* in Argentina."

Thus Mimi's ability to adapt to exile depended on the possibility of maintaining continuity with the politics she had been forced to leave behind. Resilient, she soon found a place for herself in the Argentine solidarity movement, where she and other mental health professionals carved out an important activist space on behalf of the survivors of state terror. By 1974, among the thousands of Argentine compatriots already in Mexico, a network of individuals was organizing resources to respond to the needs of refugees who continued to arrive. They arranged for housing, clothes, work, and even psychological assistance, which was secured from Argentine analysts and their Mexican colleagues in the Círculo Psicoanalítico Mexicano. In January 1976, a group of these activists met in Mimi's home to create an organization that would formalize their work. Soon they inaugurated the Committee in Solidarity with the Argentine People (COSPA) and rented an old, Spanish-style, two-story house in the heart of Mexico City to provide a center, called Casa Roma, for their activities.

COSPA had a variety of functions, ranging from practical and psychological help for Argentines just beginning their lives in exile to crisis intervention for those already established who experienced a sudden disruption in their adaptation to their new homeland. Committees of exiles gathered information about the Argentine military government in order to formally document and publicize its gross human rights violations in a variety of international professional meetings and political conferences. From its inception, COSPA sponsored weekly *peñas*, festive evenings featuring music, dancing, typical Argentine food, and often reports and discussions of current developments in Argentina. As one Mexican journalist described it, "The *empanadas* [typical Argentine meat pies] are delicious, the conversation better. [But] behind the joyfulness, the humor, the enormous solidarity, now and then one can feel the tragedy, so intense at times it is almost palpable. It happens, for example, when the person introducing the musical groups suddenly mentions, as if in passing, the death of a *compañero* in Argentina, the exile of another, the torture of yet another" (*El Día*, 1997).

Shortly after COSPA was founded, Mimi and her colleagues organized its mental health commission, the Argentine Mental Health Workers in Mexico, in order to develop a program of therapeutic assistance to adults and children from the Southern Cone. Through COSPA's Secretary of Social Assistance, their efforts were coordinated with the volunteer labor donated by family physicians, a variety of medical specialists, and sympathetic staff in Mexico City's hospitals and medical laboratories. "Because COSPA was located in a spacious house, it could serve as a temporary residence for recent arrivals or expectant mothers about to give birth. On occasion, it became an improvised residential clinic for refugees who arrived in acute states of psychological crisis or for people already living in Mexico

City who required therapeutic interventions on learning of disappearances, tortures, or deaths of loved ones still in Argentina." The mental health workers also supervised and offered treatment when needed at COSPA's preschool, where more than 100 children from different Latin American countries were cared for while their parents worked.

Exile meant other possibilities as well. In Mexico Mimi reestablished old friendships with European colleagues and made new friends with feminists from Europe, the United States, and Latin America. Young activists were drawn to her, impressed by her vitality and rare blend of wisdom and openness to new ideas. Gratifying as these relationships were, Mimi, now widowed for almost a decade, lamented the lack of people her own age able to remain involved in an activist life project and the absence of an intimate sexual relationship with a man, which she related to the social taboos against sexuality in older women. But she derived much pleasure from her family, who remained a close-knit clan. She saw her two daughters and their families often since they, too, lived in Mexico City. Her sons frequently brought their families from Buenos Aires to visit. As always, they shared Mimi with the other passions of her life. Indeed, by the late 1970s Mimi's world included growing numbers of refugees from repressive military dictatorships in Guatemala, El Salvador, and Nicaragua who were flowing into Mexico seeking asylum. Gradually the Argentine Mental Health Workers in Mexico extended solidarity activities and therapeutic assistance to these Central American exiles. In the autumn of 1978, Mimi and her colleagues had their first direct contact with the Sandinista revolutionaries, who were fighting the repressive U.S.-supported Somoza dynasty that had ruled the tiny Central American nation of Nicaragua for half a century. A group of 60 Sandinistas had been granted asylum in Mexico for several months before they returned to the struggle in their country, and many were suffering the cumulative psychological consequences of growing up in a dictatorship and fighting in the revolution to oust it from power. The young men and women had survived horrific abuse at the hands of Somoza's National Guard and were experiencing many symptoms, including alcohol abuse, depression, insomnia, and acute anxiety. The Argentine Mental Health Workers in Mexico had been contacted by an exiled Nicaraguan physician in the hope that they could help.

"We were uncertain about how they would relate to us," recalls Mimi, "so we decided to first meet with the entire group of them in the daycare center of COSPA. When we arrived, there they were, most of them so young, patiently waiting, chatting among themselves. One boy was strumming a guitar, and others were singing along. We realized that we would have to find a way to help them feel at ease and trust us, so one Argentine *compañera* began to tell of her own experience of jail and torture. Others of us spoke as well, each explaining our firsthand knowledge of political repression and why we were here in exile. Gradually the Nicaraguans, who had no familiarity with psychotherapy, warmed to the idea of being able to speak with a professional who might help them understand their emotional turmoil."[3] In the days and weeks that followed, a variety of therapeutic interventions, including private and group sessions, helped alleviate some of the Nicaraguans' symptoms, many of which were related to the fact that they had had no possibility of mourning the loss of relatives and *compañeros* who had disappeared or been killed by the National Guard. Mimi and her colleagues deepened their understanding of what she would call "frozen grief" in the context of political struggle. Although she could not know it at the time, this experience was to be but the first in an enduring connection to the Sandinista Revolution.

In later years, Mimi believed she had been fortunate that her political activism had forced her to leave Argentina before the military coup occurred "because it saved me from the experience of having to endure the dictatorship in silence, humiliation, impotence." She concluded, in fact, that those who stayed—who experienced the tribulations of internal exile—had much more courage than those who left and who had been able to benefit in many ways. In this regard, when democracy returned to Argentina in 1983, Mimi chose to remain in Mexico because she was deeply involved in the exciting project of helping the Sandinista Revolution build Nicaragua's first national system of mental health care. She was thrilled to be active as a politically committed psychoanalyst in this new context, where her focus shifted from being part of an oppositional movement to working in concert with a government whose values and goals paralleled her own.

Adaptation to exile in Mexico was facilitated for Mimi and other political refugees from the Southern Cone by the country's proximity to Latin American political struggles and its familiar language and history. But, for refugees from Argentina, Chile, and Uruguay whose flight took them to faraway continents and unfamiliar cultures, exile was experienced as a global rupture with the past and a demand to create not only a new life but a new self. They would have to begin again, learning to talk, behave, play, and work within a new cultural and social matrix.

THE VIÑARS AND FRANCE: 1976–1990

Early March seemed an appropriate time for Maren and Marcelo Viñar to arrive in Paris, for the city's late winter rains and gray, overcast skies mirrored their gloomy state of mind. Although they had chosen France as their country of exile because French colleagues had been willing to help them find a professional niche outside Uruguay, they had not foreseen the devastating impact of trying to survive in a society whose culture, language, and people they knew nothing about. It took months, indeed years, for them to adapt to exile. During their decade and a half in France, the Viñars elaborated a psychoanalytic conceptualization of exile based on their astute observations of their own experience and their clinical work with adult and child refugees from all over the world. The central issues they had engaged in Uruguay, such as the importance of social as well as individual reparation, formed the basis of the Viñars' significant contributions to the growing literature and international dialogue about the psychological impact of political repression and exile.

"Imprisonment and exile were the two most difficult experiences in my life," Marcelo says solemnly, looking at me over his reading glasses. "There were two especially painful aspects of exile. The first was what I call a narcissistic collapse, like a kind of undoing of the self. And the second was the loss of security, which is related to my origins. I was a child of the middle class, with very protective parents who supported my growth and development. As an adult, I built a successful professional life. I was *somebody*— Dr. so-and-so—who was recognized as a specific individual with a specific status in the social group. The disruption of this 'place in the world,' which I had taken for granted before it was suddenly ripped away from me in my late 30s, was devastating. We have written about how exile in this sense is a violent and decentering rupture, especially for those who have fulfilled a social role highly valued by themselves and their community. One loses the many-sided mirror in which he has created and nurtured his own image, his public persona, his celebrity, if you will. In exile, what he once was no longer exists. No one knows him, no one recognizes him. He finds himself in a new scene from an unfamiliar play with unknown actors. This is a true identity crisis."

An additional painful aspect of exile for the Viñars was economic insecurity. Although they and their children never went hungry, their economic situation during the initial years in France was precarious. "Even though as refugees we were privileged to have a group of colleagues who showed us great solidarity," Marcelo says, "the deep insecurity we felt about our very survival came as a tremendous shock. I know that I am speaking as an intellectual and a professional and that perhaps a worker who has known insecurity from birth on would respond differently. But in my case, exile plummeted me into a situation of helplessness that was extraordinary." Eventually Marcelo obtained a position in a psychiatric clinic that provided a minimal salary. His work with schizophrenics was demanding and difficult, but rewarding. "I always tell a funny story that has much of reality in it," he remarks. "After about a year in the clinic, everyone said I was the best psychiatrist there because my patients got better. Actually, I think they improved because they had a doctor to take care of rather than a doctor who took care of them! They were the nurses and therapists desperately needed by their depressed psychiatrist! This reversal of roles created a very strong link among us. My own psychological precariousness wound up facilitating a good therapeutic relationship among us."

The anguish of the first years was exacerbated by having to learn to speak and read French. Marcelo extrapolates from his own struggles that one's relationship to language is of key significance in the exile experience. His view echoes what has been noted elsewhere about the psychological impact on immigrants who are obliged as adults to learn an entirely new language. The adult must tolerate reexperiencing the initial helplessness of the child struggling to acquire language, which is the bridge to becoming an active participant in the social world. One's place in the world is ordered, after all, through the linguistic system of verbal and visual signifiers. Some adult immigrants learn the new language fairly easily, perhaps as a defensive maneuver to cope with their feelings of impotence and exclusion from social interaction. Others resist learning the new language, which may reflect their guilt for abandoning their parents' tongue.

"Each language has a code of customs, laws, relations," emphasizes Marcelo, "and to speak in a language implies knowledge of more than words—other things as well about the culture that produces it. One might be able to understand the dictionary and at the same time not know much at all. Alienation comes from not being able to interpret the meaning of words but, even more important, the meaning of gestures, references, and social relations implicit in and accompanying them. It is an unforgettable experience. Very soon after we arrived in Paris, Maren and I wrote about being strangers in a strange land. The sensation of being lost is horrible. Once you've been a stranger, a foreigner, you always carry this somewhere inside. It never goes away. One is irreversibly a stranger. One never returns to the nest, to one's home, one's homeland, nor to the illusion of completeness. That is lost forever. What remains is a rupture between the individual and his links, and there is always, forever, something lacking." When, after living in France for almost a year, Marcelo began to treat his first patient—an Argentine—they were able to conduct the analysis in Spanish. This experience represented for him the return to a state of thinking. "It gave me immense pleasure and joy to once again use my full mental capacities."

Language can become a wedge between parent and child in the exile family. The fact that children acquire the new language more easily than their parents often leads to mutual bad feelings. Marcelo recalls how his younger son would feel ashamed of him when he spoke French and would pull at his pants leg and beg him not to speak. Sometimes his children spoke French rapidly together so he and Maren could not understand them, or they spoke French between themselves and Spanish to their parents, as if to establish an authority relation that countermanded the customary one between the generations. The jealousy and envy of the older generation often turn into an accusatory and condemning attitude toward the children, whose relative ease in absorbing the codes of the host culture makes them seem like traitors to their parents' ideals. Marcelo points out that "there is often lots of conflict between parents and their adolescent kids.

With respect to the theme of political repression, for example, I remember growing up in my small Uruguayan town and being taught about the Holocaust and the oppression of Jews. But we kids would walk the streets and there was no anti-Semitism, no one pursuing the Jews. I think this discourse about the Jewish people, persecuted and forced to be immigrants, functioned in the children to secure either submission to our parents' discourse or rebellion and family misunderstandings. Now it was my turn to be a foreigner, a minority, and to demand that my children recognize and hold alive the memory of why we were exiles. I realized later that I wanted them to sustain in their minds an identification with my generation's values and struggles, with the revolutionaries who had been repressed. And they, poor things, saw nothing of this in Paris and sought only successful adaptation to their new world. Their parents' nostalgia could only create a powerful familial breach."

The family in general, the Viñars have argued, suffers many pressures in exile and is forced to play a contradictory role. On the one hand, it provides the context in which its members work through the mourning process, in which the threatened and vulnerable identity of each can be experienced as having survived the crisis. On the other, it is the stage on which is dramatically enacted all the aggression unable to be expressed elsewhere. "The family," they have written, "bears the mark of the social catastrophe. In place of the mutual support that would facilitate cohesion, miscommunication and isolation are often paradoxically unleashed among its members, dissolving the illusion that they might recover from the magnitude of...the loss" (Viñar and Viñar, 1993, p. 60).

Like elsewhere Latin Americans congregated in exile, Paris had a solidarity movement in which the Uruguayans participated. The movement generated important activities, including the exposé and denunciation of the military dictatorships across the Atlantic. As in Mexico, it provided a much-needed source of material and psychological support for Latin Americans so far from home. At times it could function as a kind of microsociety, however, where refugees shielded themselves from the demands of adaptation to their new society and culture. Some never learned more than a few words of French and refused to develop friendships with French citizens. They complained about the nation that had given them safe harbor, as if it, rather than conditions at home, was the cause of their geographic and social dislocation. Sometimes their negativism seemed justified by the ambivalent or hostile attitudes of the French, who were offended by the invasion of their politically exiled guests. Overall, though, the solidarity movement was a great source of comfort, even for those like Marcelo and Maren, who eventually succeeded in situating themselves within French culture and social relations.

Maren remembers that through the solidarity movement she joined a women's group whose members were from many Latin American countries.

The group provided much-needed emotional and practical support. "When I got sick, or my kids got sick, what could I do? My *compañeras* came; they helped me. And I helped them. We depended on one another. The strong bond of unity we built made me think a lot about how gender influences one's experience of exile. Women who remained housewives and stayed home to care for their children had something concrete to devote their energies to, something they were building for the future. We women had to deal with the schools and the parents of other children so we had a long-range project through raising the children. The men often had no equivalent psychological investment."

But in the cosmopolitan European capitals, exile also provided new opportunities for women and, in so doing, challenged traditional gender roles among the Latin American refugees. Many women who had not been involved politically in their own countries joined their activist sisters in the solidarity movements. And women now had access to work possibilities like the men, sometimes at higher wages than their partners. Maren treated many couples who experienced conflicts when the husband's sense of masculinity was undermined by his wife's superior work situation or wages. Many middle-class couples found themselves for the first time without the cheap female domestic labor so plentiful in underdeveloped Latin America, and they were forced to divide the work in the home, traditionally done by women, between husband and wife. In this regard, Marcelo recalls the pleasurable aspects of this period in Paris, when increased domestic responsibilities were tiring but emotionally fulfilling. "Evening meals, for example," he recounts nostalgically, "required the collective participation of all of us— Maren and me and the two kids. That meant that every evening we'd spend about two hours all together working, eating, and talking." Downward mobility thus provided the Viñars with a daily ritual fostering a familial intimacy not achieved in their more privileged life before or after exile.

In the end, both Maren and Marcelo recognized that each was able to use the experience of exile to grow personally, professionally, and politically. They matured intellectually through their connection to French psychoanalysis, whose unique perspectives on psychic life and psychopathology, permeated by radical political critiques of bourgeois social structures, added provocative dimensions to their writings and public presentations on the political and psychological meanings of state terror and exile. But when the military governments in the Southern Cone gave way to popular pressures for a return to democratic rule, like other exiles, the Viñars were faced with the difficult decision of whether to return to their country. In spite of the expanded horizons exile had come to represent for them, ultimately they opted to return to Uruguay.

The Viñars have written widely about the significance of returning from exile, of going home again. "It's complicated," muses Maren. "In the final analysis, we developed many connections in France and strong ties to the

French people. I also had many women friends there. To return means that you break this link; you destroy the world you've constructed. I still don't know to this day," she chuckles, "how we could do it. Sometimes I feel more intensely the rupture entailed in coming back than the original rupture of exile. The exile was obligatory, this return chosen." Marcelo listens pensively and then adds, "In reality, it's not a return. It's another departure." Maren agrees. "Yes," she says, "it's a going back to begin again. One goes back to Uruguay. But Uruguay is another country. Those who stayed are no longer those you left, and you are no longer who you were when you went away. In the final analysis, one does not go back; one actually goes away again."

JUAN CARLOS VOLNOVICH AND CUBA: 1976–1984

Juan Carlos could not know when he set foot on Cuban soil in December 1976 that he, too, would later face the choice of remaining there or returning to Buenos Aires and leaving behind the life that he would create during his eight years of exile in Caribbean socialism. At the moment of his arrival in Havana, he knew only that he felt disoriented. What was he going to do? How would he practice his profession? How would they survive? As they left the airport, one of his brother-in-law's Cuban colleagues who had come to welcome them asked what work Juan Carlos wanted to do while living in Cuba. He responded that he was a psychoanalyst and that he was worried about having to learn a new skill at his age. "I know I can't practice psychoanalysis in Cuba," Juan Carlos explained, indicating that since the early days of the revolution, when most psychoanalysts had left the country, Soviet behaviorism had been the prevailing orientation within Cuban psychology. But his Cuban acquaintance exclaimed enthusiastically and, as it turned out, quite prophetically, "Look, man, you can do anything you want here in Cuba."

And so it was. Juan Carlos and Silvia were informed that they could work within the Cuban health system where and how they chose. They surmised that their good fortune was due to the fact that Silvia's borther and sister-in-law, Leonardo and Beatriz had lived and worked in Cuba since 1960 and that they themselves had spent previous summers working in health and educational projects on the island. "This was truly a weighty decision," Juan Carlos remembers, with the usual twinkle in his eye. "Given the hostility to Cuba orchestrated by the United States and ruling elites in Latin America, we wondered what would happen to our chances of returning to Argentina someday if we lived our exile in Havana rather than in Geneva, where I'd also been offered work. The conflict was resolved in a funny way. We talked together about how if we, who considered ourselves Marxists but had failed to bring about revolutionary changes in our own country, could not adapt to socialism in a Latin American country that had made the revolution, then to hell with Geneva: We should just go to Las Vegas and never again mention Marxism! Well, we decided to stay in Cuba, to test our principles and coherence. I felt I was putting all of my pride, my integrity, on the line."

The Volnoviches took up the test of living in socialism at a propitious moment. By the mid-1970s, the quality of life for the average Cuban had improved dramatically from what it had been under the U.S.-supported dictator Fulgencio Batista. In an era of chronic unemployment through-out the rest of Latin America, the Cuban Revolution's economic develop-ment strategy provided full employment with a host of workers' benefits. Its internationally acclaimed social programs, including universal free educa-tion from kindergarten through university, free medical care, and free child care, had raised Cubans' standard of living. Even while bureaucratic cen-tralism produced inefficiencies and waste, the government's emphasis on investment in capital goods and technology had achieved long-term devel-opment goals that eluded Latin America's market-driven nations. Periodic shortages of basic necessities were dealt with through a rationing system, which was an intentional strategy to distribute available goods to all citi-zens and to avoid the price inflation that ravaged the poor in the rest of the countries of Latin America. Even so, when shortages did occur—to a good extent the intended result of the U.S. embargo of Cuba—it often meant waiting in long lines for food and other basic commodities. Daily life was also affected by the deterioration of Havana's infrastructure, with its periodic interruptions of electric, water, and gas services. At the same time, Cubans enjoyed increased access to culture through the government's encouragement and financial support of production and distribution of the arts. Cuban cinema, literature, music, and visual arts developed innovative form and subject matter that entertained international as well as Cuban audiences. The Volnoviches shared in the benefits and the difficulties of life in socialism during their years in Cuba, which brought them and their children a sense of accomplishment and pleasure in ways that were differ-ent from what they had known in cosmopolitan Buenos Aires.

"I know it's hard to believe now," Juan Carlos says, "especially given the growing difficulties in Cuba since the late 1980s with the fall of the Soviet Union and the intensification of the U.S. embargo, but life was easy on the island. Even then, people outside Cuba had the impression that we were suffering, and our friends in exile elsewhere would write, pitying us for the hard life they presumed we led. Ironically, lots of things were actu-ally better than ever for us. For example, we'd been accustomed to living in Argentine consumer culture, with our kids always demanding, 'Buy me this, buy that, buy that.' In Cuba, from the beginning, they must have intu-ited there was a difference. There were few commodities, and they simply stopped thinking about them. Instead, their attention was directed to other things. They both got very involved at school and made many new friends. Yamila enthusiastically studied art, and Roman became a champion swimmer. As they got older, they, like their Cuban *compañeritos*, learned about and felt passionately identified with struggles for social justice throughout the world. This was truly wonderful for Silvia and me, to see our kids growing up in an environment that encouraged them to care about the same things that we did. It provided us with an intergenerational continuity that was extremely gratifying."

Living in Cuba meant adjusting to the struggles being waged against traditional sexist culture and on behalf of gender equality. In 1976, the Cuban constitution had included a new Family Code legalizing a radical reordering of traditional male privilege in all domains of life, including equal pay for comparable work, access of women to traditionally male careers, reproductive rights, and paternal responsibility for all children, including those previously considered illegitimate. "Although equality between men and women was clearly not yet a reality, I did observe how in one generation the revolution represented a great change for women," Juan Carlos recalls. "There were significant differences between mothers and daughters in that regard. For example, an illiterate peasant woman might have a daughter who was the best student in her class or a youth leader who was honored by appearing alongside Fidel on television. There were many palpable differences like that."

However, the Family Code's most revolutionary article stipulated that domestic labor and child rearing were the equal responsibility of women and men whether or not women worked outside the home for wages. This article challenged the customary sexual division of labor in its most intimate domain and sparked dramatic conflicts among many Cuban couples as they struggled, negotiated, and resisted the metamorphosis it represented. Within this political context, Juan Carlos and Silvia designed a family life radically different from the one they had led in Buenos Aires. "Silvia and I get into arguments about that aspect of exile," Juan Carlos says. "She claims I was very happy, but I say she doesn't understand the effort it represented to me. I felt much more pressure to do my part to make a good home life. From the time I was two years old, we'd had two domestic workers at home, and later either Silvia or a housekeeper would take care of the housework. I didn't know what it meant to have to shop, cook, wash dishes, make beds, wash and iron clothes. This may sound strange, but it was traumatic for me!"

Juan Carlos continues, "In Cuba, we both worked as psychoanalysts in hospitals. Silvia held a responsible post at Havana's maternity hospital, where she specialized in the psychological aspects of pregnancy and childbirth. She became a highly recognized professional, probably more than I, which was the reverse of our experience in Buenos Aires. Nonetheless, we were both on tight schedules, obliged to arrive at work punctually. Like factory workers, professionals had to clock in, and if you acquired a certain number of tardies, it would be announced in hospital meetings, and you'd feel humiliated. So, in the mornings I'd wake up, take a quick shower, and rush to get to work on time. And I'd get home earlier than Silvia, who left work later and picked up the children on the way home. I'd walk in at 4 o'clock in the afternoon, and the house was exactly the same as I'd left it in the morning, exactly! I realized it had never been that way before. I'd leave the house to study or work, and when I returned, everything would be organized: the house clean, the meal ready, the clothes washed and ironed. For me, it was the most natural thing in the world. In Cuba I realized with a thud what feminists mean by 'the invisible labor of women.' I also came to understand what they mean when they say, 'The personal is political.'"

So it was that Juan Carlos developed new skills, including housework, shopping, and cooking. When Silvia and the children came home in the afternoon, the house was clean, dinner was on the table, and they all sat down for three hours of eating, chatting, reading, and studying together. "In spite of the fact that our apartment was small and the furnishings quite simple, we'd decorated it with care, and it had a real artisan feel to it," Juan Carlos says. "Silvia, Yamila, and Roman all say that this period of integrated family life represents the happiest years they can remember. And I felt proud that I was up to the task of doing my share to create this experience for us."

Juan Carlos was also "up to the task" of carving out a psychoanalytic practice within the Cuban health system. He chose to work at Havana's General Pediatric Hospital under a psychiatrist who had been trained psychoanalytically in Chicago before returning to his native land in the 1960s. "I hadn't forgotten my visit with Dr. José Perez Villar during a prior trip to Cuba. I can still see it in my mind's eye: the two of us sitting and talking together in his office, while I was transfixed by the three enlarged photographs hanging behind him on the wall. The first photo featured the founder of the Cuban Communist Party; the second, Che Guevara; and the third, Sigmund Freud! The way the photographs were arranged, Che and Freud were staring at each other! I thought, 'If Freud only knew that here in revolutionary Cuba he'd be hanging on a wall exchanging a long meaningful look with Che!'"

In the department of child psychiatry, Juan Carlos began to treat adults as well as children. His Cuban colleagues, who understood nothing of psychoanalysis, and his patients as well, who had never even heard the term, were bemused by a doctor who wanted to see his patients four times a week. Juan Carlos's esteem rose in the eyes of his Cuban colleagues, however, when successful interventions with several patients who happened to be well-known physicians resulted in "cures" of psychosomatic and hysterical symptoms. Indeed, he acquired a reputation for being somewhat of a magician! Soon he was treating adults and children who came to the hospital from the neighboring communities, as well as prominent individuals in the arts. "Because I gained prestige as an analyst among writers, artists, and musicians, Silvia used to joke that my salary should be paid by the Ministry of Culture rather than the Ministry of Health!"

Like the Viñars in France and Mimi Langer in Mexico, Juan Carlos had the opportunity to treat Latin American exiles and to develop projects that represented continuity with his psychoanalytic activism in Argentina. He treated Argentine, Chilean, and Uruguayan children whose parents had been disappeared or killed by the military and who had been sent to Cuba for safekeeping. In 1978, 400 of these "war orphans," children of Argentine disappeared, imprisoned, or murdered mothers and fathers, ranging in age from infancy through adolescence, were brought to Cuba. A residential center occupying two enormous old mansions in Havana became the new home of those children who had no relatives residing in Cuba. During the following five years, as many as 40 or 50 children at a time lived at the center with their Cuban and Argentine caregivers.

Juan Carlos supervised the work of the staff responsible for taking care of the children, including the weekly meetings of all personnel, from caregivers to janitors; these meetings dealt with the psychological and organizational aspects of the functioning of the center. The goal was to provide the children with a caring home environment—in Winnicott's terms, a holding environment—and to integrate them into Cuban society. One of the requirements was that the staff be divided equally between females and males so that the children would bond with both sexes. "It was rather like a kibbutz," recalls Juan Carlos. "We organized the program so that the very small children would be cared for by the same one or two adults, and the older ones by the adolescents in the community, much like an extended family. We were creating the model as we went along, and this pattern emerged spontaneously. The kids attended Cuban schools, and when they'd return in the afternoons, they would participate in other activities, including discussions about Argentina so they wouldn't lose their connection to their roots."

Juan Carlos was the project's chief therapist. He observed the children at play to determine which of them needed psychotherapeutic attention and then treated them at the hospital. Some of the children suffered from serious symptoms, and at times Juan Carlos had to begin treatment with children whose background—mother's and father's history, birth, infancy, traumatic event, and so on—he knew nothing about. He treated children who urinated and defecated all over themselves, who suffered panic attacks, who had psychosomatic conditions he had never before seen. Some were completely mute, and others stared into space, unresponsive to their environment. At times he was uncertain of appropriate diagnoses, and he often wondered whether he was observing symptoms of trauma or schizophrenia.

"It was very difficult to treat them, but the amazing thing was they improved very rapidly. Each one reminded me of a little dying plant that in response to sun and water begins to thrive. I was curious as to why they made such good progress, and I wrote to colleagues, including Maren Viñar, who were also treating children in exile with less positive results. I thought a good deal about how the social context interacts with individual psychology to determine the prognosis of mental health. I developed the hypothesis that an important factor was the different experience the children had in Cuba as opposed to France or other bourgeois environments. For example, the kids in other countries like France often lived with grandparents who were depressed, mourning the deaths of their children and thus unavailable emotionally to their grandchildren. In addition, the kids would learn the host country's language easily and would probably feel reluctant to bring their friends home, embarrassed by their grandparents, who spoke with accents and were fearful lest their political history and the reason for their exile be exposed. More likely than not, they would be ashamed of their parents' political activism because in Europe, Latin American exiles were often demeaned and rejected, stereotyped as guerrillas, who were mistakenly equated with terrorists. Also, many children were being raised by reactionary grandparents who told them that their parents had disappeared or were killed because of their misguided politics, blaming them for their fate instead of the armed forces and warning their grandchildren that the same would happen to them if they became activists."

Juan Carlos believes that the Cuban political environment had a positive effect on the children living there. "In Cuba," he continues, "the exiled children experienced an admiration among the Cubans for the ideals, if not the strategies, of their activist parents. Even more, their parents were considered fallen heroes in the struggle against right-wing authoritarian repression. They were respected. After all, they were like Che, who, let's not forget, was an Argentine. I concluded that this ideological coherence was an important factor in the improvement of the kids in Cuba because the environment encouraged rather than negated the children's positive identification with their lost parents and the struggle for which they had given their lives."

The children's residential program continued until 1983, when, with the return to democratic rule in Argentina, its organizers made the decision to locate the children's biological families for the purpose of reuniting them. Relatives began to come to Cuba to fetch the children, and at times the staff found it painful to relinquish them, especially when it was to grandparents or aunts and uncles who were insensitive or hostile to everything the children and their history represented. "I'll never forget a particularly difficult case," says Juan Carlos. "One child's grandparents who came from Buenos Aires to get him were wealthy industrialists who were extremely right wing. They met with me before seeing the child, and in the course of our chat told me that in the early 1970s their daughter had become involved with a Montonero, who, they were convinced, had filled her innocent head with terrible ideas about social change. These people were very influential and had friends in the military. They told me how after the coup they had decided to reveal the whereabouts of their daughter's *compañero* to their military connections, hoping to rid her of his 'evil' influence. As a result, the military had pursued the daughter along with her *compañero* and assassinated them both, leaving their infant an orphan. It was to these grandparents that we had to give the child we had nurtured for years! In cases like this, we felt terrible because we had come to love these children. They were like our own kids. We worried about the impact of relatives whose psychological ambivalence and ideological hostility toward these young people would likely trouble and confuse them, reversing the progress they'd made in dealing with the traumatic events of their early lives."

The work Juan Carlos did over the years in this unique children's project gave him extensive firsthand experience with the psychological effects of political repression and exile, which he would utilize when he reestablished his practice in Buenos Aires.

When the Argentine military relinquished the government to civilian rule in 1983, the Volnoviches faced the possibility of going home. For almost a year and a half, they struggled with their conflicting feelings about returning to Argentina. "Now, with the military back in the barracks and a democratically elected president in power, how could we not return to our culture, our home?" Juan Carlos says. "We had been very happy in Cuba, although I, more than Silvia, missed Buenos Aires and my professional life there. We anguished about it, in terrible conflict. But finally we decided to return. The key factor had to do with the kids, who were now adolescents and actively resisting the idea of leaving their life and their friends in Cuba. We concluded that we had to leave while we still had the power to decide for them because we couldn't bear the idea of a future in which we would live apart from them in different countries."

Finally, in December 1984, the Volnoviches returned to Buenos Aires. There, like the Viñars in Montevideo, they discovered that the return was more painful than the departure had been and that their fantasies of the future had been based on frozen memories of the past. In fact, what they had nostalgically clung to during their years of exile no longer existed. Everything was different: Buenos Aires, the struggle, their friends who had survived, the hole left by those who had been killed or were still in exile, and even they themselves. Only by coming to grips with this reality and mourning the multiple losses it implied—including the life they had left in Cuba—were they able to create a new one of meaning and relevance for them and their children.

MARIE LANGER AND NICARAGUA: JUNE 1984

More than a week had gone by since our arrival in Nicaragua, and I was witnessing the invigorating effects on Mimi of her participation in the creation of a national mental health program within the context of revolution. Typical of her previous trips here, our days and nights had been filled with demanding work, punctuated by lengthy midday meals and late evening dinners with colleagues and friends from all over the world. Their energetic discussions ranged from the difficulties of realizing the long-range goals of their various projects to the Sandinistas' ability to survive under the ongoing U.S. economic and military assault. Although they were anxious about the future of Nicaragua, none could know at this moment that the Sandinista experiment would collapse within just six years, undermined by the successful U.S. strategy to overturn this reformist challenge to its neoliberal hegemony in the region.

"You can see why I love it here," Mimi was saying to me as we gently swayed in our wooden rockers in the shaded central patio of the Internationalist House, where we were staying during our time in the provincial city of León. We were taking a late afternoon break, trying to escape the stifling summer heat. Outside, the sun relentlessly baked the yellow-hued stone buildings and streets of colonial León, where the Internationalist Team had been working for the past week. As we chatted amid the verdant and lush plants that overran the colorfully tiled patio, we could see the kitchen and dining area, where the two cooks were preparing the evening meal for the dozens of volunteers—agronomists, physicians, social workers, artists, engineers, filmmakers—who had come from all over the world to assist the Sandinista Revolution. These *internacionalistas* lived in the maze of rooms lining the enormous square patio. Each one contained a bed, a small bookcase, a portable radio, and boldly colored political posters. The modest accommodations of the Internationalist House were more than compensated for by the liveliness of the inhabitants, all of whom seemed delighted to be participating in the construction of a new society. Mimi looked quite content as she described what being in Nicaragua meant to her.

"You know," she reminded me, "it's been a year now since a democratic government replaced the military dictatorship in Argentina, and I could go back if I wanted to. Sometimes I miss my life there—family, friends, the special excitement of Buenos Aires. But I could never leave this work. It's the most important thing I could be doing, the most wonderful challenge of my life." She paused to sip her drink. I waited, rocking slightly in order to feel the air moving around me and thinking about how happy Mimi seemed. Then she confided, "I realized on my second trip to Nicaragua what the experience is for me. I realized that here I am not old nor young... I am atemporal...and I live it as if the Spanish Republic, the old Republic, had won, and I am collaborating in the reconstruction. It is...a continuity... and finally, and suddenly, I am there."

It was easy to see why Mimi felt this way. Nicaragua was fairly exploding with the energy of people engaged in projects they believed would develop the country and bring pleasure and productivity to their lives. It was a particularly interesting time in the brief history of the revolution, for the country had adopted a new electoral law modeled on key components of the French, Italian, Austrian, and Swedish electoral systems, and its many political parties were engaged in a spirited campaign in anticipation of the elections in early November.[4] The optimism of the people was palpable. Everyone seemed on the move, their busy days filled with long hours of work, followed by political meetings of unions, the women's and youth movements, the revolutionary neighborhood committees and the "popular" church organizations.[5] "*Compañero*" was the familiar greeting used by everyone identified with the revolution, indicating closeness and mutual respect for all who shared the values and goals of the difficult and exhilarating political process.

In truth, there was much to be done. When the Sandinistas ousted the repressive Somoza dictatorship on July 19, 1979, they inherited a country whose class and ethnic relations bore the weight of five centuries of colonialism and neocolonialism. In the 50 years leading up to the Revolution, Nicaragua had been characterized by extreme economic inequities, brutal political repression, and subservience to U.S. geopolitical interests. The majority of its nearly three million inhabitants lived in abject poverty, with a per capita annual income of $897 and an illiteracy rate that reached 70 percent in some areas. Those conditions had produced a mass-based revolutionary movement whose goal was to overturn the structural inequalities in Nicaraguan society. When the revolution triumphed, about 1.5 percent of the population had been killed, with an additional 110,000 disabled and almost 50,000 children orphaned. Crops had been ruined; and schools, hospitals, medical centers, and houses had been damaged or entirely destroyed. In response to these conditions, the Sandinistas designed a strategy to reconstruct the country within the context of their Marxist conceptualization of the structural causes of underdevelopment. The model they chose was based on the principles of political pluralism, a mixed economy, and a nonaligned foreign policy.[6]

Although the Sandinistas represented the largest constituency in the country, minority parties to the left and right battled over their different points of view in the National Assembly, each pressuring the government to go faster or slower in the implementation of reforms. The private sector resented the new taxes that had been imposed by the Sandinistas to pay for the many social programs aimed at improving the health, education, work, and living conditions of the Nicaraguan people. The achievements were notable. By 1984, illiteracy had been reduced from 70 to 13 percent. Women were taking part actively in political affairs, and in 1983 the high priority given to health won Nicaragua the World Health Organization's praise for the greatest achievement in health care by a third-world country.

Mimi was continually incensed by U.S. policy toward Nicaragua. "That cold warrior Reagan you have in the White House," she would say indignantly, "just can't bear it when a tiny country whose fate has been determined by the 'monster to the north' since the mid-19th century finally says 'enough'—*basta*! *We* determine what goes on in our country!" Indeed, in spite of the political democracy and economic reformism instituted by the Sandinistas, the United States had declared Nicaragua to be a communist threat in the Western Hemisphere. In order to avoid out-and-out invasion by U.S. forces, which the Pentagon believed would be unpopular with U.S. citizens, Reagan implemented an alternative strategy known as Low Intensity Conflict (LIC).[7] LIC was a combined psychological, economic, and military assault used against governments considered to be a threat to U.S. interests. In echoes of the U.S. strategy to undermine the Allende government in Chile, Reagan sabotaged the Nicaraguan economy with an embargo that made traditionally imported goods scarce in the hope that the erosion of the Nicaraguan people's standard of living would alienate them from their government. The United States also organized and armed the Contras, Nicaraguan mercenaries led by the ex–National Guard who were attacking and destroying newly built rural schools, clinics, and agricultural cooperatives. The Contras killed and wounded not only soldiers but also hundreds of civilians, Nicaraguans and foreigners alike, in the process. The tortured and butchered bodies were purposely paraded in order to psychologically terrorize those who survived.[8]

Hardly anyone escaped the emotional turmoil produced by the country's volatile conditions. Alongside the obvious exhilaration of many Nicaraguans actively involved in the revolution's many social projects, there was also tension and conflict. In fact, when the revolution triumphed, it inherited the psychological as well as the political and economic contradictions of a country ruled for more than half a century by dictatorship. Thousands of adults and children suffered the traumatic sequelae of having lived under the terror and repression of Somoza's fearsome National Guard. And many were severely depressed in response to multiple losses of loved ones sustained during the revolutionary struggle. Symptoms associated with trauma were commonplace, including listlessness, emotional withdrawal, anxiety, intellectual impairment, paranoia, and damaged self-esteem.

After the triumph, some of the more transient disorders diminished, especially among activists whose participation in revolutionary reconstruction projects offered a form of psychological reparation because they were achieving the goals of those who had died. But the revolution also exacerbated psychological problems because of the profound alteration it was stimulating in the traditional hierarchical relations of class, gender, and the generations. For example, as Mimi had pointed out to me numerous times, "the Sandinista commitment to the struggle for women's equality is noteworthy, and feminists in North America and Europe are right to admire it. But we must remember that while change creates benefits, it stimulates fears and anxieties as well. By challenging traditional male dominance in Nicaraguan culture, the Sandinista platform adds stress to the most intimate emotional relationships of the men and women whose collaboration with one another is needed in the difficult task of developing their country."

However, another characteristic of the Sandinista Revolution was its recognition of the importance of people's psychological health, and it set about to develop a national system of mental health care for all Nicaraguans. At the time of the triumph only one psychiatric hospital, one medical school, 12 psychiatrists, 30 to 40 psychologists, and one electroencephalograph machine were in the entire country. The Sandinistas immediately initiated the construction of a number of health facilities and programs to train a new generation of mental health professionals, social workers, nurses, and educational psychologists. The Ministry of Health (MINSA) endorsed a strategy of preventive care, which became available through a network of hospitals, community clinics, the newly established Centers for Psychosocial Attention, and the Sandinista mass organizations, such as the women's movement, the peasant unions and the neighborhood committees. Putting psychology at the core of the revolutionary state's health policy was a strategy that Mimi and her colleagues heartily endorsed. According to MINSA, mental health is the product of a dialectical relationship among the biological, psychological, and social aspects of life, and psychology should therefore be a part of all the health services and should be taught as an aspect of all specialized training. This perspective was the theoretical basis for the Internationalist Team's collaboration in Nicaragua.

"We began our work," Mimi had explained to me, "when the dean of the León Medical School attended a conference in Mexico, where he heard us speak about our work in Argentina during the late sixties and early seventies and requested that we come to León to train and supervise physicians, psychiatrists, and students at the medical school. We agreed, but since none of us could move to Nicaragua because of work and family responsibilities in Mexico, we devised this team effort that permits us to come in twos and threes for 10 days each month. All 12 of us meet every Monday evening in Mexico to provide continuity in our work. We started in 1981 and developed projects at the psychiatric hospital and children's hospital in Managua and the university hospital in León. But since then we have also worked directly with MINSA and are involved in all kinds of mental health projects." The Nicaraguan work was being financed partially by the Pan American Health Organization, and in addition Mimi raised funds through annual trips to Europe, where she reported on the Internationalist Team to enthusiastic audiences of progressive psychoanalysts willing to donate money to a project they believed had great social value.

The complex and contradictory process of reconstructing a society under conditions of extreme poverty was challenging Mimi and her colleagues to reassess their political and psychoanalytic posture, which had been devised years earlier under different circumstances. Now they were absorbed in the thorny practical problem of how to adapt psychoanalysis to the conditions and urgent needs of a tiny, poor Central American country undergoing radical social transformation, with few resources and many competing priorities. As Mimi put it, "Now we ask, 'How can one be useful to Nicaragua with certain psychoanalytic concepts?'"[9] As I saw during our several weeks' stay in Nicaragua, Mimi and her colleagues in the Internationalist Team were interested in elaborating central concepts in psychoanalytic theory and technique that would provide the basis for training and treatment within the specific culture of Nicaragua, the limited economic conditions of underdevelopment, and the financial constraints of the revolutionary government. I had observed her in a variety of settings during the previous week in Managua as she taught classes to psychiatric residents, social workers, psychologists, and nurses. She was especially gifted as a teacher, one who could make the fascinating—but often fantastic sounding—fundamentals of psychoanalytic thought accessible to students who were introduced to them for the first time. She told me during our stay in Nicaragua that the team was drawing up a list of the basic psychoanalytic concepts they believed to be essential to an understanding of how the mind works. These concepts provided the foundation of the psychoanalytic training of the Nicaraguans, who had to develop therapeutic modes feasible in their country, such as brief individual, group, and family treatment. "We call them our 10 commandments," she joked, and added that she planned to write an article called "Psychoanalysis Without the Couch" to elucidate the ideas.[10]

"Ten basic concepts?" I laughingly responded. "Well, just think about what you'd have to include," she told me, now serious. "We teach about the unconscious and how it may be demonstrated through interpretations of slips, dreams, fantasies, and delusions, and how even our ideology is partly unconscious. Then we elaborate how the human mind is characterized by conflict and how even while people fight for change, they are simultaneously frightened of it. We explain how all symptoms have a primary and secondary benefit. It is also important to see that the mind is essentially contradictory and that, as Winnicott shows us, even the mother who loves her baby also hates it. We teach that the history and sexuality of our childhood are important because they are repeated in the present, mostly without our conscious awareness. The same is true for transference, in which we project internal representations of important early figures in our lives onto those in the present, distorting current relationships in the process. We think it is essential to teach about countertransference because every therapist should understand what he or she brings unconsciously to the therapeutic relationship. As we've always argued, no one is neutral. And finally, we believe it is very important, especially in a revolutionary situation like Nicaragua's, to show how every individual has many aspects to his or her personality. Each of us is wonderful, but also a bit mad. Each loving, but also perverse. We are all heroes, but also cowards. And we need to accept rather than deny this so we can learn how to deal with conflict and fear. We also have to understand guilt and how to diminish it because guilt usually paralyzes people and doesn't serve as a good basis for commitment to anyone or anything."

I realized I was observing Mimi and Nacho practice what they preached. I was reminded of how they supervised two cotherapists doing group therapy in a community clinic in Managua the previous week. Both therapists believed that their patients all manifested the sequelae of the collective trauma of Nicaraguan life under the Somoza dictatorship. Mimi and Nacho painstakingly showed the Nicaraguan therapists how to pursue the unique meaning that each individual attributed to his or her traumatic symptoms and how it was related to early life experiences and constitutional endowment. They also emphasized the importance of intervening through interpretation rather than by using the directive approach favored by the Nicaraguans.

I recalled, as well, the supervision sessions in the psychiatric hospital in Managua during which Dora, an astute young social worker, presented a case to Mimi and Nacho. Their interpretations captured the essence of their psychoanalytic conceptualization of psychopathology and treatment interventions, as well as their appreciation of the centrality of the social context of individual mental illness and reparation. Mimi brought to her supervision of Dora her special interest in the role of women in Central American societies, which she had learned about through her treatment of Salvadoran and Guatemalan refugees in Mexico and through her friendships with some of the Sandinista Revolution's famous women leaders, such as Dora María Tellez.[11] She learned even more through her clinical interventions with female patients in Nicaragua who sought treatment for depression, anxiety, and psychosomatic symptoms. Here she observed the psychological manifestations of the problematic family structure in Nicaragua, which was characterized historically by male abandonment. The widespread pattern of female-headed and female-centered households had produced contradictory patterns. As feminists from the United States and Europe noted, this phenomenon had strengthened women by promoting independence and self-sufficiency, enabling them to care for themselves and their children as well as preparing them to participate in large numbers—and in leadership positions—in the revolution. But Nicaraguan women also felt disempowered by the widespread practice among men of forming more than one family—la familia grande and la familia chica—either simultaneously or sequentially. Consequently, many women harbored intense feelings of resentment toward men, the result of which was their tendency to form their closest affective ties with their children, whose strivings for independence were often experienced by their mothers as a threat and were thus resisted. Mimi believed that the revolution's support of women's rights would help women to struggle together against these entrenched patterns, and she was glad to have the opportunity to provide psychological treatment to female patients living in a society whose government supported the fight against patriarchal structures and values.

Mimi listened to Dora's case presentation with this political context in mind. Dora reported that her patient was a 17-year-old girl who had become agoraphobic after suffering two psychotic episodes. Dora was treating the patient, her mother, and her two married sisters in family therapy because they all lived together along with the sisters' husbands and children. All three daughters claimed to adore their dominating mother and viewed their family as loving and conflict free. The father, who also had a common-law wife and children with whom he currently lived, was participating in the therapy sessions as well. The patient's older brother had been killed in battle by the National Guard just prior to the triumph of the revolution, but his death had not been recognized by the community, which had chosen to rename its street to honor another fallen combatant.

Mimi discussed the unconscious mechanisms at work in Dora's patient and her family. She suggested that the patient's psychotic episodes might be understood as the container for the otherwise denied aggression of her mother and siblings. The married daughters' dependence on their mother had prevented them from establishing their own households, and they were unable to express any aggressive feelings toward the mother, who relied on her children for fulfillment of her emotional needs. The patient's symptoms, which kept her regressively dependent on her mother, also unconsciously legitimized the mother's overprotective hovering. In addition, the patient's agoraphobia, which was sometimes reflected in the fear that her mother might be harmed if she left her alone in the house, was a manifestation of her desire to protect her mother from her own unconscious aggression by never leaving her side. In addition, the patient's illness had succeeded in bringing the father home in order to participate in the treatment. Mimi indicated that the therapeutic work needed to address the mother's feelings toward her rejecting husband, the unconscious conflict between mother and daughters and the guilt related in part to the unexpressed desire of the daughters to attain psychological independence. Mimi went on to demonstrate how the patient's symptoms should also be explored as a manifestation of frozen grief related to the death of her brother. "Your identified patient," she told Dora, "cannot go outside, but the rest of the family can't 'come outside' themselves to mourn their loss."

Treatment for the family therefore would also have to encourage grieving for the dead brother.

In a society where the state, political ideology, and mass organizations encourage people's involvement in social struggle to improve the quality and substance of their lives, Mimi was convinced that psychologically disturbed individuals can benefit from political activism. Thus, an assessment of the social context was also a part of the suggested treatment plan. "We are lucky here in Nicaragua," Mimi reminded Dora, "for in addition to psychotherapy, this family can rely on political resources as well. We can encourage the patient, her mother, and her sisters to become involved with AMNLAE." Mimi was referring to the Association of Nicaraguan Women, the Sandinista mass organization that took a special interest in education, child care, family life, and employment of women that was spearheading the struggle for women's legal and political equality. AMNLAE had developed consciousness-raising groups for women, successfully fought to require men who abandoned their children to pay child support, and won passage of a new law that required both men and women to participate equally in household and childrearing tasks. By becoming involved in the organization's many activities, both mother and daughters would have an opportunity to develop a new sense of autonomy and self-esteem through mutual supportive relations with other women engaged in the social world outside the family.

Mimi also recommended to Dora that she think about the community resources for this family to help them deal with the problem of frozen grief. "This family has not yet experienced the community's recognition of the deceased brother, and their capacity to mourn him can be greatly helped through public acknowledgment of his death and his importance to the revolution. The Neighborhood Committees for the Defense of the Revolution and the popular church," she advised her supervisee, "can both be mobilized to provide community rituals that can facilitate private mourning."

Mimi and her colleagues were working directly with the mass organizations in their primary prevention campaigns. One example was the Sandinista brigade program, through which individuals from different sectors of Nicaraguan society could be trained to participate in specific health and mental health projects. The brigade workers—*brigadistas*—worked among the people of their sector, providing services such as vaccinations against infectious diseases, education in sanitation, instruction in mother and infant health care, and therapeutic intervention for psychological problems. The Internationalist Team taught the *brigadistas* basic principles of how to help individuals experiencing emotional difficulties. The *brigadistas* became involved with specific psychological issues and brought people together in groups to share common problems. They were involved, for example, in establishing such groups for mothers whose children were fighting in the war against the Contras and who needed a chance to share their anxieties and fears. The *brigadistas* also organized people who were working two and three jobs to replace those who had gone to the front to protect the country against the Contras. Many were under extreme stress and were burnt out with symptoms that included headaches, hypertension, alcoholism, insomnia, anxiety attacks, and family distress. The *brigadistas* were trained to help them in simple ways by providing them the chance to participate in group discussions and relaxation classes. *Brigadistas* were also trained to recognize individuals who might be suffering from trauma and to offer them the opportunity to speak about their feelings in an emotionally safe environment.

While we had been in Managua, Mimi and Nacho met with psychologists who worked with *brigadistas* in the squatter settlements around Managua. The target population in this project was refugees from El Salvador, mainly women and children. Their flight from the civil war raging in their country had separated them from husbands and fathers who had either been disappeared or killed by the military or who were fighting with the revolutionary opposition, their fate unknown.

The psychologists' specific task was to train *brigadistas* to recognize the psychodynamics of persons suffering from frozen grief. After studying with the Internationalist Team, they helped the *brigadistas* design comic books that taught their cohorts how to detect the symptoms characteristic of people whose functioning was impaired by their inability to mourn. The comic books demonstrated basic techniques the *brigadistas* could employ to encourage such individuals to express their feelings and to gradually feel less isolated and more connected to their current situation and social relations. The psychologists proudly showed Mimi and Nacho a sample of their instructional comic books and related a poignant story about how a *brigadista*'s interventions with several depressed Salvadoran mothers had resulted in their becoming more psychologically available to their small children and actively involved in their new community in Nicaragua. As I was listening to their discussion, I began to leaf through the comic book. My attention was caught by a frame in which the cartoon character representing the *brigadista* suggests to the depressed peasant he is trying to help, "I understand, *compañero*; it's okay, you may cry without feeling embarrassed. I want to hear your story; I understand, for I, too, have lost people I love. I will listen as long as you need me to." In the next frame, the peasant begins to weep, and the *brigadista* gently touches his shoulder, patiently waiting.

"Here in León," Mimi was saying, and her words brought me back to the present, "the most fascinating experiment is the university medical school's work-study program. I think it is a brilliant approach to training future physicians in a holistic approach to illness. I wish medical training programs everywhere would incorporate it." She smiled as she recollected the morning's lengthy meeting with the university medical school's staff and how they had planned the Internationalist Team's psychological component for the third and fourth years of medical school. The work-study strategy challenged traditional medical training models in that it focused on a specific theme each year—physician attitudes toward patients in the first year, school-aged children's needs in the second year, contagious diseases in the third year, and mother and child health in the fourth year—and involved students in a variety of research and collaborative activities in the community so as to familiarize them with the social context of physical disease. "The students learn about the psychological dimension of each year's focus through our classes," Mimi told me, "and then their internships take them out into community organizations and schools for practical experience directly related to the psychosocial theory we teach them."

As I observed Mimi working in the different programs the Internationalist Team was developing in Nicaragua, I was struck by her boundless energy and buoyant spirits. The tiny Central American country's revolution did seem to be the perfect environment in which this Viennese-Argentine analyst could integrate her politics and professional expertise. Mimi was passionately committed to Nicaragua, and I was slowly realizing that her dedication emerged from a mature assessment of what is possible rather than a naïvely romantic sentimentality. She deeply believed in the need to create social structures that nourish all human beings in an environment of equality and justice, and for that reason she was angered by U.S. efforts to overturn the Sandinista government. As a psychoanalyst, she understood that even human beings committed to the most radical goals might fail to achieve them for psychological reasons, and so she was not disillusioned when the Sandinista leadership or its followers manifested personal or political limitations or contradictions. "If I am asked what psychoanalysis is for, beyond transforming symptoms, I always say 'in order not to lie to oneself anymore,'" she said. "If I go to Nicaragua I think I am not lying to myself, although I know of the existing contradictions. I try to weigh things up and say that, despite the contradictions, I am in favor of the Sandinista Revolution, because the positive far outweighs the negative."[12]

Sitting together in the momentary tranquility of that late afternoon in León, neither one of us was thinking about the future. We did not yet know that in several years Mimi would be diagnosed with inoperable cancer. But some time earlier in Mexico when we had spoken about aging and death, Mimi had told me, "I don't want to die without meaning. I want to live until the end. So when the dangers of the Nicaraguan work become undeniable, [I think about how] there is an important difference between a worthwhile death and one that has no value. I believe this very much, and I believe that my life has been worthwhile, within my own limits."

Mimi Langer lived intensely and with meaning until the end. In the three years following our trip to Nicaragua, she continued in her role as the Co-coordinator of the Internationalist Team. She returned to Nicaragua many times and traveled to Europe to raise money and counteract the disinformation campaign against the Sandinista Revolution. As she continued the work that gave value to her life, by 1986 she was also battling the cancer that was consuming her. Experimental cancer treatments gave intermittent hope to family, friends, colleagues, and *compañeros* who found it painfully difficult to contemplate the world without her. When she and I were together, our discussions revealed the shifts between her desire to live and her rational acceptance of death.

Finally, in the fall of 1987, Mimi returned to Buenos Aires to live out her life in the home that she had been forced to flee 13 years earlier. Just before she left Mexico, she received an invitation to participate in a conference, "The Driving Out of Reason and Its Return," organized by the Austrian government to honor prominent figures in the arts and sciences who had been forced to leave the country after the *Anschluss* in 1938. Mimi was saddened that she could not attend, but she was now too ill to travel. Her letter to the organizers expressing her regret was read publicly to the participants in the conference, who responded with an ovation acknowledging her contributions to psychoanalysis and human rights.

Once again in Buenos Aires, Mimi was in the familiar environment of her home, now also occupied by her older son and his family. Although in an increasingly weakened state, she stubbornly resisted her doctors' orders to rest. In the final several months of her life, she welcomed her many friends and colleagues who came to visit and even agreed to be interviewed at length on film by several members of the Internationalist Team about her work in Nicaragua. Although exhausting, this was a precious opportunity, on the brink of her death, to achieve continuity with the values by which she had lived her life. On December 22, 1987, Mimi Langer died at home, surrounded by her family. To the end, she was an active participant in history.

Memorials took place in Argentina, Mexico, and Nicaragua, honoring Mimi's contributions to psychoanalysis and Latin American social struggles. She would have been especially moved to know that her *compañeros* renamed themselves the Marie Langer Internationalist Team of Mental Health Workers.[13]

* * *

When exile ended for our other protagonists, the politics of psychoanalytic activism in the Southern Cone were to face new challenges. For those who returned from abroad and those who had lived through the dictatorships in internal exile, the new democratic regimes would come to represent another chapter in the Latin American story of oppression and struggle.

Popularly elected presidents in Argentina, Chile, and Uruguay would negotiate the reintegration of former military violators of human rights into
civil society and become the overseers of ever-deepening economic crises
and social violence arising from the growing gap between the haves and
the have-nots. Our protagonists would become actively engaged in human
rights struggles, whose aim would be to address the psychological legacy
of the culture of fear and to posit a politics aimed at individual and social
reparation.

ENDNOTES

1. Author interviews with Mimi Langer and Nacho Maldonado, Mexico City
   and Nicaragua, various times, 1983–1987. The two also coauthored a manu-
   script about their experience in Mexico and Nicaragua, a copy of which Mimi
   gave me. It was never published.
2. For an exploration of the psychological meanings of the experience of
   exile from a psychoanalytic perspective, see Grinberg and Grinberg (1984).
   León Grinberg was an analysand of Mimi Langer's; his scholarly analysis is
   informed by his own personal experience of exile. He and his wife/colleague
   left Argentina in the late 1970s and have lived in Spain ever since. See also
   Akhtar (1995) and Hollander (2000b). For a description of the impact of exile
   on Central American refugees, see Bottinelli and Maldonado (1990).
3. Many therapists who work with Holocaust survivors point out that the
   patient's awareness that the therapist repudiates the Nazi project or that
   the therapist has had some direct or indirect personal experience with the
   horrors of the Holocaust (or both) has a positive impact on the patient's
   capacity to trust the therapist and to develop a "therapeutic alliance." See,
   for example, Pines (1985).
4. In November of that year, the elections took place and were certified by international observers as meaningful, clean, and competitive; in a contest with
   political parties to the right and the left of them, in which 75 percent of the
   registered voters cast ballots. The Sandinistas won 65 percent of the vote. The
   presidency and vice-presidency went to Sandinistas Daniel Ortega and Sergio
   Ramirez, respectively, and 61 of the 96 seats in the new National Assembly
   were won by the Sandinista Front; see Walker (1987).
5. The popular church was involved with the Sandinista government; "between
   revolution and religion, there is no contradiction" was a popular slogan during the revolution.
6. The Reagan administration attacked the Sandinista government, even breaking
   U.S. law to do so, not because it was a communist threat but because it represented a legitimate model for sovereignty and development in the Americas,
   much akin to the welfare capitalist model of the Scandinavian countries: a number of political parties functioned legally—the right wing was even financed by
   the "new right" in the United States—and in the economy, by design, the private
   sector controlled at least 60 percent of industrial and agricultural production.

For an analysis of the kind of politics and socioeconomic order the Sandinistas were developing, see Burns (1987), Walker (1987), Harris and Vilas (1985), and Kovel (1988).

7. To understand LIC, see Klare and Kornbluh (1988), especially chapter 6. According to a Defense Department official, the project in Nicaragua was to "keep some pressure on the Nicaraguan government, force them to use their economic resources for the military, and prevent them from solving their economic problems—and that's a plus" (George, 1991, p. 19).

8. The Contras got training in psychological torture from the United States; an example was what they learned from a 1968 lessons book, *Armed Psyop*, used at the Army Special Warfare School at Fort Bragg, North Carolina, which called for the use of selected violence against civilians, as reported in the *Washington Post*, October 24, 1984. According to Edgar Chamorro, who testified before the World Court on September 5, 1985, FDN (a Contra army) "would assemble all the residents in the town square and then proceed to kill—in full view of the others—all persons suspected of working for the Nicaraguan government." Also see the CIA training manual on psychological warfare, including torture (Omang & Neier, 1985). As a U.S.-trained and supported anti-Sandinista counterinsurgency operative expressed his sentiments about work, "I love killing; I have been killing for the past seven years. There's nothing I like better. If I could, I'd kill several people a day" (Americas Watch, 1985). In Mimi's mind, U.S. policy in Nicaragua constituted a form of state terror perpetrated from abroad.

9. Mimi and I had lengthy discussions about this priority shift from the experience in Argentina, and this concise expression of it appears in Langer (1989, p. 229).

10. In fact, Mimi did write the article about a year later and presented it as an invited paper to people in the arts and literature in Havana at Casa de las Américas. Her presentation was followed by a renewed interest in psychoanalysis on the part of the Cubans. Subsequently, Mimi and other colleagues organized the Latin American Congress of Marxist Psychology and Psychoanalysis (Encuentro Latinoamericano de Psicología Marxista y Psicoanálisis), which has met biannually since 1986 at the University of Havana, Department of Psychology. Mental health professionals from all over Latin America and Europe, with some participation from U.S. colleagues, meet to discuss their ideas about the intersection between individual psychology and social structures. Mental health and social issues are examined by those attending, all of whom share a progressive view of the world and a commitment to mental health and a politics of justice and equality.

11. I would later interview Dora María for my radio program on "Pacifica," KPFK, Los Angeles. She made a complex critical assessment of the Sandinistas' struggle with male chauvinism to the effect that although they had initially supported women's equal rights and had launched an important AIDS-awareness campaign, their willingness to sustain women's issues as primary and their ability to support gay rights paled as other priorities emerged during the war against the Contras. Dora María and other Sandinistas interested in feminist issues criticized the Sandinista leadership for its resistance to allowing women an equally prominent role in the organization. To see the shift in many

women's views about how their gender interests were being represented by the Sandinistas, see Margaret Randall's (1981, 1992) two studies, separated by 11 years; see also Randall (1995), especially chapter 4.

12. Mimi had told me this many times, and this concise version of her sentiment is quoted in Langer (1989, p. 221).

13. Mimi died before the U.S. economic and military aggression against the Sandinistas succeeded in dislodging them from power. When the 1990 elections in Nicaragua took place, the U.S.-funded conservative candidate, Violeta Chamorro, won on the basis of a campaign that presented her as the only hope to stop the war with the Contras and the vehicle through which the United States would send much-needed money instead of arms to her country. The Sandinistas honored the outcome of the elections, which brought to power a Chamorro-led coalition whose rule did not attract the promised U.S. dollars and whose policies have unraveled all the Sandinista social programs developed during the 1980s. The standard of living has declined for Nicaraguans, and social violence has escalated. The Sandinistas remain the best organized political force in the country and often ally themselves with the president in her struggles against the more reactionary elements in her ruling coalition. After years of remaining in the opposition, the 2006 presidential election was won by the Sandinista National Liberation Front candidate, Daniel Ortega. Although there are deep divisions within the Sandinista movement, in part reflecting political as well as personal tensions, the Nicaraguan government allies itself with the continent-wide progressive trend toward Latin American self-determination.

Chapter 7

Neoliberal democracy in Latin America

Impunity and economic meltdown

> I live with a circumstantial pessimism and a fundamental historical optimism.
>
> — Diana Kordon

The third floor office of the Grandmothers of the Plaza de Mayo is a converted apartment that fronts the busy Avenida Corrientes in the commercial center of Buenos Aires. The drone of the congested traffic below provides a steady acoustic background to the sounds of women answering telephones, typing letters, and organizing an upcoming event of solidarity with the Haitian people. The walls of the rooms are covered with large photographs, colorful artwork, and posters from human rights groups from all over the world. They are visual testimonies to the valiant struggle the Grandmothers have waged since the late 1970s to locate their grandchildren who forcibly disappeared by the military during Argentina's Dirty War. It is the fall of 1998, and I am here with Estela Carlotto, a retired primary-school teacher and the president of the organization, and she has been telling me her personal history and how, 17 long years ago, she came to be an activist in the opposition to state terror.

It is impossible not to be impressed by this woman, whose age and tragic experiences are hidden by her composure, attractive elegance, contagious vitality, and sense of purpose. She emanates the intelligence and determination that have molded her emotional pain into an effective activism on behalf of human rights. Like so many of the Grandmothers who are busily at work in this office, Estela experienced the trauma of her pregnant daughter disappearing by force and then being assassinated after giving birth, and her newborn grandchild appropriated by the Argentine armed forces. Like many other grandmothers, she has spent years using all legal and scientific means at her disposal to try to locate her disappeared grandchildren. She has yet to be successful, but because of the efforts of their organization, more than 50 of the estimated 400 babies who suffered similar fates have been located and returned to their legitimate families.

As we pause for several minutes to have a *café*, we reminisce about the human rights conference the Grandmothers had organized several years earlier.[1] Estela comments appreciatively about the presentations of the psychoanalysts and psychologists who had described their work with the restituted (reunited) children and their biological families. She feels they helped the public to become aware of the complex psychological issues involved in this unique situation, especially the impact on the children of learning the truth about their history and about the families with whom they grew up. As she speaks, I recall the several psychoanalysts who had elaborated the idea of trauma and its different meanings in the particular situation in which children disappeared and were located years later by their families of origin. They had distinguished between the nature and meaning of two different traumas. The first was the "destructive original trauma" suffered by the children when they were stolen right after birth or as small infants or toddlers and raised on the basis of a family secret, the lies they were told about their origins by their appropriators, who were often the assassins of their biological parents. The second was the "reconstructive trauma," an inevitable aspect of the revelation of the truth about their origins and their abductor "parents," but nevertheless the kind of traumatic experience that facilitates the psychic and social reconstruction of one's existence and provides the foundation for an identity and life based on the truth.[2] I tell Estela that I vividly remember the moving final plenary session, when many of the restituted grandchildren came up on the stage with flowers to embrace each of the Grandmothers present. One boy read a poem to the audience describing how much the children love these women, whose collective struggle had given them back their true identity; all of the women have become these children's grandmothers. Estela smiles. "Yes," she says, "these are the gratifying results of our hard work."

As we speak, I think about how the Mothers and Grandmothers were the first organizations to actively resist the culture of fear in Argentina. I remember as well that other individuals and groups eventually emerged to protest all aspects of the terrorist state's economic and social policies. At some point, in each of the Southern Cone dictatorships, people like Estela found a collective voice to demand that the military relinquish its hold on the government and return to the barracks.

THE UNDOING OF STATE TERROR

It is difficult to pinpoint the precise moment when the tables turned on those whose arbitrary rule seemed absolute. In the three Southern Cone nations, various factors were at work by the early 1980s, moving them inexorably back to constitutional rule: (1) international pressures for the return to democracy because the military had fulfilled their historical purpose, (2) internal rifts among the armed forces, and (3) the strength of an opposition bent on reasserting a democratic alternative. These forces were rapidly converging to press for the military's return to the barracks. The specific political and cultural history of each country affected the tempo and character of the reassertion of constitutional rule. While in Chile and Uruguay the transition to democracy was protracted and tightly controlled by the military leaders, in Argentina the military regime literally collapsed under the weight of its extraordinary corruption and humiliating defeat in a military confrontation with Great Britain over the long-disputed Malvinas/Falkland Islands.

The devastating results of neoliberalism sponsored by the armed forces provided the important context for political change in all three nations. Each was characterized by high rates of unemployment, the reduction and impoverishment of the urban working classes and their labor movements, the pauperization of the peasantry and rural working classes, the downward mobility of the middle classes, and the displacement of the industrial sector by the speculative finance sector within the ruling elites. By the time the military exited, the quality of life of the majority of people had painfully deteriorated.

When protests against the economic and social impact of state terror emerged, the participants in all three countries included the human rights communities, labor unions, democratic political parties, grassroots community organizations, activist intellectuals, and individuals from all social sectors. Tato Pavlovsky recalls this transitional period well. He returned to Buenos Aires from exile in 1981 and realized that the consensus imposed by the culture of fear was being challenged. He felt more free to speak out and even began to publish articles critical of Argentina's authoritarian environment. "At the time I returned, it seemed as if there were two Argentinas. In one, people manifested a fascist mentality, a kind of subjective complicity: 'There's nothing problematic happening here.' But there was also another Argentina, full of very courageous people who had stayed here. Many whom I had known welcomed me back happily, overjoyed to be together again, to struggle side by side, with an intense fervor to do something worthwhile."[3] In Uruguay, Marcelo Viñar's friend, imprisoned playwright Mauricio Rosencof (1993b), described the Uruguayan people's growing ability to resist the military government:

> None of us, however alone we may be, is ever really alone. And in the most extreme situations, we are saved by our human condition, the cornerstone of which is not a particular ideology but rather a sense of solidarity: the strength of character which prevents us from transferring the weight of the crosses we bear to the shoulders of our brothers and sisters. That notion is common to Christians, Marxists, atheists and Buddhists precisely because it lies at the heart of our shared humanity. (p. 131)

By the mid-1980s, citizens in both Argentina and Uruguay used the ballot box to vote in civilian governments. Although the Pinochet regime in Chile continued intact, new collective struggles permitted thousands of people to emerge from their isolation and to share together their personal responses to years of living in the culture of fear. Elizabeth Lira studied the salutary psychological effects of group experience on the individual capacity to resist authoritarian rule. In *The Psychology of Political Threat and Fear*, Elizabeth (Lira & Castillo, 1991) writes that the "deprivatization" of feelings of terror facilitates the recuperation of subjectivity, by which she means the transition from passive victimization to individual autonomy and the ability to confront the private and social impact of the culture of fear. "Making visible what had been hidden and covert," she asserts, "meant that the Chilean people could collectively search for a solution" (p. 239).

In fact, growing resistance to the military's hard line after a decade and a half provoked the Chilean right and the United States to worry that the conditions might be ripe for all-out revolution. By 1988, this concern, plus a flagging economy that desperately needed loans from the International Monetary Fund and World Bank, which were now more favorably disposed toward constitutional rather than authoritarian regimes, converged to pressure Pinochet to agree to a democratization process,[4] which ultimately produced the country's first democratic election since the military coup. In 1990, Christian Democrat Patricio Aylwin became Chile's new president. When he was inaugurated as the chief executive in early 1990, he was obliged to share real political power in his country's fragile democracy with a parliament that was dominated by right-wing parties and that contained six senators appointed by Pinochet, who continued as commander-in-chief of an armed forces that would remain one of the major players in Chilean politics.

PSYCHOANALYTIC ACTIVISM AND HUMAN RIGHTS

In each of the three countries, successful democratic elections produced a momentary euphoria. But after the celebrations were over, the people of the Southern Cone settled down to deal with the legacy of the terrorist state. A focal point of the struggle centered on the widespread wish to legally indict the torturers for their human rights abuses. But in each country, the armed forces had made it clear that they would oppose any judicial investigation of their policies, which they maintained had been justified because their nations had been in a state of war. Now, in response to the outcry for human rights tribunals, the armed forces threatened a return to the past should civil society embark on such a foolhardy undertaking.

The conflict between those who advocated bringing the military to justice and those who wanted to leave the human rights issue behind was articulated as a confrontation between the advocates of forgetting about the past—*olvido*—and the proponents of remembering and understanding it—*memoria*. Psychoanalytic activists became articulate critics of the dangers of individual and social amnesia and joined the fight against amnesty for the former military rulers (Kordon, 1995).

As the political struggle between the forces arrayed for and against prosecuting the military continued, the Argentine people were dealing with other aspects of the legacy of state terror. Many people were experiencing the complex emotional journey of return: They came back from exile abroad, they emerged from internal exile ("inxile"), or they were released from prison. The reencounter of these three groups often generated a new kind of distress. Marcelo and Maren Viñar noted the phenomenon in Uruguay in their book *Fracturas de Memoria*:

> Between those who suffered torture and exile—interior and exterior—the dialogue has been difficult or impossible to resume, and instead of capitalizing on the rich diversity of experience, insults prevail, and difference is condemned. Our hypothesis...is that when extreme violence is endured, but not symbolized, it results in the internalization of the aggressor's ways of operating, which reinforces the system of exclusion imposed by the dictatorship. (Viñar & Viñar, 1993, p. 125)[5]

For Juan Carlos Volnovich, the return to Argentina was deeply painful because "we weren't the same; Argentina wasn't the same. Many of our friends weren't here, some because they were dead and others because they were in exile. Still others, with whom we'd shared our ideals and commitments, were no longer as we'd remembered them." This political disillusionment was compounded by the practical difficulties of repatriation; and Juan Carlos and Silvia, like thousands of other returnees, lived through a period of economic duress as they reconstituted their lives. Over time Juan Carlos acquired a high profile in the professional and academic communities and also became a familiar voice in the mass media, where he was repeatedly interviewed about the psychological impact of diverse social and political developments in the country. New intellectual opportunities presented themselves as well when Juan Carlos and Silvia began to explore the feminist scholarship that was emerging within U.S. and European psychoanalysis. They revised their own psychoanalytic thinking through the new lens of gender, writing articles and organizing conferences to open a dialogue among their Argentine colleagues. Their growing feminist sensibilities also added a dimension to their political analysis, which permitted a new understanding of the failures of the revolutionary movements of the 1960s and 1970s.

In addition to their assessment of the objective interests and psychology of the dominant classes who had embraced state terror to deal with their political opposition, Juan Carlos and Silvia were also interested in the role played by the left leaders themselves in their failure to successfully sustain the mass movement for change. In applying a feminist analysis, they saw that the strategic mistakes made by the mainly male left leaders were due in part to a psychology associated with traditional patriarchal values, whose contours often constrained their ability to develop political strategies based on a realistic evaluation of the existing power relations in their societies. Juan Carlos believed that although the left leaders had successfully mobilized a mass movement that challenged class and race oppression, they had uncritically and unconsciously reproduced among themselves elements of the authoritarian mentality associated with male chauvinism, which led them to overemphasize the military aspects of the political struggle for change. "In so doing," he argues, "they weakened their struggle in many ways, not the least important of which was falling victim to the grandiose and omnipotent fantasy that they could take on a militarized state disposed to defend the status quo with a cruelty that knew no bounds." The male reluctance to tolerate feelings of weakness and vulnerability had led the leaders to deny their own and their followers' powerlessness in relation to their enemy, especially as systematic repression increased. This denial contributed to their inability to recognize their imminent defeat and thus did not permit them to develop a defensive strategy to protect the movement. They thereby left hundreds of thousands of activists vulnerable and less prepared to safeguard themselves at the key moment of all-out military and paramilitary assault.

Each of our protagonists found ways to actualize a socially committed psychoanalysis in this new period, haunted as it was by the problem of the *desaparecidos*. Juan Carlos began to collaborate closely with the human rights work of Estela Carlotto and the Grandmothers of the Plaza de Mayo, which permitted him to retain a connection to the progressive ideals of previous times. Diana Kordon, Lucila Edelman, and Darío Lagos of the Equipo continued to treat families whose loved ones had disappeared, working with the Mothers of the Plaza de Mayo as they had during the dictatorship. After the return to democracy, they also organized "reflection groups" of professionals, students, and mental health workers as the need arose to elaborate collectively, in both a personal and an intellectual way, the painful legacy of political repression and the complex implications of possible amnesty for the perpetrators. These groups, which the Equipo organized among other sectors of society as well, "permitted the psychological processing of traumatic situations that had a social origin in a more effective way than other modalities...The group environment enables the participants to put into concrete words, articulated collectively, the different ways a social experience affects people subjectively and the personal manner in which each *afectado* negotiates the traumatic situation" (Kordon, 1995, pp. 189, 194). The three Equipo activists noted the following benefits of the groups' work in articulating the experience of trauma: the reduction of anxiety and an increased capacity to tolerate it; the lessening of guilt feelings, which are more frequent in families of *desaparecidos* than in other mourners; the strengthening of protective ego defenses; and the increase of self-esteem.

Julia Braun also found group psychotherapy an effective way for individuals and families to elaborate emotional problems whose origins were linked to the social trauma of the *desaparecidos*. When the Argentine Ministry of Health took the unprecedented step of establishing a special psychological service for the victims of military repression, Julia was appointed its director, marking the first time a psychoanalyst had assumed a leadership position within the ministry. Julia organized therapy groups for the families of the *desaparecidos*, which focused on the special mourning required of persons affected by this perverse political policy. Julia also extended the psychological services of the Ministry of Health to the educational system, aiding school directors and teachers to make appropriate interventions with children whose psychological symptoms were not only the cumulative response to the period of state terror but also a reaction to the rash of violence perpetrated by the right wing around the country as it tried to intimidate human rights activists in their efforts to seek accountability on the part of the military.

During this period, Julia had the dubious privilege of learning the truth of what had happened to her son Gabriel. Julia discovered that Gabriel had been in the very police station where his father had initially gone to look for him the night he was abducted. Then he had been taken to a clandestine prison, where he was taunted for being a Jew and a subversive and subjected to terrible torture. He was later murdered along with two other prisoners in a way that was made to look as though they were juvenile delinquents who had been killed during an armed confrontation with the police. Like thousands of others, this political murder had gone through the theatrics of a police criminal investigation, followed by the burial of Gabriel and the two other victims in anonymous, unmarked graves. "Knowing the truth, even with its horrific details, gave me a certain amount of peace," says Julia. "Mothers of other *desaparecidos* called to tell me how lucky I was. My 'luck' was to know that they'd killed my son with machine guns. The mothers told me that they wished they were in my place. That's how important the truth, the knowing, is."

Estela Carlotto of the Grandmothers confirms Julia's assertion. "Knowing concretely is important. I have the terrible certainty of knowing about Laura's death. In my experience, the certainty that comes from having the body and being able to bury your loved one helps in the mourning process. It's impossible in the situation of the *desaparecidos*; many families leave a place set at the dinner table, celebrate the birthday, leave the clothes hanging in the closet. They are frozen." In Estela's case, her persistence to learn about her daughter Laura's disappearance paid off. In 1985 she succeeded in locating her daughter's body, which she had exhumed in order to disprove the military's story that Laura was a criminal who had been killed trying to escape from the police and that she had not had a baby in captivity. The examination of the body demonstrated that Laura had been in a concentration camp, that she had been subjected to torture, and that she had been shot at close range. It also proved that she had given birth to a baby before she met her death. "With the truth confirmed," says Estela, "my bereavement was possible. I saw her; I saw what remained. My mourning was now linked to reality. And I am still searching for my grandchild. Witnesses who saw Laura when she gave birth in a military hospital have told me the baby was a boy whom Laura named Guido after her father. But even if I find him someday," she adds, "I'll continue with the Grandmothers. This is a commitment for life."

In their concern for justice, the Mothers and Grandmothers took the position that the military should be prosecuted and then prevented from participating in politics altogether. This radical posture led them to criticize traditional Argentine political structures. When, on a trip to Europe, President Alfonsín publicly declared that he did not think the Mothers' political agenda coincided with the "national interest," the Mothers published a reply in their newspaper:

> To this president, who claims to be democratic, it is necessary to explain...what the meaning of "national" is to us. What is authentically national is a population that develops the wealth of this country for its own benefit; it is to receive an adequate wage, to have enough food, to have a home; it is to be able to educate our children, to have health protection, to improve our intellectual and technical capacity, to have our own culture and to have freedom of expression; it is to have armed forces to drive lorries, planes and boats that transport troops and materials to places of natural disaster, who work with the people in an efficient and rapid way; it is to have a police force that protects freedom and respects all citizens; it is to have impartial judges who guarantee justice; it is to have duties and rights that can be exercised freely; it is, simply, to have the right to life, but with dignity. (Fisher, 1989, pp. 142–143)

The Mothers were speaking for millions of their compatriots.

In December 1985, Julia and other psychoanalysts from the Argentine Psychoanalytic Association studied the psychological effects of political repression and presented papers at a symposium held in Buenos Aires's most important cultural center. The following year, a collection of the papers was published as *Argentina psicoanálisis represión política*. In the book's prologue, the editor wrote the following:

Psychoanalysis permits the patient to recover aspects of his life and his personality that have been repressed, denied, or dissociated. While what is "overcome" through these defenses is erased from one's memory, it always returns through symptoms, character problems, and inhibitions in love and work, which make one's life painful. In the same way, a people has a memory that is necessary to recover. The suppression of memory, the disinformation, the forgetting—all are enemies of individual and collective mental health. That which is forgotten makes itself present through repetition, which compromises the future and keeps people defenseless and in a state of desperation. Only the clarification of memory and knowledge of reality, however painful at the moment, permits us to recover those aspects of ourselves from which we have been alienated. It is urgent that we all take responsibility for the importance and value of the historical truth of what we as a people have suffered and its sequelae of horror, death, and deterioration...The patient is only able to stop repeating his neurotic behavior by remembering, resignifying, and elaborating [the past]. We believe that a people should also remember and signify, so as not to repeat. (Abudara et al., 1986, p. 16)[6]

This argument on behalf of *memoria* became the battle cry of those who believed in the fundamental necessity of confronting and understanding the painful reality of the past so as to diminish the likelihood of repeating it.

Closely connected to the effort on behalf of *memoria* was another issue that fueled the attempts to bring the military to trial. It had to do with the role of justice in society. The progressive psychoanalysts and psychologists in Argentina, along with their counterparts in Chile and Uruguay, agreed on the fundamental principle that without the rule of law citizens live together unprotected, defenseless, and in a permanent state of anxiety. They quoted Freud, who in *Civilization and Its Discontents*, written in 1929 after World War I and on the eve of the rise of fascism, examined the origins of human social organization.

Human life in common is only made possible when a majority comes together which is stronger than any separate individual and which remains united against all separate individuals. The power of this community is then set up as "right" in opposition to the power of the individual, which is condemned as "brute force"...The first requisite of civilization, therefore, is that of justice—that is, the assurance that a law once made will not be broken in favor of an individual. This implies nothing as to the ethical value of the law. The further course of cultural development seems to tend towards making the law no longer an expression of the will of a small community—a caste or a stratum of the population or a racial group—which, in its turn, behaves like a violent individual towards other, and perhaps more numerous, collections of people. The final outcome should be a rule of law to which all...have contributed by a sacrifice of their instincts, and which leaves no one...at the mercy of brute force. (in Kordon, 1995, pp. 74–75)

The military dictatorships in all three Southern Cone countries, whose authoritarian discourse had ignored established law, had through brute force inflicted the arbitrary and brutal rule of a minority on the majority of citizens, thus countermanding what Freud had argued was one of the essential pillars of civilization.

This violation of the rule of law demanded an accounting. As Diana, Lucila, and Darío argued, formal judgment of the military's wrongdoing was a necessary prerequisite for the recovery from state terror. Rather than vengeance, the human rights movement sought acknowledgment of the law, an admission that citizens' human rights had been violated, and some form of reparation. Only then was forgiveness possible, and only then could members of society feel they were protected. But the military did not seek pardon. They denied or justified their actions; and many civilians, frightened about the possible consequences of pursuing justice, believed that it was better to forget the past than to upset their fragile new democracies. They supported amnesty for the military. "Don't live in the past," they urged. "There has already been so much damage. Let us forget and move on to what lies in the future" (Kordon, 1995, p. 22). Nobel Prize winner and human rights activist Adolfo Pérez Esquivel countered on behalf of remembering. "To recapture memory does not signify remaining in the past but the possibility of illuminating the present in order to construct critical consciousness and to recuperate values that sustain life, culture, and identity. It means that people stop being spectators and assume their role as protagonists of history" (Weschler, 1990, p. 94).

This call for grassroots activism on behalf of justice was taken up in Argentina, Uruguay, and Chile during the ensuing years. One Uruguayan activist opposed to amnesty in his country argued, "You can't pardon someone who's convinced he has behaved well. Someone asks for a pardon [after] having repented. I don't care whether anyone is incarcerated, as long as he confesses, repents, and *then* is pardoned" (Weschler, 1990, p. 98). Meanwhile, Uruguayans, like their counterparts in Argentina and Chile, now lived in the same society with those who had actively colluded with the military and with many others who had passively submitted to the authoritarian state. They were living with the torturers among them—traveling in the same subways, eating in the same restaurants, enjoying the same concerts. They inhabited an environment whose physical reminders of terror—the public buildings, the factories, the private mansions where people had been tortured and murdered—were inescapable. Yet they were asked to forget about the past. As Marcelo and Maren have written,

In response to the experience of terror, Uruguayan society is split into two irreconcilable camps. For some, life simply continued, and the terror was a detail in the course of history. For others, it was a convulsion that broke the continuity of their destinies, obliging them to form scar tissue over wounds that were irreparable. We propose that this horror and violence have imposed a fragmentation of memory and of collective identity, whose dissociative mechanism corrodes and corrupts the social bond. (Viñar & Viñar, 1993, p. 125)

According to the Viñars, the intrapsychic and interpersonal conflicts thus generated required a reparative process, one that was impeded by amnesty.

Like Argentines and Uruguayans, Chileans lived through the complex adjustment to the return of democratic government during the struggle over amnesty. In Chile, too, social trauma had created a legacy of deep wounds that affected every domain of life. As Elizabeth Lira notes, "The difficult unraveling of dictatorship is never a return to the democracy imagined but to another democracy that has incorporated the conflictual structural and institutional aspects of the regime that proceeds it." Although a subsequent reparation law for the families of the victims helped to resolve concrete problems in their daily lives, these monetary compensations have been viewed as insufficient given the social and juridical impunity enjoyed by the armed forces. As Elizabeth argues, "Because the culprits were not sanctioned for their criminal deeds, there are ethical and subjective sequelae that remain irresolvable. Amnesty highlights the irreparable nature of the crimes that were committed and at the same time it underscores the persistence of their impact on social relations."

In Argentina, the struggles on behalf of *memoria* and justice culminated in convictions of a small number of commanding officers who had administered the Dirty War. But in spite of public opposition, President Alfonsín secured congressional support for several bills that resulted in exemption from prosecution of officers with rank of lieutenant colonel and below because their human rights violations had been carried out under orders. Thus, the unprecedented conviction of military commanders was tarnished when amnesty was accorded to the middle-ranking officers who had carried out the disappearances, torture, and murder of tens of thousands of Argentine citizens. They were thus free to become the generals of the future.

In mid-1989, Alfonsín eagerly passed the presidential sash several months early to President-elect Peronist Carlos Menem, who inherited a country embattled by hyperinflation and a dissatisfied armed forces still seeking complete amnesty and moral vindication. During his first year in office, President Menem, the man who had campaigned as a populist on the side of the people, allied himself with the powerful in society. Menem expanded the neoliberal solution to his country's economic woes, including the sale of state-owned enterprises to mainly foreign-owned private corporations, which only exacerbated the gap between the elites and the rest of society. He also delivered a blow to the ideal of justice and human rights by definitively closing the Dirty War with a blanket amnesty (*impunidad*) for the military, pardoning the few junta officers who had been prosecuted and imprisoned. Menem's impunity came down on the side of social amnesia, which would have not only juridical but cultural and moral consequences as well.

HEGEMONY IN THE 1990S: IMPUNITY AND SOCIAL VIOLENCE

We can say that in Gramsci's terms, hegemony took the form of impunity in all social domains, with a consequent erosion in the quality of intersubjective and intrapsychic experience. In the three countries of the Southern Cone, impunity has facilitated the psychological defenses of repression, denial, and dissociation in citizens who were obliged to adjust to the new political situation which, while nominally democratic, nonetheless constituted a permanent state of latent threat. The conditions necessary to facilitate a mourning process for the many losses caused by state terror were undermined by impunity, and thus a genuine working-through of social trauma was compromised.

Moreover, as our protagonists have argued, the effects of impunity infused all realms of life and were manifested in the intensification of social violence. Diana and Lucila believe that impunity legitimized the generalized violation of the rights of others.

> Impunity is reflected in criminal economic behavior—the corruption of government and corporate executives—and the murders—especially of our youth—carried out or covered up by the police, the army or groups protected by the powers that be...[When] crime is sanctioned, justice and law do not function to provide a moral climate, symbolic reparation or social cohesion. Thus, in conditions of impunity, there has been a modification in habits, in definitions of what is permissible and what is forbidden, what is legal and what is illicit, to which the members of society universally respond. These habits and definitions have been internalized over time...In the past fifteen years, we can attest to the fact that there has been a profound change in the fundamental norms of society. (Kordon, 1995, p. 27)

Julia agrees that life in her country reflects patterns that were developed during the military dictatorship. "Impunity is manifested not only in a higher degree of corruption but in the open flaunting of it," she says, "and I relate this to the rupture of traditional restraints. Now anyone can do anything and get away with it. Before, the powerful used to kill with machine guns, and now they do the same thing but with laws and decrees. Political decadence and individualism are omnipresent. For instance, can you imagine that in this country, with its traditions of working-class consciousness, today a union leader can give a speech in which he tells workers, 'Whoever works is an ass because no one makes money working!' He isn't offering a critical discourse, mind you; it's an identification with corruption. And it represents the level of social decomposition that results from living through the Dirty War, when they killed people as if they were ants and then were pardoned. There is a profound legacy of violation of the law, which before was committed against the body and now is committed against the mind." From Elizabeth's point of view, similar conditions obtain in Chile. She speaks of the internalization of impunity, which reinforces traditionally overt and covert forms of authoritarianism in politics and in daily life. She gives the example of the impunity of male violence. In the private sphere of the family, men's abuse of their wives and children has been traditionally justified by custom and law, and now it is further legitimized by the impunity of political violence. "Impunity," argues Elizabeth, "has also imposed a pervasive conservatism in the mentality of the Chilean people." In other words, internalized hegemonic values and attitudes, a psychological default position, emerge as prominent among people who have been traumatized into passivity in the face of the social challenges that feel irresolvable.

Progressive psychoanalytic activists have consistently endorsed struggles for *memoria* and the need to develop a critical discourse about the historical role played by state terror in the Southern Cone. From their perspective, state terror was the handmaiden that ensured the maturation of neoliberalism in Latin America, which has succeeded in increasing profits and consumerism for an elite international capitalist class while expanding poverty, marginalization, and social violence for the majority of Latin Americans. Elizabeth expressed it this way:

> The massive and serious violation of the right to life and personal integrity [by state terror] tended to cover up its coexistence with the violation of social-economic rights. Political repression was able to generate diverse forms of subjugation that prepared people to accept unemployment, super-exploitation and the lack of basic necessities (health, housing, education). It smashed any manifestation of social resistance until it seemed as if the majority had resigned themselves to the loss of rights and hope. (Lira, 1994, p. 171)

This view of the historical role of state terror is shared by all of our protagonists and by many of their *compañeros* in the human rights movement.

Hebe de Bonafini, president of the Mothers of the Plaza de Mayo, echoes this view when she proclaimed:

> The torture, the murders, the genocide were for one thing only: to apply an economic plan that would bring misery to the majority of the people...Economic repression is the strongest form of repression...There are so many recessions. Wages and salaries aren't enough to live on. There is unemployment. There is hunger...We still have the same problems that our children were fighting to change. (Fisher, 1989, p. 145)

VICTIMS OF NEOLIBERAL DEMOCRACY

Political democracy has overseen the steepest decline in social and economic democracy in recent memory. In fact, the 1980s were dubbed "The Lost Decade" because they produced the highest number of poor people in a single decade in Latin American history. Despite the change from military to constitutional regimes during these years, the mammoth debt crisis and a continent-wide 10 percent decline in the standard of living condemned 44 percent of the region's population to live below the official poverty line. The new democratic regimes throughout Latin America found themselves held hostage by the terms imposed by the International Monetary Fund and the World Bank. In exchange for renegotiating outstanding loans, the International Monetary Fund demanded that governments implement "structural readjustment" policies, including austerity measures, that facilitated the full implementation of the neoliberal economic model. This Faustian bargain between the powerful international lending agencies and Latin American democratic states included the deregulation of the economy, the liberalization of trade, the dismantling of the public sector through privatization of state-owned enterprises, the elimination of the social "safety net," and the predominance in the economy of the financial sector over production and commerce. Thus the state abandoned its role as the agent of social development and equitable distribution and instead supported the redistribution of the wealth upward.

During the 1980s and 1990s, wherever social movements arose to challenge this model, as in Nicaragua, El Salvador, Guatemala, and Haiti, they became targets of the Doctrine of National Security. The United States and its elite allies in Central America and the Caribbean employed a new strategy called Low Intensity Conflict that uses a combination of economic, psychological, and political pressures, often via local mercenary forces, to liquidate opposition to neoliberalism and its economic agenda.[7] Throughout the 1980s, in her work as the co-coordinator of the Internationalist Team, Mimi Langer actively opposed this policy and helped to treat the psychic trauma in response to the U.S.-sponsored international economic campaign and Contra military and psychological warfare against the people of Nicaragua.

All our protagonists believe that neoliberal economics and conservative politics were the twin factors responsible for the exacerbation of the psychological and social problems of Latin America during the 1980s and 1990s. Impunity was manifested in the irresponsible policies of the transnational corporations, whose uncontrolled investments in Latin America raised exports, enriching local elites and global capital, but leaving in their wake land that was drying out and sinking and workers who were sick from the large-scale use of insecticides and chemical fertilizers prohibited in the United States and Europe. Over 200 pesticides on the World Health Organization's blacklist were being used with impunity in Uruguay, which developed one of the highest cancer rates of any country in the world. In Chile, free-market impunity resulted in ever-escalating unemployment, which pushed 40 percent of the workforce into the dirty, dangerous, and unregulated environment of the informal economy. The rapacious export-based economy in Chile resulted in deforested hills, fished-out shorelines, and chemical-ridden fields in the country's fruit belt. The indiscriminate use of fertilizers has been linked to alarming rates of birth defects in children of farm workers.[8]

In Argentina, impunity was expressed in a variety of ways, including the manner in which the president and Congress extended the implementation of the free-market economic model. They demolished the country's traditional welfare capitalism through a privatization policy, selling off nationally owned enterprises to foreign transnational corporations and severely downsizing employment and social services in the public sector. By the early 1990s, luxury malls thrived in bourgeois neighborhoods, while 33 percent of the population was driven below the poverty line. By the mid-1990s, the unemployment rate rose to an unprecedented 20 percent. Another manifestation of impunity was the ongoing abuse of authority by the police, who continued to act with free rein: In a two-year period—1988 to 1990—police officers committed more than one-third of the homicides in the Greater Buenos Aires area. They also made Argentine youth the new enemy, targeting them at rock concerts and on the streets, especially in working-class neighborhoods, for arbitrary detention and murder.

In this era of neoliberal impunity, children suffered especially. Education levels throughout Latin America declined, and the impunity of the market, reflected in the widespread elimination of customary social protections, resulted in a breakdown of the family. More and more children were forced to contribute to family incomes or to fend for themselves on the streets. As traditional structures like the family, church, and schools were no longer protected and nurtured, millions of children were forced to survive in alternative structures of authority and community—often illicit—that made them the victims of drug lords, pimps, and right-wing death squads. They became the targets, as well, of rising numbers of vigilantes, whose lawless form of crime prevention was aimed at "social cleansing." The vigilantes' self-declared "war against the disposable people" was aimed not only at children but at the homeless, gang members, and addicts, and it also extended to prostitutes, gays, and political activists.

In Nicaragua, the electoral victory of opposition candidate Violeta Chamorro in 1990 was part of the overall goal of reintegrating the country into the neoliberal political model and of dismantling the Sandinista social projects. By the mid-1990s, free-market economic policies were exacerbating the social and economic crises that had been provoked earlier by the Contra war. As Nicaragua's debt to the International Monetary Fund and other international lending agencies expanded and its markets opened up in response to new free-trade strategies, its tiny elite sector increased access to consumer goods, while the rest of its population experienced rising unemployment, lowered nutritional levels, less access to decent housing, education, and medical care and exposure to expanding social violence, which included an escalation in drug use and juvenile delinquency.[9]

By the late 1990s, when my colleagues and I are discussing these horrific conditions, it is still several years before the political tide will turn. Diana tells me, "I live with a circumstantial pessimism and a fundamental historical optimism." And no wonder. She and her colleagues witness people's psychological duress in response to the deterioration of social life. As a Uruguayan colleague describes life in the 1990s, "Whereas during the dictatorship our motto was 'Everyone against them,' now it is 'Everyone against everyone else'" (Achugar, 1993, p. 234). In Argentina, public culture, with its traditional values of a just and cooperative society, has been replaced by the growing influence of the mass media, whose morality and aesthetics are driven by a market "survival of the fittest" that encourages an ethic of individualism and noncooperation. In Chile, where strong traditions of community life show signs of disintegration, the psychological deterioration is notable. Between 1970 and 1991, suicides increased threefold and alcoholism quadrupled. Family breakdowns are multiplying and crime rates are soaring. More than half of all visits to the country's public health system, for example, involve psychological ailments, mainly depression. This dramatic impact of neoliberalism on Latin America moved the Grandmothers of the Plaza de Mayo to organize a human rights conference, at which the vice-rector of the University of Buenos Aires told an enthusiastic audience that, in agreement with the Grandmothers, he believed there is a need for a new agenda for human rights, especially for the child victims of neoliberalism: "This is a new form of torture, a new form of disappearance. The new *desaparecidos* of the 1990s are the poor, and the majority of them are children. These are the victims of democracy" (Abuelas de Plaza de Mayo, 1995, p. 166).

The "economic terrorism" of neoliberalism administered by democratic states has been facilitated by another important development: the emergence of a unipolar world. The fall of the Soviet bloc has, for the historical moment, seemed to obliterate any alternative to global capitalism. Although the authoritarianism and centralized command economy of the Soviets were unappealing to most on the left throughout Latin America, nonetheless the mere existence of the Soviet bloc and thus of a bipolar world had served as a deterrent to all-out U.S. economic, military, and political aggression in the region. The triumph of capitalism has been interpreted in the United States as the historic victory of a superior system and has been presented by conservative intellectuals as the "end of history," by which they mean the victory of a system that is the final and crowning achievement in the long evolution of human social organization. South of the border, however, the new unipolar world is viewed by many not as an achievement but as a defeat in the struggle to build a political economy characterized by equity and social justice. The problem facing the contemporary world, from the point of view of progressive Latin Americans, is that we now live in a singular international system that draws human beings inexorably into a profoundly exploitative social order or marginalizes them into abject poverty. This system appears at this historical period to be invincible. But in a prescient moment, Tato puts it this way: "I think it's like a boxer who's lost the fight in a knockout...Really existing socialism failed, and that has favored the free-market economic model because there is no alternative. It's disillusioning—this lack of an alternative, the lack of hope that there is something else besides capitalism, besides the consumer culture. But I believe that Soviet-style socialism failed, not socialism in and of itself. I'm not an economist, but to me it seems that capitalism is driving a significant percentage of the population to disaster, certainly here in Latin America, but even in the United States. From my perspective, we are getting close to a global crisis, and as intellectuals, we have a choice: We can either put our heads in the sand or get involved in every way possible, to raise the issues of a new morality, a new ethic, a new future."

The collapse of Soviet-style socialism has had a paradoxical effect on Latin America. While it eliminated a bipolar world, it simultaneously opened up the possibility for the emergence of new forms of radical thinking and practice. Toward the end of the 20th century, it is clear that the wish for a life of dignity, justice, and liberty did not fall with the Berlin Wall. Some of the victims of neoliberalism are rising up as its critics, turning themselves from objects of history into its social subjects. Amid the widespread alienation of Latin Americans from politics sprouts a new radical praxis, one that is more local and more democratic and that involves civil society in new ways. Since the late 1980s, new grassroots movements have developed, not only among organized labor but in other sectors as well. The contemporary left is undergoing a rebirth based on a critical assessment of traditional ways of doing politics. A new appreciation for the class, race, and gender identities that motivate people to build political movements has emerged. There is a growing recognition that even though the current struggles are responses to the deterioration of life under global capitalism, they are multifaceted and often organize people around issues of individual freedoms, living conditions, and environmental concerns. Movements that address class oppression, moreover, are often fought in terms of gender, gay, and ethnic rights. Women are becoming visible players, not only in new feminist groups sprouting up throughout the continent but increasingly as leaders in political parties, labor unions, neighborhood organizations, and the ecology movement. It is often argued that the increased activism of women has spurred the renewed commitment to democratic process and grassroots involvement.

Electoral politics are once again the site of activism but now with a new emphasis on mobilizing civil society. However, even while engaged in radical political struggles, many activists all too often manifest a psychological conservatism that is expressed in a wish for stability and a fear of confrontation with authority, as described by Elizabeth. All too often activists can forget about the long-range goal of social transformation in the struggle to meet immediate, specific objectives. Moreover, they have difficulty sustaining the optimism required to deal with the demoralization, competitiveness, and opportunism that inevitably emerge in oppositional movements and weaken the struggle for a decent society. However, with all these limitations, by the new millennium, these social movements will become influential enough to bring to power genuinely progressive governments throughout the region to challenge the hegemony of the United States and elite-driven neoliberal agenda.[10]

Alongside these movements for social change, the wounds of state terror are sustained as a latent threat, ready to be reactivated in the public psyche. Such is the case with the impact of the public confessions made by torturers in Chile and Argentina. In July 1995, disturbing memories of Pinochet's culture of fear were stimulated for Chileans when Osvaldo Romo, a carpenter and former agent of the Directorate of National Intelligence (DINA), spoke publicly about how he had tortured political prisoners, often to death, during the military regime. Romo showed no remorse for his crimes, but rather claimed that DINA's biggest error had been not killing all its torture victims. "I wouldn't leave a parakeet alive," the torturer declared (Hollander, 1997, p. 212). His publicized remarks not only reawakened anxieties, terrors, hatreds, and bitter feelings of impotence among Chileans but reminded them that because of impunity, hundreds of torturers were still free, living and working among them.

Romo's public declarations came on the heels of the confession in Argentina several months earlier by Adolfo Francisco Scilingo, a former navy lieutenant commander who disclosed his participation in the murder of suspected "subversives" during the Dirty War. Scilingo, who had been in charge of a notorious center for the detention and torture of political prisoners in Buenos Aires, chilled the Argentine public by describing how political prisoners had been stripped naked, drugged, and hauled unconscious onto airplanes to be flown over the South Atlantic and thrown out to meet their deaths in the freezing ocean waters. Scilingo described his participation in these "death flights," during which he had seen in his mind's eye photographs of the Nazi death camps as he pushed the bodies of his victims into the darkened night sky. Almost two decades after the Dirty War, Scilingo filed a complaint in the federal court charging the head of the navy with illegally covering up "the methods that superiors ordered used in the Navy Mechanics School for detaining, interrogating and eliminating the enemy during the war against subversion" (Hollander, 1997, p. 212). He argued that, given the amnesty laws, there was no sense in hiding the facts; and moreover, because he and other military officers had merely been following orders from above, it was only fitting that his superior officers should share the terrible guilt from which he was suffering.

The human rights movement in Argentina welcomed his confession because, for the first time, the perpetrators had publicly acknowledged the truth of the crimes of which they were accused by their victims. It also stimulated a debate about the previously unexamined role of the Catholic Church during the Dirty War, forcing the hierarchy to acknowledge that it had been complicit through silence and, in all too many instances, actual collaboration with the repression. Moreover, the army chief of staff now was obliged to declare on national television that "it's time to assume the responsibility and no longer deny the horrors of the past." He went on to clarify that the army had "employed illegitimate methods, including the suppression of life, to obtain information." The Mothers of the Plaza de Mayo responded with outrage. "Let them go to hell with their repentance," declared their president, Hebe de Bonafini. "We will continue struggling so that someday we may see them in jail." Bonafini's militant declaration is typical of the Mothers and Grandmothers of the Plaza de Mayo, whose voices rise above the din of compromise and adaptation to an unacceptable status quo, in which economic exploitation, social injustice, political repression, and psychological alienation continue to characterize the neoliberal enterprise in Latin America.

THE CALM BEFORE THE STORM

During the late 1990s, like the Mothers and Grandmothers, our Latin American psychoanalytic protagonists continued to forge their political analyses and social activism on the basis of their understanding of the intensifying exploitative relations and social- and psychopathology that are endemic throughout Latin America. They believed that the mode of analysis they developed from the late 1960s—namely, a psychoanalysis that takes account of convergences between psychological processes and social forces—was as relevant in the contemporary period as it had been more than two and a half decades earlier. They pointed to the process by which globalization enriches an international elite as it simultaneously lowers the standard of living and the expectations of working people, not only in the Global South but in the United States and Europe as well. Misery, anxiety, and social violence are the universal byproducts.

Each of our Latin American protagonists is an intellectual who has read and digested postmodernist political, social, and psychological theories, whose critical essence they believe is a direct outgrowth of the traditions of Marx and Freud: Marxism because of its insistence that modes of production, class relations, and dominant ideologies affect the nature of mental life and psychological experience of individuals; and Freudianism because of its assertion that the apparent unity and "knowability" of the human mind is an illusion hiding the essential discontinuity and multiplicity of the self that lies below the surface. The postmodern impulse, which pervades scholarly research and popular culture alike, stresses the need to expose the assumptions within all systems of thought and to reject the tendencies of all theoretical models to construct exclusive bipolar categories because conceptualizing the world in this way overlooks the shared and overlapping attributes that move fluidly back and forth between such categories. Postmodernism focuses on knowing the social context that determines any individual narrative of reality and encourages a critical awareness of the kaleidoscope of perspectives and points of view that together constitute the multiplicity of human experience. Although our protagonists have embraced the postmodernist insistence on the need to deconstruct all assumptions in the process of analyzing any object of study, they argue that in contemporary—postmodern—capitalism, class, race, and gender relations continue to be governed by general patterns that can be known, understood, and struggled against. For them, the specificities of contemporary social pathology and psychopathology should be understood in ways that lead to an emancipatory practice.

"It's what's happening in your country as well as in Latin America," Juan Carlos told me in the late 1990s, "that for me makes Marx's insights still relevant today. For example, Marx argued that no social formation disappears before all its productive forces are fully developed. I think he anticipated what we see today through the globalization of neoliberalism. The intersystemic contradictions between capitalism and socialism, which evolved throughout the 20th century, from the Russian Revolution in 1917 to the fall of the Berlin Wall in 1989, have collapsed; and in their place we are experiencing the intrasystemic contradictions in the crisis of global capitalism. For the first time in history, capitalism constitutes an autonomous and mature entity whose determinants, tensions, and conflicts—insoluble contradictions—reside within the system itself. In the 21st century, capitalism will guarantee one constant reality: more than three-quarters of humanity will live in extreme misery."

But Juan Carlos suggested that we also have to understand how it is that this same humanity suffers profound inhibitions when it comes to developing an ideological alternative to hegemony, that is, the official story of those in power. "The lack of critical consciousness among so many requires us to deepen our understanding not only of historical processes but of the history of each subject, whose complex unconscious workings need to be analyzed in order to be known. Psychoanalysis deepens our exploration into the historicity of each subject and thus can teach us who we are at this historical juncture and how each of us is limited and restricted in ways we are not conscious of by internal and external forces. For me, in spite of all the seductive qualities of postmodernist thinking, it is the new scholarship in contemporary psychoanalysis, along with radical social criticism, that has the best chance to help us understand the world we live in and how—call me old-fashioned—to change it by assuming our position as the subjects of our own history."

The return of the repressed: Economic meltdown and rebellion

In December 2001, while we in the United States were absorbed with the terrifying aftermath of 9/11, a global traumatic cataclysm hit Argentina. The unfathomable, the unsymbolizable—much like the Lacanian Real—happened: The entire economy collapsed, plummeting millions of Argentines into boundless states of insecurity and panic. In the weeks leading up to this unprecedented crisis, the symptoms had multiplied: Alongside an unemployment rate of 20 percent and growing, incomes plunged by 30 percent, and foreign-owned banks transferred more than $40 billion to their home offices. All savings and checking accounts were frozen, and when banks declared insolvency, the savings of pensioners and the middle class were virtually destroyed. Wages and salaries were reduced by 65 percent, and unemployment continued to soar. But then something extraordinary happened.

A spontaneous mass uprising erupted, one of the most explosive upheavals of multiple social sectors in Argentina's history. The people found their collective voice, and beginning on December 19, hundreds of thousands of pot-banging, impoverished, middle-class people, pensioners, unemployed workers, and trade union activists converged on the Presidential Palace to demand that all those responsible for the disaster that had ruined their lives leave the country—the politicians, the bankers, the transnational corporations, the International Monetary Fund (IMF), and the military. *Que se vayan todos*—"all of you get out now"—was the battle cry that became the symbol of the challenge waged by the middle and working classes united against a system that robbed them of their jobs, savings, retirement, dignity, and hope. Confrontations with authorities ensued, and the economy continued to be totally paralyzed. Over a two-week period, Argentina saw a rapid turnover of three different presidents, each forced to resign by the protesters. In the frenzied period that followed, Argentines built an oppositional movement that for a while challenged the state and the very bases of capitalism itself.

Unprecedented collective organizing of alternative strategies for survival occurred throughout the country. Neighborhood assemblies were spontaneously organized in middle- and working-class communities to deal collectively with families' basic needs. Commercial markets sprouted up where neighbors could deal with the scarcity of money by bartering goods and services among themselves. Militant protests by unemployed workers escalated that included a wave of factory occupations by workers whose bosses had fled the country, taking their capital, cheating the creditors out of their indebted businesses, and abandoning their workers who had not been paid in months. Grissinopoli, a factory that manufactures bread products in the heart of a working-class community in Buenos Aires, was the site of one of those occupations.

* * *

It is December of 2003, a sunny, spring, Saturday afternoon in Buenos Aires, two years following the economic collapse. I am about to present a talk about psychoanalysis and politics. I have done so over the years in a variety of venues here, but this one is unique, and I am very excited. We are in Grissinopoli, now a worker-occupied-and-run factory, whose cultural center within the core of the factory itself has been developed through the efforts of a group of psychoanalysts and artists in solidarity with the Grissinopoli worker cooperative, La Nueva Esperanza (The New Hope). I am to elaborate a psychoanalytic perspective on living in the post–9/11 United States.

For months, on the ground floor of this factory, the cultural center has featured a number of speakers from other countries who have come to share their views on contemporary social and political crises and to learn about the incredible grassroots movements that exploded in Argentina several years earlier in response to the country's catastrophic economic meltdown. I begin my talk to an audience that includes psychoanalysts, social scientists, middle-class intellectuals, artists, people from the lower middle-class community surrounding the factory, and workers with little more than an elementary school education.

Those who are assembled, having lived through their own extreme social situations, are interested in learning about how we in this country are psychologically managing the multiple threats of terrorism, war without end, and a right-wing assault on our democracy. In the lively discussion after my presentation, despite their collective and individual traumatogenic history, these Argentines are clearly evidencing the reparative effects of participation in a popular rebellion against the past. As some of them point out, for the first time in years they feel they are taking control over their own lives and recreating vital social bonds that had been ruptured during the previous three decades. Juan Carlos has collaborated with the New Hope Cooperative in the factory, and he captures this sense when he tells me: "I would say that there are three discourses within psychoanalysis in Argentina, all of which I've identified with: The first one has to do with suffering, and for years I treated the victims of torture, the families whose loved ones had been disappeared by the military, those who returned from exile suffering from survival guilt and a range of other socially induced pathologies. Then there's the discourse of resistance, and I have been active in many of the human rights struggles, where I have provided treatment to activists and to victims of human rights abuses. But now we are at a turning point, which is the discourse of struggle, and that's what you are seeing now in Argentina. It is very rewarding to be working with people who are trying to create something new, something different, whose very psychology is being changed in the act of becoming protagonists of their own lives. It makes me feel very hopeful to think that a new world is possible."

Indeed, in 2003 Argentina is a veritable laboratory for anyone interested in the potential for democratic and grassroots radical change in a society with a history of political and psychological trauma. During the 1990s, Argentina had been the poster child of neoliberalism, but its status as one of the wealthiest countries in Latin America hid the structural inequities endemic to that economic model. Only when it collapsed in December 2001 did the inherent weaknesses of the unregulated market become visible, prompting spontaneous protest movements that demonstrated the people's rejection of what neoliberalism had to offer them. For psychoanalysts interested in understanding the social as well as the psychic forces responsible for human suffering and in investigating how a new subjectivity can emerge to challenge the existing social order and its hegemonic ideology through demands for a redistribution of power, Argentina in 2003 is the opportunity of a lifetime.

In the Grissinopoli factory the afternoon of my presentation are psychoanalysts I have known and worked with for years, each with a long history of interest in such a project. They have gone beyond the consultation room into the streets to learn from and to offer their skills to the poor, the disenfranchised, and participants in oppositional movements—to engage in, as Mimi Langer used to put it in the 1980s, a "psychoanalysis without the couch." Today these activist psychoanalysts are interested theoretically in the nature of subjectivity as it is constituted in neoliberal capitalism and in the complex factors that explain how and why the subject identifies with a symbolic order whose institutions and ideology inevitably demand, alienate, and decenter. The social movements that emerged in December 2001 have spurred a renewed interest among these psychoanalysts in theory that can locate the gaps or ruptures through which emerge alternative libratory ideologies. As the Argentines argue, the relationship of the subject to the social and political world and one's role as citizen is so central to identity that it is inevitably a legitimate part of the psychoanalytic enterprise.

Julia Braun emphasizes that subjectivity is constituted through the links with significant others throughout the life span. Relationships, events, and even social catastrophes may be significant enough to profoundly alter the subject. This process is called *subjectification* and, in the context of Argentina's experience with state terror and the culture of impunity, has constituted a pathogenic one for its citizens. Braun (2004) describes what is observable in the clinical setting about the nature of the environment against which the social movements have rebelled:

> Clinical practice now confronts us not only with the discontents of civilization as described by Freud, but also with the demands of a culture that destroys the social sense of belonging and the social links between generations, both of which have devastating effects for subjectivity. This culture of discontent forces us to think about a new kind of existence, new subjects and the conflicts generated by the new social conditions. (p. 217)

Diana, Lucila, and Dario of the Equipo have also written about subjectivity in the context of the collective signification of a social order that assaults psychic stability, predictability, and continuity. Anxiety, depression, and the overreliance on defenses such as denial, disavowal, dissociation, and splitting are widespread in the population and are manifested in a variety of symptomatologies seen in individual and group treatment. These three psychoanalysts and their colleagues write and publish their research on the ways that a subjectivity inscribed by social pathology has been positively impacted by the new social movements, which from their inception challenged the fundamental institutions and principles of a pathogenic social order.

The slogan *que se vayan todos* expressed the conviction that the capitalist system—based on the sacrosanct protection of private property, the hegemony of the market, and the commodification of all human relationships—had failed to respond to basic human rights. Thus, many Argentines were willing to venture beyond the prevailing ideological foundation of this system to try to create alternative structures responsive to their needs. In "Group

Psychology and the Analysis of the Ego," Freud (1921) stressed the regressive nature of group psychology, which, he argued, involved a diminishing of the conscious individual personality, the predominance of the affective and unconscious aspects of the psyche, and the projection of each individual's ego ideal onto a leader, whose idealized authority produced a collectively experienced infantilized dependency. However, as German psychoanalyst Alexander Mitscherlich pointed out in regard to the radical political movements in Latin America in the 1960s, far from a loss of identity or a regression such as Freud identified, when people break out of apathetic acceptance of an oppressive social order into some kind of commonality in struggle, there is a gain in identity, a progress toward self-awareness, and a strengthening of the critical ego faculties (Mitscherlich, 1968). In Argentina in 2003, progressive psychoanalytic activists take the same position as Mitscherlich, stressing that in an unprecedented way the grassroots movements surged up spontaneously from among the people themselves and did so without any leaders. They represented a group reassertion of libidinal social links and bonds in a critical and autonomous act of rebellion against the rupturing and fracturing nature of Argentina's version of neoliberal capitalism and its culture of impunity (see Hollander, 2004).

The specific experience of the Grissinopoli workers is illustrative. Grissinopoli is among about 200 factories that are occupied and administered by workers. The two pioneering and most famous are Brukman, a clothing factory in Buenos Aires of mainly women workers, and Zanon, a ceramics factory in the south of Argentina. Both have provided inspiration to other workers, especially in light of the fact that they are functioning successfully in economic terms despite the state's multiple repressive efforts to sabotage them. Grissinopoli is a small factory, and the experience of its workers and their New Hope cooperative demonstrate important lessons articulated by several psychoanalysts, including Cesar Hazaki and Silvia Yankelevich, who have worked with New Hope since its inception.

The plight of these workers predated December 2001, when for years their employer had consistently underpaid them, sometimes giving them just enough money to travel between home and work. Their desperate situation was exacerbated after December 2001, and the workers initiated the difficult legal struggles with the state to keep the indebted and abandoned factory running and to obtain the right to own and administer it. In the beginning, their involvement in this kind of activism came from economic need rather than political ideology, and for a time they sustained a belief in the state's willingness to meet their just requests. In the process, they were gradually learning that those in authority tended to align with the owners of property and could not be trusted much more than their former boss to be concerned about their rights as workers. They were simultaneously experiencing the solidarity and support shown them by the social movements struggling to develop alternatives to existing institutions. Grissinopoli stirred particular passions because for the first time in Argentina's history, children were suffering from hunger on a massive scale. The media was replete with reports that young people were fainting from malnutrition during classes. So the workers and their sympathizers were outraged that a factory that produced a variety of bread products was lying idle.

Realizing they had to take matters into their own hands and inspired by the militancy of other workers, the Grissinopoli workers eventually occupied their factory and began to manufacture its products. Along the way, specialists of various kinds, including economists and experts in public administration, offered their help. Early on, the psychoanalysts associated with the magazine *Topia* held a fund-raiser for the workers. Afterward, a large solidarity meeting was organized, in which the various social movements, including the unemployed workers' movement *los piqueteros*, workers from other occupied factories, activists in the neighborhood assemblies, artists, and a variety of professionals, demanded that rather than award the factory to the former boss's creditors the state nationalize it to permit the workers to run it and share the profits of their labor.

Psychoanalysts Silvia Yankelevich and Cesar Hazaki were approached early on by some of the workers, and each became involved in different ways. They both describe how timid the workers were at the beginning of their struggle, humiliated by their economic need and filled with inhibitions regarding their right to assert themselves with those in power. For both psychoanalysts, the workers' attitudes revealed the mark in unconscious life of hegemonic ideology and how, even when those in power have been exposed as corrupt and completely self-serving, too often the oppressed continue to suffer from their identification with authority. Yankelevich recalls that the workers, about one-third of whom were women, at first felt profoundly vulnerable and hesitant. After they occupied the factory, many of them began to experience physical maladies, and they asked Yankelevich and Hazaki to help them. Some suffered a number of psychosomatic symptoms that revealed the tremendous pressure they were under. They were defying the discourse of power at many levels, ranging from their collective challenge to the state and its property laws to their individual violations of the cultural norms at the most intimate level of the family. As the workers became more involved in the struggle and were benefiting from the solidarity of the social movements, for example, some of the male workers endured terrible guilt that their involvement in the factory occupation meant that they were eating and had a roof over their heads while they had no idea what was happening to their wives and children who lived in the distant suburbs, penniless and without resources. All of the female workers had to deal with their husbands, some of whom were anxious, threatened, and angry that their wives were cohabitating with male workers in the factory. They also experienced guilt with respect to their children, who missed their mothers and exhibited a number of problematic psychological reactions.

Some of the workers, mostly women, asked to unburden themselves with Yankelevich. "The women developed a transference to me," she says, "and wanted to talk. And I, being a psychoanalyst, wanted to listen." She began to accompany the workers when they had to appear in court as part of their legal negotiations, and was an invaluable resource as well as a role model to these working-class people who had never dared to assert their rights or insist on their entitlement to work and to earn a decent living.[11]

Hazaki describes how the factory floor itself became a consultation room and that the male workers, who were unaccustomed to being self-revealing or reflective about their psychological experience, began to engage him in casual conversations or exchanges over a cup of coffee that would often lead to a significant therapeutic intervention. The presence of these psychoanalysts was also useful in that they frequently assisted the workers in developing new capacities to function in a group and to resolve differences and negotiate conflicts in the process of learning to administer a factory. Like the other occupied factories, the New Hope Cooperative established a nonhierarchical and democratic approach to decision making, allocation of positions within the factory, and distribution of the income their labor earned. With the aid of other professionals and the artistic community, Hazaki was instrumental in helping the workers launch the factory's cultural center. He was also an important resource in their establishing multiple links with the surrounding community, an example of which were the popular weekly Saturday night screenings of free movies and popcorn for the neighborhood children and adolescents. These experiences aided the workers' growing awareness of their importance to others in the neighborhood and contributed to their increased individual and collective self-esteem.[12] As one of the workers described it,

> This experience changed our mentality. From now on, we don't give ourselves away and we don't sell ourselves out. Now we know that as workers, we provide a service and we have to get paid. And that's because this work is an essential part of our dignity and the respect that we owe ourselves. (Hazaki, 2002, p. 36)

In general, the workers claimed they were learning that they did not need the capitalists to operate the factories, especially since it was they who had the know-how and skills.

The psychoanalysts who have been involved with Grissinopoli and active in the other social movements speak of a change in the subjectivity of the participants. According to Hazaki, "Without doubt, psychoanalysis can collaborate in developing a new subjectivity, one that aspires to be more autonomous and critical." Juan Carlos points to some significant lessons being learned by workers who engage in these radical political struggles: (1) They rebel against superego mandates to consider the bosses as the only legitimate owners of the factories, mandates that serve to shore up the laws that defend private property and a repressive system, thereby enslaving them; (2) they defy being depicted as needy and incapable people who, if they just behave themselves, will be in a position to receive aid from the state, the church, or other charitable organizations; (3) they eliminate the sensation of being helpless and without protection when they join a health network composed of doctors and social workers who have organized themselves in a similar fashion in response to their own workplaces being shut down; (4) they break with the assumption that only capitalist bosses and their technical experts know how to administer a business and make it productive; and (5) the women overcome the social expectation that they should passively wait for men to take the initiative (see Volnovich, 2004).

We all agree that these lessons garnered in the context of struggle will be put to the test as the social forces representative of power resist the collective demands for change in the hegemonic structures of Argentine society.

* * *

In December 2004, one year after my talk in the cultural center of Grissinopoli, I returned to Buenos Aires to research developments over the subsequent year. I was interested in the impact on the social movements of the presidency of politically progressive Nestor Kirchner, whose election in May 2003 marked a substantial attack on the culture of impunity and the neoliberal economic model. His willingness to prosecute high-ranking individuals from the former military dictatorship and corrupt democratic regimes that followed, as well as his nationalist economic policies, brought hope to many Argentines through a renewed sense of identification with and pride in a political system that seemed at last to uphold human rights and the law. Moreover, Kirchner's nationalist policies that reasserted the role of the state in stimulating economic growth and providing a social net for citizens began to produce some degree of personal and national recovery from the December 2001 debacle. Indeed, immediately following his election, Kirchner's public presentation and his actions as head of state seemed to merit citizens' optimistic expectations. At the time of his inauguration he proclaimed, "I am part of a generation that was decimated and castigated by painful absences [of the 30,000 disappeared]. I joined the political struggle believing in values and convictions that I don't intend to leave at the door of the presidential palace...we arrive without rancor but with memory" (Hollander, 2004, pp. 231–232). This language firmly established Kirchner's identification with the victims of the military dictatorship and his rejection of the prior regimes' official discourse of silence and denial about state terror. In dramatic distinction from his predecessor, the disreputable Carlos Menem, he announced his commitment to complete transparency in government, a purge of the military, the impeachment of the entire Supreme Court, and abolition of the law that had granted amnesty to former perpetrators of the Dirty War. In the months that followed, Kirchner's impassioned rhetoric, nationalistic defense of the interests of the Argentine people in negotiations with the IMF, and impeccable honesty garnered him the affectionate nickname of "Hurricane K."

Kirchner became one of the most vocal leaders among a wave of new, progressive presidents who have emerged in Latin America to confront the entrenched interests of neoliberalism, increasingly known as the "Washington Consensus." Because of his friendly diplomatic relations with progressive presidents Lula of Brazil and Chavez of Venezuela and his unwillingness to join the hostile diplomacy toward Cuba mounted by the United States, Kirchner was maligned by Roger Noriega, the U.S. State Department's Assistant Secretary for Western Hemisphere Affairs. In the worn-out Cold War rhetoric still used by the State Department to criticize progressive and nationalist trends in Latin America, Noriega accused Kirchner's nationalist stance as indicative of "a certain leftward drift" in Argentina's foreign policy. Kirchner responded indignantly that the days are gone when Argentina would jump every time the U.S. waved its scolding finger." Taking a position that was applauded by the Argentine public, he declared that his country was no longer a "carpet to be trampled on by foreign nations" because it is "an independent country with dignity" (Hollander, 2004, p. 233).

Even as many Argentines continued to remain optimistic and to find pleasure in their president's leadership and audacity, others were becoming critical of what they viewed as the emerging contradictions between Kirchner's rhetoric and his policies. For example, while some sectors of the middle class enjoyed a return to their customary privileged lifestyle, redistributive policies were not yet making much of a dent in the deplorable conditions of the 50 percent of the population that remained in poverty and the more than 20 percent that were still unemployed or underemployed.

Progressive Argentines were divided in their assessment of the role of Kirchner: Some believed he was stifling the radical movements in his country by offering a minimal program of reforms to contain the threatening level of disenchantment with the system among millions of people provoked by the economic meltdown in 2001. Others were grateful to be returning to a culture of accountability and some progressive reforms that increased opportunities for working people, even if the price was a brake on what might have been a gradual, radicalized challenge to the system itself. From their perspective, Kirchner's policies and ideology were the best they could hope for at that moment in history. In fact, Kirchner's policies were economically stimulative enough so that sectors of the middle class experienced a return to their customary opportunities and stability, and their involvement in the social movements had consequently flagged. Simultaneously, the militant unemployed workers' movements and factory occupations were under constant threat due to a variety of factors: the lack of an effective movement within the traditional left to provide support and valuable political experience to those engaged in the spontaneous radical mobilizations; diminishing support from a recovering middle class more focused on its own sectoral interests than solidarity with other less fortunate social classes; the complex political maneuverings by the state whose progressive reforms were compelling enough to diminish the apparent need for the alternative projects that had emerged in response to the economic crisis; and the state's periodic repression of those militant workers and unemployed who continued to confront authorities in their struggles for economic justice. Equally important, as one social scientist pointed out to me, especially for those Argentine middle-class people who were not involved in any of the alternative movements, the 2001 economic meltdown represented in some ways a worse traumatic stressor than state terror, for their entire world and possibilities for survival collapsed. The ontological fears that the experience provoked remained as an internal reservoir to be tapped at any sign of instability, which motivated a conservative, security-seeking impulse that in political terms translated into absolute support for the stability, even in the short term, that Kirchner could offer.

The fate of the New Hope Cooperative at Grissinopoli is one example of what happened to the grassroots radical projects as they were impacted by these general developments. In addition, the Grissinopoli workers fell victim to the pressures applied by officers of a right-wing union, who argued convincingly that given their close relationship with the government, they, rather than the radical social movements, could alone guarantee the survival of the New Hope Cooperative. To the dismay of all, including the progressive psychoanalysts who had labored so hard to help these workers develop a critical consciousness, the twin forces of an internalized hierarchical ideology and submissive psychology won, and the workers were seduced away from counterhegemonic ideologies and movements. The discourse of power proved, at least in the short run, to be stronger than these workers' newly evolving radical consciousness.

By 2004, Argentina was a kaleidoscope of conflicting trends impacting citizens in a variety of ways that made subjectivity a contested arena for the contradictory claims of the ego and the unconscious, of rationality and desire, of hegemony and rebellion. Where did that leave the activist psychoanalysts? A bit dispirited, they acknowledged, with regard to Grissinopoli, but only, as they saw it, for the present. They were proud of what psychoanalysts had been able to contribute to the social movements in general and to the New Hope Cooperative in particular. Silvia Yankelevich suggested that psychoanalysts must focus our efforts so as to understand subjectivity in relationship to the means of reproduction of the discourse of power. Only through participation as citizens with social struggles, she emphasized, can we have direct experience and the raw material to postulate answers to questions regarding the tenacity of our attachments to the hegemonic sociosymbolic order. Juan Carlos added that it is essential to understand the subjective bases of power, especially in terms of the processes through which power captures the conscious and unconscious complicity of the subject. He posited that the important goal is to find the gaps in hegemony, to which a radical psychoanalysis is particularly well suited. For example, one of the myths of power in the contemporary world is that no alternative to neoliberal capitalism and its deplorable inequities is possible. Psychoanalysis, he asserted, can help to create new meanings and to resignify such myths so as to dismantle the subject's relationship to authority. He stressed that the transference relationship, which can facilitate the patient's development of alternative representations and an increased detachment from unconscious repetitive enactments symbolic of submission to an internalized discourse of power, can be an important tool in the social sphere as well.

In a related vein, what has the experience of psychoanalysis beyond the couch brought to Argentine psychoanalysts interested in questions of change in the overlapping domains of psychic and social reality? Hazaki (2002) pointed out that it permits them to accomplish important concrete tasks for a broader range of people, and in the process it provides an opportunity to turn their ideals into realities. Moreover, he added, "the Grissinopoli workers were not the only beneficiaries of our relationship. As a result of our direct experiences, we psychoanalysts were able to produce a series of concepts and analyses that have allowed us to grow with respect to our understanding of the convergence of theory and practice in the context of social crises and catastrophes."[13]

On a final note, a question arose as to how much the Argentine experience is relevant for us in this country. Juan Carlos emphatically pointed out that psychoanalysts throughout the world would do well to pay close attention to events in his country. He suggested that with respect to the internal contradictions of neoliberal capitalism, for the Global North as well as the Global South, "Argentina is like the canary in the mines."

Given the intensifying nature of the social, political, and economic crises in the United States and their profound and contradictory effects on our own subjectivity, I took his admonition to heart. In addition to growing concerns about the authoritarian trends of the Bush administration, we were at that very moment seeing signs of the economic fallout of the president's "crony capitalism," as many of his critics called his neoconservative implementation of neoliberal principles. It was, indeed, a propitious time for us in this country, as professionals and as citizens, to continue refining our own versions of psychoanalysis without the couch.

ENDNOTES

1. The conference commemorated the 15th anniversary of the Grandmothers of the Plaza de Mayo in April 1992. A book that includes the proceedings and presentations at the conference was subsequently published under the same title as the conference (Abuelas de Plaza de Mayo, 1995).
2. See especially Silvia Bleichmar (1995). This perspective represents the most optimistic assessment of the ultimately benign effects of this human drama; some mental health professionals are less sanguine about the impact on young people who learn they are the children of *desaparecidos*, and they are concerned about what happens to children and their biological families who do not seek professional help to negotiate the difficult emotional states produced by these painful circumstances. Because of the uniqueness of this situation, there is no knowledge about the long-term psychological effects on these young people, who must grapple with the knowledge that their biological parents were disappeared and were probably tortured and murdered and that the people with whom they grew up and whom they called Mama and Papa were either direct collaborators or childless couples willing to close their eyes and not ask questions when the possibility of "adopting" a child presented itself. Some mental health professionals have noted in these children symptoms associated with an inability to mourn and with guilt connected to having survived or to having (unknowingly) betrayed their parents by loving the family who brought them up (or both). There is a growing literature in Spanish on this topic, but for a source in English that tells the moving story of the first restituted grandchild, see Carlson (2008).
3. The statistics throughout this section come from the following issues of NACLA (1992b, 1993a, 1993b, 1994a, 1994b, 1996).
4. This shift in international financial support from authoritarian right-wing governments to the constitutional regimes that would succeed them and institutionalize the essential aspects of their rule is too complex to detail here but is examined in Sigmund (1993).
5. For an analysis of the differences in the experience of repatriation among Argentines and Uruguayans because of their respective governments' policies, see Mámora and Gurrieri (1988).
6. During the late 1980s and 1990s, other studies were published that analyzed various aspects of the psychological impact of state terror on individuals, children, and families. See, for example, Puget and Kaes (1991), *Revista de Psicoanálisis* (1985), and Movimiento Solidario de Salud Mental, Familiares de Detenidos y Desaparecidos por Razones Políticas. (1987). There is much literature on specific extraordinary events that marked the advance of the draconian policies of the military; see, for example, Seoane and Núñez (1992). Many individuals whose children disappeared published books about them and their experience under state terror; see Echave (1986), Herrera (1987), and Nosiglia (1985).

7. Low Intensity Conflict begins with counterinsurgency and extends to economic, political, military, and psychological operations, both overt and covert. It represents a commitment by U.S. policymakers to employ force in its global attempts to suppress third-world revolutionary movements and governments; see Klare and Kornbluh (1988).

8. The specific data used in this description of the various indicators of impunity in the Southern Cone are from the following issues of North American Congress on Latin America (1992b, 1993a, 1993b, 1994a, 1994b, 1996). See also Verbitsky (1997) and Giussani (1990).

9. For monthly reports and analyses of the situation in Nicaragua, see *Envío* (Universidad Centroamericana, Managua, Nicaragua).

10. Information on the new social movements in Latin America can be found in North American Congress on Latin America (1992a, 1993a, 1994a). I want to thank Juan Carlos Volnovich and my colleague Marjorie Bray, both of whom cautioned me not to idealize peoples' struggles and the role they play in changing history. Juan Carlos, for example, is cautious about the import of peoples' struggles in the elimination of the military dictatorships, arguing that although people did mobilize to oust them, the militaries had, in fact, fulfilled their historical function and could withdraw to the barracks with the conviction that the articulate opposition to the neoliberal project had been eliminated and that their civilian heirs to political power would continue their basic policies. Marjorie reminded me that although new social movements have indeed appeared, they have been fraught with problems that should not be ignored. I thank them both for their measured assessments—especially given that each identifies with these movements for social change—but in defense of my highlighting people's struggles, I quote renowned U.S. historian Howard Zinn (1980), who writes in his preface: "If history is to be creative, to anticipate a possible future without denying the past, it should, I believe, emphasize new possibilities by disclosing those hidden episodes of the past when, even if in brief flashes, people showed their ability to resist, to join together, occasionally to win. I am supposing, or perhaps only hoping, that our future may be found in the past's fugitive moments of compassion rather than in its solid centuries of warfare" (p. xi). By the early 21st century, history would prove that these social movements were effective enough to produce elections of progressive governments whose policies and discourse represented oppositional movements that challenge the "Washington Consensus."

11. Personal interview, November 27, 2003.

12. Personal interview, December 4, 2003.

13. Personal interview, March 23, 2005.

Chapter 8

U.S. neoliberal / neoconservative democracy

Psychoanalysis without the couch

No one can live with a death inside: She has to choose between tossing it far away like a rotten fruit or keeping it and dying from contamination.

— Alicia Partnoy (2004)

Silence is the real crime.

— Hanna Segal (2002)

It is April 2006, and a troubled United States is increasingly beleaguered by a crippled democracy, interminable war, and growing signs of economic dislocation. Hedda and I have maintained an ongoing dialogue about these troubling trends, some of which have been addressed over the past several years in the day-long conferences organized by our Uprooted Mind Committee.

Now we are in Philadelphia at the annual meetings of the Division of Psychoanalysis (Division 39) of the American Psychological Association. Hedda is a presenter on a panel whose subject is an appraisal of the achievements of second-wave feminism. Among the other speakers is Jane Fonda, and she and her discussant have both just presented powerful analyses of the significance of the women's movement and its contributions to our understanding of how gendered subjectivity organizes experience and relationships. They have addressed the multiple effects of the movement on several generations of women since the 1970s, and Fonda has candidly used personal testimony to illustrate her main ideas. I am in the overflow audience, which has just enthusiastically applauded Fonda and her discussant.

It is Hedda's turn to speak, and I wait with anticipation, for I have grown to know what is important to her. Now 97 and casually elegant as always, she slowly and gracefully gets up from her chair behind the presenters' table and approaches the audience to speak about the terrible crises that are gripping the country. She talks about the growing political and economic problems most families face that have been brought on by the war and other misguided policies of the Bush administration. She insists that social class along with gender ought to be an important analytic category because life is vastly different for working-class and Black women than for middle- and upper-class Euro-American women. She urges the audience to recognize that we must do something about the terrible condition of our body politic and that we ought to be in the streets demanding change, demonstrating by the millions on behalf of all the women and children who are suffering in this country and in Iraq because of the ill-conceived priorities of the present government. I smile in agreement. The audience is excitedly applauding, and there are even some supportive whoops to boot.[1]

Hedda's focus on class rather than gender is consistent with her life-long orientation that stems from her familial and social roots. She once remarked to me that her parents were Marxists and that she had read Marx for the first time when she was nine years old. She told me she had always identified with a radical critique of capitalism, which for her was simply a matter of fact. "I'll tell you something," she had added, "Marie Langer and I both attended the same private girls' school in Vienna, though we never knew one another because I was one year ahead of her. And while we both got the advantage of studying at a Social Democratic and feminist school in Red Vienna, I think Marie was able to live her life more than I in tune with what she believed in. I couldn't always act on what I believe. But I'll tell you one thing: I've always had a knee-jerk reaction that left is better than right, no matter what."

Hedda may be correct about the difference between Marie Langer and herself, but her commitment to expressing a radical perspective and her ability to affect others come through in what she has chosen to say in this professional setting and in the audience's enthusiastic response. Their applause after Hedda insists that we should be out in the streets demanding social justice for the most oppressed in our society is also indicative of an awakening of oppositional consciousness throughout the country as critical voices and movements protest ever louder the deleterious social impact of the Bush administration's rightist policies. Although we don't yet realize it, within several years this rumble will produce a groundswell of repudiation that will successfully end the neoconservative hold on government.

As psychoanalysts, we are accustomed to assuming an interpretive sensitivity to our patients' unconscious conflict that underlies the manifest content of dreams and symptoms. But just as Juan Carlos Volnovich warned, it is also imperative that we understand the causes of the symptoms of social malaise. Our challenge is to perceive the underlying dynamics and historical forces responsible for the social illness that has produced the human suffering Hedda has critiqued.

DIAGNOSIS OF A DISORDERED SYSTEM

How is it that Juan Carlos could suggest that we in the Global North need to interpret his country's economic collapse as the canary in the mines?

What do the causes of the Argentine meltdown have to do with our economic troubles in the heart of empire? The answer lies in the nature of the neoliberal paradigm that was conceptualized in this country and implemented throughout much of the world. In previous chapters I analyzed the nature and effects of neoliberalism in the history of Latin America. Now I want to explore how this system and its ideology evolved and was put into practice in this country, with profound social and psychological implications. It was implemented in the 1970s, but the neoconservative movement extended and deepened its problematic characteristics by creating a U.S. culture of impunity and an economic meltdown of global proportions.

Neoliberalism is a social theory and practice organized around the notion of individualism, a core feature of the culture out of which this country was originally fashioned. Individualism arose historically in relation to the political principles of individual rights and liberties associated with the French Revolution and the Enlightenment. These developments were an integral part of the end of the old order of absolute monarchy and feudal privileges of the aristocracy and the emergence of capitalism and a new social order ruled by the bourgeoisie. The formation of the United States occurred as an aspect of this historical shift in that Europeans fleeing state or religious oppression were committed to establishing a new society whose government would protect individual inalienable rights and the values of citizenship. In the context of U.S. expansionism from the 19th century on, rugged individualism became a cultural ideal well suited to the entrepreneurial ethic that accompanied the unimpeded development of capitalism and its domination of the resources and peoples of a vast continent. However, as historian Stephanie Coontz (1992) shows, the ideological embrace of individualism, competition, and private property hid the reality that an activist state invested public funds and established laws that facilitated the accumulation of capital and power by specific groups at the cost of the majority in the social hierarchy. By the early 20th century, due to the growing disparities within U.S. society, the cultural ideal of individualism was being challenged by militant trade union struggles that fought for working-class rights and a progressive political movement that organized on behalf of middle-class demands for state-sponsored reforms to redistribute power and resources from corporate oligarchies. Collective oppositional movements and their politics of social and economic democracy contradicted the ethic of individualism and threatened corporate rule. These factors, along with the capacity of industry to produce unprecedented quantities of goods and services, required a corporate strategy that would expand markets and create a citizenry oriented to associate aspirations for individual rights and democracy with consumerism. The emerging public relations field and its most prominent representative, Freud's nephew, Edward Bernays, utilized psychological principles garnered from psychoanalysis and social psychology to develop a new and highly successful advertizing industry. Their stipulated goal was the construction of an individualistic, consumer-based, large group psychology among U.S. citizens whose yearnings for democracy would be reframed: The experience of individual self-esteem, success in personal and work relationships, and general well-being would now be identified with the products they could purchase rather than with shared struggles for political power and economic justice (see Ewen, 1977).[2]

In the ensuing decades, the ideology of individualism functioned to undercut notions of the common good and rights of the larger community and to hide the history of collective struggles in this country, with corrosive effects on social relations.[3] Let us recall that Zizek captured the power of ideology as a lived daily practice by asserting that "they do not know it, but they are doing it" (Myers, 2003, p. 63). By way of illustrating what I think Zizek means, I share a joke told by Bob Rae, the former Premier of Ontario, as he spoke to the Ontario Chamber of Commerce about what from his perspective is a problematic ideological feature of capitalism:

> This fellow is going to go camping with a friend, and in preparation he goes to a sporting goods store to buy various pieces of equipment and a pup tent. He selects all of his purchases and is about to leave the store when the salesman says to him, "How about a pair of running shoes?"
>
> The fellow responds, "Listen, I'm going camping, I don't need a pair of running shoes."
>
> The salesman says: "What if you run into a bear?"
>
> The fellow, perplexed and a bit irritated, answers, "Come on, I'm not going to outrun a bear."
>
> To which the salesman replies: "You don't have to; you just have to outrun your friend!"[4]

What we do not know as we do it—in this case when we share and laugh at the joke—is that we reproduce and reinforce an unquestioned piece of ideology that we have internalized. While we do not necessarily think about it, our shared chuckle at the joke relieves the unconscious anxiety produced by the assumption that we are each pitted against one another, that we really cannot rely on our friends, that we will be abandoned at the first sign of danger, or that in our own self-interest we are willing to sacrifice our valued others. It permits a vicarious expression of sadism as well, in the victorious experience of vanquishing the other to survive. While there is pleasure in subverting the repressions of such behavior, it emphasizes that each of us individuals is on our own and encourages a fatalistic acceptance of this inevitability. There are profound psychological implications of living in a culture that places such a high value on individualism and narcissism, one that implicitly denigrates cooperation in the face of threat. This jocular depiction of the principle of survival of the fittest satirizes a central component of the dominant ideology that is so pervasive it usually goes without question. The ubiquitous cynical phrase "it's a dog-eat-dog world" is itself a fatalistic view of life uttered by people who are not conscious of its pathogenic effects on their self-esteem and intersubjective experience. The unquestioned identification with the notion of individualism symbolized in this joke leaves people vulnerable to the conservative ideology and the economic agenda that have dominated this country since the 1970s. It emphasizes that our insertion into capitalism—whether as members of the working and middle classes or members of that segment of the wealthy class who own and control capital and the means of production—forces us all to be engaged in the competitive struggle for jobs or profits in which we either vanquish others or are vanquished by them. This social reality that cannot provide a containing holding environment produces psychic states of vulnerability that must be disavowed unconsciously if they cannot be symbolized, that is, thought about and resisted. In this sense, the joke does its job by reinforcing an unquestioned view of human nature that erases the rich history of people's collective struggles in this country and facilitates what Russell Jacoby (1997) calls "social amnesia." Because this view is part of hegemony and to a degree unconscious, it impedes citizens' critical awareness. We become vulnerable to identifying with political discourses that oppose social welfare policies aimed at protecting our shared human rights to food, shelter, work, education, pleasure, and genuine participatory democracy.

While notions of individualism and social Darwinism are endemic to capitalism itself, they have played a significant ideological role in the rise of neoliberalism and its implementation since the 1970s, when it emerged as the paradigmatic free-market economic model imposed in this country and around the world. Although neoliberal intellectual roots can be found in part in the post–World War II German "Freiburg School" economic movement, it is most commonly associated with the ideas developed by Milton Friedman and his colleagues at the University of Chicago. The "Chicago School" critiqued social welfare policies and advocated a radically free market with maximized competition and free trade through an active state that fosters deregulation, elimination of tariffs, and a range of monetary and social policies that are, as political theorist Wendy Brown (2003) suggests, "favorable to business and indifferent toward poverty, social deracination, cultural decimation, long term resource depletion and environmental destruction" (accessed January 28, 2009). As we have seen, neoliberalism was initially implemented in Latin America under military dictatorships that eliminated all advocates of progressive political ideas and government policies favoring working people over foreign corporations and national elites. Recall that following the U.S.-supported military coup in Chile on September 11, 1973, that country's economy was reconstructed under the stewardship of Milton Friedman and his colleagues, known as "the Chicago boys." In her internationally acclaimed book *The Shock Doctrine:*

The Rise of Disaster Capitalism (2007), Naomi Klein shows how neoliberalism has been effectively implemented in countries during periods of political or economic distress because, as she argues, it would not be tolerated by people under ordinary circumstances. For example, neoliberalism was able to be employed in Chile following the military coup precisely because Pinochet's policies of disappearing, torturing, and murdering his own citizens terrorized the Chilean population into regressed states of extreme fear and anxiety that overcame their ability to organize, protest, and fight back. As I argued in earlier chapters, in similar fashion, the military dictatorships throughout Latin America played midwife to this neoliberal agenda.

We have seen how in the context of Latin America, neoliberalism is not only an economic policy but embodies a social analysis and a prescriptive cultural matrix that extend market values to all institutions, social practices, and individual psychology. It is internalized to become a constituent of identity among citizens who live it on a daily basis. Neoliberal ideology was critiqued and fought against by our Latin American psychoanalytic colleagues and other progressives because of its destructive effects on social relations and community. In order to understand the impact of neoliberalism in our own country, let us look at its essential characteristics as conceptualized by noted political philosopher Michel Foucault: In neoliberal theory (1) every facet of existence is submitted to the principles of economic rationality, so that all human action is assessed in terms of rational entrepreneurial objectives based on principles of utility, benefit, supply and demand, and moral value-neutrality; (2) the economy is not naturally given to rational behavior but needs an activist state to intervene to assure competition, free trade, and rational economic action by every member and institution of society; thus the basis of state legitimacy is the health and growth of the economy, rather than, as in liberal democracy, the representation and realization of all citizens' rights and needs; (3) citizens are called upon by the neoliberal state and social institutions (interpellated, to use Althusser's notion) to develop a subjectivity based on an entrepreneurial ethic and a moral autonomy reflected in the capacity for "personal responsibility" and "self-care" (see Lemke, 2005).

As Foucault points out, when the state privatizes important functions, the process does not mean the dismantling of government, but rather a technique of governing in which regulatory functions are transferred to individual citizens who are encouraged to live their lives based on entrepreneurial values and goals. The model neoliberal citizen strategizes a life plan for him- or herself based on individual responsibility for success or failure, regardless of impediments of social class, education, rates of unemployment, and limited welfare benefits. Scholar Thomas Lemke (2005) writes that the culture of neoliberalism is characterized by a harmonious value system "in which not only the individual body, but also collective bodies and institutions (public administrations, universities, etc.), corporations, and states have to be 'lean,' 'fit,' 'flexible,' and 'autonomous': It is a technique of power" (p. 13). Sociologist Pierre Bourdieu calls the essence of neoliberalism the "utopia of endless exploitation," in which the absolute reign of flexibility means that employees are hired through fixed-term contracts or on a temporary basis, and autonomous divisions and teams within corporations are forced to compete with each other for survival. Self-exploitation is increased among individual workers, who must practice self-discipline as a requirement of employment on the basis of individual performance objectives, merit, career paths, and ability to delegate responsibility. Bourdieu (1998) suggests that these neoliberal patterns, which he calls "structural violence," converge to weaken or abolish collective standards or solidarities, producing massive insecurity, suffering, and stress.

Because the psyche is constituted in part by the internalization of hegemonic ideology and practices, the neoliberal paradigm fashions what psychoanalyst Lynne Layton calls a "normative unconscious," characterized by the delinking between the individual and the social. Particularly in the U.S. context, the ideology of the "free individual" is closely connected with self-reliance and an extreme individualism that denies connections of all kinds. According to Layton (2004b), a narcissistic character is thus fostered in which "a split in the relation between attachment capacities and agentic capacities...emerges because of the mutually exclusive way each set of capacities is defined and because of the higher value placed on agentic capacities." An unconscious association develops that equates autonomy with self-reliance, which is highly esteemed, and attachment with submission, which is devalued. Layton postulates that those individuals who achieve dominant positions in the various hierarchies of class, race, and gender do not have to recognize neediness, want, or dependency, all of which can be demeaned, split off, and projected in order to sustain a privileged identity. The "free" individual at the heart of the neoliberal paradigm thus represents an attack on linking that has serious political implications.

The neoliberal isolated self is activated within the elite, whose position in the class hierarchy requires a competitive and self-serving egoism that can sustain power, defended by a manic omnipotence that eschews acknowledgement of need and empathy for others. The majority of citizens come to identify with and are burdened by similar values and attitudes, but with little to show for their culturally induced psychic isolation in either emotional well-being, material wealth, social status, or political power. A passive, depoliticized citizen becomes the ideal feature of the system as neoliberalism erodes collective struggles along with public-mindedness. Furthermore, as genuine liberal democracy is undermined, the principles associated with it, including liberty and justice, are used ideologically to justify neoliberal policies but are drained of their meaning in the process.

The social/economic project of neoliberalism has been imposed in different countries under a variety of unique social and political circumstances that prevented people from developing intelligible narratives independent of the official story that justified it.[5] In the United States and Great Britain, neoliberalism was successfully implemented during the 1970s through ideological consensus rather than coercion, a process Noam Chomsky (2002) calls "the manufacturing of consent." Ronald Reagan and his British colleague Margaret Thatcher set about to build an ownership society based on individualistic principles. Having declared that "there is no such thing as society, only individual men and women" (Harvey, 2009, p. 23); Thatcher, along with Reagan, developed policies aimed at eliminating all forms of social solidarity associated with the welfare state and trade union activism that had characterized both countries since the Great Depression. Thatcher understood the important role of ideology and its impact on psychology in securing the acquiescence of citizens whose lives would be deeply affected. She put it like this: "Economics are the method, but the object is to change the soul" (Harvey, 2005, p. 23).

What did this political and economic shift mean in the case of the United States? The redistributive policies known as Keynesianism that had emerged in response to the Great Depression were implemented by President Roosevelt through government support for social programs and infrastructural investments that kept employment high and provided needed services. This economic strategy could be sustained beyond the Great Depression as long as high rates of capital accumulation could exist alongside welfare state social policies. It survived through war and the economically expansionist period of the 1950s and 1960s, when profit rates were high and the capitalist class was thus willing to share a reasonable percentage of its profits with the middle and working classes, whose standard of living rose as a result. But by the mid-1970s a series of economic crises ushered in a period of stagflation, to which the capitalist class responded by adopting a neoliberal economic policy. In the United States, the neoliberal state sought to reassert the power of capital and its accumulation capacities through the imposition of a deflationary policy that caused the United States and much of the rest of the world to plunge into recession and relatively high rates of unemployment. While Reagan famously declared that government was not the solution but rather the problem, he used the government to deregulate the flow of capital and profits through tax and budget cuts. And he assaulted trade union and professional sectors, the symbol of which was his destruction of PATCO, the Professional Air Traffic Controllers Organization. Since that time, the mission of the neoliberal state has been to create a favorable climate for capital profits regardless of the deleterious effects on employment or social well-being. The privatization of assets, deregulation of economic and social activities formerly administered by the government, and unencumbered mobility of capital have been its primary achievements. According to noted anthropologist David Harvey (2006), neoliberalism is hostile to all forms of social solidarity, and while claiming to encourage competition, fosters the interests of monopoly and centralized economic power.

These regressive economic policies required an ideological strategy that could secure consensus by turning citizens' attention away from the social origins of the new economic and class realities and mobilizing a subjectivity based on neoliberal notions of citizenship. In chapter 1 we saw how, beginning with Reagan, the Republican Party became the political instrument of the wealthy who built a popular base of support among the very people most hurt by its policies but who identified with the neoliberal values of individualism, rights of property, and patriotism. Facilitated by the rise of the Christian right, the socially and economically disenfranchised were mobilized politically through appeals to the "traditional values" allegedly threatened by the social movements of the 1960s that had developed collective struggles on behalf of gender, class, and ethnic equity and against imperialist war making. As the financial sector of capital replaced industrial production to become the major generation of profit in the U.S. economy, millions of working people's lives throughout the South and Midwest were decimated. Many of these citizens, in order to defend themselves against their loss of jobs, quality of life, and self-esteem, sought refuge in the battle for a return to the reliable, clear boundaries of the traditional family, woman's domestic role, and religious fundamentalism in order to shield themselves from the undefined ambiguity of the values associated with liberal America. In his critical study *American Fascists: The Christian Right and the War on America* (2006), award-winning journalist Chris Hedges has empathically captured the motivation of citizens who make up the base of the neoconservative Christian evangelical movement:

> The pain, the dislocation, alienation, suffering and despair that led millions of Americans into the movement are real...The democratic traditions and the values of the Enlightenment, they believe, have betrayed them. They speak of numbness, an inability to feel pain or joy or love, a vast emptiness, a frightening loneliness and loss of control. The rational, liberal world of personal freedoms and choice lured many of these people into one snake pit after another. And liberal democratic society, for most, stood by passively as their communities, families and lives splintered and self-destructed...these believers have abandoned, in this despair, their trust and belief in the world of science, law and rationality. They eschew personal choice and freedom. They have replaced the world that has failed them with a new, glorious world filled with prophets and mystical signs. (p. 35)

Thus ideology and psychological defenses joined forces to ward off feelings of helplessness in the face of the complex systemic sources of the new neoliberal political and economic assault on the status and security of millions of working people (see Frank, 2004; Bageant, 2007).

In parallel fashion meanwhile, by the mid-1970s, many of the leaders and activists who had participated in the 1960s radical movements that fought against a corporate state and its racist, sexist, and imperialist policies were gradually retreating from political activism. In response to the overwhelmingly difficult task of altering institutionalized power, many turned toward a more personal, libratory journey. Frustrated with the difficulties of changing social reality, they looked inward to transform psychic reality through the search for individual authenticity and liberation from socially repressive expectations and values. Their emphasis on the personal path to change dovetailed with the neoliberal emphasis on individual responsibility for self-management and success. Self-actualization as a life goal fit well with the market-driven consumer values of neoliberal capitalism that marked the eighties and nineties in what some scholars have dubbed "the culture of narcissism."[6] The problematic effects of the values of consumer culture and the mass media have been analyzed critically by scholars, including psychoanalysts. Many have noted the disturbing impact on people of living in a mass-mediated society, in which the relationship with machines, themselves an integral aspect of consumerism, has come to rival in importance relationships between people. Philip Cushman (1995) suggests that the complex web of meanings through which traditional cultures taught wisdom and healing has been replaced by advertising and a pseudo-culture based on the concept of lifestyle. This consumer culture has become the source of meaning and identity and self-esteem, which Cushman argues has contributed to the development of the "empty self." Transformative experience is sought through repetitive consumption of commodities. Psychoanalytic scholars have analyzed another dimension of the negative impact of the powerful role of the mass media. They maintain that the radical shift from socialization in the family and through the written word toward socialization by images in various kinds of virtual realities results in the erosion of our capacity for independent thought, self-discipline, and self-reliance. Normal ego and superego development is compromised, as is the capacity to discriminate between reality and fantasy and between who we are as distinct from what we consume. It is more difficult to resist the constant mass-mediated stimulation for instantaneous narcissistic gratification, which, it is argued, leads to psychic structures analogous to an adolescence that is never outgrown (Eizirik, n.d.).

Within this general pattern of retreat into an individualistic paradigm, some progressives interested in libratory ideas and strategies continued to persist in their passions. Hedda Bolgar was among them, and by the early 1970s she felt the need to "fill the hole" in her life that was the product of a profession dominated by an ethic of the separation between psychic and social reality. Hedda had spent some seven years involved in a research project with Franz Alexander assessing the efficacy of the psychoanalytic process, after which she had joined what became a successful struggle to secure licensure in the State of California for psychologists to practice as clinicians. By the early 1970s, she turned toward a project that would integrate her professional and social interests. Together with a group of postdoctoral students with whom she had previously worked, Hedda developed a model of what from her perspective would be an ideal graduate training program for psychologists based on the integration of a social and psychodynamic paradigm. "I wanted the degree to be a social clinical Ph.D., which was the beginning for me of thinking about internal and external reality and how they affect one another." In Berkeley, Hedda's friend and colleague Nevett Sanford, a coauthor of the groundbreaking Frankfurt School study *The Authoritarian Personality* (Adorno et al., 1982), had founded the Wright Institute, an independent graduate research institute. With his initial support, in 1974, Hedda and her postdoctoral colleagues developed a doctoral and postdoctoral program, which they launched as the Wright Institute in Los Angeles. Occurring shortly after Hedda's husband, Herbert, had died, for her the Wright Institute would be in part, "an homage to him because it incorporated all of his fundamental values and interests." The Wright Institute was composed of a graduate school, a postdoctoral program, a low-fee clinic, and a research component. "Lots of people wanted to come to get a Ph.D. in this unique training program. It was feminist and Marxist and strongly psychoanalytic. After about 120 very good Ph.Ds graduated, by the early 1980s we were under such financial duress that we had to close the graduate program. But the postdoctoral program still exists and sustains an important link between psychoanalytic ideas and social preoccupations."

In general, notwithstanding the Wright Institute and other social projects of various kinds organized throughout the country by individuals committed to sustaining a vision of a more just society, progressive activism on a larger scale diminished during this period. The political right, however, organized in multiple ways. Backed and funded by corporate money, conservative operatives built think tanks and circulated their ideas and strategies throughout society in corporations, universities, professional associations, churches, school boards, and finally in electoral politics at local, state, and federal levels of government (Harvey, 2005; Frank, 2004).

The historical process that occurred over the past several decades appears to have developed two Americas, but the essential principles underlying these divisions have been relatively stable in the sense that most citizens continued to share assumptions basic to the dominant ideology. As Gramsci argued, within hegemony a variety of competing creeds, doctrines, and modes of perception jostle for authority, but together they tend to generate a belief in the existing system. So it has been since the 1970s in this country. The neoliberal state and its ideological features have become entrenched and their dominance secured in both mainstream political parties. In truth, U.S. citizens had been abandoned by most political leaders, who, Republican and Democrat alike, rallied around their own self-interested allegiance to the moneyed classes, weakening the political principle of universal representation that had been foundational to liberal democracy. In point of fact, after the Democratic Party suffered dramatic electoral losses to Reagan, a group of prominent Democrats argued that their party was out of touch and in need of a radical shift in economic policy and ideas of governance. In 1985, they founded the Democratic Leadership Council (DLC) and advocated a political "third way" to compete with Reagan's electoral successes. By the time the Democratic Party returned to power under Bill Clinton, who was a "New Democrat" and a major figure in the DLC, it had adopted neoliberal principles in both domestic and foreign policy that continued to strengthen U.S. corporate interests internationally while structurally weakening policies that in previous periods had assured a reasonable level of employment, living standards, and social welfare for U.S. citizens.

Clinton provided a culturally permissive mask whose New Deal rhetoric obfuscated the policy spirit of Reagan. In fact, Clinton's political strategies were profoundly neoliberal in nature, reflected in his leadership role in privatization and outsourcing policies in welfare, education, prisons, the police, and the military. Clinton and his New Democrats were more open to deregulation than the previous Democratic leadership had been. This shift was especially evident in the large-scale deregulation of agriculture and the telecommunications industries, as well as the ratification of the North American Free Trade Agreement (NAFTA), in spite of widespread progressive and union opposition. Although it was not obvious at the time, the short-lived affluence of the Clinton presidency was, argues David Harvey (2005), based mainly on the privileged position of U.S. capital in the global market and the "flow of tribute" from the rest of the world, rather than on domestic growth. This reality is only now becoming clear as we understand the historical context of our current economic meltdown.

What does the rise of neoconservatism represent in the context of neoliberal hegemony? This movement constituted a reaction against some cultural and political aspects of neoliberalism, all the while it expanded the basic processes of privatization and deregulation. The intellectual roots of neoconservatism were multiple, and thus as a political formation it is not unified ideologically or socially. It emerged from a convergence of interests among evangelical Christians, Jewish followers of the political and philosophical critique of liberalism by University of Chicago scholar Leo Strauss, secular Cold Warriors, conservative "feminist" family moralists, converted liberals, and individual politicians and intellectuals, all of whom advocated U.S. political and military expansion (Brown, 2006). During the Cold War, the followers of Strauss, many of whom would later found the Project for a New American Century, believed that in order for the United States to bring good to the world, it had to overcome its own fundamental weaknesses that were the product, from their perspective, of relativism, liberalism, absence of self-confidence, and lack of belief in its own value. One of their main political projects was to reinforce the conviction that the United States was the only force for good in the world. In order to mobilize citizens to support that idea, as well as the military might and policy to implement it, the myth of an evil Soviet empire able and determined to vanquish this country was developed.[7] After the fall of the Berlin Wall and the emergence of a unipolar world, a new enemy—the "axis of evil"—was created in order to sustain support for the U.S. military-industrial-congressional complex basic to the neoconservative agenda realized during the Bush administration.

Although neoconservatism is unevenly religious, religion is understood to be an instrument that promotes morality. In the tradition of what Plato called a *noble lie*, for many neoconservatives, religion is viewed as a necessary myth told to the majority of citizens by a philosophical elite that in so doing can rule to ensure social order. In fact, Christian fundamentalism has facilitated the appeal of neoconservatism among its base and has helped to foster receptivity to its authoritarian political character. In its angst about the declining status of morality in the West—alongside an idealized view of the West's traditional values—neoconservatism has represented an impulse to unite state power and morality. The state has been given the task of establishing the moral-religious compass for this society and for the world, an impulse that fashioned the discourse of Bush's rationale for preemptive war abroad and repressive measures on the home front.

Neoliberalism and neoconservatism *collide* in many ways—one difference is that the former values a market model of the state and the latter a theological model of the state. But they *converge* in their rejection of the key principles long associated with constitutional democracy, including egalitarianism, civil liberties, fair elections, and the rule of law. They also share a commitment to the capitalist principles of individualism, competition, and private property. Neoliberalism views society in terms of winners and losers based on entrepreneurial skill; neoconservatism emphasizes the importance of preserving what one has and militantly protecting one's own, either at the individual family level or in the broader sense of "U.S. interests" worldwide. Wendy Brown (2006) posits that the neoliberal ideological conversion of socially produced problems into individual problems with market solutions resulted in a general depoliticization in this country that created a citizen-subject receptive to the authoritarian features of neoconservative governance. And Christian fundamentalism, by making a virtue of submission to religious truth, facilitated an acceptance of government ruled by an enlightened political elite that makes unilateral decisions on behalf of citizens who willingly acquiesce to its authority.

Thus it was that the neoconservative Bush administration deepened the antidemocratic tendencies within neoliberalism. In spite of the fact that the neoconservatives appeal to rule by consent through moral values centered on cultural nationalism, Christian family values, and right-to-life issues, in practice those neoconservatives in decision-making positions under Bush emphasized the authoritarian tendencies of the movement through their escalation of militarism, the unprecedented centralization of power in a unitary executive branch of government, the creation of a surveillance society, and an assault on civil liberties in the name of national security. Thus, in our country, neoliberalism and neoconservatism have represented different emphases between rule by consent and rule by coercion in sustaining unquestioned acceptance of the legitimacy of unregulated capitalism and U.S. superpower strivings.

These constituents of hegemony reinforced the ideological and psychological factors I described in chapter 1 that predisposed citizens to support the Bush administration's bellicose policies following the traumatogenic events of 9/11. Neoliberal capitalism had produced growing divisions in this society in which workers, racial groups, social classes, and regions were pitted against each other to produce a profound sense of loss of community and social links. Following 9/11 these chronic stressors seemed to diminish for a time in the symbolic reparation that was experienced because the identifiable threat to our "American way of life" shifted from internal factors to an external source, permitting U.S. citizens to unite in directing their aggression outward against a foreign enemy rather than inward against themselves. Moreover, the neoconservative link between theology and the state, reflected in Bush's "crusade" against evil, resonated for citizens identified with hegemonic notions of American exceptionalism and the Christian rationale of Manifest Destiny that have for centuries defined this country's position in the world and its relationship to other cultures and nations.

The Bush administration implemented a single strategy from Iraq to New Orleans aimed at expanding under the shock and awe of war and natural disaster the neoliberal deregulated market and privatization schemes favorable to its corporate allies. Its policies were developed in an unprecedented secretive fashion through the gutting of the Freedom of Information Act and the declaration as "classified" of more than 1,000 contracts with its most-favored corporate ally, Halliburton. Naomi Klein (2007) shows how under Bush, the corporatist state flourished. The traditional "revolving door"—between the private and public spheres, in which former government officials leave office to become corporate chief executive officers and then return to public service in a mutually enhancing information and profit feedback system—became an "archway" in the sense that public officials sustained their corporate connections while they were in office, thus making more efficient the transfer of taxpayers' monies to private coffers. One specific example in the many instances researched by Klein is the emergence of a new industry following 9/11, which she calls the "war on terror bubble." She describes the Bush administration's awards of noncompetitive contracts to favored corporations (often managed and/or owned by past and even sitting government officials) who used tax dollars to develop a host of new technologies that have facilitated the development of a surveillance society. She writes of the unethical and unprecedented alliance of government and corporate capital and concludes:

> What is striking is how little the security boom is analyzed and discussed as an economy, an unprecedented convergence of unchecked police powers and unchecked capitalism, a merger of the shopping mall and the secret prison…it changes the values of a culture. Not only does it create an incentive to spy, torture and generate false information but it creates a powerful impetus to perpetuate the fear and sense of peril that created the industry in the first place. (p. 306)[8]

The privatization of the military, the best known case of which is Blackwater (Scahill, 2007), also strengthened the unitary executive branch that could now use a private army to expand its overseas preemptive invasions and occupations and to impose "law and order" in domestic emergencies, such as the social crisis produced by Hurricane Katrina.

During the Bush years, U.S. superpower strivings became transparent and undeniable, its global "interests" protected by more than 725 U.S. military bases in 35 countries scattered throughout the world, alongside expanded surveillance networks via various forms of telecommunications and spy satellite systems (Johnson, 2004). The military-industrial-congressional complex drove an integrated strategy of unilateral aggressive foreign policy and expansion of U.S. corporate investments, especially to guarantee access to and control over international strategic and increasingly scarce resources like oil, natural gas, and water.

It is understandable that until the financial crisis of 2008, citizens tended to experience the policies of deregulation and privatization as normative and unquestioningly accepted rhetorical attacks on big government. They did not understand that both neoliberal and neoconservative policies were creating what economist Dean Baker (2006) calls "the conservative nanny state," that is, big government whose function was to ensure the interests of the wealthy and privileged. Indeed, Bush expanded the government to the breaking point with a war budget and entitlement programs for financial corporations, while drastically reducing social programs that in the past benefited the middle and working classes as well as the poor. The growing gap between a wealthy elite and the rest of U.S. citizens continued apace, so that by the end of the second Bush term, we were living in a society in which the top 1 percent of families held more than a third of the country's total wealth, or, put another way, 1 percent owned more than the wealth held by 90 percent of the rest of American families (Economic

Policy Institute, 2009). Moreover, during the past three decades, poverty was increasing by an average of more than 12 percent per year,[9] leaving more and more citizens enslaved by the "free" market. Citizens living in the midst of these social conditions conducive to paranoid-schizoid states of persecutory anxiety and hampered by internalized ideological constraints to critical consciousness were fated to play out the role of bystander to their own ignoble fate.

However, this erosion of political and economic democracy was producing as well signs of a shift in consciousness among some citizens. Fewer people were willing to remain silent in the face of a hegemonic discourse that justified authoritarian governance. Indeed, intensifying contradictions brought on by administrative policies that were in open violation of domestic and international law and a devastating war economy riddled with corrupt financial practices produced an outpouring of protest that grew into a veritable din. Alongside a bystander population, more citizens declared "not in our name" and openly opposed aggressive war abroad and attacks on peoples' human rights and civil liberties at home. As it turned out, Bush's post–9/11 antiterrorism discourse had only temporarily marginalized the global justice movement that had been active throughout the world during the 1990s. In this country that movement had made its biggest impact during its militant protests—known as the "Battle in Seattle"—at the 1999 corporate-dominated World Trade Organization's first meeting on U.S. soil. Now the global justice movement, with its ecological, peace, workers', women's, community, civil liberties, and immigrants rights constituent organizations, was back in the center of ideological struggle. Not only at the grassroots level but in popular culture as well, progressive perspectives were being increasingly represented. Bestseller lists featured books whose authors offered scathing and well-researched critiques of Bush's political, economic, and military policies and denunciations of the impunity with which the government was undermining the constitution and democratic institutions.[10] Beginning with one of the early critical voices in the mass media, *The Daily Show's* host Jon Stewart on Comedy Central, a new space opened up in prime-time television programming on channels like MSNBC and a new radio outlet called Air America, whose progressive content began to compete with Fox News and right-wing talk radio for mainstream viewers and listeners. The blogosphere was increasingly filled with exchanges from every ideological perspective, and progressive points of view drew increasing attention from citizens eager to engage in interactive online dialogues. Moreover, although the corporate-dominated media did not cover progressive political activism, organizations dedicated to a variety of environmental, community, health, antiwar, human rights, civil liberties, and more were multiplying throughout the country. The change was beginning to mirror what Ernesto Laclau had observed in Latin America some years earlier to the effect that new subjectivities were extending the meaning of democracy from an occasional participation in voting to activism around a whole new series of social issues and relations.[11] And many U.S. citizens, like activists throughout the world, were opposing war as a solution to international conflict, including the threat of terrorism. Increasingly, they were critiquing the foundational structures of neoliberal and neoconservative capitalism (Negri & Hardt, 2004).

PSYCHOANALYSIS: FROM NEUTRALITY TO SOCIAL RESPONSIBILITY

When Hedda commented that Mimi Langer was able to realize her political principles in ways that she herself had not been able to, perhaps she believed it was because Mimi lived in the more radicalized conditions of the third world or that Mimi had fewer inhibitions to act in accord with her deepest convictions. However, it seems to me that Hedda has found ways to actualize her political values within the more constraining social and cultural milieu of this country, even while over the decades she felt frustrated in her endeavors to interest her psychoanalytic colleagues in significant political and social issues. In one of our discussions over the previous several years, Hedda confided that the most important social movements to her from the 1960s on were what she calls "the life and death" struggles, including the antinuclear, civil rights, and antiwar movements. She said that for years she was most deeply committed to the antinuclear movement and that she gave as much time, energy, and money as she could to the cause. She found that for decades the psychoanalytic community was loath to take up social issues and struggles, even this overridingly important one. In the early 1970s, Hedda was one of the founders of a psychoanalytic institute, the Los Angeles Institute and Society for Psychoanalytic Studies, (LAISPS), which challenged the medical model of psychoanalytic training to include psychologists and individuals with advanced degrees from allied fields. In line with Hedda's orientation, the Web site of LAISPS, which became a component society of the International Psychoanalytic Association, announces that its goal is to train candidates to become knowledgeable and skillful psychoanalysts "capable of practicing, teaching, conducting research, and applying psychoanalytic principles to the broad spectrum of human endeavor." But that "broad spectrum" took many years to evolve into a commitment to do outreach into the community beyond the couch. For the many years before that development, Hedda told me, she felt rather alone as a psychoanalyst deeply concerned about the social context of psychological distress. "During the anti-Vietnam War movement, for example, I felt pretty isolated from institutional psychoanalysis. I didn't know too many analysts who were actively participating in opposing that war. And in the years following that, there continued to be a real split for me between my political principles and my profession. I think we always had to obey the rule that politics had no place in our psychoanalytic theory or practice. I struggled with that preposterous idea always. Actually, the Uprooted Mind conference in 2004 was the first time I was really able to bring those two facets of my life together." Hedda's experience is a window into the history of psychoanalysis in this country in the second half of the 20th century.

As we have seen, the political culture of the United States was not a propitious one in which psychoanalysis could sustain important radical trends that had characterized the origins of the profession. Following World War I in Europe, a socially critical tradition had emerged because psychoanalysis was connected to bohemian and artistic critiques of repressive bourgeois culture and values and leftist political analyses of oppressive class-related sources of psychological misery. Freud himself was the inspiration for the development in Vienna and Berlin of free clinics that provided treatment free or on a sliding scale to a wide range of patients from among the social classes that could not have afforded private treatment. In his keynote address to the Fifth Congress of the International Psychoanalytic Association held in September 1918 in Budapest at the close of World War I, Freud told his colleagues:

> It is possible to foresee that the conscience of society will awake and remind it that the poor man should have just as much right to assistance for his mind as he now has to the life-saving help offered by surgery; and that the neuroses threaten public health no less than tuberculosis and can be left as little as the latter to the impotent care of individual members of the community. Then institutions and out-patient clinics will be started to which analytically-trained physicians will be appointed so that men who would otherwise give way to drink, women who have nearly succumbed under the burden of their privations, children for whom there is no choice but running wild or neurosis, may be made capable, by analysis, of resistance and efficient work. Such treatments will be free... (Danto, 1998, p. 287; see also 2005)

Psychoanalyst Stephen Portuges (2009) summarizes the nature of the early psychoanalytic project:

> Psychoanalysis began as a radical critique of the illness-producing effects of the social suppression and consequent psychological repression of human sexuality...many among the first and second generation psychoanalytic pioneers, which included Freud, Francis Deri, Otto Fenichel, Edith Jacobson, Barbara Lantos, Annie and Wilhelm Reich, Ernest Simmel and many others, saw themselves as social-change agents whose politically progressive values obliged them to participate in move-

ments for social justice and equality while developing and applying their theories and techniques of psychotherapeutic treatment. (p. 63)

The radical social orientation thrived especially in the environment of Red Vienna, where from a young age both Marie Langer and Hedda Bolgar developed their political and psychological sensibilities, and in Berlin, where the Psychoanalytic Institute in that city developed a project of providing free psychoanalytic treatment for men, women, and children from many social classes (Danto, 2005). This psychoanalysis inspired by social responsibility was eviscerated throughout Europe by the Nazis. When prominent psychoanalysts, including Edith Jacobson and Otto Fenichel, fled fascism and emigrated to the United States, they tended to censor their radical political views for a variety of reasons. Their fate mirrored in some ways the experience in postwar Argentina of Marie Langer and other European psychoanalysts whose insecurities as immigrants in the enigmatic political environment of that country motivated them to silence their leftist politics. In the United States the psychoanalytic émigrés struggled to adapt to the conservative political culture dominated by Cold War ideology and McCarthyism (Jacoby, 1983). The United States was managing the legacies of multiple traumas, including the Great Depression, massive losses in wartime, fears of human destructiveness mobilized by the Nazi Holocaust and the atomic bomb and anxieties stimulated by the need to reassert traditional gender roles as soldiers reintegrated into civilian life. Thus predictability and stability became highly prized goals in the culture of conformity that emerged during that period. Also eclipsed in this environment were the critical cultural concerns and humanistic traditions within psychoanalysis that had emerged in this country during prior decades. Clara Thompson, Karen Horney, Erich Fromm, Henry Stack Sullivan, and the members of the Frankfort School, especially Max Horkheimer and Theodor Adorno, were all theorists working in the United States who had developed a critical perspective that linked individual psychology to a pathogenic social order. Many had critiqued the dominant characteristics of capitalist society as an inherently oppressive system that created a troubled subjectivity. But, as Philip Cushman (1995) shows, theirs was "the road not taken" in the postwar environment. Indeed, their work would remain marginalized from mainstream psychoanalysis for several decades before being reappropriated by the generation of psychoanalysts coming of age in the late 1960s in a U.S. culture much more volatile and contested.

Meanwhile, in the social pull toward conformity and stability in the postwar period, mainstream psychoanalysis was organized around the conservative medical model of training and practice. The prevailing orientation was ego psychology, which neglected those aspects of Freud's conflict model of the mind that included a critical appreciation of the inevitable identification with and *resistance* to oppressive social relations and cultural mores. Ego psychology favored an emphasis on the autonomous ego's adaptive capacities, which were conceptualized in an ahistorical, universal, and apolitical manner. Adaption to existing social structures and values in an uncritical fashion was considered to be an important individual achievement and a goal of psychoanalytic treatment. In this sense, ego psychology was a good "fit" with the cultural emphasis on compliance to hegemonic power structures and values typical of this historical period. When the critical visions within psychoanalysis reemerged, it was in the context of the political ferment of the 1960s, at first through the work in academic settings by critical social theorists such as Herbert Marcuse and Norman O. Brown, rather than within institutional psychoanalysis itself. Ultimately, the feminist and antiwar movements influenced a new generation of psychoanalysts to return to an exploration of the relationship between psychic and social reality,[12] especially regarding the social production and psychic reproduction of gender inequity and the social construction of war-induced trauma. Within the citadel of psychoanalysis proper, by the 1980s and 1990s, classical psychoanalysis was being challenged by new intellectual approaches; first influenced by British object relations and then by a return to interest in the work of Sullivan and Thompson, which led to the development of interpersonalist and relational approaches that seek in a variety of ways to integrate a structural analysis of the intrapsychic world with an elaboration of the intersubjective (social) context of psychological experience. Thus, both within professional psychoanalysis as well as radical social theory's applications of psychoanalytic ideas, a return to a critical social inquiry during the past several decades has created a rich literature, now replete with writings that engage the social, especially in regard to the illness-producing effects of inequitable power hierarchies of gender, class, race, and national chauvinism.[13]

By the late 1990s, and especially following 9/11, more psychoanalysts in this country began to turn their attention to the psychological meanings of an increasingly persecutory and violent world and to the psychic costs of human destructiveness that are threatening the survival of the species as well as the planet. Some have focused attention on the systemic and ideological forces that represent important features in the multigenerational transmission of trauma. Still others have centered their analyses on the psychological and social sequelae of living in an increasingly authoritarian political environment.

They have also organized. And that has meant coming to terms with the sacrosanct rule of neutrality, a mandate that has tended to keep politics out of the clinical setting and psychoanalysts out of politics.

PSYCHOANALYSTS REACH BEYOND THE COUCH

In the tradition of our Latin American psychoanalytic protagonists who have developed within the clinic and beyond a praxis that Elizabeth Lira calls "ethical nonneutrality," more psychoanalysts in this country have become engaged in the significant social issues of our time. They have challenged the traditions within training institutes that mandate analysts to interpret patients' concerns about or focus on politics as resistance to the "real" psychoanalytic material or as merely symbolic of unconscious conflict stemming from personal etiology and interpersonal relationships. They have also eschewed the traditional assumption that the analyst should refrain from political activism or from publicly taking political positions lest it interfere with the "neutrality" of the analyst and patients' ability to use the analyst as a transference object. We have seen how Hedda decried this ideology of "neutrality" within the field, and she has been joined over the past decade by increasing numbers of psychoanalysts who have assumed a critical stance toward these institutional inhibitions. Increasingly, psychoanalysts are thinking in relational terms of how their respective socially constructed subjectivities and relationships to prevailing political values and structures are aspects of the analytic process to be analyzed just like any other material. They are also exploring ways of taking seriously on their own terms political themes as they enter the transference/countertransference dynamic. As well, more analysts have become involved in projects beyond the couch that publicly critique and remediate the social sources of psychological malaise brought on by neoliberal culture and state abandonment of responsibility for the welfare of citizens. They have also organized politically to challenge specific public policies they believe to be unethical and illegal and that undermine the psychological well-being of people.

It is worth noting that this activism beyond the couch has developed in a different context than that of our Latin American colleagues, whose activist experience was nurtured in a social matrix of a tradition of wide-ranging multiparty politics, highly politicized populations, and the existence of large-scale progressive and radical political organizations and union movements that were demanding radical change in the structures of capitalism. In this country, psychoanalytic activism has emerged as one site of progressive political engagement within a social matrix dominated by an ideologically narrow two-party system, an eviscerated working- and middle-class union movement, and a progressive political activism that has been organized locally and around single-issue struggles focusing on the multiple *symptoms* of neoliberal capitalism.

A forerunner of the contemporary refusal among psychoanalysts to remain quiet in the face of critical social issues was the position that British psychoanalyst Hanna Segal took in 1985 in her presentation at the inauguration of the organization, International Psychoanalysts Against Nuclear Weapons. She called her presentation "Silence Is the Real Crime" and warned against the danger of silence in the face of the nuclear arms race. She advocated an activist role for psychoanalysts to confront denial: "...there are situations in which...an attitude [of psychoanalytic neutrality] can also become a shield of denial. To be acquainted with facts and recognize psychic facts, which we of all people know something about, and to have the courage to try to state them clearly is in fact the psychoanalytic stand. We must face our fears and mobilize our forces against destruction. And we must be heard." A little over 15 years later, following 9/11, Hanna Segal wrote a postscript to her 1985 paper in which she criticized the omnipotent grandiosity of America's response to the 9/11 terrorist attacks. She argued that U.S. policy represents the superpower's defense against intolerable vulnerability and the need to replace the traditional Cold War enemy with a new one that functions as a receptacle for the projection of evil. Her message is consistent with her earlier position when she argues, "We are all members of some group or other and share responsibility for what 'our group' does. Even when we are passive and feel detached our apathy abandons the group to its fate. But speaking our minds takes courage because groups do not like outspoken dissenters." Segal concludes with an admonition: "We are told, 'ours is not to reason why, ours is to do (to kill) and die.' But we have minds of our own. We still have choices. We could say, 'ours *is* to reason why, ours is to live and strive.' And I think that silence is still the real crime" (Segal, 2002, p. 284).

Several years before 9/11, some U.S. psychoanalysts were already feeling the need to eschew silence in favor of addressing problematic social conditions, about which psychoanalysis has a lot to say. For example, in 1999, Lewis Aron, then president of the Division of Psychoanalysis (Division 39) of the American Psychological Association, was troubled, as he puts it, "by the fact that since the post–World War II period psychoanalysis in this country had become too much a part of the establishment and had thus lost the radical edge of the early generation of psychoanalysts who had been much more socially and politically active."[14] He decided to address the problem by forming a section within the Division called "Psychoanalysis for Social Responsibility" and invited psychoanalysts Neil Altman and Rachael Peltz to organize this effort. Altman (1995) had already published important contributions within psychoanalysis to the dialogue about race and racism in this country. Peltz had long been interested in "bridging the gap between psychoanalysis and critical social theory," and had earlier formed a committee on social responsibility in Division 39. According to Peltz, "the committee had offered programs that showed how psychoanalysis and critical theory could explore everyday life themes in the U.S."[15] At Aron's invitation, Altman and Peltz eagerly launched Section IX, "Psychoanalysis for Social Responsibility," within Division 39, which they hoped would bring together a network of psychoanalysts doing work "off the couch." They established a Section IX board of like-minded colleagues and thus began a multifaceted journey, which over the years has included a variety of endeavors that have had an impact on the profession and on the general public as well.[16] I enthusiastically became an active participant in this experience, which has permitted me to adapt much of what I have learned with my Latin American psychoanalytic colleagues to the political conditions in this country and the struggles for social justice within our profession. The psychoanalysts who have been active in Section IX have developed a sense of community and purpose with a group of colleagues who strive to develop a critical social psychoanalysis and to take seriously our ethical nonneutrality in the face of our own culture of impunity.

Section IX has been organizing panels and presentations at annual meetings of Division 39 since the late 1990s. These events have featured prominent figures within psychoanalysis and critical theory to speak from a variety of perspectives about the interface between psychic and social reality. Examples of these presentations include Fred Alford, who showed how Kleinian concepts can be applied to an analysis of a troubled social order; Juan Carlos Volnovich, who explored the significance of psychoanalytic activism in the radical movements that arose after the Argentine economic meltdown; Robert Jay Lifton, who spoke about how Vietnam shadows current policies in Iraq and whom the Section honored for his lifelong integration of professional expertise with a commitment to progressive political activism; Hedda Bolgar, who examined the erosion of constitutional rule and the rise of European Fascism from the perspective of a psychoanalyst as witness; an empathic dialogue among a group of Israeli, Palestinian, and North American Arab and Jewish psychoanalysts who work together on themes related to the psychodynamics of trauma in the Israeli–Palestinian conflict. A variety of panels over the years have included Section IX members whose presentations have covered topics related to the social matrix of psychic experience and its manifestations in clinical work and the psychological meanings of post–9/11 political culture. One Section IX board member, Lynne Layton, who reports that she "became active in the section out of despair about the political situation in the U.S.," had been writing about the damaging effects within psychoanalysis of conformity to the social norm that keeps the psychic and the social separate."[17] Layton initiated a project to develop a syllabus, "Psychoanalysis and Culture," that could be used as a course in analytic training. It includes examples of the growing number of clinical papers addressing cultural inequities, unconscious collusions, and social symptoms. Section IX's membership participated though our e-mail list in a year-long online discussion of the readings in the syllabus, which was made available for all who wanted to propose such a course in their psychoanalytic institutes. In order to reach a wider audience, Section IX has cosponsored, together with the online conference producer PsyBc (www.psybc.com), an annual online seminar called "Ideology and the Clinic." The 2007 papers and discussion among presenters and participants on PsyBc were published in the British journal *Psychotherapy and Politics*.[18]

As the Bush administration's policies became more authoritarian, the Section IX e-mail list provided a venue for its members to engage in a series of psychoanalytically informed analyses of the political situation and to share information about local oppositional activities around the country. Over the years, members of Section IX have cosponsored community events in their various regions, one example of which was a conference in 2002 held in San Francisco, "The Crisis of Health Care in America," in which a single-payer strategy was debated.

In addition to Section IX's efforts, a variety of other psychoanalytic community projects have evolved in the past several decades. They represent different kinds of interventions in communities plagued by the social and economic problems of neoliberal society whose policies and ideology have abandoned responsibility for the welfare of its citizens. One example is the work of Stuart Twemlow, who has developed a model for intervention in violent situations that can be applied to schools, workplaces, and organizations. Along with other significant contributions to community psychoanalysis, Twemlow's model was elaborated in a collection of articles, *Analysts in the Trenches: Streets, Schools, War Zones* (Sklarew, Twemlow, & Wilkinson, 2004). The book's authors document a variety of experiences and explain how they counter a tradition in which psychoanalysts who are engaged in community activism stress their professional identity so as to demonstrate to the public the relevance of psychoanalysis in the amelioration of mental suffering. Instead, the progenitors of these projects advocate being helpful to the various constituencies with whom they work without stressing professional affiliation. As the book's editors put it, "Being helpful may be the best way psychoanalysts can make their mission known to the lay public. When people feel they are being helped, they often become curious about the background and training of the person who has been helpful" (p. xviii). Taken together, the articles demonstrate how psychoanalytic concepts can be used innovatively in a variety of programs and practices developed to intervene in this era's violent and traumatic situations, including forced migration, crime, and homelessness. The book testifies to the authors' clinical and personal courage as they engage as activist citizens in their communities. Most recently, the American Psychoanalytic Association has organized a syllabus on Psychoanalysis in the Community, which, along with speakers like Twemlow, provides speakers to institutes that organize conferences on this theme. Elsewhere, Twemlow and Henri Parens, in their coauthored *Might Freud's Legacy Lie Beyond the Couch?* have written that "We hold the position that until psychoanalysis is recognized as a body of knowledge that can be applied to understanding and solving pressing community and social problems, rather than hold to its limited application to the treatment of patients with specific psychiatric diseases, or in training those who treat them, it will lose its pioneering relevance in the 'social brain' initiative in the 21st century" (Twemlow & Parens, 2006, p. 434).

A different model of community outreach, one example among many in the country, has been organized in Los Angeles through LAISPS, the psychoanalytic institute that Hedda cofounded. In response to the major mental health challenges within the larger Los Angeles community, in 1999 LAISPS established the Ernest S. Lawrence Trauma Center. Its mission is to provide community service and outreach through psychoanalytically informed treatment of emotional/physical trauma. Its brochure states that "…a psychoanalytic perspective can be helpful moving outside its traditional frame in confronting cycles of trauma, child abuse and neglect, and transgenerational violence within the community. It is also believed that psychoanalysis itself could be enhanced by an active engagement with these issues." The Trauma Center's first project, Parents and Infants Developing Together, offers psychological services for "at risk" populations by volunteer clinicians from among members of LAISPS. They travel to the diverse Echo Park section of Los Angeles, where they treat mothers, fathers, and other family members who are referred through the Center for Non-Violent Parenting, a nonprofit organization in that community. Other Trauma Center therapists provide psychotherapy through the Venice Family Clinic in West Los Angeles, which offers health services to a diverse low-income population that includes many immigrants from Central America and Mexico. The current Trauma Center director, Carol Tannenbaum, brings to this community work her experience travelling to Bosnia on a yearly basis, where since 1996 she has worked as a volunteer with the Global Children's Organization. "That first summer in Bosnia was a life-altering experience," Tannenbaum says. "I was riveted by the firsthand exposure to the war, and I understood the responsibility one undertakes when engaging in humanitarian work, whether it be in the consulting room, the community, or the world." Of the Trauma Center's work, she adds that psychoanalysis can be enriched by the connection to diverse cultures within Los Angeles. Another component of the Trauma Center is the Soldiers Project, which consists of an extensive network of volunteer clinicians who offer pro bono counseling and support for service men and women, children, spouses, and parents struggling with the overwhelming trauma of war, from deployment to homecoming to postwar readjustment.[19]

One unique effort to bring psychoanalysis to the community is The Women's Therapy Centre Institute (WTCI) in New York, a training institute that represents an intersection of the psychoanalytic and feminist communities and the public at large. The WTCI was founded in the early eighties as a sister organization to The Women's Therapy Centre in London

(1976) by Carol Bloom, Luise Eichenbaum, and Susie Orbach to explore the intimate relationship between personal and political experience, with particular focus on the gendered psyche. According to Eichenbaum, "Our feminist critique of psychoanalysis led us to a practice of psychoanalytic psychotherapy that we believed more adequately addressed the gender-specific intersubjective needs of women patients. The mission of The Women's Therapy Centre Institute is to publicize and educate both the public and the psychotherapy community about the psychology of gender, its impact on psychic life, and the difficulties of living in a female body. Our public campaigns and training programs for psychotherapists are based in our understanding of how contemporary culture's monolithic ideal for women, especially as promoted in consumer/visual culture, is detrimental to their physical and mental health. The epidemic of body/self dissatisfaction and disordered eating are the inevitable outcomes."[20]

WTCI programs are designed to educate about the ways women's psychological conflicts are expressed in and through their bodies and more specifically in their relationships to food, feeding, and disciplining the female body. Luise Eichenbaum and Susie Orbach published several books, including *What Do Women Want: Exploding the Myth of Female Dependency* (1999) and *Understanding Women: A Feminist Psychoanalytic Approach* (1983), and Orbach authored *Fat Is a Feminist Issue* (1998) with the goal of popularizing psychoanalytic and feminist perspectives on female experience. The WTCI faculty's groundbreaking, coedited *Eating Problems: A Feminist Psychoanalytic Treatment Model* (Bloom et al., 1994) has made a significant contribution to the mental health community's understanding of the cultural as well as the unconscious meanings and clinical treatment of eating and body image in women.[21]

Interest in the academic community in the potential of psychoanalysis to contribute to an interdisciplinary dialogue on the pressing social issues of our times, including violence and war, evolved during this period as well. For example, the Association for the Psychoanalysis of Culture & Society organizes an annual conference that meets every fall at Rutgers University, where it brings together international scholars and clinicians to present papers and exchange ideas informed by psychoanalysis and critical theory. Its journal, *Psychoanalysis, Culture & Society*, publishes some of these presentations, along with a wide variety of psychoanalytically informed analyses of subjectivity, ideology, and social crises submitted by contributors from all over the world. Another example of the academic interest in psychoanalytic understandings of political conflict and war was a conference organized in May of 2005 by Greg Forter, Professor of English at the University of South Carolina, called "Psychoanalysis, the Iraq War, and the Prospects for a Lasting Peace." The presentations were subsequently published in the June 2006 issue of *The International Journal of Applied*

Psychoanalytic Studies. As the invited editor of the collection, Dr. Forter wrote in his introduction:

> The following essays are...unusually "conjunctural" essays, in the Marxist sense of that term: They were written to address a particular historical moment from a specific social location (psychoanalytically informed critique), and they thus exhibit a particular kind of political and theoretical urgency. The historical event that precipitated them was, of course, the Iraq war. More specifically, the authors of the essays were responding to a feeling that I believe all of us shared, and that motivated my organizing the symposium in the first place: that mainstream discourse about the Iraq war has lacked the psychological sophistication necessary to understanding and effectively resisting it, while psychoanalytic responses to it have often been limited by a tendency to reduce historical factors to psychic ones. A central aim of the conference was thus to fuse psychological and historical modes of analysis. That aim was wedded to the project of developing effective strategies of resistance—strategies that needed to rest, in our view, on an adequately rich understanding of the psychopolitical "ground" of the war. (p. 113)

Forter's comment captured not only the critical perspective that characterized the authors' essays but also the sensibility of a number of psychoanalysts who, even before the United States made war on Iraq, were interested in fusing psychological and historical modes of analysis and in developing effective strategies of resistance to the U.S. government's discourse and policies based on retaliatory vengeance. Some of them were among the mental health professionals who lived in New York City and who, immediately following 9/11, participated in a variety of posttraumatic interventions that included going to firehouses, police stations, hospitals, and places of worship, as well as sites designated for survivors' and victims' families. Nina Thomas, a psychoanalyst with a specialty in trauma whose research has included interviews with war survivors in Bosnia, describes her experience at Ground Zero as one that bore an ominous resemblance to that country in the immediate postwar period: "...Although in New York, the noise of equipment and backlit smoke that made the pile [at Ground Zero] look like some *noir* Hollywood film set distinguished the setting from Sarajevo, the empty streets, buildings hanging from strands of steel, and faces lined by tragedy and bone-crushing exhaustion were very reminiscent." Thomas and a group of colleagues at the New York University Postdoctoral Program in Psychotherapy and Psychoanalysis initiated a pilot program called the "Firehouse Clinician Project," in which each participant analyst became "the house shrink" for a firehouse. "We made regular rounds of our firehouses to be available as the firefighters needed us," Thomas remembers. "The project was enormously successful, shortly expanding to include a clinician in each firehouse that had lost someone on 9/11." Much like the Argentine psychoanalysts who practiced psychoanalysis under many diverse crisis situations, Thomas and her colleagues carried out a psychoanalysis beyond the couch in nontraditional ways. "I sat with the men in their kitchen where the life of the house is centered...and did nontraditional 'therapy' to be sure, but which was still valued and valuable to '*my* guys.' I came to know the widows, children, mothers, fathers, brothers, fears, delights, and dreads and shared them with the men for the almost two years I was a continuous presence in the house...They didn't need interpretations, and even empathy could be suspect. They did need someone to listen. That's what I did." This experience was repeated by the many mental health professionals who made themselves available to the survivors of the 9/11 catastrophe.

Just four months after 9/11, in January 2002, at the annual conference of the International Association of Relational Psychotherapists and Psychoanalysts (IARPP) in New York, a panel of psychoanalysts was hastily organized to address the significance of 9/11 and the U.S. response. The overflow crowd that attended the early morning session made it clear that there was a need among psychotherapists for an ongoing organization that offered the possibility of sharing concerns and deciding together how to shift feelings of helplessness in the face of social trauma toward an activist response to the rapidly developing culture of fear and aggressive foreign policy being designed by the Bush administration. Psychoanalysts who were members of IARPP, including Neil Altman and Jessica Benjamin; and the New York–based feminist psychoanalytic WTCI, including Susan Gutwill, Luise Eichenbaum, and others, many of whom also belonged to Section IX, established a steering committee in order to organize meetings and coordinate actions of a group that ultimately became Psychotherapists for Social Responsibility (PSR). Psychotherapists from other organizations from the New York area joined PSR. According to Katie Gentile and Susan Gutwill (2005), activists in PSR who published a psychoanalytically informed analysis of this experience, the motivation for initiating the group was related to a critical perception of the general political environment:

> As therapists, we understood the power and danger of splitting off aggression in order to be identified as the good, virtuous victim. We knew that collapsing the potential space limits reflection, thinking and the capacity to question. In this atmosphere all wrongdoing on behalf of the US, for example, the history of our support for dictators in the Middle East, could be erased, as the Taliban and then Iraq and others were cast as the "evil enemy" who threatened us...we explored how to expand the analytic vision from being an exclusively individualistic form

of inquiry, to one more responsive to the escalating political situation and the "large group" (societal) psychodynamics it created. (p. 122)

During the next three or four years, PSR organized speak-outs for mental health professionals to dialogue about the ways they understood the mutual impact of psychic and social reality in an increasingly threatening world. They sponsored educational evenings featuring speakers and films that provided important background on the developing political crisis. And members participated in many local and national protests against Bush's march toward war, including the international demonstrations of February 11, 2003, in which they united together under the banner "Peace of Mind." PSR also organized online Web conferences, including an international one that was cosponsored by PsyBc, in an attempt to educate mental health professionals around the intersection of the personal and the social unconscious. They were especially interested in exploring how and why sectors of the population at large responded to, identified with, or opposed the politics of fear and aggression, as well as how these politics were finding their way into or being avoided in clinical work. In their opposition to neoconservatism, many of the members actively participated in the 2004 election campaign of Democratic candidate John Kerry. In their article assessing the strengths and limitations of PSR, Gentile and Gutwill apply a historical and psychoanalytic interpretation of the patterns and values of the external social environment, which they argue was characterized by "attacks on linking" that acted as an impediment to the organization's capacity to expand and sustain an energized membership. Similarly, they candidly evaluate the internal factors that were also obstacles to group effectiveness, including the hierarchies that developed in a number of ways: between psychoanalytically trained members and other mental health professionals; between the more articulate or politically experienced and those less so; and between those whose views and language in written materials were politically radical and others who did not agree or felt that the language would alienate the very people they were attempting to reach. The authors conclude that despite the group's problems, they made a significant contribution as they evolved into a loosely organized, large group of mental health professionals committed to critically speaking out on behalf of social change.

Meanwhile, a battle was brewing within the American Psychological Association that would put psychoanalytic activism at the heart of a controversy around Bush's torture policies and the institutional relationship of psychology to U.S. foreign policy. By Bush's second term in office, debates about his "global war on terror" included exposés of his administration's practice of disappearing and torturing people at Guantanamo, Abu Ghraib, and Central Intelligence Agency (CIA) "black sites" in unnamed countries likely to endorse torture. When evidence began to emerge that psychologists and other health professionals were playing a central role in planning, conducting, and standardizing abusive interrogations, pressure built on the relevant professional organizations to curtail such activities. That this issue assumed such importance is significant because for many years U.S. citizens have played bystander to the decades-long contribution of the United States to torture beyond our borders and the collaboration of health professionals in state-organized violence. Citizens in the United States are only recently learning that their government has been practicing torture, and this exposé has been ideologically framed as a violation of "American values." However, it is important to remember that the U.S. military and CIA have played a prominent role since the 1960s in the training, funding, and arming of Latin American repressive states, including their implementation of torture that I described in an earlier chapter.[22] Moreover, like the cooperation of health professionals with the military in this country, the collaboration of individual physicians and mental health professionals with interrogators and torturers throughout the repressive state apparatuses in countries like Argentina, Chile, and Uruguay is publicly documented (see Miles, 2008). One of the most well-known in the psychoanalytic world has to do with the case that was first publicly denounced by Marie Langer in 1973 about a Brazilian torturer of the military dictatorship who was not only a physician, but a candidate at the Psychoanalytic Society of Rio de Janeiro and an analysand of the society's president. The ethical issues involved in this case were highly controversial and plummeted the two Rio societies and the International Psychoanalytic Association (IPA) into divisive struggles for years. As the author of a historical review and psychoanalytic account of the case writes, "…it is not acceptable for the president of an analytic society, or for any analyst, to permit the acceptance, let alone the training, of a candidate who is sworn to alleviate human suffering and instead contributes to the imposing of physical or psychological pain in the interrogation of any human being, including prisoners, whether criminal or political" (Villela, 2005, p. 815).[23]

So it is especially praiseworthy that in response to the revelations about current U.S. engagement in human rights violations of detainees and the collaboration of health professionals, health organizations in this country are taking principled positions to impose ethical standards of nonparticipation on their members. By mid-2006 the American Medical Association banned its members from conducting or directly participating in interrogations on the basis of its abrogation of the physician's role as healer. The American Psychiatric Association, as well, banned its members from direct participation in interrogations, whether in the United States or elsewhere, on the grounds that it violated the Hippocratic ethic. In contrast, a reluctant American Psychological Association would join their professional counterparts only after a lengthy institutional struggle by its members. In 2005, it established a special task force, the Presidential Task Force on Psychological Ethics and National Security (PENS), to evaluate the participation of psychologists in interrogations of detainees. Many of the members of the task force were psychologists with long-standing ties to the military/intelligence interrogation programs, so it was not surprising that the task force concluded: "It is consistent with the APA Ethics Code for psychologists to serve in consultative roles to interrogation and information-gathering processes for national security-related purposes."[24]

But even as the American Psychological Association leadership clung tightly to this policy, concerned members refused to be silent in their opposition to what was considered to be an unethical practice in violation of national and international law and human rights conventions. Around the time of the PENS report, the Section IX e-mail list began to function as a venue for a critical dialogue about psychologists' involvement in military and CIA abusive interrogations. In the process, individual members researched the history of the intimate relationship between psychology and the military, which we came to understand as the context for the tenacity of the association's position on this issue. We discovered that this collaborative relationship goes back at least as far as the Cold War, during which the U.S. government, and especially the CIA, had an interest in developing specialized techniques for mind control. Psychologists received extensive funding to do research into potentially effective interrogation techniques, including the use of hypnosis, drugs, isolation and extreme sensory deprivation, brain stimulation, and so forth. During the following decades, partly on the basis of research done by psychologists, the military developed a number of special programs, including the systematic use of psychological torture, such as prolonged isolation, sleep deprivation, sensory distortion, and sexual and cultural humiliation. Long before their use in the "war on terror," these techniques were set forth in CIA training manuals distributed throughout Latin America in the 1970s and 1980s. In addition, the military's Survival, Evasion, Resistance, Escape (SERE) program, initially developed to teach U.S. officers counterresistance training in case of capture by an enemy that did not respect the Geneva Conventions, was "reverse-engineered" to be exported to Guantanamo and elsewhere as techniques to be practiced by U.S. personnel.[25] A 2006 report by the Defense Department Office of the Inspector General was declassified in 2007, and it showed that SERE staff taught SERE-based techniques to Behavior Science Consultation Teams (BSCTs) composed of psychologists and others who participated in interrogations at Guantanamo and later consulted to interrogators in Iraq and Afghanistan.

With definitive indications of the involvement of psychologists in abusive interrogation techniques, individual members of Section IX began to lead a multipronged strategy to fight the association's leadership on behalf of a new ethics code banning such practices among its members. When in June 2006 Steven Behnke, Director of Ethics for the American Psychological Association, was quoted in *The New York Times* to the effect that psychologists involved in military interrogations were making an important contribution toward combating terrorism, many members of the association wrote outraged letters to elected and appointed officials in the organization. According to Section IX member and trauma specialist Ghislaine Boulanger,[26] writing these letters was "...an inadequate form of protest. I felt the need to take some action that would make it clear that I was no longer complicit in APA policies, so I decided to stop paying APA dues." With the recognition that more than a personal protest was needed, Boulanger began an e-mail list for like-minded psychologists. "I reasoned that if enough psychologists withhold their dues, the loss of revenue would be a cause of concern to the APA. I also felt that the e-mail list could provide an organizing forum to plan effective demonstrations, make our concerns known to rank-and-file psychologists who were unaware of the policies being carried out in their names, and get media coverage for our protest." WithholdAPAdues.com has served all of these functions admirably throughout the struggle within the association.

Cofounder of Section IX, Neil Altman, in his role as a Division 39 representative on the APA's governing body, the Council of Representatives, provided important pressure from within the organization. As he was finishing his term in August of 2006, Altman submitted a resolution asking the association to call for a moratorium on the participation of psychologists in interrogations taking place at U.S. detention centers that were holding so-called enemy combatants. His resolution was based on the fact that since 1986, APA has been a nongovernmental organization accredited to the United Nations and thus was bound to affirm and promote the Declaration on Human Rights and the Geneva Conventions. Altman recognized that it defined torture in line with the qualifications and reservations the United States had used in its ratification of the Geneva Conventions, so his moratorium resolution declared that psychologists should refrain from working in detention sites until the ambiguity was clarified. Because the Military Commissions Act of 2006 left it to the U.S. president to decide what constitutes a breach of the Geneva Conventions, Altman argued that psychologists working in detention sites were at legal risk if those rulings were at variance with the international standard. Moreover, in response to the argument that psychologists should be present in such interrogations because they have the expertise to resist "behavior drift" toward abusive treatment and could therefore be whistle-blowers, Altman (2008) claimed that this view amounted to an overvaluing of cognition "as opposed to emotional forces like fear, rage, helplessness, and sadism" to which we are all vulnerable regardless of professional training. He saw his resolution as a request that

> people on the APA Council of Representatives...swim against the current on this issue to acknowledge that psychological expertise and good

intentions have such a limited impact in the face of the brutal U.S. response to 9/11...On a deeper level, my resolution suggests that none of us is immune to the emotional dynamics that produce torture and that it behooves us to avoid circumstances that have been set up, more or less deliberately, to foster abuse. (p. 660)

In August of 2007, at its national convention in San Francisco, the association's Council of Representatives voted down Altman's moratorium resolution. The prior month, the Board of Directors had submitted a substitute motion which, if adopted, would replace Altman's motion. The substitute motion improved existing policy to prohibit certain interrogation techniques, such as waterboarding, and formally recognized that certain cruel, inhuman, and degrading treatment could be a function of the setting in general, not just of specific techniques. This substitute motion was a strategy to head off the mounting pressure from the membership that the association adopt a new ethics code and to reduce the public controversy being stirred up by critical reporting in the popular media (Hersh, 2004; see also Goodman, 2008; Meyer, 2007). Psychologist/psychoanalyst Steven Reisner (Reisner, Losi, & Salvaticio, 2002), one of the central figures and a prominent spokesperson in the media for this struggle within the association, says of the successful mobilization of a critical mass of support for a change in the ethics code: "[this is] the story of how a small group of psychoanalysts used psychoanalytic methods to overcome resistance and join the resistance." Reisner describes his own growing involvement in this struggle, which he sees as having made a strategic contribution toward the exposé of the Bush administration's illegal torture policies: "[A]s it happens, the story we were presented with—from the Bush administration and from the American Psychological Association—about the role of psychologists and psychology in national security interrogations didn't make sense...for me, at least, the story aroused skepticism and curiosity *as a psychoanalyst*. I found myself listening to the material that the government and the American Psychological Association were presenting clinically, much like I listen to my patients' stories. I found myself listening for the hidden story— the story that was being obscured precisely as the surface narrative was being perfected."

Reisner dedicated almost full-time energies to the struggle within the association. Others joined him, including Boulanger through the "withhold dues" campaign, psychoanalyst and public health researcher Stephen Soldz, and activist members of the Divisions of Social Justice (which includes Division 39) within the American Psychological Association. Soldz, who is a founding member of the Coalition for an Ethical Psychology,[27] reports that "as a long-time antiwar activist, I was not surprised when word first came that our government was abusing detainees at Guantanamo and Iraq...When articles started appearing describing the roles of psychologists and other mental health workers...I decided to speak out...this brought me in contact with colleagues who shared my rapidly developing passion to confront this perversion of psychology head on." Soldz researched and organized relentlessly on behalf of information-gathering, keeping contact with journalists who were publishing significant information for the public and updating colleagues through the Section IX e-mail list and his online Psyche, Science, and Society blog (http://psychoanalystsopposewar.org/blog/).

In March 2007, five months before the American Psychological Association convention, the Psychoanalytic Institute of Northern California organized a conference, "Unfree Association: The Politics and Psychology of Torture in a Time of Terror," at which Soldz, Altman, and Boulanger presented papers analyzing various aspects of this struggle. I spoke, as well, about how the more extreme example of the Argentine terrorist state's use of torture could be instructive for our understanding of the drift toward authoritarianism in this country and how the state's use of torture should be seen as a piece of a larger political project aimed at silencing opposition to arbitrary assaults on democratic process and civil liberties. These papers were published as part of a special issue of *Psychoanalytic Dialogues* (Vol. 18, No. 5, 2008) and, along with additional articles, including a history of the role of psychology in the U.S. military by former Section IX president, Frank Summers, they provide psychoanalytic explorations of the psychodynamics of torture, the psychosocial impact of living in a torture society, and the kinds of unconscious defenses citizens employ in order to deal with the threatening implications of living in a country whose president has the right to arbitrarily declare any individual an "enemy combatant" and virtually kidnap, incarcerate without charges, and torture him or her for an indeterminate amount of time.

During the months preceding the August 2007 American Psychological Association convention in San Francisco, Reisner and Soldz, along with Brad Olson and others, worked with Physicians for Social Responsibility regarding the legal aspects of a new ethics code. A cadre of Section IX psychoanalysts and other association members in the Bay Area prepared for the convention by organizing a rally and demonstration that would bring the controversial issue to public awareness. They mobilized local and national media coverage of the many panels that were scheduled for discussion of this issue at the convention,[28] which included presenters ranging from the critical voices within the association to representatives of the military and military psychologists.

"I still find it unfathomable," says Reisner, "that pulling on the threads of the role of psychologists unraveled the Bush administration's covert torture program—its development, its execution, its legal justifications, and its dissemination—and unfathomable that all of these involved psychologists and/or psychology."[29]

It is true that this struggle contributed to the ultimate exposé of Bush's criminal torture policies. But the American Psychological Association continued steadfast in its resistance to changing its ethics code; and the Council of Representatives, probably influenced by the leadership's arguments that psychologists' presence protects detainees, did not vote at the convention to prohibit psychologists from being present in military or CIA detention sites. Thus, during the following year a new strategy was developed in which the dissident association members bypassed their leadership and organized a petition that secured enough signatures for a referendum to be voted on directly by the membership. The referendum authors, Brad Olson, Ruth Fallenbaum, and Dan Aalbers, urged their colleagues to change association policy by prohibiting the presence of psychologists at detention sites at which detainees are denied the basic protections of the Geneva Conventions and the Convention Against Torture, with the exception of psychologists who are either providing treatment for military personnel or working directly for the benefit of the detainees (e.g., through the Red Cross). On September 17, 2008, it was announced that the referendum had passed with 58.8 percent of the votes. Thanks to the efforts of all those involved in this struggle, the turnout for this vote was the highest ever in the association's history. Aalbers stated: "This is a decisive victory for the membership of the American Psychological Association and for human rights advocates everywhere. This new policy will ensure that psychologists work for the abused and not the abusers at places like Guantanamo Bay and the CIA black sites."[30]

Believing that it was important for the association to communicate this change to the relevant government entities, the referendum authors worked with the American Psychological Association president to write a letter that embodied the spirit and meaning of the referendum. It was signed and sent by the association's president to the White House, the Department of Defense, and the CIA. Even with this enormous victory, the struggle within the association continues as concerned members, aware of the current vagaries of U.S. law and its divergence from international human rights principles justified in terms of "national security" interests, demand that the association modify its ethics code to remove clauses that still permit ethical violations when psychological ethics are in conflict with "law, regulations, or other governing legal authority" (Fallenbaum, 2008).

* * *

While psychoanalysts and psychologists were fighting the American Psychological Association and the state on the question of torture, other aspects of a growing authoritarianism were emerging and being denounced by a variety of U.S. citizens increasingly anxious about the political direction of the country. Evidence was accumulating that the repressive measures being implemented by Bush and his neoconservative colleagues were aimed at the U.S. population itself. Concerns over the national security state could no longer be seen as a paranoid vision of the left because now mainstream political figures, print and other media journalists, and scholars from a variety of disciplines were voicing alarm about the rightward trend of the government. "It can't happen here," the customary assertion that nothing quite as sinister as dictatorship could ever emerge in the United States, was forgotten amid the indications that, quite to the contrary, we were drifting rapidly in just that direction. For the growing numbers of citizens who were no longer turning a blind eye to the ominous signs, the picture was becoming clear.

ENDNOTES

1. These presentations were subsequently published in *Studies in Gender and Sexuality*, 10(4), Bolgar 2009. Hedda's article was titled "A Century of Essential Feminism" (pp. 195–199).
2. This classic study traces the effects of turn-of-the-20th-century industrial capitalism and its consumer values on the changing family structure and gender roles.
3. For an exploration of the history of the corporation and its legal status as an individual with inalienable rights, see Bakan (2004). *The Corporation* is an award-winning feature documentary version of the book.
4. Psychologist/psychoanalyst Morris Eagle, Ph.D., conveyed this joke as told to him by his friend Bob Rae, August 18, 2008.
5. In *The Shock Doctrine*, Naomi Klein brilliantly documents the diverse impositions of neoliberal practices in countries from Russia to Poland to South Africa to China, all in the context of transitional periods of extreme disruption during which citizens could not adequately protect themselves from its nefarious effects.
6. For the classic popular version of this analysis, see Lasch (1978).
7. See the extraordinary documentary by British filmmaker Adam Curtis (2004), *The Power of Nightmares: The Rise of the Politics of Fear*. See also Bronsther (2009): "The most crucial feature of neoconservatism is its Manichean worldview, wherein the Earth is pitted in an urgent struggle between purely good and purely evil nations. As George W. Bush famously told then Sen. Joe Biden: 'I don't do nuance.'"
8. See especially chapter 14, "Shock Therapy in the USA."
9. For this and other information about growing inequality in this country and the deteriorating conditions of people living below the poverty line, see Penn State's *Poverty in America Project*: http://www.povertyinamerica.psu.edu/.
10. Authors such as Noam Chomsky, Mark Danner, Chalmers Johnson, Naomi Klein, and Howard Zinn, who had been previously read by a small, highly educated, and politically progressive sector of the population, were appearing increasingly on best-seller lists and even featured by the checkout stands in airport bookstores.

11. For elaborations of his views on contemporary political struggles, see Laclau and Mouffe (2001) and Laclau (2007).
12. For an elaboration of this history, see the introduction in Layton, Hollander, and Gutwill, *Psychoanalysis, Class and Politics* (2006).
13. Although there are too many authors to provide an inclusive list here, they include Judith Herman, Nancy Chodorow, Jessica Benjamin, Neil Altman, Andrew Samuels, Susi Orbach, Victor Wolfenstein, Lynne Layton, and Slavoj Zizek. Several journals that feature psychoanalytic perspectives on the social are *Psychoanalysis, Culture and Society*; *The International Journal of Applied Psychoanalytic Studies*; *Gender and Sexuality*; *Psychotherapy and Politics International*; and *Free Associations: Psychoanalysis Groups Politics Culture*.
14. In this section, all direct quotes by individual psychoanalysts come from written exchanges and personal conversations between them and the author for the express purpose of this text. Lew Aron is the former director and a current faculty member of the New York University Postdoctoral Program in Psychotherapy and Psychoanalysis. He was the founding president of the International Association for Relational Psychoanalysis and Psychotherapy (IARPP) and a past president of the Division of Psychoanalysis (39) of the American Psychological Association. Among his many publications is *A Meeting of Minds: Mutuality in Psychoanalysis* (2001).
15. Rachael Peltz is Faculty Member, Psychoanalytic Institute of Northern California, and has authored varied publications (e.g., 2004, 2005). She is in private practice in Berkeley, California.
16. Presidents of Section IX have been Neil Altman, Rachael Peltz, Nancy Hollander, Arlene Lu Steinberg, Frank Summers, and currently Alice Shaw.
17. Lynne Layton is Assistant Clinical Professor of Psychology, Harvard Medical School, and Faculty and Supervisor, Massachusetts Institute for Psychoanalysis. She is editor of the journal *Psychoanalysis, Culture & Society*; author of *Who's That Girl? Who's That Boy? Clinical Practice Meets Postmodern Gender Theory* (2004a); and coeditor (with Hollander and Gutwill) of *Psychoanalysis, Class and Politics* (2006).
18. Stephen Soldz and several others, including an interview with Neil Altman and Nancy Hollander about their papers, were discussed on PsyBc (2007).
19. Carol Tannenbaum is Chair, Ernest S. Lawrence Trauma Center of The Los Angeles Institute and Society for Psychoanalytic Studies; adjunct faculty, Pacifica Graduate Institute, Carpenteria, California; Art Director, Global Children's Organization; and volunteer with the Soldiers Project.
20. Luise Eichenbaum is cofounder (with Susie Orbach) of the Women's Therapy Centre Institute, London and New York, and is on the institute faculty. She is in private practice in New York.
21. The newest project of the WTCI is a worldwide forum for feminist organizations to study and politically challenge the reality that the female body is an endangered species, as endangered as the earth it represents. Just as the female body is alternately starved and stuffed, so too is the earth: Globally, real food is being destroyed by the profit motive of corporate technological innovation,

while human beings are either stuffed or starved. The project plans to relate the assault on women's bodies to the rape of the earth through advertising and agribusiness.

22. See Marks (1999), McCoy (2006), Perkins (2005), and Harbury (2005). See also Ireland (2004): School of the Americas Watch (SOA) is an organization that has been fighting for years to close this center that trains military officers from Latin America; for ongoing reports on the SOA, see their Web site at www. soa.org.

23. In the early 1970s, Marie Langer published a denunciation of the participation of the Brazilian psychoanalytic candidate in the military state's torture of detainees, with little response from the international community. For a complete history and analysis of this controversial case and the resistance of the International Psychoanalytic Association to fully investigate it and implement consequences to those involved, see Villela (2005).

24. The information in this section is taken from the years-long information-gathering efforts that were part of the Section IX e-mail list discussions, as well as the following secondary sources that include bibliographies of primary resources and works by scholars and investigative journalists on the subject of the relationship between the profession of psychology and the U.S. military. See Soldz (2008), Summers (2008), Altman (2008), and Mayer (2005).

25. There are a plethora of books published on this issue; see, for example, Klein (2007) and Danner (2004).

26. Ghislaine Boulanger is a clinical psychologist/psychoanalyst in private practice in New York City and a faculty member of the New York University Postdoctoral Program in Psychotherapy and Psychoanalysis. She is a member of Section IX and has most recently authored "Witnesses to Reality: Working Psychodynamically with Survivors" (2008) and the groundbreaking *Wounded by Reality* (2007).

27. Stephen Soldz is a professor at the Boston Graduate School of Psychoanalysis and co-chair of the End Torture Action Committee. He is active in Psychologists for Social Responsibility, whose Web site (http://psysr.org/) features analyses and a variety of national activities that socially concerned psychologists and colleagues promote. Soldz's important blog for information about psychoanalysis and social issues is Psyche, Science, and Society at http://psychoanalystsopposewar.org/blog/.

28. End Torture Action Committee cochair and Steering Committee member of Psychologists for Social Responsibility; for those interested, see the *Democracy Now* Web site archives at http://www.democracynow.org/ for its extensive coverage and for interviews with participants from both sides of the question.

29. Steven Reisner is the cofounder of the Coalition for an Ethical Psychology (see Reisner, Losi, & Salvaticío, 2002). He is a central figure in the struggle within the American Psychological Association around the question of torture. In 2008, he ran as a candidate for the association's presidency, and although he lost the election, he succeeded in raising issues important to activist psychoanalysts with the rest of the membership. Reisner is in private practice in New York City.

30. Press release, September 17, 2008, Coalition for an Ethical Psychology and Psychologists for an Ethical APA. An August 1, 2002, memo said the CIA relied on its "on-site psychologists" for help in designing an interrogation program for Abu Zubaida and ultimately came up with a list of 10 methods drawn from a U.S. military training program known as Survival, Evasion, Resistance, and Escape, or SERE. That program, originally used to help prepare pilots to endure torture in the event they are captured, is loosely based on techniques that were used by the Communist Chinese to torture American prisoners of war. The role played by psychologists in adapting SERE methods for interrogation has been described in books and news articles in major newspapers, including *The Washington Post*. Author Jane Mayer and journalist Katherine Eban independently identified James Mitchell and Bruce Jessen, two psychologists in Washington State who worked as CIA contractors after 2001 and had extensive experience in SERE training. The CIA psychologists had personal experience with SERE and helped convince CIA officials that harsh tactics would coerce confessions from Abu Zubaida without inflicting permanent harm. Waterboarding was touted as particularly useful because it was "reported to be almost 100 percent effective in producing cooperation," the memo said. The agency then used a psychological assessment of Abu Zubaida to find his vulnerable points. One of them, it turns out, was a severe aversion to bugs. For more detail, see Stephen Soldz (2008).

Chapter 9

Impunity and resistance

Saving democracy in the heart of empire

Cultures that cannot distinguish between illusion and reality die.

— Chris Hedges (2009a)

Inevitable in life, the new life dawns in me: a small sun with roots that I will have to water deeply and push to fight their own battle against the weeds...

— Roque Dalton (1984)

Hedda and I are having coffee in her office on an early autumn day in 2007, and we are commiserating with one another. We are both distressed as the political realities become increasingly foreboding, but encouraged by what appears to be a rising tide of critical opposition to neoconservative ideology among citizens willing to acknowledge the grave state of our tarnished democracy. Hedda has suddenly remembered an article she wrote when she turned 90 years old, and she goes to hunt for it amid the piles of articles and papers bursting at the seams of her challengingly disordered filing cabinet. A miracle occurs, and she returns victorious with it in hand.

I try not to get distracted by its main theme, which is about Hedda's own aging and what it feels like to be old, facing death and still a full-time psychoanalyst. She writes that the self-disclosure required of such an endeavor feels somewhat like taking visiting friends on a sight-seeing tour of her city:

> There is the scenic route of parks, the endless vista of the open sea, of gardens, outdoor sculptures, famous architecture, elegant shopping streets, and picturesque ethnic enclaves. Those are the things I really want them to see. But there is also what used to be called the "wrong side of the tracks," now the "inner city," with its treeless streets, its neglected houses and ugly vacant lots serving as playgrounds, the old dilapidated cars, and the overloaded shopping carts of the homeless.

If the visitors are close friends, perhaps I can overcome the temptation to take them only through the scenic part; perhaps I can overcome
my pride in my beautiful city and my shame about the ugly city and let
my friends see where I really live... (2002, p. 641)

It occurs to me that Hedda might be describing not only a universal ambivalence about self-revelation, but also a ubiquitous reluctance to acknowledge
the dark side of our experience with others. In the context of our current
preoccupation, Hedda's metaphor might be an apt description of how we
cling to the idealized version of our society and thus protect ourselves from
seeing its ugly side, "where we really live." While we both still worry about
how this psychological predilection contributes to a bystander population,
it is incontrovertible that just as Hedda is emboldened to expose many
aspects of herself in her article, so too, at this point in the Bush administration's second term, more individuals are writing and speaking publicly to
expose the ugly reality of a national security state whose repressive policies
are aimed at "us"—U.S. citizens—as much as at "them"—the terrorists.

For example, in 2005 and 2006, James Risen and Eric Lightblau (2009)
reported in the *New York Times* that a secret government program developed by President Bush had been approved by Congress giving the National
Security Agency the right to wiretap citizens' phones, read their e-mails,
and follow international financial transactions. Citizens' groups around the
country were being infiltrated and harassed, an example of which was the
progressive All Saints Church in Pasadena, whose minister preached that
Jesus was in favor of peace. This church found itself being investigated by
the Internal Revenue Service, while churches that mobilized Republicans
to vote in local and national elections, which is illegal under U.S. tax law,
were being left alone. The American Civil Liberties Union (2007) reported
that thousands of ordinary American antiwar, environmental, and other
groups were being infiltrated by agents and that a secret Pentagon database included more than four dozen peaceful antiwar meetings, rallies, or
marches by U.S. citizens in its category of 1,500 "suspicious incidents."
The equally secret Counterintelligence Field Activity (CIFA) agency of the
Department of Defense was busy gathering information about domestic
organizations engaged in peaceful political activities: CIFA was supposed to
track "potential terrorist threats" as it watched ordinary U.S. citizen activists. A little-noticed new law redefined activism such as the animal rights
protests as "terrorism." The definition of "terrorist" slowly expanded to
include citizens involved in activities that could be construed as being part
of the opposition to neoconservative principles and policies.

By 2004, the U.S. Transportation Security Administration confirmed
that it had a list of passengers who were targeted for security searches or
worse if they tried to fly. The net was cast wide enough to include two mid-
dle-aged women peace activists in San Francisco, liberal Senator Edward

Kennedy, a member of Venezuela's government, and thousands of ordinary U.S. citizens. On March 1, 2007, Walter F. Murphy, one of the foremost constitutional scholars in the nation, author of the classic *Constitutional Democracy* (2006), and a decorated former marine, was denied a boarding pass at Newark International Airport because he was on the "terrorist watch list." When the airline employee enquired whether he had attended a peace demonstration, he replied in the negative, but remembered that some six months prior he had "given a lecture at Princeton critical of George Bush for his many violations of the constitution," which had been televised and put on the Web. The employee responded, "That'll do it" (Wolf, 2007).

In 2007, the Committee to Protect Journalists reported that arrests of U.S. journalists were at an unprecedented level: Josh Wolf, a blogger in San Francisco, was imprisoned for a year for refusing to turn over video footage of an antiwar demonstration; investigative journalist Greg Palast was accused by Homeland Security in a criminal complaint against him of threatening "critical infrastructure" when he and a TV producer were filming victims of Hurricane Katrina in Louisiana. Palast (2006) had written a best-seller critical of the Bush administration.

Even more alarming, in September 2006, Congress had passed the Military Commissions Act, giving the president the authority to define and designate any individual an "enemy combatant," who then could be seized accordingly. This bill was adopted rapidly, even though it authorized Bush to include U.S. citizens as "unlawful enemy combatants." Kellogg Brown & Root, a subsidiary of Vice President Cheney's Halliburton corporation, was granted millions of dollars to construct an elaborate facility at an undisclosed location to hold tens of thousands of "undesirables" (Cohn, 2006, 2007).[1] A series of secret memos written by the Office of Legal Counsel authorized memoranda to legitimize the Bush administration's unlawful national security policies, including one memorandum that related to military detention of U.S. citizens and another that addressed the domestic use of military force to combat terrorist activities (Cohn, 2009).

When such violations of rights are cast in terms of "national security," in part their function is to intimidate citizens and inhibit dissent. And when national security includes the state's torture practices, accompanied by an enigmatic alternation between denial and justification of this illegal and immoral practice, it is a further disincentive for citizens to challenge authority.

In addition, the administration's political manipulation of the fear of outsiders, the xenophobia inherent in the "war on terrorism" ideology, exacerbated the nativist antagonism stimulated by the increasing competition for jobs in this country. A new protracted war on the home front was being fought against a domestic enemy: undocumented immigrants. Repressive laws and increased budgets put more drones, weapons, and troops inside the country. The Department of Homeland Security agency gave new powers to the Immigration and Customs Enforcement (ICE), which in the fall of 2006 launched a campaign of workplace and home raids that over time detained hundreds of thousands of immigrants, who constituted the fastest-growing part of the U.S. prison system. Multibillion-dollar Homeland Security contracts for border security created a new market for aerospace companies like General Electric, Lockheed Martin, and Boeing. Calling this marriage between the state and global corporations the "migration-military-industrial complex," Latin American specialist Roberto Lovato (2008) concludes:

> Like other nation states, the United States suffers from strains wrought by the free hand of global corporations that have abandoned large segments of its workforce. Such a situation necessitates the institutionalization of the war on immigrants in order to get as many armed government agents into a society that may be teetering on even more serious collapse as seen in the recession and economic crisis devastating core components of the American Dream like education, health care and home ownership. (p. 20)

Most insidious because it was below the radar of public awareness was the Bush administration's strategy to use executive agencies to protect corporate interests over those of the public welfare. In their mandates to protect the workplace and the environment, the Environmental Protection Agency and the Occupational Safety and Health Administration were repeatedly constrained by the Bush administration. The pro-business decisions these two agencies were forced to make had cumulatively damaging effects on the health and working conditions of tens of thousands of citizens in the country's factories, mines, offices, schools, and communities (Shakir, Pitney, Terkel, & Schwin, 2007).

And through it all, war without end, two wars that were becoming increasingly unpopular among a citizenry whose opposition was noted in national polls but was too passive to be effective in changing official policy. Since the Vietnam War era, when the draft had directly affected millions of U.S. soldiers and their families and provoked a massive antiwar movement that brought that war to an end, now most citizens were isolated from the experience of war, which was being fought by a professional military augmented by privatized mercenary forces like Blackwater.[2] Over the past four decades the customary connection in a democratic society between the majority of citizens and the military was eliminated, and only a small minority of our society was being exposed to war and its psychological and physical sequelae. Moreover, citizens did not often recognize the indirect negative effects of war on their lives as tax dollars were redirected from education, health care, and infrastructure into war appropriations. In effect, the neoliberal values of individualism and policies of privatization that have eroded our democracy in general were reflected in the U.S. military and military policy.

Until recently, the sons of presidents, bankers, and oilmen regularly served in the military. Now, even though privileged citizens are claiming to be "proud of the troops," the influential tend not to serve and to maintain class-based deprecatory attitudes toward military culture (Roth-Douquet & Schaeffer, 2006). Studies show that most military people are from working- and middle-class families, with second-generation military providing an increasing percentage of recruits. The majority are coming from the Midwest and the South, or as Aaron Glantz writes in *The War Comes Home* (2009), the rural areas and inner cities of this country provided the new warrior class. It is becoming common for upper-middle- and upper-class communities, as well as Ivy League universities, to protect themselves from the military's access to their sons and daughters by organizing recruitment-free zones. This pattern is contrasted with the literal invasion by military recruiters into the high schools of the working class and Black communities.[3]

In her analysis of neoliberal culture, scholar Wendy Brown (2006) interprets the meanings of the bumper sticker "Support Our Troops" in light of its implicit demand and reprimand that reflect a "channeling of authority." The command is without content and its position of moral rectitude is conveyed without any clarity about what the support would entail. "...The contentlessness is the content: the vacuity of the bumper sticker expresses the very lack of action or participation that is contemporary citizenship..." (p. 709). Brown adds that the disinvitation to deliberate about the nature of the war and what the troops are doing corresponds to an uncritical patriotism and a refusal to think or invite others to think independently. Indeed, citizens' isolation from military realities meant they had little awareness of Bush's policies or the treatment of soldiers. Troops were sent into battle without body armor or armored Humvees to protect them; stop-loss policies extended troops' battle duty two and three times over; much-needed medical attention to soldiers returning from the war front was often withheld or dangerously delayed; and the guarantees of a college education promised by recruitment officers frequently evaporated.

A professional army is seen by the military to be more cost efficient than a draft, especially when augmented by private militaries like Blackwater, which have come to represent a larger percentage of U.S. military occupations than in any previous era. This delinking of government accountability and military service from citizens empowers the government to (mis)use military force in foreign policy even when the majority of citizens oppose it. In psychological terms, by being able to disavow responsibility for the aggression perpetrated in their name, citizens' capacities for experiencing guilt in the service of reparative action is eviscerated and the status quo reinforced. The vet becomes the holder of this disavowed guilt, a projective phenomenon that can increase the motivation on the part of citizens to maintain the gulf between themselves and perpetrator/victim soldier.

This situation has had multiple consequences. One primary effect is the psychological sequelae suffered by U.S. veterans who have been sent to Iraq, who for the most part are being left to deal privately with the knowledge of their murderous assaults on Iraqi men, women, and children in the atrocity-producing situation of war.[4] Thousands of veterans from the battlefields of both Iraq and Afghanistan have been returning home with extreme posttraumatic stress disorder (PTSD) and, finding too little help from the military and Veterans Administration or from communities with little capacity or motivation to understand their experience, cannot often bear the psychic wounds alone. Violent resolution of intolerable states of mind are frequently ending in homicidal or suicidal tragedies (Associated Press, 2009).

Countless testimonies of soldiers and their families reveal the tragedy of individual responsibility shouldered by family members who must often quit their jobs to become full-time advocates for their wounded warrior relatives in a government bureaucracy whose economic and political raison d'être is to sabotage access to medical care. In the post–9/11 era of warmaking, the historical pattern of government abandonment of vets is even more problematic because the need for medical and mental health interventions has grown (Glantz, 2009). Advanced technology and improved battlefield medical interventions have meant that many more soldiers are returning alive, but with more serious wounds, including severe PTSD and traumatic brain injury (TBI). They are returning to a neoliberal government that disinvested in the military medical system and the Veterans Administration (VA) has even privatized aspects of their delivery system, constituting a cruel abandonment of this disenfranchised sector of the population.

Hedda has spoken about the psychological meanings of this bifurcation between war politics and the society at large. "There is," she told me at an Uprooted Mind conference related to this subject, "an increasing disregard for human life in the context of the Iraq war and what the U.S. occupation is doing to the Iraqi population. When people speak of death and the dying, I don't see much affect in what they say unless it's about their own families. I don't see any mourning or grief or any feeling that perhaps the most important thing is not to add more dead to existing losses. What are our fundamental values in this country? That we have to win? That we dictate to the rest of the world how they have to live? Is that worth the loss of all these dead Iraqis and Americans? Maybe it's a defensive reaction to Iraq, but I'm worried about trends in this culture of mindlessness and unwillingness to relate to and examine death."

This culture of resistance to dealing with war has meant that our soldiers and their families have been ruthlessly used and then discarded by the body politic. Perhaps by holding the threat of death and killing, they serve as a container of what Robert J. Lifton calls "death anxiety" for the civilian population, who then experiences the triumph or at least the relief of safety in a dangerous world. Viewed from this perspective, not only the Iraqis or Afghans or any other foreign object of U.S. aggression become a container for projected death anxiety as well as aggression, but our own soldiers as well. It is they who are subjected by the government to the terrifying conditions of war that unleash behavior otherwise prohibited by civil society. They thereby become the socially chosen vehicles through which not only trauma but also guilt are expressed and individual violence repeated on behalf of society in general, which is thereby relieved from having to experience group responsibility. As noted journalist and war correspondent Chris Hedges (2009b) puts it:

> What happens when the corporate state says that you can die in its wars but at home you are human refuse, that there is no job, no way to pay your medical bills or your mortgage, no hope? Then you retreat into your private hell of rage, terror and alienation. You do not return from the world of war. You yearn for its sleek and powerful weapons, its speed and noise, its ability to abolish the lines between sanity and madness. You long for the alluring, hallucinogenic landscapes of combat. You miss the psychedelic visions of carnage and suffering, the smells, sounds, shrieks, explosions and destruction that jolt you back to the present, which make you aware in ways you never were before. The thrill of violence, the God-like power that comes when you can take a human life with impunity, is matched against the pathetic existence of waiting for an unemployment check. You look to rejoin the fraternity of killers. Here. There. It no longer matters. (accessed October 1, 2009)

PSYCHOANALYTIC ACTIVISTS CONTINUE IN THE TRENCHES

In March 2009, a group of U.S. soldiers and veterans gathered in Washington, D.C., to recount their experiences in Iraq and Afghanistan. They spent three days testifying, confessing, and mourning. They revealed atrocities never before spoken of—their brutal murders of civilians, the destruction of homes and villages, the rape and sexual assault of both civilians and U.S. military women—and displayed photographs and video footage to back up their confessions. In the tradition of the 1971 Winter Soldier Investigation, in which another generation of veterans gathered in Detroit to give testimony about war crimes they had committed or witnessed in Vietnam, this contemporary event, also called Winter Soldier, detailed U.S. troops' actions in Iraq and Afghanistan. Like its predecessor, this generation of soldiers charged with carrying out U.S. military policy offered firsthand accounts of that policy's devastating effects. Their public testimonies demonstrated what psychoanalysts understand about the human psyche and how aggression and violence emerge in response to conditions that produce terror and helplessness. Moreover, as psychoanalyst Adrienne Harris (2006) points out, shame and humiliation "play a crucial role in the extremes of brutality, damage and self-damage in military experiences, training and combat" (p. 1156).

In April 2005, Sean Huze was performing *The Sand Storm: Stories From the Front*, the critically acclaimed play he authored based on his experiences serving in the U.S. Marine Corps from 2001 to 2005. While in Iraq, Huze had been awarded a Certificate of Commendation citing his "courage and self-sacrifice throughout sustained combat operations," and in 2005 he received an honorable discharge from the Marine Corps. *The Sand Storm* is a series of 10 monologues of recently returned veterans from Iraq that take the audience into the immediate posttraumatic aftermath of war. It depicts psychological disruptions characterized by chaos, confusion, adrenalin, night sweats, claustrophobic nightmares, and moments of human goodness that intercept the evils of war so threatening to the psyche. The audience does not know whether the play's 10 young men, haunted by their distressing memories, will wind up in psychotic states, psychic numbness, denial, homicide, addictions, or reparative action and resolution.

In the audience one evening sat psychoanalyst Judith Broder,[5] who was so moved by Sean's depiction of war trauma that she felt compelled to act. Broder spent the next several years mobilizing a network of psychoanalysts and other mental health care professionals to offer pro bono mental health services to military service people and their families. She founded The Soldiers Project, which became a constituent organization of the Los Angeles Institute and Society for Psychoanalytic Studies (LAISPS) Trauma Center, although its participating therapists and supporters include members of several psychoanalytic institutes, as well as other licensed clinicians in the Los Angeles community. Broder and The Soldiers Project steering committee began by developing working relationships with Sean Huze and several veterans' organizations, some from the Vietnam War era as well as those formed since the wars in Iraq and Afghanistan. Although convinced that psychoanalytic training was sufficient to offer quality help to soldiers and their families, Broder also arranged for an ongoing series of workshops featuring experts on trauma, including psychiatrists and psychologists from the VA and the military. Several one-day conferences included mental health speakers, vets, and active-duty service people to raise consciousness for the community at large about the experience and impact of war.

When The Soldiers Project was forming, studies indicated that upwards of 35 percent of Iraq war veterans sought access to mental health services within a year of their return from combat, only a partial representation considering those who resisted seeking help because of the stigma associated with it. Reservists and National Guard members, who made up 40 percent of the forces in Iraq, were returning to their communities ineligible for the same medical coverage as active-duty service members. An estimated 1.6 million soldiers and 10 times that number of family members would be affected by the disruption of war, precipitating a potential public health problem. The Soldiers Project's roughly 150 volunteers in the Los Angeles area provided pro bono therapy to a range of individuals and family members. They reached out to veterans groups, the VA, military bases, and community venues to raise awareness of the psychological consequences of war and their availability for free, confidential, individualized counseling. The Soldiers Project Web site offers a mission statement that indicates: "We provide help to service members and families struggling with issues related to the overwhelming trauma of war including the cycle from predeployment to deployment to homecoming and reentry to civilian life. Our services are entirely free of charge. We do not report to any government agency." Typically, either a vet, active-duty soldier, or mother or girlfriend calls The Soldiers Project 24-hour phone line with presenting complaints for vets or active-duty personnel that include anxiety, depression, drug or alcohol abuse, and difficulty reestablishing customary family interactions. Spouses and children typically describe anxiety, depression, or school problems following the deployment or return of the soldier.

In May of 2008, The Soldiers Project organized a national conference, "Hidden Wounds of War: Pathways to Healing," which featured nationally recognized experts in the field. A principal objective was to bring mental health professionals from throughout the United States together with veterans and their families to discuss and share information on the psychological consequences of U.S. wars. In part as a result of this conference and also in response to requests from colleagues from other cities across the country, The Soldiers Project has a national network of 300 clinicians who offer pro bono services to service people and their families.

I spoke with Judith Broder about this challenging and illuminating experience.[6] She told me that at first one question arose among the clinicians about how they could work effectively with a population that had been affected by the extreme situation of war that they themselves had not experienced. How could they convey to their patients that they could understand their experience? As she spoke, I remembered what Julia Braun had encountered after a terrorist bomb blew up the Argentine Israeli Center (AMIA) in downtown Buenos Aires in 1994, killing 100 people and wounding hundreds more. "Many psychoanalysts asked what they could do in such a crisis," Julia had told me, "and we reminded them that Freud wrote about how in critical moments an analyst can listen and contain terrible anxieties. Many of us worked with the survivors, and I reminded the candidates I was supervising that even though the Argentine Psychoanalytic Association doesn't offer a course 'What to Do if a Bomb Explodes,' as psychoanalysts we have the necessary tools to treat these people." Judith Broder shares this perspective, so that in addition to the many training workshops and relevant bibliographies The Soldiers Project offers, the foundational proto-col is engaged in listening. Although some therapists also add a variety of specific techniques, such as eye movement and desensitization and repro-cessing (EMDR), the basic approach is the psychoanalytic tool of listening well. "I am convinced that in most cases what's needed is a witness to hear the stories, which helps to undo the sense of isolation and horror at what they've seen and what they've done. These soldiers are damaged in terms of the idea of a shattered self as a response to their war experience. It's also true of the families, who seem to have more access than the soldiers to psychological education that helps them understand what they are going through as spouses or kids of those directly affected."

The Soldiers Project patient population is divided approximately into 40 percent returning vets, 40 percent extended family members, and 20 per-cent active-duty personnel who are returning to war. Clinicians may have an antiwar perspective or be supportive of the government's military poli-cies, but the treatment is organized so as to give the servicemen and women an opportunity to clarify for themselves the complex emotions evoked by being in a war zone. Often clinicians help an individual who is absent with-out leave return to base to avoid facing criminal charges, or they intervene on behalf of individuals suffering acute depression so as to help them avoid returning to combat. The Soldiers Project receives referrals from military and VA health professionals when these professionals cannot provide care for service people, see them intensively for an extended period of time, or respond quickly enough in family crises. Soldiers Project clinicians also do community outreach by speaking in a variety of venues, including churches, schools, rotary clubs, and synagogues. Broder points out that most com-munities know very little about the crisis of our service people: "This is the bad part of the professional army," she emphasizes. "There is a split: The service people experience terrible things, they do terrible things, and it's hard for us to recognize that they are doing it for us. So it divides the population psychologically and socially."

Over time, The Soldiers Project has become a legitimate organization from the perspective of the upper ranks of military bureaucracies. "And," reports Broder, "I have learned that most of the people we've come in contact with among the military and VA providers are good hearted and that each wants to provide the best care possible for the troops and their families." She adds, "In our work we still encounter obstacles related to the huge stigma regarding mental health care, seen as a sign of weakness, expressed especially among the ground troops. People will often be ridi-culed and treated badly if they seek it. So from my perspective, the stigma operates at a personal rather than an institutional level." She stresses that this is especially problematic given the current military buildup and lack of troops, because many soldiers are forced to repeat tours of duty that only exacerbate chances of suffering the psychological sequelae of war trauma.

One of the workshops that The Soldiers Project organized early on featured two psychoanalysts, Kenneth Reich, president of the Psychoanalytic Couple and Family Institute of New England, and Jaine Darwin, a former president of American Psychological Association Division 39.[7] They presented a history of their organization, SOFAR (Strategic Outreach to Families of All Reservists), which they cofounded in Massachusetts to aid the families of reservists suffering secondary trauma in response to their relatives' war-related traumatic states. As Reich has written, "The 'secondary trauma' associated with war is extremely far-reaching...separation and anxiety put stress on troops' marriages and relationships, and often make children anxious or sad in response to the separation and fears of their parent being hurt or not returning." The model developed by Reich and Darwin was a pilot program they proposed to the Army Reserves that began implementation in April 2005. Volunteer SOFAR psychoanalysts and psychologists began to work with the Family Readiness Group of the Army Reserves' 883rd Medical Company and other units to help families deal with the stresses associated with deployment, alert, mobilization, and reunion. Darwin, Reich, and other volunteers typically led a discussion group for families, followed by facilitated breakout groups for parents, spouses, significant others, and children.

Ken Reich explains that his motivation to engage in this work was an outgrowth of his experience 17 years prior when he cofounded the Psychoanalytic Couple and Family Institute in New England. That organization's mission was to train clinicians to do outreach and prevention in underserved communities. Volunteers from psychoanalytic institutes took part in a range of activities, including The Child Witness to Violence project at Boston Medical Center. Others worked with foster care and adoption programs, as well as with probate court officers. Reich tells me, "We wanted to train clinicians to work with families and couples and to do community outreach. In order to make every hour of a clinician's impact meaningful and for it to multiply geometrically to reach more people, our model was to find the caregivers in an organization working with underserved people whose lives could be improved as a result of our interventions. For me, SOFAR was a natural outgrowth and extension of that experience. Two events were the catalyst: The first was 9/11, when I went to New York in response to my 23-year-old daughter's request that I come and stay with her. I realized how difficult it was to leave when it was still uncertain about whether or not there would be another attack and when we had no idea about the circumstances under which we would see one another again. At one point most of my New York family was together in one synagogue, which was very scary and painful because leaving evoked such strong feelings of separation, which surprised me. I thought about how other people would be having a hard time as well. That led me to think about doing a conference for clinicians and the public. So the Psychoanalytic Couple and Family Institute in New England, Boston Medical Center, and Brandeis University organized the conference in 2002. During this experience I read an article about the difficult situation of army families, who were given one free mental health session so long as their loved one was deployed and one if their loved one remained deployed. After that, they could pay if they wanted more treatment. I realized that if the wars in Afghanistan and Iraq were to continue, it would likely be for a long time and would have a significant impact on a large sector of our population."

Reich emphasizes that when a soldier goes to war the entire family serves—mom, dad, husband, wife, grandparents, cousins, nieces, aunts, close friends, colleagues, and so forth. Thus the death of one soldier impacts 30 to 40 people. "With e-mails and cell phones, it would happen within a matter of hours and so the impact of this country's wars would include the extended family members in addition to the service people themselves." Because such a limited number—less than 2 percent—of the population serves, these victims would become the invisible casualties of war. The idea to create a group of highly trained clinicians, including many psychoanalysts, to treat these families pro bono was developed in 2003, with the hope that it would become a national program. In 2005, Jaine Darwin joined Reich and they named the project SOFAR.

SOFAR bases its work on the family therapy model. Its strategy at first was to work within the military system, which resulted in a two-and-a-half-year vetting process with the Judge Advocate General's office of the New England Reserves. They won the commanding general's permission to begin a pilot program in the Boston area, which developed initially with the reserves and then with the National Guard. "In the beginning," Reich told me, "we would be invited to attend family readiness group meetings called by family members under the umbrella of the military. They were run on bases or military installations, and we would meet once or twice a month for the duration of their loved ones' deployment. We worked to put a real face on mental health workers, while normalizing what they felt, helping them to build resilience within their families." Over time, SOFAR's work expanded to other activities, including the development of psychoeducational tools for military families, as well as for physicians and teachers. Their booklet, the SOFAR *Guide for Helping Children and Youth Cope With the Deployment and Return of a Parent in the National Guard and Other Reserve Components*, describes the impact of war on children from a developmental perspective. It is used in classrooms, pediatricians' offices, and homes. It has been distributed by authorization of the governor's office to every school in North Carolina and Massachusetts, with expanding possibilities in New York and New Jersey. SOFAR has a network of approximately 225 clinicians, distributed among Massachusetts, New York, Michigan, and Florida, with plans for expanding to additional states.

Because stigmatization functions to prevent people from taking advantage of SOFAR's pro bono services, their focus has shifted to the provision of psychoeducational tools and workshops for caregivers and the training of families to become gatekeepers for their loved ones who serve or have served. As the Department of Defense has become more concerned about the high suicide rate among soldiers and vets, SOFAR is examining the relational issues within their family structures as a key to the high suicide rate. According to Reich, now president of SOFAR, "Separation is ubiquitous and powerful, and it shapes and reshapes one's internal landscape as well as what happens within a family structure surrounding its members' relationship issues with one another. The impact of the war on each individual's unique capacity to deal with separation is one key factor, along with others, that can help us better understand the high suicide rate. But we have to remember as well that every time a soldier deploys, a wife becomes a single parent and has to deal with economic, educational, psychological, and medical issues, and often with children's problems as they face the change in the family system. Although many families may have dealt resiliently with the deployment of a soldier, many other family members have to deal with the return of their loved one, who may be experiencing anxiety, depression, PTSD, and TBIs, and they can develop similar symptoms we call 'secondary trauma.' So there are a large number of people affected in addition to the soldiers and marines themselves, and that's why our work to help these 'invisible casualties of war' develop more resilience is so important."

Secondary trauma affects not only family members of military personnel but the therapists who work with them as well. For that reason, The Soldiers Project offers its clinicians an opportunity to participate in peer supervision groups that provide feedback regarding psychotherapeutic interventions as well as a holding environment for expectable psychological disruptions that are stimulated by the work with this population that has been exposed to extreme situations of terror and violence. Judith Broder indicates that this work has affected her by "increasing my personal revulsion and horror about war. It has made me a pacifist. When I see these young people with shattered lives, it feels unconscionable that this is what we do to our young and our poor people." In terms of the theme of military service and social class, Judith remarks, "These young people are hyped about signing up and about what they will gain. This is another way they are taken advantage of. Many people who are poor don't know that there are other ways to get an education. And while the new GI bill includes money for tuition, once you've suffered from combat stress or traumatic brain injury, it's not so easy to pursue that education. On the other hand, those who have served learn a lot of discipline in the military, so it's not all negative. They can now do things they couldn't do before. Perhaps the important context of the plight of service people is something we all have to deal with, which is the general societal problem that there aren't enough jobs for everyone."[8]

These two psychoanalytic projects were begun as efforts to take social responsibility for the direct U.S. victims of the state's war-making policies. Together, the individuals, families, and communities suffering from the sequelae of war were visible signs of the dark side of life during the Bush years. As we have seen, the neoconservative era gave this country in addition to a professional and privatized military split off from the larger community of citizens, secret government programs that invaded citizens' right to privacy; secret government information gathering on domestic organizations; repressive legislation like the Military Commissions Act, extended ICE raids into factories, offices, and homes; and pro-business federal agencies overseeing environmental and labor conditions. Together they signified our society's slide toward authoritarian governance and culture. Like Hedda's essay on self-disclosure and the reluctance of human beings to expose the ugly side "where we really live," we too were having to struggle with our resistance to knowing about our tarnished democracy.

VIEWS FROM LATIN AMERICA

These disturbing developments were being observed and their implications thought about throughout Latin America. For many Latin Americans, conditions in the U.S. superpower seemed uncannily reminiscent of the transitional periods leading to their own experiences with dictatorship. They were alarmed because while this country was frequently resented as an imperialist force whose most recent imposition throughout the hemisphere was neoliberalism, its stable democratic institutions and commitment to individual rights and civil liberties were admired and served as an example to be emulated. For many, the political and social shifts represented by the Bush administration were disconcerting. In periodic visits to Argentina during those years, I informally discussed these issues with my psychoanalytic colleagues. In December 2007, I returned to Buenos Aires to formally interview them about themes related to impunity, militarism, *memoria*, and human rights in the context of the U.S. response to 9/11 and the changing horizons within Latin America, much of which was now governed by progressive regimes critical of the neoliberal Washington Consensus.

I am delighted, as always, to be back in the frenetic sights and sounds of Buenos Aires, where not everyone tangos, but no one sleeps. And so it is that among the elaborate lunches, late-night dinners, and smorgasbord of cultural events, I once again sit down with my psychoanalytic friends and colleagues, tape recorder on the ready, to document their perspectives on the psychological implications of recent political developments in both of our countries.

December in Buenos Aires brings humid, hot winds, and for that reason, Juan Carlos Volnovich, his wife and colleague, Silvia Werthein, and I are relaxing in his air-conditioned office. Its low-key, calming interior is complemented by French doors that open onto a lovely garden in full bloom. Mimi Langer gazes down from her photograph on the wall as Juan Carlos and Silvia animatedly disagree about the relative success of President Kirchner's challenge to the neoliberal paradigm in Latin America. This is a favorite and controversial topic among progressive Argentines. Juan Carlos believes that through his institution of enough budget, trade, and infrastructural reforms to bring stability to the middle class, Kirchner's role has been to deflate the radical challenges to the existing order that arose in response to the 2001 economic meltdown. He argues that Kirchner has undermined the strong human rights movement by driving a wedge among its various groups, co-opting and privileging some over others and restricting the human rights discourse to the violations of the past only rather than to the contemporary violations of people's economic as well as political rights. "No," Silvia replies vociferously, "that's not right. Before Kirchner, we couldn't reform anything in this country because of the culture of impunity, so his human rights discourse and his strategy to undo the legal framework of impunity and indict and prosecute the perpetrators of state terror were a fundamental rupture with the past 30 years. That was important to relegitimize the state in citizens' minds. Not only that, the modicum of economic stability his policies have brought to the country really matters." Juan Carlos agrees that this economic stability is very important to a people traumatized by the global systemic collapse just five years prior. "But," he says, "what's terrible is that we are in a moment of great prosperity, due in large measure to the raw materials Argentina can cultivate and sell in a temporarily advantageous international market, but in no way does this translate into a more just distribution of the wealth... For me," he adds, "the important thing is that neoliberal globalization is based in political and military domination, economic privatization, and the mass media's conquest of minds so that we all are collaborationists and complicit in a system destructive to human beings and the earth."

And while Juan Carlos agrees with Silvia that before Kirchner nothing substantive could be done about social justice in a culture of impunity, he argues that behind the facade of all the apparently democratic states that govern in the era of neoliberalism, mafias with economic power use the government to manage their own rules of the market. "So the neoliberal democratic state with its discourse of human rights covers up the fact that never in history has there been so much violation of human rights. In Argentina today we have political assassinations, many political prisoners, and kids killed in the streets by the police, just like during the dictatorship."

We move to the question of contemporary subjectivity within neoliberal culture. The idea of the domination of the subject by a homogenized international market-based culture and values leads Juan Carlos to comment that "for some Lacanians the 'Other' as a referent has disappeared. For example, given the lack of anything that represents a dynamic-enough force—power and authority in the traditional sense of the terms—to compete with the market as the referent, we're in a postsymbolic order era. Within Argentine psychoanalysis there is a growing interest in identities, fantasies, and unconscious experience related to the body, the embodied psyche." He gives the example of interest in exploring the meanings of the popularity among contemporary youth of *raves*, large-scale dances featuring ear-splitting hard rock music where the main objective is an encounter of bodies, not of persons. "It's a trance-like experience, transitory, corporeal in nature. Much of the time the participants never even get each other's phone numbers." Silvia Bleichmer, a prominent psychoanalytic cultural critic, argues that such culturally sanctioned activity points to a different kind of subject than the one framed by the sexually repressive civilization that Freud theorized. Today's cultural practice is organized around the search for narcissistic stimulation, including sexual pleasure, independent of emotional contact with another. "What is important is that one experiences pleasure. A patient who cannot tolerate his own conflicted experience of being in a relationship with others recently said he suspects that I don't approve of his participating in raves and wonders if it's because I'm very repressed. I responded that it doesn't really matter if I am or am not repressed; the important thing is that he is lonely and his embrace of this kind of life is a justification to stay alone and to resist exploring why he cannot allow himself to look for someone with whom he can experience love and a shared sexual pleasure. And then there's the other version of pleasure, also imported from the United States through the media, associated with uninhibited aggression. In these same raves, youth often crowd into a 'mosh pit,' a lowered area of the dance floor, where to the booming, hard rock music they fling their bodies against one another's pummeling fists and elbows, as if this will enliven deadened psychic experience." Returning to the notion that the Other no longer exists, Juan Carlos comments, "Even if we look at all the political struggles in the world today, we could say that rather than comprising the symbolic order, the great monotheistic religions, like Christianity and Islam, mirror corporate ventures that buy and sell arms and lure their clients to sign up to be the foot soldiers in their grandiose aspirations to extend exclusive control over populations and resources."

This idea stimulates associations to 9/11, and I ask about its impact on Argentines.[9] "On the one hand it was disorganizing," Juan Carlos answers, "because we are used to thinking about the United States as a signifier of omnipotent power. And regardless if power is good or bad, one feels protected by the fact of its existence. 9/11 revealed that the United States is actually vulnerable. It can make one feel like an orphan, which was stimulated by the media that transmitted the images of the planes crashing into the towers over and over again. A patient asked me if that could happen here. I thought, 'Have you forgotten so easily?' In fact, it had already happened here with state terror, and his question is an example of a kind of disavowal. It reminds me of how when the dictatorship ended, some citizens who were interviewed about the secret concentration camps located in their neighborhoods denied knowing about them. But then when they were asked about specific details—had they noticed funny smells or sounds of people screaming or comings and goings of unmarked cars?—they could recall those individual facts without ever having let themselves put it all together to know that they were living among the state's torture chambers. This is one example of the famous bystander phenomenon."

There were additional meanings of 9/11 as well, and Juan Carlos continues: "For many Argentines there was a kind of forbidden pleasure, an identification with the terrorists' assault as a retaliatory fantasy for the feelings of resentment toward the United States accumulated over decades. Of course, this was not appropriate to talk about. So alongside the feelings of distress experienced by some, there was also a kind of elation provoked by the idea that the symbol of absolute power is vulnerable, which opened up the idea that one could challenge it. Of course, this was related to the customary cynicism in Latin America about U.S. motives, which was reinforced by the invasion and occupation of Iraq. It's my impression that Argentines are skeptical and thus did not believe anything the United States said to justify its wars. We thought that the United States needs to control the oil and that all the rhetoric about democracy and liberation was mere pretext. The war was carried out to occupy the space, the territory; it's about domination. And this relates to the antiterrorism discourse; it seems to me the international system needs some form of violence and war because there's nothing left to conquer. Capitalism needs to expand, and there's nothing left in the world to swallow up. There's a kind of self-colonialism occurring in which capitalism destroys the environment, the very thing it needs to survive. Also, most governments now share a strategy that has fear at the center of politics: Who can infuse the most fear in their own population? The problem is that all current terrorisms, state or nonstate, take a partial truth and make it the whole, and the whole is an absolute that permits the enactment of terrorism 'for people's own good,' an abstraction that becomes in effect evil."

Inevitably the discussion turns toward Latin America's new progressive governments that have emerged in the last decade. To Silvia's positive assessment that the governments of Venezuela, Bolivia, Ecuador, Brazil, Chile, Argentina, and Uruguay are effectively confronting neoliberalism, Juan Carlos insists that the most we can hope for is that they can use the state to return us to the Keynesian welfare state policies of the 1960s rather than fundamentally challenge neoliberal economic policies and market ideology.

These issues occupy all my exchanges with my Argentine colleagues, and among the most optimistic about this historical moment is Tato Pavlovsky, who receives me in his sprawling Mediterranean-style home in one of the older, quiet, residential neighborhoods of the city. He is still handsomely imposing and as passionately interested in the world as he has been since his youth. He has stopped writing and performing in the theater to focus on his therapeutic work with groups. He is also studying the new social movements throughout the region, from the Brazilian landless peasant movement to the Chiapas-based Zapatistas in Mexico, and their contribution to what he calls the new revolutionary subject. From his perspective, these movements produced this generation of progressive Latin American leaders who constitute a new Latin American identity and discourse that confronts U.S. hegemony. Tato inclines toward Silvia's position about Kirchner, because even though his reformist policies have helped mainly the middle class while ignoring the poorer 30 percent of Argentines, his commitment to human rights and his ability to challenge the International Monetary Fund (IMF) and World Bank are reason for optimism.

For Tato, contemporary subjectivity is complex, and one of the most disturbing developments in his country is the obsessive preoccupation with personal security that overshadows social consciousness. He criticizes the media and the government, which pay more attention to an incident in which young people rob and kill a middle-class family than to all the hundreds of thousands of poor, starving youth of the country. "But," he says, "with social crime rising, even with my critical awareness I'm afraid as much as anyone else. For example, one young kid was hanging around my house, ringing the bell at all hours, and I told him, 'Look, if you agree, you come every Tuesday at 6:00 P.M. and I'll give you 15 pesos.' He agreed and even though it seemed to be working, he still came in one afternoon and robbed me. I understood it, even though I didn't appreciate it happening to me. Delinquency has increased at a shocking rate, but society has to provide children and youth with legitimate possibilities for survival and a meaningful life."

Tato tells me that the fear and insecurity that dominate middle-class consciousness stem from their wish to preserve their property. "They can only think of their own situation, not of the poor in the provinces or urban slums who are hungry and have no opportunities whatsoever. They are preoccupied with losing what they have or being attacked because of it." While a number of middle-class progressives continue to ally themselves with the political struggles of the workers and unemployed, Tato suggests that the majority of middle-class people are hostile to the unemployed workers' organizations that have obtained small governmental survival subsidies. "Middle-class people claim the workers just don't want to work, and they resent the help they receive from the state. This is a *petit bourgeois* mentality," Tato insists. "The majority of people want to work, but can you imagine the miserable work and unsustainable wages they have access to? And there's a parallel feeling among kids' disillusionment with education. 'Why study?' they ask. 'For what? What will we be able to do once we've graduated?'" Tato indicates that a significant sector of Latin American youth is demoralized and increasingly using drugs to ward off profound anxieties provoked by an insecure social world. A dramatic rise of illegal drug trafficking is inducing serious addictions among young people of all social classes. I inquire whether or not Tato is pessimistic about the younger generation. "No," he answers. "There is another extremely motivated sector with an incredible imaginative capacity, especially in comparison with European youth who are so dominated by the market. Here there are 150 theater pieces every weekend, much of which are the creative efforts of our young people. They are involved in searching for a meaningful identity in the context of the contemporary world."

The topic of the new Latin American identity reminds Tato of Venezuelan President Hugo Chavez, the most outspoken critic of U.S. policy and advocate of a Latin American–wide strategy to use Latin American resources to redistribute wealth and power among all Latin Americans and to curtail U.S. economic and military power in the region. His ideology and charismatic confrontational personality make him popular among the traditionally disenfranchised working classes, peasants, indigenous peoples, and their radicalized middle-class allies and a foe of the powerful and those afraid of losing their privileged positions and status. Tato tells me that because Chavez is demonized in the U.S. media, it is hard for U.S. citizens to understand how he could be appreciated in Latin America. He had the chance to spend time with Chavez during his recent trip to Buenos Aires, where he was received by huge flag-waving, adoring audiences. "I trust him and have confidence in his ability to be the leading spokesperson for a much-needed new direction for Latin America. I was very impressed when he told me that he isn't only angry at the United States for its exploitative policies, but that he admires the intelligence of the U.S. political strategy and laments our failure to figure out how to deal with it. Chavez insists that we need to elaborate a capacity to more effectively respond to the neoconservative intellectuals who surround Bush."

With regard to Argentines' reactions to 9/11, Tato suggests they have to be understood in the context of the strong anti-imperialist sentiment throughout Latin America. "On the one hand, we see the Iraq fiasco as a drive to control the oil. To destroy an entire country and then say you want to leave them in peace and with democracy is ridiculous, and virtually no one believes it. Only the extreme right here believes Bush's antiterrorism rhetoric. More and more people here also know that the U.S. state has control over the minds of its citizens, but we can see a growing resistance and criticism within the United States, including the many internationally acclaimed actors who are speaking out. On the other hand, there is the whole issue of the suicide bombers, which is a phenomenon that we in Latin America don't understand because it isn't part of our experience. It's a form of resistance that we don't have here. But who knows, from the point of view of those who practice it, perhaps it is appealing because there really aren't options, given the powerful forces organized to maintain the status quo."

As we finish our conversation, Tato scours his library for copies of his latest publications on these and related topics. When I leave his home to walk the several blocks to a busy intersection, I note that small groups of youth are aimlessly hanging out between parked cars and in front of the neighborhood's small businesses. I wonder if one of them is the kid who robbed Tato's house. I suddenly recall all my friends' warnings to protect my purse while walking in the streets because of the recent wave of robberies in Buenos Aires. So as I proceed, I watch these young men staring at me and my ideology and emotional state part ways: I am thinking empathically about the global economic forces that have robbed them of productive lives, and I am simultaneously feeling anxious and endangered. Like the middle-class people preoccupied with personal security that Tato has just critiqued, I hold my tape recorder and purse tight to my body and guiltily walk rapidly to the busy intersection where a cab will liberate me from this unpleasantly contradictory experience.

The next day is another scorcher. Julia Braun is offering me an iced drink as we settle into our scheduled interview in her 20th-floor condominium. The floor-to-ceiling windows reveal the busy plaza below and in the distance the sparkling waters of the La Plata River and high-rises of Montevideo, just as I remember them from times past. Julia tells me that her psychoanalytic writing continues to focus on the social violence intrinsic to neoliberalism in Latin America. She reminds me that from her perspective, the subject is constituted by both psychic and social reality and that the social world does not represent externality or the individual world internality; rather, both are spaces in which different meanings coexist and are always present. So when she speaks of current political developments in her society, she is referring to identity and core aspects of subjective meaning-making experience.[10] For example, Julia's enthusiasm about the latest political developments in the region takes into account the psychological significance of a world turned on its head. "Imagine," she observes, "for so many years we in Latin America were the ones living under state terror, and the democratic countries of Europe and the United States denigrated us because of our violently repressive regimes. Now it's the reverse. We have been electing progressive governments that advocate indigenous rights, land reform, and economic autonomy and have now established a regional bank so we can fund these objectives and become independent of the IMF. The seven presidents who are forming this bank recently met in Buenos Aires, and their pledge that this bank will help the Latin American people who are fighting for development and for human rights moved us to tears. These are the very goals...the same values...of the young people who fought for them decades ago, believing then that they were only achievable through armed struggle. Now they are represented by the democratically elected governments that are trying to use the state to attain them. And so, ironically, now it is we who embody democracy, and the United States, under Bush, authoritarianism."

"And the controversial Hugo Chavez?" I ask Julia. She laughs as she responds, obviously more circumspect about her assessment than Tato: "Look, he's very provocative and irritating, but for the moment, he is mobilizing opposition to U.S. hegemony. I like him a lot because he's very intelligent and clear. But I don't know if it's a great political strategy to irritate the behemoth to the north. Sometimes I think it's too much, but sometimes I find it really amusing. Among the Argentines, the conservatives are very hostile toward him, and the left is divided, some identifying with him and others worrying that his confrontational personality will polarize hemispheric relations in a destructive way. But just like with Cristina [the wife of Nestor Kirchner, who recently won the presidential election], who's a very capable leader but at the same time a bit hysterical and preoccupied with her physical appearance in ways that can be off-putting, I think it's important to be able to separate the personality from the politics. Chavez's four- and five-hour speeches are a bit ridiculous, for example, but he is really very intelligent and is managing to sustain a popular following throughout Latin America by articulating a critique of U.S. economic and military objectives in the region. I think that means a lot."

Julia's clinical experience demonstrates that these larger economic and political questions are not just of intellectual interest but felt intimately by people who are either consciously preoccupied by them or unconsciously affected and live them only through anxieties or symptoms. Such was the case during state terror, but is also true of the impact of the economic meltdown of 2001. "Patients dwelled on their deep anxieties and terrible anguish related to disappearing jobs, escalating unemployment, and inept governments that could not create an environment of safety. Each patient was preoccupied with how he or she would be affected personally, and there was a sense of catastrophic danger. I witnessed a decline of patients' experience of helplessness in response to the political movements that emerged, even if they were not personally involved. That's why the grassroots radical struggles were so important. They became a signifier that another Argentina is possible, which helped alleviate people's desperation and disillusionment. There's much more hopefulness at the present."

When I ask about her understanding of the impact of 9/11 in her country, Julia responds that "the terrible attacks of 9/11 permitted Bush to carry out this so-called war on terror, and that has shifted what we used to think about the United States. We always assumed that even though lots of bad things could happen within the United States or be perpetrated by it internationally, at least democracy existed there. We always believed that in the United States the law is respected, justice functions; kids even learn to debate this in the schools and so forth. Now everything has been turned around." Julia says that immediately after 9/11, most Argentines identified with and supported the American people. But Bush's aggressive policies ended that sympathy. She agrees with Tato that only the most right wing agree with Bush's discourse and that most of her compatriots think that Bush's policies are a political strategy to extend U.S. power. Some even think that the Iraq war was a military calculation to help a failing economy.

Our attention turns to the concerns of contemporary psychoanalysis in Argentina. Julia tells me that the majority of congresses now focus on psychoanalysis and society, including themes related to memory and testimony. She points out that this social orientation is very different from the prevailing one during the period of state terror when psychoanalysis was isolated from social concerns. Since the return to democracy all the institutes and different schools within psychoanalysis organize study groups and meetings related to problematic social issues. Many psychoanalysts are involved in these activities, especially, Julia adds, since Kirchner developed a variety of interesting social programs in health and psychology that deal with specific problems such as homelessness, the plight of children of unemployed families, the growing problems associated with addiction, and so forth. Like all her colleagues, Julia is distressed about the increasing drug trafficking and delinquency, especially among the lower-class youth who consume the strongest and more toxic drugs that are less expensive than those consumed by their upper-class counterparts. She believes that although the children of the poor suffer more because of a combination of unemployed and demoralized parents, inadequate schools, malnutrition, and toxic drugs, drug consumption in all social classes is rising due to the lack of opportunity and belief in a meaningful future. The corporate, globalized culture, she argues, propagates an enticingly transgressive version of the rock and underground culture that lures Argentine youth into drugs and a profound kind of fatalism about the world.

"Let's end on a positive note," she says, "lest we also fall into a seductive pessimism. We began with the affirmative political direction in Latin America. Another development in Argentina in this regard has been the legitimization of the human rights and *memoria* discourse, which is providing the possibility of thinking about the past and what it means for us and our future as a people. There is even a park dedicated to *memoria* that features an enormous monument with the names and ages of all the disappeared and dead. Imagine: 30,000 names! This is a place of recognition by the society of what we lived through and what continues to live in us.

The gratitude toward the government and the fact that the president was present at the monument's inauguration are notable. The Mothers of the Plaza de Mayo are invited to all official acts related to human rights, which indicates official endorsement of the human rights struggles and society's need for truth and memory. This stance on the part of state authority significantly affects the social imaginary, including even those citizens who aren't directly involved."

Julia's view is corroborated when I meet with Estela Carlotto, the President of the Grandmothers of the Plaza de Mayo. We are in the organization's headquarters, where its many volunteers, young and old, are engaged in so many diverse political activities that the environment is as frenetic as it was during my prior visit a decade ago. The Grandmothers continue the work of searching for their disappeared grandchildren and also engage in a number of additional struggles related to the multiple human rights violations that are the trademark of neoliberal society. Estela is as elegant as ever, dressed to the hilt even as she fans herself in the debilitating heat of the late afternoon. She is graciously slowing down for an hour from her demanding nonstop schedule to speak with her North American *compañerita*.

Estela reports that since Kirchner was elected the Grandmothers have worked in the government through the National Commission for the Right to Identity. The legacy of the Dirty War is still very much with them, and their organization helps young people who suspect that they might be children of the disappeared to obtain DNA tests that can be matched with data in the central genetic bank. "Most of these young people don't want to sue their appropriators; they just want to know their real identity. So this government intervenes to help this process. The kids who grow up with doubts about their origins because there are biological or cultural differences between them and their 'parents' or because they are badly treated now have recourse. But this problem has become complicated due to a growing trafficking in babies. Because of so much poverty, people often sell their babies, and middle-class families take advantage of this because the adoption laws are ponderous and complex. So of those who come to us to search for their identity, it turns out that some were born in clandestinity, others were stolen from their disappeared parents, and still others were sold by desperately impoverished families. And here's the psychological irony: The kids prefer to find out they were children of the disappeared, because that means they weren't abandoned. It was the state that separated them from parents who loved them. And they find new families who have been looking for them for years, sustaining loving wishes to integrate them into their families. But those who discover the contrary—that their impoverished mothers sold them or delivered them in clinics for the poor where traffickers steal the newborns—are disappointed, and for them it's really a shock. They want to know who their mother is, why they were given up, and if they have siblings. And we help them, along with the support from psychoanalysts and psychologists who collaborate with us in this work."

Estela says there are additional ways Argentines live with the consequences of the dictatorship and the policies of impunity toward the perpetrators. "We are struggling against the groups that the dictatorship left intact who operate as gangs that carry out the terrifying *secuestros express* [express kidnappings], as we call them, of human rights activists and witnesses that plan to testify in the new court cases against the torturers." Importantly, the Grandmothers have expanded the meaning of human rights to include the economic and social problems that plague their country that they insist are the legacy of the dictatorship's installation of free-market economics. They are involved with women's rights organizations and struggles on behalf of the elderly for a life of dignity, including decent living conditions and access to art and culture. Estela insists that the Kirchner government has supported this wider definition of human rights, and his commitment to the theme of identity means that it has been integrated into school curricula. Identity is complex, she says, and includes one's relationship to the larger group, which means, in the face of values imported from the United States and propagated by the mass media, the preservation of Argentine language, culture, music, art, and history.

Is there a new Argentine generation that is politically progressive and engaged? "Yes," Estela replies emphatically. "It's remarkable. The adolescents who work with us go into the schools and the neighborhoods to speak of these important things. When someone says, 'But the dictatorship didn't affect me,' we say, 'Yes, it did; maybe you didn't lose someone who disappeared, but your economic security, your social security, and peace of mind disappeared, along with your savings. You were a victim, too.' We are contributing to an understanding that we all need to work toward a better society. And our young people are some of our most effective activists." An urgent phone call marks the end of our interview, but I am glad to have had this chance to catch up with *la presidenta*, who along with the other Grandmothers is a magnet for young people whose engagement in constructive social activism provides them with an important sense of agency to counter the negative forces in their society.

It takes some doing, but Diana Kordon, Darío Lagos, Lucila Edelman, and I finally manage to coordinate schedules so that I can interview them. We are at their offices in the busy center of the city, stuffing ourselves into a small, hot room off the main office, because just as in the Grandmothers' headquarters, there is too much going on to be able to hear ourselves speak. Therapists and staff alike are engaged in the many facets of the work of the organization, renamed from the original Team of Psychological Assistance to the Mothers of the Plaza de Mayo to its current title, the Argentine Team of Psycho-Social Work and Research (EATIP).[11] We are laughing at our stuffy, makeshift arrangement so unpropitious for serious thought, but soon enough we are caught up in our discussion. They begin by telling me that they are still working with individuals affected by the dictatorship, an increasing number of whom are the young adult children of the disappeared, the exiled, and former political prisoners. Their patients also include witnesses in the current trials of the Dirty War's torturers, many of whom have been retraumatized since the September 2006 kidnapping of 77-year-old Julio Jorge Lopez, a witness whose gripping testimony of torture helped convict a former police officer of crimes committed during the dictatorship. Lopez has never been found, and this kidnapping challenges the idea of "Never Again" in Argentina. Darío says that the theme of "Never Again" emerged after the end of the dictatorship and was a very forceful signifier in the popular imagination. Among some groups of the children of the disappeared its obliteration has reinforced the terrors associated with their traumatic loss. Lucila adds that "because the government didn't protect the participants in these prosecutions and trials and make certain that something like this couldn't happen, it was as if the old impunity had raised its ugly head. The sense of vulnerability, of the lack of protection, has returned for many people." I ask the three if this disappearance of Lopez has successfully resurrected the bystander phenomenon among a scared population, to which Diana responds, "No. It was intimidating, but not paralyzing. In spite of the many ongoing threats to those involved, including human rights activists and judges, the witnesses remain involved in the judicial process, and the mass mobilizations supporting the trials of the torturers have continued."

The importance of the trials, the three agree, can be understood in both personal and social terms. The experience of attending the trials, for example, fills a very important need for the children of the disappeared, who literally yell at the accused, "Sons of bitches, where are our parents?" For the larger society, it represents a process that instills the values of group responsibility for the state's violations of citizens' rights and the social need for a legal form of accountability. The right wing still argue that reconciliation, by which they mean forgetting about the past, is necessary because the main problem is not human rights or accountability but the economic problems that plague peoples' lives.

"But," Diana says, "progressives stand fast that the only form of genuine reconciliation is based on the truth. In terms of the popular imagination, it has been very important that in public places, like hospitals and schools, there are homages to human rights and the disappeared. I remember at the inauguration of the public monument to the disappeared, it was a gray overcast day, and there were thousands of school-aged kids there. Just at the very moment before the inauguration ritual was beginning, the sun suddenly appeared, and these kids began to applaud and shout, as if the appearance of the sun were a symbol of the importance of this public acknowledgement of our collective losses. So *memoria* has become a significant constituent of the social imaginary."

However, like Juan Carlos, Diana, Darío, and Lucila believe that this focus on human rights endorsed by the Kirchner government is a progressive aspect of a very complicated political phenomenon. They explain that on the one hand, the government has fostered an ideology that secures support among citizens interested in the human rights theme, in part by encouraging its diffusion in the media. One example is the popular TV series *Monte Cristo*, based on the stories of the children of the disappeared, aimed at creating a consensus around the crimes of the dictatorship. Simultaneously, the government hides its own repressive policies, especially those aimed at the workers who still wage militant struggles for their rights. "So today," says Darío, "we experience something that is ongoing, a kind of eternal triad: brutal repression, impunity of the authorities, and popular resistance...We don't think that this is a progressive government. The number of people who are impoverished and marginalized grows daily, even while the state's discourse is critical of impunity and supports human rights. In fact, Kirchner has divided the human rights movements, some of which support the government and others maintain a critical distance. This kind of thing happens all over the world when the official ideology captures what the popular sectors have been struggling for and dilutes their capacity for genuine change. It's essentially a process of co-optation."

I wonder with them about the significance of 9/11 for Argentines. "It was shocking," recalls Diana, "completely disorienting, and I think that at first our reaction was disavowal: We knew it happened but we couldn't believe it. So we kept watching the TV images over and over to confirm that it had actually occurred. It was so awful that in the first few days it was impossible to think analytically about its significance." Lucila remembers that everyone commented about having a foreboding sense of threatening violence because even though it had occurred in a distant place, the televised images made the tragedy feel so close and experience-near. In those first days, there was a lot of fear about its implications for the future. Even though in Argentina there is a strong collective anti-Yankee sentiment, the violent assault and the magnitude of the people affected provoked an overriding sense of empathy for the victims. At the same time, the assault represented a vulnerability of empire that had never been considered." Darío continues: "You have to understand, though, that Bush's government stimulates a lot of hatred here, exacerbated by his militaristic policies. Many people ridiculed his 'axis of evil' formulation. The invasion of Iraq provoked lots of demonstrations, and people carried signs that read 'Bush is a fascist' and 'Bush the terrorist.'" For perspective, Lucila adds that "with the exception of political activists, Bush's policies had little psychological significance for people's everyday experience, except when it was ruptured by dramatic events like the exposé of the photographs of Abu Ghraib. Then everyone felt profound repugnance and condemned the behavior and what it demonstrated about U.S. policy." Diana interrupts, "But, we have to remember that this experience converged with a psychological and social elaboration of a reality constructed historically by the actions of the United States in our country, which is that 'nothing good can come from the United States.' This is a conviction about U.S. governments, about 'American power' and not about the people." Darío provides a recent example in the decisive role played by U.S. pressure in the Argentine government's institution of a series of antiterrorism laws, "which most Argentines suspect will be used to repress the progressive movements that continue to demand more radical reforms than the present government is disposed to permit."

And the legacy of the 2001 economic meltdown? From their perspective, while it appears that in Argentina conditions have returned to a kind of "normality," in essence the grassroots movements have lost their role as protagonists of the historical process. "They scared the dominant sectors," Diana states, "who have won by displacing the powerful mobilization of so many sectors in the country. The psychological effect is significant because if you can see that your collective struggle yields change from your own effort, it gives you a sense of empowerment and agency. In effect, that experience alters subjectivity. In the aftermath of 2001, there was a collective sense of power, and everyone felt like a protagonist of history. But Kirchner's policies have succeeded in dividing the different sectors that had been acting in solidarity during that period."

For these three colleagues, contemporary subjectivity is marked by the dialectics of fear, insecurity, and struggle. Diana points out that in the recent presidential election, many people did not vote because they questioned the nature of how citizens are actually represented politically by any and all of the candidates. "This is very important because it represents a challenge to the bourgeois interpretation of democracy, which is a narrow one of electoral politics rather than of economic and social justice. And this is only one example of what causes the elites to have an ongoing anxiety that we could return to a situation in which popular resistance is once again uncontainable."

* * *

I selected from these interviews with my Latin American colleagues the material that seemed most salient for us in the United States as we struggled with similar social problems and their complex psychological meanings. I had been writing for some years about how in spite of the conventional wisdom that the developing countries would inevitably come to emulate the advanced industrial nations that, on the contrary, the social and economic structures of U.S. society and thus group anxieties, as well, were actually devolving to resemble those of the Global South (see Hollander, 1997). However, what I could not know at the time of these conversations in Buenos Aires was that in a few short months, Juan Carlos Volnovich's earlier warning that Argentina was the canary in the mines would be explosively demonstrated in this country's terrorific economic meltdown. This crisis would even more dramatically narrow the gap between the psychological and social experience of Latin American and U.S. citizens.

THE RETURN OF THE REPRESSED: REBELLION ALONG THE ELECTORAL ROAD

In early 2008, I arrived from Buenos Aires to witness a rising chorus of voices that were similar to my Latin American colleagues' concerns about the nature of the Bush administration. Best-selling feminist writer Naomi Wolf was one important cultural critic to articulate warnings of what from her perspective represented a growing threat of fascism in this country. In 2007 she published *The End of America: Letter of Warning to a Young Patriot*, an analysis of the shifts in governance that for her mirrored the same strategies that have characterized other nations in the process of succumbing to dictatorship. In the *Guardian* newspaper in that same year, she wrote:

> ...it is a mistake to think that early in a fascist shift you see the profile of barbed wire against the sky. In the early days, things look normal on the surface; peasants were celebrating harvest festivals in Calabria in 1922; people were shopping and going to the movies in Berlin in 1931. Early on, as W. H. Auden put it, the horror is always elsewhere— while someone is being tortured, children are skating, ships are sailing: "dogs go on with their doggy life...How everything turns away/ Quite leisurely from the disaster. (April 24)[12]

Was Wolf being hysterical and hyperbolic in her concern about the Bush regime's danger to U.S. democracy? If so, she was in good company, for there were many dispassionate voices speaking with equal concern, including political insiders like John Dean, who was arguing that Republicans were imposing their authoritarian political philosophy on everyone in the country. In *Conservatives Without Conscience* (2006), Dean elaborated the characteristics of the authoritarian leader based on psychologist Robert Altemeyer's (1996) research on right-wing authoritarianism.[13] Altemeyer argued that not only was the U.S. neoconservative leadership characterized by authoritarian traits, but approximately 25 percent of the U.S. adult population was solidly authoritarian in their outlook and would uncritically "...march America into a dictatorship and probably feel that things had improved as a result" (Dean, 2008).

As the extended 2008 presidential election campaign season approached, alongside the neoconservative leadership and its followers allegedly authoritarian in disposition, millions of other citizens had had enough of neoconservative rule to say a collective "basta" as they joined the fight to make progressive change a reality. Like the protests that emerged to overturn Latin American state terror several decades earlier, so, too, in this country a wide-ranging movement was coalescing to challenge the U.S. version of authoritarian governance and its culture of impunity.

Let us summarize some of the ways we can explain this capacity of people to rebel against hegemony. Freud himself posited that from our earliest relationships on, we are ambivalently attached to authority. This conflictual relationship provides the foundation for a subjectivity constituted by resistance to as well as identification with power, which is so deep-seated that it is destined to be repeated throughout life within the family as well as in one's relationship to the larger social group. Detachment from hegemony is rooted in this ambivalence so that at crucial times and in specific circumstances resistance can trump identification. As German psychoanalyst Alexander Mitscherlich had observed of the radical political movements in Latin America during the 1960s, when individuals reject their apathetic acceptance of an oppressive social order and engage in a shared political struggle, they move from ignorance and disavowal toward self-awareness and a strengthening of critical ego faculties. Argentine psychoanalytic activists saw this process take place within the social movements that arose following the economic meltdown in 2001, which they believed represented a group reassertion of libidinal social links in a critical and autonomous act of rebellion against the rupturing and fracturing nature of Argentina's version of neoliberal capitalism. Let us recall that Lacanian Zizek has noted that it is only within the opposition to the interpellation by hegemonic ideological apparatuses that the subject emerges. He argues that "...for psychoanalysis, the subject emerges when and in so far as interpellation...fails. Not only does the subject never fully recognize itself in the interpellative call: Its resistance to the symbolic identity provided by interpellation *is* the subject" (Butler, Laclau, & Zizek, 2000, p. 121). For Zizek, challenging hegemony requires the recognition of and engagement in actions that redefine what is possible. In the context of the political crisis produced by neoconservatism, this notion meant the collective capacity to imagine and then to fight on behalf of an alternative to the prevailing structures and ideology that had decimated the social fabric and subjective experience of living in this country.

As the 2008 presidential campaign advanced, the Democratic candidacy of Barack Obama mobilized all the left progressive organizations in the country and unleashed the latent yearning for a constructive answer to the ever-mounting threats to liberal democracy and economic stability. While the neoconservative violations of the constitution were central concerns articulated by Obama, the country slid into a deep economic recession, the product of a speculative fever and a collectively shared manic search for consumption without limits made possible by the neoliberal deregulated free-market policies. The addiction to speculative bubble economics was being exposed as inherently irrational and threatening to the collective welfare of U.S. citizens. At least at the rhetorical level, hegemony was being challenged by the critical idea that governmental, publicly regulated oversight and accountability mechanisms were needed to contain the unrestrained search for profit and unchecked competition of a financial elite whose behavior had been destructive to this country and the global economy as well. One underlying ideological principle, in addition to individualism, that was being contested politically was the neoliberal and neoconservative conceptualization of freedom, critiqued by political theorist Karl Polanyi as "…the freedom to exploit one's fellows, the freedom to make inordinate gains without commensurable service to the community, the freedom to keep technological inventions from being used for public benefit, or the freedom to profit from public calamities secretly engineered for private advantage" (Harvey, 2005, p. 36). Polanyi suggested another perspective, one that tied freedom to social justice so that the rights of a few were extended to include everyone in a society regulated to guarantee that all citizens freely share in the benefits of their labor, talent, and skills. Such a society would more easily be able to balance potential tensions between individual freedoms and social justice in order to embrace both as defining principles of the social contract.

This expanded definition of freedom was a driving sentiment behind the increasing number of voices that arose to confront the neoconservative agenda. The left progressive ideas and organizations within the militant global justice and environmental movements that had been eclipsed by the post–9/11 discourse of the "war on terrorism" reemerged, this time constituting what Gramsci called an oppositional ideology, now closer to the center of the political stage. In the electoral arena, they gave their activist energies and resources to the young senator from Illinois. Suddenly many of their ideals and goals were being articulated by a charismatic leader who could reach out to the millions of citizens disaffected from politics as usual and yearning to believe that another world is possible—a political leader who just might be able to win a national election.

As election day approached, the political situation was increasingly intense and unpredictable. The economic crisis loomed as a catastrophic threat, and for many citizens, it mobilized the psychic reservoir of terror provoked by 9/11, often overwhelming capacities to think critically about the nature of the emergency and the policies that would best address it. The ideology of individualism, privatization, and small government deeply embedded in the culture constrained imaginative solutions. In this political environment, like other progressives, the psychoanalysts engaged in social projects and political activism hoped that the crisis would provide a space for a new political direction in the country, and many participated in the campaign for an Obama victory. In October, with less than a month before the election, Andrew Samuels and I presented papers at the San Francisco Jungian Institute's conference, "Psyche, Politics and Transformation." Just four short years earlier, on the eve of the 2004 election, we had participated together in the Uprooted Mind conference. Now each of us was presenting a social psychoanalytic appraisal of the dynamics underlying the political crisis facing this country. In my remarks, I presented the debate among progressives regarding how to assess the historical significance of Barack Obama and the extent to which he represented an authentic ideological challenge to U.S. unregulated capitalism and empire. The most cautious argued that Obama had emerged in reaction to the crisis of legitimacy of neoconservative governance and that his political objectives fit the goals of the liberal wing of the ruling elites associated with neoliberalism. His presidency from this perspective would sustain U.S. financial corporate monopoly and military global hegemony and reinvigorate consensus by instituting modest reforms in domestic policies that would actually sustain the overall status quo. More optimistic progressives viewed Obama as a political leader who was giving voice to the inchoate rage aimed at government policy and politicians whose loyalty to corporate interests threatened citizens' well-being and security. According to prominent activist Tom Hayden (2008), Obama's candidacy and discourse were reminiscent of what Gandhi once said of India's liberation movement: "There go my people. I must follow them, for I am their leader." Obama was seen as the heir to the years of political organizing by thousands of grassroots progressive organizations, and it was hoped that he would assert a new direction for the United States in a globalized multipolar world, one that would foster values of equal opportunity, a living wage for all, diplomacy rather than war, and environmental sustainability.

The growing economic crisis threatening to bring on another Great Depression was the trigger for the Bush administration's final gift to its corporate allies: It awarded almost a trillion dollars of taxpayers' money to the largest financial institutions deemed "too big to fail." In contrast to Republican presidential candidate John McCain's erratic and uninformed comments on the economic debacle, Obama's measured interventions and thoughtful discourse conveyed the quality of a competent leader in times of crisis, even while he uncritically allied himself with the transfer of billions of dollars from the public to the private sector with no governmental regulations or oversight. Meanwhile, the Republican vice-presidential candidate, Sarah Palin, was mobilizing the religious fundamentalist base among white working class voters—"rednecks," as journalist Joe Bageant called his brethren in *Deerhunting With Jesus*—to protest the liberal Obama's candidacy. At McCain/Palin rallies, regressive group dynamics were reflected in the racism, homophobia, anti-Muslim hatred, and xeno-phobia that colored the vitriolic outbursts against Obama. Crowds yelling "Arab," "Terrorist," "off with his head," "kill him," and "bomb Obama" were a visceral manifestation of a psychological inability to deal with the uncertainty and ambiguity characteristic of U.S. social reality. Hysteria was compromising the capacity for rational thought about the complex political issues facing the country. Psychologist Bryant Welch (2008) called these emotionally laden politics "the battleground states" of mind, characterized by paranoia, envy, and sexual perplexity, effectively manipulated by con-servatives. The ideological confusion of the Republican base was evidenced at many rallies in which voters screamed their protest at "the socialists tak-ing over our country." Understandably frightened and angry, these voters could not see that it was the conservative financiers bailing themselves out through a strategy of socialism for the wealthy that was leaving them and their families in the dust—literally, as millions began to lose their homes to those same financial elites.

Noted linguist George Lakoff (2004, 2008a) was publicly encouraging Obama to recognize that political ideas are not exchanged at the rational level only, but are filtered through an unconsciously internalized ideologi-cal frame. He warned Obama to resist the temptation to convey his mes-sage by moving to the political center and adopting the language that had been framed by conservative think tanks for the previous 30 years. Lakoff urged the Democratic candidate to create a new conceptual frame that reinterpreted in progressive terms the central issues of our time. Rather than accepting, for example, the right-wing ideological position on taxes communicated linguistically through the term *tax relief*, Obama needed to argue that paying taxes to solve social and economic problems is the best kind of American patriotism. A progressive frame could convey the idea that taxes are democratic, that they offer opportunity and guarantee the infrastructure—the highway system, Internet, telecommunications, public education, power grid, subsidies for training scientists, and medical care provisions—we all use in a civilized society. "A progressive frame," asserted Lakoff (2008b), "presents taxes as the dues we pay to be an American."

Obama was facing a daunting task, battling deeply engrained racism and political confusion, aspects of hegemony internalized and practiced by his organized opposition and operating within the so-called independents as well. In his emphasis on bipartisan hope that citizens could cooperate to make the country better, Obama was proving himself to be a responsible political leader who could provide a reparative containment of destructive impulses. C. Fred Alford (1990) has written that because any group suf-fers from its own anxieties that foment paranoid-schizoid defenses of split-ting, reparative leadership offers the positive option of "turning the group's attention towards the restoration and protection of its own goodness—that is, toward the restoration of threatened group values" (p. 27). Such political guidance reaffirms a reparative morality for the group itself. In political terms, the Kleinian notion of reparation was reflected in Obama's stance to defend the country against the further erosion of democracy. His growing popularity lay in his capacity to remain steady in the face of the economic turmoil threatening our society and the destructive passions expressed by his opposition. His admonition that the United States needed to adopt a strategy that combined personal and governmental responsibility was an attempt to integrate the U.S. cultural emphasis on individualism with a progressive acknowledgement of the importance of an activist state that regulates resources in the interests of all citizens. His discourse consistently appealed to the best within people by emphasizing the importance of hope and stimulating among many citizens the wish to collectively recreate an America based on the positive passions of empathy, solidarity, and willingness to sacrifice for the common good. He aroused desires to recreate an America that engages in negotiated compromise of conflicted values and goals and a government whose regulatory policies assure a level playing field for all citizens. In contrast to his Republican opponents' inducement of persecutory states in their followers that produced black-and-white interpretations of the world, Obama encouraged his supporters to deal with the complexity of reality. He appealed to an ideal that in times of crisis, recognition and negotiation of differences rather than violent confrontation could produce the cooperation necessary to solve collective problems. Further, he addressed the role of the United States in the community of nations by taking responsibility for misguided policies that exacerbated international tensions and by advocating dialogue rather than military solutions to conflict.

However, it was already clear that if elected, Obama would be able to convert his discourse into action only if a strong and vigorous progressive movement remained mobilized to empower him to move in a reformist direction. It would be the task of such a movement to demand that our government develop a long-range economic strategy to deal with the structural weaknesses inherent in the dramatic concentration of wealth and growing national debt. On the eve of the election, citizens were losing their jobs at alarming rates and drowning in overextended home and credit card debt. Cities and states were near bankruptcy and the federal government was indebted to other countries who owned a significant percentage of U.S. treasuries and growing percentages of U.S. corporations and property. Without courageous leadership committed to challenging entrenched interests, these social crises would continue, regardless of how much taxpayers' money was pumped into the private financial institutions considered "too big to fail."

* * *

During the week before the election, Hedda tells me that she hopes that the progressive interpretation of Obama is the right one. We talk about her concerns that the economic catastrophe is now driving the election. She confides that although she understands why this is so and that it increases the likelihood of an Obama victory at the polls, she is dismayed that the war seems to be receding as an urgent issue. From her perspective, the war policy of the Bush administration is unpopular now with U.S. citizens not necessarily based on political principle or an ideological commitment to diminish the violence in the world but because it is too costly and has had a devastating impact on the U.S. economy and on the soldiers themselves. I remind Hedda of Juan Carlos's notion of the Argentine meltdown being the canary in the mines and that one possible outcome of this economic disaster may be a turn toward progressive political consciousness here as occurred in Argentina. Hedda agrees, but then pauses, and the psychoanalyst in her speaks: "If this country votes for Palin, I've got to do something. I'm too old to emigrate, but I feel disgust for her, especially how that poor Down syndrome baby is being carted around. The baby doesn't cry, wiggle, or smile, and she doesn't touch it or relate to it. She's a terrible mother, without empathy or caring, and she hasn't a clue about her own limits." She charges McCain with irresponsibility for having chosen Palin as a running mate. "Palin," says Hedda, "reminds me of the Nazis in that she appeals to the lowest instincts in people and knows how to mobilize them on that basis. And this is really dangerous. I am banking on the American people," she says, "to once again, like in the thirties and then in the fifties, to go to the edge and not jump, but to find their balance at the last moment."

As I listen to her, I find myself smilingly recalling an event that had occurred several months earlier on August 24, 2008, a very special date. It was a balmy late afternoon in Los Angeles, and Hedda's backyard was in full radiant bloom. Colorfully decorated tables surrounded the pool, whose water glittered lazily among the many trees and multihued flowerbeds. The yard was filled with many guests, 99 of them to be exact, because Hedda had been sure to invite exactly that number of friends and colleagues to help her celebrate her 99th birthday. When it came time for the champagne toast, we all gathered around her, and many took their turn to offer appreciation and congratulations for Hedda's special qualities and her many contributions to our community. Then she spoke and expressed her gratitude for all the people in her life who had, each in his and her way, cared about the world and done something to ameliorate its serious problems. As the cake was brought into the circle, its many candles ablaze, Hedda said that even while it was supposed to be bad luck to share aloud one's birthday wish, she always does so anyway. "And it's always the same," she declared. "It's that the world become a more just and decent one for all people everywhere." Then, as she leaned down to blow out the candles, she paused, looked up impishly, and murmured, "May the elections go well."

ENDNOTES

1. There has been reporting on a master military contingency plan since the Iran Contra hearings in 1987; see Roland (2006).
2. See the brilliant documentary *Sir No Sir!* (Zeiger, 2005) for an analysis through direct testimonies from servicemen about why they refused to fight in Vietnam and their motivations for organizing a massive movement against the war from within the military itself.
3. In 2002, recruiters benefited when then-Representative David Vitter (Republican from Louisiana) included a provision into the No Child Left Behind Act requiring high schools to give recruiters the names and contact details of all juniors and seniors. Schools that do not comply risk losing their NCLB funding. This unpublicized regulation turned an education bill into an aggressive military recruitment tool, and while students can sign an opt-out form, they have to know about it to request doing so. Moreover, in 2005, privacy advocates revealed that the Pentagon had been collecting records from Selective Service, state Motor Vehicle Departments, and data brokers to create a database of tens of millions of young adults and teens. For information on these and other nefarious tactics by the military to go after young people to sign up for military service, see Goodman (2009b).
4. Robert Jay Lifton has analyzed a variety of atrocity-producing situations in his many books (e.g., 2005). See also the online interview with Lifton, "Evil, the Self and Survival" (Kreisler, 1999).
5. Judith T. Broder is a Training and Supervising Analyst at the Los Angeles Institute and Society for Psychoanalytic Studies and founder of The Soldiers Project.
6. Personal interview, July 24, 2009.
7. Personal interview with Kenneth Reich, August 31, 2009.
8. Judith Broder was one of this year's recipients of the Purpose Prize in recognition of her contribution to the welfare of the community through her role as the founder and administrator of The Soldiers Project. TSP was awarded a $100,000 grant for its work with members of the military and their families.
9. The contextual reference in Spanish to the date September 11 makes it clear as to whether one is speaking about the U.S. 9/11 or Chile's September 11th.
10. For an elaboration of this and related themes, see Braun (2004).
11. For the group's publications and updates of their professional projects, see their Web site at http://www.eatip.org.ar/textos/equipo.php.
12. Wolf's article summarized the central points of her book *The End of America*, which analyzed the factors Wolf argued characterized a move toward authoritarianism under Bush, including the centralization of power in the executive branch, surveillance of groups and individuals, control of the press, and the criminalization of dissent.
13. See also Stenner (2005) for her argument that degrees of authoritarianism fluctuate with shifting social conditions.

Chapter 10

The future's uprooted minds

And what rough beast, its hour come round at last,
Slouches towards Bethlehem to be born?

— W. B. Yeats
The Second Coming (1920)

You may say I'm a dreamer
But I'm not the only one
I hope someday you'll join us
And the world will be as one

— John Lennon
Imagine

The 2008 U.S. presidential election proved to be historic. The first Black candidate in U.S. history was voted into the highest office in the land, an event that seemed to demonstrate the ability of this country to repair its reprehensible legacy of slavery and racism. Obama became a signifier that this nation was, indeed, the harbinger of democracy and equality of opportunity. And this election that brought to power the candidate who rejected unilateralism in favor of a collaborative approach to international relations potentially redeemed the United States within the community of nations. On January 20, 2009, almost two million people from every corner of the country travelled to Washington to cheer the inauguration of the popular Barack Obama as he took the oath of office. At that moment Obama embodied hope that we could emerge from the dark years of the Bush administration with a new lease on distributive justice and reparation of the institutional sources of instability and violence at home and abroad.[1] The welcome end to the authoritarian trends of the neoconservative era was captured in the collective sigh of relief and hoots of victory that emerged from those who watched as the presidential helicopter took off from the nation's capitol to transport George Bush and his family to a marginalized Texas retirement.

The optimism expressed in the celebratory spectacle of Barack Obama's inauguration was soon challenged by the sobering reality that he was inheriting a catastrophic economy and a political culture of impunity that would prove resistant to change. Equally important, he was now in the leadership of citizens who, while politically divided, shared a group experience of years of chronic social trauma rendering them vulnerable to the acute stressor of living with intensifying economic insecurity. In this first year of Obama's administration, the convergence of these elements of reality and the president's character and political convictions have raised significant questions about the nature of his leadership. Obama's discourse of dialogue, compromise, and bipartisanship and his assumption of responsibility for past U.S. missteps in the international arena have reflected a capacity for responsible leadership. Obama, in other words, promises to be a very different kind of leader from Bush, who, as I have argued, provoked regressed group dynamics and ideological splitting, both of which functioned in the service of destructive political aims. As Obama maneuvers within the constraints of countervailing interests, he appears committed to containing the political polarizations that accrued during the Bush years and to reinvigorating a collaborative spirit as we face unprecedented perils, ranging from ongoing economic deterioration to terrorist threats with weapons of mass destruction to potentially irreversible environmental devastation.

We recall that psychoanalysis can contribute to our understanding of the role of leaders and group dynamics that can shed light on Obama's impact and role at this early stage of his presidency. From a Kleinian perspective, responsible leaders do not exaggerate the goodness of their own group and the badness of others because it encourages paranoid-schizoid splitting and projection. Responsible leaders can recognize that a threatening social reality such as we experience today produces group fears and anxieties often expressed in aggressive attitudes and behaviors that can be as dangerous as external enemies. Such leaders help citizens understand that their own anxiety is also an enemy because it impedes their capacity to experience and engage in a reparative morality (Alford, 1990). In Bion's terms, in response to traumatic stimuli, responsible leadership guides the group away from regressed dynamics, such as the manic flight into consumption and war making that characterized the Bush years. Obama's willingness to articulate truths, his urging of citizens to think about our complex reality, and his stress on the need for a shared individual and governmental responsibility to repair our disordered society encourage citizens' capacities to work together to solve real problems. However, from a Bionian perspective, the leader can be a potential trigger rather than a container for regressive group dynamics, an example of which is Obama's charismatic appeal that runs the risk of stimulating group fantasies of having a savior who can miraculously resolve all our problems with little effort on our part. As time elapses it is compelling to think that Obama's present leadership function is paradoxical. Just as he urges us to develop our capacities to deal with reality and to work together to solve collective problems, his enigmatic actions as president threaten to stimulate on the one hand disillusionment among those progressives whose regressed wish to be saved by a powerful messiah/leader are frustrated, and on the other, intensifying antagonism among the base of his right-wing opposition whose regressed paranoid attraction toward hatred and splitting are enflamed.[2]

This Kleinian and Bionian perspective on the relationship between leaders and the groups they direct and reflect is illuminated by the accounts of subjectivity in the Lacanian and group psychoanalytic tradition, which explicate how the unconscious is partially constituted by the power relations and hegemonic ideology of the social world. Thus, the group dynamics described above are structured by and reflect the institutional and ideological matrix that contextualizes them. Through this lens, we can think about how Obama in part reflects and reinforces the very ideological hegemony and power relations his discourse appears to challenge. His economic and military policies so far are characterized by continuity with the institutional foundations of neoliberalism and U.S. superpower strivings. A case in point is the battle currently raging over health care reform. As president, contrary to linguist George Lakoff's advice, Obama has increasingly adopted core concepts of neoliberal ideology in his linguistic framing of this significant political battle. His argument on behalf of reform has emphasized the neoliberal values of competition and choice rather than the human right all citizens have to affordable quality health care. While he criticizes the self-serving aspects of for-profit insurance oligopolies, his weak support of a robust national health care strategy (single payer or public option) falls far short of a pledge to protect citizens' health needs from the incontrovertible greed of corporate practice. Further, he has stipulated that any health care legislation he signs must not add a penny to the rising national deficit, but to date he has not applied the same criterion with regard to his increasing military budget, which is now the largest in U.S. history (Hellman, 2009). To the extent that Obama's strategic decisions constitute his own reluctance to confront the collusion between corporate power and the state or his hesitancy to challenge his entrenched political opposition, his leadership will be less likely to achieve a reparative morality or reformation of institutional corruption and inequity.

Seven months into Obama's presidency, Hedda and I have lunch on the Fourth of July to talk politics before the evening's celebrations begin. The summer's battle around health care reform has already begun, and I am eager to hear Hedda's impressions of this new political era about which we had felt so much hope. I ask her how she assesses our young president at this early stage. "My heart sank when he first made his cabinet appointments," she responds wryly. "They were the same people who had made the mess in the first place." I ask what she thinks motivated this decision, and she muses that because of his own inexperience, he might feel compelled for a while to have people accustomed to being close to power as his advisors. "It's related to his insistence so far on bipartisanship as well. Perhaps Obama thinks he can unite everybody and even civilize the Republicans! If so, he is revealing a grandiosity that does not bode well, because in the process he is making too many compromises that might prove irrevocable." She wonders if "he manifests a kind of omnipotence as a defense against insecurity and the need for everyone's approval." It is a confusing picture, we agree, and perhaps too early to tell definitively what this election will mean for the country. "On my good days," Hedda remarks, "I think he is doing a fabulous job and that he is making little conciliations now to pave the way for fundamental changes he will endorse later on. I tell myself that after the immediate economic crisis is muted, he will change these advisors, and that he is maneuvering so as to position himself to be effective in his long-range reformist objectives." And on her bad days, I question? "Then I think that Washington has co-opted him, that it's a bad sign that he did not choose at least several progressive economists, like Paul Krugman or Joseph Stiglitz, among his economic advisors. And his support of preventive detention appalls me. His position is straight out of Cheney, and Obama is a lawyer who should know better. If he continues like this, it could be like living under Bush again. I think that actually no one knows for sure who he is beyond the calm, efficient, and unflappable persona he presents. As for his position on Afghanistan, I don't like what I hear, but my hope is that once he has gotten his balance, he will make major changes in the future."

Like so many progressives at this point, Hedda vacillates in her appraisal of Obama, while tending to remain hopeful even in the face of worrisome developments. "One thing is clear," she states emphatically. "My subjective feeling is really different since Obama became president: I'm not angry every day, and I feel less threatened. And let's remember that the right wing is still deeply entrenched and is actively pressuring on many fronts. It's naïve to think Obama could step into the presidency and immediately change everything. And I think his charisma, while inspirational in some ways, can be a problem. We need to be realistic, and anything that diminishes citizen activism is bad. We need to be engaged politically. This doesn't exclude having an idealized figure at the helm, but I think it can distract and inhibit action. I can see it in myself," she says, "in my willingness to make excuses: I tell myself that his individual decisions I don't like are just down payments for a bigger change later on." As we finish lunch and conclude our discussion before the evening's celebratory fireworks, Hedda offers the following apt metaphor: "In the long run, we might face the choice that if Obama is the wonderful mortgage on a house we can't afford, maybe we'd be better off not buying it."

Hedda's observations some months ago captured the contradictory quality of current political realities. As the year moves on, this early phase of the Obama presidency is proving to be a time of collective emotional upheaval, demonstrating the ways in which the social matrix affects psychological states. The majority of citizens who are not actively engaged in the political process are learning, often quite painfully, that "the political is personal" indeed, as their livelihoods and economic futures continue to be threatened. Some 10 months earlier, in September 2008, an American Psychological Association poll had already indicated growing anxieties among the public: 80 percent of respondents stated that the economy was a significant source of stress, with 49 percent reporting feeling nervous or anxious and 48 percent feeling depressed or sad. By December, another American Psychological Association poll showed that 82 percent of those questioned experienced stress with regard to money and the economy, while 69 percent were worried about work (American Psychological Association, 2008). Percentages for households with children were even higher, as were those for female-headed households (see Roan, 2009). A Rutgers University national poll some months later found an equally despondent response among the unemployed about the potential for economic recovery, concluding that "Americans believe that this is the Katrina of recessions. Folks are on their rooftops without a boat" (Herbert, 2009, A33).

President Obama's strategy for dealing with the systemic causes of citizens' deepening anxieties was not reassuring, beginning with his choice of Wall Street–friendly economic advisors. Their names, including Larry Summers and Timothy Geithner, read like a "who's who" of politicians directly connected to the nation's largest financial corporations and neoliberal ideologues whose policies are responsible for the current economic debacle. As Norman Solomon of the Institute for Public Advocacy reminds us, "You choose your advisors, you choose your advice."[3] In a manner reminiscent of what Naomi Klein describes as the shock therapy of disaster capitalism, these advisors rescued the nation's largest financial institutions "too big to fail" by transferring over a trillion dollars of private debt to public debt without any governmental regulations or oversight of how this money would be used or recovered.[4] Finance capital appropriated these funds, after which they continued to practice their high-risk ventures and to manufacture bloated profits that have had little positive impact on the real economy. Meanwhile, Obama's stimulus package has been too small to deter the ongoing loss of jobs, health care, homes, savings, and retirement plans of millions of working- and middle-class citizens, who are increasingly dispirited or enraged.[5] Even while federal monies have helped stem the loss of jobs and services provided by state and county governments, it is nonetheless estimated that the actual current unemployment rate is much greater than official statistics, nearing 20 percent if the unemployed, underemployed, and despondent individuals who have given up looking for work are included.[6] Among them are the unprecedented numbers of executives, professionals, and managers who have lost their jobs and are joining those sectors of the population most deeply affected, especially Blacks, who are living in perilous conditions customarily associated with the Great Depression. As German sociologist Rudolf Goldscheid observed some decades ago: "The budget is the skeleton of the state stripped of all misleading ideologies" (Solomon, 2008). These cold statistics demonstrate his assertion: By November 2009, according to government reports, one year after the economic meltdown, Wall Street profits are exceeding the record set three years ago; the Chief Executive Officer of Goldman Sachs, Lloyd Blankfein, defended the bank's massive profits by saying Goldman is "doing God's work." At the same time, the Department of Agriculture revealed that more people are going hungry than previously thought, some 50 million citizens, including a quarter of all children, who struggled to get enough to eat last year. The number of children who live in households in which food at times was scarce last year stands at 17 million, an increase of four million children in just one year. An angry Robert Sheer demanded, "Where is the community organizer we elected?" (A. Goodman, 2009).

The financial reforms put forth by the Obama administration and Congress have so far been relatively ineffective. The few limits on executive salaries and bonuses at the largest corporate beneficiaries of taxpayer bailout dollars and weak regulation of risky derivatives trading are being criticized as window dressing because they contain large loopholes. And the economy is still vulnerable to another downturn, in part because the Obama administration has not sought to reinstitute the Glass-Steagall Act that had until the late 1990s separated commercial banking from investment banking that involves risky securities holding and trading. Nor has it addressed the problem of companies the government is obliged to rescue because they are ostensibly too big to fail. In fact, Neil Barofsky (2009), special inspector general of the Treasury Department's Troubled Asset Relief Program, recently claimed that not only do we lack meaningful regulatory reform, but because the government has sponsored several mergers of the country's largest banks, "The idea that the government is not going to let these banks fail, which was implicit a year ago, is now explicit...Potentially, we could be in more danger now than we were a year ago" (p. 2).

These worrisome indicators are complicated by divisive issues on the constitutional and juridical front. For example, Obama has proved resistant to demands that former Bush administration officials be investigated for what many legal experts deem war crimes, including the illegal invasion and occupation of Iraq and the use of torture in Abu Ghraib, Guantanamo, and Central Intelligence Agency "black sites." Obama's claim some months ago that he did not want to dwell on the past but rather to focus on the future was eerily reminiscent of the argument made in postdictatorship Latin America by those who fought investigations of the previous regimes' torturers by arguing on behalf of social amnesia and calling it reconciliation. As constitutional law professor Jonathan Turley argues, Obama's stance violates the principle of accountability and the possibility of asserting a moral component in U.S. political life.[7] Putting the problem in psychological terms, recall the Argentine Psychoanalytic Association's perspective on the importance to society of the acknowledgement of historical truth and accountability:

> The suppression of memory, the disinformation, the forgetting—all are enemies of individual and collective mental health. That which is forgotten makes itself present through repetition, which compromises the future...It is urgent that we all take responsibility for the importance and value of the historical truth...The patient is only able to stop repeating his neurotic behavior by remembering, resignifying, and elaborating [the past]. We believe that a people should also remember and signify, so as not to repeat. (Abudara et al., 1986, p. 16)

The repetition compulsion seems an apt descriptor of aspects of current U.S. military policy. Candidate Obama's criticism of Bush's "war of choice" in Iraq and its cost to the U.S. economy will be equally applicable to any decision leading to a U.S. military escalation in Afghanistan and Pakistan. While the majority of citizens wish their government to scale down its military engagements in the Middle East and Southeast Asia, Obama has been under pressure by the hawkish military advisors he appointed to make "Af-Pak" his chosen war.[8] Many critics of escalation view it as a quagmire that would recommit the United States to its permanent war policy and budget that eviscerate citizens' welfare at home and multiply their enemies abroad. Outspoken progressives view as a paradox the fact that Obama has been awarded the Nobel Peace Prize just as he appears to be continuing what they argue is a warfare state. During October and November 2008 discord about strategy in Afghanistan raged between, on the one hand, pro-escalation generals and their Republican and Democratic political allies, and on the other, key advisors warning Obama against an ill-begotten counterinsurgency strategy (COIN) related to the Long War, a new national security policy devised during the Bush administration, which they consider doomed to fail (Bacevich, 2009; Dreyfuss, 2009). According to Pulitzer Prize–winning author Seymour Hersh (2009), the military establishment was actively pressuring a president whom "they think [is] weak and the wrong color. Yes, there's racism in the Pentagon. We may not like to think that, but it's true and we all know it."[9] Hersh argued that the Pentagon tried to corner Obama so that whether or not he decided to increase the troop presence in Afghanistan he would lose politically. If he chose escalation, rising U.S. casualties and endless war would increasingly antagonize war-weary citizens, and if he decided to redirect foreign policy by withdrawing or limiting U.S. troops in favor of regional diplomacy and investment in social services and infrastructure, an organized backlash from the right would be mounted, attacking him as wimpy, unpatriotic, and incapable of protecting American lives and interests. Obama decided on a "surge" strategy aimed at satisfying as many constituencies as possible, further entangling the United States in a country that has never lost a war to its occupiers. Even more alarming is the increasing evidence of the so-called "secret" CIA drone operations over Pakistan, as well as the even more secret Obama-approved U.S. military units and private army Blackwater contractors also operating in Pakistan in an undeclared war in that country, where intensifying violence is dangerously destabilizing the political situation (Skahill, 2009).[10]

To be sure, our civilian and military leaders are obliged to address legitimate U.S. security concerns. But as those opposed to the Pentagon-industrial-congressional complex point out, U.S. security is threatened as long as civilians in other countries continue to be killed by U.S.-occupying forces or sophisticated technology in the form of remote-controlled drones. Even if U.S. military campaigns succeed in killing terrorists or terrorist leaders, they recruit more terrorists from among survivors and witnesses, who become convinced of the legitimacy of the anti-U.S. discourse of Islamic fundamentalists.[11] Meanwhile, Obama has also inherited other aspects of established U.S. military practices less visible to the average citizen. The United States contributes to international levels of violence in its role as the number one arms supplier worldwide and first in sales to nations in the developing world. In 2008 alone, the United States signed weapons agreements valued at $37.8 billion dollars, or 68.4 percent of all business in the global arms bazaar, up significantly from the previous year. Italy followed as a distant second with $3.7 billion, and Russia in third place with $3.5 billion (*New York Times*, 2009, A4; see also Bauman, 2007). Further, the United States continues to maintain more than 737 military bases, located on every continent in well more than 130 countries. This aspect of foreign policy antagonizes peoples whose experience is one of foreign domination rather than salvation. According to scholar and CIA analyst Chalmers Johnson, the purpose of this "baseworld" is "force projection," or the maintenance of U.S. military dominance around the world to ensure that no other nation can ever represent an effective military challenge. "We talk about the spread of democracy, but we're talking about the spread of democracy at the point of an assault rifle. That's a contradiction in terms. It doesn't work. Any self-respecting person being democratized in this manner starts thinking of retaliation" (Englehardt, 2006).[12] Johnson called his last book in a trilogy about U.S. imperial reach *Nemesis*, a reference to the ancient Greek goddess of revenge, the punisher of hubris and arrogance in human beings. "You may recall," Johnson (*Truthdig*, 2009) has said, "she is the one that led Narcissus to the pond and showed him his reflection, and he dove in and drowned. I chose the title because it seems to me that she's present in our country right now, just waiting to...carry out her divine mission." In addition to national narcissism, current U.S. policy sustains the ideological and psychological splitting that Christopher Bollas calls "violent innocence." This country's aggressive foreign policy continues to be justified as wholly defensive in nature or motivated by the generous wish to liberate other peoples suppressed by their own rulers. U.S. geopolitical aims, including access to and control over strategic resources throughout the world, are denied as a contributory factor to global violence and threat.

Johnson's perspective is demonstrated in the current tensions developing between the United States and Latin America, as this country attempts to recover its influence in a region that during the Bush years had assumed secondary importance to the Middle East. Latin America's progressive governments remain determined to chart a course independent of the Washington Consensus and are alarmed at evidence of increased U.S. military ambitions in their countries. For example, in August 2009, presidents of the Union of South American Nations (UNASUR) met to discuss a provisional U.S.–Colombia Defense Cooperation Agreement, which, if signed, will facilitate U.S. access to three Colombian air force bases, two naval bases, two army installations, and other Colombian military facilities. The pact followed upon Ecuador's termination of a U.S. military base in its territory, and UNASUR presidents expressed concern that it could have serious consequences for their sovereignty. UNASUR has developed a regional approach to security, which emphasizes national capacity, nonproliferation, and nonintervention from the United States. The group warned that "the presence of foreign military forces—with their means and resources linked to their own objectives—must not threaten the sovereignty and integrity of any other South American nation, and in consequence threaten the peace and security of the region" (Phillips, 2009).[13] An additional source of tension between regional leaders and the United States came on the heels of the June 2009 military ouster of the democratically elected president of Honduras, which evoked fears of the reappearance of the era of state terror and threatened the continent's commitment to "never again." The Obama administration's tepid and toothless critical response fell dramatically short of the Southern hemispheric–wide unqualified condemnation of the elite-driven military coup's ongoing human rights abuses and demands for the return of President Manuel Zalaya to power. The U.S. stance has isolated it from all but the few conservative countries in the hemisphere, such as Peru and Colombia. The rest of Latin America, ranging from social liberal regimes, like Chile and Uruguay, or democratic socialist, like Venezuela, Bolivia, and Ecuador, stand as one in opposition to Washington's business as usual.

It is too early to definitively assess the domestic and international significance of the Obama presidency, although various perspectives are already being expressed among politically engaged citizens. Many progressives have become disillusioned because after having worked for Obama's election, they find themselves marginalized from the White House decision-making process regarding core economic, financial, and foreign policy strategies. They are critical of what they see as Obama's abandonment of an authentic reformist stance, either because of political expediency or character weakness, that impedes his ability to stand up to entrenched interests. In a facetious vein, Drew Westen, professor of psychology and psychiatry and author of *The Political Brain* (2007), wrote that the essence of the president's approach to leadership—Obamaprise—is "the art of compromising when you don't have to...The president is fortunate that Martin Luther King did not share his conflict-averse approach to leadership, or Obama himself would be sitting in the middle of a bus somewhere, not on Air Force One" (2009). Some progressives are demoralized enough to withdraw from political engagement, rationalizing it as a legitimate wait-and-see strategy related to a disappointing leader or a realistic assessment that the nation's corrupt political system cannot be reformed. The many progressives who continue to try to influence public policy are frustrated when ignored or placated by the Obama White House, but they remain actively engaged.[14] Some think of themselves as more realistic in their expectations about what is possible to achieve given the powerful forces that are arrayed against change, while others claim to have had fewer illusions about Obama in the first place (Solomon, 2009). These progressives' efforts, including online letter-writing campaigns and public demonstrations on behalf of health care, environmental issues, economic recovery, and diplomatic resolution of international conflict, provide a much-needed pressure from the left for a president they hope desires to use it. Even though their activism receives scant coverage by the corporate media, their hard work has effectively influenced a growing number of Congresspersons and Senators as well as public opinion. Polls show that in two of the most controversial issues facing this country, a majority of citizens consistently supports a robust government health care option as well as an end to U.S. military action in Afghanistan. Indeed, at this writing, the battle over health care rages on, in the process revealing that the private health insurance industry operates in the interest of profits for shareholders rather than the health needs of citizens. So far Obama's role has been disappointing: He never permitted single-payer to be explored as a reform possibility and has offered only halfhearted presence in the struggle for a solid public option. Instead, he has engaged in negotiations with pharmaceutical and for-profit health insurance companies and deferred to the Congress the extent and terms of the reform that will constitute the health care legislation he signs. There is great concern among progressives that, should it pass, the health care reform law may have a private mandate that guarantees for-profit insurance companies millions of new customers without a strong public option that finally protects citizens from corporate abuse.

On the other side of the political spectrum, conservatives are reacting antagonistically to the Obama presidency. Even as Obama's moderate and bipartisan discourse and strategy alienate many progressives, the Republican Party is unresponsive, determined to sabotage any success he might have in hopes that the country's escalating problems will return them to power in 2012. Meanwhile, the conservative base, fearful of change and the uncertainty it brings, has been mobilized by right-wing cable and radio talk show hosts. They demonstrate against Obama, who continues to be derided in racist and xenophobic diatribes as a fascist, socialist, dictator, and Hitler, a foreigner who is destroying this country. As they march against health reform they reveal the intensification of the terror and rage that have developed during the past 40-plus years among people whose desperation is matched by their ideological confusion. Even as they see more clearly the inordinate corporate influence on government, by blaming it as well as big government in general on Obama, they fail to recognize the history of their own Republican Party's use of state power to rule on behalf of the privileged. This stance represents a perverse relationship to reality in the service of defending against painful truths that threaten ideological and psychological disequilibrium. Ironically, the participants in anti-Obama demonstrations often do not realize that the conservative entities organizing their mobilizations, such as Americans for Prosperity and Freedom Works, are funded by right-wing corporations whose policies have been so destructive to their welfare.[15] Their corporate funders keep a low profile, which enables the conservative media to misrepresent right-wing activism as spontaneous grassroots movements.[16] Alongside the sparse media coverage of progressive activism, it is too often the right-wing base that has become the spectacle and implicit signifier of the state of U.S. political subjectivity in 2009.

AMERICAN EXCEPTIONALISM MEETS THE PERFECT STORM: ECONOMICS, ENERGY, ENVIRONMENT

In late October 2009, Bono, Irish singer and musician admired for his humanitarian work, wrote in his occasional editorial column for the *New York Times* that "America is not just a country but an idea, a great idea about opportunity for all and responsibility to your fellow man." He went on to claim that in these dangerous times, the notion of America "rings like a bell...Why? Because the world sees that America might just hold the keys to solving the three greatest threats we face on this planet: extreme poverty, extreme ideology and extreme climate change" (Bono, 2009). Bono argued that since the United States is tired of being the world's policeman and cannot afford to be its philanthropist, it could become the world's partner.

Ironically, Bono's statement reveals a perhaps unintended ambivalence about the very country he is applauding. Moreover, his perspective is based on uncritical assumptions about "American Exceptionalism," an ideology related to Manifest Destiny that asserts the uniqueness of this country's history and its superior cultural values and institutions, which the United States has generously attempted to extend to the rest of the world (see chapter 1). Bono's editorial replicates this ideology by appealing to his U.S. readers to see ourselves as an exceptional people who can continue to actualize our well-deserved reputation as the only nation that holds the key to solving the world's problems. Would it not be preferable for U.S. citizens to think beyond our own cultural narcissism to a realistic assessment of our nation's contradictory role in the world and its complex effects on others? Would we not be in a more psychologically resilient state if we risk seeing clearly our own changing reality in a dramatically changing world? Would such an effort not help us understand the specific social context of our psychological experience as we face multiple challenges in these unprecedented times?

In a related vein, can psychoanalysts who have much to contribute to our understanding of the psychodynamics of individual and group conflict not also learn from an interdisciplinary approach to the analysis of systemic and institutional factors that influence psychological processes? After all, identity is framed by the social matrix of ideology and power relations. Elsewhere, Susan Gutwill and I (Hollander & Gutwill, 2006) have suggested that psychoanalysts can provide a transitional space in which both patient and analyst may question the normative split between psyche and social, between the individual and the collective, so as to reflectively explore their points of convergence. Psychoanalysis aims in part to make the unconscious conscious so that the individual has more freedom and increased choices, and this process ideally includes making conscious politically unconscious material that permeates the contours of relational conflicts. When patients express anxieties about declining work possibilities or unemployment, difficulties in sustaining relationships with loved ones, low self-esteem in response to frustrated aspirations, fears about losses due to local manifestations of climate change, concerns about inadequate medical care, distrust or naïve acceptance of the media's presentation of political reality, and so forth, they are responding to symptomatic evidence of the destruction of the social template of our lives. Psychoanalysts can create the opportunity to explore how these conflicts manifest larger social processes as well as private pain. The reluctance to participate in such an endeavor leaves intact the ideological domination and exploitation of psychic life that forecloses critical awareness and individual options. As British group psychoanalyst Earl Hopper (1996) suggests, "An analyst who is unaware of the effect of social facts and forces…will not be able to provide a space for patients to imagine how their identities have been formed at particular historical and political junctures, and how this continues to affect them throughout their lives" (p. 7). Moreover, Hopper points out that understanding the ways in which patients' reactions to social, political, and economic forces are not only central to the constitution of identity but are also reproduced unconsciously within the patient–therapist relationship makes for a more nuanced and thorough psychoanalytic treatment. I would caution us to include in Hopper's argument what our Latin American colleagues insist on, and that is the fantasy aspect of the psychoanalytic principle of neutrality. Far from being neutral or representing neutrality in relation to patient material, analysts, like every human being, are subjectivized, both in and by the sociosymbolic world in general as well as by unquestioned hegemonic assumptions in psychoanalytic theory and training that affect their experience and interpretations of their patients' unconscious dynamics and conscious conflicts. From this perspective, optimal psychoanalytic treatment eschews the idea of neutrality in the service of understanding how hegemony, in all its ramifications, is reinforced or interrogated in the intersubjective process between both participants.

I am not advocating that psychoanalysts proselytize their patients. Quite the contrary: our patients' political attitudes and social values may be similar to or very different from our own. But it is precisely the psychoanalytic frame that offers the possibility of an intersubjective experience in which, through the analyst's careful monitoring of transference and countertransference dynamics, both analyst and patient can create the possibility to be separate and different within a respectful relationship. The psychoanalytic process can thus provide for the emergence of a more sturdy subject with the capacity to critically negotiate affective and cognitive responses to the social order, so much of which is too often unthought, unquestioned, and unconscious. Such patients might not be obliged to rely on disavowal or manic certainty to manage the multiple threats in the world around them. As we help to make the unconscious conscious, we open up the potential space for observation of our relationships to hegemony and thus help to make the movement between submission and resistance to authority a more fluid one.

With these observations in mind, I would like to briefly take note of several of the discourses related to the important "social facts and forces" that from my perspective represent our biggest challenges in today's world. In this book I have been examining the times of terror in the Americas symbolized by Latin America's September 11 and the U.S. 9/11. But there are additional concerns—we might even say terror-producing realities— that we will be increasingly obliged to deal with. Too many of us will be aware of only the symptomatic evidence of the forces responsible for altering the social matrix of our lives. If we are not grounded in a critical understanding of their fundamental causes, we are more vulnerable to feeling helpless, confused, and anxious. These regressed states of mind promote a bystander posture or fear- and rage-driven reactive behavior that do not favor adaptive resolutions. I believe that hope lies in our willingness to tolerate the anxiety associated with knowing what is real in order to develop a sense of agency that enables constructive engagement in forward-looking solutions and reparative action.

Among the themes I wish to examine are (1) the fate of the United States as the world's superpower; (2) the status of global capitalism; (3) the significance of unprecedented risks emerging from industrial society and its relationship to the environment; (4) and the potential for authoritarian and progressive responses to these multiple challenges. From my perspective, discourses about these subjects contribute to a psychoanalytic appreciation of contemporary social conditions and how they will increasingly affect individual and group anxieties, defenses, and more or less adaptive resolutions of the conflict between desire and the limits of reality.

Hegemonic notions that the United States is and will continue to be the world's singular superpower are challenged by evidence that points to our being in the midst of a paradigm shift. A substantive debate about imperial decline has been under way for several decades. But since the recent U.S. economic meltdown with its global repercussions it has expanded beyond academic discussion to become a theme in intelligence circles and even popular culture as well. The economic and military supremacy of the United States is being successfully challenged not only by religious fundamentalism but by a realignment of international power. A new, multipolar world is emerging that will have profound material and psychological implications for subjects living in the heart of a failing empire. This development has resulted from systemic weaknesses in the U.S. economy produced by the neoliberal deregulation policies of the last three decades that permitted capital to secure ever-rising profits by exporting the production of U.S. goods and services offshore. By the 21st century, this country stopped producing jobs in traditional export industries and in industries that compete with imports. The thriving industrial sector that made this economy the most powerful in the world has dramatically shrunk: The national income share of manufacturing has declined from 21 percent in 1980 to 12 percent in 2005, so that job creation in the United States is primarily in low-paying, low-security positions rather than the traditionally high-productivity, high-waged occupations that until the 1980s had created the middle and upper-middle classes and fueled consumption. The superpower, once the major producer and exporter of capital goods, now suffers a trade deficit in machinery, machine tools, computers, and telecommunications equipment. U.S. citizens are dependent for their essential needs on imports that range from foods, feeds, and beverages to industrial supplies and materials, automotive vehicles, parts, engines, manufactured durable and nondurable goods, and oil. The country's resulting massive trade deficit is supported by foreign creditors who accept dollars for U.S. goods and services, which they then use as an international medium of exchange or investment in U.S.

treasuries and other dollar-denominated assets that finance our government's budget deficit (Roberts, 2007; see also Krugman, 2009).

This dramatic weakness in the U.S. economy is exacerbated by heavy military expenditures that channel limited resources away from investment in the social and physical infrastructure. For years "military Keynesianism" has been responsible for subsidizing such bloated military budgets that in 2008, the U.S. Department of Defense spent more than all other nations' military budgets combined. In that same year, the supplementary budget to pay for the wars in Iraq and Afghanistan was larger than the combined military budgets of Russia and China (Johnson, 2008).[17] Contrary to the customary wisdom that wars and military spending are good for the economy, the Center for Economic and Policy Research (CEPR) studied the long-term economic impact of increased military spending and, according to CEPR economist Dean Baker (2008), "while the model shows that increased spending initially provides an economic boost, the spending soon becomes a drain on the economy. The United States has over decades robbed investment possibilities from civilian sectors of the economy for military investments." A current example is provided by Baker, who shows that if the United States escalates the war in Afghanistan, by the 10th year the increase in military spending is projected "to lead to a loss of 460,000 jobs. Twenty years of increased military spending is projected to lead to a loss of 670,000 jobs...The model also projects that higher military spending leads to a large increase in the trade deficit." Norman Solomon (2008) reveals how in California, taxpayers have paid more than $66 billion to directly pay for their share of the war in Iraq, which is more than four times greater than California's current enormous budget deficit of $15 billion. He points out that as long as military spending remains astronomical, domestic programs for human needs are at a severe disadvantage. Not unrelated to this conundrum, the standard of living and quality of life of the majority of U.S. citizens today is so compromised that measured by indexes such as health, poverty, and wealth inequality, this country has the status of a third-world nation, third from the bottom of a ranking of 30 countries, ahead of only Mexico and Turkey (Einhorn, 2009).[18]

Empires cannot maintain both a global military presence and a strong domestic economy forever, and sooner or later the standard of living and social equity erode at home. There is also a multifaceted resistance abroad. Many political economists argue that the United States is facing this dilemma now: domestic economic meltdown on the home front at the same time that countries throughout the world are no longer willing to finance their own economic subordination to the superpower. The U.S. balance-of-payments deficit, a large percentage of which is due to military expenditures, ends up in the hands of foreign banks and central banks whose only choice is to recycle the dollars by buying U.S. government debt (treasuries). From the point of view of Asian countries, they have been financing their own economic subordination and military encirclement (Hedges, 2009c; Hudson, 2009). The signs of opposition are everywhere: New economic/military alliances have been forming, composed of countries that want to abandon the dollar as the global reserve currency and develop trading zones based on other currencies. One example is the six-nation Shanghai Cooperation Organization (SCO), composed of China, Russia, Kazakhstan, Tajikistan, Kyrgyzstan, and Uzbekistan, with observer status for Iran, India, Pakistan, and Mongolia. In 2005, the SCO requested that the United States set a timeline to withdraw from its military bases in Central Asia. This alliance is in the oil-rich area of the globe, which investigative journalist Pepe Escobar (2009a) fallaciously calls "Pipelineistan," where much of the political and military tension is related to the struggle to control regional energy supplies. Escobar (2009b) warns us to "forget the mainstream media's obsession with al-Qaeda, Osama 'dead or alive' bin Laden, the Taliban—neo, light or classic—or that 'war on terror,' whatever name it goes by. These are diversions compared to the high-stakes, hardcore geopolitical game that follows what flows along the pipelines of the planet." The SCO is also interested in changing the nature and functioning of international financial institutions, such as the U.S.-dominated International Monetary Fund and the World Bank, so that no individual country or its political issues and motives will dominate. Another alliance with aspirations toward more economic autonomy from the United States is the BRIC countries, which includes Brazil, Russia, India, and China, with similar goals of replacing the dollar as their trading currency. The Latin American continental alliance against U.S. economic and military intrusions is an additional front of opposition to U.S. global hegemony. Even the G20 organization, when it met in April 2009, formally declared the death of the Washington Consensus as it established new regulatory functions for the International Monetary Fund (IMF) and included new countries, such as China, India, and Brazil, in the control over the IMF and other international agencies. Joseph Stiglitz said of the meeting, "It's a historic moment when the world came together and said we were wrong to push deregulation...it is a major step forward" (Saunders, 2009). British Prime Minister Gordon Brown, who convened the summit, declared, "Today we have reached a new consensus...I think a new world order is emerging."

While few debate the inevitability of a multipolar world, they differ with respect to its effect on the United States. Some observers argue that even with the displacement of the dollar internationally, the United States will not suddenly fade into irrelevance because it still represents the largest economy and military presence in the world, at least for the foreseeable future. Further, as long as investors are willing to hold 10-year treasury bonds at a 3.5 percent interest rate, they apparently are not so concerned about the U.S. deficit. Europe, Japan, and China are motivated to keep the dollar stable because its sudden plunge would cut their exports to the

United States, devastating their economies (Baker, 2009). Others argue the opposite, that other countries are abandoning the dollar in favor of more stable currencies like the euro or yen and will be demanding higher interest rates to buy U.S. treasuries. Either or both of these developments would be devastating to the U.S. economy. Indeed, China is already less willing to buy treasuries and is using its plethora of dollars in good Keynesian fashion to finance a dramatic expansion and modernization of its infrastructure and to acquire assets throughout the world. A dynamic Chinese economy, in contrast to a lengthy U.S. recession, could attract more global suppliers of raw materials into the Chinese trade orbit and lessen the relative significance of the United States in international trade. The effect would be to accelerate the flow of wealth from West to East, with significant social consequences. If this were to transpire, according to David Harvey (2009), "The supreme irony...is that the political and ideological barriers in the United States to any full-fledged Keynesian program will almost certainly hasten loss of U.S. dominance in global affairs even as the elites of the world...would wish to preserve that dominance for as long as possible" (see also Jacques, 2009).

I would argue that it is advantageous to the world that the powerful United States is reduced to one nation among many. But unless there are dramatic shifts in the distribution of power and privilege within this country, the end of empire threatens to create life conditions for U.S. citizens similar to the vicissitudes traditionally suffered by Latin Americans in their inequitable capitalist economies. We might wonder if citizens in this country can foster a government with similar principles of redistributive equity and social justice that characterize most contemporary Latin American regimes. Before I indicate how I think the foreclosure of the "American Dream" will affect political subjectivity, I want to make mention of a related discourse that represents even bigger challenges—new terrors, we might say—in the current period. This discourse has evolved around the question of peak oil and its impact on industrial society. Peak oil was originally a concern of geologists and a variety of other scientific analysts, but the debate about its significance has reached governments and popular culture alike. There is some agreement that, sooner or later, the cheap energy source that fueled the development over the last century and a half of industrial society, including our oil-driven transportation, agricultural, and manufacturing activities, will decline. Most modern industrial societies are dependent on the relatively low cost and high availability of oil, which makes them vulnerable to its inevitable postpeak production decline that in all likelihood will cause high prices and extreme inflation. Without a government and private sector commitment to putting in place programs for conservation and alternative energy sources, great economic and social dislocation on a global scale are inevitable. The debate is not about if, but when, global oil decline will begin, and estimates range from an optimistic date of 2020 to more pessimistic views that peak oil has already begun or is about to occur in the very near future. In 2005, the U.S. Department of Energy published a report on peak oil, in which it argued:

> The peaking of world oil production presents the US and the world with an unprecedented risk management problem. As peaking is approached, liquid fuel prices and price volatility will increase dramatically, and, without timely mitigation, the economic, social, and political costs will be unprecedented. Viable mitigation options exist on both the supply and demand sides, but to have substantial impact, they must be initiated more than a decade in advance of peaking. It is a matter of risk management—early mitigation will be less damaging than delayed mitigation. (Hirsch et al., 2005; see also Kunsler, 2005)

The report argues that government intervention will be required to contain the otherwise economic and social chaos that will result from rapidly declining oil availability. While it is comforting to see that the government has been put on notice, the time frame seems dangerously casual, pushed into the future. To the extent that neither public nor private actors are ideologically and psychologically able to grapple with this objective demand to alter life as usual and develop a proactive collaborative strategy to use remaining oil and natural gas resources to develop energy alternatives, it is feared that global industrial society could collapse. A warning sign, it is argued, about what lies in store was seen in the first two quarters of 2008, when the global recession was made worse by record high oil prices. However, alongside the grave concern about the potentially catastrophic implications of peak oil is the perspective that it contains potentially positive implications.[19] Many critics who hold this view suggest that as oil supplies diminish and oil prices rise, nations will be forced to develop and use alternative clean fuels that will contribute to the effective control of fossil fuel pollution and thus mitigate global warming. Further, they point out that if governments recognize the reality of peak oil and act to creatively plan adaptive strategies, such as the construction of local food networks, alternative energies, and dense population centers conducive to walking and nonfuel-dependent modes of transportation, they will constitute an ethical response to the acknowledgment of finite fossil resources.

The peak oil debate is directly connected to the discourse on global warming and the ecological crisis. Since the United States has consistently been the largest per capita emitter of carbon dioxide from the burning of fossil fuels, this country has a significant role to play in constructively addressing the urgent crises represented by global warming. Unfortunately the United States does not have a good record of cooperation in international efforts, never having ratified nor withdrawn from the Kyoto Protocol. In April 2009, President Obama announced that it did not make sense for the

United States to sign Kyoto because the agreement was about to end, even though that target date will not occur for almost three years. And while the latest scientific studies show that the planet is warming faster than had been realized, the implications of which are potentially calamitous, neither the long anticipated Senate climate bill nor the climate treaty likely to emerge from the December 2009 Copenhagen meeting promise to be substantive enough to meet the challenge. It is unclear as of this writing whether there will be a binding agreement on greenhouse gases, for example. Naomi Klein (2009) reports that the global justice movement is planning a series of events and protests that will mirror in some ways the anti–World Trade Organization (WTO) Battle of Seattle events. Climate-justice activists point out that the current focus on the strategy of carbon trading not only fails to solve environmental problems, but more importantly, it is an unprecedented privatization of the atmosphere. This "market-based solution" approach is a potential resource grabbing that will deepen poverty and inequality because the poorest people are the primary victims of climate change and the guinea pigs for these emissions-trading schemes. This approach by the world's prominent decision makers in the face of mounting evidence of looming ecological disaster represents the convergence of irresponsibility and denial. As sociologist Zygmunt Bauman puts it, in our negatively globalized planet, "The roots of our vulnerability are of a *political* and *ethical* nature."

The ecological crisis is related to yet another discourse, which has to do with the fate of capitalism as a global mode of production, not only in terms of whether it can respond to human needs in an equitable fashion, but whether it can adapt to the changing requirements of the earth.

In the 1960s, John Lennon sang,

> Imagine no possessions
> I wonder if you can
> No need for greed or hunger
> A brotherhood of man
> Imagine all the people
> Sharing all the world...

When these words were written, they were a poetic wish. Today we might say they are a reality-based imperative. They remind us that in spite of all the reformist ideas about growing a green economy, if humanity does not reassess the economic priorities of industrial society itself, we may not be able to respond to the demands of a rapidly debilitating planet. We can say that globalization began in 1492, the inauguration of an international division of labor in which the Global South would furnish the industrializing world of Europe and later the United States with essential resources and cheap/free labor that would consistently enrich the former and impoverish the latter. In fact, the privilege of those living in the Global North was based on the suffering of the inhabitants of the Global South: two inevitably linked parts of a single system. Until recently it was assumed that the Global South could ultimately develop and utilize the infinite resources of the earth to emulate the living standards of their advantaged brethren in the industrialized world. Now we know this assumption to be fantasy, that in fact, these resources are quite finite. It is essential, therefore, that we reexamine the future adaptability of the individualism, competitiveness, and accumulative impulse of capitalist expansion that we have taken for granted, for it is this system that may, indeed, threaten the survivability of humanity and kindred ecosystems. Psychoanalyst and social critic Joel Kovel has studied the scientific, sociological, and psychological aspects of the relationship of human beings to nature. He shows how nature is not static, but on the contrary, has a history bound up with the gradual emergence of a species—*homo sapiens*—that has been distinguished from other species by the capacity for production—that is, the conscious transforming of nature for human purposes. While humans are technically but one ecosystem in relation to all other ecosystems, early on, humans came to think of themselves as separate from and above nature, which they thought of as an environment external to humanity whose resources could be utilized for our needs and desires. We can say, writes Kovel (2002), that human beings have a pathological relation to nature, reflected in "the anthropocentric delusion that sees nature, in all its intricate glory, existing like so many planets around the human sun" (p. 102). Indeed, the great span of human prehistory is a story of the many facets of human–natural transformations characterized by man's gradual domination of nature.

Central to the evolution of man's domination over nature is the corresponding history of male domination over woman. Many scholars argue that gender constitutes the first split in human society and that the initial division of labor was woman as giver of life and man as taker of life. The original male groupings for the hunt with its death-dealing tools evolved into the raid that included the seizure of women and children from neighboring groups. Social violence grew out of retaliatory or defensive attacks and the compulsion among groups to achieve power over other groups, which in turn produced property relations as a way of holding on to what had been acquired violently. Patriarchy emerged as a complex system of the exchange of women in order to link different groups together in reciprocal relations, which included apportioning women to men and assuring ownership and control over children. Over tens of thousands of years, this process, alongside the conquest of nature, generated civilization. Thus, property and domination in society and over nature were gendered from the beginning and provided a template for universal male domination with its multiple cultural renderings (Hollander, 2009).[20] Ultimately, science, technology, and industry became the pillars of a capital accumulation process that began with agriculture and the domestication of animals and evolved into an economic developmental process based on constant and inexorable growth and expansion. Kovel and others demonstrate that it is both the law of expansion that defines the capitalist mode of production, along with its hegemonic presumption that growth and expansion are the correct and necessary aims of economic life, that constitute the barrier to imagining not only the possibility but the necessity of reorganizing society so as to adopt an ecologically sound relationship with the earth. The command economies of the Soviet bloc provided no alternative to expansionist assumptions embedded in the capitalist model and replicated its devastating impact on the environment. While that system imploded, the contemporary deep social divisions that each day are exacerbated by a victorious global capitalism are matched only by the system's destructive impact on the physical environment that ultimately implicate its ability to serve human needs.

Economist William Greider (2003) argues that while capitalism is forward-looking and ingeniously creative, it has one large incapacity: "As a matter of principle, it cannot take society's interests into account...In the economic sphere, efficiency trumps community" (pp. 35, 39). Greider agrees with Kovel that capitalism kills, not only human beings, but perhaps most importantly, multiple and increasing ecosystems in nature that sustain life and the planet itself. The social irresponsibility that is a foundational characteristic of corporate capitalism is taken up from another perspective by Joel Bakan (2004), who traces the history of the corporation in U.S. culture. By the late 19th century it had acquired the legal status of a "person," separate from the real people who are its owners and managers. In 1886, a Supreme Court decision determined that corporations were "persons" under the protection of the 14th Amendment, with the right to due process and equal protection under the law. Through the years, progressive organizations struggled to make corporations act with social responsibility, with periodic successes until the era of neoliberalism, when deregulation permitted corporations to go offshore to seek the means of producing goods and services at the lowest possible cost. In 1993, the WTO was created to bar governments' regulatory measures that might restrict the flow of international trade and to establish a supranational legal entity to countermand local laws protecting labor rights and environmental safety. Governments competed with each other to offer the cheapest labor and lowest taxes in order to attract corporate investment. Corporations now dictated economic policy to governments, a turnabout that provoked an international global justice movement. Bakan argues that since the corporation has the legal status of an individual, it makes sense to give its ruthless self-serving behavior and inability to act with concern for others a psychological diagnosis. To this end, he queried Dr. Robert Hare, an internationally renowned expert on psychopathology, who agreed that the institutional character of corporations is, indeed, psychopathological. They are characterized by irresponsibility, extreme grandiosity, a lack of empathy, asocial tendencies, and the compulsion to manipulate everyone and everything. Corporations refuse to accept responsibility for their actions and cannot feel remorse for wrong-doing. According to Hare, corporations relate to others superficially and duplicitously: "Their whole goal is to present themselves to the public in a way that is appealing…[but] in fact may not be representative of what th[e] organization is really like" (Bakan, 2004, p. 57).

The political consequences of corporate globalization are profound in that a single system has produced *both* transnational capitalist giants and religious fundamentalism, two polarized opposites that are hostile to democracy. It is often assumed that democracy requires capitalism to exist, but as I have argued in the chapters on Latin American neoliberal authoritarian societies, there is no direct relationship between the market and democracy. "Nation state capitalism once contributed to democracy's founding," writes political scientist Benjamin Barber (1996), but

> Today McWorld's global capitalism may signal its demise…McWorld's global strategy…cannot serve American or global public interests such as full employment, the dignity of work, the creative civic use of forced leisure, environmental protection, social safety nets, and pension protection. McWorld's advocates will argue that the "market" does "serve" individuals by empowering them to "choose" but the choice is always about which items to buy and consume, never about *whether* to buy and consume anything at all… (p. 77)

Barber stresses that the mass media have caused increasing isolation of individuals from one another and from community: "McWorld calls on us to see ourselves as private and solitary," he writes, "interacting primarily via commercial transactions where 'me' displaces 'we'; and it permits private corporations whose only interest is their revenue stream to define by default the public goods of the individuals and communities they serve" (p. 98).

All of the above contemporary crises and the terrors they produce, from religious fundamentalism to weapons of mass destruction to ecological disaster, have been analyzed by German sociologist Ulrich Beck and Polish sociologist Zygmunt Bauman as the unexpected and paradoxical effects of modernity itself. Within this framework, premodern cultures suffered all kinds of terrifying threats like famines, plagues, floods, and the perennial darkness that enshrouded most humans' lives. The forces responsible for stimulating ubiquitous states of fear and anxiety appeared to come from outside, attributable to the gods, demons, or nature. With the advent of modernity between the 16th and 18th centuries, it was assumed that through industry and scientific knowledge, rational man would take control over nature to enjoy a newfound security and predictability. All the calamities and catastrophes to which human beings had been subjected, both natural and moral, would be predictable and preventable, responsive to the powers of human reason. With the shift to a secular perspective, social risk presupposed human decisions, and along with it, uncomfortable questions about human accountability and responsibility. Some centuries later, we find that modernity only succeeded in producing new problems, this time manmade, such as newly discovered illnesses, crime, economic marginalization, terrorism, weapons of mass destruction, war, and climate change. These manufactured risks are produced by human agency and are paradoxically the very triumph of modernity. Moreover, in agreement with Freud, Zygmunt Bauman believes that the era of what he calls "solid modernity" brought security to human beings at the cost of their freedom. Postmodernity, or what Bauman calls "liquid modernity," marks the shift in capitalism to a culture of consumerism, in which security was sacrificed in order to enjoy increased freedoms to consume and enjoy life. This process created new unprecedented challenges stemming from rapid changes of every aspect of life. Social forms and institutions have little time to solidify, and thus instability marks peoples' lives, lending a fragmentation that requires individuals to be flexible and adaptable to constantly shifting circumstances. In liquid modernity, citizens everywhere live and must react to conditions of endemic uncertainty that produce inescapable apprehension that Bauman (2007) calls "liquid fears." In Ulrich Beck's terms, modernity produced a "risk society," and we are all members of a global community of global threats, in part the result of the shared risks produced by science itself as well as by the ubiquitous conflict of social inequalities. Beck stresses that risk is different from catastrophe in that the latter is an experience that has already happened. *Risk* refers to future events that may or will threaten us, which create an environment conducive to chronic fear and longings for security. "...Because this constant danger shapes our expectations, lodges in our heads and guides our actions," claims Beck (2009), "it becomes a political force that transforms the world" (p. 9). Beck and Bauman agree that in globalized society the need for security is displacing a prior period's focus on freedom and equality as the highest value that the state could hope to provide its citizens. They both worry that our growing fears motivate a willingness to accept a "tightening of laws, a seemingly rational 'totalitarianism of defense against threats.'" Bauman's eloquent description of the globalization of "liquid modern fears" is his version of what I have been describing as today's uprooted minds and the states of dislocation, anxiety, and fear that characterize our daily experience. He argues that in our negatively globalized planet, which is a mosaic of ethnic and religious diasporas, we can no longer speak of "inside" versus "outside" or the "center" versus the "periphery." Globalization means that all on the planet suffer the same multiple threats that mobilize the prototype of all fears: the meta-danger of death. "On a negatively globalized planet," Bauman (2007) writes, "all the most fundamental problems—the genuinely *meta*-problems which condition the chances and the ways of tackling all other problems—are global, and being global they admit of no *local* solutions" (pp. 125–128). It follows that the principles of democracy and freedom in a world saturated with billions of human beings deprived of justice and dignity can never be achieved in one country or group of countries but depend on its universal implementation.

The universal implementation of democracy and freedom seem to scholars who have studied the history of capitalism an unlikely achievement within existing negative globalization. David Harvey, Immanuel Wallerstein, Eric Hobsbawm, Michael Hudson, Jared Diamond, Arundhati Roy, and, more recently, Minqui Li, for example, agree that we are at a stage of great uncertainty about what is to come, but that deregulated capitalism will have to yield to a more benign global economic system. Some believe that capitalism will have to evolve into a more stable, equitable, and environmentally friendly mixed public/private mode of production, while others argue that capitalism is not "sustainable" and will have to be replaced by new alternative economic orders dedicated to a more equally shared but modest use of resources and a benign carbon footprint. Even while scientists and scholars have pointed to industrial capitalism as the major culprit of escalating global inequities and ecological crisis, corporate and government leaders, as well as citizens, are "habituated" to the ideological claims that this economic system is the best and highest achievement of humanity. In a painful and ironic observation, cultural critic Fredric Jameson has noted that it is easier to think about the idea of the end of the world and ecological destruction than it is to think about the end of global capitalism and the possibility of a different form of social, economic, and political organization of human existence. Echoing Jameson, Zizek has written, "It seems easier to imagine 'the end of the world' than a far more modest change in the mode of production, as if liberal capitalism is the 'real' that will somehow survive even under conditions of a global ecological catastrophe" (Wright & Wright, 2000, p. 55).

I suggest that the corporate and governmental leaders who enjoy the accumulation of capital and profits and whose economic, social, and cultural power are primarily responsible for the continued destructiveness toward the earth operate with impunity and manifest a predilection for grandiosity and an inability to adapt to the reality principle. Their disavowal of responsibility operates on the basis of what Bion saw as an omnipotence originating in the inability to tolerate the recognition of the limits of reality and the narcissistic need to control one's objects. In social terms, these objects include markets, commodities, profits, workers, resources, and capital. Moreover, such omnipotence represents the subordination of truth to self-interest in what Bion called "basic assumption" types of regressed group behavior. In this case omnipotent fantasies are sustained by the ideological defense of industrial capitalism as the only way of organizing production and distribution and the denial of the urgent need to alter its priorities of profit-making expansion. Together they constitute an attack on knowledge.

Bion saw these mechanisms as a particular aspect of malfunction and perversion, a social pathology taking the form sometimes of lies or of the total
refusal to enter the treacherous field of communication through language.
The disavowal practiced by elites and reinforced ideologically sets the stage
for the rest of us, who struggle with, on the one hand, pressure to identify
with the system's prevailing values and our participation in its expansion
and growth, and on the other, the impulse to protect ourselves from knowing what we know about its destructiveness because the enormity of the
crisis subjects us to overwhelming feelings of helplessness and terror. As
author and environmental activist Derrick Jensen puts it,

> All of the so-called solutions to global warming take industrial capital-
> ism as a given...The natural world is supposed to conform to indus-
> trial capitalism. This is insane. It is out of touch with physical reality.
> What's real is real. Any social system—it does not matter if we are
> talking about industrial capitalism or an indigenous Tolowa people—
> their way of life, is dependent upon a real, physical world. Without a
> real, physical world you don't have anything. When you separate your-
> self from the real world you start to hallucinate. (Hedges, 2009d)[21]

A symbolic convergence of these discourses emerged at the Copenhagen
Climate Summit in December 2009, which has been called the most important diplomatic gathering in the world's history. In addition to the formal
meeting among government and corporate representatives, tens of thousands of activists from social movements around the world met in parallel meetings and protests that critiqued the values and practices of an
economic model based on inexorable growth responsible for destructive
global warming. Many participants came from the poorest countries in
Africa, Latin America, and Asia, whose resources have been appropriated
over the centuries by the industrialized world. They bore testimony to how
their homelands are the site of the gravest impact of climate change so far,
including unprecedented droughts and rising sea levels that are robbing
people of their traditional sources of water, food, income, and housing. As
climate justice activists objected to the rich countries' reliance on a market-based remedial strategy, a leaked draft of a climate agreement among
the United States, Britain, and Denmark, called the "Danish Text," was
published in the British newspaper *The Guardian*. The revelation drove
a wedge between rich and poor nations because the draft proposal made
significant changes to the Kyoto Protocol and was interpreted to remove
the United Nations' process from any future climate decisions, placing it
within a framework that would effectively stifle the growth of poor nations
while allowing wealthy nations to continue their disproportionate levels of
carbon pollution. Alternatively, the social activists from the Global North
and the Global South were introducing concepts of social justice and class

exploitation into the climate change debate, arguing that the industrialized world, which accounts for the historical production of the vast majority of harmful carbon production and has benefited from fossil fuel exploitation, should shoulder a bigger percent of the burden of emissions reduction and financially support efforts in the developing countries to adopt a growth strategy using alternative sources of energy.

During the conference news was also leaked that the United States would not sign a binding agreement in Copenhagen to limit carbon emissions. Meanwhile, in nearby Oslo, President Obama accepted the Nobel Peace Prize. Saying little about climate change, he addressed the contradiction between being honored as a peacemaker and his decision to escalate the war in Afghanistan. Pundits claimed his speech reflected a political position of realism given the complexities of a conflicted world. Indeed, he held the tension between articulating a rationale for "just war" and arguing that in our imperfect world, we must reach for ideals that make it better. Although Obama is reputed to be critical of the national security strategy known as the Long War, for many progressives, his speech was marred by its continuity with an all-too-familiar hegemonic narrative of American Exceptionalism and an ideological splitting that demonized others and idealized the United States. He spoke of evil in the world, locating it out there in others—in Al Qaeda and those who have defiled Islam and used religion to justify attacking the United States and killing innocent people. While decrying Islamic extremism that kills in the name of God, the closest he came to equating a similar abuse of religion in the West was noting the Crusades, leaving glaring the omission of any reference to contemporary Christian motives for waging war and proselytizing throughout the world. In contrast to evil, Obama portrayed this country as the embodiment of good, asserting that our citizens and servicemen and women have shed blood for more than six decades to underwrite global security and promote peace, prosperity, and democracy. "We have borne this burden," Obama declared, "not because we seek to impose our will. We have done so out of enlightened self-interest—because we seek a better future for our children and grandchildren, and we believe that their lives will be better if other peoples' children and grandchildren can live in freedom and prosperity."[22] Significantly, several terrorism experts responded to Obama's rationale of "just war" by insisting that a prime motive for Muslim violence is the occupation of their countries by the United States (Shane, 2009). Seen in the context of the discourses explored above, Obama's speech has the effect of foreclosing our capacity as citizens to develop critical awareness and psychological insight about our contributions to violence and instability in the world and it encourages us to identify with superpower strivings and militarized solutions to global problems. One wonders if this is the U.S. version of Latin America's culture of impunity that dominated the region for three decades.[23]

CONTEMPORARY SUBJECTIVITIES:
DESPAIR AND HOPE

I believe a critical and reflective knowledge of the significant social issues I have described is important not only for us as citizens, but for a psychoanalytic understanding of contemporary subjectivity. When people function by disavowing a threatening reality they suffer the inevitable dissociated anxieties in the form of symptoms that often appear to have nothing to do with their source. In this country, psychoanalysts are trained to interpret patients' presenting complaints and conflicts exclusively in terms of frustrated personal desires, relationships, and goals manifested in a variety of psychic and bodily dysfunctions. However, I am arguing that the plethora of liquid fears that Bauman writes about also emerge in derivative fashion in treatment, often left unattended because they are not considered to be a legitimate aspect of the psychoanalytic frame. I am suggesting that psychoanalysis take account of internalized hegemonic structures and values that are the social matrix of the subject's unresolved losses of childhood and inform the vulnerabilities and resiliencies with which the subject experiences and engages the social.

In the current period, I suggest that our states of mind will be dramatically affected by increasingly traumatogenic stressors as this country undergoes a shift in its status and endures increasingly polarizing social conditions. We are faced with important questions that none of us can escape. How will the United States manage a transition from its status as hegemon to a diminished role internationally in which it is one nation among many to collaborate in dealing with economically and politically destabilizing events? How will it contribute to the global need for a reality-based strategy to repair the socioeconomic inequities of global capitalism and its destructive effects on the earth? Can we act to contribute to the containment of the liquid fears generated by our risk societies? Chris Hedges (2009a) wonders:

> Will we cling to the absurd dreams of a superpower and the fantasies of a glorious tomorrow, or will we responsibly face our stark, new limitations? Will we heed those who are sober and rational, those who speak of a new simplicity and humility, or will we follow the demagogues and charlatans who rise up in moments of crisis and panic to offer fantastic visions of escape? Will we radically transform our system to one that protects the ordinary citizen and fosters the common good, that defies the corporate state, or will we employ the brutality and technology of our internal security and surveillance apparatus to crush all dissent? (p. 145)

Hedges' query leads us to an exploration of the state of political subjectivity in the contemporary United States. How deeply embedded in our social structures and collective consciousness are democratic principle and process? Does this country have the capacity to move toward a more inclusive and equitable sharing of power and resources, or does it still have the potential to turn toward a repressive governance and political culture? Although these questions may seem outmoded since the departure from power of the neoconservative movement, there is much on the political landscape that continues to be preoccupying. Some analysts worry that another global economic collapse could bring reactionary, xenophobic movements to power in many countries, including in the compromised heart of empire. Indeed, there are provocative signs suggesting a growing concentration of political power and a rightward turn of the body politic.

Naomi Klein's contention that the revolving door between the corporate world and government has become a bridge solidifying the collusive relationship between the two is confirmed by scholar Janine Wedel's (2009) analysis of what she calls the "shadow elite." Wedel spent years in Russia studying the nature of the governing clique that assumed power after the fall of the Soviet Union. She thinks she sees similarities in the dynamics of who now rules the United States. Wedel analyzes the coterie of financial and policy decision makers who, following Wall Street's economic meltdown, have permeated virtually all arenas of government. Backed by billions of taxpayers' dollars, this clique is establishing the financial structures of the future. Moreover, during the past 15 years the contracting out of government work to private companies has been so extensive that it has hollowed out the regulatory and monitoring functions of the state. Many public priorities and decisions are made by private companies instead of government officials and agencies, dangerously compromising accountability to citizens. These developments represent a profound challenge to the healthy functioning of democracy.

Alongside this and other substantial structural shifts threatening democratic culture are recent political trends. Conservatism, the main ideological orientation among U.S. citizens, has increased one year after the election of President Obama. In September 2009, a Gallup Poll found that 40 percent of respondents described their political views as conservative, 36 percent as moderate, and 20 percent as liberal, marking a shift from 2005, when moderates were tied with conservatives as the most prevalent group. A move toward the right was revealed in the following categories: the belief that there is too much government regulation of business and industry, the preference for less influence by labor unions, the desire for less strict laws governing the sale of firearms, support for a decrease in immigration, the wish for government to promote "traditional values," support for prolife on abortion, and the belief that global warming is "exaggerated" in the news.

The different sectors of the organized right in this country have effectively influenced the attitudes of increasing numbers of citizens. The neoconservative movement, although voted out of power, continues to be active. Their Project for the New American Century has been converted into the Foreign Policy Initiative, where its members warn that the United States must continue in its hegemonic role in the international community. Its program states: "The challenges we face requires 21st-century strategies and tactics based on a renewed commitment to American leadership. The United States remains the world's indispensable nation—indispensable to international peace, security, and stability, and indispensable to safeguarding and advancing the ideals and principles we hold dear." This neoconservative vision resists the idea of a multipolar world and is committed to a hefty military with a sturdy defense budget that can assure a strong America ready to confront contemporary threats to its position in the world (Duss, 2009).

The evangelical movement has infiltrated popular culture, its ideology influencing the 141 million citizens who daily watch Christian television channels and listen to Christian radio stations. Moreover, the Christian right political agenda has moved into the Congress and the courts, with hundreds of senators and representatives winning 80 to 100 percent approval ratings from influential Christian rights advocacy groups. The Christian fundamentalist movement has successfully used spectacle to deliver its organizing principles and religious ideology to millions, in the process shattering the Republican Party that once encompassed moderates as well as conservatives. Authoritarian and colorful personalities who use their mass media pulpits to preach to their eager followers are delivering convincing messages of the end days and Armageddon. James Dobson, perhaps the most influential leader of the Christian right, was trained as a child psychologist and has won millions of followers through his radio programs that offer listeners advice about common, mundane problems like bedwetting or sexuality in children. According to award winning journalist Max Blumenthal's research on the evangelical movement, Dobson advocates deliberate violence to discipline children, which helps to shape among his followers and their progeny a predisposition to an authoritarian personality. Those who join do so in order to resolve inner turmoil and self-doubt, becoming its most ardent, rigidly ideological, and loyal leaders and followers alike. Blumenthal (2009) posits that the essential character of the Christian base is marked by sadism, in that they wish to lash out at people who are weaker than they, including homosexuals, immigrants, foreigners, and progressives. Their masochism is reflected in their uncritical subservience to a higher cause or a strong leader with magical appeal, most visible in "the macho Jesus archetype" they worship. This view is corroborated by Chris Hedges (2006), who grew up steeped in the Bible and Christian tradition and has also researched and analyzed Christian fundamentalism. He worries about its growing influence in the government and the military and warns progressives that tolerance is not a characteristic of this movement, which he believes has fascistic inclinations: "Debate with the radical Christian Right is useless," he insists. "This movement seeks, in the name of Christianity and American democracy, to destroy that which it claims to defend...In the event of a crisis...the movement stands poised to manipulate fear and chaos ruthlessly and reshape America in ways that have not been seen since the nation's founding" (pp. 202, 207).

Another trend within evangelical Christianity, which scholar Jeff Sharlet (2009) calls "elite fundamentalism," has deep roots in the political leadership of this country. For the past 70-plus years this movement, known as the Family (sometimes also referred to as the National Fellowship Foundation, The National Fellowship Council, and C Street Center), has cultivated the powerful, key individuals they believe have been chosen by God to direct the affairs of the nation. The Family is associated with many influential leaders, including a number of senators and congresspersons, corporate executives, military officers, heads of religious and humanitarian aid organizations, ambassadors, and foreign leaders. According to David Kuo, former Special Assistant to Bush: "The Fellowship's reach into governments around the world is almost impossible to overstate or even grasp" (pp. 24–25). Many members of the Family who are prominent in the Washington political elite either reside in or frequent a residential center called C Street, situated close to Congress. Family congresspersons work to insert their Christian evangelical principles into legislation, as witnessed in their recent successful bipartisan effort to add an antiabortion amendment to the House Health Care Reform Bill. It is not likely to succeed because of the progressives in both houses, but it represents a strategy aimed at either sabotaging the passage of the health care bill because prochoice lawmakers will not vote for it or achieving a health care bill that contains a ban on public and private coverage for therapeutic abortions, thereby becoming the first legal impediment of a woman's right to choose since *Roe v. Wade* became the law of the land.

The political right are connected to and financially supported by conservative corporate financial interests active behind the scenes of these evangelical impingements on the political life of this country. In addition, Rush Limbaugh and other right-wing media figures circulate conspiracy theories and extremist ideas in the mainstream that create paranoia and hysteria and instigate militantly violent groups that advocate armed confrontation with the enemies they believe have stolen America from them. According to the Southern Poverty Law Center (2009), almost a decade after largely disappearing from public view, right-wing militias are emerging in large numbers around the country. Nativist organizations, like the Council of Conservative Citizens, have multiplied in many states to assail all those who are not part of European Christian America and its values. Militias are arming themselves, encouraged by right-wing media personalities predicting doom or the rise of socialism or a take-over of this government by a Marxist dictator. One law enforcement agency reports 50 new militia training groups, one composed of present and former police officers and soldiers.

Authorities around the country describe an increase in Patriot activities and propaganda. The radical right movement views the federal government as its primary enemy, especially since it is headed by a Black man. Obama's ethnicity dovetails with high levels of non-White immigration and a decline in the percentage of Whites in the United States to invoke a racist theme in the Patriot movement. Vigilante groups, such as the Minutemen Civil Defense Corps, have proliferated along the border as Whites defend themselves from what they view as the polluting effects of the Latino invasion of their music, their foods, their jobs, and their land. In April 2009, three Pittsburgh police officers were ambushed and murdered by an assailant who had written beforehand, "The only way we can rid ourselves of this evil is kill them in the streets. Kill them where they gather...if life ain't worth living anymore don't just kill yourself. Do something for your Country before you go. Go Kill Liberals!" (Pitt, 2009). This homegrown Christian fundamentalist terrorism is unsettling and could expand to infect the base who make up the Tea-Baggers, Birthers, and their kindred movements, whose fear of a centralized state with military power has them more convinced than ever of their right and need to arm themselves. Some are already threatening to return armed in future demonstrations against progressive Democratic representatives whom they mistakenly believe represent a socialist takeover of the government. Frank Schaeffer, whose father was a prominent figure in the evangelical movement during the 1980s, warns that these groups are like the U.S. Taliban. They make bumper stickers and T-shirts quoting psalms from the Old Testament demanding the elimination of the Obama presidency and the widowhood of Michelle Obama that function as thinly veiled death threats. Such activities are their version of a holy war, says Schaeffer (2009), who laments the fact that the Republican Party and religious leaders are not denouncing these scary religious fanatics.[24]

What are the long-range implications of this multifaceted right-wing movement that is growing in response to dislocating social and economic realities? One perspective raises concern about the potential for fascism in this country and bases its analysis on the work of historian Robert Paxton, a preeminent scholar of how countries become fascist. Paxton (1998) writes that while each fascist movement has its own national characteristics and particular evolution, they are all characterized by the fact that the passions rather than the intellect propel them. Their organizing principles include a conviction that their group is victimized, a dread of the group's potential decadence brought on by cosmopolitan liberalism, the unity and purity of a community forged by certainty and violence if necessary, the group's elevated and embellished status that bolsters individual self-esteem, and a presumed authority of natural leaders who incarnate the group's destiny. Factors that have facilitated the rise of fascism include polarization within civil society and an ineffectual, deadlocked performance of the political system. Some argue that this analysis is applicable to the United States today: The characteristics of fascist movements come close to describing the radical right that has taken over the Republican Party, as well as its economically disenfranchised, increasingly racist, and xenophobic Christian fundamentalist base. And given the dearth of potential leaders among the Republicans, Sarah Palin—whose psychology betrays regressed paranoid states that converge with simplistic ideological endorsements of patriotism, patriarchy, and religiosity—remains a charismatic attraction for the right wing in this country (see Kim & Reed, 2009). Most significantly, the Democratic Party fits the qualification of a liberal party in power that oversees a deadlocked political system: Even while it occupies the White House and has a majority in the Congress, it is proving itself ineffective in developing and implementing progressive reforms that adequately address the grave problems confronting most people in the country (see Robinson, 2009). Its incompetency—or complicity—and internal divisions may end up contributing to a future electoral victory by a more mobilized and passionately vigorous right-wing movement.

Another perspective on the possible political direction of this country is offered by political philosopher Sheldon W. Wolin (2003, 2008), who posits that the current political landscape may develop into what he calls "inverted totalitarianism." He examines the structural nature of the state and sees a picture somewhat different from classic totalitarianism constructed around a charismatic leader or demagogue. He suggests that our current situation is characterized by an anonymous corporate-run state that manipulates the electoral process so that the appearance of democracy is sustained. The state utilizes the ideology of patriotism to dominate a population effectively distracted by a mass media that controls all information and mystifies through illusion and spectacle. Wolin has recently articulated his fears that mounting discontent and social unrest might prompt greater state control and repression. He worries about the apolitical character of the majority of citizens whose bystander function could move the country in a dictatorial direction.[25] And as I have also argued, the goals of the political right are facilitated by how easily their rhetoric can simplistically connect with and reinforce internalized hegemonic ideology so as to mobilize the understandable fears of disenfranchised citizens in a self-defeating direction.

These sobering warnings about the potentially dangerous implications of the current political situation in this country are important to heed. However, they are only a piece of the story. There is also reason for hope in this time of despair. As Bauman (2007) puts it, "…it is the task of the living to keep hope alive; or rather to resurrect it in a rapidly changing world prominent for rapidly changing the conditions under which the ongoing struggle to make it more hospitable to humanity is conducted" (p. 160). Indeed, the dual delegitimization of empire and of market fundamentalism has created a bigger space for progressive global alternatives than has existed since the end of the Cold War. This is an opportune moment for the spread of progressive political and economic visions emerging from below. In the United States today, hundreds of thousands of left and progressive activists sustain many of the principles and values of the 1960s' antiwar, civil rights, and feminist movements, which they apply now to the new political challenges in this country. It is a multifaceted oppositional movement, demographically diverse in terms of age, ethnicity, genders, and geography, and it is active on a multiplicity of issues via many different organizations that mobilize locally and at the state and national level. The struggles against hegemony are decentralized and, as expected, less funded than the right wing. The 1960s' oppositional movements were visible in the popular imaginary, while today's activists, both more numerous and in some ways more politically sophisticated, are "disappeared" by a much more centralized corporate media hostile to their values and goals. Thus the general public has to be much more proactively engaged to learn about the movement, its critical perspectives, and its many activities. Its existence is ubiquitous on the more democratized Web-generated communication system, and in local venues it is visible throughout the country in public meetings, experiments in sustainable lifestyles, economic collectives, demonstrations demanding a host of progressive changes, and peace vigils.

In the course of writing this book, I began to collect articles, books, and online examples of the organizations and kinds of political struggles progressives are engaged in throughout the United States. My plan was to include them so as to demonstrate that there is, indeed, much to be hopeful about and to feel proud of. Alas, as I sit with them piled high on my desk, I realize that this task is much beyond the scope of these final pages. But for me one important theme that runs through all this activism is articulated by award-winning author Rebecca Solnit in her new book, *A Paradise Built in Hell: The Extraordinary Communities That Arise in Disaster* (2009). Solnit analyzes disasters that have occurred in the country and how, in contradistinction to expectations, while government often fails to constructively intervene, people themselves rise to the occasion and through improvisation form engaged communities and save lives, and do so with joy. Solnit writes of these spontaneous communities that act following disasters: "...The constellation of solidarity, altruism, and improvisation are within most of us and reappear at these times" (p. 10). I believe this to be true of progressive activism in general, and anyone who has been to a peace vigil or marched against war or participated in phone bank efforts on behalf of health care or in support of workers' rights or women's reproductive choice can attest to the positive feelings of self and group identity based on respect and caring rather than on hatred and fear.

This kind of activism is also transnational. Ulrich Beck (2008, 2009) postulates that the world risk society produces a reflexive capacity and a "cosmopolitan moment" that awakens actors of many kinds throughout the world to act on behalf of a globally endangered humanity. Because the anticipated state of emergency we face is global, not national or local, it activates and connects actors across borders in response to the uncontrollable liabilities that befall us all and motivate us to make border-transcending new beginnings outside the context of the agendas of particular nation-states. Beck (2008) suggests that

> ...the historical power of global risk is found in the recognition that the perceived risks facing humanity, which can be neither denied nor externalized...are capable of awakening the energies, the consensus, the legitimation necessary for creating a global community of fate, that will demolish the walls of nation-state borders and egotisms... (accessed July 15, 2009)

He critiques a Eurocentric cosmopolitanism and describes the many signs of what he sees as new forms of internationalism. According to Beck (1996), "subpolitics" sets all areas of society in motion in which "direct" politics or *ad hoc* individual participation bypasses formal institutions of opinion-formation to shape society from below. He describes successful coalitions of what are customarily assumed to be "forces 'totally' incapable of allying with one another" that win important ecological struggles against deregulated free-market capitalism (p. 18). Beck's analysis captures the current reality of many different kinds of organizations with international connections that collaborate in forums without borders and use the global reach provided by new information technologies to exchange data and analyses and to mobilize their constituencies. One good example of subpolitics is depicted in the extraordinarily compelling documentary film, *Crude* (Berlinger, 2009), a *cinéma-vérité* feature that follows the history of one of the largest and most controversial environmental lawsuits on the planet.[26] The case takes place in the Amazon jungle of Ecuador, pitting 30,000 indigenous rainforest dwellers against the U.S. oil giant Chevron. The filmmaker guides the audience through a high-stakes legal drama in which the plaintiffs claim that Texaco—which merged with Chevron in 2001—systematically contaminated one of the most biodiverse regions on earth, poisoning the water, air, and land and ruining the health and the culture of the local indigenous population. The film shows how this struggle has brought together a convergence of forces across national borders that include the environmental movement, celebrity activism, human rights advocacy and legal teams, the media, and the indigenous community. As of this writing the suit has not yet been settled, but the impact of the multi-faceted movement can be seen in a significant recent political development: Under the leadership of Ecuador's progressive indigenous President Rafael Correa, the Ecuadoran people just voted for a new national Constitution that contains articles guaranteeing nature the "right to exist, persist, maintain and regenerate its vital cycles, structure, functions and its processes in evolution" and mandating that the government take "precaution and restriction measures in all the activities that can lead to the extinction of species, the destruction of the ecosystems or the permanent alteration of the natural cycles" (Nueva Constitucion del Ecuador, 2009, articles 72 and 73; see also Community Environmental Legal Defense Fund, 2008). This struggle and one of its outcomes are indeed representative of what Ulrich Beck denotes as the "cosmopolitan moment."

There are also examples of a psychoanalysis beyond the couch that activates transnational efforts on behalf of peace and justice. An important example is the work of Vamik D. Volkan, M.D., Professor Emeritas of Psychiatry at the University of Virginia School of Medicine and Past President of the International Society of Political Psychology. Volkan has been working for many years on the project of integrating psychoanalytic concepts with historical and political analyses of large group behavior in conflict situations. His theoretical contributions are born in part out of his experiences in leading interdisciplinary teams to a number of trouble spots in the world, where he has facilitated ongoing dialogues among important representatives from contesting sides of large group conflicts. This activity, known as second-tier diplomacy, is a strategy designed to help members of opposing sides speak and listen to one another over time so as to recognize that they share similar emotional experiences, which motivate their violent engagement. The objective is to develop the empathy necessary to move from violence to peaceful negotiated resolutions of conflict. Second-tier diplomacy works with influential representatives of conflicting parties (ethnic, religious, or national groups) with the goal of influencing the primary decision makers. Volkan's work has produced many publications, in which he elaborates his theory that large groups suffer from chosen traumas, mental representations of a past event that by having caused groups to experience dramatic losses and humiliation at the hands of another group produce injured self-images and accompanying psychological needs for vengeance and hatred that can be mobilized by leaders who are intent on violent confrontation with an enemy (Volkan, 1999a,b,c, 2004, 2006). His most recent contribution to understanding the psychological aspects of political conflict is *Killing in the Name of Identity: A Study of Bloody Conflicts* (2006). Another important effort of psychoanalysts to affect national and international policy in a progressive direction that respects human rights is the International Psychoanalytic Association nongovernmental organization (NGO) that functions through the United Nations. A founding member of the group is Egyptian-born, New York–based Afaf Mahfouz. She is of Muslim background and was a political scientist and lawyer by training before she became a psychoanalyst. For the past 16 years Mahfouz has facilitated a discussion group on prejudice at the American Psychoanalytic Association (APsaA) annual meetings. The group's participants have explored topics such as anti-Semitism, sexism, racism, Islamaphobia, and Arabphobia. With a history of involvement in multiagency change internationally and substantial experience at the United Nations, when in 1998 the International Psychoanalytic Association (IPA) became an NGO with consultative status at the United Nations, Mahfouz was asked to be the chair. She and colleague Argentine-born New York psychoanalyst Isaac Tylim have worked to assure that the IPA is present when the United Nations discusses issues relevant to mental health concerns, including human rights, women's rights, and children's rights. Their efforts are also dedicated to assuring that the mental health dimension will be included in international treaties, such as the U.N. Treaty for the Protection of Children. The IPA committee, composed of five psychoanalysts residing in New York, enjoys the input of colleagues from all over the world who send feedback and attend meetings during the IPA and APsaA conferences in New York. Mahfouz and her colleagues advocate and lobby enthusiastic and reluctant governments alike to support women's reproductive health rights and to protect women against domestic violence. "Mainly," says Mahfouz, "we bring the perspective of psychoanalysis to the various U.N. committees and government representatives, all of whom are very receptive to our psychoanalytic perspectives that in part we convey through presentations of individual cases and interpretations that are meant to teach how to think about the psychological implications of problematic institutions and structures in the social world."[27]

Another example of a psychoanalysis beyond the couch that attends to international issues is a group called Psychoanalytic Work Group for Peace in Palestine/Israel. The group was formed by Nadia Ramsy, a clinical psychoanalyst in private practice in St. Louis, Missouri, and Faculty Member of the St. Louis Psychoanalytic Institute. She is also editor-in-chief (with Stuart Twemlow) of the *International Journal of Applied Psychoanalytic Studies* and leads a discussion group at APsaA annual meetings on the application of psychoanalytic thinking to social problems. Always interested in the psychosocial dynamics of the "intractable conflict" between Israeli Jews and Palestinians, after meeting George Awad, a Toronto-based Palestinian psychoanalyst, at the IPA meeting in New Orleans in 2004, Ramsy organized several public dialogues between Awad and Israeli psychoanalytic psychologist Carlo Strenger at the APsaA meetings and an interdisciplinary conference on prejudice in Utah in 2005. With consultation from Lord John Alderdice, a trained mental health professional crucial during a 10-year period in the process leading to a resolution of the "troubles" between Britain and Northern Ireland, Ramsy formed a group of psychoanalysts and psychologists that over several years came to include North American Arab and Jewish psychoanalysts, Palestinian and Jewish Israeli psychoanalysts, and psychoanalytically oriented Palestinian psychologists. Informed by Alderdice's experience, the group's guiding principles are mutual respect, empathy, and inclusion. The goal has been to engage in commentary and discourse with other psychoanalysts that have the potential to lead to social action in the interest of peace and justice in the Middle East. In their presentations at the APsaA and Division 39 meetings, group members have offered dialogues among themselves so as to model empathic speaking and listening among individuals with different perspectives on this highly contentious subject. Over the course of almost five years of presenting at professional meetings, the group has witnessed a change in attitudes, including some alteration of prejudice in hitherto automatic pro-Israel and anti-Palestinian attitudes. The group process is focused on the application of a psychoanalytic attitude as a source of understanding the nature and functions of prejudice. According to Ramsy, "The group process is an in-depth experience in the conscious and unconscious dynamics involved in this geopolitical conflict. It is in the microcosm of the group process that we experience and sometimes enact at the personal level the lived experience of this complex social conflict. By engaging in and observing the process of the small group we gain a deep level of understanding of the dynamics of the large-scale social process as it is experienced and expressed by two traumatized peoples." Ramsy believes that over time the group's activities have enhanced the capacity of its audiences to reflect on their own attitudes and to understand the dynamics in which we all participate that move our society in the direction of conflict and war rather than peace. The group has been engaged in defining its own version of second-tier diplomacy,[28] whose goal is to facilitate citizens becoming active in pressing the U.S. government to assume a more reasoned and tolerant discourse and policy in the region.[29]

This is the kind of psychoanalysis in which Hedda Bolgar finds great solace. Several months ago in August 2009, Hedda marked her 100th birthday. There were many celebratory gatherings in Los Angeles and at the International Psychoanalytic Association meeting in Chicago. After the partying subsided, Hedda settled in to this period of her life, ready for new projects and for taking stock of her personal century on this earth. "I'm spending lots of time reviewing my life," she told me, "sometimes in the middle of the night when I can't sleep, and it's dark and quiet and there's nothing else I have to do. I go through things in my mind that I'd never considered important before and I have the feeling that everything is very clear about the past, about my life, about me. Sometimes I think about how some psychoanalytic values in my earlier years, including the American emphasis on self-reliance or its unquestioned assumptions about gender, for example, not infrequently made my personal choices more conflicted." When I asked her about the psychological impact of reviewing one's life, she answered, "Well, it requires a willingness to take the risk of feeling regretful. You know, 'I wish I'd been more aware of...' or 'I wish I'd made the time for...' You have to be able to live with regret about what you see as your failings with others who have been significant in your life. There are reparative compensations, you could say. In my case, I have built a world of relationships and I feel there are a lot of people I have given to or impacted on or helped. I have learned to listen very carefully to people and to be really available to them. So while there's no way of directly repairing some things one feels regretful about, there's reparation in the humanity of a life well lived." As I listened to Hedda, I thought of Mimi Langer, whose untimely death at the age of 76 came when she was experiencing the optimism of her socially relevant psychoanalytic work in the context of the Sandinista Revolution. And I wondered aloud with Hedda what it feels like to be 100 in a world that seems so filled with problems that deeply uproot our minds. "Well, we haven't talked about my Buddhism," she replied. "It's a sense of connectedness to everything in the universe: with nature, people, animals, even trees! I can't define it exactly, but for me this is an extremely benign experience that in some completely irrational way makes it possible to endure this complex, painful, disorganizing and disorganized political situation. I am looking at the future with ideas and with hope and curiosity. But I do feel that I live very much in the present, and this is connected to something else Buddhism has taught me: the impermanence of things. Everything changes, everything passes, so that when bad or good things happen they don't last forever. When you get to be 100, I think wisdom comes from not being too attached to things and learning to live with complexity."

Meanwhile, Hedda's professional life continues apace, with her clinical practice and a new interest in developing a much-neglected track in psychoanalytic training programs dealing with the challenges and meanings of aging. She is also engaged as a member of the Uprooted Mind Committee in the coalition of groups invited by the Los Angeles Institute and Society for Psychoanalytic Studies (LAISPS) Trauma Center to organize a conference in Los Angeles on Psychoanalysis in the Community for the fall of 2010. It should come as no surprise that Hedda continues to endorse a militant politics of the streets to achieve much-needed change in our society. She recently wrote in the context of women's struggles:

> I would like to really become an activist again and let me remind you that our ancestors, the suffragettes, were activists, they were out in the streets, they were chained to trees, they were force-fed, they really put their bodies on the line. I would like to see the women's movement become active again and really try to do what it was supposed to do originally—improve society and improve the world. (2009, p. 199)

Indeed, the women's movement is active throughout this country and around the globe, with a surfeit of struggles organized on behalf of female legal, cultural, sexual, reproductive, domestic, and psychological rights. Some of the most significant contributions to the ecology movement are coming from feminist narratives and activism that explain from different perspectives the inevitable link between the liberation of women from patriarchy and the liberation of nature from technical-industrial domination. (see Plant, 1989; Shiva, 1988; Haraway, 1971)

* * *

Following upon the horrors of World War I and continuing evidence of the human capacity for destructiveness, Freud published *Civilization and its Discontents* (1929), in which he postulated:

> The fateful question for the human species seems to me to be whether and to what extent their cultural development will succeed in mastering the disturbance of their communal life by the human instinct of aggression and self-destruction...[Men] know this, and hence comes a large part of their current unrest, their unhappiness and their mood of anxiety. (p. 145)

Freud went on to wonder whether the other force that drives humanity—eros, the capacity for love and connection—could contain the aggression that might otherwise be our undoing. Although we may approach Freud's question from a variety of theoretical perspectives, it is *our* fateful question as well. It is difficult to be positive in these often despairing times. But it is equally difficult to live without hope that we may bequeath to our children a world in which they can flourish and find meaning and pleasure in new social arrangements. But this hope requires effort. To be a bystander is to inadvertently take a stand, one that we cannot afford in this negatively globalized world. Perhaps historian Howard Zinn says it best: You can't be neutral on a moving train.

Although it is important to sustain awareness of the difficult challenges we face, I have found through my experiences in Latin America and in the United States that it is empowering to have a belief in a more just and equitable world and to engage with others in trying to actualize it. With all the frustrations that come along the way—and there are many—there is great gratification in the experience. I always remember what Mimi Langer told me about her ongoing commitment to her version of psychoanalysis without the couch in the context of the Sandinista Revolution: "If I go to Nicaragua I think I am not lying to myself, although I know of the existing contradictions. I try to weigh things up and say that, despite the contradictions, I am in favor of the Sandinista Revolution, because the positive far outweighs the negative." Mimi was willing to struggle with the complex reality that we imperfect souls live in an imperfect world and our reparative endeavors are themselves imperfect. In a related vein, Hanna Segal writes of the distinction between operating on the basis of idealization and acting in a manner that is guided by ideals. The first constitutes a distortion inevitably accompanied by splitting and projection. To possess ideals is different, she argues: "It is not pathological to hope for a better future, for instance, for peace, and to strive for it, whilst recognizing how hard it is to attain, and that the opposition to it comes not only from others but also has its roots in ourselves" (Peltz, 2005, p. 348). Segal is referring to depressive position capacities that permit the subject to tolerate the ambiguity and complexity of reality, to rely less on splitting, projection, and omnipotent control over others, to take responsibility and feel guilt for one's own aggressive impulses, and to make creative reparation. These capacities can be realized in part through engagement in efforts to move society toward structures and relations of equity and justice.

Psychoanalysts are contributing to this movement as citizens; and as clinicians, they can participate in the process our Latin American colleagues call "ethical nonneutrality" by opening up the psychoanalytic endeavor to considerations that include the social. This stance permits the psychoanalytic relationship to provide a crucial environment in which the unthinkable can be thought and elaborated in order to promote the integration of knowledge and affective experience on behalf of agency. Moral imagination and hope reside in the detailed and caring cultivation of knowing in the service of achieving reparative capacities, not only in intimate relationships but in one's connection with the social world and the earth as well. So, when my attention is grabbed by the inexplicably awesome beauties of life or the extraordinary actions of ordinary people that demonstrate human goodness, joy rather than terror triumphs. At such times it seems possible that we human beings will be able to contain our aggression so that empathy and understanding prevail enough of the time to dig down roots of new sustainable social relations and respect for the earth. And it is then that I take comfort and pleasure in the words of Indian feminist writer and activist Arundhati Roy: "Not only is another world possible, she is on her way. On a quiet day, I can hear her breathing."

ENDNOTES

1. For an analysis of the 2008 election voting trends by race, class, gender, and geography, see Davis (2009).
2. See Ashbach (2009) and Bion (1959a). For several different psychoanalytic perspectives on leadership, see the International Journal of Applied Psychoanalytic Studies, 5(3) and 6(2), and also Volkan (2004).
3. Public lecture sponsored by Robert Greenwald Brave New Films, November 10, 2009, Santa Monica, CA.
4. See Prins and Hayes (2009) for the argument and analysis of the full Troubled Asset Relief Program (TARP) payment and subsidy being close to $17.5 trillion and the implications for average citizens. There is some indication as of late

October 2009 about a crack in the ideological consensus that the banks must be saved and enabled to prosper. Although it is too early to tell if this is mere rhetoric, former Chairmen of the Federal Reserve Bank Alan Greenspan and Arthur Volker are calling for a break-up of big banks. Greenspan condemned Wall Street executives for "reckless speculation and deceptive practices and short sightedness and self-interestedness from a few" (Schechter, 2009).

5. Progressive economists, including Jack Rasmus, James Galbraith, Joseph Stiglitz, Dean Baker, Paul Krugman, and Michael Whitney, all argued that the strategy and amount of the stimulus package were inadequate, especially since it contained no massive public works and conservation projects to employ the millions of citizens without jobs and still losing them. This lack reflected an underappreciation for the magnitude and structural nature of what threatens to be a long recession with true "recovery" not even on the horizon.

6. Ian Masters' radio interview with Michael Lind of the New American Foundation, who argues that the real unemployment rate is nearing 20 percent (Background Briefing, KPFK-FM, October 25, 2009); see also Lind (2009). Elizabeth Warren (2009), Chair of the Congressional Oversight Panel, warns that the United States is losing the middle class: "Today, one in five Americans is unemployed, underemployed or just plain out of work. One in nine families can't make the minimum payment on their credit cards. One in eight mortgages is in default or foreclosure. One in eight Americans is on food stamps. More than 120,000 families are filing for bankruptcy every month. The economic crisis has wiped more than $5 trillion from pensions and savings, has left family balance sheets upside down, and threatens to put ten million homeowners out on the street."

7. Turley went further to criticize citizens who watch the nightly exposé of the Bush administration's illegal rush to war and its use of torture: "What's in question is the politics, and most importantly, whether the citizens of this country will understand that they can't simply treat Cheney like some Darth Vader who controls their thoughts and actions. It is equally immoral to stand silent in the face of a war crime and do nothing, and that is what the citizens are doing" (December 16, 2008). Critics of President Obama's changes to the regulations governing military commissions are characterizing these changes as "cosmetic improvements," amid a growing consensus among human rights organizations that these tribunals are designed to produce convictions, while trials in civilian courts are far more likely to produce justice. Investigative journalist William Fisher (2009) writes, "It is immoral to stand silent in the face of a war crime and do nothing. Because, you see, the bodies were burned and dumped. They—the CIA—are Nazis for committing the crimes. And we are Nazis for not giving a damn" (accessed November 12, 2009).

8. For an analysis of the histories of Obama's selected military advisors and their involvement in prior decades of U.S. adventures from Nicaragua to Indonesia to Iraq, see Zunes (2009).

9. For a discussion of Rand Corporation and other think-tank analyses of the pressures and perils on the Afghanistan strategy, see McGovern (2009).

10. Obama's speech announcing his Afghanistan policy utilized traditional themes of American Exceptionalism, rationalizing the escalation of the war in a self-congratulatory, idealized interpretation of a U.S. humanitarian and selfless foreign policy.

11. Scott Atran, anthropologist at the National Center for Scientific Research in Paris, John Jay College, and the University of Michigan, and author of the forthcoming *Listen to the Devil*, is one example of many social scientists who study a variety of cultures and their belief systems, social networks, and psychological patterns and argue that military occupation is the wrong strategy to combat contemporary terrorism among Muslims. They suggest instead intelligence and security operations that can constructively intervene on the basis of educated awareness and respect for indigenous cultural practices and perspectives that motivate retaliatory violence. See, for example, Atran (2007).

12. Johnson (2009) notes one of our most abject failures as a government and a democracy: "There is virtually no news coverage—no journalists' or editors' curiosity—about the pressures or lures at work when the U.S. government seeks to persuade officials of Romania, Aruba or Ecuador that providing U.S. military-basing access would be good for their countries." Of the some 865 bases located in all the continents except Antarctica, Johnson laments that "the American public, if not the residents of the territories in question, is almost totally innocent of the huge costs involved, the crimes committed by our soldiers against women and children in the occupied territories, the environmental pollution, and the deep and abiding suspicions generated among people forced to live close to thousands of heavily armed, culturally myopic and dangerously indoctrinated American soldiers."

13. The Bolivarian Alliance for the Peoples of Our America (ALBA) is another hemispheric cooperation strategy aimed at regional economic integration based on principles of social welfare. For information on current developments in Latin America, see monthly publications of the North American Congress of Latin America's Report on the Americas, upsidedownworld (http://upsidedownworld.org/main/), and ZNet (http://www.zmag.org/znet). See also the James Petras Web site (http://lahaine.org/petras/).

14. Several examples are Progressive Democrats of America, MoveOn.org, Office of the Americas, Interfaith Coalition for Peace and Justice, Iraq Vets Against the War, ANSWER Coalition, Public Citizen, Campaign for America's Future, Progressives for Obama, Code Pink, and Global Exchange.

15. Freedom Works has mobilized the movement known as the "Tea-Baggers" and is chaired by former U.S. House Majority Leader Dick Armey.

16. For example, see the Americans for Prosperity Web site, which is funding the mobilization of anti–health care reform activities from the right, like "Hands Off My Health Care Bus Tour"; a multimillionaire activist pays for much of this. The World Net Daily, a right-wing group that has ties to Republican representatives, is waging an anti-Muslim campaign in the Congress.

17. In this article Johnson elaborates what he calls the budgetary sleight of hand that accounts for much unrecorded military allocations of tax dollars.

18. For a number of flagging quality of life indexes for the United States, see American Human Development Project of the Social Science Research Council (2009). See also Klare (2009) for a summary of the events that demonstrate the more rapid decline of U.S. preeminence than predicted by the CIA.

19. See Beyondpeak.com (www.beyondpeak.com/scenarios/winners.html), which includes many articles arguing on the positive potential of peak oil.

20. Psychologists for Social Responsibility recently wrote a letter to members of Congress, urging them to take measures to contain global warming and elucidating for them the psychological costs of climate change already observable in the population and likely to become worse. For information on this letter and campaign, as well as additional activities of this important national organization, see their Web site, http://psysr.org/.

21. The U.S. Defense Department has sponsored various studies to assess many of the issues under discussion. However, the lens through which they view these threats to humanity is the limited one of national security. For them the main question has to do with how the U.S. military will protect U.S. interests and maintain stability. One example is the study by the Strategic Studies Institute of the U.S. Army War College (Freier, 2008, p. 16). It suggests that the changing nature of the world is defined mostly by its unpredictability, so that the defense of the United States should be thought about outside the traditional box. Titled "Known Unknowns: Unconventional 'Strategic Shocks' in Defense Strategy Development," the report warns the Defense Department that the likeliest and most dangerous future challenges will be unconventional, demanding a reevaluation of defense-relevant strategies. The report concludes: "The most challenging defense-relevant shocks might emerge from...the unguided forces of globalization, toxic populism, identity politics, underdevelopment, human/natural disaster, and disease. In the end, shocks emerging from contextual threats might challenge core U.S. interests more fundamentally than any number of prospective purposeful shocks." Michael Klare reports that based on CIA forecasts for 2025, it seems that the government is interested in determining national security issues and what the defense forces will have to do to protect the country rather than initiating a constructive international reparative effort. The U.S. government and the think tanks it employs are concerned about the status of the United States and busy assessing the nature and extent of future challenges. Some intelligence sources agree that there will be a significant international realignment over the next several decades. For example, in early 2005, the National Intelligence Council (2005) released a report, "Mapping the Global Future," in which it predicted that while the United States will remain an important actor in the global community in 2020, its relative power position will have eroded. This process, they predict, will be facilitated by an exclusion or isolation of the United States by emerging powers, including China, India, Brazil, Indonesia, and others. After noting many problematic shifts and challenges represented by political and economic developments in the next several decades, the report concludes with the optimistic view that "for all the challenges ahead, the United States will nevertheless retain enormous advantages, playing a pivotal role across the broad range of

issues—economic, technological, political, and military—that no other state can or will match by 2020. Even as the existing order is threatened, the United States will have many opportunities to fashion a new one" (p. 119).

The Oath Keepers began as an apparently contrary development in the military and police forces, a nonpartisan association of currently serving military, reserves, National Guard, peace officers, fire fighters, and veterans who swore an oath to support and defend the Constitution against all enemies, foreign and domestic: "We won't 'just follow orders.'" The Web site lists orders the group will not follow, including any order to detain American citizens as "unlawful enemy combatants" or to subject them to trial by military tribunal. For more information on this group, see http://oathkeepers.org/oath/2009/03/03/declaration-of-orders-we-will-not-obey. Since Obama's election, new members increasingly include right-wing military and police identified with the birthers, truthers, tea partiers, and their ilk. Their interpretation of the Constitution as well as their perspective on Obama's dubious presidential authority will be seen through that lens. They are armed and organizing. See Justine Sharrock, "Oath Keepers," *Mother Jones*, March/April 2010.

22. The full text of this speech can be found online at http://www.msnbc.msn.com/id/34360743/ns/politics-white_house/page/4/.

23. Alfredo Astiz, an ex-navy captain dubbed the "Blond Angel of Death," has gone on trial in Argentina with 18 others for kidnapping and torture during the military's "Dirty War." Human rights activists point out that the years of amnesty for Astiz and other defendants provided by former Argentine governments has cost untold human effort and money to bring these perpetrators to justice. It may be that human rights advocates in the United States face a similar problem because the clear abusive techniques, including waterboarding, used by the Bush administration to extract information from detainees clearly violated the Convention Against Torture, which should have triggered a governmental investigation and prosecution of the offenders. However, that treaty obligation has so far been violated by the Obama administration, which is resisting calls for government investigations; instead it is going to court to block lawsuits that demand release of torture evidence or seek civil penalties against officials implicated in the torture. Jameel Jaffer, director of the American Civil Liberties Union's National Security Project, said to reporters that although "the Bush administration constructed a legal framework for torture, now the Obama administration is constructing a legal framework for impunity...On every front, the [Obama] administration is actively obstructing accountability. This administration is shielding Bush administration officials from civil liability, criminal investigation and even public scrutiny for their role in authorizing torture" (Leopold, 2009).

24. Schaeffer was interviewed on The Rachael Maddow Show, November 17, 2009.

25. Bauman (2007, chapter 5) discusses the devolution of the "social state" to the "security state," which he views as conducive to a new type of totalitarianism.

26. For screening and purchase information on *Crude*, see www.crudethemovie.com. One continual source of audio and visual reportage that communicates the diverse progressive voices and movements throughout the world is the

acclaimed program, "Democracy Now," hosted by Amy Goodman on radio and television. The Web site for current programming and archival research is www.democracynow.org/.

27. Interview, September 22, 2009.
28. Second-tier diplomacy refers to the work done by mental health professionals, mediators, and others with individuals who are members of groups in conflict situations. The objective is to help those motivated to collaborate in understanding the psychopolitical dynamics of conflict so that they may in turn positively influence those in power. One well-known psychoanalyst who has worked in this capacity is Vamik D. Volkan (1999a, 1999b, 1999c).
29. Interview, September 14, 2009.

References

Abudar, O., Amati, S., Aragones, R. J., Arias, L. R., Berkowiez, L. B., & Bodni, O. (1986). *Argentina psicoanálisis represión política*. Buenos Aires, Argentina: Ediciones Kargieman.

Abuelas de Plaza de Mayo. (1995). *Filiación, identidad, restitución: 15 años de lucha de Abuelas de Plaza de Mayo*. Buenos Aires, Argentina: El Bloque Editorial.

Achugar, H. (1993). Postdictatorship, democracy, and culture in the Uruguay of the eighties. In S. Sosnowski & L. B. Popkin (Eds.), *Repression, exile, and democracy*. Durham, NC: Duke University Press.

Adorno, T. W., Frenkel-Brunswik, E., Levinson, D. J., & Sanford, R. N. (1982). *The authoritarian personality*. New York: W. W. Norton & Co.

Agosín, M., & Galmozzi, M. B. (2008). *Surviving beyond fear*. Buffalo, NY: White Pine Press.

Akhtar, S. (1995). A third individuation: Immigration, identity, and the psychoanalytic process. *Journal of the American Psychoanalytic Association, 4*, 1051–1083.

Alford, C. F. (1989). *Melanie Klein and critical social theory*. New Haven, CT: Yale University Press.

Alford, C. F. (1990). Reparation and civilization: A Kleinian account of the large group. *Free Associations, 1*, 7–30.

Altemeyer, R. (1996). *The authoritarian specter*. Cambridge, MA: Harvard University Press.

Althusser, L. (1984). Ideology and ideological state apparatuses (Notes towards an investigation). In S. Zizek (Ed.), *Mapping ideology* (pp. 100–140). London: Verso, 1994.

Altman, N. (1995). *The analyst in the inner city: Race, class, and culture through a psychoanalytic lens*. Hillsdale, NJ: The Analytic Press.

Altman, N. (2008). The psychodynamics of torture. *Psychoanalytic Dialogues, 18*(5), 658–670.

American Civil Liberties Union. (2007, January 17). No real threat: The Pentagon's secret database on peaceful protest. Retrieved April 20, 2009, from http://www.aclu.org/national-security/no-real-threat-pentagons-secret-database-peaceful-protest.

American Human Development Project of the Social Science Research Council. (2009). Factoids. www.measureofamerica.org/2008-2009-report/factoids/.

American Psychological Association. (2008, December 4). Financial concerns top list of holiday stressors for women, families with children. Retrieved January 26, 2009, from http://www.apa.org/releases/holiday-1208.html.

Americas Watch (1985). *Human rights in Nicaragua: Reagan, rhetoric and reality.* New York: Author.

Amnesty International. (1982). *Disappearances: A workbook.* London: Author.

Amnesty International. (1984). *Torture in the eighties.* London: Author.

Argentine National Commission on the Disappeared (1986). *Nunca más.* New York: Farrar, Straus & Giroux.

Aron, L. (2001). *A meeting of minds: Mutuality in psychoanalysis.* Hillsdale, NJ: The Analytic Press.

Ashbach, C. (2009). A group dynamics approach to understanding America's current "collapse." *Psychologist-Psychoanalyst,* 9–12.

Asociación Psicoanalítica Argentina. (1982). *APA, 1942–1982.* Buenos Aires, Argentina: Author.

Associated Press. (2009, July 15). Army: Violence by GIs at home tied to combat. Retrieved August 29, 2009, from www.commondreams.org/headline/2009/07/15-10.

Atran, S. (2007). Terrorism and radicalization: What not to do, what to do. Retrieved December 1, 2009, from www.edge.org/3rd_culture/Atran07/index.html.

Bacevich, A. J. (Ed.). (2009). *The long war: A new history of U.S. national security policy since World War II.* New York: Columbia University Press.

Bageant, J. (2007). *Deerhunting with Jesus: Dispatches from America's class war.* New York: Crown Publishers.

Bakan, J. (2004). *The corporation: The pathological pursuit of profit and power.* Free Press: New York.

Baker, D. (2006). *The conservative nanny state: How the wealthy use the government to stay rich and get richer.* Raleigh, NC: Lulu.

Baker, D. (2008). CEPR fact sheet: The cost of war. Center for Economic Policy Research. Retrieved September 20, 2009, from www.cepr.net/index.php/dean-bakers-publications/.

Baker, D. (2009, October 7). Debunking the dumping-the-dollar conspiracy. Center for Economic Policy Research. Retrieved November 2, 2009, from www.cepr.net/index.php/op-eds-&-columns/op-eds-&-columns/debunking-the-dumping-the-dollar-conspiracy/.

Balán, J. (1991). *Cuéntame tu vida: Una biografía colective del psicoanálisis argentine.* Buenos Aires, Argentina: Planeta Espejo de la Argentina.

Barber, B. (1996). *Jihad vs. McWorld: How globalism and tribalism are reshaping the world.* New York: Random House.

Barofsky, N. (2009, October 25). *New York Times Week in Review,* 2.

Bauman, Z. (2007). *Liquid fear.* Cambridge, UK: Polity Press.

Beck, U. (1996). World risk society as cosmopolitan society? Ecological questions in a framework of manufactured uncertainties. *Theory, Culture & Society, 13,* 18.

Beck, U. (2008, November 12). Risk society's "cosmopolitan moment." Lecture at Harvard University, Cambridge, MA.

Beck, U. (2009). *World at risk.* Cambridge, UK: Polity Press.

Bendfeldt-Zachrisson, F. (1988). Torture as intensive repression in Latin America: The psychology of its methods and practice. *International Journal of Health Services, 18*(2), 201–310.

Berlinger, J. (Director). (2009). *Crude* [Motion picture]. United States: Entendre Films.

Bigliani, C., Bigliani, L., & Capdouze, L. E. (1971). Dependencia y autonomía en la formación psicoanalítica. In M. Langer, *Cuestionamos I*. Buenos Aires, Argentina: Gránica Editor.

Binion, R. (1976). *Hitler among the Germans*. New York: Elsevier.

Bion, W. R. (1959). *Experiences in groups*. New York: Basic Books.

Bion, W. R. (1961). *Experiences in groups: And other papers*. New York: Routledge.

Bion, W. R. (1962). *Learning from experience*. New York: Basic Books.

Bion, W. R. (1967). *Second thoughts*. New York: Aronson.

Black, G. (1988). *The good neighbor: How the U.S. wrote the history of Central America and the Caribbean*. New York: Pantheon.

Bleichmar, S. (1995). Traumatismo: Apropiación—Restitución. In Abuelas de Plaza de Mayo, *Filiación, identidad, restitución* (pp. 107–114). Buenos Aires, Argentina: El Bloque Editorial.

Bloom, C., Gitter, A., Gutwill, S., Kogel, L., & Zaphiropoulos, L. (1994). *Eating problems: A feminist psychoanalytic treatment model*. New York: Basic Books.

Blumenthal, M. (2009). *Republican Gomorrah: Inside the movement that shattered the party*. New York: Nation Books.

Boggs, C. (1984). *The two revolutions: Gramsci and the dilemmas of Western Marxism*. Cambridge, UK: South End Press.

Bolgar, H. (2001). An endless becoming. In J. Reppen (Ed.), *Why I became a psychotherapist* (pp. 39–49). Northvale, NJ: Jason Aronson.

Bolgar, H. (2002). When the glass is full. *Psychoanalytic Inquiry, 22*, 640–651.

Bolgar, H. (2009). A century of essential feminism. *Studies in Gender and Sexuality, 10*(4), 195–199.

Bollas, C. (1992). *Being a character*. Scarborough, ON: HarperCollins.

Bono (2009, October 17). *New York Times*. Retrieved October 15, 2000, from www.nytimes.com/2009/10/18/opinion/18bono.html.

Bottinelli, M. C., & Maldonado, I. (1990). *Psychological impacts of exile: Salvadoran and Guatemalan families in Mexico*. Washington, DC: Hemispheric Migration Project, Center for Immigration Policy and Refugee Assistance, Georgetown University.

Boulanger, G. (2007). *Wounded by reality: Understanding and treating adult onset trauma*. Mahwah, NJ: The Analytic Press.

Boulanger, G. (2008). Witnesses to reality: Working psychodynamically with survivors. *Psychoanalytic Dialogues, 18*(5), 638–657.

Bourdieu, P. (1998, December). Utopia of endless exploitation: The essence of neoliberalism. *Le Monde Diplomatique*.

Braun, J. (2004). Argentina: A laboratory of social experience. *Mind and Human Interaction, 13*(3), 214–221.

Bronstein, A. (1982). *The triple struggle: Latin American peasant women*. Birmingham, UK: WOW Campaigns.

Bronsther, J. (2009, 29 September). What do neocons have to do with Obama? *The Christian Science Monitor*.

Brown, C. (1985). *With friends like these*. New York: Pantheon Books.

Brown, W. (2003). Neoliberalism and the end of liberal democracy. *Theory & Event, 7*(1).

Brown, W. (2006). American nightmare: Neoliberalism, neoconservatism, and de-democratization. *Political Theory, 34,* 696.

Bunster, X. (1993). Surviving beyond fear: Women and torture in Latin America. In M. Agosín, (Ed.), *Surviving beyond fear: Women, children, and human rights in Latin America.* Fredonia, NY: White Pine Press.

Burns, E. B. (1987). *At war in Nicaragua: The Reagan doctrine and the politics of nostalgia.* New York: Harper & Row.

Burns, E. B. (1990). *Latin America: A concise interpretive history.* Englewood Cliffs, NJ: Prentice-Hall.

Butler, J., Laclau, E., & Zizek, S. (2000). *Contingency, hegemony, universality: Contemporary dialogues on the left.* London: Verso.

Cardoso, F. H., & Faletto, E. (1979). *Dependency and development in Latin America.* Berkeley, CA: University of California Press.

Carlson, M. (2008). A tragedy and a miracle: Leonor Alonso and the human cost of state terrorism in Argentina. In M. Agosín & M. B. Galmozzi (Eds.), *Surviving beyond fear* (pp. 71–85). Buffalo, NY: White Pine Press.

Caruth, C. (1995). An interview with Robert Jay Lifton. In *Trauma: Explorations in memory* (pp. 128–150). Baltimore: Johns Hopkins University Press.

Caruth, C. (2001). An interview with Jean LaPlanche. Retrieved March 13, 2009, from http://pmc.iath.virginia.edu/text-only/issue.101/11.2caruth.txtLaplanche.

Castañeda, J. G. (1994). *Utopia unarmed: The Latin American left after the Cold War.* New York: Vintage Books.

Castillo, M. C. (1979). *Fuerzas armadas: Etica y repression.* Buenos Aires, Argentina: Editorial Nuevo Orden.

Chavkin, S. (1982). *The murder of Chile.* New York: Everest House.

Chavkin, S. (1989). *Storm over Chile: The junta under siege.* Chicago: Hill.

Chomsky, N. (1985). *Turning the tide: U.S. intervention in Central America and the struggle for peace.* Boston: South End Press.

Chomsky, N. (2002). *Manufacturing consent: The political economy of the mass media.* New York: Pantheon.

Chomsky, N. (2003). *Hegemony or survival? America's quest for global domination.* New York: Henry Holt and Co.

Cohn, M. (2006, October 13). American prison camps are on the way. Retrieved October 30, 2007, from http://www.alternet.org/.

Cohn, M. (2007). *Cowboy republic: Six ways the Bush gang has defied the law.* Sausalito, CA: PoliPoint Press.

Cohn, M. (2009, March 4). Memos provide blueprint for police state. *Truthdig.* Retrieved April 3, 2009, from http://www.truthdig.com/report/item/20090304_nine_torture_memos_released/.

Collins, J. (1986). *What difference could a revolution make? Food and farming in the new Nicaragua.* San Francisco: Institute for Food and Development Policy.

Community Environmental Legal Defense Fund. (2008, September 28). Ecuador approves new constitution: Voters approve rights of nature. Retrieved November 22, 2009, from www.celdf.org/Default.aspx?tabid=548.

Constable, P., & Valenzuela, A. (1991). *A nation of enemies: Chile under Pinochet.* New York: Norton.

Coontz, S. (1992). *The way we never were*. New York: Basic Books.

Corradi, J. E. (1985). *The fitful republic: Economy, society, and politics in Argentina*. Boulder, CO: Westview Press.

Curtis, A. (Director). (2004). *The power of nightmares: The rise of the politics of fear* [Television broadcast]. London: BBC.

Cushman, P. (1995). *Constructing the self, constructing America: A cultural history of psychotherapy*. New York: Perseus.

Dalal, F. (2001). The social unconscious: A post-Foulkesian perspective. *Group Analysis, 34*(4), 547–548.

Dalton, R. (1984). *Poemas clandestinos (clandestine poems)*. San Francisco: Solidarity Publications.

Danner, M. (2004). *Torture and truth: America, Abu Ghraib, and the war on terror*. New York: New York Review of Books.

Danto, E. A. (1998). The ambulatorium: Freud's free clinic in Vienna. *International Journal of Psychoanalysis, 79*, 287–300.

Danto, E. A. (2005). *Freud's free clinics: Psychoanalysis and social justice, 1918–1938*. New York: Columbia University Press.

Davies, J. M. & Frawley, M. G. (1994). *Treating the adult survivor of childhood sexual abuse*. New York: Basic Books.

Davis, M. (2009). Obama at Manassas. *New Left Review, 56*, 5–40.

Dean, J. (2006). *Conservatives without conscience*. New York: Penguin Group.

Dean, J. (2008, November 1). It is now absolutely crystal clear that Republican rule is dangerous and authoritarian. Retrieved November 1, 2008, from http://www.alternet.org/.

Debray, R. (1971). *The Chilean revolution conversations with Allende*. New York: Pantheon Books.

Deere, C. D., & León, M. (1987). *Rural women and state policy*. Boulder, CO: Westview Press.

Dery, M. (1999). *The pyrotechnic insanitarium*. New York: Grove.

Dicks, H. (1972). *Licensed mass murder: A socio-psychological study of some SS killers*. New York: Basic Books.

Drake, P. W. (1978). *Socialism and populism in Chile, 1932–1952*. Urbana, IL: University of Illinois Press.

Dreyfuss, R. (2009, October 28). The generals' revolt. *Rollingstone.com*. Retrieved November 15, 2009, from www.rollingstone.com/politics/story/30493567/the_generals_revolt.

Duhalde, E. L. (1983). *El estado terrorista argentine*. Buenos Aires, Argentina: Argos Vergara.

Duss, M. (2009, March 26). Project for the rehabilitation of neoconservatism. *Think Progress*. Retrieved April 22, 2009, from http://wonkroom.thinkprogress.org/2009/03/26/project-for-the-rehabilitation-of-neoconservatism/.

Eagleton, T. (1994). Ideology and its vicissitudes in Western Marxism. In S. Zizek (Ed.), *Mapping ideology* (pp. 179–226). London: Verso, 1994.

Echave, N. U. H. (1986). *Después de la noche: Diálogo con Graciela Fernández Meijide*. Buenos Aires, Argentina: Editorial Contrapunto.

Economic Policy Institute (2003). *The state of working America 2002–2003*. Washington, DC: Author.

Economic Policy Institute (2009). *The state of working America 2008–2009.* Washington, DC: Author.

Eichenbaum, L., & Orbach, S. (1983). *Understanding women: A feminist psychoanalytic approach.* New York: Basic Books.

Eichenbaum, L., & Orbach, S. (1999). *What do women want: Exploding the myth of female dependency.* New York: Barkley Trade.

Einhorn, B. (2009, October 13). Income inequality around the world. *Business Week.* Retrieved November 2, 2009, from http://images.businessweek.com/ss/09/10/1013_biggest_rich_poor_gap_globally/1.htmTheUN.

Eizirik, C. L. (n.d.). Freud's group psychology: Psychoanalysis and culture. Unpublished paper.

El Día (June 5, 1997).

Elliot, A. (1939). *Social theory and psychoanalysis in transition: Self and society from Freud to Kristeva.* London: Free Association Books.

Ellis, P. (Ed.). (1986). *Women of the Caribbean.* London: Zed Books.

Elshtain, J. B. (1992). The mothers of the disappeared: Passion and protest in maternal action. In D. Bassin, M. Honey, & M. M. Kaplan (Eds.), *Representations of motherhood* (pp. 75–91). New Haven, CT: Yale University Press.

Escobar, P. (2009). *Obama does globalistan.* Ann Arbor, MI: Nimble Books.

Etchegoyen, R. H. (1996). Some views on psychic reality. *International Journal of Psychoanalysis, 77,* 1–14.

Ewen, S. (1977). *Captains of consciousness: Advertising and the social roots of the consumer culture.* Basic Books: New York.

Fagen, P. W. (1992). Repression and state security. In J. E. Corradi, P. W. Fagen, & M. A. Garretón (Eds.), *Fear at the edge: State terror and resistance in Latin America.* Berkeley, CA: University of California Press.

Fallenbaum, R. (2008). You spoke: The making of a small revolution. *Psychologist/Psychoanalyst,* Fall.

Ferla, S. (1985). *El drama político de la Argentina contemporánea.* Buenos Aires, Argentina: Paídos.

Fisher, J. (1989). *Mothers of the disappeared.* Boston: South End Press.

Fisher, J. (1993). *Out of the shadows: Women, resistance and politics in South America.* London: Latin American Bureau.

Fisher, W. (2009, November 10). Military commissions create "second-class" justice system, lawyers charge. *Truthout.* Retrieved December 2, 2008, from www.truthout.org/1110098.

Fitzgibbon, R. H. (1954). *Uruguay: Portrait of a democracy.* New Brunswick, NJ: Rutgers University Press.

Fleming, D. F. (1961). *The cold war and its origins, 1917–1960.* Garden City, NY: Doubleday.

Fonagy, P. (2002). *Attachment theory and psychoanalysis.* New York: Other Press.

Foner, P. (1963). *A history of Cuba and its relations with the U.S.* New York: International Publishing.

Forter, G. (2006). Introduction. *International Journal of Applied Psychoanalytic Studies, 3*(2), 113.

Foucault, M. (1979). *Discipline and punish: The birth of the prison* (A. Sheridan, Trans.). New York: Vintage Books.

Foulkes, S. H. (1990). *Selected papers: Psychoanalysis and group analysis.* London: Karnac Books.

Frank, A. G. (1974). *Lumpenbourgeoisie, lumpendevelopment: Dependence, class, and politics in Latin America.* New York: Monthly Review Press.

Frank, T. (2004). *What's the matter with Kansas? How conservatives won the heart of America.* New York: Henry Holt.

Fraser, N., & Navarro, M. (1980). *Eva Perón.* New York: Norton.

Freier, N. (2008). Known unknowns: Unconventional "strategic shocks" in defense strategy development. Retrieved January 14, 2009, from www.StrategicStudiesInstitute.army.mil/.

Fresonke, K. (2003). *West of Emerson: The design of Manifest Destiny.* Berkeley: University of California Press.

Freud, S. (1921). Group psychology and the analysis of the ego. In J. Strachey (Ed. & Trans.), *The standard edition of the complete psychological works of Sigmund Freud* (Vol. 18, pp. 67–143). London: Hogarth Press.

Freud, S. (1929). *Civilization and its discontents.* In J. Strachey (Ed. & Trans.), *The standard edition of the complete psychological works of Sigmund Freud* (Vol. 21, pp. 59–145). London: Hogarth Press.

Frontalini, D., & Ciati, M. (1984). *El mito de la guerra sucia.* Buenos Aires, Argentina: CELS.

Frosh, S. (1987). *The politics of psychoanalysis: An introduction to Freudian and post-Freudian theory.* New York: NYU Press.

Galeano, E. (1973). *Open veins of Latin America: Five centuries of the pillage of a continent.* New York: Monthly Review Press.

Galeano, E. (1992). *The book of embraces.* New York: W. W. Norton.

Gente, H. P. (Ed.). (1972). *Marxismo, psicoanálisis y sexpol.* Buenos Aires, Argentina: Gránica Editor.

Gentile, K., & Gutwill, S. (2005). To create social activism: Turning the passive to active without killing each other. *Psychotherapy and Politics International, 3*(2).

George, A. (Ed.). (1991). *Western state terrorism.* New York: Polity Press.

Gil, F., Lagos, R., & Landsberger, H. (Eds.). (1979). *Chile at the turning point: Lessons of the socialist years, 1970–1973.* Philadelphia: Institute for the Study of Human Issues.

Gilbert, G. M. (1950). *The psychology of dictatorship.* New York: Ronald Press.

Giussani, P. (1990). *Menem: Su lógica secreta.* Buenos Aires, Argentina: Editorial Sudamericana.

Glantz, A. (2009). The war comes home: Washington's battle against America's veterans. Berkeley, CA: University of California Press.

Godwin, R. (1993). On the deep structure of conservative ideology. *Journal of Psychohistory, 20*(3), 289–304.

Golden, R. (1991). *The hour of the poor, the hour of women: Salvadoran women speak.* New York: Crossroad.

Goodman, D. (2008, March 1). The psychology industry's long and shameful history with torture. *Mother Jones.* Retrieved April 10, 2009, from http://motherjones.com/news/feature/2008/03/the-enablers.html.

Goodman, A. (2009a, November 19). Interview with Robert Sheer. *Democracy Now.* Retrieved December 1, 2009, from http://www.democracynow.org/.

Goodman, D. (2009b, September). A few good kids? How the No Child Left Behind Act allowed military recruiters to collect info on millions of unsuspecting teens. *Mother Jones*. Retrieved August 31, 2009, from http://motherjones.com/.

Gramsci, A. (1971). *Selections from the prison notebooks*. New York: International Publishers.

Graziano, F. (1992). *Divine violence: Spectacle, psychosexuality, and radical Christianity in the Argentine "Dirty War."* Boulder, CO: Westview Press.

Greider, W. (2003). *The soul of capitalism: Opening paths to a moral economy*. New York: Simon and Shuster.

Grinberg, L., & Grinberg, L. (1984). *Psychoanalytic perspectives on migration and exile*. New Haven, CT: Yale University Press.

Gutwill, S. (2009, March). Toward social and economic relationalism: Will Obama change our alienation from ourselves, each other and the earth? Discussion of Andrew Samuels' "The Economic psyche." Paper presented at the American Association for Psychoanalysis in Clinical Social Work conference, New York, NY.

Halebsky, S., & Kirk, J. M. (Eds.). (1990). *Transformation and struggle: Cuba faces the 1990s*. New York: Praeger.

Halebsky, S., & Kirk, J. M. (Eds.). (1992). *Cuba in transition: Crisis and transformation*. Boulder, CO: Westview Press.

Haraway, D. (1971). *Simians, cyborgs and women: The reinvention of nature*. London: Free Association Press.

Harbury, J. (2005). *Truth, torture, and the American way: The history and consequences of U.S. involvement in torture*. Boston: Beacon Press.

Hardt, M., & Negri, A. (2001). *Empire*. Boston: Harvard University Press.

Harvey, D. (2005). *A brief history of neoliberalism*. Oxford: Oxford University Press.

Harvey, D. (2009, February 12). Why the U.S. stimulus package is bound to fail: Radical perspectives on the crisis. Retrieved February 21, 2009, from http://sites.google.com/site/radicalperspectivesonthecrisis/news/harvey-whytheusstimuluspackageisboundtofail.

Harris, A. (2006). *Trained to kill: Soldiers at war* by Theodore Nadelson Baltimore, Baltimore, MD: John Hopkins University Press, 2005, 208. *International Journal of Psychoanalysis*, (87), 1154–1157.

Harris, R., & Vilas, C. M. (1985). *Nicaragua: A revolution under siege*. London: Zed Books.

Haugaard, M. (2008). Power and liquid modernity: A dialogue with Zygmunt Bauman. *Journal of Power*, 1(2), 112.

Hayden, T. (2008, January 27). An endorsement of the movement Barack Obama leads. *Huffington Post*. Retrieved July 25, 2008, from http://www.huffington-post.com/tom-hayden/an-endorsement-of-the-mov_b_83478.html.

Hazaki, C. (2002). Grissinopoli: Crónica de una lucha obrera. In E. Carpintero & M. Hernández (Eds.). *Produciendo realidad: Las empresas comunitarias*. Buenos Aires, Argentina: Colección Fichas.

Hedges, C. (2006). *American Fascists: The Christian right and the war on America*. New York: Free Press.

Hedges, C. (2009a). *Empire of illusion: The end of literacy and the triumph of spectacle*. New York: Nation Books.

Hedges, C. (2009b, September 14). Stop begging Obama and get mad. *Truthdig*. Retrieved October 1, 2009, from http://www.truthdig.com/report/item/ 20090914_stop_begging_obama_to_be_obama_and_get_mad/.

Hedges, C. (2009c, June 14). The American empire is bankrupt. *Truthdig*. Retrieved June 15, 2009, from www.truthdig.com/report/item/20090614 _the_american_empire_is_bankrupt/.

Hedges, C. (2009d, October 18). A reality check from the brink of extinction. *Truthdig*. Retrieved November 2, 2009, from www.truthdig.com/report/ item/20091019_a_reality_check_from_the_brink_of_extinction/.

Hellman, C. (2009, March 3). President Obama's first defense budget: The end of an era. The Center for Arms Control and Non-Proliferation. Retrieved April 2, 2009, from http://www.armscontrolcenter.org/policy/securityspending/ articles/030309_obamas_first_budget_ends_era/.

Herbert, B. (2009, September 15). A world of hurt. *New York Times*, A33.

Herman, J. (1992). *Trauma and recovery: The aftermath of violence—From domestic abuse to political terror*. New York: Basic Books.

Herrera, M. (1987). *José*. Buenos Aires, Argentina: Editorial Contrapunto.

Hersh, S. M. (2004). *Chain of command: The road from 9/11 to Abu Ghraib*. New York: HarperCollins.

Hersh, S. M. (2009, October 23). Military is waging war against the White House. *Huffington Post*. Retrieved October 28, 2009, from http://www.huffington-post.com/2009/10/23/seymour-hersh-military-is_n_332139.html.

Hirsch, R. C., Bezdek, R., & Wendling, R. (2005). Peaking of world oil production: Impacts, mitigation, and risk management. *Post Carbon Institute Energy Bulletin*. Retrieved June 2, 2009, from www.energybulletin.net/node/4638.

Hodges, D. (1973). Argentina: The protracted struggle. *NACLA Report on the Americas*, 7(7).

Hodges, D. (1976). *Argentina 1943–1976: The national revolution and resistance*. Albuquerque, NM: University of New Mexico Press.

Hodges, D. (1991). *Argentina's "Dirty War": An intellectual biography*. Austin: University of Texas Press.

Hollander, N. C. (1974). Si Evita viviera... *Latin American Perspectives*, 1(3), 42–57.

Hollander, N. C. (1977). Women workers and the class struggle: The case of Argentina. *Latin American Perspectives*, 12/13(1/2), 180–193.

Hollander, N. C. (1990). Buenos Aires, Argentina: Latin Mecca of psychoanalysis. *Social Research*, 57(4), 889–919.

Hollander, N. C. (1996). The gendering of human rights: Women and the terrorist state in Latin America. *Feminist Studies*, 22(1), 41–80.

Hollander, N. C. (1997). *Love in a time of hate: Liberation psychology in Latin America*. New York: Other Press.

Hollander, N. C. (2000). Introduction. In M. Langer, *Motherhood and sexuality* (pp. 12–14). New York: Other Press.

Hollander, N. C. (2004). Argentine economic meltdown: Trauma and social resistance. *Mind and Human Interaction*, 13(4).

Hollander, N. C. (2006). Psychoanalysis and the problem of the bystander in times of terror. In L. Layton, N. C. Hollander, & S. Gutwill (Eds.), *Psychoanalysis, class and politics: Encounters in the clinical setting* (pp. 154–165). London: Routledge.

Hollander, N. C. (2009). When not knowing allies with destructiveness: Global warming and psychoanalytic ethical non-neutrality. *Journal of Applied Psychoanalytic Studies, 6*(1), 1–11.

Hollander, N. C., & Gutwill, S. (2002). Zero tolerance or media literacy: A critical psychoanalytic perspective on combating violence among children. *Journal of Psychoanalysis of Culture and Society, 7*(2), 263–273.

Hollander, N. C., & Gutwill, S. (2006). Despair and hope in a culture of denial. In L. Layton, N. C. Hollander, & S. Gutwill (Eds.), *Psychoanalysis, class and politics: Encounters in the clinical setting* (pp. 81–91). London: Routledge.

Hollander, N. C. (2010). The gendering of human rights: Women and the Latin American terrorist state. In Harris, A., & Botticelli, S. (Eds.), *First do no harm: The paradoxical encounters of psychoanalysis, warmaking, and resistance* (pp. 279–301). London: Routledge.

Hook, D. (2008). Articulating psychoanalysis and psychosocial studies: Limits and possibilities. *Psychoanalysis, Culture and Society, 13*, 351.

Hopper, E. (1996). The social unconscious in clinical work. *Group, 20*(1).

Huberman, L., & Sweezy, P. M. (1961). *Cuba: Anatomy of a revolution.* New York: Monthly Review Press.

Hudson, M. (2009, June 13). De-dollarization: Dismantling America's financial-military empire: The Yekaterinburg turning point. *Global Research.* Retrieved June 19, 2009, from http://michael-hudson.com/articles/globalism/090614De-DollarizationDismantlingEmpire.html.

Immerman, R. H. (1982). *The CIA in Guatemala: The foreign policy of intervention.* Austin, TX: University of Texas Press.

Ireland, D. (2004, July 22). Teaching torture: Congress quietly keeps School of the Americas alive. *LA Weekly.* Retrieved June 14, 2007, from http://www.laweekly.com/content/printVersion/38688.

Jacoby, R. (1983). *The repression of psychoanalysis.* New York: Basic Books.

Jacoby, R. (1997). *Social amnesia: A critique of contemporary psychology.* New Jersey: Transaction Publishers.

Jacques, M. (2009). *When China rules the world: The end of the western world and the birth of a new global order.* New York: Penguin.

Jaquette, J. (Ed.). (1989). *The women's movement in Latin America, feminism, and the transition to democracy.* Boston, MA: Unwin.

Jelin, E. (Ed.). (1990). *Women and social change in Latin America.* London: Zed Books.

Johnson, C. (2004). *The sorrows of empire: Militarism, secrecy, and the end of the republic.* New York: Metropolitan Books.

Johnson, C. (2008, April 26). The Pentagon strangles our economy: Why the U.S. has gone broke. *Le Monde Diplomatique.*

Johnson, C. (2009, May 15). On the cost of empire. *Truthdig.* Retrieved June 2, 2009, from www.truthdig.com/arts_culture/item/20090514_chalmers_johnson_on_the_cost_of_empire.

Johnson, D. L. (Ed.). (1973). *The Chilean road to socialism.* New York: Anchor Books.

Johnson, J. J. (1958). *Political change in Latin America: The emergence of the middle sectors in Latin America.* Stanford, CA: Stanford University Press.

Katz, M. (2006). The beheading of America: Reclaiming our minds. In L. Layton, N. C. Hollander, & S. Gutwill (Eds.), *Psychoanalysis, class and politics: Encounters in the clinical setting* (pp. 141–153). London: Routledge.

Kaufman, E. (1979). *Uruguay in transition: From civilian to military rule*. New Brunswick, NJ: Transaction Books.

Keen, S. (1986). *Faces of the enemy: Reflections of the hostile imagination*. New York: Harper and Row.

Khan, M. (1963). The concept of cumulative trauma. *Psychoanalytic Study of the Child, 18*, 286–306.

Kijak, M., & Pelento, M. L. (1986). Mourning in certain situations of social catastrophe. *International Review of Psycho-Analysis, 13*(4), 468.

Kim, R., & Reed, B. (Eds.) (2009). *Going rouge: Sarah Palin: An American nightmare*. New York: OR Books.

Klare, M. (2009, October 26). The great superpower meltdown. *TomDispatch. com*. Retrieved November 2, 2009, from www.tomdispatch.com/blog/175113/tomgram:_michael_klare,_the_great_superpower_meltdown/.

Klare, M., & Kornbluh, P. (Eds.). (1988). *Low intensity warfare: Counterinsurgency, proinsurgency, and antiterrorism in the eighties*. New York: Pantheon Books.

Klare, M., & Stein, N. (1978). *Armas y poder en América Latina*. Mexico City: Era.

Klein, M. (1935). A contribution to the psychogenesis of manic-depressive states. *International Journal of Psychoanalysis, 16*, 145–174.

Klein, M. (1937). Love, guilt and reparation. In M. Klein & J. Riviere (Eds.), *Love, hate and reparation* (pp. 57–91). London: Hogarth Press.

Klein, N. (2007). *The shock doctrine: The rise of disaster capitalism*. New York: Metropolitan Books.

Klein, N. (2009, November 11). Copenhagen: Seattle grows up. *The Nation*. Retrieved November 26, 2009, from www.thenation.com/doc/20091130/klein.

Kordon, D. R. (1995). *La impunidad: Una perspectiva psicosocial y clinica*. Buenos Aires, Argentina: Editorial Sudamericana.

Kordon, D. R., & Edelman, L. I. (Eds.) (1986). *Efectos psicológicos de la represión política*. Buenos Aires, Argentina: Sudamérica Planeta.

Kovel, J. (1988). *In Nicaragua*. London: Free Association Books.

Kovel, J. (2002). *The enemy of nature: The end of capitalism or the end of the world?* London: Zed Books.

Kreisler, H. (1999). Evil, the self and survival: Conversation with Robert Jay Lifton, MD. http://globetrotter.berkeley.edu/people/Lifton/lifton-con0.html.

Krugman, P. (2009). *The return of depression economics and the crisis of 2008*. New York: W. W. Norton.

Kunsler, J. (2005). *The long emergency: Surviving the end of oil, climate change, and other converging catastrophes of the twenty-first century*. New York: Atlantic Monthly Press.

Laclau, E. (2007). *On populist reason*. London: Verso.

Laclau, E., & Mouffe, C. (2001). *Hegemony and social strategy: Towards a radical democratic politics*. London: Verso.

LaFeber, W. (1983). *Inevitable revolutions: The United States in Central America*. New York: Norton.

Lakoff, G. (2004). *Don't think of an elephant! Know your values and frame the debate—The essential guide for progressives*. White River Junction, VT: Chelsea Green Publishing Company.

Lakoff, G. (2008a). *The political mind: Why you can't understand 21st-century American politics with an 18th-century brain*. New York: Penguin Group.

Lakoff, G. (2008b, July 6). The mind and Obama magic. *The Huffington Post.* Retrieved September 4, 2000, from http://www.huffingtonpost.com/george-lakoff/the-mind-and-the-obama-ma_b_111105.html.

Langer, M. (1971). Psicoanálisis y/o revolución social. In *Cuestionamos I* (pp. 262–263). Buenos Aires, Argentina: Gránica Editor.

Langer, M. (1989). *From Vienna to Managua* (M. Hooks, Trans.). London: Free Association Books.

Langer, M. (2000). *Motherhood and sexuality.* New York: Other Press.

LaPlanche, J. (1999). *Essays on otherness.* New York: Routledge.

Lasch, C. (1978). *The culture of narcissism: American life in an age of diminishing expectations.* New York: W. W. Norton & Co.

Latin American and Caribbean Women's Collective. (1977). *Slaves of slaves: The challenge of Latin American women.* London: Zed Press.

Layton, L. (2004a). *Who's that girl? Who's that boy? Clinical practice meets post-modern gender theory.* Hillsdale, NJ: The Analytic Press.

Layton, L. (2004b, February). Psychoanalysis and the free individual. Paper presented at the conference "The Desire of the Analysts: Psychoanalysis and Cultural Criticism in the 21st Century," University of South Carolina, Columbia.

Layton, L., Hollander, N. C., & Gutwill, S. (Eds.) (2006). *Psychoanalysis, class and politics: Encounters in the clinical setting.* London: Routledge.

Lemke, T. (2005). The birth of biopolitics: Michel Foucault's lecture at the Collège de France on neo-liberal governmentality. *Economy & Society, 30*(2), 190–207.

Leopold, J. (2009, 12 December). Blistering indictment leveled against Obama over his handling of Bush era war crimes. *Truthout.* Retrieved December 12, 2009, from www.truthout.org/12110911.

Lifton, R. J. (1973). *Home from the war: Vietnam veterans: Neither victims nor executioners.* New York: Simon & Schuster.

Lifton, R. J. (2003). *Superpower Syndrome: America's apocalyptic confrontation with the world.* New York: Nation Books.

Lira, E. (Ed.). (1994). *Psicología y violencia política en América Latina.* Santiago, Chile: ILAS.

Lira, E., & Castillo, M. I. (1991). *Psicología de la amenaza política e del miedo.* Santiago, Chile: ILAS.

Lovato, R. (2008). Terror incognita: Immigrants and the Homeland Security state. *Report on the Americas, 41*(6).

Mámora, L., & Gurrieri, J. (1988). *Return to Rio de La Plata: Response to the return of exiles to Argentina and Uruguay.* Washington, DC: Center for Immigration Policy and Refugee Assistance, Georgetown University.

Manz, B. (1982). *Refugees of a hidden war: The aftermath of counterinsurgency in Guatemala.* Albany, NY: State University of New York Press.

Marks, J. (1999). *The search for the "Manchurian Candidate," The CIA and mind control: The secret history of the behavioral sciences.* New York: W. W. Norton & Co.

Martín-Baró, I. (1994). *Writings for a liberation psychology.* Cambridge, MA: Harvard University Press.

Mayer, J. (2005, July 11). The experiment: Is the military devising new methods of interrogation at Guantánamo? *New Yorker.* Retrieved January 25, 2008, from http://www.newyorker.com/archive/2005/07?11/050711fa_fact4.

McCoy, A. W. (2006). *A question of torture: CIA interrogation, from the Cold War to the War on Terror*. New York: Metropolitan Books.

McGovern, R. (2009, November 10). Kipling haunts Obama's Afghan war. Information Clearing House. Retrieved November 2, 2009, from http://www.huffingtonpost.com/2009/10/23/seymour-hersh-military-is_n_332139.html.

McLeod, M. (1986). *GAM-Comadres: Un análisis comparative*. Mexico City: Citgua.

Media Reform Information Center (2004). Retrieved June 22, 2005, from http://corporations.org/media.

Menchú, R. (1992). *I Rigoberta Menchú* (A. Wright, Trans.). London: Verso.

Meyer, J. (2007, August 13). The black sites. New Yorker. Retrieved June 10, 2009, from http://www.newyorker.com/reporting/200713fa_fact_mayer?printable=true.

Miles, S. H. (2008). Torture: The bioethics perspective. In M. Crowley (Ed.), *From birth to death and bench to clinic: The Hastings Center bioethics briefing book for journalists, policymakers, and campaigns* (pp. 169–172). Garrison, NY: The Hastings Center.

Miller, J., Engelberg, S., & Broad, W. (2002). *Germs: Biological weapons and America's secret war*. New York: Touchstone.

Mitchell, S. A. (1993). *Relational concepts in psychoanalysis*. New York: Basic Books.

Mitchell, S. (1998). Aggression and the endangered self. *Psychoanalytic Inquiry*, 18, 21–30.

Mitscherlich, A. (1968). Group psychology and the analysis of the ego: A lifetime later. *Psychoanalytic Quarterly*, 47.

Movimiento Solidario de Salud Mental, Familiares de Detenidos y Desaparecidos por Razones Políticas. (1987). *Terrorismo de estado: Efectos psicológicos en los niños*. Buenos Aires, Argentina: Paídos.

Murphy, W. F. (2006). *Constitutional democracy: Creating and maintaining a just political order*. Baltimore: Johns Hopkins University Press.

Myers, T. (2003). *Slavoj Zizek*. London: Routledge.

Nash, J., & Safa, H. (1985). *Women and change in Latin America*. New York: Bergin & Garvey.

National Intelligence Council. (2005). Mapping the global future. Retrieved October 30, 2009, from www.dni.gov/nic/NIC_2020_project.html.

North American Congress on Latin America. (1983). Chile: Beyond the darkest decade. *NACLA Report on the Americas*, 15(5).

North American Congress on Latin America. (1988). Pinochet's plebiscite: Choice with no options. *NACLA Report on the Americas*, 22(2).

North American Congress on Latin America. (1992a). *Report on the Americas*, 25(5).

North American Congress on Latin America. (1992b). *Report on the Americas*, 26(4).

North American Congress on Latin America. (1993a). *Report on the Americas*, 27(3).

North American Congress on Latin America. (1993b). *Report on the Americas*, 27(6).

North American Congress on Latin America. (1994a). *Report on the Americas*, 28(1).

North American Congress on Latin America. (1994b). *Report on the Americas*, 28(2).

North American Congress on Latin America. (1995). *Report on the Americas*, 29(1).

North American Congress on Latin America. (1996). *Report on the Americas*, 29(6).

Nosiglia, J. E. (1985). *Botin de guerra*. Buenos Aires, Argentina: Cooperativa Tierra Fértil L Tada y Julio E. Nosiglia.

Nueva Constitucion del Ecuador (2009). Retrieved November 22, 2009, from http://pdfdatabase.com/index.php?q=nueva+constitucion+del+ecuador+2009.

O'Donnell, G. A. (1973). *Modernization and bureaucratic-authoritarianism: Studies in South American politics*. Berkeley, CA: Institute of International Studies, University of California.

O'Donnell, G. A. (1978). Reflections on the patterns of change in the bureaucratic-authoritarian state. *Latin American Research Review*, *12*(1), 33–38.

O'Donnell, G. A., Schmitter, P. C., & Whitehead, L. (Eds.). (1986). *Transitions from authoritarian rule*. Baltimore: Johns Hopkins University Press.

Ogden, T. H. (1986). *The matrix of the mind*. Northvale, NJ: Aronson.

Omang, J., & Neier, A. (1985). *Psychological operations in guerrilla warfare: The CIA's Nicaragua manual*. New York: Vintage Books.

Oppenheim, L. H. (1993). *Politics in Chile: Democracy, authoritarianism, and the search for development*. Boulder, CO: Westview Press.

Orbach, S. (1998). *Fat is a feminist issue*. London: Arrow Books Ltd.

Page, J. (1983). *Perón: A Biography*. New York: Random House.

Partnoy, A. (2004). *Dialogue with Alaíde Foppa*. In Hollander, N. (Ed.), Argentine economic meltdown: Trauma and social resistance. *Mind and Human Interaction*, *13*(3), 238.

Paxton, R. O. (1998). The five stages of fascism. *The Journal of Modern History*, *70*(1).

Pelento, M. L., & Braun, J. (1985). La desaparición: Su repercusión en el individuo y en la sociedad. *Revista de Psicoanálisis*, *42*, 1391–1397.

Peltz, R. (2004). My father's flags: Psychoanalytic perspectives on being an American from the streets and the consulting room. *Psychotherapy and Politics International*, *2*(3), 174–183.

Peltz, R. (2005). The manic society. *Psychoanalytic Dialogues*, *15*(3), 347–366.

Perelli, C. (1992). Youth, politics, and dictatorship in Uruguay. In J. E. Corradi, P. W. Fagen, & M. A. Garretón (Eds.), *Fear at the edge: State terror and resistance in Latin America*. Berkeley, CA: University of California Press.

Pereyra, D. (1994). *Del moncada a chiapas: Historia de la lucha armada en América Latina*. Madrid, Spain: Los Libros de la Catarata.

Perkins, J. (2005). *Confessions of an economic hit man*. San Francisco: Berrett & Koehler.

Perkins, J. (2007). *The secret history of the American empire: Economic hit men, jackals, and the truth about global corruption*. New York: Dutton.

Petras, J., & Veltmeyer, H. (2001). *Globalization unmasked: Imperialism in the 21st century*. London: Zed Books.

Phillips, T. (2009, September 14). South American nations question U.S.–Colombia military base agreement. Americas Program. Retrieved September 22, 2009, from http://americas.irc-online.org/am/6411.

Pines, D. (1985). Working with women survivors of the Holocaust: Affective experiences with transference and countertransference. *Revista de Psicoanálisis*, *42*(4).

Pitt, W. R. (2009, April 10). Appomattox again. *Truthout*. Retrieved April 22, 2009, from www.truthout.org/041009R.

Plant, J. (Ed.) (1989). *Healing the wounds: The promise of ecofeminism*. Gabriola Island, BC: New Society Publishers.

PNAC (2007). Project for a new American century. Retrieved January 21, 2003, from http://www.newamericancentury.org/statementofprinciples.htm.

Pollack, S. (Director). (2005). *The interpreter* [Motion picture]. United States: Universal.

Portuges, S. (2009). The politics of psychoanalytic neutrality. *International Journal of Applied Psychoanalytic Studies, 6*(1).

PsyBc. (2007). *Psychotherapy and Politics International, 5*(3), 163–214.

Puget, J., & Kaes, R. (Eds.). (1991). *Violencia de estado y psicoanálisis.* Buenos Aires, Argentina: Bibliotecas Universitarias Centro Editor de América Latina.

Randall, M. (1981). *Sandino's daughters: Testimonies of Nicaraguan women in struggle.* Toronto, CA: New Star Books.

Randall, M. (1992). *Gathering rage.* New York: Monthly Review Press.

Randall, M. (1995). *Our voices our lives: Stories of women from Central America and the Caribbean.* Monroe, ME: Common Courage.

Reisner, S., Losi, M., & Salvaticio, S. (2002). Psychosocial and trauma response in war-torn societies: Supporting traumatized communities through theatre and the arts. *Psychosocial Notebook, 3.*

Revista de Psicoanálisis. (1985). Acerca del malestar en la cultura. *Revista de Psicoanálisis, 42*(6).

Risen, J., & Lightblau, E. (2009, April 15). Officials say U.S. wiretaps exceeded law. *New York Times.* Retrieved April 16, 2009, from www.nytimes.com/2009/04/16nsa.html.

Roan, S. (2009, March 23). A rising slump. *Los Angeles Times,* E6.

Roberts, P. C. (2007, September 9). American economy: R.I.P. Information Clearing House. Retrieved October 20, 2008, from www.informationclearinghouse.info/article18350.htm.

Robinson, S. (2009, August 7). Is the U.S. on the brink of fascism? *Truthout.* Retrieved August 27, 2009, from www.truthout.org/080909A?n.

Roland, A. L. (2006, August 20). Rex 84: FEMA's blueprint for martial law in America. Retrieved November 3, 2007, from http://www.salon.com/src/pass/sitepass/spon/sitepass_website.html.

Rosencof, M. (1993a). *Memorias del Calabozo.* Nafarroa/Navarra, Uruguay: Txalaparta Editorial.

Rosencof, M. (1993b). On suffering, song, and white horses. In S. Sosnowski & L. B. Popkin (Eds.), *Repression, exile, and democracy: Uruguayan culture.* Durham, NC: Duke University Press.

Roth-Douquet, K., & Schaeffer, F. (2006). *AWOL: The unexcused absence of America's upper classes from military service and how it hurts our country.* New York: HarperCollins.

Rouquié, A. (Ed.). (1983). *Poder militar y sociedad política en la Argentina.* Buenos Aires, Argentina: Emecé.

Roxborough, I. (1977). *Chile: The state and revolution.* New York: Holmes & Meier.

Roy, A. (2001). *Power politics.* Cambridge, MA: South End Press.

Ruskin, M. (1991). *The good society and the inner world: Psychoanalysis, politics and culture.* London: Verso.

Russell, J. (1975). *Social amnesia: A critique of conformist psychology from Adler to Laing.* Boston: Beacon Press.

Samuels, A. (2001). *Politics on the couch: Citizenship and the internal life.* New York: Other Press.

Saunders, D. (2009, April 3). U.S. takes back seat as power balance shifts. *Globe and Mail*. Retrieved April 5, 2009, from www.theglobeandmail.com/servlet/story/RTGAM.20090403.wg20analysis03/BNStory/International/?page=rss&id=RTGAM.20090403.wg20analysis03.

Scahill, J. (2007). *Blackwater: The rise of the world's most powerful mercenary army*. New York: Avalon.

Scarry, E. (1985). *The body in pain: The making and unmaking of the world*. New York: Oxford University Press.

Schaeffer, F. (2009). *Patience with God: Faith for people who don't like religion (or atheism)*. Cambridge, MA: Da Capo Press.

Schechter, D. (2009, October 27). Downrising. *ZSpace*. Retrieved November 11, 2009, from http://www.zcommunications.org/zspace/commentaries/4025.

Schlesinger, S., & Kinzer, S. (1983). *Bitter fruit: The untold story of the American coup in Guatemala*. Garden City, NY: Doubleday.

Segal, H. (2002). Silence is the real crime. In C. Covington, P. Williams, J. Arundale, & J. Knox (Eds.), *Terrorism and war: Unconscious dynamics of political violence* (pp. 263–284). London: Karnac.

Seminario Internacional. (1987). *La tortura en América Latina, 2–5 diciembre 1985*. Buenos Aires, Argentina: Codesedh.

Servicio Paz y Justicia. (1992) *Uruguay: Nunca más: Human rights violations, 1972–1985* (E. Hampsten, Trans.). Philadelphia: Temple University Press.

Shakir, F., Pitney, N., Terkel, A., & Schwin, P. (2007). Administration under the radar: An unsafe America. Center for American Progress Action Fund, *The Progress Report*. Retrieved October 20, 2008, from http://www.americanprogress.org/issues/2007/10.

Shane, S. (2009, December 12). Domestic insecurity: Recent cases shake the comforting idea that radical U.S. Muslims pose few risks. *New York Times*, 1.

Sharlet, J. (2009). *The Family: The secret fundamentalism at the heart of American power*. New York: Harper.

Sharrock, J. (2010, March/April). The Oath Keepers. *Mother Jones*. Retrieved March 7, 2010, from http://motherjones.com/politics/2010/03/oath-keepers.

Shiva, V. (1988). *Staying alive: Women, economy and development*. London: Zed.

Sigmund, P. E. (1993). *The United States and democracy in Chile*. Baltimore: Johns Hopkins University Press.

Simpson, J., & Bennett, J. (1985). *The disappeared and the mothers of the plaza*. New York: St. Martin's Press.

Skahill, J. (2009, November 23). The secret US war in Pakistan. *The Nation*. Retrieved November 25, 2009, fromwww.thenation.com/doc/20091207/scahill.

Sklarew, B., Twemlow, S., & Wilkinson, S. (Eds.) (2004). *Analysts in the trenches: Streets, schools, war zones*. Hillsdale, NJ: The Analytic Press.

Soldz, S. (2008). Healers or interrogators: Psychology and the United States torture regime. *Psychoanalytic Dialogues, 18*(5), 592–613.

Soler, C. (2006). *What Lacan said about women: A psychoanalytic study*. New York: Other Press.

Solnit, R. (2009). *A paradise built in hell: The extraordinary communities that arise in disaster*. New York: Penguin.

Solomon, M. (2009, October 13). Barack Obama, right wing frenzy—And the left. Progressives for Obama. Retrieved October 14, 2009, from http://progressives-forobama.blogspot.com/.

Solomon, N. (2008, September 18). Our tax dollars and the Iraq War. Progressive Democrats of America. Retrieved November 11, 2009, from http://pdamerica.org/articles/news/2008-09-18-10-08-51-news.php.

Sosnowski, S., & Popkin, L. B. (Eds.). (1993). *Repression, exile, and democracy: Uruguayan culture*. Durham, NC: Duke University Press.

Southern Poverty Law Center. (2009, August 12). Return of the militias. Retrieved September 4, 2009, from www.splcenter.org/news/item.jsp?aid=392.

Sperling, J. (2004). *The great divide: Retro vs. metro America*. Sausalito, CA: Polipoint Press.

Spooner, M. H. (1994). *Soldiers in a narrow land: The Pinochet regime in Chile*. Berkeley, CA: University of California Press.

Staub, E. (1989). *The roots of evil: The origins of genocide and other group violence*. Cambridge, UK: Cambridge University Press.

Stein, S. J., & Stein, B. H. (1970). *The colonial heritage of Latin America*. New York: Oxford University Press.

Stenner, K. (2005). *The authoritarian dynamic*. Cambridge, MA: Cambridge University Press.

Stockwell, R. (Senior Producer). (2008, December 16). *Countdown with Keith Olberman* [Television broadcast]. New York: MSNBC.

Stockwell, R. (Senior Producer). (2009, March 5). *Countdown with Keith Olberman* [Television broadcast]. New York: MSNBC.

Suarez-Orozco, M. M. (1987). The treatment of children in the 'Dirty War': Ideology, state terrorism and the abuse of children in Argentina. In N. Scheper-Hughes (Ed.), *Child survival*. Dordrecht, The Netherlands: Reidel.

Summers, F. (2008). Making sense of the APA: A history of the relationship between psychology and the military. *Psychoanalytic Dialogues, 18*(5), 614–637.

Thomas, N. (2004). An eye for an eye: Fantasies of revenge in the aftermath of trauma. In D. Knafo (Ed.), *Living with terror, working with trauma: A clinician's handbook* (pp. 297–311). New York: Aronson.

Thomas, N. (2006). Psychological effects of America's war on terrorism. In P. Kimmel & C. Stout (Eds.), *Collateral damage: The psychological consequences of America's war on terrorism* (pp. 131–144). Westport, CT: Praeger Publishers.

Thomson, M. (1986). *Women of El Salvador: The price of freedom*. Philadelphia: Institute for the Study of Human Issues.

Timmerman, J. (1982). *Prisoner without a name, cell without a number*. New York: Vintage Books.

Turner. F. C., & Miguens, J. E. (Eds.). (1983). *Juan Perón and the reshaping of Argentina*. Pittsburgh, PA: University of Pittsburgh Press.

Twemlow, S. W., & Parens, H. (2006). Might Freud's legacy lie beyond the couch? *Psychoanalytic Psychology, 23*, 430–451.

Verbitsky, H. (1997). *La posguerra sucia: Un análisis de la transición*. Buenos Aires, Argentina: Editorial Legasa.

Villela, L. (2005). The chalice of silence and the case that refuses to go away. *Psychoanalytic Review, 92*, 807–828.

Viñar, M. (1993). Pedro o la demolición: Una mirada psicoanalítica sobre la tortura. In M. Viñar & M. Viñar, *Fracturas de memoria: Crónicas para una memoria por venir*. Montevideo, Uruguay: Ediciones Trilce.

Viñar, M., &Viñar, M. (1993). *Fracturas de memoria: Crónicas para una memoria por venir*. Montevideo, Uruguay: Ediciones Trilce.

Volkan, V. (1999a). Psychoanalysis and diplomacy, part I: Individual and large-group identity. *Journal of Applied Psychoanalytic Studies, 1*, 29–55.

Volkan, V. (1999b). Psychoanalysis and diplomacy, part II: Large-group rituals. *Journal of Applied Psychoanalytic Studies, 1*, 223–247.

Volkan, V. (1999c). Psychoanalysis and diplomacy, part III: Potentials for and obstacles against collaboration. *Journal of Applied Psychoanalytic Studies, 1*, 305–318.

Volkan, V. (2004). *Blind trust: Large groups and their leaders in times of crisis and terror*. Charlottesville, VA: Pitchstone Publishing.

Volkan, V. (2006). *Killing in the name of identity: A Study of bloody conflict*. Pitchstone Publishing, kurt@pitchstonepublishing.com.

Volnovich, J. C. (2004). Psychoanalysis and hope in the epicenter of despair: A view from Argentina. *Mind and Human Interaction, 13*(3), 194–195.

Waisman, C. H. (1988). *Reversal of development in Argentina*. Princeton, NJ: Princeton University Press.

Walker, T. W. (Ed.). (1987). *Reagan versus the Sandinistas: The undeclared war on Nicaragua*. Boulder, CO: Westview Press.

Warren, E. (2009, December 3). America without a middle class. *Huffington Post*. Retrieved December 3, 2009, from www.huffingtonpost.com/elizabeth-warren/america-without-a-middle_b_377829.html.

Wedel, J. (2009, November 8). Wall Street's bailout gives me déjà vu. *Salon.com*. Retrieved November 23, 2009, from www.salon.com/opinion/feature/2009/11/08/berlin_wall/index.html.

Weinberg, H. (2007). So what is this social unconscious anyway? *Group Analysis, 40*(3), 307–322.

Weinstein, M. (1988). *Uruguay: Democracy at the crossroads*. Boulder, CO: Westview Press.

Welch, B. (2008). *State of confusion: Political manipulation and the assault on the American mind*. New York: St. Martin's Press.

Weschler, L. (1990). *A miracle, a universe: Settling accounts with torturers*. New York: Penguin Books.

Westen, D. (2007). *The political brain: The role of emotion in deciding the fate of the nation*. New York: Perseus Books.

Westen, D. (2009, November 2). Leadership, Obama style. *Huffington Post*. Retrieved November 15, 2009, from www.huffingtonpost.com/dfrew-westen/leadership-obama-style b 342269.html.

Wickham-Crowley, T. P. (1992). *Guerrillas and revolution in Latin America*. Princeton, NJ: Princeton University Press.

Winnicott, D. W. (1965). *The maturational processes and the facilitating environment*. New York: International Universities Press.

Winnicott, D. W. (1971). *Playing and reality*. New York: Basic Books.

Winnicott, D. W. (1975). Primary maternal preoccupation. In *Through paediatrics to psycho-analysis* (pp. 300–303). New York: Basic Books.

Wolf, N. (2007). *The end of America: Letter of warning to a young patriot*. White River Junction, VT: Chelsea Green Publishing Co.

Wolf, N. (2007, April 24). Fascist America, in 10 easy steps. *The Guardian*. Retrieved April 20, 2009, from www.theguardian.co.uk.

Wolin, S. (2003, May 1). Inverted totalitarianism. *The Nation*. Retrieved August 24, 2009 from www.thenation.com/doc/20030519/wolin.

Wolin, S. (2008). *Democracy incorporated: Managed democracy and the specter of inverted totalitarianism*. Princeton, NJ: Princeton University Press.

Women's Therapy Centre Institute. (1994). *Eating problems: A feminist psychoanalytic treatment model*. New York: Basic Books.

Wright, E., & Wright, E. (Eds.). (2000). *The Zizek reader*. Oxford, UK: Blackwell.

Wyden, P. (1980). *Bay of Pigs: The untold story*. New York: Touchstone Books.

Yeats, W. B. (2009). Literature Network. Retrieved August 12, 2009, from www.online-literature.com/yeats/780/.

Zeiger, D. (Director). (2005). *Sir! No sir!* [Motion picture]. United States: Displaced Films.

Zinn, H. (1980). *The twentieth century: A people's history*. New York: Harper & Row.

Zinn, H. (1990). *A people's history of the United States*. New York: Harper Perennial.

Zizek, S. (2002). *Welcome to the desert of the real*. London: Verso.

Zunes, S. (2009, January 30). Obama gathering a flock of hawks to oversee U.S. foreign policy. *AlterNet.org*. Retrieved March 24, 2009, from www.alternet.org/politics/all/.

Index

A

Aalbers, Dan, 259
Abadi, Mauricio, 89 n.1
Absolutist attitudes, defensive, 27
Abudar, O., 199, 307
Abuelas de Plaza de Mayo; *See*
    Grandmothers of the Plaza de
    Mayo
Abu Ghraib, 6, 253, 290, 306; *See also*
    Torture
Abuse of transference, 89 n.3
Abusive interrogations; *See* Torture
Academic community
    interdisciplinary dialogues,
        250–251
    U.S. right-wing organization, 235
Accountability; *See also* Impunity
    Bush–Cheney Administration
        policies, Obama
        Administration policy,
        306–307, 344 n.23
    grassroots opposition to amnesty,
        200
    social amnesia; *See* Amnesia, social
Achugar, H., 206
Activism, political
    contemporary trends and
        challenges, 332–338
    and new subjectivities, 240–241
    redefinition as terrorism, 266–267
    right-wing organization, 311
    therapeutic benefits of, 129–130,
        152, 153, 155 n.18, 183
    transnational, 333–338
Activism, psychoanalytic community, 2
    in Latin America, 194–202

Equipo, 121, 124, 140, 147–153,
    155 n.18, 196–197, 299 n.11
    in late 1990s, 209–210
    meltdown and rebellion,
        211–221
    memory and human rights,
        194–202
    in new millennium, 208
    therapeutic benefits of, 129–130
    in U.S., 245–260, 272–278
Adaptation, psychology of social
    trauma, 123
Adorno, T. W., 235, 243
Advertising industry, 227–228
Affects, social power relations and, 10
Afghanistan strategy, 341 n.9, 342
    n.10
Agents provocateurs, 123
Aggression, 143–147
    depressive position and, 18
    hegemony, disengagement from, 28
    identification with the aggressor,
        125–126, 141
    psychology of social trauma, 126
    psycho-social aspects of subjectivity,
        11
    responsible leadership, 302
    social matrix effects on expression
        of libidinal and aggressive
        impulses, 8–9
    splitting, 252–253
Agosin, M., 155 n.16
Akhtar, S., 187 n.2
ALBA (Bolivian Alliance for the
    Peoples of Our America), 342
    n.13
Alcoholism, 206

Alderice, John, 337–338
Alexander, F., 235
Alfonsin, Raul, 111, 198, 201
Alford, C. F., 90 n.10, 247, 296, 302
Algeria, 104
Alienation, Marx–Freud correlations, 84
Allende, Salvator, 48, 49, 50, 60 n.14, 99, 101, 118 n.1
Alliance, therapeutic, 187 n.3
Alliances, geopolitical, 316, 342 n.13
Altemeyer, Robert, 292
Althusser, Louis, 12, 81, 230
Altman, N., 90 n.10, 246–247, 252, 256–257, 261 n.13, 261 n.16, 261 n.18, 262 n.24
Amati, S., 199, 307
Ambiguity, depressive position and, 18
Ambivalence, Kleinian approach, 85
American Exceptionalism, 16–17, 22, 238, 311–326
American Medical Association, policy on participation in interrogations, 254
American Psychoanalytic Association, Psychoanalysis in the Community syllabus, 248
American Psychological Association
Division 39, 225–226, 246–247
Section 9, 31 n.9
torture issue, 256–258, 262 n.29, 262–263 n.30
complicity and participation of professionals with torture, 253–254
Ethics Code, 254–255
Amnesia, social
amnesty issues, 195–202
identification with hegemonic ideology, 229
Obama Administration policy, 306–307, 344 n.23
Amnesty, 200; See also Impunity
Analysts; See Activism, psychoanalytic community
Analysts in the Trenches: Streets, Schools, War Zones (Skarlew, Twemlow, Wilkinson), 248
Analytic categories, gender and class as, 225–226
Analytic neutrality; See Neutrality, analytic

Anger, contemporary challenges, 313–314
Annan, Kofi, 30 n.6
Annihilation anxiety, 9, 27
Anthrax attack, 14
Anticipatory anxiety, 123–124
Antiwar activists, 299 n.2
Bush–Cheney surveillance programs and, 266
contemporary trends, 333
Iraq War demonstrations, 29
Anxieties, 122
bystander situation, 27, 28
dynamics of response to 9/11, 21
psychology of social trauma, 123, 124
therapeutic approaches with families of desaparecidos, 197
Apathy, 122, 215
Appropriation, psycho-social subjectivity, 10
APU (Uruguayan Psychoanalytic Association), 97, 98
Aragones, R. J., 199, 307
Argentina, 60 n.15, 60 n.16, 89 n.4, 103–104, 278, 344 n.23
as canary in the mine, 221, 226–227, 292, 298
economic meltdown and rebellion, 211–221
election of civilian governments, 194
emigration/migration/political exile from, 161–164, 169–175
Langer's migration to, 66
lessons to be learned from, 258
lives during transition to dictatorship
Braun family, 92–95
Pavlovsky family, 95, 97
Volnovich family, 95–97
neoliberal democracy and meltdown; See Neoliberal democracy in Latin America
progressive governments, emergence of, 281
psyche and social revolution, 66–72
class struggle and psychoanalysis, 82–89
Peronist political culture in 1930s and 1940s, 67–71

social commitment to
psychoanalysis, 74–75
refugees from Uruguay, 138
repatriation of exiles, 222 n.5
results of free-market impunity, 205
state terror
aftermath of, 187
collaboration of health
professionals in torture, 254
comparison with Nazis, 140–142
disappearances and torture,
112–113
fate of disappeared, 134
historical context of, 34–38
historical context of emergence
of state terror in Latin
America, 38–41
justice/retribution/amnesty
issues, 200
locating missing grandchildren,
191–192
Marie Langer, 35–38
monument to casualties of Dirty
War, 286–287
National Commission for the
Right to Identity, 287
paradox of populism, 50–57
public confessions by torturers
in, 208–209
rhetoric of pathology, 105
U.S. assistance in training of
military, 118 n.2
U.S. role in, 119 n.2
transition to democracy, 193
Argentine Anticommunist Alliance
(Triple A), 56, 61, 88, 94
Argentine Feminist Union (UFA),
86–87, 90 n.11
Argentine Mental Health Workers in
Mexico, 163
Argentine Psychiatric Federation
(FAP), 83
Argentine psychoanalysts, on
sociocultural elements/aspects
psychic reality, 8
Argentine Psychoanalytic Association
(APA), 72, 92, 98, 149, 161,
307
Argentina psicoánalisis represión
política, 198–199
foundation of, 66–67
institutional debate, 75–79

institutional rupture, 79–82
Langer's work in, 69
political and theoretical struggles of
60s, 74
Viñar campaign, 135
Argentine Team of Psycho-Social Work
and Research (EATIP), 288
Ariasm L. R., 199, 307
Armed Psyop, 188 n.8
Armey, Richard, 342 n.15
Aron, L., 246, 261 n.14
Ashbach, C., 340 n.2
Assassinations, state terror strategies,
108, 111; See also State terror
Association for the Psychoanalysis of
Culture and Society, 250
Astiz, Alfredo, 344 n.23
Atran, Scott, 342 n.11
Austria and Europe during 1930s, 2–4
Authoritarianism
contemporary trends and
challenges, 314, 329
feminist analysis, patriarchal values
and, 195–196
Freud on group psychology,
214–215
historical development and
evolution of neoliberalism/
neoconservatism, 238
historical/strategic functions of
Latin American dictatorships,
103–104
impunity and social violence, 203
Latin America; See Dirty Wars
Latin American military and, 104
lives during transition to
authoritarian rule, 92–101
neoconservatism and, 237
political trends in U.S., 2
post 9/11 trends, 7
psychological and social sequelae,
244
social conditions and, 299 n.13
United States
attitude trends, 292
National Security Doctrine, 114
torture policy implications, 258,
260
Authoritarian Personality, The
(Adorno et al.), 235
Authority
hegemony (Gramsci model), 11

hegemony, disengagement from, 28
Authority structures, free-market
    impunity and, 205–206
Autonomy, torture objectives, 132
Awad, George, 336
Axis of evil, 18, 26, 237
Aylwin, Patricio, 194

B

Baby trafficking, 117, 287
Bacevich, A. J., 307
Bageant, J., 234, 295
Bakan, Joel, 321, 322
Baker, Dean, 239, 315, 341 n.5
Balán, J., 89 n.1
Baranger, Madelaine, 72
Baranger, Willy, 72
Barber, Benjamin, 322
Barish, Samoan, 30 n.2
Barofsky, Neil, 306
Barrutia, Antonio, 90 n.8
Batista, Fulgencio, 40, 170
Bauleo, Armando, 79
Bauman, Zygmunt, 12, 308, 319, 322,
    323–324, 327, 332, 344 n.25
Bay of Pigs, 40, 54
Bechtel, 17
Beck, Ulrich, 322, 323, 333–334, 335
Behavior Science Consultation Teams
    (BSCTs), 255
Behaviorism
    in Chile during 1950s and 1960s,
        73
    Cuban mental health care system,
        110
    official Communist Party policy in
        1930s and 1940s, 68
    and state terror victim therapy, 147
Behaviors
    psychology of social trauma, 123
    unconscious function of dominant
        ideology, 12
Behnke, Steven, 255–256
Bekker, H., 3
Belief, hegemony (Gramsci model), 11
Bendfeldt-Zachrisson, F., 116, 154 n.8
Benjamin, J., 252, 261 n.13
Bennett, J., 116
Berkowicz, L. B., 199, 307
Berlinger, J., 334, 344–345 n.26
Bernays, Edward, 227

Bernfeld, S., 63
Betrayal, 123, 144, 145
Bettelheim, Bruno, 116–117
Bezdek, R., 318
Bigliani, C., 76
Bigliani, L., 76
Bion, W. R., 9, 69, 154 n.6, 159, 302,
    303, 324, 325, 340 n.2
Birth rate, decline in, 70
Blackwater, 17, 239, 269
Blankfein, Lloyd, 306
Bleger, J., 68, 76, 98
Bleichmar, Silvia, 222 n.2, 280
Bloom, Carol, 250
Blumenthal, Max, 329
Bodni, O., 199, 307
Boggs, C., 11
Bolgar, Hedda, 1–6, 15, 25, 27, 30 n.2,
    225–226, 234–235, 241–242,
    243, 247, 260 n.1, 265–266,
    270, 298, 337–338
    Austria and Europe during 1930s,
        2–4
    on neutrality, 245
    on Obama Administration,
        303–305
    in U.S. after 9/11, 4–6
Bolgar, Herbert, 235
Bolivia, 281, 309, 342 n.13
Bollas, C., 15, 309
Bonafini, Hebe de, 204, 209
Bono, 311–312
Book burning, in Argentina, 57
Border security, 268
Bosnia, 249, 251
Bottinelli, M. C., 187 n.2
Boulanger, G., 30 n.4, 154 n.1, 256,
    262 n.26
Braun, Julia, 89 n.4, 122, 127–130,
    139, 143–144, 154 n.2, 155
    n.18, 197, 214, 273, 284–287,
    299 n.10
    life during transition to
        dictatorship, 92–95
    psychodynamics of state terror, 91
Bray, M., 223 n.10
Brazil, 45, 343 n.21
    progressive governments, emergence
        of, 281
    psychologist participating in
        torture, 117, 254, 262 n.23

Brazil, Russia, India, China (BRIC), 316
Brazilian Psychoanalytic Society, 82
BRIC countries, 316
Brigadistas, Nicaragua, 183–184
Broad, W., 19
Broder, Judith, 272, 273, 274, 277, 299 n.5, 299 n.8
Brown, Gordon, 316
Brown, Norman O., 244
Brown, Wendy, 120 n.10, 154 n.1, 229, 236, 237, 269
Burn (Pontecorvo film), 59 n.2
Burns, E. B., 59 n.2, 188 n.6
Bush, George W., 15, 260 n.7
Bush–Cheney Administration policies, 4–6, 237, 265–299
   activism by psychoanalytic community, 271–278
      SOFAR, 275–278
      Soldiers Project, 272–275
   analysis of consensual support for, 12–24
   domestic social impact of wars, 268–269
   election of 2008, 292–298
   government–corporate sector nexus, 268
   historical development and evolution of neoliberalism/ neoconservatism, 237–239
   human rights violations, 341 n.7
   immigration issues, 267–268
   Latin American perspectives on, 278–292
      Braun, 284–287
      Carlotto, 287–288
      Kordon, Lagos, and Edelman, 288–291
      Pavlovsky, 282–284
      Volnovich and Werthein, 279–282
   military
      composition of, 269
      treatment of soldiers, 269–271
   national security apparatus, 265–267
   neoconservative ascendancy, 24
   Obama Administration policy, 344 n.23
   psychologists participating in torture, 253–254
   Section IX activism, 248
   violent innocence, 15–16
Butler, J., 29, 293
Bystander position, 24–30, 281
   contemporary challenges, 313–314
   memory and, 200
   psychology of social trauma, 126
   U.S. social changes since 1980, 240

C

C Street Center, 330
Cabinet appointments, Obama Administration, 304
Camps, Ramon J., 119 n.3
Canary in the mine, Argentina as, 221, 226–227, 292, 298
Capital
   flow of tribute, 236
   neoliberalism and, 232
Capitalism; *See also* Neoconservative movement; Neoliberal democracy in Latin America
   Argentine analyst study groups, 81
   disaster, 305
   future prospects, 319–326
Capodouze, L. E., 76
Cardoso, F. H., 60 n.10
Carlotto, Estela, 191–192, 197–198, 287–288
Caruth, C., 21
Castaneda, J. G., 59 n.9
Castillo, Maria Isabel, 89 n.5, 154 n.3, 194
Castillo, M. C., 119 n.8
Castro, Fidel, 40
Catholic Church, 108–109, 150, 209
Catholic Foundation of Social Aid, 146–147, 155 n.14
CDI; *See* Research and Traning Centers, Organization of Mental Health Workers
Censorship, 126
Center for Economic Policy Research (CEPR), 315
Central America, 204
Central American exiles, 163, 187 n.2
Central American immigrants, 249
Central Intelligence Agency (CIA), 25
   assistance to Latin American militaries, 102
   black sites, 253, 259, 306

Chilean operations, 48, 118 n.1
Guatemalan coup, 40
Nicaraguan Contra training in U.S., 188 n.8
Obama Administration policy, 308
psychologists participating in torture, 262–263 n.30
SERE program, 255
Chamorro, E., 188 n.8
Chamorro, Violetta, 189 n.13, 206
Chavez, Hugo, 219, 283, 285
Chavkin, S., 102, 118 n.1
Cheney, Richard, 267, 304, 341 n.7
Chicago School of economics, 103, 119 n.4, 229
Children
    culture of fear, 154 n.4
    psychoanalytic 10 commandments of Nicaraguan training program, 180
    psychological impact of state terrorism, 222 n.6
    psychology of social trauma, 123
    victims of neoliberalism, 206
Children of disappeared, 222 n.2
    adoption of, 117
    locating and reuniting with families, 191–192
    pathogenic effects of parental lies, 135
    types of trauma, 192
Children's project, in Cuba, 172–175
Chile, 37, 60 n.13, 60 n.14, 89 n.5
    cultural status of psychoanalysis in 50s, 72, 73
    current opposition to U.S. policies, 309
    FASIC, 146–147, 155 n.14
    justice/retribution/amnesty issues, 200, 201, 203
    progressive governments, emergence of, 281
    psyche and social revolution, 73
    psychoanalysis, social preconditions for, 145–146
    results of free-market impunity, 205
    September 11 events, 299 n.9
    state terror
        aftermath, 187
        collaboration of health professionals in torture, 254
        culture of fear, 124–125

demise of democratic socialism, 45–50
    disappearances and torture, 113
    fate of disappeared, 134
    historical context of emergence of, 38–41
    lives during transition to dictatorship, 99–101
    migration from to Argentina, 87–88
    public confessions by torturers in, 208
    U.S. assistance in training of military, 118 n.2
    transition to democracy, 193
Chilean Psychoanalytic Association (APC), 73
China, 317, 343 n.21
Chirac, J., 30 n.6
Chodorow, N., 261 n.13
Chomsky, N., 30 n.5, 59 n.4, 119 n.2, 232, 260 n.10
Christian fundamentalism, 24, 233, 236
    contemporary trends and challenges, 329–330, 332
    elite fundamentalism, 330
    neoconservatism and, 237
Church Committee, U.S. Senate, 118 n.1
Ciati, M., 120 n.10
Citizen, subjectivity, 214
Citizen-subject, creation of, 237
Civil rights, contemporary trends, 333
Civilian governments, election of in Latin America, 194
Civilization and Its Discontents (Freud), 73, 199–200, 214, 339
Clandestine operations, 125
Class, social
    as analytic category, 225–226
    class struggle
        as dangerous idea, justification of state terror, 105
        psyche and social revolution, 82–89
    composition of military, 269
    neoliberal isolated self, 231
    political manipulation of class rage, 23–24

psycho-social aspects of subjectivity, 10
radical critiques of political and social repression, 242–243
reemergence of class identity, 208
torturers, 115
traditional values, rhetoric of, 105–106
Classical psychiatry, in Chile during 1950s and 1960s, 73
Clean, rhetoric of terrorist state, 107
Climate issues, 325–326, 343 n.20
Clinical neutrality; See Neutrality, analytic
Clinton, W. J., 24, 102, 236
Coalition for Ethical Psychology, 262 n.29, 262–263 n.30
Coercion, manufacturing of consent versus, 232
Coherence, unconscious function of dominant ideology, 12
Cohn, M., 267
Cold War, 236
    Latin American policy, 40, 41
    psychologist collaboration with military, 255
Cold War ideology, 101, 102–103, 243, 246
Collective identity, human rights violations and, 201
Collier, 60 n.11
Colombia, 309
Colonialism, 39–41, 59 n.2
Committee in Solidarity with the Argentine People (COSPA), 162–163
Communique from Argentina, 34–35
Communism, rejection of psychoanalysis and adoption of behaviorism, 68
Community structures
    free-market impunity and, 205–206
    ideology of individualism, 228
    neoliberalism and, 206, 230
Competition, neoliberal values, 227, 230
Complexity, depressive position and, 18
Complicity, 209, 253–254
Conflict
    Kleinian approach, 85
    psychopolitical dynamics, 335, 337, 345 n.28
    resistance to authority, 28
Consciousness, false, 11
Consensus, neoliberalism implementation in U.S. and Britain, 231
Consent, manufacturing of, 232
Conservatism, 311
    contemporary trends and challenges, 328–329
    ideology of individualism, 229
    political exploitation of cultural divisions, 23–24
Conservative nanny state, 239
Conservatives without Conscience (Dean), 292
Constable, P., 60 n.14, 113
Constitutional government
    Latin American elections of 1980s, 194
    neoconservative models of state, 237
Consumerism, 260 n.2
    Bush Administration recommendations, 13
    conversion of Uruguayan prison to shopping mall, 42
    historical development and evolution of neoliberalism/ neoconservatism, 227–228, 234
Container/contained concept, 8–9, 21, 125, 154, 154 n.6, 182, 271, 302
Contradiction, psychoanalytic 10 commandments of Nicaraguan training program, 181
Control systems, hegemony (Gramsci model), 11
Coontz, Stephanie, 227
Cooperation, ideology of individualism, 228
Coping mechanisms, psychology of social trauma, 123–126
Corporate hegemony, 332
    Bush–Cheney Administration policies
        economic meltdown and bailouts, 295–296
        government-corporate sector nexus, 268

historical development and
     evolution of neoliberalism/
     neoconservatism, 227,
     229–230, 234, 238–239
history and legal status of
     corporations, 260 n.3
impunity of transnational
     corporations, 205
Obama Administration policy, 303,
     310
right-wing mobilization in U.S., 311
Corporate media; See Media
Corporation, The (Bakan), 260 n.3
Corporations
     border security operations, 268
     institutional character of, 321–322
     personhood of, 321
     state terror support, 105, 119 n.2
Corradi, J. E., 60 n.15, 75
Correa, Rafael, 334–335
Corruption, 52, 202
Cosmopolitan moment, 335
Council of Conservative Citizens, 330
Counterinsurgency programs, 101–
     102, 104, 307
Countertransference; See Transference/
     countertransference
Coups, political
     Argentina, 74–75, 88
     Chile; See Allende, Salvator
     Guatemala, 40, 59 n.6
     historical context of emergence of
          state terror in Latin America,
          38–41
     Uruguay, 45
Creeds, hegemony (Gramsci model), 11
Criminal economic behavior, impunity
     and, 202–204
Crises, implementation of
     neoliberalism during,
     229–230
Cristeller, Gabriella, 90 n.11
Critical theory, 244, 247
Critical thinking, psychology of social
     trauma, 125
Crony capitalism, 221
Crude (Berlinger), 334, 344–345 n.26
Crusade, state terror rhetoric, 105
Cuba
     Volnoviches exile in, 109–110,
          169–175
Cuban Revolution, 40, 45, 48, 54, 101

Cuestionamos, 82, 90 n.9
Cuestionamos II (Langer), 117, 155
     n.13
Cultural nationalism, neoconservative
     appeal, 238
Culture
     authoritarianism in Latin America,
          104
     of consumption; See Consumerism
     contemporary trends in
          psychoanalysis, 89 n.6
     historical development and
          evolution of neoliberalism/
          neoconservatism, 227
     Latin American state terror,
          depiction of, 104
     neoliberal, postsymbolic order, 280
     neoliberalism and, 230
     pathological public sphere, 23
     socially constructed trauma,
          intergenerational transmission
          of, 8
     social matrix effects on expression
          of libidinal and aggressive
          impulses, 8–9
Culture of fear
     children, impact on, 154 n.4
     psychology of social trauma,
          124–125
     recovery of capacity for resistance,
          193
     reminders of, 208–209
     and social trauma; See Social
          trauma, culture of fear and
Culture of impunity, 214, 215, 218,
     279, 326
Culture wars, 23–24
Cumulative trauma, 22
Curtis, Adam, 260 n.7
Cushman, P., 234, 243
Custom
     impunity and social violence, 203
     unconscious function of dominant
          ideology, 12

D

Dalal, F., 10
Danger, psychology of social trauma,
     123
Danner, Mark, 260 n.10, 262 n.25
Darwin, Jaine, 275, 276

Darwinism, social, 206
historical development and
evolution of neoliberalism/
neoconservatism, 228–229
Davies, J. M., 154 n.1
Davis, M., 340 n.1
Dean, John, 292
Death anxiety, 21, 271
Death squads; See also State terror
Argentina, 56, 61, 88, 94
free-market impunity and, 206
Debray, R., 60 n.13
Debt crisis, 204, 314–315
Decentered subject, 8, 11
Defenselessness, 125
Defenses
adaptations to state terror, 110–111
bystander situation, 26, 27–28
containment of destructive
impulses, 296–297
need for enemy, 18
neoliberal revolution, 233–234
political repression, psychological
effects of, 199
psychology of social trauma, 123,
124, 125, 139–140
psycho-social definition, 10
social power relations and, 10
Deficits, U.S.
funding, 315, 316–317
Obama Administration policy, 303
de Groot, Jeanne Lampl, 64
Delinquency, 282, 286
Delusion, adaptations to state terror,
110
Democracy
nation state capitalism and, 322
U.S., 332
Democracy Now, 344–345 n.26
Democratic Leadership Council (DLC),
236
Democratic Party, U.S., 236, 332, 342
n.14
Democratization, Latin American
elections of 1980s, 194
Demolition, psychic, 131
Denial, 6
adaptations to state terror, 110
versus analytical neutrality, dealing
with political repression,
81–82
exile, psychological impact, 158

of human rights violations, by
miliitary, 200
Marx–Freud correlations, 84
political repression, psychological
effects of, 199
psychology of social trauma, 124,
126, 139–140
rationalization of policy, 18–20
responses to Bush–Cheney policies,
26, 27
Viñar on, 7
Dependency
Freud on group psychology, 215
hegemony, disengagement from, 28
resistance to authority, 28
Dependency theory, 60 n.10
Depoliticized citizen, neoliberal
isolated self, 231
Depression, social breakdown and, 206
Depressive position, Kleinian, 18,
21–22, 340
resistance to authority, 28
Deregulation
Clinton Administration and, 236
historical development and
evolution of neoliberalism/
neoconservatism, 236, 238
neoliberalism and, 232
victims of neoliberal democracy,
204
Deri, Francis, 242
Dery, Mark, 23
Desaparecidos; See also
Disappearances;
Grandmothers of the Plaza de
Mayo; Mothers of the Plaza
de Mayo
children of, 173, 222 n.2
therapeutic approaches to families
of, 196–197
Destructive original trauma, 192
Destructiveness, human, 139–143
hegemonic institutions and, 9
helplessness, responses to, 26
Kleinian approach, 85
paranoid/schizoid defenses, 104,
106
political activism and, 28
Deutsch, H., 64
Diagnosis of disordered system,
225–241
Diamond, Jared, 324

Dictatorship
  historical/strategic functions of,
    103–104
  lives during transition to, 92–101
Diplomacy, second-tier, 335, 337, 345
  n.28
Dirty, rhetoric of terrorist state, 107
Dirty Wars, 33–59, 103–104, 344 n.23
  aftermath of; See Neoliberal
    democracy in Latin America
  Argentina
    paradox of populism, 50–57
    precursors to, 74–75
  Chile, demise of democratic
    socialism, 45–50
  historical context of emergence of
    state terror in Latin America,
    38–41
  identification with the aggressor,
    141
  justice/retribution/amnesty issues,
    199–202
  Marie Langer, 35–38
  monument to casualties of, 286–287
  National Commission for the Right
    to Identity, 287
  public confessions by torturers
    in Chile and Argentina,
    208–209
  Uruguay, assault on welfare state
    politics, 41–45
  U.S. role in, 119 n.2, 119 n.5
Disappearances; See also State terror
  children of desaparecidos, 173, 222
    n.2
  children of disappeared, treatment
    of in Chile, 173
  identification with the aggressor
    and, 126
  psychodynamics of state terror,
    112–118
  psychology of social trauma, 125,
    126
  rhetoric of terrorist state, 107
  and social trauma, 127–130
  state terror strategies, 107–108
  therapeutic approaches to families
    of desaparecidos, 196–197
Disaster capitalism, 305
Discourse
  media, language distortion in,
    17–18

reductive/demonizing, 18
  state terror justifications, 104–106
Disease rates, among exiles, 159–160
Disillusion, Obama policies and,
  302–303, 309–310
Disorientation, torture methods,
  133–134
Displacement, Marx–Freud
  correlations, 84
Dissent, stigmatization of, 17–18
Dissident movements, APA, 75–79
Dissociation/dissociated states
  adaptations to state terror, 110
  political repression, psychological
    effects of, 199
  psychology of social trauma, 124,
    139–140
Division 39, APA, 225–226, 246, 247
Dobson, James, 329
Doctrines, hegemony (Gramsci model),
  11
Documento, 79
Domestic surveillance, Bush–Cheney
  Administration policies,
  266–267
Dominant ideology; See also
  Neoliberalism
  false consciousness, 11
  identification with, 24, 235
  survival of the fittest principle,
    228–229
  unconscious function of, 12
Doubling phenomenon, 142–143
Drake, 60 n.13
Dread, bystander situation, 27, 28
Dreyfuss, R., 307
Drives, social power relations and, 10
Drug trafficking/drug abuse, 206, 286
Duhalde, E. L., 102
Dunayevich, Bernardo, 127
Dunayevich, Gabriel, 92–95, 118,
  127–130, 143–144, 197
Dunayevich, Mariano, 93–95, 127–130
Duss, M., 329

E

Eagle, Morris, 260 n.4
EATIP (Argentine Team of Psycho-
  Social Work and Research),
  288
Eban, Katherine, 263 n.30

Echave, N. U. H., 222 n.6
Ecological crisis, 319–320
Economic conditions
    emotional impact of, 285
    social stresses contributing to
        response to 9/11, 21–23
Economic corruption, impunity and,
    202–204
Economic crisis
    21st century, 2
    Argentina
        as the canary in the mine, 221,
            226–227, 292, 298
        meltdown and rebellion,
            211–221
        implementation of neoliberalism
            during, 229–230
        Menem and, 201–202
        neoliberal democracy in Latin
            America, 211–221
    U.S., 341 n.6
        Bush–Cheney bailout, 295–296
        election of 2008, 295–297, 298
        Obama Administration policy,
            341 n.5
Economic hegemony, impunity of
    transnational corporations,
    205
Economic philosophies, historical
    development and
    evolution of neoliberalism/
    neoconservatism, 229–230
Economic rationality, 230
Economic system
    consumerism; See Consumerism
    contemporary crises in energy,
        environment, and economy,
        311–326
    Latin America
        flow of tribute, 236
        Nicaragua, 178
        women in Argentine workforce,
            70–71
    neoliberalism, 103; See also
        Globalization; Neoliberalism
    U.S.
        current trends in, 305
        Obama Administration policy,
            303, 304
        Obama policy, 294
Economic terrorism, neoliberalism as,
    207

Ecuador, 281, 309, 334–335
Edelman, Lucila, 121, 149, 155 n.15,
    196, 200, 202, 214, 288–291
Equipo, 147–148
    psychology of social trauma, 124
Education
    free-market impunity and, 205
    in Nicaragua, 177
Ego function
    mass media impact, 234
    political activism and, 215
    psychology of social trauma, 125
    therapeutic approaches with
        families of desaparecidos, 197
Ego ideals
    adaptation to exile, 161–162
    bystander situation, 27
Ego psychology
    doubling phenomenon, 142–143
    mainstream psychoanalysis in
        postwar (World War II)
        period, 243–244
Eichenbaum, L., 250, 252, 261 n.20
Eichmann, Adolf, 154 n.12
Einhorn, B., 315
Einstein, A., 104
Eizirik, C. L., 234
El Salvador, 163, 181, 204
Elections
    Latin America, 194, 291
    U.S.
        2004, 253
        2008, 292–298
        contemporary trends and
            challenges, 332
Elite fundamentalism, 330
Elites
    complicity with state terror, 150
    financial sectors displacement of
        industrial sectors, 193
    neoliberalism and, 229
    Obama policy, 294
    shadow, 328
Elliot, A., 10
Elshtain, J. B., 155 n.16
Emigration/migration/political exile
    into Argentina, 87–88
    from Argentina, 161–164, 169–175
    from Chile, 73, 87–88
    escape from state terror, 109–112
        Pavlovsky family, 110–112
        Volnovich family, 109–110

from Europe in 1930s, 3–4, 243
Latin American social revolutions,
    61–62, 88–89
Marie Langer in Mexico, 1974–
    1987, 161–164
Marie Langer in Nicaragua,
    176–186
psychological impact and
    psychosomatic sequelae,
    157–160
repatriation, Argentines versus
    Uruguayans, 222 n.5
from Uruguay, 45, 87–88, 164–169
Viñars in France 1976-1990, 139,
    164–169
Volnoviches to Cuba, 109–110,
    169–175
Employment/unemployment
in Argentina, 219
contemporary challenges, 314
free-market impunity and, 205
Latin American issues, 286
U.S., 305–306, 341 n.6
Empty self, 234
*End of America: Letter of Warning to
    a Young Patriot* (Wolf), 292,
    299 n.12
End Torture Action Committee,
    Psychologists for Social
    Responsibility, 262 n.28
Enemy, need for, 18, 246, 252–253
Enemy combatant designation, 267
Energy, 311–326
Energy crisis, 317–318
Engagement, capacity for, 28
Engdahl, Bonnie, 30 n.2
Engelberg, S., 19
Englehardt, 308
Enhanced interrogation; *See* Torture
Environment
    contemporary crises in energy,
        environment, and economy,
        311–326
    free-market impunity and, 205
    neoliberalism and, 229, 319, 325
Environmental Protection Agency, 268
Envy–greed–destructiveness, Kleinian
    approach, 85
Equipo, 121, 124, 140, 147–153, 155
    n.18, 196–197, 299 n.11
Ernest S. Lawrence Trauma Center,
    249

Eroticism, torture and, 115
Escobar, Pepe, 316
Esquivel, Adolfo Perez, 200
Etchegoyen, R. H., 8
Ethical nonneutrality, 245–260, 340
Ethics, collaboration of health
    professionals in torture,
    253–255
Ethics Code, APA, 254–259
Ethnic identity, reemergence of, 208
Europe, rise of fascism in, 2–4, 62–65
European culture, 67, 334
Evangelical Christianity; *See* Christian
    fundamentalism
Evil, rhetoric of, 238, 260 n.7, 290
Ewen, S., 228
Exceptionalism, American, 16–17, 22,
    238, 311–326
Executive branch expansion, Bush–
    Cheney policy, 20
Exile; *See* Emigration/migration/
    political exile
Expectations, Obama presidency and,
    302–303
Exploitation, historical
    development and
    evolution of neoliberalism/
    neoconservatism, 231
Extraordinary rendition; *See* Torture/
    extraordinary renditions
Eye movement and desensitization and
    reprocessing (EMDR), 274

F

Fagen, P. W., 102
Faletto, E., 60 n.10
Falk, Richard, 119 n.2
Falklands War, 193
Fallenbaum, Ruth, 259
False consciousness, 11
False self, 123
False sense of well being, 124
Family, the (National Fellowship
    Council/Foundation), 330
Family structure
    consumerism and, 260 n.2
    historical development and
        evolution of neoliberalism/
        neoconservatism, 234
    impact of torture, 137
    impunity and social violence, 203

neoliberal values and, 206
Nicaragua, 181–183
psychological impact of state
    terrorism, 222 n.6
Family therapy model, SOFAR, 276
Fanon, Franz, 22
Fantasy, mass media impact, 234
Fascism
    European (1930s), 2–4
    potential for in U.S., 331–332
Fascist mentality, Argentina, 193
FASIC, 146–147, 155 n.14
Fear, politics of, 260 n.7
Fears
    bystander situation, 27, 28
    contemporary challenges, 313–314
    liquid, 323, 327
    manic defense, 4
Fellowship, The, 330
Female sexuality and reproduction,
    69–70, 171–172
Feminist movement, 260 n.1; See also
    Gender
    achievements of second-wave
        feminism, 225–226
    Argentina, 86, 87, 90 n.11
    contemporary trends, 333
    contemporary trends and
        challenges, 338–339
    Cuban Family Code, 171–172
    Nicaragua, 181–182, 188–189 n.11
    reemergence of gender identity, 208
    theoretical approaches, 244
    Vienna in 1920s and 1930s, 63
    women's reproductive disturbances,
        Langer's interest in, 65
    Women's Therapy Center Institute
        (WTCI), 249–250, 261–262
        n.21
Feminist theory
    convergence with psychoanalysis
        and Marxism in Langer's
        work, 82
    role of patriarchal value in
        authoritarian regimes,
        195–196
Fenichel, O., 63, 74, 242, 243
Ferla, S., 120 n.10
Fernandez Meijide, Graciela, 129–130
Figner, Vera, 62
Finance sector

displacement of industrial sectors,
    193, 233
Obama Administration policy, 294,
    305, 306
Financial support, for authoritarian
    regimes, 222 n.4
Firehouse Clinician Project, 251–252
Fisher, J., 155 n.16, 198, 204
Fisher, W., 341 n.7
Fitzgibbon, R. H., 60 n.12
Fleming, J., 118 n.2
Fonagy, P., 15
Fonda, Jane, 225
Forced disappearances; See
    Disappearances
Ford factory, 109
Foreign policy, U.S.; See United States
    foreign policy
Foreign Policy Initiative, 329
Fort Bragg, 102
Fort Gulick, 102
Forter, G., 250–251
Foucault, Michel, 154 n.5, 230
Foulkes, S. H., 9
France, 119 n.3
Franco, Francisco, 48
Frank, T., 31 n.7, 234, 235
Frankfort School, 243
Fraser, N., 60 n.16, 87
Frawley, M. G., 154 n.1
Free association (analytical), 64, 143,
    145
Free trade, 230
Freedom, delinking individual from
    social, 231
Frei, Eduardo, 48, 50
Freiburg School of economics, 229
Frenkel-Brunswick, E., 235
Freud, A., 64
Freud, S., 30 n.1, 37, 63, 172, 242, 323
    Argentine CDIs and, 83–84
    Civilization and Its Discontents,
        73, 199–200, 214, 339
    conflict model of mind, 243
    on decentered subject, 8
    "enemies of Western Christian
        Civilization," 57, 104
    and female sexuality/reproduction,
        69, 70
    "Group Psychology and the
        Analysis of the Ego," 214–215

"Psychoanalysis and/or Social
Revolution" (Langer), 78–79
Freudian analytic schemes, neoliberal
democracy in Latin America,
209–211
Friedman, Milton, 103, 119 n.4, 229
Fromm, Erich, 74, 81, 85, 243
Frondizi, Silvio, 94
Frontalini, D., 120 n.10
Frosh, Stephen, 8
Frozen grief, 164, 182–183, 184,
197–198
Funding, right-wing think tanks, 235
Future prospects, U.S.; See United
States, future prospects

G

Galbraith, James, 341 n.5
Galeano, Eduardo, 39, 59 n.1, 108,
121
Galmozzi, M. B., 155 n.16
Geithner, Timothy, 305
Gender, 320; See also Feminist
movement
as analytic category, 225–226
consumerism and, 260 n.2
Cuban Family Code, 171
and exile experience, 168
impunity and social violence, 203
psycho-social aspects of subjectivity,
10
and responses to state terror, 155
n.17
role of patriarchal value in
authoritarian regimes,
195–196
social hierarchy, Nicaragua,
178–179
social production and psychic
reproduction of inequities,
244
state terror ideology, 119 n.9
traditional values, rhetoric of,
105–106
Gender identity, reemergence of, 208
Geneva Conventions, 26, 255, 256,
259
Gente, H. P., 155 n.13
Gentile, K., 252, 253
George, A., 118 n.2, 188 n.7
Getino, Octavio, 79

Gil, F., 60 n.14
Gilbert, G. M., 155 n.12
Gitter, A., 250
Giussani, P., 223 n.8
Glantz, Aaron, 269
Glass-Steagall Act, 306
Global warming, 328, 343 n.20
Globalization, 22
contemporary challenges, 314
and democracy, 322
Marxist, Freudian, and
postmodernist analysis,
210–211
negative, 323–324
social matrix of psychic experience,
22–23
transnational activism, 333–334
Godwin, R., 116
Going-on-being, 27
Golden, R., 155 n.16, 155 n.17
Goldscheid, Rudolf, 306
Goodman, Amy, 306, 344–345 n.26
Goodman, D., 257, 299 n.3
Government–corporate sector nexus,
268
Government corruption, 202–204
Graduate training program, social
clinical Ph.D., 235
Gramsci, A., 11, 12, 28, 202, 235–
236, 294
Grandmothers of the Plaza de Mayo,
51, 150, 191–192, 196, 206,
222 n.1, 287
Graziano, E., 60 n.18, 114, 119 n.7,
120 n.10, 125
Great Depression, 232, 243
Greenspan, Alan, 341 n.4
Greenwald, Robert, 340 n.3
Greider, William, 321
Grief, frozen, 164, 182–183, 184,
197–198
Grinberg, L. and Grinberg, L., 160,
187 n.2
Grissinopoli workers, 212–221
Group behavior
human destructiveness, 140–141
political conflicts, psychology of,
335, 345 n.28
Group dynamics
institutional and ideological matrix,
303

regressive, responsible leadership and, 302
social matrix of psychic experience, 9–10
Group psychology
 Freud on, 214–215
 historical development and evolution of neoliberalism/ neoconservatism, 227–228
Group treatment, 77
 Equipo and, 196–197
 in Nicaragua, 181
 Pavlovsky work in, 282
 psychoanalytic community beliefs, 69
Group values, containment of destructive impulses, 296–297
Guantanamo Bay, 253, 259, 306; See also Torture
Guatemala
 coup in, 40, 59 n.6
 refugees/migrants, 163
 U.S. National Security Doctrine, 204
Guatemalan refugees, 181
Guevara, Ernesto, 40, 54, 172
Guillen, Nicolas, 48
Guilt
 depressive position and, 18
 Grissinopoli workers, 216
 psychology of social trauma, 124
 survivor, 158–159
 therapeutic approaches with families of desaparecidos, 197
 torture victims, 131
Gurrieri, J., 222 n.5
Gutwill, S., 6, 21, 23, 30 n.3, 250, 252, 253, 261 n.12, 261 n.17, 312
Guzzetti, Cesar A., 105

H

Haiti, 204
Halebsky, S., 59 n.7
Halliburton, 17, 238, 267
Haraway, D., 339
Harbury, J., 31 n.10, 119 n.3
Hardt, M., 30 n.5, 241
Hare, Robert, 321–322
Harris, R., 188 n.6

Harvey, D., 232, 235, 236, 294, 317, 324
Hasbury, J., 262 n.22
Hate; See Destructiveness, human
Hayden, Tom, 295
Hayes, Nomi, 340–341 n.4
Hazaki, Cesar, 215, 216, 217, 221
Health
 EPA and OSHA enforcement under Bush–Cheney, 268
 free-market impunity and, 205
 in Nicaragua, 177
 medical school work–study program, 184–185
 Sandanista brigade program, 183–184
Health care policy, 303, 310, 330, 342 n.16
Health professionals, interrogators' interest in, 137
Hedges, C., 233, 271, 316, 325, 327, 329–330
Hegemonic values, 313
 alternatives to, 211
 bystander situation, 27–28
 consensual support of Bush–Cheney policies, 12–24
 demonized other, 326
 disengagement from, 28
 future prospects for U.S., 303
 historical development and evolution of neoliberalism/ neoconservatism, 238
 identification with, 229
 identification with the aggressor, 126
 ideology of state terror, 101–106
 impunity and social violence, 203
 internalization of, 231
 Latin American policy, 40
 Marx–Freud correlations, 84
 neoconservative discourse, 17
 neoliberal isolated self, 231
 neoliberal state, 235–236
 neoliberalism and, 227
 unconscious function of dominant ideology, 12
 U.S. Latin American policy, 29
Hegemony, Argentina in 1990s, 202–204
Hellman, C., 303
Helplessness, 122

bystander situation, 27, 28
manic defense, 4
psychology of social trauma, 125
responses to Bush–Cheney policies,
    26
torture objectives, 132
Herbert, B., 305
Herman, E. S., 118 n.2
Herman, J., 154 n.1, 154 n.10, 261
    n.13
Herrera, M., 222 n.6
Hersh, Seymour, 257, 307
Hierarchy, 178–179
Hiroshima, 18–19
Hirsch, R. C., 318
History
    neoliberal/neoconservative
        democracy in U.S., 225–241
    socially constructed trauma,
        intergenerational transmission
        of, 8
Hobshawm, Eric, 324
Hodges, D., 60 n.15, 60 n.17, 75, 119
    n.6, 119 n.7, 120 n.10
Hollander, N. C., 6, 21, 23, 30 n.3,
    70, 87, 89 n.1, 116, 119 n.9,
    155 n.17, 187 n.2, 208, 209,
    215, 218, 219, 261 n.12, 261
    n.16, 261 n.17, 261 n.18, 291,
    312, 320
Holocaust, European, 53, 147, 154–
    155 n.12, 167, 187 n.3, 243
Homeland Security Department,
    267–268
Hook, D., 10
Hope, 28, 153
Hopper, Earl, 312–313
Horkheimer, Max, 243
Horney, K., 243
Hour of the Furnaces (Getino and
    Solanas), 79
Huberman, L., 59 n.7
Hudson, M., 316, 324
Human rights
    in Argentina
        kidnapping of witnesses, 288,
            289
        Kirchner policy and, 290
    culture of impunity and, 279
    impunity and, 202–204
    market hegemony and, 214

neoliberal democracy in Latin
    America, 194–202
and psychoanalytic practice,
    preconditions for, 143–147
U.S. violations of, 254
Human trafficking, 287
Huze, Sean, 272
Hyperactivity, psychology of social
    trauma, 124
Hysteria, 71

I

Idealization, 9
    versus ideals, 339–340
Identification with the aggressor,
    125–126, 141
Identity
    in Argentina, Kirchner policy, 287,
        288
    collective, human rights violations
        and, 201
    constitution of, 312–313
    formation by social matrix of
        ideology and power relations,
        312
    Freud on group psychology, 215
    hegemonic ideology
        disengagement from, 28
        internalization of, 27–28
    interpellation, 28–29
    Latin American military culture,
        104
    neoliberal isolated self, 231
    political activism and, 215
    psychic and social realities,
        constitution of subject, 284
    psychology of social trauma, 124
    social and political world and, 214
    torture methods, 134
Ideology
    consensual support of Bush–Cheney
        policies, 12–24
    contemporary trends in U.S., 312
    defensive significance of ideological
        response to 9/11, 18–20
    dominant, unconscious function
        of, 12
    future prospects for U.S., 303
    historical development and
        evolution of neoliberalism/
        neoconservatism, 225–241

identity formation by social matrix of ideology and power relations, 312
ideologized modes of thinking, 15
media and, 16
multigenerational transmission of trauma, 244
oppositional, 294
psychoanalysis as substitute for, 71–72, 74
radical right, 332
resistance to authority, 28
social matrix effects on expression of libidinal and aggressive impulses, 9
state ideological apparatus, Althusser analysis, 12
state terror, 101–106
justifications of, 104–105
U.S. role in, 118 n.2
taxation, 296
U.S. National Security Doctrine, 30
ILAS (Latin American Institute of Mental Health and Human Rights), 147
IMF; See World Bank and International Monetary Fund
Immerman, R. H., 59 n.6
Immigration, 267–268, 328, 331
Immigration and Customs Enforcement (ICE), 267–268
Impotence; See Helplessness
Imprisonment, and social trauma, 130–139
Impunity, 223 n.8, 288
culture of, 214, 215, 218, 279, 326
justice/retribution/amnesty issues, 202–204
public confessions by torturers in Chile and Argentina, 208–209
and social justice, 279
transnational corporations, 205
India, 343 n.21
Individual
delinking from social, 231
social power relations and, 10
Individualism, 11
historical development and evolution of neoliberalism/neoconservatism, 227–228, 234

isolation, mass media effects, 322
neoliberal values, 206
ownership society, 232
Indochina, 104
Indonesia, 341 n.8, 343 n.21
Industrial sectors
contemporary challenges, 314
replacement by financial sector, 193, 233
Infantilization, 125, 215
Infertility, female, 70, 71
Infrastructure projects, 232
Inhibition, psychology of social trauma, 123
Innocence, radical/violent, 15–16
Integrity, psychic, torture objectives, 132
Intellectual roots of neoconservatism, 236–237
Intergenerational issues
exile experience, 166–167
social hierarchy, Nicaragua, 178–179
Intergenerational transmission, socially constructed trauma, 8
Internal Revenue Service, 266
Internal security, 102
Internalization
bystander situation, 27–28
hegemonic values, 231
impunity and social violence, 203
International Association of Relational Psychotherapists and Psychoanalysts (IARPP), 252
International Medical Brigade, 65
International Monetary Fund; See World Bank and International Monetary Fund
International Psychoanalysts Against Nuclear Weapons, 246
International Psychoanalytic Association, 71, 241
and Brazilian psychologist participating in torture, 262 n.23
counter-congresses of 1969 and 1971, 78–79
NGO, 335, 336
psychic reality theme, 8
recognition of Argentine Psychoanalytic Association, 67

Internationalist Team of Mental
Health Workers, Mexico–
Nicaragua, 36, 157
Internet conferences and resources,
262 n.28
activism, contemporary trends, 333
Equipo, 299 n.11
Latin American issues and
developments, 342 n.13
PSR, 253
School of the Americas (SOA)
Watch, 119 n.3
Stephen Soldz blog, 262 n.27
Interpellation, 12, 28–29, 230
Interrogation, enhanced; See Torture
Intersubjectivity, 89 n.6, 313
ideology of individualism and, 229
psycho-social definition, 10
social context of psychological
experience, 244
Inverted totalitarianism, 332
Invulnerability, psychological defenses,
27
Isolation
political prisoners, 131
psychology of social trauma, 123
torture methods, 134
Israel, 119 n.2
Israeli–Palestinian conflict, 247,
336–337

J

Jacobson, Edith, 63, 242, 243
Jacoby, R., 243
Jacques, M., 317
Jaffer, Jameel, 344 n.23
Jameson, Frederic, 324
Japan, 18–19
Jelin, E., 155 n.16
Jensen, Derrick, 325
Jessen, Bruce, 263 n.30
Jewish analysts, persecution of in
1930s, 65
Johnson, C., 239
Johnson, Chalmers, 260 n.10, 308–
309, 315, 342 n.12, 342 n.17
Johnson, D. L., 60 n.14
Johnson, J. J., 59 n.8
Journalists, criminal complaints and
imprisonments in U.S., 267

Judiciary, complicity with state terror,
150
Just war, 105, 326
Justice; See also Impunity
in Argentina
fear of pursuing, and amnesty
for military, 200
kidnapping of witnesses, 288
rule of law, Freud on, 199–200
Justification, of human rights
violations, 200

K

Kacs, R., 222 n.6
Katz, Maureen, 6
Kaufman, E., 60 n.12
Kellogg, Brown, and Root, 267
Kennedy, Edward, 266–267
Kernberg, Otto, 73
Kerry, John, 253
Kesselman, Hernan, 79
Keynsianism, 232
Khan, M., 22
Kidnappings, 288–289; See also
Disappearances
lives during transition to
dictatorship, 94
Mothers of the Plaza de Mayo
members, 150
state terror strategies, 107–108
Killing in the Name of Identity: A
Study of Bloody Conflicts
(Volkan), 335
Kim, R., 332
Kinzer, S., 59 n.6
Kirchner, Cristina, 285
Kirchner, Nestor, 218–219, 279, 282,
286, 287, 288, 290
Kirk, J. M., 59 n.7
Klare, M., 118 n.2, 188 n.7, 223 n.7,
343 n.21
Klein, Melanie, 9, 18, 69–70, 85, 302,
303
Klein, Naomi, 119 n.4, 229–230,
238–239, 260 n.5, 260 n.10,
262 n.25, 305, 319, 328
Kogel, L., 250
Kollontai, Aleksandra, 62
Kordon, Diana, 121–122, 148–149,
151–152, 196, 200, 202, 206,
214, 288, 289, 290, 291

Kordon, D. R., 121, 122, 140, 155
    n.15, 195, 196, 200, 202,
    288–291
Kornbluh, P., 188 n.7, 223 n.7
Kovalsky, Juana, 89 n.5
Kovel, J., 321
Kreisler, H., 299 n.4
Krugman, Paul, 304, 315, 341 n.5
Kunstler, James, 318
Kuo, David, 330
Kyoto Protocol, 318–319, 325

L

Lacan, J., 9, 28
Lacanian analysis, 130–131
    leadership, 303
    "Marx and Freud are the two main
        enemies of Western Christian
        Civilization," 60 n.18
    social matrix of psychic experience,
        10, 11
Lacanian view, social matrix of psychic
    experience, 12, 14–15
Laclau, E., 29, 240, 261 n.11, 293
LaFeber, W., 59 n.4
Lagos, Dario, 121, 122, 147–148, 196,
    200, 214, 288, 290
Lagos, Ricardo, 30 n.6, 60 n.14,
    288–291
Lakoff, George, 296, 303
Landsberger, H., 60 n.14
Langer, Marie, 2, 35–38, 61–65, 79,
    87, 89 n.1, 89 n.3, 90 n.10,
    94, 98, 129, 138, 146, 149,
    155 n.13, 187 n.1, 188 n.9,
    189 n.12, 189 n.13, 226, 243,
    262 n.23, 279, 338, 339
    APA institutional conflicts, 75–76
    on collaboration of mental health
        professionals with torture,
        254
    Cuestionamos II, 117
    death of, 185–186
    exile experience, 160
    flight from Argentina, 61–62,
        88–89
    flight from Europe, 66
    on human destructiveness, 140–141
    Latin American Congress of
        Marxist Psychology and
        Psychoanalysis, 188 n.10

in Mexico 1974–1987, 161–164
    in Nicaragua, 157, 176–186
    opposition to neoliberal agenda,
        204–205
    psychology of social trauma, 124
    state terrorism from abroad, U.S.
        policy as, 188 n.8
    Viñar campaign, 135
Langer, Max, 65, 66
Language
    distortion of in media discourse,
        17–18
    euphemisms and justifications for
        torture, 24–26
    exile experience, 166
    psycho-social aspects of subjectivity,
        10
    reductive/demonizing, 18
    state terror strategies, 107
Lantos, Barbara, 242
LaPlanche, Jean, 9, 10, 11
Lasch, C., 260 n.6
Latin America, 2, 7, 12, 31 n.10
    bystander problem, 29–30
    collaboration of health professionals
        in torture, 254
    current tensions developing with
        U.S., 309
    Dirty Wars, 33–59; *See also* Dirty
        Wars
    hemispheric cooperation initiatives,
        342 n.13
    interviews on Bush–Cheney
        Administration responses to
        9/11
        Braun, 284–287
        Carlotto, 287–288
        Kordon, Lagos, and Edelman,
            288–291
        Pavlovsky, 282–284
        Volnovich and Werthein,
            279–282
    neoliberal democracy and
        meltdown; *See* Neoliberal
        democracy in Latin America
Latin America, psychoanalysis in New
    World, 66–73
    Argentina, 66–72
    Argentina, social commitment to
        psychoanalysis, 74–75
    Chile, 73

class struggle and psychoanalysis, 82–89
exile, 61–62, 88–89
institutional debate, 75–79
institutional rupture, 79–82
Uruguay, 72–73
Latin American Congress of Marxist Psychology and Psychoanalysis, 188 n.10
Latin American Institute of Mental Health and Human Rights (ILAS), 147
Latin American perspectives, on Bush–Cheney Administration policies, 278–292
Law, rule of, 199–200
Lawrence Trauma Center, 249
Layton, L., 231, 247, 261 n.12, 261 n.13, 261 n.17
Leadership, responsible, 302, 340 n.2
Lemke, T., 230
Leopold, J., 344 n.23
Levinson, D. J., 235
Li, Minqui, 324
Liberalism
  hegemonic assumptions, 11
  political exploitation of cultural divisions, 23–24
Liberation theology, 45
Libidinal and aggressive impulses; See Aggression
Lifestyle, 234
Lifton, Robert Jay, 6, 14, 21, 154 n.1, 247, 299 n.4
Lightblau, Eric, 266
Limbaugh, Rush, 330
Lind, Michael, 341 n.6
Liquid fears, 323, 327
Lira, Elizabeth, 45–50, 57, 113, 154 n.3, 194, 201, 203, 245
  life during transition to dictatorship, 99–101
  psychoanalysis, social preconditions for, 145–146
  psychology of social trauma, 124–125, 142–143
  social trauma of state terror, 132
  torture psychodynamics, 116
Listen to the Devil (Atran), 342 n.11
Liwsky, Norberto, 129–130, 154 n.7
Long War, 307
Lopez, Julio Jorge, 289

Los Angeles Institute for Psychoanalytic Studies (LAISPS), 241, 249, 299 n.5
Soldiers Project, 272–275
Losi, M., 257, 262 n.29
Loss
  adaptation to exile, 160
  psychology of social trauma, 124
  themes in Argentinian psychoanalysis, 82
Lovato, Roberto, 268
Low Intensity Conflict (LIC), 178, 188 n.7, 204, 223 n.7
Lula da Silva, Luiz Inacio, 22, 30 n.6, 219

M

Machismo, 105–106
Mahfouz, Afaf, 335–336
Malaise, social, 226
Maldonado, Ignacio (Nacho), 37, 157, 159, 187 n.1, 187 n.2
Malvinas War, 193
Mamora, L., 222 n.5
Manic defense, 27
  Europe in 1930s, 4
  psychology of social trauma, 124
  responses to exile, 159
Manifest Destiny, 16–17, 29, 39, 238, 312
Manufacturing of consent, 232
Manz, B., 155 n.16
Marcuse, H., 73, 74, 244
Market economy
  historical development and evolution of neoliberalism/ neoconservatism, 227–228; *See also* Neoliberalism
  impunity of transnational corporations, 205
Marks, J., 262 n.22
Martín–Baró, Ignacio, 33
Marx, K., 37
  Argentine CDIs and, 83–84
  "enemies of Western Christian Civilization," 57, 104
Marxism
  class as analytic category, Bolger on, 225–226
  Europe, 1920s and 1930s, 3, 4, 62–63

Latin America, 59 n.9
and psychoanalysis, 37, 68
    APA ideological struggles, 76–77
    in Chile, 73
    "Psychoanalysis and/or Social
        Revolution" (Langer), 78–79
Marxist analysis, neoliberal democracy
    in Latin America, 209–211
Mass Psychology of Fascism, The
    (Reich), 141
Masters, Ian, 341 n.6
Matte–Blanco, Ignacio, 73
Mayer, J., 262 n.24, 263 n.30
Mayhew, Carol, 30 n.2
McCain, John, 295, 298
McCarthy (Joseph) era, 25–26, 243
McClintock, Michael, 119 n.2
McCoy, Alfred, 30, 119 n.3, 262 n.22
McGovern, R., 341 n.9
McLeod, M., 155 n.16
McNamara, Robert, 102
Meaning(s)
    multiple, coexisting, constitution of
        subject, 284
    psychoanalytic training program in
        Nicaragua, 181
    psycho-social definition, 10
    therapeutic benefits of activism, 153
Media
    Christian evangelical movement,
        329
    concentration of ownership, 17
    and contemporary activism in U.S.,
        310
    contemporary trends and
        challenges, 329, 342 n.12
    corporate dominated, 240
    culture of fear, 125
    historical development and
        evolution of neoliberalism/
        neoconservatism, 234
    impact on community and social
        organizations, 322
    Latin American filmmaking in
        1960s and 1970s, 79–80
    Latin American state terror,
        depiction of, 104
    neoconservative discourse, 5
    neoliberal values, 206
    official ideology, 16
    opposition journalists with criminal
        charges and arrests, 267

pathological public sphere, 23
political role of, 312
reports on torture and
    extraordinary rendition, 25
right wing, 330
    and neoconservative ascendancy,
        24
    organization, 240
    social matrix of psychic experience,
        16
    state terror strategies, 107
    traditional values, rhetoric of,
        105–106
    WTC image replays, 13
Medical model, psychoanalysis, 243
Medical training, Nicaraguan medical
    school work–study program,
    184–185
*Meeting of Minds, A: Mutuality in
    Psychoanalysis* (Aron), 261
    n.14
Meijide, Graciela Fernandez, 129–130
Memory
    amnesty issues, 194–202
    Bush–Cheney Administration
        policies, Obama
        Administration reconciliation
        policy, 306–307
    and collective mental health, 199
    monument to casualties of Dirty
        War, 286–287
Menchu, R., 155 n.16
Menem, Carlos, 201–202, 218
Mental health professionals
    interrogators' interest in, 137
    participation in torture
        Brazil, 117, 254, 262 n.23
        U.S., 253–258
    PSR and, 253
    Sandanista policies, 179, 183–184
Mental processes, psychology of social
    trauma, 123, 124
Mentalization, 15
Mexican immigrants, Ernest S.
    Lawrence Trauma Center
    services, 249
Mexico, 59 n.4
Mexico, exiles in, 36, 62
    Argentine Center, 36
    Langer, 1974-1987, 161–164
Meyer, J., 257
Middle class

Argentina economic collapse effects,
    219–220
  Latin American issues, 282–283,
    284
  U.S., 341 n.6
*Might Freud's Legacy Lie Beyond
    the Couch?* (Twemlow and
    Parens), 248–249
Migration, political; *See* Emigration/
    migration/political exile
Miguens, J. E., 60 n.16
Miles, S. H., 254
Militarism, neoconservative
    ascendancy, 236–237
Military, Latin America
  draconian policies, literature on,
    222 n.6
  paternalistic gender values, 105–106
  U.S. assistance to and training of,
    102, 118 n.2
  worldview, 119 n.7
Military, U.S.
  budgets, contemporary challenges,
    315
  Bush–Cheney Administration
    policies
    composition of, 269
    privatization of, 239, 269–270
    sequelae of service, 270–278
    SOFAR, 275–278
    Soldiers Project, 272–275
    treatment of soldiers, 269–271
  master contingency plan, 299 n.1
  Obama Administration policy, 303,
    307–308, 341–342 nn.7–12,
    342 n.17, 343–344 n.21
  recruitment activity, 299 n.3
  and state terror, 120 n.11
Military Commissions Act of 2006,
    256, 267, 278
Military coups; *See* Coups, political
Military dictatorships, and
    implementation of
    neoliberalism, 230
Militias, 330–331
Miller, Barry, 30 n.2
Miller, J., 19
Mind, models of, 243–244
Minqui Li, 324
Minutemen Civil Defense Corps, 331
Mitchell, James, 263 n.30
Mitchell, S. A., 9

Mitscherlich, Alexander, 215, 293
Mobility of capital, 232
Modernity, solid, 323
Mom, Jorge, 89 n.1
Montoneros, 55, 56, 80, 83, 87, 96
Moral values, 230, 237
Mosh pits, 280
Motherhood and Sexuality (Langer),
    71
Mothers of the Plaza de Mayo, 124,
    155 n.15, 155 n.16, 155 n.18,
    196, 209, 287
  Argentine Team of Psycho–Social
    Work and Research, 288
  Equipo, 299 n.11
  social trauma and culture of fear,
    121, 147–153
Mouffe, C., 261 n.11
Mourning
  disappeared, 128–129
  psychology of social trauma, 124
  therapeutic approaches with
    families of *desaparecidos*,
    197, 198
Multigenerational transmission of
    trauma, 244
Multipolar world, emergence of, 316
Murder, state terror strategies,
    107–108
Murphy, Walter F., 267
Myers, T., 12, 228

N

"Nacho" Maldonado, Ignacio, 157
NAFTA, 236
Nagasaki, 18–19
Nanny state, conservative, 239
Narcissism, 309
  historical development and
    evolution of neoliberalism/
    neoconservatism, 228–229,
    231
  postmodern culture; *See*
    Postmodern culture
  responses to neoliberal changes,
    234, 260 n.6
Narcissistic vulnerabilities, 13
Nation state capitalism, and
    democracy, 322
National Commission for the Right to
    Identity, 287

National Fellowship Council/
    Foundation, 330
National Intelligence Council, 343
    n.21
National Reorganization, Process of,
    105
National Security Agency, 266
National Security Doctrine, U.S., 30,
    101, 108
    social matrix of psychic experience,
    7–24
    torture as element of, 114, 116
National security policy
    Bush–Cheney Administration,
    265–267
    contemporary challenges, 343 n.21
    Long War, 307
    from social state to security state,
    344 n.25
National Socialism, 63–64, 140–142
Nationalism, cultural, 238
Nationalist movements, Latin America,
    39
Nativism, 330
Navarro, M., 60 n.16, 87
Nazis, 154–155 n.12
Negative globalization, 323–324
Negri, A., 30 n.5, 241
Neier, A., 188 n.8
Nemesis (Johnson), 308–309
Neocolonialism, 59 n.2
Neoconservative movement, 5
    authoritarianism, U.S. attitudes,
    292
    evolution of, 24
    hegemonic assumptions, 11
    intellectual roots, 236–237
    social matrix of psychic experience,
    17–18, 24
Neoliberal democracy in Latin
    America, 191–223
    economic meltdown and rebellion,
    211–221
    modes of analysis, Freudian,
    Marxist, postmodernist,
    209–211
    progressive governments, emergence
    of, 281–282
    psychoanalyst activism and human
    rights, 194–202
    social violence and impunity,
    hegemony in 1990s, 202–204

state terror, undoing, 192–194
    victims of, 204–209
Neoliberal/neoconservative democracy
    in U.S., 225–263
    activism of psychoanalysts,
    245–260
    historical development and
    evolution of, 225–241
    psychoanalysis, from neutrality to
    social responsibility, 241–244
Neoliberalism, 23, 29, 103
    and Latin America, 39
    Obama Administration policy, 303,
    305
    and state terror, 119 n.4
Neruda, Pablo, 48
Neutrality, analytic, 313
    APA institutional conflicts, 75,
    81–82
    ethical nonneutrality, 245–260, 340
    social preconditions for
    psychoanalysis, 144–145, 147
    U.S. psychoanalytic community,
    from neutrality to social
    responsibility, 241–244
New Democrats, U.S., 236
New Hope Cooperative, 212–221
New World Order, 22, 52
New York, Firehouse Clinician Project,
    251–252
Nicaragua, 37, 157, 187–188 n.6, 223
    n.9, 339, 341 n.8
    Contra training in U.S., 188 n.8
    elections 1990, 189 n.13
    Internationalist Team of Mental
    Health Workers, Mexico–
    Nicaragua, 36
    Langer work in, 164, 176–186
    neoliberalism, effects of, 206
    refugees/migrants, 163–164
    U.S. National Security Doctrine,
    204, 205
Nihilism, postmodern culture; See
    Postmodern culture
Nixon, Richard, 99–100
No Child Left Behind Act, 299 n.3
No fly lists, 266–267
Noisiglia, J.E., 222 n.6
Nonneutrality, ethical, 245–260, 340
Noriega, Roger, 219
Normative unconscious processes, 231

North American Congress on Latin
    America, 60 n.9, 60 n.14, 223
    n.8, 223 n.10
North American Free Trade Agreement
    (NAFTA), 236
Nuclear weapons, 18–19
Nunca mas, 119 n.5, 154 n.7
Nunez, H. R., 222 n.6

O

Oath keepers, 344 n.21
Obama, Barack, 29, 292–298
Obama Administration policy,
    301–311, 326, 341–345
Obamaprise, 310
Object relations theory, 9
Occupational Safety and Health
    Administration, 268
O'Donnell, G. A., 60 n.11
Office of Public Safety, 102
Ogden, T., 13, 154 n.6
Oil supplies, 317–318, 343 n.19
Oligarchy, 227
Olivdo, 194–202; *See also* Amnesia,
    social
Olson, Brad, 259
Omang, J., 188 n.8
Online resources, PsyBc seminar,
    Ideology and the Clinic, 248
Oppenheim, L. H., 118 n.1
Opposition, political
    absence of, 24
    antiwar demonstrations of 2003, 29
    Argentina, death squad activity, 88
    Bush–Cheney surveillance programs
        and, 266
    culture of fear, 126
    historical/strategic functions of
        Latin American dictatorships,
        103–104
    Obama Administration policy, 311
    to Obama policies, 303
    psychology of social trauma, 125
    state terror strategies, 107
    torture policy as deterrent to, 258
    United States
        right-wing activism, 329–331
        right-wing organization, 344
        n.21
    in U.S. after 9/11, 240
Oppositional ideology, 294

Oppression
    acceptance of, 215
    ego psychology and, 244
Orbach, S., 244, 250, 261 n.20
Order, language distortions, 107
Organization of Mental Health
        Workers, 83–84, 149
Ortega, Daniel, 187 n.4, 189 n.13
O'Sullivan, Gerry, 118 n.2
Ownership society, 232

P

Page, J., 60 n.16
Palast, Greg, 267
Palin, Sarah, 295, 298, 332
Panama, 102, 118 n.2
Panic, 122
*Paradise Built in Hell, A: The
        Extraordinary Communities
        That Arise in Disaster*
        (Solnit), 333
Paramilitary forces, 56, 61, 82, 83, 85,
        88, 102–103, 106, 107, 111,
        196
Paranoia, psychology of social trauma,
        123
Paranoid/schizoid position
    bystander situation, 27
    containment of destructive
        impulses, 296–297
    Klein on, 9
    responsible leadership, 302
    U.S. social changes since 1980, 240
Paranoid/schizoid splitting, 15
Parens, Henri, 248–249
Participant–observer role, psychology
        of social trauma, 125
Passivity
    neoliberal isolated self, 231
    psychology of social trauma, 125
Pathological public sphere, 23
Pathology, rhetoric of, 105
Pathology of the potential space, 13
Patriarchy, 119 n.9, 320
    and authoritarianism, 195–196
    Mothers of the Plaza de Mayo and,
        150
    political ideology of U.S. right wing,
        332
    traditional values, rhetoric of,
        105–106

Patriot Act, 14
Patriotism, political ideology of U.S. right wing, 332
Pavlovsky, Eduardo, 76–78, 79, 80, 86, 90 n.7, 124, 141–142, 193, 282–284
    escape from state terror, 110–112
    life during transition to dictatorship, 95, 97
Pax Americana, 17
Paxton, Robert, 331
Peak oil, 317–318, 343 n.19
Pelento, M. L., 128
Peltz, Rachael, 9, 246–247, 261 n.15, 261 n.16, 340
Pena, Rudolfo Ortega, 95
People's Revolutionary Army (ERP), 83
Perception, modes of, 11
Perelli, C., 154 n.3
Pereya, D., 59 n.9
Perez Esquivel, Adolfo, 200
Perez Villar, Jose, 172
Perkins, J., 31 n.10, 262 n.22
Peron, Evita, 70
Peron, Juan, 71
Peronism, 53–54, 55, 56, 60 n.16, 87
    Buenos Aires in 1940s and 1950s, 67
    Montoneros; See Montoneros
    repression of opposition in 1970s, 88
Persecutory anxieties, 116, 141, 143, 240
    dynamics of response to 9/11, 21–22
Personal security, Latin American issues, 282, 284
Personality, impact of torture, 137
Personhood of corporations, 321
Peru, 309
Petras, J., 30 n.5, 342 n.13
Phillips, T., 309
Pines, D., 187 n.3
Pinochet, A., 105, 118 n.1, 194, 208
Pitney, N., 268
Pitt, W. R., 331
Plant, J., 339
Plataforma, 79, 80, 81, 98
Plunder, 117
Plutocracy, 227
PNAC, 17–18, 24

Political activism; See Activism, political; Activism, psychoanalytic community
Political Brain, The (Westen), 310
Political conflict, psychoanalytically oriented academic conferences, 250–251
Political corruption, impunity and, 202–204
Political crises, implementation of neoliberalism during, 229–230
Political culture
    Buenos Aires in 1940s and 1950s, 67–68
    social matrix effects on expression of libidinal and aggressive impulses, 9
    U.S.
        culture war strategies of political parties, 23–24
        right-wing organization, 235
        social stresses contributing to response to 9/11, 22, 23–24
        social trauma and; See Social trauma, and post–9/11 political culture
Political economy; See Neoliberal democracy in Latin America
Political ideology; See also Ideology
    contemporary trends and challenges, 328–332
    psychoanalysis as substitute for, 71–72, 74
    psychological and social sequelae, 244
Political subjectivity, 6
Politics of fear, 260 n.7
Politics on the Couch (Samuels), 6
Pontecorvo, G., 59 n.2
Popkin, L. B., 154 n.3
Populism, conservative, 23, 24
Portuges, Stephen, 242–243
Postmodern culture, 8
Postmodernist analysis, neoliberal democracy in Latin America, 209–211
Postsymbolic order era, 280
Posttraumatic stress disorder (PTSD), 122
    returning military, 270
    torture sequelae, 132

Potential space, pathology of, 13
Poverty
    in Argentina, 219
    neoconservative ascendancy and,
        239–240
Poverty in America Project, 260 n.9
Power
    hegemony (Gramsci model), 11
    historical development and
        evolution of neoliberalism/
        neoconservatism, 230–231
    identity formation by social matrix
        of ideology and power
        relations, 312
    unconscious function of dominant
        ideology, 12, 221
*Power of Nightmares: The Rise of the
    Politics of Fear* (Curtis), 260
    n.7
Power relations, social, 10
    feminist analysis, patriarchal values
        and, 195–196
    future prospects for U.S., 303
Preemptive war, 237
Presidential Task Force on
        Psychological Ethics and
        National Security (PENS),
        254–255
Prins, Christopher, 340–341 n.4
Prison system, U.S., 268
Private property, 11, 227
Privatization
    border security operations, 268
    historical development and
        evolution of neoliberalism/
        neoconservatism, 230, 236,
        238, 239
    military, 268
    neoliberalism and, 232
    U.S. military, 269–270
Process of National Reorganization,
    105
Professional associations, right wing,
    235
Professional military, U.S., 269–270
Professionals, interrogators' interest
    in, 137
Project for a New American Century
    (PNAC), 17, 236–237,
    328–329
Projection, 9, 15
    idealization versus ideals, 339–340

    need for enemy, 18
    psychological defenses, 27
Projective identification, 9
PSR; *See* Psychotherapists for Social
        Responsibility (PSR)
PsyBc, 248, 253, 261 n.18
Psychic demolition, 131
Psychic experience, social matrix of,
        7–24
    ideological and rhetorical responses
        to 9/11, 12–17
    globalization impacts and,
        22–23
    media, 16
    PNAC and neoconservative
        movement, 17–18, 24
    theoretical perspectives
        Gramsci perspective, 12
        group dynamics, 9–10
        Lacanian view, 10, 11
        LaPlanche perspective, 10, 11
        Lifton perspective, 14, 21
        object relations theory, 9
        psychoanalytic research, 8–9
Psychic numbing, 21
Psychic reality
    constitution of subject, 284
    exploration in psychoanalysis,
        social preconditions for,
        143–147
    interplay with social forces, 8
    social reality and, 247, 305
Psychoanalysis
    dissident movements in Argentina,
        78–79
    and Marxism, in Chile, 73
    from neutrality to social
        responsibility, 241–244
    official Soviet rejection of, 68
    social matrix of psychic experience,
        8–9
    social preconditions for exercise of,
        143–147
Psychoanalysis, Class, and Politics
        (Layton, Hollander, and
        Gutwill), 261 n.12, 261 n.17
Psychoanalysis, Culture & Society,
        250
Psychoanalysis and Culture, 247
"Psychoanalysis and/or Social
        Revolution" (Langer), 78, 82

Psychoanalysis for Social
    Responsibility section, APA
    Division 39, 246–247
Psychoanalysis without the couch, 180,
    213–214, 221, 339
Psychoanalytic Dialogues, 89 n.6
Psychoanalytic Work Group for Peace
    in Palestine/Israel, 336
Psychodrama, 77
Psychological warfare, Nicaraguan
    Contra training in U.S., 188
    n.8
Psychologists for Social Responsibility,
    343 n.20
Psychology
    culture of fear and practice of
        psychoanalysis, 143–147
    individual, linkage to social
        pathology, 243
    psychology of social trauma,
        139–140
    torture sequelae, 132
Psycho-social, defined, 10
Psychosocial dynamics of state terror,
    91–120
    flight/escape from, 109–112
    forced disappearances and torture,
        112–118
    ideology of state terror, 101–106
    lives during transition to, 92–101
        Braun family, 92–95
        Lira family, 99–101
        Pavlovsky family, 95, 97
        Viñar family, 97–99
        Volonvich family, 95–97
    strategies, 107–109
Psychosomatic problems
    responses to exile, 159–160
    responses to state terror, 178
Psychotherapists for Social
    Responsibility (PSR),
    252–253
Public culture
    advertising industry and, 227–228
    social breakdown and, 206
Public discourse
    state terror justifications, 104–106
    state terror strategies, 107
Public health projects, Argentina, 87
Public interests, corporate interests
    versus, 268

Public relations, public cultural ideals,
    227
Public sphere
    historical development and
        evolution of neoliberalism/
        neoconservatism, 230–231
    pathological, 23
Puget, J., 222 n.6
Pyrotechnic Insanitarium, The (Dery),
    23

Q

Quality of life indices, U.S., 343 n.18

R

Race, psycho-social aspects of
    subjectivity, 10
Radical free market ideology, 229
Radical innocence, 15–16
Radical right; *See* Right-wing activism
Radical social criticism, 211
    applications to psychoanalysis, 244
    Vienna in 1920s and 1930s,
        242–243
Rae, Bob, 228, 260 n.4
Ramirez, S., 187 n.4
Ramsy, Nadia, 336, 337
Randall, Margaret, 189 n.11
Rand Corporation, 341 n.9
Rascovsky, Arnaldo, 89 n.1
Rasmus, Jack, 341 n.5
Rationality, neoliberal theory, 230
Reagan, Ronald, 157, 178, 187 n.6,
    232, 233, 236
Realities
    exploration in psychoanalysis,
        social preconditions for,
        143–147
    psychic and social, constitution of
        subject, 280
    psychic-social interface, 247
    social and psychic, linkages,
        243–244
Reality
    Lacanian view, 130–131
    mass media impact, 234
    psychology of social trauma, 125,
        126
    responsible leadership, 302
    torture methods, 133–134

Reconstructive trauma, 192
Recruitment, military, 299 n.3
Reed, B., 332
Refugees, political; *See* Emigration/
    migration/political exile
Regressed states, contemporary
    challenges, 313–314
Reich, A., 242
Reich, Kenneth, 275–276, 299 n.7
Reich, W., 63, 64, 73, 74, 81, 141, 242
Reisner, Steven, 257, 258, 262 n.29
Relational perspectives, 9, 89 n.6, 244
Relativism, postmodern culture; *See*
    Postmodern culture
Religion, 187 n.5
    Christian fundamentalism,
        233; *See also* Christian
        fundamentalism
    hegemony (Gramsci model), 11
    neoconservatism and, 237
    state terror justifications, 105–106
Religiosity, political ideology of U.S.
    right wing, 332
Reparation
    containment of destructive
        impulses, 296–297
    Kleinian approach, 85
    responsible leadership, 302
Repetitive trauma, 122–123
Repression, economic, 204
Repression, emotional
    Marx–Freud correlations, 84
    political repression, psychological
        effects of, 199
    psychoanalysis, social preconditions
        for, 143–147
    psychology of social trauma, 126
    responses to Bush–Cheney policies,
        26
Repression, political
    Argentina, 81–82, 198–199
    conversion of prison to shopping
        mall in Uruguay, 42
    impunity and social violence, 203
    psychoanalysis, social preconditions
        for, 143–147
    state terror strategies, 108
    U.S. political climate of 1950s,
        25–26
Reproduction; *See* Women's
    reproduction
Republican Party, 233, 311, 332

Research, psychological, 102
Research and Training Centers,
    Organization of Mental
    Health Workers, 83–84, 85,
    149
Resistance; *See also* Opposition,
    political
    recovery of capacity for, 193
    torture objectives, 131–132
Responsible leadership, 302
Retribution; *See* Impunity
Revolutions
    Europe, rise of Fascism, 62–65
    in Hungary, 4
    Latin America, psychoanalysis in
        New World, 66–73
    Argentina, 66–72, 74–75
    Chile, 73
    class struggle and
        psychoanalysis, 82–89
    exile, 61–62, 88–89
    institutional debate, 75–79
    institutional rupture, 79–82
    Uruguay, 72–73
    Nicaraguan popular church, 187
        n.5
    psychoanalytic analogues, 84
Rhetoric
    Argentinian military, 105
    state terror justifications, 105–106
Right-wing activism, 311, 342 n.15,
    342 n.16
    contemporary trends and
        challenges, 329–332, 344
        n.21
    Obama Administration and, 304
Risen, James, 266
Risk, social preconditions for
    psychoanalysis, 144–145
Risk society, 323
Roberts, P. C., 315
Robinson, S., 332
Roosevelt, Franklin D., 232
Rosencof, Mauricio, 142, 154 n.9, 193
Roth-Douquet, K., 269
Rouquie, A., 120 n.10
Roxborough, I., 60 n.13
Roy, A., 30 n.5, 324, 340
Rule, hegemony (Gramsci model), 11
Rule of law, 199–200
Ruskin, M., 9, 90 n.10
Russia, 328

S

Sadism, 115, 116, 143–147, 228, 329
Salvadoran refugees, 181
Salvaticio, S., 257, 262 n.29
Samuels, Andrew, 6, 261 n.13, 295
Sand Storm, The: Stories from the Front (Huze), 272
Sandanista Front, 187 n.4
Sandanista National Liberation Front, 189 n.13
Sandanista Revolution, 164, 339; *See also* Nicaragua
    brigade program, 183
    U.S. Latin American policy, 187–188 n.6
Sanford, Nevett, 235
Sanford, R. N., 235
Saunders, D., 316
Scahill, J., 239
Scapegoating, 126
Scarry, E., 117
Schaeffer, F., 269, 331, 344 n.24
Schechter, D., 341 n.4
Schlesinger, S., 59 n.6
Schmitter, P. C., 60 n.11
School of the Americas (SOA), 102
School of the Americas (SOA) Watch, 119 n.3, 262 n.22
Schwin, P., 268
Scilingo, Adolfo Francisco, 208–209
Second-tier diplomacy, 335, 337, 345 n.28
Secondary trauma, SOFAR program, 277
Secrecy, Bush–Cheney Administration policies, 238
Section 9, APA, 31 n.9
Section IX, 247–248, 255–256, 261 n.16, 262 n.24, 262 n.26
Security seeking, responses to economic crisis, 220
Security state, devolution to, 344 n.25
Segal, Hannah, 18, 19, 245–246, 339, 340
Self
    psycho-social subjectivity, 10
    social reality and, 8
Self-actualization, 234
Self-censorship, psychology of social trauma, 123, 126

Self-defense, justification of arms trade, 19
Self-determination, political, 40
Self-esteem
    adaptation to exile, 161–162
    ideology of individualism, 228, 229
Self-repression, psychology of social trauma, 125
Self-states
    empty self, 234
    neoliberal isolated self, 231
Señor Galindez (Pavlovsky), 78, 80, 86, 90 n.7, 97, 142
Sense of going-on-being, 27
Seoane, M., 222 n.6
SERE program, 263 n.30
Sexuality
    and motherhood, Langer's interest in, 65
    psycho-social aspects of subjectivity, 11
    Vienna in 1920s and 1930s, 63
Shadow elite, 328
Shakir, F., 268
Shane, S., 326
Shanghai Cooperation Organization (SCO), 316
Shared experience, social trauma as, 123
Sharlet, Jeff, 330
Sharrock, Justine, 344 n.21
Shary, Joy, 30 n.2
Shaw, Alice, 261 n.16
Sheer, Robert, 306
Shiva, V., 339
Shock and awe, 18, 238
Shock Doctrine, The: The Rise of Disaster Capitalism (Klein), 119 n.4, 229–230, 260 n.5
Sigmund, P. E., 222 n.4
Silence, psychology of social trauma, 123
Simmel, Ernest, 242
Simpson, J., 116
Sir No Sir! (Zeigler), 299 n.2
Skahill, J., 308
Skarlew, B., 248
Slavoj, Zizek, 261 n.13
Social amnesia; *See* Amnesia, social
Social brain initiative, 249
Social cleansing, 206

Social conditions
  and authoritarianism, 299 n.13
  and psychoanalytic practice,
    preconditions for, 143–147
Social construction of war-induced
    trauma, 244
Social context of mental illness, 181
Social context of psychological
    experience, 244
Social Darwinism, 206, 228–229
Social decay, and responses to 9/11,
    21–23
Social dislocations, neoliberalism and,
    193
Social factors, contemporary trends in
    psychoanalysis, 89 n.6
Social impact of Bush–Cheney
    Administration wars,
    268–269
Social issues, emotional impact of in
    Latin America, 286
Social movements, activism in new
    millennium, 208
Social neutrality, APA institutional
    conflicts, 81
Social pathology, 324–325
  ego psychology and, 243–244
  individual psychology linkage, 243
  responsible leadership, 302
Social policy
  Great Depression, response to, 232
  historical development and
    evolution of neoliberalism/
    neoconservatism, 229–230
Social power relations, 10
Social process, delinking individual
    from, 231
Social programs
  Great Depression, response to, 232
  Nicaragua since 1990, 189 n.13
Social psychiatry, 76
Social psychology
  advertising industry, 227–228
  social clinical Ph. D. program, 235
Social reality
  constitution of subject, 284
  psychic reality and, 243–244, 247
  psychoanalysis, social preconditions
    for, 143–147
Social services, Great Depression, 232
Social structures
  culture of impunity and, 279

ideology of individualism, 228
neoliberalism and, 230, 232–233
and psychological states,
    contemporary trends, 305
Social symbols, 9
Social trauma, and post–9/11 political
    culture, 1–30
  bystander position, problem of,
    24–30
  Hedda Bolgar, 1–6
    in Austria and Europe, 2–4
    in U.S. after 9/11, 4–6
  social matrix of psychic experience,
    7–24
  social matrix of psychic experience,
    ideological and rhetorical
    responses to 9/11, 12–17
    Bush Administration responses,
    4–6
    globalization impacts and,
    22–23
    media, 16
    PNAC and neoconservative
    movement, 17–18, 24
  social matrix of psychic experience,
    theoretical perspectives
    Gramsci perspective, 12
    group dynamics, 9–10
    Lacanian view, 10, 11, 12, 14–15
    LaPlanche perspective, 10, 11
    Lifton perspective, 14, 21
    object relations theory, 9
    psychoanalytic research, 8–9
Social trauma, culture of fear and,
    121–155
  Equipo and Mothers of the Plaza de
    Mayo, 147–153
  forced disappearances and, 127–130
  human destructiveness, 139–143
  imprisonment, torture, and social
    trauma, 130–139
  justice/retribution/amnesty issues,
    199–202
  nature of trauma and definitions,
    122–123
  psychoanalytic practice under state
    terror, 143–147
  psychology and dynamics of social
    trauma, 123–126
Social unconscious, 9–10
Social violence, 202–204, 320
Social welfare policies, 229

Socialization, historical
    development and
    evolution of neoliberalism/
    neoconservatism, 228, 234
Socially constructed trauma,
    intergenerational transmission
    of, 8
Sociosymbolic order, 7, 13
SOFAR, 275–278
Solanas, Fernando, 79
Soldiers Project, 272–275, 299 n.5,
    299 n.8
Soldz, Stephen, 257–258, 261 n.18,
    262 n.24, 262 n.27, 263 n.30
Soler, C., 10
Solid modernity, 323
Solnit, Rebecca, 333
Solomon, Norman, 305, 306, 310, 315
Somatic disturbances, psychology of
    social trauma, 123
Somoza, Anastasio, 177, 178
Sosnowski, S., 154 n.3
South Africa, 119 n.2
Southern Cone, Dirty Wars, 33–59;
    See also Dirty Wars
Soviet Union, 40, 207, 328
Spanish Civil War, 65, 66
Sperling, J., 31 n.7
Splitting, 9, 15
    containment of destructive
        impulses, 296–297
    demonized other, 326
    idealization versus ideals, 339–340
    life during transition to
        dictatorship, 99
    psychology of social trauma, 124,
        139–140
    responsible leadership and, 302
    and victimhood, 252–253
Spooner, M. H., 118 n.1
Stagflation, 232
Stalinism, 68, 81
State
    neoconservative models, 237
    neoliberal theory, 230
    from social state to security state,
        344 n.25
State ideological apparatus, 12
State terror
    Latin America; See also Latin
        America

aftermath, reminders of,
    208–209
Dirty War in Argentina, 33–59;
    See also Dirty Wars
impunity and social violence,
    202–204
memoria versus olvido, 194–
    202; See also Impunity
migration from Chile and
    Uruguay to Argentina, 87–88
psychological impact on
    individuals, children, and
    families, 222 n.6
themes in Argentinian
    psychoanalysis, 82
undoing, 192–194
Nicaraguan Contra training in U.S.,
    188 n.8
psychoanalysis, social preconditions
    for, 143–147
psychosocial dynamics of, 91–120
    flight/escape from, 109–112
    forced disappearances and
        torture, 112–118
    ideology of state terror, 101–106
    lives during transition to, 92–101
    strategies, 107–112
Staub, Ervin, 24, 27, 57
Stein, B. H., 59 n.2
Stein, N., 118 n.2
Stein, S. J., 59 n.2
Steinberg, Arlene Lu, 261 n.16
Stenner, K., 299 n.13
Stewart, Jon, 240
Stiglitz, Joseph, 304, 316, 341 n.5
Strategic Outreach to Families of All
    Reservists (SOFAR), 275–278
Strategic Studies Institute, U.S. War
    College, 343 n.21
Strategy, state terror, 107–112, 118 n.2
Strauss, Leo, 236
Strenger, Carlo, 337
Structural analysis of intrapsychic
    world, 244
Suarez-Orozco, M. M., 154 n.4
Subject
    decentered, 8, 11
    hegemony, disengagement from, 28
    identity, relation to the social and
        political world and, 214
    interpellation, 28–29

psychoanalytic exploration of
    unconscious, 211
Subjectification, 214
Subjectivity
    contemporary, 327–340
    contemporary challenges, 327–328
    doubling phenomenon, 142–143
    gendered, as analytic category,
        225–226
    Lacanian and group psychoanalytic
        tradition, 303
    Latin American perspectives on,
        280, 291
        Braun, 284–285
        personal security issues and, 282
    neoliberal culture and, 280
    new, political opposition and,
        240–241
    oppressive systems and, 243
    political, 6, 7
    psychoanalysis and, 217–218
    socially constructed, 9–10
    torture policy implications, 114
Subpolitics, 334
Subversion, 137
Subversive ideology
    counterinsurgency program
        definitions of, 101–102
    psychoanalysis as, 64
    state terror, justifications of,
        104–105
Suicide, returning veterans, 277
Suicide bombers, 284
Suicide rates, 206
Sullivan, H. S., 243, 244
Summers, Frank, 258, 261 n.16, 262
    n.24
Summers, L., 305
Superego
    adaptation to exile, 161
    bystander situation, 27
    mass media impact, 234
    psychoanalysis and, 217–218
    and responses to Bush–Cheney
        policies, 26
Superpower role, 11
Superpower syndrome, 14, 239, 246
    contemporary challenges, 314
    Obama Administration policy, 303
*Superpower Syndrome: America's
    Apocalyptic Confrontation
    With the World* (Lifton), 6

Survival, Evasion, Resistnce, Escape
    (SERE) program, 255, 263
    n.30
Survival of the fittest ethos, 206,
    228–229
Survivor guilt, 158–159
Suspicion, psychology of social trauma,
    123
Sweezy, P.M., 59 n.7
Symbolic order, 10, 11
    postsymbolic order era, 280
Symbols, social, 9
Symptoms
    economic and political insecurities
        and, 285
    Grissinopoli workers, 216
    Nicaraguan Contra conflict,
        183–184
    psychoanalytic 10 commandments
        of Nicaraguan training
        program, 180
    psychoanalytic training program in
        Nicaragua, 181
    social breakdown and, 206
    of social malaise, 226
    social trauma and culture of fear,
        122, 123
    torture sequelae, 132
Symptoms, neoliberal capitalism, 245
Systemic forces, multigenerational
    transmission of trauma, 244

T

Tannenbaum, Carol, 249, 261 n.19
Taxation, 296
Tea Party movement, 342 n.15, 344
    n.21
Team of Psychological Assistance to
    the Mothers of the Plaza de
    Mayo; *See* Equipo
Telarañas (Pavlovsky), 111, 141
Tellez, Dora Maria, 181, 188–189 n.11
Terkel, A., 268
Terror
    manic defense, 4
    state; *See* State terror
Terrorism, Bush–Cheney
    Administration definition of,
    266–267
Thatcher, Margaret, 232
Theatre, 77–78, 86

Theological model of state, 237
Therapeutic alliance, 187 n.3
Therapeutic benefits of activism,
    129–130, 152, 153, 155 n.18,
    183
Think tanks, right-wing organization,
    235
Thomas, Nina, 25, 31 n.8, 251–252
Thompson, Clara, 243, 244
Thomson, M., 155 n.16
Thought, ideologized modes of
    thinking, 15
Threat, manic defense, 4
Threat assessment, social, 28
Timmerman, Jacobo, 108, 131
Topia, 216
Torture, 120 n.10
    American Psychological Association
        on, 256–258, 262–263 nn.
        24–30
    activism by members, 256–259
    complicity and participation of
        professionals with torture,
        253–254
    Ethics Code, 254–255, 258, 259
    Bush–Cheney Administration
        policies, Obama
        Administration reconciliation
        policy, 306–307
    bystander problem, 24–30
        Bush–Cheney war on terror,
            24–29
        U.S. Latin American policy,
            29–30
    human destructiveness, 139–143
    justice/retribution/amnesty issues,
        199–202
    Nicaraguan Contra training in U.S.,
        188 n.8
    Obama Administration policy, 344
        n.23
    psychodynamics of state terror,
        112–118
    psychodynamics of torturers,
        116–117
    psychologists' complicity in Brazil,
        82, 262 n.23
    psychology of social trauma, 125
    public confessions by torturers
        in Chile and Argentina,
        208–209
    qualifications of torturers, 114–116

    and social trauma, 130–139
    state terror strategies, 107–108
    themes in Argentinian
        psychoanalysis, 82
    trials, kidnapping of witnesses, 287,
        288
    U.S. advisors and, 102
    U.S. policy, 258, 260
    U.S. psychologists participation
        and complicity, 253–255,
        262–263 n.30
    women, 119 n.9
Torture/extraordinary renditions, 4–5
Totalitarianism, inverted, 332, 344
    n.25
Trade, NAFTA, 236
Trade deficits, 314
Trade unions; *See* Union activism/
    activists
Training, Women's Therapy Center
    Institute (WTCI), 249–250
Training program, Wright Institute,
    235
Transference/countertransference, 75,
    82, 147, 313
    defined, 89 n.3
    Marx–Freud correlations, 84
    neutrality and, 245
    psychoanalytic 10 commandments
        of Nicaraguan training
        program, 180
    social preconditions for practice of
        psychoanalysis, 143–144
    therapeutic alliance formation, 187
        n.3
Transnational activism, 333–338
Trauma
    children of the disappeared,
        191–192
    cumulative, 22
    Ernest S. Lawrence Trauma Center,
        249
    multigenerational transmission of,
        244
    nature and definitions, 122–123
    ongoing nature of, 154 n.1, 154 n.2
    responses to state terror, 178
    socially constructed,
        intergenerational transmission
        of, 8
    socially constructed subjectivity,
        9–10

therapeutic approaches with
    families of *desaparecidos*,
    196–197
    war-induced, social construction
    of, 244
Traumatic brain injury, 270
Treatment interventions, victims of
    state terror, 146–147
Treatment settings, underground
    activism in Argentina, 85–86
Trials, kidnapping of witnesses, 288,
    289
Triple A (Argentine Anticommunist
    Alliance), 56, 61, 88, 94
Troubled Asset Relief Program
    (TARP), 306, 340–341 n.4
Truman era policy, 102
Trust
    betrayal, risk of, 123, 144, 145
    pathogenic effects of parental lies,
    135
Tupamaros, 44–45, 99, 132, 135
Turley, Jonathan, 306–307, 341 n.7
Turner, F. C., 60 n.16
Twemlow, Stuart, 248, 249
Tylim, Isaac, 336

U

UFA (Argentine Feminist Union),
    86–87
Ulricksen de Viñar, Maren, 41–42,
    43–45
Uncertainty, bystander situation, 28
Unconscious, 313
    interplay with social forces, 8
    myths of power, 221
    psychoanalysis and, 211
    psychoanalytic 10 commandments
    of Nicaraguan training
    program, 180
    social, 9–10
Union activism/activists, 108
    Argentina, 34, 53, 55, 74, 83, 85,
    87, 90 n.11
    desaparecidos, 130
    Grissinopoli workers, 220
    neoliberalism and, 103
    uprising in 2001, 211
    Chile, 47
    desaparecidos, 130

historical development and
    evolution of neoliberalism/
    neoconservatism, 227, 232
lives during transition to
    dictatorship, 95
Nicaragua, 177, 179
scapegoating, mechanisms of, 140
United States
    conservative trends, 328
    neoliberalism and, 227, 232,
    236, 245
Uruguay, 43, 44, 97, 108
Union Feminista Argentina (UFA),
    86–87, 90 n.11
Unions, neoliberalism and, 232
Unipolar world, emergence of, 207
United Nations, 336
United States
    historical development and
    evolution of neoliberalism/
    neoconservatism, 225–241
    neoliberal/neoconservative
    democracy in, 225–263;
    See also Neoliberal/
    neoconservative democracy
    in U.S.
    Peronist policy, 67
    superpower syndrome, 2
United States, future prospects,
    301–345
    American Exceptionalism, global
    realities and, 311–326
    contemporary subjectivities,
    327–340
    Obama Administration policy,
    301–311
United States foreign policy, 5–6;
    See also Bush–Cheney
    Administration policies
    consensual support of Bush–Cheney
    policies, 12–24
    Cuban embargoes, 170
    Latin America, 29–30, 39–41, 59
    nn.4–7
    Argentina, 55, 119 n.5
    Chile, 48, 49–50, 99–101
    Guatemala, 40
    National Security Doctrine,
    101–106
    Nicaragua, 178, 187–188 n.6,
    188 n.8

Low Intensity Conflict (LIC), 178,
    188 n.7, 223 n.7
    state terror strategies, 118 n.2, 119
        n.5
U.S. National Security Doctrine,
    204
Unity, unconscious function of
    dominant ideology, 12
Universities, U.S. right-wing
    organization, 235
University of Chicago, 229; See also
    Chicago School of Economics
"Uprooted Mind, The: Psychoanalytic
    Perspectives on Living in an
    Unsafe World," 6, 25, 30 n.2
Uruguay, 7, 37, 60 n.12
    cultural status of psychoanalysis in
        1950s, 72–73
    current opposition to U.S. policies,
        309
    disappearances and torture,
        113–114
        collaboration of health
            professionals in torture, 254
        fate of disappeared, 134–135
        justice/retribution/amnesty
            issues, 200
    election of civilian governments,
        194
    emigration/migration/political exile
        from, 164–169
    Langer's migration to, 66
    migration from/to Argentina, 87–88
    progressive governments, emergence
        of, 281
    psyche and social revolution, 72–73
    repatriation of exiles, 222 n.5
    state terror
        aftermath of, 187
        assault on welfare state politics,
            41–45
        historical context of emergence
            of state terror in Latin
            America, 38–41
        lives during transition to
            dictatorship, 97–99
    transition to democracy, 193
    transition to dictatorship, 97–99
Uruguayan Psychoanalytic Association
    (APU), 97, 98, 135

V

Valenzuela, A., 60 n.14, 113
Values
    hegemony (Gramsci model), 11
    historical development and
        evolution of neoliberalism/
        neoconservatism, 227,
        230–231
Veltmeyer, H., 30 n.5
Venezuela, 281, 309
Verbitsky, H., 223 n.8
Veterans' Administration, 270
Victimhood
    psychology of social trauma, 125
    splitting and, 252–253
Videla, Jorge, 88, 105
Vienna Psychoanalytic Institute, 64
Vigilance, psychology of social trauma,
    123, 125
Vigilantism, 206, 331
Vilas, C. M., 188 n.6
Villar, Jose Perez, 172
Villela, L., 254, 262 n.23
Viñar, Marcelo, 7, 41–45, 57, 72–73,
    102, 131, 154 n.11, 193, 195,
    200–201
    exile experience, 160
    in France 1976–1990, 164–169
    life during transition to
        dictatorship, 97–99
    psychoanalysis, social preconditions
        for, 144–145
    psychology of social trauma, 124
    on responses to social trauma, 153
    on social preconditions for talking
        cure, 143–147
    torture and sequelae, 132–139
Viñar, Maren, 73, 133, 134, 135, 137,
    138, 139, 154 n.11, 195,
    200–201
    exile experience, 160
    in France 1976–1990, 164–169
    life during transition to
        dictatorship, 97–99
    psychology of social trauma, 124
    on responses to social trauma, 153
Violence
    bystander situation, 126
    globalization impacts, 210
    intervention model, 248
    language distortions, 107

pathological public sphere, 23
Violent innocence, 15–16
Vitter, David, 299 n.3
Volkan, Vamik, 335, 340 n.2, 345
    n.28
Volker, P., 341 n.4
Volnovich, Juan Carlos, 51, 52–57,
    68, 76, 79, 80–81, 85–86,
    109–110, 139–140, 210, 213,
    218, 221, 223 n.10, 247,
    279–282
  in Cuba 1976–1984, 169–175, 324
  exile experience, 160
  life during transition to
      dictatorship, 95–97
  psychoanalysis, social preconditions
      for, 145
  psychology of social trauma, 124
  return to Argentina, 195–196
  social illness, symptoms and
      dynamics of, 226
Volnovich, Silvia; See Werthein, Silvia
Vulnerability
  bystander situation, 27, 28
  superpower syndrome and, 14

W

Waisman, C. H., 60 n.15
Walker, T. W., 187 n.4, 188 n.6
Wallerstein, I., 324
War
  costs of, 315
  opposition to, 241
  preemptive, 237
  psychoanalytically oriented
      academic conferences,
      250–251
War Comes Home, The (Glantz), 269
War crimes, Bush–Cheney
      Administration, 306
War economy, 23
War on terror
  media and, 16
  PNAC agenda, 17
Warren, Elizabeth, 341 n.6
Washington Consensus, 219, 278, 316
Waterboarding, 263 n.30
Wealth, redistribution upward,
      239–240
Weapons of mass destruction, 19
Wedel, Janine, 328

Weinberg, H., 9
Weinstein, M., 60 n.12
Welch, Bryant, 296
Welcome to the Desert of the Real
    (Zizek), 14–15
Welfare state, 232, 239
Wendling, R., 318
Werthein, Leonardo, 54
Werthein, Silvia, 54–57, 68, 76, 80,
    95–97, 109–110, 169–175,
    195–196, 279–282, 324
Weschler, L., 200
Westen, Drew, 310
Western Hemisphere Institute for
    Security Cooperation; See
    School of the Americas (SOA)
Whitehead, L., 60 n.11
Whitney, Michael, 341 n.5
Wickham–Crowley, T. P., 118 n.2
Wiesenthal, Simon, 154 n.12
Wilkinson, S., 248
Winnicott, D. W., 9, 27, 154 n.6, 159,
    180
Wiretaps, 94, 266
Withdrawal, 122
Witness kidnappings, in Argentina,
    288–289
Wolf, Josh, 267
Wolf, Naomi, 267, 292, 299 n.12
Wolfenstein, V., 261 n.13
Wolin, Sheldon W., 332
Women's movement
  contemporary trends and
      challenges, 338–339
  Peronist, 70
Women's reproduction
  Langer's work in, 69–70
  psychosomatic disturbances in,
      Langer's interest in, 65
Women's Therapy Center Institute
    (WTCI), 249–250, 252, 261
    n.20, 261–262 n.21
Women's Therapy Centre, London,
    249–250
Work
  in Nicaragua, 177
  unemployment; See Employment/
      unemployment
Work–study program, Nicaraguan
    medical school, 184–185

World Bank and International
Monetary Fund, 103, 194,
219, 316
Argentina, mass uprising in 2001,
211–212
social and economic crises in Latin
America, 206
state terror strategies, 108
victims of neoliberal democracy,
204
World Trade Organization, 240, 321
Wright, E. and Wright E., 324
Wright Institute, 235
Wyden, P., 59 n.7

X

Xenophobia, 267–268

Y

Yankelevich, Silvia, 215, 216, 217, 219,
220

Z

Zalaya, Manuel, 309
Zaphiropoulos, L., 250
Zimmerman, Edmundo, 89 n.4
Zinn, H., 59 n.4, 223 n.10, 260 n.10,
339
Zizek, Slavoj, 12, 14–15, 28–29, 130,
228, 293, 324